MINORITIES,
AGING, AND
HEALTH

MINORITIES, AGING, AND HEALTH

Edited by
Kyriakos S. Markides
Manuel R. Miranda

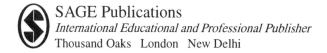
SAGE Publications
International Educational and Professional Publisher
Thousand Oaks   London   New Delhi

For information:

 SAGE Publications, Inc.
2455 Teller Road
Thousand Oaks, California 91320
E-mail: order@sagepub.com

SAGE Publications Ltd.
6 Bonhill Street
London EC2A 4PU
United Kingdom

SAGE Publications India Pvt. Ltd.
M-32 Market
Greater Kailash I
New Delhi 110 048 India

Printed in the United States of America

Library of Congress Cataloging-in-Publication Data

Main entry under title:

Minorities, aging, and health / by Kyriakos S. Markides, Manuel R.
    Miranda (editors).
        p. cm.
    Includes bibliographical references and index.
    ISBN 0-8039-5973-7 (cloth). — ISBN 0-8039-5974-5 (pbk.)
        1. Minority aged—Health and hygiene—United States. 2. Minority
    aged—Medical care—United States. I. Markides, Kyriakos S.
    II. Miranda, Manuel, 1939-
    RA408.M54M55 1997
    613'.0438'08900973—dc21   97-4841

This book is printed on acid-free paper.

97 98 99 00 01 02 10 9 8 7 6 5 4 3 2 1

Acquiring Editor:	Margaret Zusky
Editorial Assistant:	Corinne Pierce
Production Editor:	Astrid Virding
Production Assistant:	Karen Wiley
Typesetter/Designer:	Rebecca Evans
Indexer:	L. Pilar Wyman
Cover Designer:	Candice Harman
Print Buyer:	Anna Chin

Contents

PART IV. *Mental Health*

PART VI. *Health Policy*

Preface

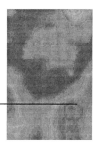

As we approach the end of the 20th century, it seems appropriate to take stock of the knowledge on the health of America's minority elderly. The rapid growth of the elderly population in general has been well-documented. Less documented and appreciated is the current and projected growth of the elderly in the major ethnic minority populations: African Americans, Hispanics, Asian/Pacific Islanders, and Native Americans.

The growth in numbers and increasing diversity of America's ethnic minority populations, coupled with political and scientific considerations, has led the National Institutes of Health to mandate the inclusion of minorities in research with human subjects. There has been a realization that knowledge on the population's health and health care needs is incomplete without special attention to the problems and needs of ethnic minorities. As most researchers have had little experience studying ethnic minority groups, they often encounter difficulties in getting their research funded and carrying it out when they do.

This volume is aimed primarily at these researchers in the field of aging. We felt that a comprehensive volume covering the health and health care needs of ethnic minority elderly would be an invaluable resource to all gerontologists. We assembled a distinguished group of experienced researchers and asked them to review state-of-the-art knowledge on major ethnic groups in six general areas: Mortality and life expectancy; chronic diseases and disabilities; diet and nutrition; mental health; health services and long-term care; and health policy. As a collection, the chapters in this volume, we believe, provide an excellent overview of special health problems of certain groups, and of socioeconomic, historical, and cultural factors influencing these health problems. At the same time, they also document how little knowledge exists in many areas, particularly with respect to Asian/Pacific Islanders and Native Americans. Difficulties in studying these and other groups are also outlined and, hopefully, make a compelling case why more and more targeted research is needed.

This volume is also aimed at students in gerontology, the health sciences, the social sciences, and related fields. In addition to providing basic information on a growing segment of the population, we hope that the following chapters provide ideas for researchable areas as part of masters' and doctoral dissertations.

Finally, we hope that policymakers find this volume useful as they make important decisions affecting the lives of older Americans as we enter the next century.

Acknowledgments

In addition to the contributors to this volume, we would like to thank Kathlynn Joel, Julie Morreale, and Myrna Díaz for their expert editorial assistance.

Minorities, Aging, and Health

An Overview

Kyriakos S. Markides
Manuel R. Miranda

Growing Diversity

Gerontologists are paying increasing attention to diversity and hetero-geneity in the aged population, especially with respect to gender, race, ethnicity, and minority status. No doubt an impetus behind this attention to ethnicity and minority status has been the rapid pace of growth in the numbers and proportions of people of color and diverse ethnic origins in the United States as well as in other Western societies. In 1980, for example, 80% of the elderly population in the United States were Whites of non-Hispanic origin. By 1995, this proportion dropped to approximately 74% and is projected to decline to only 67% by the year 2050 (U.S. Bureau of the Census, 1993).

As we approach the end of the 20th century, African Americans continue to be the largest ethnic minority population of the United States, and their numbers are projected to increase by 150% over the next 40 years. Projected increases during the same period are considerably larger for the elderly in other major ethnic minority populations: over 200% among Native Americans, almost 500% among Hispanics, and by well over 500% among Asians/Pacific Islanders. The impact of this growth in numbers of minority elderly is expected to be especially strong in the South and Southwest (U.S. Bureau of the Census, 1992). Hispanic elderly are expected to outnumber

African American elderly by the year 2050, and Asian/Pacific Islander elderly will constitute approximately 7% of the older population by the year 2050, up from 2% in 1995 (U.S. Bureau of the Census, 1993).

Researchers as well as policymakers often ignore the diversity within these minority populations, especially among Hispanics and Asians/Pacific Islanders. Approximately 49% of Hispanic elderly are of Mexican origin and reside primarily in the southwestern states; 15% are of Cuban origin and reside mostly in south Florida; 12% are of Puerto Rican origin and are concentrated in the New York City area and other urban areas in the Northeast; finally, approximately 25% are of Central American and other Hispanic origin and are found throughout the country, but especially in the Northeast.

Although lumping Hispanics into one category is often based on political reasons, the various components are in fact rather diverse. While they share a common language and are predominantly Roman Catholic, they vary substantially on many other important characteristics. Older Mexican Americans, for example, are more likely to have been born in the United States but have had limited occupational opportunities, only average English language ability, the lowest educational levels, and relatively high poverty rates. On the other hand, older Cubans, who are virtually all foreign-born, have the highest educational levels and include a disproportionate number of professionals who immigrated to the United States after the Cuban revolution. Despite their higher socioeconomic status, older Cubans have the lowest English ability (Portes & Bach, 1986). Older Puerto Ricans share the low socioeconomic and occupational backgrounds of Mexican Americans, but few were born on the United States mainland, as much of the Puerto Rican migration to the mainland began after World War II (Sánchez-Ayéndez, 1988). Finally, little is known about the rapidly growing segment of Hispanic elderly originating in Central America.

The diversity of the Asian/Pacific Islander population is even greater than that of the Hispanic population, but like the Hispanic population it contains disproportionate numbers of young immigrants that contribute to a relatively small overall percentage of older people. In 1990, 30% of the older population were of Chinese, 24% of Japanese, 24% of Filipino, 8% of Korean, 5% of Asian Indian, and 5% of other Asian and Pacific Islander origins (U.S. Bureau of the Census, 1992, 1993). Because the Filipino, Korean, Asian Indian, and other categories are younger than the Japanese- and Chinese-origin populations, we can expect rapid growth in the numbers and proportions of the elderly in these more recent immigrant groups in the next several decades. The vast cultural, religious, linguistic, and immigration experience variation in the 26 plus Census-recognized Asian and Pacific Islander populations makes lumping them together for research purposes even more inappropriate than aggregating the various Hispanic groups. For example, while on the aggregate Asian/Pacific Islander elderly have high educational and income levels, a number of subgroups have a disproportionate number of elderly with low education and income. In addition, the more recent immigrant groups contain a disproportionate number of elderly, who face linguistic and cultural barriers that often are associated with intergenerational tensions within the family (Markides & Black, 1996).

Finally, the great diversity of the Native American population remains unappreciated. The approximately two million American Indians, Eskimos, and Aleuts in the United States originated from approximately 500 tribes that differ in cultural, religious, social, and economic characteristics. However, the elderly in most of these groups experience particularly high rates of poverty (U.S. Bureau of the Census, 1993). The Native American population is still relatively young, with only 5% being 65 years or older. Their numbers and proportions of the elderly should increase rapidly in the next several decades (U.S. Bureau of the Census, 1993).

Studying the Health of Minority Elderly

As will become clear from the chapters contained in this volume, we know the most about the health of the African American elderly compared with the health of other populations. National data on the health and health needs of African Americans have been available for some time and have consistently shown a health disadvantage in this population relative to other groups. We are also beginning to learn more about the health of Hispanic elderly, especially Mexican Americans. Much of this is owed to the Hispanic Health and Nutrition Examination Survey (HHANES) conducted in the early 1980s and to recent funding initiatives of the National Institute on Aging (Markides, Rudkin, Angel, & Espino, 1997).

When it comes to Asian/Pacific Islander and Native American elderly, our knowledge is rather limited by the absence of national data and the plethora of small ethnic subgroups that make large-scale epidemiologic studies impractical.

Purpose and Organization of the Volume

Despite gaps in knowledge on the health status and health needs of most ethnic minority populations, we felt that sufficient information had emerged in recent years to allow us to compile this volume. In many cases, the chapters outline more gaps in knowledge than firm knowledge per se. Yet, identifying gaps will, we hope, provide an impetus for needed research on this rapidly rising segment of the American elderly population.

The remainder of this volume is organized into six parts: Part I contains chapters on aging and mortality among African Americans, Asian and Pacific Islander Americans, and American Indians. Part II includes chapters on aging, chronic conditions, and disabilities among African Americans, Hispanics, Asian and Pacific Islander Americans, and American Indians. Part III consists of chapters on aging, diet, and nutrition among African Americans and Hispanics. Part IV contains chapters on aging, health services, and long-term care among African Americans, Hispanics, and American Indians. Part V includes chapters on aging and mental health among Hispanics and Asian/ Pacific Islander Americans. Finally, Part VI consists of a chapter on public policies relevant to all major ethnic minority populations in the United States.

Next, we provide a brief overview of each of the six parts of the book.

Part I. Mortality and Life Expectancy

Manton and Stallard note that it has been well established that mortality ratios of African Americans relative to Whites are high, peak in middle age, and decline in old age. However, the often observed mortality "crossover," where Black/White mortality ratios at advanced ages decline to less than 1.0, has been the subject of some debate in recent years because of questions regarding the quality of age reporting by African Americans at advanced ages. The authors examined total and cause-specific mortality for five cohorts followed for 43 years and found evidence of a racial total mortality crossover for three of the cohorts. No trend toward a crossover was evident in total cancer mortality in any of the five cohorts. They argue that if the crossover was the result of age misreporting, cancer victims' ages, at death would have to be reported accurately at advanced ages, whereas deaths from all other causes of death would not. They conclude that the crossover and other patterns observed are consistent with insights obtained from genetic and molecular epidemiology of cancer risks.

Elo points out that mortality estimates have pointed to a marked advantage for Asian and Pacific Islander Americans, but there remained questions about the reliability of the evidence. She examines mortality estimates for Chinese, Japanese, Filipinos, other Asian and Pacific Islanders, all Asian and Pacific Islanders combined, and for Whites using data from vital statistics and the U.S. Census for 1989-1991 and from the National Longitudinal Mortality Survey. It is found that Asian and Pacific Islanders have lower mortality rates at ages 25 and above relative to Whites. Most of the mortality differential at ages 45 and over is explained by lower death rates from heart disease and cancer in Asian and Pacific Islanders. However, there remains a great deal of uncertainty about the reliability of mortality rates for Asian and Pacific Islanders in the United States.

John provides an overview of aging and mortality in the American Indian population. He notes that available data suffer from misclassification of the underlying cause of death, misidentification of race of the decedents, and inaccuracies in population estimates of the American Indian population. Yet, when using even the most conservative estimates, life expectancy at birth for American Indians increased from 51 years in 1940 to 70.3 years in 1991. This remarkable improvement is attributed to efforts of the Indian Health Service to eliminate infectious diseases and better address acute care needs of American Indians. However, the mortality profile of American Indians has been changing dramatically toward chronic and degenerative diseases that are concentrated in old age. Clearly, more accurate data on mortality and life expectancy for American Indian populations are needed.

The mortality and life expectancy experience of Hispanic populations was reviewed recently in another volume (Markides et al., 1997). The evidence continues to support the "epidemiologic paradox" identified more than a decade ago (Markides & Coreil, 1986) whereby Hispanic populations have an equal to or higher life expectancy than other Whites at all ages despite the relatively poor socioeconomic circumstances. Hispanic advantages in mortality appear to be more characteristic of males and result primarily from advantages in mortality from cardiovascular diseases and cancer. One potential explanation for such an advantage relates to the positive impacts of selective immigration that results in a "healthy immigrant" phenomenon (Markides et al., 1997; Sorlie, Backlund, Johnson, & Rogot, 1993).

Part II. Chronic Diseases and Disabilities

Clark and Gibson document large disadvantages of African Americans in early old age in chronic conditions and disabilities. These disadvantages decline or disappear among persons aged 80 and over except with respect to obesity and disability as measured by Activities of Daily Living (ADLs). The authors also suggest that the impact of hypertension and diabetes on disease-related outcomes is probably greater among elderly African Americans than among Whites.

Hazuda and Espino review evidence on prevalence of chronic conditions and disability in Hispanic elderly. They note, for example, that the excess prevalence of diabetes among Mexican Americans persists to the older years, with self-reported prevalence ranging from 22% to 25%. Clearly, the true prevalence is probably twice as high given the high rate of undetected diabetes in this population.

Prevalences of other chronic conditions are not very different from those in the general population of the elderly. However, rates of disability in most Hispanic elderly groups are high. Difficulties in performing Activities of Daily Living and lower body actions are influenced by most major medical conditions, especially stroke and disability. They argue that longitudinal data now becoming available in several studies should be used to examine the "disablement process" model in order to gain a better understanding of how medical conditions influence rates of dependency and disability in Hispanic elderly.

Kagawa-Singer, Hikoyeda, and Tanjasiri review the limited evidence on aging, chronic conditions, and physical disabilities in Asian and Pacific Islander elderly (APIA). They argue that the APIA label hides a great deal of heterogeneity in the health status and needs of the various ethnic groups subsumed under it. Significant predictors of disability in addition to chronic conditions include low rates of insurance coverage and rapid rates of modernization that lead to the adoption of high-fat diets, low-fiber diets, and sedentary lifestyles. They predict a trend toward higher mortality from hypertension, diabetes, cardiovascular disease, and cancer in most APIA elderly populations.

Kramer reviews the limited and scattered evidence on the burden of chronic conditions in American Indian and Alaska Native elderly populations. She notes a gradual shift away from infectious diseases to chronic conditions common in the general population, including cardiovascular diseases, diabetes, and cancer. However, there appears to be great diversity in health problems and health behaviors within the various Native American cultures. Dramatic increases for many tribes have been especially observed in diabetes, with high rates of complications. Again, the small numbers of American Indian and Alaska Native elderly, along with the great heterogeneity of the various tribes and cultures, have made the study of the health of the elderly quite difficult.

Part III. Diet and Nutrition

Kumanyika provides an overview of diet and nutrition issues affecting older African Americans. She notes that a number of diet-related chronic conditions such as overweight, hypertension, and diabetes are disproportionately more prevalent among older African Americans than among other elderly. Overnutrition in terms of high-fat, low-fiber diets as well as suboptimal intakes of vitamins and minerals are highlighted. Poverty is seen as a key contributor to poor diets and nutrition. Research is needed on certain sociocultural characteristics related to family relations and other factors in order to examine how such factors might compensate for the negative influences of poverty. Studies are also needed on how successful interventions might be implemented.

Tucker, Falcón, and Bermúdez evaluate knowledge on nutritional issues affecting Hispanic elderly. They highlight differences in diets across the various Hispanic populations, such as the higher fat content of Mexican American elderly diets than those of Puerto Rican and Dominican elderly, who consume more rice, potatoes and other root crops, and plantains. Nevertheless, average micronutrient intakes are lower among Puerto Ricans and Dominicans than among Mexican Americans. Data from HANES III show lower micronutrient intakes among older Mexican Americans than among non-Hispanic Whites.

As with African Americans, obesity is a major problem among Hispanic elderly, especially women. Obesity is implicated in high rates of diabetes among most Hispanic groups. Future research should focus on differences in obesity and nutrient intakes among the various Hispanic groups. Identification of socioeconomic and cultural factors influencing diet and nutrition should facilitate the development of interventions aimed at improving the nutritional and health status of Hispanic elderly.

Part IV. Mental Health

Aranda and Miranda present an overview of how acculturation and related
processes influence the mental health of older Hispanics. They note that the
literature has proposed several hypotheses suggesting a linear positive, a linear negative, and a curvilinear relationship between acculturation and mental
health. Unfortunately, the literature has given little attention to whether these
hypotheses apply to the experience of older Hispanics, the majority of whom
are at the lower end of the acculturation continuum. In addition to measurement problems of acculturation among older people, there is the problem of
confounding socioeconomic status and health status with acculturation, making meaningful analyses difficult.

The chapter also discusses the importance of other related concepts,
such as immigrant status, living arrangements, social support, minority status,
and type of Hispanic origin. Researchers must bring these and other variables
into their analyses when examining how acculturation influences mental
health. Large-scale population-based studies are needed in order to estimate
the prevalence and incidence of psychiatric disorders among the elderly in the
various Hispanic populations. Finally, culturally appropriate interventions
targeting at-risk elderly are needed.

Kitano, Shibusawa, and Kitano note at the outset that Asian American
populations have often been lumped together and have been subject to stereo-
typing, including that mental illness is not a major problem and that Asians
take care of their own. However, there is substantial diversity within and
among the various Asian groups in mental health characteristics and their
correlates. One generalization can be made, however: that the elderly in Asian
American groups underutilize community professional mental health services. An important challenge for mental health researchers and practitioners
is the need to understand mental illness in the culture of origin because so
many Asian Americans are recent immigrants.

Part V. Health Services and Long-Term Care

Keith and Long review issues related to health care services and long-term
care in African American elderly. They note that although racial differences
in access to health care have been reduced by Medicare and Medicaid, many
older African Americans continue to face barriers in obtaining medical care.
An important factor is absence of supplementary coverage. In addition, older

African Americans do not have equal access to sophisticated diagnostic procedures and are less likely to use preventive services. The authors' analysis of data from the Health Interview Survey (HIS) shows that older African American men are particularly less likely to visit physicians, have general checkups, or have cholesterol screenings. Using data from the Medicare Current Beneficiary Survey (MCBS) they found that satisfaction with health care services is low among African American women, those in "fair" or "poor" health, those with Medicare only, and those with low evaluations of their place of care.

The authors also address the issue of the lower use of nursing homes by African American elderly. They suggest that financial factors are important. However, the extent to which cultural factors related to family supports are important is not clear based on the research reviewed. They also review evidence that discrimination in nursing home placements continues partly to explain lower use. Clearly, these factors deserve more attention by researchers.

Angel and Angel argue that data point out that older Hispanics face serious barriers to acute and long-term care because of low income and lack of supplemental insurance coverage. Older Hispanics, especially Mexican Americans, have low Medicare coverage. Older Puerto Ricans exhibit high rates of physician use, while older Mexican Americans have the lowest rates of use of community-based services. Factors explaining low nursing home use include lack of facilities in Hispanic communities, cultural differences between Hispanics and providers, cultural factors related to caring for the elderly, and low financial resources. Understanding the complex patterns of health care use among older people in the various Hispanic populations will require more sophisticated analyses of socioeconomic, cultural, and health care delivery system factors.

Chapleski undertakes the difficult task of reviewing the literature on American Indian long-term care. After documenting tribal differences and demographic trends pointing toward rapid aging of the population in the foreseeable future, she provides an overview of socioeconomic and health characteristics that documents the current and future need for long-term care. Clearly, American Indian elders have many problems and needs, yet systematic studies on key characteristics are lacking. This is particularly so in the areas of mental health and cognitive functioning. Data from her research on Great Lakes Indian elders suggest that the concept of long-term care is foreign to American Indians. In addition, long-term care has not been a priority for the Indian Health Service.

Defining the need for long-term care is hampered by the absence of appropriate data, especially if one is interested in generalizing across the various tribal groups, levels of acculturation, residential locations, and socioeconomic and demographic conditions.

Part VI. Health Policy

Wallace and Villa present an overview of current health policies affecting the elderly in minority populations. They argue that minority elderly have been invisible in public policy. An important trend has been increased hostility toward immigrants and minorities and a federal policy increasingly dominated by budget considerations. While increases in the numbers of minority elderly in the 21st century may increase a public awareness of the health policy issues affecting minority elderly, rising costs of health care may very well cause public policy to ignore the health care needs of the elderly in minority populations.

Conclusion

As the various chapters in this text outline, population estimates of current as well as future age-group structuring in the United States clearly demonstrate that the elderly are among the subgroups whose numbers are most rapidly increasing. It is not merely the *growth rate* of the aging population, however, that compels us to give it attention. The dimension of *diversity* must be added if we are to understand the enormous implications of these two trends for the health and well-being of our minority elderly.

The minority elderly face a number of negative outcomes during the later years of life. The elderly are confronted by multiple losses, which may occur simultaneously: death of a partner, older friends, colleagues, relatives; decline of physical health and coming to personal terms with death; loss of status, prestige, and participation in society; and, for large numbers of the older population, the additional burdens of marginal living standards. The process of aging, even in the absence of health problems or loss, can be acutely distressing. Coupled with a lifetime of racial discrimination and severely reduced economic opportunities, the ethnic elderly are at triple jeopardy—old, poor, and of minority status. Confusion and uncertainty confront the elderly as they attempt to deal with the variety of changes that accompany the aging process.

With the aging of our population, maintaining the quality of life among the elderly—minority as well as nonminority—will continue to be one of our major societal goals. The extension of life and the compression of morbidity serve as ideal objectives in assuring that our elderly citizens lead full, productive, and satisfying lives marked by only minimal dependency and physical and mental deterioration prior to death.

Solutions to the continuing problem of life-quality inequities between mainstream older Americans and elderly minorities must arise from economic and social changes, as well as health services in both the public and private sectors. The present volume describes some of those changes and provides a variety of insightful and in-depth responses to the problems confronting the minority elderly. The data presented in this book are intended to assist those individuals charged with the responsibility of responding to the complex and diverse needs of the elderly minority population.

References

Markides, K. S., & Black, S. (1996). Race, ethnicity and aging: The impact of inequality. In R. H. Binstock & L. K. George (Eds.), *Handbook of aging and the social sciences* (4th ed.). San Diego: Academic Press.

Markides, K. S., & Coreil J. (1986). The health of southwestern Hispanics: An epidemiologic paradox. *Public Health Reports, 101,* 253-265.

Markides, K. S., Rudkin, L., Angel, R. J., & Espino, D. V. (1997). Health status of Hispanic elderly in the United States. In L. J. Martin, B. Soldo, & K. Foote (Eds.), *Ethnic differences in late life health.* Washington, DC: National Academy Press.

Portes, A., & Bach, R. (1986). *Latin journey.* Berkeley: University of California Press.

Sánchez-Ayéndez, M. (1988). Elderly Puerto Ricans in the United States. In S. R. Applewhite (Ed.), *Hispanic elderly in transition.* Westport, CT: Greenwood.

Sorlie, P. D., Backlund, M. S., Johnson, N. J., & Rogot, F. (1993). Mortality by Hispanic status in the United States. *Journal of the American Medical Association, 270,* 2646-2668.

U.S. Bureau of the Census. (1992). *Sixty-five plus in America* (Current Population Reports, Special Studies, P23-178). Washington, DC: Government Printing Office.

U.S. Bureau of the Census. (1993). *Racial and ethnic diversity of America's elderly population: Profiles of America's elderly* (No. 3, POP/31-1). Washington, DC: Government Printing Office.

PART 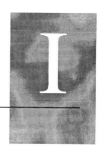 I

Mortality and Life Expectancy

Non-White and White Age Trajectories of Mortality

Evidence From Extinct Cohort Analyses, 1950 to 1992

Kenneth G. Manton
Eric Stallard

Gender-specific age trajectories of total, and cause-specific, mortality rates in Blacks and Whites are different. There is higher Black infant mortality, mortality from external causes (especially for young Black males), and mortality in middle-aged Black males and females due to hypertension and diabetes-related heart disease and stroke. The age-specific relative mortality ratio between Blacks and Whites reaches a peak in middle age and then begins to decline after about age 45 (National Center for Health Statistics [NCHS], 1995).

The question of whether there is a real age-related decline in the relative mortality ratio between Blacks and Whites, beginning in middle age, is little in doubt (e.g., Manton & Stallard, 1994; Markides & Keith, 1995). The issue of whether there exists a mortality "crossover," where the Black-to-White mortality ratio reaches 1.0 at some late age (e.g., above age 75) and then declines to less than 1.0 (i.e., Black q_xs are lower than for Whites at some late age x), has been, however, a topic of debate. One issue is how the quality of age reporting for Blacks at later ages (e.g., 75+) on census and death certificate data affects the age trajectory of their estimated mortality rates.

One study that endeavored to examine the quality of age reporting on death certificates and censuses by examining ages reported by decedents in

much earlier censuses (e.g., 1900 and 1910), for both Black and White decedents in two states (Pennsylvania and New Jersey), found that, for mortality
rates for 5-year age groups, White mortality rates up to age 100 seem to be of
good quality (i.e., no rate deviating by more than 2% from the corresponding
rate adjusted for estimates of age misreporting). Though the relative size of
errors in Black age reporting on mortality rates was larger, it was unclear
whether the effects of those errors produced a systematic bias until above age
90 in 1970 (Rosenwaike & Logue, 1983). If errors below age 90 were due to
a greater tendency to report "rounded" ages, than systematically to over- or
underreport age, that suggests that Black mortality trajectories could be un-
biased up to age 90 (the age by which the Black/White mortality crossover
has usually occurred) with respect to the form of their dependence on age. A
problem with that study, as with most efforts directly to validate age reports
at late ages, is that a large proportion of both the U.S. White and Black elderly
populations cannot be tracked (due to a lack of birth certification; or to geographic mobility between states over the life span; or early immigration to the
United States for Whites) back to early census records (e.g., the censuses of
1900 or 1910) with sufficient accuracy to generate the census-based age reporting data to match to ages reported on death certificates.

       Consequently, despite such efforts at record validation, there is no sin-
gle U.S. demographic data source that can unequivocally determine whether
the U.S. Black/White mortality crossover at late ages is due to differentials in
data quality—or is primarily a result of racial differences in the age-specific
biology of particular chronic disease and mortality mechanisms. The necessary data to validate age as reported on death certificate and census records
from direct documentary sources (e.g., birth certificates) do not now exist in
the United States. Countries that have long-standing population registries of
high quality (e.g., Sweden; select other Scandinavian countries) have few
Blacks (or, until relatively recently, other racially distinctive groups) in their
populations. It is only recently that efforts have been made to register births
in the United States by requiring Social Security numbers to be issued before
a child's first birthday.

       As a consequence, researchers have had to examine the U.S. Black/
White mortality crossover using several other types of data. A study of the
correspondence of age reporting on death certificates, and in Medicare data,
for 1987 showed that the quality of ages reported on death certificates for
Blacks and Whites seemed good up to about age 100 in that the ages reported
on death certificates were similar to those recorded for the 187,000 cases in

the two states where Medicare records and death certificates were matched (Kestenbaum, 1992). It was concluded in that study that a real crossover in U.S. Black/White mortality rates occurred about age 86 (males) to 88 (females).

A Black/White mortality crossover was also found at about age 81 (both sexes) in extinct cohort life tables based solely on death certificate data recorded for all U.S. deaths occurring from 1960 to 1990, with the crossovers evaluated for calendar years 1962, 1967, and 1972 (Manton & Stallard, 1994). The Kestenbaum (1992) study suggests that these observations are unlikely to be due to the overreporting of age on the death certificates filed for Blacks. In addition, the use of extinct cohort life table procedures has the advantage that the denominators and numerators of mortality rates are necessarily internally consistent—both being formed from age-specific counts of U.S. deaths.

A Black/White mortality crossover was also found in a study based on an analysis of multiple years of the U.S. Current Population Survey, with the income-adjusted rates crossing at ages 75 to 79 (males) to 85+ (females). In that study (the National Longitudinal Mortality Study), mortality crossovers were also manifest for specific causes of death (e.g., heart disease, cancer) with the age trajectory of the relative mortality ratios (and the age at crossover) varying by cause of death (Sorlie, Rogot, Anderson, Johnson, & Backlund, 1992). If the crossover were simply due to age misreporting, we would not expect the age at which the crossover occurs to vary by cause of death.

Black/White crossovers have also been found at ages 85 (males) and 92 (females) in two closed cohort epidemiological studies in which most persons were enrolled in the study cohort before age 70 (i.e., at an age below which significant age misreporting is much less likely—those enrolled before age 75 contributed 90% of the exposure at or above age 75) and then followed continuously for 25 to 30 years: the Charleston Heart Study and the Evans County Study (Keil et al., 1993; Manton, Stallard, & Wing, 1991; Wing, Manton, Stallard, Hames, & Tyroler, 1985).

Black/White crossovers were also found at ages 80 to 84 (males) and 90 to 94 (females) among the 49,469 mostly middle-class participants (1,135 Blacks) of the Cancer Prevention Study who attained age 75 or older after 1960 (Lew & Garfinkel, 1990).

Another approach is to examine the physiological basis of racial mortality and morbidity differentials in a variety of different studies of risk factors, disease mechanisms, and their natural histories, to determine if the epidemiological, biological, and clinical evidence is consistent with different Black and White patterns of age dependence for the incidence and risk of death from specific diseases (Manton, Patrick, & Johnson, 1989; Manton & Stallard, 1996). For example, considerable epidemiological evidence suggests that the risk of hypertension and stroke in middle age is much higher for Blacks than Whites (Bronner, Kanter, & Manson, 1995). Clinical data also suggest that the biological mechanisms underlying hypertension differ between Blacks and Whites because different antihypertensive drugs (e.g., beta blockers, diuretics, calcium channel blockers, ACE-II inhibitors), and different combinations of those drugs, work better in different racial (as well as gender- and age-specific) subpopulations (Materson et al., 1993).

Epidemiological studies also suggest that differences in circulatory disease risks may be related to definable racial differences in genetic susceptibility to specific disease processes; for example, genetic factors have been implicated in the higher risk of hypertension for African Americans (Cooper & Rotimi, 1994; Jeunemaitre et al., 1992). Diabetes mellitus type II has a greater prevalence among African Americans than Whites (Cowie, Harris, Silverman, Johnson, & Rust, 1993). Diabetes is a risk factor for circulatory disease, stroke, hypertension, and renal dysfunction (Keil et al., 1993; Manton et al., 1989; McKeigue, Shah, & Marmot, 1991; Qualheim, Rostand, Kirk, & Luke, 1991). However, diabetes may have less effect on hypertension in Blacks than Whites (Svetkey, George, Burchett, Morgan, & Blazer, 1993). Hypertension has an earlier age at onset in Blacks than Whites (Perneger et al., 1993)—as does renal disease. The rate at which African Americans utilize the Medicare ESRD (end-stage renal disease) program is much higher than for Whites. In the dialysis portion of the ESRD program in 1991, 34.9% of participants were Black—almost 3 times their proportion in the U.S. population. The dominant, and increasing, disease risks identified as causing chronic renal failure, and hence the need for renal dialysis, are diabetes (25.7%) and hypertension (26.5%) (Greer, 1993).

In addition, there is epidemiological evidence that lipid metabolism and fibrinolytic mechanisms contributing to circulatory disease risks may differ by race. Indeed, there had been some confusion about the contribution of cholesterol to coronary heart disease in Blacks because, at least for Black males, HDL cholesterol levels were higher than in Whites. Recently, however, other types of lipoproteins have been identified that may play a significant role in atherogenesis in Blacks. For example, there was a significant (nearly double) elevation (relative to Whites) of the blood lipid Lp(a) among

African Americans—especially females—in both the CARDIA (Marcovina et al., 1993) and Atherosclerosis Risk in Communities (ARIC; Brown, Morrisett, Boerwinkle, Hutchinson, & Patsch, 1993) studies. The role of Lp(a) in causing circulatory diseases may be multifactorial. One of its possible roles in circulatory disease is that one of Lp(a)'s components, Apo(a), is structurally similar to plasminogen—a protein important in fibrinolysis (i.e., the process by which blood clots are dissolved; clot formation at the site of an atherosclerotic plaque is often the final stage in the natural history of atherogenesis leading to potentially lethal occlusive circulatory events in the heart or brain). Lp(a) may thus block the action of plasminogen by occupying its receptor site and thereby increasing the risk of thrombosis (Rader & Brewer, 1992). Recently, it has been questioned if the Apo(a) portion of Lp(a) is responsible for much of the variation in Lp(a) levels across racial groups (Sandholzer et al., 1992).

Lp(a) may also be directly involved in atherogenesis as a lipid that is oxidized and trapped in macrophages forming foam cells in atherosclerotic plaques. Lp(a) is also associated with renal disease and diabetes—two other diseases with elevated prevalence in Blacks (Jenkins et al., 1989; Parra, Luyeye, Bouramoue, Demarquilly, & Fruchart, 1987).

Lp(a) levels appear to be strongly genetically determined. The intraclass correlations of Lp(a) were so high in one study of female twins (.94 in Whites; .96 in Blacks) that too little nongenetically determined variation remained to study (Selby et al., 1994). Lp(a) is associated with coronary heart disease (CHD) and stroke (Schaefer et al., 1994), as well as premature atherosclerosis (Schreiner et al., 1993). In that latter study, no differences in Lp(a) effects were noted over race or sex. Thus, the very different distribution of Lp(a) in Blacks and Whites (high Lp[a] levels being much more common in Blacks; Sandholzer et al., 1992) may explain much of the Black/White age differences in atherosclerosis and circulatory disease risks. If so, given Lp(a)'s known relation to premature atherosclerosis, it could partly explain (along with the early onset of hypertension) the relative (to Whites) elevation of circulatory disease mortality risks in younger African Americans.

Another group of diseases that has been examined in epidemiological and clinical studies for possible racial differences in physiological mechanisms are cancers. A complication in studying racial differences in cancer risks is that there are many different types. These are generally defined by the type of tissue within which the tumor initiates—as well as the ways in which cells in the target tissue change function. Furthermore, even within a given tissue type there is considerable heterogeneity in the set of specific genetic errors occurring that triggered neoplastic growth (e.g., Fearon & Vogelstein, 1990). Nonetheless, large Black/White differentials in mortality risks have been documented for a number of cancers—for example, multiple myeloma (Bowden, Crawford, Cohen, & Noyama, 1993), prostate cancer (Ross & Henderson, 1994), and cervical cancers. Breast cancer has a higher mortality risk, and incidence, in young (up to age 40) Black females but a lower overall incidence—and incidence at later ages (Elledge, Clark, Chamness, & Osbourne, 1994). Overall, African Americans have a disproportionate burden of cancer, with higher incidence rates, earlier age at onset, and poorer survival than Whites—a heightened susceptibility that is correlated with biological markers such as mutagen sensitivity (Spitz et al., 1995).

We next examine racial differences in the gender-specific risks of mortality for all cancers, and separately for lung and breast cancer. We chose breast and lung cancer as specific causes of death to assess the Black/White mortality crossover for several reasons. First, lung and breast tumors are highly prevalent. Second, both genetic and behavioral risk factors have been identified for lung and breast cancers. Third, new data suggest that some physiological mechanisms involved in the natural history of both these cancers may also be involved in specific phases of atherogenesis. Finally, a number of theories now suggest that commonalities exist between the genetic alterations found in these (and other) cancers that may be important in biological senescence (e.g., Bacchetti, 1996; Cutler & Semsei, 1989; Morin, 1996; Warner, Fernandes, & Wang, 1995).

Possible Theoretical Foundations of Racial Differences in the Age Dependence of Cancer Risks

Understanding individual susceptibilities to various cancers is now accelerating as the techniques of molecular epidemiology mature (Perera, 1996). One classic type of susceptibility involves highly penetrant, dominant genetic mutations. Though well understood, this type of susceptibility is rare and explains little of the risk of cancer in the overall population. For example, the Li-Fraumeni syndrome, where there is a germline deletion of one allele of the p53 tumor suppressor gene, produces a nearly 100% risk of breast cancer. However, the Li-Fraumeni syndrome is extremely rare (less than 0.1%). Such genetic mechanisms as a group likely explain only about 5% of all cancers.

Often sporadic, nonhereditary forms of cancer involve the same genetic alterations (e.g., p53 mutations; Blaszyk et al., 1994) as for the inherited syndromes, but in sporadic disease, mutations are generated by environmental exposures.

More common genetic traits predisposing to cancer involve, instead, differences in the metabolism and detoxification of specific chemicals. That is, given equal exposure to an ingested carcinogen, individuals vary dramatically in their ability to metabolize the carcinogen without biologic risk. This type of model suggests that genetic susceptibility is often a necessary, but not sufficient, factor in carcinogenesis. The degree of exposure to environmental carcinogens thus is often a rate-determining step in carcinogenesis.

One way this genetic environmental interaction can occur is due to differences in the super family of cytochrome p450 enzymes. There are two basic types of p450 enzymes—phase I, or functionalization, and phase II, or conjugation enzymes (Gonzalez & Nebert, 1990). Phase I enzymes attach a chemical "handle" on both endogenous (e.g., steroid hormones, fatty acids) and exogenous chemicals. This is done so phase II enzymes can combine those functional groups with other chemicals, so that those chemicals become hydrophilic, and, therefore, excretable. In doing so, however, the phase I enzymes often convert chemicals that are often not intrinsically reactive with DNA into DNA-binding intermediate forms (by the addition of a functional group) that are genotoxic and carcinogenic. For example, 10% of the Caucasian population is highly susceptible to the induction of the p450 CYPIA1 enzyme, which catalyzes many smoking-related chemicals (Taioli et al., 1995). The level of this gene's expression ranges over individuals by 20-fold in the liver to 50-fold in the lung. These large differentials in tissue-specific p450 enzyme activity help determine where (i.e., in what organ) a tumor is induced. For example, the greater variation of p450 CYPIA1 in the lung is consistent with its association with lung cancer.

The balance of phase I and II cytochrome p450 enzyme activity is a strong determinant of the molecular dose of carcinogens—thereby substantially controlling cancer risks (Guengerich & Shimada, 1991). For example, 50% of Caucasians have a deletion in the GSTM1 gene, reducing the phase II capacity to detoxify a number of carcinogens—including many associated with smoking (Yu et al., 1995). Only 35% of Blacks carry the GSTM1 null genotype. The significance of environmental interactions with such genetic susceptibilities is shown in that, in persons with the GSTM1 null genotype, there is little lung or bladder cancer risk in nonsmokers (Bell et al., 1993). In smokers with the GSTM1 null genotype there is a strong, graded increase in bladder cancer risk associated, in a dose-related fashion, to increases in cigarette consumption. It is suggested that 25% of bladder cancer is due to the effects of this null genotype.

Of interest is that, in persons with the GSTM1 null genotype, there is an earlier age at onset for both lung and breast cancer (Ambrosone et al., 1995). Though there was little relation to the amount of cigarettes smoked, there was a link to the duration of smoking (Ryberg, Hewer, Phillips, & Haugen, 1994). GSTM1 activity was reduced by 30% in heavy smokers, suggesting they have a reduced capacity to detoxify smoking constituents. In addition to the GSTM1 null genotype, cancer risks have been found to be higher for slow "acetylators." Slow acetylators (the highest risk group) were found to represent 54% of Whites, 34% of Blacks, and 14% of Asians. The combined risk of being a slow acetylator and having a null GSTM1 was 27% in Whites, 15% in Blacks, and 2.7% in Asians (Yu et al., 1994; Yu et al., 1995). The slow acetylator genotype is associated with higher bladder cancer but lower colo-rectal cancer risks. Some evidence suggests that vitamin E may mitigate the effect of the GSTM1 null genotype effects (Grinberg-Funes et al., 1994).

At least four other genetic mechanisms affect cancer risks. One is the efficiency of DNA repair. One DNA repair enzyme (0^6-alkyldloxy guanine DNA alkyl transferase) shows interindividual variability in activity of 180-fold. The activity of a second repair enzyme (uracil DNA glycosylase) varies by more than 300-fold among individuals. Mutagen sensitivity, as a measure of DNA repair efficiency, indicated a greater risk in African Americans for lung cancer. The proportion that were mutagen sensitive was about 25% in African Americans versus 18% in Caucasians (Spitz et al., 1995).

A second mechanism involves differences in cell membrane receptor binding. This may be especially prominent in hormonally dependent cancers, for instance, breast, prostatic, or ovarian tumors. Breast and prostate cancer both show large variation in risk across racial groups (i.e., Caucasians, Blacks, and Asians).

The occupation of a receptor site by a chemical with the correct structure stimulates a message to nuclear DNA to form specific proteins. These proteins may be growth factors stimulating the proliferation of specific cell types. Some genes implicated in stimulating cancer cell growth (e.g., the c-myc oncogene) are also active in certain phases of atherogenesis (e.g., the growth of smooth muscle cells in artery walls; Yi, Stone, & Dao, 1993). Thus, some physiological processes elevating the rate of progression of specific stages in atherogenesis may also accelerate certain stages in carcinogenesis. For example, Lp(a), implicated in accelerated (and premature) atherogenesis, is also elevated in breast cancer patients (Kokoglu, Karaarslan, Karaarslan, & Baloglu, 1996)—the more advanced the stage of breast cancer, the higher the level of Lp(a). For controls, the Lp(a) level was 48.9 (mg/dl), for stage I breast cancer, 88.4, and for stage IV breast cancer, 145.0. Lp(a) may accelerate atherogenesis by blocking fibrinolysis. Such blockage of fibrinolysis could also allow tumors to form an intercellular matrix more readily so that systemically disseminated tumor cells can "seed" in metastatic sites and grow. The fact that Lp(a) is elevated in Black women could be one reason why they have higher risks than White women of early breast cancer (that tends to be more systemically aggressive) incidence and mortality.

Differences in hormonal levels may also affect the risk of both circulatory and neoplastic disease. The level of circulating and free (not bound to albumin or Sex Hormone Binding Globulin [SHBG]) testosterone in healthy Black males is 15% higher than in White males (Ross, 1994). Because prostate cancer incidence increases as the 4th to 5th power of time since the start of exposure, assuming testosterone exposure begins at puberty, a 15% higher testosterone level in African American males would translate into a 15% difference in prostate tissue aging ($1.15^{4.5}$), which produces a 1.88 higher risk of prostate cancer in Blacks—similar to the 1.91 to 1 risk ratio for prostate cancer actually observed in U.S. Black and White populations (Ross, 1994).

The elevation of testosterone may be determined prenatally in males in that Black females also have higher testosterone levels than White females (Ross & Henderson, 1994). High endogenous levels of testosterone in females, which is a chemical precursor in the production of estrogen, also appears to increase the risk of breast cancer by stimulating tumor growth (Berrino et al., 1996). A higher level of testosterone could also serve to increase lean body mass in Black females, reducing their osteoporosis risk. It might also shift female fat deposition patterns toward androgynous patterns, which are associated with higher heart disease risk and potentially higher risks of diabetes (McKeigue, Laws, Chen, Marmot, & Reaven, 1993; McKeigue et al., 1991).

A third mechanism is age changes in the immunological response to tumor cells. Tumor growth and metastases can be promoted by inappropriate immunological responses. For example, macrophages may stimulate the production of local growth factors in triggering inflammatory responses (Kundu, Beaty, Jackson, & Fulton, 1996). In breast cancer, the presence of epidermal growth factor (EGF) is indicative of aggressive tumors. EGF is not secreted by normal or malignant epithelial cells, however; it is secreted by activated macrophages drawn to the tumor by substances released by malignant cells. These substances may cause macrophages to respond physiologically to the tumor as if it were a wound to be healed (O'Sullivan, Lewis, Harris, & McGee, 1993). Such inflammatory mechanisms may also be important in circulatory diseases—especially in stimulating smooth muscle cell growth in an arterial endothelium (Buja & Willerson, 1994). Autoimmune responses also appear to be involved in malignant hypertension (Hilme, Hansson, Sandberg, Söderström, & Herlitz, 1993), which could also be related to the high risk of multiple myeloma among Blacks (Bowden et al., 1993).

A fourth recently discovered biological mechanism, which may be related to aging, has to do with the expression of telomerase. This is an enzyme that helps regulate the length of the telomere—the end portion of the chromosome that protects the DNA in a cell during cell division. In normal cells, the telomere shortens as the cell replicates. At a certain telomere length, the cell can no longer replicate. In cancer cells, however, errors occur during cell division, a crisis state is provoked, and the production of the enzyme, telomerase, which does not occur in most normal somatic cells, is stimulated. Telomerase allows the telomere to lengthen and the cell to become immortalized. This immortalization by telomerase of the malignant cell line appears to be a near universal phenomenon in human cancers (Bacchetti, 1996; Morin, 1996). Given the disparity in the risk of tumors in specific tissues between Blacks and Whites, there may be differences in how telomerase becomes expressed during cell crises. This is suggested by differences in hemopoietic cancer types among Caucasians, Asians, and Blacks (e.g., in multiple myeloma; Bowden et al., 1993). As a major factor in carcinogenesis, and important in cell replication senescence, telomere and telomerase activity could potentially affect the "rate of aging" at the cellular level in different tissue types. This mechanism, if different between Whites and Blacks, could generate racially distinct rates of aging. The expression of telomerase has been confirmed in both lung and breast cancer (e.g., Hiyama et al., 1995; Hiyama et al., 1996)—the two types of cancers whose cohort-specific mortality we examine next in detail.

Data

Cohort mortality analysis requires a lengthy time series of cause-specific mortality and population data. For cancer mortality, we had data on 35 types of cancer in individuals for the period 1950 to 1992, with race coded as White versus non-White. The Black population accounts for about 88% of the U.S. non-White population, so that trends in non-White mortality are dominated by the Black mortality experience.

Census population estimates are of uneven quality, with the White population having greater reliability at older ages and for more recent years. Published estimates of total age-specific (5-year age groups up to 75+) population counts were available for the censal years 1950, 1960, 1970, and 1980 and were used to correct the official counts for errors of undercount, race misclassification, and illegal residents (Fay, Passel, & Robinson, 1988). We applied the 1980 correction factors to the uncorrected 1990 Census counts. Single-year-of-age estimates were adjusted to match the corrected 5-year totals.

Above age 80, additional adjustments were performed to improve the accuracy of the single-year-of-age estimates. We used extinct cohort population estimates for both race groups for ages 90 to 118 for the period 1950 to 1992 (see Manton & Stallard, 1994, 1996; Stallard & Manton, 1995, for details). For ages 81 to 89 in 1950 to 1992, a blending of the products of both extinct cohort and intercensal projection methods was done using weights ranging from 0.1 to 0.9 applied over the 9-year linkage period. For ages 2 to 80, we used age-specific mortality counts to project from one census year to the next for the periods 1950-1960, 1960-1970, 1970-1980, and 1980-1989. The projection error at the end of each period was used to correct each inter-period projection count (e.g., half the 1970 error was added to the projected count for 1965 on a cohort-specific basis). A similar method was used for 1991 and 1992. Alaska and Hawaii were excluded for the 1950-1959 period.

Cohorts were defined for 5-year age groups in 1950 ranging from 23-27 to 63-67, corresponding to central birth years of 1925, 1920, . . . , 1885. Mortality and population counts were tabulated for these cohorts from 1950 to 1992, with smoothed central death rates computed using 5-year moving averages of these annual central death rates (i.e., deaths/population).

Using these data, we examined gender- and race-specific cohort mortality for the period 1950 to 1992 for lung and breast cancer, all cancer sites combined, and total mortality. We examined lung cancer because of evidence that the biological susceptibility of females to lung cancer is greater than for males (Risch et al., 1993; Ryberg et al., 1994; Wynder, 1992). We also assessed if there are Black/White differences in lung cancer risks specific to gender (e.g., as suggested by differences in Ha-ras-1 alleles; Weston et al., 1991; the Ha-ras-I VTR is 18% prevalent in African Americans and 3% prevalent in Caucasians). We examined breast cancer because it is one of the leading causes of female cancer mortality, and because there are racial differences in the age trajectory of mortality that may be explained by a two-disease (early, premenopausal; late, post-menopausal) model of breast cancer (Manton & Stallard, 1992). There is also a well-established Black/White crossover of breast cancer risks occurring at about age 40 (Krieger, 1990). We examined trends in total cancer mortality because there are risk factors that affect both many neoplastic diseases and specific phases of the process of atherogenesis. Those that cause specific mortality differentials were related to the age patterns for total mortality.

Results

Cohort Changes in Mortality 1950 to 1992

In Table 2.1 we present the gender-specific average change in smoothed (5-year moving average) single-year-of-age mortality rates for Whites and non-Whites. This statistic is similar to the cohort-specific slope of age changes in mortality rates that we could get from regression. A statistic is calculated for each cohort over the 43 years of observed mortality. Thus, the statistic is calculated over different age ranges for each of the five White and non-White birth cohorts.

For total mortality, there is a faster rate of increase in mortality rates for non-Whites than Whites for the first two birth cohorts (i.e., for persons born in 1925 and 1915; observed up to age 77 by 1992). For the three older birth cohorts, Whites have a faster average age rate of mortality increase over the 43 years of follow-up. Thus, for the 1905 birth cohort (observed from age 45 to 87) both male and female non-Whites show a slower average rate of mortality increase than Whites. It may be that at later ages (experienced after 1992) that a slower average non-White rate of increase will emerge in the two younger cohorts because not only is there a difference among the cohorts, but

TABLE 2.1 Average Change in Mortality Probability for Age x to $x + 1$ Over
the Period 1950-1992 for Five Non-White and White Birth Cohorts

Central Birth Year (y) of Cohort	Ages Observed for Cohort y	MALES Whites (%)	MALES Non-Whites (%)	MALES Percentage NW Excess (+) or Deficit (−)	FEMALES Whites (%)	FEMALES Non-Whites (%)	FEMALES Percentage of NW Excess (+) or Deficit (−)
			TOTAL MORTALITY				
1925	26-67	0.05430	0.07235	+33.2	0.03057	0.04342	+42.0
1915	35-77	0.13061	0.14577	+11.6	0.07314	0.07781	+6.4
1905	45-87	0.30061	0.28717	−4.5	0.20209	0.18608	−7.9
1895	55-97	0.62581	0.51316	−18.0	0.49390	0.41148	−16.7
1885	65-107	0.71998	0.58497	−18.8	0.64970	0.45147	−30.5
			TOTAL CANCER				
1925	26-67	0.01976	0.02693	+36.3	0.01315	0.01447	+10.0
1915	35-77	0.03783	0.04784	+26.5	0.02024	0.01889	−6.7
1905	45-87	0.05675	0.06732	+18.6	0.02603	0.02563	−1.5
1895	55-97	0.06241	0.07019	+12.5	0.02647	0.02969	+12.2
1885	65-107	0.05835	0.05589	−4.2	0.02518	0.02350	−6.7
			LUNG CANCER				
1925	26-67	0.00836	0.01061	+26.9	0.00389	0.00347	−10.8
1915	35-77	0.01341	0.01502	+12.0	0.00509	0.00376	−26.1
1905	45-87	0.01304	0.01320	+1.2	0.00390	0.00358	−8.2
1895	55-97	0.00807	0.00477	−40.9	0.00266	0.00243	−8.6
1885	65-107	0.00463	0.00696	+50.3	0.00185	0.00380	+105.4
			BREAST CANCER				
1925	26-67	—	—	—	0.00245	0.00226	−7.8
1915	35-77	—	—	—	0.00299	0.00222	−25.8
1905	45-87	—	—	—	0.00329	0.00288	−12.5
1895	55-97	—	—	—	0.00408	0.00476	+16.7
1885	65-107	—	—	—	0.00514	0.00340	−33.9

there is a systematic gradient in the slope over birth cohorts with the older birth cohorts, observed at older ages, having the largest non-White mortality advantage. This pattern is consistent with a mortality crossover but based on cohort (rather than the usual cross-sectional) data, with the trend manifest across 43 years of observation on each of five birth cohorts.

In the second panel of Table 2.1 we present the same statistics for total cancer mortality. For males there is a consistent pattern, with older non-White male cohorts having a smaller adverse trend, with the slope finally being lower for non-White males in the oldest cohort (followed from ages 65 to

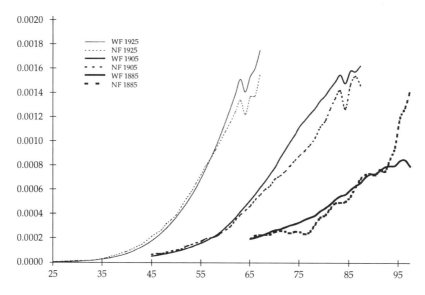

Figure 2.1. Female Lung Cancer Mortality by Cohort With Five-Year Moving Average for Whites and Non-Whites

107). For females, the age patterns are more complex. This may be partly explained by examining the slopes for lung and breast cancers.

For lung cancer, four of five birth cohorts show a non-White male disadvantage in the average rate of change in mortality with age. Only for the 1895 cohort (the primary cohort of males serving in World War I) is there a large non-White male advantage. For females, the cohort pattern is different. Non-White females have, for the four youngest cohorts, a slower average rate of lung cancer mortality increase with age than White females—a slope that is largest for the two youngest birth cohorts. Only the 1885 non-White female cohort shows a large disadvantage.

The mortality patterns for three White-non-White female cohorts are plotted in Figures 2.1 and 2.2. In Figure 2.1, there is a mortality crossover for lung cancer in the 1905 and 1925 cohorts. Mortality from lung cancer increases at about the same rate for both White and non-White females, though there is a crossover at age 57 for the 1905 birth cohort, and at age 54 for the 1925 birth cohort. The pattern for the oldest cohort is less clear with both an early and a late crossover. The numbers of non-White lung cancer deaths for females, however, is small above age 90.

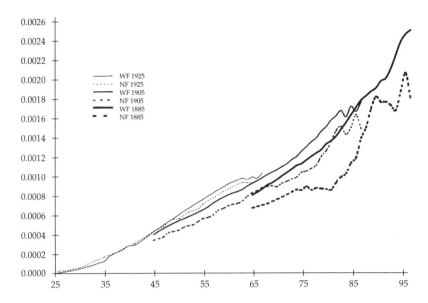

Figure 2.2. Female Breast Cancer Mortality by Cohort With Five-Year Moving Average for Whites and Non-Whites

In studying lung cancer, an area of recent interest is gender differences in susceptibility to smoking. This is because recent data suggest that females may be more susceptible to lung cancer than males. In female smokers, there was a 50% higher risk of lung cancer than in male smokers (Zang & Wynder, 1996). The differences appear to result from two mechanisms. One is gender differences in cytochrome p450 enzyme activity. This is supported by the finding that DNA adduct levels were higher for females than males with smoking dose controlled. A second mechanism involves the effects of hormones on tumor development. It was found, for older women with adenocarcinoma of the lung, that many were never smokers.

For breast cancer (Figure 2.2) we see the expected pattern, with non-White females having a slower average increase of mortality with age than for White females for the three birth cohorts. In Figure 2.2, the crossover occurs about age 45 for the 1925 birth cohort. For the other two cohorts, the crossover has already occurred with there being much higher mortality rates for White females at all ages.

Breast cancer, below age 40, has a higher incidence in non-White than White females. This shifts above age 40. This is consistent with a two-disease model of breast cancer in which early disease is more strongly genetically determined, more aggressive, and more likely to show a higher degree of histological disorganization. Late-stage breast cancer, in contrast, tends to be linked to fertility behavior, slower growing, less metastatically aggressive, and more likely estrogen receptor positive. The risk of early, premenopausal breast cancer seems to be higher for non-White females, which apparently causes the crossover for female breast cancer mortality. A similar type of pattern, with Blacks expressing more aggressive early disease, is found in prostate cancer for males (Yatani, Chigusa, Akazaki, Stemmermann, & Welsh, 1982).

There are several factors that might explain the higher risk of early breast cancer in Black females. One is that they may express a higher level of testosterone than White females. Higher testosterone levels in females have recently been shown to precede breast cancer occurrence (Berrino et al., 1996). In addition, it appears that early pregnancy stimulates breast cancer risk—especially in women with a family history of breast cancer. It is speculated that pregnancy induces hormonal changes stimulating genetically programmed predispositions to breast cancer (Colditz, Rosner, & Speizer, 1996). Testosterone is also argued to be a factor affecting male prostate cancer risks—which are higher in Black males (Ross & Henderson, 1994). These hormonal differences could also explain the lower risk of osteoporosis in Black females, for example, by producing a higher lean body mass in non-White females. Another factor, possibly related to lessened osteoporosis risk in Black females, is the lower susceptibility of Blacks to the actions of vitamin D (Moon, Bandy, & Davison, 1992), which is a potent regulator of cell differentiation. A third factor is that there are different patterns of mutations for important cell growth regulatory genes such as p53 (Blaszyk et al., 1994).

Mortality Levels for Whites and Non-Whites

Table 2.1 showed how mortality rates change within cohort over 43 years (1950 to 1992) for White and non-White males and females. To complete the picture of mortality changes, we examined the level of mortality for the set of cohorts at fixed points in time. This is like the "constant" in a regression—which complements the "slope" estimates in Table 2.1. This is shown in Table 2.2 for the year 1970, roughly the mid-point of the 1950 to 1992 time series.

In Table 2.2, for total mortality, shortly after age 75, non-White males have an advantage that, in 1970, reaches 18.1% by age 85. For females the

TABLE 2.2 Mortality Probability in 1970 for Five White and Non-White Birth Cohorts

Central Birth Year (y) of Cohort	Age of Cohort y 1970	MALES			FEMALES		
		Whites (%)	Non-Whites (%)	Percentage NW Excess (+) or Deficit (−)	Whites (%)	Non-Whites (%)	Percentage NW Excess (+) or Deficit (−)
			TOTAL MORTALITY				
1925	45	0.642	1.185	+84.6	0.355	0.754	+112.4
1915	55	1.662	2.380	+43.2	0.802	1.431	+78.4
1905	65	3.911	4.684	+19.8	1.855	3.031	+63.4
1895	75	8.363	8.687	+3.9	4.956	5.368	+8.3
1885	85	18.125	14.837	−18.1	13.688	10.983	−19.8
			TOTAL CANCER				
1925	45	0.120	0.187	+55.8	0.137	0.176	+28.5
1915	55	0.385	0.537	+39.5	0.298	0.342	+14.8
1905	65	0.885	1.022	+15.5	0.495	0.565	+14.1
1895	75	1.483	1.617	+9.0	0.772	0.718	−7.0
1885	85	2.007	1.910	−4.8	1.137	0.956	−15.9
			LUNG CANCER				
1925	45	0.046	0.074	+60.9	0.018	0.021	+16.7
1915	55	0.150	0.199	+32.7	0.041	0.037	−9.8
1905	65	0.322	0.305	−5.3	0.052	0.047	−9.6
1895	75	0.382	0.326	−14.7	0.054	0.051	−5.6
1885	85	0.259	0.224	−13.5	0.060	0.055	−8.3
			BREAST CANCER				
1925	45	—	—	—	0.043	0.044	+2.3
1915	55	—	—	—	0.075	0.062	−17.3
1905	65	—	—	—	0.093	0.083	−10.8
1895	75	—	—	—	0.115	0.083	−27.8
1885	85	—	—	—	0.163	0.114	−30.1

crossover occurs about the same time, between ages 75 to 85, with the non-White female advantage being 19.8% by age 85.

For total cancer, a roughly similar pattern is noted with the oldest non-White male cohort and the two oldest non-White female cohorts, advantaged relative to overall cancer mortality. For lung cancer, however, the pattern is different, with the non-White male and female advantages emerging earlier—between ages 55 to 65 for males, and between ages 45 to 55 for females. For breast cancer, for the cohorts examined, there is only one age (i.e., age 45) at which White females have a mortality advantage in 1970. To confirm the

TABLE 2.3 Mortality Probability in 1980 for Five Non-White and White Birth Cohorts

Central Birth Year (y) of Cohort	Age of Cohort y 1980	MALES Whites (%)	Non-Whites (%)	Percentage NW Excess (+) or Deficit (−)	FEMALES Whites (%)	Non-Whites (%)	Percentage NW Excess (+) or Deficit (−)
		TOTAL MORTALITY					
1925	55	1.307	1.941	+48.5	0.698	1.150	+64.8
1915	65	3.206	4.026	+25.6	1.658	2.360	+42.3
1905	75	7.323	7.632	+4.2	4.074	4.848	+19.0
1895	85	16.065	14.494	−9.8	11.081	9.756	−12.0
1885	95	28.889	23.629	−18.2	22.762	17.743	−22.0
		TOTAL CANCER					
1925	55	0.391	0.571	+46.0	0.310	0.340	+9.7
1915	65	0.927	1.212	+30.7	0.567	0.596	+5.1
1905	75	1.658	1.889	+13.9	0.840	0.859	+2.3
1895	85	2.347	2.604	+11.0	1.178	1.142	−3.1
1885	95	2.526	2.678	+6.0	1.333	1.321	−0.9
		LUNG CANCER					
1925	55	0.164	0.231	+40.9	0.070	0.073	+4.3
1915	65	0.367	0.441	+20.2	0.120	0.096	−20.0
1905	75	0.519	0.485	−6.6	0.114	0.089	−21.9
1895	85	0.437	0.411	−5.9	0.092	0.094	+2.2
1885	95	0.265	0.253	−4.5	0.085	0.121	+42.4
		BREAST CANCER					
1925	55	—	—	—	0.076	0.072	−5.3
1915	65	—	—	—	0.102	0.085	−16.7
1905	75	—	—	—	0.126	0.104	−17.5
1895	85	—	—	—	0.166	0.133	−19.9
1885	95	—	—	—	0.238	0.187	−21.4

stability of these patterns, we performed the same calculations 10 years later in 1980 (see Table 2.3).

For non-White males the crossover occurs at about the same age—between 75 and 85—with the two oldest non-White cohorts now having an advantage (as opposed to only the oldest cohort in 1970). For non-White females the advantage is expressed again for the two older cohorts. In addition, for the three younger cohorts, the White female and male advantage has dropped markedly in size between 1970 and 1980 (e.g., for the 1905 non-White female cohort at age 65 from 63.4% to 19.0% at age 75; likewise the

TABLE 2.4 Proportion of Mortality From Cancer Relative to Total Mortality or Total Cancer Mortality for Five Non-White and White Birth Cohorts in 1970

Central Birth Year (y) of Cohort	Age of Cohort y in 1970	MALES			FEMALES		
		Whites (%)	Non-Whites (%)	Percentage NW Excess (+) or Deficit (−)	Whites (%)	Non-Whites (%)	Percentage NW Excess (+) or Deficit (−)
		TOTAL CANCER/TOTAL MORTALITY					
1925	45	18.7	15.8	−15.6	38.6	23.3	−39.5
1915	55	23.2	22.6	−2.6	37.2	23.9	−35.7
1905	65	22.6	21.8	−3.6	26.7	18.6	−30.1
1895	75	17.7	18.6	+5.0	15.6	13.4	−14.1
1885	85	11.1	12.9	+16.3	8.3	8.7	+4.8
		LUNG CANCER/TOTAL CANCER					
1925	45	38.3	39.6	+3.2	13.1	11.9	−9.2
1915	55	39.0	37.1	−4.9	13.8	10.8	−21.4
1905	65	36.4	29.8	−18.0	10.5	8.3	−20.8
1895	75	25.8	20.2	−21.7	7.0	7.1	+1.5
1885	85	12.9	11.7	−9.1	5.3	5.8	+9.0
		BREAST CANCER/TOTAL CANCER					
1925	45	—	—	—	31.4	25.0	−20.3
1915	55	—	—	—	25.2	18.1	−28.0
1905	65	—	—	—	18.8	14.7	−21.8
1895	75	—	—	—	14.9	11.6	−22.4
1885	85	—	—	—	14.3	11.9	−16.8

White female advantage at age 65 in 1980 for the 1915 cohort has dropped to 42.3%—from 78.4% at age 55 in the 1905 cohort in 1970).

For total cancer, the patterns differ, with non-White males being disadvantaged at all ages for all cohorts in 1980, though the differentials for the younger cohorts declined. An increase in risks is noted for non-White females from 1970 to 1980 for the two oldest cohorts; the three younger female cohorts show a smaller non-White disadvantage. The pattern for lung cancer differs from that observed for total cancer. For non-White males the excess mortality of the two youngest cohorts has declined, while the non-White advantage for the two older cohorts moderated. For females the risk is clearly elevated for Whites for the 1915 and 1905 cohorts in 1980. For breast cancer the elevation of White mortality rates is now present for all five cohorts.

TABLE 2.5 Proportion of Mortality From Cancer Relative to Total Mortality or
Total Cancer Mortality for Five Non-White and White Birth Cohorts
in 1980

Central Birth Year (y) of Cohort	Age of Cohort y in 1980	MALES			FEMALES		
		Whites (%)	Non-Whites (%)	Percentage NW Excess (+) or Deficit (−)	Whites (%)	Non-Whites (%)	Percentage NW Excess (+) or Deficit (−)
		TOTAL CANCER/TOTAL MORTALITY					
1925	55	29.9	29.4	−1.7	44.4	29.6	−33.4
1915	65	28.9	30.1	+4.1	34.2	25.3	−26.2
1905	75	22.6	24.8	+9.3	20.6	17.7	−14.1
1895	85	14.6	18.0	+23.0	10.6	11.7	+10.1
1885	95	8.7	11.3	+29.6	5.9	7.4	+27.1
		LUNG CANCER/TOTAL CANCER					
1925	55	41.9	40.5	−3.5	22.6	21.5	−4.9
1915	65	39.6	36.4	−8.1	21.2	16.1	−23.9
1905	75	31.3	25.7	−18.0	13.6	10.4	−23.7
1895	85	18.6	15.8	−15.2	7.8	8.2	+5.4
1885	95	10.5	9.4	−9.9	6.4	9.2	+43.6
		BREAST CANCER/TOTAL CANCER					
1925	55	—	—	—	24.5	21.2	−13.6
1915	65	—	—	—	18.0	14.3	−20.7
1905	75	—	—	—	15.0	12.1	−19.3
1895	85	—	—	—	14.1	11.6	−17.4
1885	95	—	—	—	17.9	14.2	−20.7

Changes in the Importance of Cancer as a Cause of Death

Another way to view the mortality risk of cancer is to examine how much it represents of the total mortality risk by age and cohort. This is presented in Table 2.4 for the year 1970. In Table 2.4 we see that cancer as a proportion of all mortality is higher for non-Whites only for the 1885 cohort for females; and for males only in the 1885 and 1895 birth cohorts.

In terms of the proportion of all cancer risk that is due to lung cancer, we see different patterns for males and females. Non-White males tend to have lower risks, relative to Whites, for older cohorts, while lung cancer risks for non-White females tend to be lower for younger cohorts. For breast cancer, the non-White deficit as a proportion of total cancer occurs for all five cohorts.

As before, we can compare the 1970 patterns to the patterns observed 10 years later in 1980 (see Table 2.5). For total cancer as a proportion of total mortality there has been an increase in the excess mortality of non-White males over cohorts that is also consistent with the basic age pattern. A similar change occurred for non-White females, although the three youngest non-White female cohorts continue with a significant advantage. Though there is an increase in the non-White excess cancer risk, it is of interest that, overall, cancer is a proportionally less important cause of death at age 85 than it is at age 55.

Lung cancer decreases, and contributes less to non-White male total cancer in 1980. Non-White females maintained a similar pattern of relatively lower age-specific lung cancer mortality for the three youngest cohorts— though at ages 10 years older. The patterns of much lower non-White breast cancer mortality contribution to total cancer remains for all five female cohorts.

Conclusions

We examined total and cause-specific mortality patterns for Whites and non-Whites for five birth cohorts followed for 43 years, that is, from 1950 to 1992. In those data, we saw clear evidence of a Black/White mortality cross-over for the three oldest cohorts in terms of the overall age pattern of decline in each of the cohort mortality rates. The absolute levels of mortality cross over at about age 76 for males and between ages 65 and 75 for females in 1970 in the two older cohorts. The crossovers were manifest in the same two co-horts, to a greater degree, in 1980.

In contrast to total mortality, total cancer mortality showed no evidence of a trend toward crossover in any of the five cohorts. Thus, if the crossover were due to age misreporting, the ages at death for cancer victims presumably would have to be accurately reported to late ages while the ages reported for all other causes of death would have to be relatively unreliable. Further com-plicating the argument that the crossover might be due to age reporting error is that female lung and breast cancer show generally lower mortality slopes for non-Whites than Whites—as opposed to the pattern for, say, lung cancer in males. Finally, the patterns observed seemed to be consistent with a number of insights from the genetic and molecular epidemiology of cancer risks and their differences by both gender and race.

References

Ambrosone, C. B., Freudenheim, J. L., Graham, S., Marshall, J. R., Vena, J. E., & Brasure, J. R. (1995). Cytochrome P4501A1 and glutathione S-transferase (M1) genetic polymorphisms and postmenopausal breast cancer risk. *Cancer Research, 55,* 3483-3485.

Bacchetti, S. (1996). Telomere dynamics and telomerase activity in cell senescence and cancer. *Seminars in Cell & Developmental Biology, 7,* 31-39.

Bell, D. A., Taylor, J. A., Paulson, D. F., Robertson, C. N., Mohler, J. L., & Lucier, G. W. (1993). Genetic risk and carcinogen exposure: A common inherited defect of the carcinogen-metabolism gene glutathione S-transferase M1 (GSTM1) that increases susceptibility to bladder cancer. *Journal of the National Cancer Institute, 85,* 1159-1164.

Berrino, F., Muti, P., Micheli, A., Bolelli, G., Krogh, V., Sciajno, R., Pisani, P., Panico, S., & Secreto, G. (1996). Serum sex hormone levels after menopause and subsequent breast cancer. *Journal of the National Cancer Institute, 88*(5), 291-296.

Blaszyk, H., Vaughn, C. B., Hartmann, A., McGovern, R. M., Schroeder, J. J., & Cunningham, J. (1994). Novel pattern of p53 gene mutations in an American Black cohort with high mortality from breast cancer. *The Lancet, 343,* 1195-1197.

Bowden, M., Crawford, J., Cohen, H. J., & Noyama, O. (1993). A comparative study of monoclonal gammopathies and immunoglobulin levels in Japanese and United States elderly. *Journal of the American Geriatrics Society, 41,* 11-14.

Bronner, L. L., Kanter, D. S., & Manson, J. E. (1995). Primary prevention of stroke. *New England Journal of Medicine, 333*(21), 1392-1400.

Brown, S. A., Morrisett, J. D., Boerwinkle, E., Hutchinson, R., & Patsch, W. (1993). The relation of lipoprotein[a] concentrations and apolipoprotein[a] phenotypes with asymptomatic atherosclerosis in subjects of the Atherosclerosis Risk in Communities (ARIC) study. *Arteriosclerosis and Thrombosis, 13*(11), 1558-1566.

Buja, L. M., & Willerson, J. T. (1994). Role of inflammation in coronary plaque disruption. *Circulation, 89*(1), 503-505.

Colditz, G. A., Rosner, B. A., & Speizer, F. E. (1996). Risk factors for breast cancer according to family history of breast cancer. *Journal of the National Cancer Institute, 88*(6), 365-371.

Cooper, R., & Rotimi, C. (1994). Hypertension in populations of West African origin: Is there a genetic predisposition? *Journal of Hypertension, 12,* 215-227.

Cowie, C. C., Harris, M. I., Silverman, R. E., Johnson, E. W., & Rust, K. F. (1993). Effects of multiple risk factors on differences between Blacks and Whites in the prevalence of non-insulin-dependent diabetes mellitus in the United States. *American Journal of Epidemiology, 137*(7), 719-732.

Cutler, R. G., & Semsei, I. (1989). Development, cancer and aging: Possible common mechanisms of action and regulation. *Journal of Gerontology, 44*(6), 25-34.

Elledge, R. M., Clark, G. M., Chamness, G. C., & Osbourne, C. K. (1994). Tumor biologic factors and breast cancer prognosis among White, Hispanic, and Black women in the United States. *Journal of the National Cancer Institute, 86*(9), 705-712.

Fay, R. E., Passel, J. S., & Robinson, J. G. (1988). *The coverage of population in the 1980 Census* (Evaluation and Res. Rep. PHC80-E4, U.S. Department of Commerce). Washington, DC: Government Printing Office.

Fearon, E. R., & Vogelstein, B. (1990). A genetic model for colo-rectal tumorigenesis. *Cell, 61,* 759-767.

Gonzalez, F. J., & Nebert, D. W. (1990). Evolution of the P450 gene superfamily: Animal-plant "welfare" molecular drive, and human genetic differences in drug oxidation. *Trends in Genetics, 6,* 182-186.

Greer, J. (1993). End stage renal disease. In *Health care financing review 1992 annual supplement* (chap. 9). Baltimore, MD: U.S. Department of Health and Human Services.

Grinberg-Funes, R. A., Singh, V. N., Perera, F. P., Bell, D. A., Young, T. L., Dickey, C., Wang, C., Wang, L. W., & Santella, R. M. (1994). Polycyclic aromatic hydrocarbon-DNA adducts in smokers and their relationship to micronutrient levels and the glutathione-S-transferase M1 genotype. *Carcinogenesis, 15*(11), 2449-2454.

Guengerich, F. P., & Shimada, T. (1991). Oxidation of toxic and carcinogenic chemicals by human cytochrome P-450 enzymes. *Chemical Research Toxicology, 4,* 391-407.

Hilme, E., Hansson, L., Sandberg, L., Söderström, M., & Herlitz, H. (1993). Abnormal immune function in malignant hypertension. *Journal of Hypertension, 11,* 989-994.

Hiyama, E., Gollahon, L., Kataoka, T., Kuroi, K., Yokoyama, T., Gazdar, A., Hiyama, K., Piatyszek, M., & Shay, J. W. (1996). Telomerase activity in human breast tumors. *Journal of the National Cancer Institute, 88*(2), 116-122.

Hiyama, E., Yokoyama, T., Tatsumoto, N., Hiyama, K., Imamura, Y., Murakami, Y., Kodama, T., Piatyszek, M. A., Shay, J. W., & Matsuura, Y. (1995). Telomerase activity in gastric cancer. *Cancer Research, 55*(15), 3258-3262.

Jenkins, D. J. A., Woleve, T. M. S., Spiller, G., Buckley, G., Lam, Y., Jenkins, A. L., & Josse, R. G. (1989). Hypocholesterolemic effect of vegetable protein in a hypocaloric diet. *Atherosclerosis, 78,* 99-107.

Jeunemaitre, X., Soubrier, F., Kotelevstev, Y. V., Lifton, R. P., Williams, C. S., Charru, A., Hunt, S. C., Hopkins, P. N., Williams, R. R., Lalouel, J. M., & Corvol, P. (1992). Molecular basis of human hypertension: Role of angiotensinogen. *Cell, 71,* 169-180.

Keil, J. E., Sutherland, S. E., Knapp, R. G., Lackland, D. T., Gazes, P. C., & Tyroler, H. A. (1993). Mortality rates and risk factors for coronary disease in Black as compared with White men and women. *New England Journal of Medicine, 329*(2), 73-78.

Kestenbaum, B. (1992). A description of the extreme aged population based on improved medicare enrollment data. *Demography, 29*(4), 565-581.

Kokoglu, E., Karaarslan, I., Karaarslan, H. M., & Baloglu, H. (1996). Elevated serum Lp(a) levels in the early and advanced stages of breast cancer. *Cancer, Biochemistry and Biophysics, 14,* 133-136.

Krieger, N. (1990). Social class and the Black/White crossover in the age-specific incidence of breast cancer: A study linking census-derived data to population-based registry records. *American Journal of Epidemiology, 131,* 804-814.

Kundu, N., Beaty, T. L., Jackson, M. J., & Fulton, A. M. (1996). Anti-metastatic and anti-tumor activities of Interleukin 10 in a murine model of breast cancer. *Journal of the National Cancer Institute, 88*(8), 536-541.

Lew, E. A., & Garfinkel, L. (1990). Mortality at ages 75 and older in the Cancer Prevention Study (CPSI). *Cancer Journal for Clinicians, 40*(4), 210-224.

Manton, K. G., Patrick, C. H., & Johnson, K. (1989). Health differentials between Blacks and Whites: Recent trends in mortality and morbidity. In D. P. Willis (Ed.), *Health policies and Black Americans* (pp. 129-200). New Brunswick, NJ: Transaction Books.

Manton, K. G., & Stallard, E. (1992). Demographics (1950-1987) of breast cancer in birth cohorts of older women [Special issue]. *Journal of Gerontology, 47,* 32-42.

Manton, K. G., & Stallard, E. (1994, December). *Ethnic health and disability differences in the U.S. elderly population.* Paper presented at the Workshop on Racial and Ethnic Differences in Health in Late Life, sponsored by the National Institute on Aging and the National Research Council Commission on Behavioral and Social Sciences and Education, Washington, DC.

Manton, K. G., & Stallard, E. (1996). Longevity in the U.S.: Age and sex specific evidence on life span limits from mortality patterns: 1962-1990. *Journal of Gerontology: Biological Sciences, 51A*(5), B362-B375.

Manton, K. G., Stallard, E., & Wing, S. (1991). Analyses of Black and White differentials in the age trajectory of mortality in two closed cohort studies. *Statistics in Medicine, 10,* 1043-1059.

Marcovina, S. M., Albers, J. J., Jacobs, D. R., Perkins, L. L., Lewis, C. E., Howard, B. V., & Savage, P. (1993). Lipoprotein[a] concentrations and apolipoprotein[a] phenotypes in Caucasians and Africans: The CARDIA Study. *Arteriosclerosis and Thrombosis, 13,* 1037-1045.

Markides, K. S., & Keith, V. M. (1995). Race, aging and health in the USA. *Review in Clinical Gerontology, 5,* 339-345.

Materson, B. J., Reda, D. J., Cushman, W. C., Massie, B. M., Freis, E. D., Kochar, M. S., Hamburger, R. J., Fye, C., Lakshman, R., Gottdiener, J., Ramirez, E. A., & Henderson, W. G. (1993). Single-drug therapy for hypertension in men: A comparison of six antihypertensive agents with placebo. *New England Journal of Medicine, 328*(13), 914-921.

McKeigue, P. M., Laws, A., Chen, Y. D., Marmot, M. G., & Reaven, G. M. (1993). Relation of plasma triglyceride and ApoB levels to insulin-mediated suppression of nonesterified fatty acids: Possible explanation for sex differences in lipoprotein pattern. *Arteriosclerosis and Thrombosis, 13*(8), 1187-1192.

McKeigue, P. M., Shah, B., & Marmot, M. G. (1991). Relation of central obesity and insulin resistance with high diabetes prevalence and cardiovascular risk in South Asians. *The Lancet, 337,* 382-386.

Moon, J., Bandy, B., & Davison, A. J. (1992). Hypothesis: Etiology of atherosclerosis and osteoporosis: Are imbalances in the calciferol endocrine system implicated. *Journal of the American College of Nutrition, 11*(5), 567-583.

Morin, G. B. (1996). The structure and properties of mammalian telomerase and their potential impact on human disease. *Seminars in Cell & Developmental Biology, 7,* 5-13.

National Center for Health Statistics. (1995). *Health, United States, 1994.* Washington, DC: Public Health Service.

O'Sullivan, C., Lewis, C. E., Harris, A. L., & McGee, J. O. (1993). Secretion of epidermal growth factor by macrophages associated with breast carcinoma. *The Lancet, 342,* 148-149.

Parra, H. J., Luyeye, I., Bouramoue, C., Demarquilly, C., & Fruchart, J. C. (1987). Black-White differences in serum Lp(a) lipoprotein levels. *Clinica Chimica Acta, 168*(1), 27-31.

Perera, F. P. (1996). Molecular epidemiology: Insights into cancer susceptibility, risk assessment, and prevention. *Journal of the National Cancer Institute, 88*(8), 496-509.

Perneger, T. V., Klag, M. J., Feldman, H. I., & Whelton, P. K. (1993). Projections of hypertension-related renal disease in middle-aged residents of the United States. *Journal of the American Medical Association, 269*(10), 1272-1277.

Qualheim, R. E., Rostand, S. G., Kirk, K. A., & Luke, R. G. (1991). Changing patterns of end-stage renal disease due to hypertension. *American Journal of Kidney Disease, 18,* 336-343.

Rader, D. J., & Brewer, H. B., Jr. (1992). Lipoprotein (a): Clinical approach to a unique atherogenic lipoprotein. *Journal of the American Medical Association, 267*(8), 1109-1112.

Risch, H. A., Howe, G. R., Jain, M., Burch, J. D., Holowaty, E. J., & Miller, A. B. (1993). Are female smokers at higher risk for lung cancer than male smokers? A case-control analysis by histologic type. *American Journal of Epidemiology, 138*(5), 281-293.

Rosenwaike, L., & Logue, B. (1983). Accuracy of death certificate ages for the extreme aged. *Demography, 20,* 569-585.

Ross, R. K. (1994). Prostate cancer. In D. Schottenfeld & J. F. Fraumeni (Eds.), *Cancer epidemiology and prevention*. New York: Oxford University Press.

Ross, R. K., & Henderson, B. E. (1994). Do diet and androgens alter prostate cancer risk via a common etiologic pathway? *Journal of the National Cancer Institute, 86*(4), 252-254.

Ryberg, D., Hewer, A., Phillips, D. H., & Haugen, A. (1994). Different susceptibility to smoking-induced DNA damage among male and female lung cancer patients. *Cancer Research, 54,* 5801-5803.

Sandholzer, C., Saha, N., Kark, J. D., Rees, A., Jaross, W., Dieplinger, H., Hoppichler, F., Boerwinkle, E., & Utermann, G. (1992). Apo(a) isoforms predict risk for coronary heart disease. *Arteriosclerosis and Thrombosis, 12*(10), 1214-1226.

Schaefer, E. J., Lamon-Fava, S., Jenner, J. L., McNamara, J. R., Orodovas, J. M., Davis, C. E., Abolafia, J. M., Lippel, K., & Levy, R. I. (1994). Lipoprotein(a) levels and risk of coronary heart disease in men: The Lipid Research Clinics Coronary Primary Prevention Trial. *Journal of the American Medical Association, 271*(13), 999-1003.

Schreiner, P. J., Morrisett, J. D., Sharrett, A. R., Patsch, W., Tyroler, H. A., Wu, K., & Heiss, G. (1993). Lipoprotein [a] as a risk factor for preclinical atherosclerosis. *Arteriosclerosis and Thrombosis, 13*(6), 826-833.

Selby, J. V., Austin, M. A., Sandholzer, C., Quesenberry, C. P., Zhang, D., Mayer, E., & Utermann, G. (1994). Environmental and behavioral influences on plasma lipoprotein(a) concentration in women twins. *Preventive Medicine, 23,* 345-353.

Sorlie, P., Rogot, E., Anderson, R., Johnson, N., & Backlund, E. (1992). Black-White mortality differences by family income. *The Lancet, 340,* 346-350.

Spitz, M. R., Hsu, T. C., Wu, X., Fueger, J. J., Amos, C. I., & Roth, J. A. (1995). Mutagen sensitivity as a biological marker of lung cancer risk in African Americans. *Cancer Epidemiological Biomarkers Prevention, 4,* 99-103.

Stallard, E., & Manton, K. G. (1995, October). *The trajectory of mortality from age 80 to 110.* Paper presented at the Southern Demographic Association Annual Meeting, Richmond, VA.

Svetkey, L. P., George, L. K., Burchett, B. M., Morgan, P. A., & Blazer, D. G. (1993). Black/White differences in hypertension in the elderly: A epidemiologic analysis in central North Carolina. *American Journal of Epidemiology, 137*(1), 64-73.

Taioli, E., Crofts, F., Trachman, J., Demopoulos, R., Toniolo, P., & Garte, S. J. (1995). A specific African-American CYP1A1 polymorphism is associated with adenocarcinoma of the lung. *Cancer Research, 55,* 474-478.

Warner, H. R., Fernandes, G., & Wang, E. (1995). A unifying hypothesis to explain the retardation of aging and tumorigenesis by caloric restriction. *Journal of Gerontology Bioscience, 50*(3), B107-B109.

Weston, A., Vineis, P., Caporaso, N. E., Krontiris, T. G., Lonergan, J. A., & Sugimura, H. (1991). Racial variation in the distribution of Ha-ras-1 alleles. *Molecular Carcinogenesis, 4,* 265-268.

Wing, S., Manton, K., Stallard, E., Hames, C., & Tyroler, H. (1985). The Black/White mortality crossover: Investigation in a community-based study. *Journal of Gerontology, 40,* 78-84.

Wynder, E. L. (1992). The dose makes the therapy. *Journal of the National Cancer Institute, 84*(9), 658-659.

Yantani, K., Chigusa, I., Akazaki, K., Stemmermann, G. N., & Welsh, R. A. (1982). Geographic pathology of prostatic carcinoma. *International Journal of Cancer, 29,* 611-616.

Yi, G., Stone, S., & Dao, B. (1993). Low ventricular performance and high resistance in established hypertension in adults. *Journal of Hypertension, 11*(11), 1243-1251.

Yu, M. C., Ross, R. K., Chan, K. K., Henderson, B. E., Skipper, P. L., & Tannenbaum, S. R. (1995). Glutathione S-transferase M1 genotype affects aminobiphenyl-hemoglobin adduct levels in

White, Black and Asian smokers and non-smokers. *Cancer Epidemiological Biomarkers Prevention, 4,* 861-864.

Yu, M. C., Skipper, P. L., Taghizadeh, K., Tannenbaum, S. R., Chan, K. K., Henderson, B. E., & Ross, R. K. (1994). Acetylator phenotype, aminobiphenyl-hemoglobin adduct levels, and bladder cancer risk in White, Black, and Asian men in Los Angeles, California. *Journal of the National Cancer Institute, 86*(9), 712-716.

Zang, E. A., & Wynder, E. L. (1996). Differences in lung cancer risk between men and women: Examination of the evidence. *Journal of the National Cancer Institute, 88*(3/4), 183-192.

Adult Mortality Among Asian Americans and Pacific Islanders

A Review of the Evidence

Irma T. Elo

Mortality estimates based on vital statistics and census data have consistently pointed to a sizable health advantage for Asian Americans and Pacific Islanders compared to White Americans. The Census Bureau's estimates of life expectancies at birth for 1995, which are the basis for the Bureau's latest population projections, for example, show life expectancies at birth of 79.3 and 84.9 years for Asian and Pacific Islander males and females, respectively, compared to 73.6 and 80.1 for White males and females, respectively (Day, 1996). The above estimates for Asian and Pacific Islanders place them above those recorded for Japan, which has the highest documented life expectancies in the world based on good quality data: 76.6 for males and 83.0 for females in 1994 (Japan Aging Research Center, 1996). The question is, of course, whether the U.S. estimates are reliable. Inconsistencies in the coding of race on birth, death, and census records raise serious questions about the reliability of mortality estimates for Asian Americans and Pacific Islanders based on these data sources (Elo & Preston, in press; McKenney & Bennett, 1994).

This chapter reviews and evaluates recent evidence on mortality estimates among Asian Americans and Pacific Islanders in the United States by age, sex, and ethnic origin. The emphasis is on mortality at adult ages in the

AUTHOR'S NOTE: This research is supported by grants from the National Institute of Aging, AG10168 and 5P20AG12836. I would like to thank Samuel Preston for valuable comments and suggestions.

41

1989-1991 period in comparison to White Americans. Main attention is given to mortality from all causes combined, although reference will also be made to cause-specific differentials. Several recent studies have drawn attention to the limited availability of data for the study of health and mortality among Asian Americans and Pacific Islanders, particularly among the many cultural subgroups that make up this population in the United States (e.g., Hahn & Stroup, 1994; Yu & Liu, 1992). The large influx of Asian immigrants since the liberalization of U.S. immigration laws in 1965 has greatly diversified the composition of the Asian and Pacific Islander population in the United States relative to what it was in earlier decades of the 20th century. Due to lack of data on health conditions among the many Asian and Pacific Islander subgroups, however, relatively little is known about the variability in health conditions among them. The lack of available data also necessarily restricts the scope of this investigation.

I begin by discussing the ethnic and demographic composition of the Asian and Pacific Islander population in the United States and the availability of national-level data for the study of health and mortality among this population subgroup to set the subsequent discussion of mortality in a broader context. I then examine mortality differentials at adult ages among Chinese, Japanese, Filipinos, Other Asians and Pacific Islanders, and all Asian and Pacific Islanders combined with reference to White Americans. The availability of data dictates the focus on the above Asian Pacific Islander subgroups. As will become clear from the following discussion, the "Other Asian and Pacific Islander" category is a composite of numerous Asian and Pacific Islander-origin populations whose mortality experience may vary substantially. In the discussion of mortality among Asians and Pacific Islanders, I also review issues related to data quality. Here I examine evidence of studies that have investigated the consistency of reporting of race in vital statistics and census data among Asian and Pacific Islanders, including Japanese, Chinese, and Filipinos. The focus then shifts to an analysis of mortality among Asians and Pacific Islanders based on linked data files, and I end with a discussion of cause-specific mortality differentials.

Demographic Structure

Asian Americans and Pacific Islanders are the fastest growing racial/ethnic group in the United States. The Asian American population grew by 141% between 1970 and 1980 and by 99% between 1980 and 1990. Respective figures for the United States as a whole were 11% and 9% (Barringer, Gardner, & Levin, 1993, table 2.4A). The absolute number of Pacific Islanders, who make up only about 5% of the Asian and Pacific Islander population, increased by 46% between 1970 and 1980 and by 41% between 1980 and 1990 (Barringer et al., 1993, p. 268; U.S. Bureau of the Census, 1992). The rapid growth of Asian Americans and Pacific Islanders is expected to continue well into the 21st century. The Census Bureau's latest population projections estimate faster growth for this population subgroup than for any other for which separate projections are made. According to the Bureau's medium-range projections, the number of Asian Americans and Pacific Islanders will increase by 267.1% between 1995 and 2050, compared to 35.1% and 82.8% projected increases for Whites and African Americans, respectively. Only the projected growth of the Hispanic-origin population, estimated at 258.3% between 1995 and 2050, approaches that of Asian Americans and Pacific Islanders (Day, 1996, table K). According to the Census Bureau's medium range projections, Asian Americans and Pacific Islanders will make up 8.7% of the total U.S. population by 2050, up from 2.9% in 1990 (Day, 1996, table J; U.S. Bureau of the Census, 1992).

The key factor determining the growth and composition of the Asian and Pacific Islander population in the United States has been and continues to be immigration. It has been estimated, for example, that close to 3.5 million Asian immigrants and refugees entered the United States between 1971 and 1990 (Barringer et al., 1993, tables 2.1 and 2.3). The continued net inflow of immigrants in the early decades of the 21st century is also the main factor in the Census Bureau's projections discussed above. Shifts in immigrant flows among various Asian countries and the rapid increase in the total number of in-migrants during the past two decades in turn has dramatically changed the composition of the Asian and Pacific Islander population relative to what it was in earlier decades of this century (see Barringer et al., 1993, for a discussion of Asian immigration to the United States).

For most of this century, the Japanese were the largest Asian-origin population, representing more than half of all Asian Americans as late as 1960 (Barringer et al., 1993, p. 38). By 1980, however, both Chinese and Filipinos had surpassed the size of the Japanese population due to the large increase in the number of Chinese and Filipino immigrants following the liberalization of the U.S. immigration laws in 1965, while immigration from Japan during this period remained modest. By 1990, the Chinese made up about 23% of all

Asian Americans and Pacific Islanders, Filipinos 19%, and Japanese only about 12% (Table 3.1). The remaining 46% consists of many diverse subgroups, among whom the most prominent are Asian Indians, Koreans, and Vietnamese, whose numbers in the United States had been relatively small prior to 1970. Others include many relatively small Asian-origin populations, including Cambodians, Hmong, Laotians, Thais, and many others.[1] Among Pacific Islanders, Hawaiians dominate, accounting for about 58% of the total (Table 3.1). Other groups in this category include relatively small numbers of individuals from Samoa, Guam, and Micronesia, and individuals from other islands in the Pacific.

Because net immigration from Asia has been the predominant factor in the growth of the Asian and Pacific Islander population in the United States, a very large percentage of this population is foreign-born compared to other racial and ethnic groups enumerated in the 1990 Census. More than 60% of all Asian Americans and Pacific Islanders were foreign-born, compared to only 6.3% of the rest of the U.S. population (Table 3.1; see also U.S. Bureau of the Census, 1993). The percentage foreign-born also varies among the Asian and Pacific Islander subgroups. Among the three largest Asian populations, the Japanese stand out in having a relatively small percentage of their population enumerated as having been born outside the United States in comparison with the Chinese and the Filipinos. Overall, 32.4% of the Japanese are foreign-born compared to 69.3% of the Chinese and 64.4% of the Filipinos. Among the Japanese, the percentage foreign-born seems particularly low at ages 65+; only 17.2% of Japanese Americans in this age range were foreign-born in contrast to over 80% and over 90% of the Chinese and the Filipinos, respectively.[2] An extremely high proportion of Other Asian Americans is also foreign-born, 74.0% overall and more than 90% at ages 25 and above (Table 3.1). In contrast to Asian Americans, the percentage foreign-born among Pacific Islanders residing in the United States is low, only 13% (Table 3.1).

The growing heterogeneity of the Asian and Pacific Islander population calls into question the logic of grouping these population subgroups under the rubric of Asian and Pacific Islander. Of all federal data collection agencies, however, only the Census Bureau has substantially changed the way it collects and publishes information for Asian Americans and Pacific Islanders over time. The race question in the 1970 Census, for example, included nine separate so-called race items, five of which pertained to Asian Americans and/or Pacific Islanders, namely Chinese, Filipino, Japanese, Korean, and

TABLE 3.1 Asian and Pacific Islanders and Selected Asian and Pacific Islander Subgroups, United States, 1990

Ethnic Origin	Number	Foreign-Born
All API	7,273,622	63.1%
Age 25+	4,300,113	78.5%
Age 65+	454,458	69.7%
Median age	29.8	35.2
All Asian	6,908,638	65.6%
Age 25+	4,117,839	81.1%
Age 65+	439,723	71.6%
Median age	30.1	35.2
Chinese	1,645,472	69.3%
Age 25+	1,067,213	83.6%
Age 65+	133,977	83.5%
Median age	32.1	36.7
Filipino	1,406,770	64.4%
Age 25+	852,405	84.7%
Age 65+	104,206	94.6%
Median age	31.3	38.7
Japanese	847,562	32.4%
Age 25+	607,463	35.4%
Age 65+	105,932	17.2%
Median age	36.3	38.5
Other Asian	3,008,834	74.0%
Age 25+	1,590,758	95.7%
Age 65+	95,605	92.6%
Pacific Islanders	365,024	13.0%
Age 25+	182,274	17.9%
Age 65+	14,735	13.6%
Median age	25.0	31.6
Hawaiian	211,014	2.9%
Age 25+	110,763	2.6%
Age 65+	10,233	2.3%
Median age	26.3	30.5

SOURCE: U.S. Bureau of the Census (1992, table 23; 1993, table 1).

NOTE: The percentage foreign-born and the median age of the foreign-born are based on sample data; the size of the population and the median age of the entire population are based on 100% count data.

Hawaiian. Separate tabulations were also published for these population subgroups (U.S. Bureau of the Census, 1973). In the 1980 Census, the race question was expanded to include 15 items, 9 of which pertained to Asian

Americans and Pacific Islanders—Japanese, Chinese, Filipino, Korean, Vietnamese, Asian Indian, Hawaiian, Guamanian, and Samoan—with space for write-in responses provided under a category "Other" (U.S. Bureau of the Census, 1983). The 1990 race question was similar to the one included in the 1980 Census, except that an "Other API" category with space for a write-in response was added (U.S. Bureau of the Census, 1992). Separate tabulations in both years were published for 19 Asian- and Pacific Islander-origin populations, namely Chinese, Filipino, Japanese, Korean, Asian Indian, Vietnamese, Laotian, Thai, Cambodian, Pakistani, Indonesian, Hmong, Polynesian, Hawaiian, Samoan, Tongan, Micronesian, Guamanian, and Melanesian (U.S. Bureau of the Census, 1988, 1993).

Other federal agencies for the most part follow the Office of Management and Budget Directive No. 15, which sets standards for the collection of federal statistics and for administrative reporting on race and ethnicity. According to this directive, race must be classified into at least four broad categories—White, Black, American Indian or Alaskan Native, and Asian and Pacific Islander (Office of Management and Budget, 1978; see also Hahn, 1992).[3] This classification is used by the National Center of Health Statistics (NCHS) in its survey programs, including the Health Interview Survey and the National Health and Nutrition Examination Survey, two key sources of information on health status and prevalence of selected chronic conditions among the U.S. civilian noninstitutionalized population. Because Asians and Pacific Islanders represented only about 2.9% of the entire U.S. population in 1990, routine tabulations of health status or prevalence of chronic conditions, even for the Asian and Pacific Islander population as a whole, is problematic based on these or other NCHS surveys (see, e.g., Yu, Drury, & Liu, 1982; Yu & Liu, 1992, 1994).

Only in NCHS vital statistics data is it possible to make some distinctions among Asian Americans and Pacific Islanders. Since 1979, the NCHS has published data separately for the three largest Asian American populations, Chinese, Filipino, and Japanese. In some prior years, data were available for Chinese and Japanese. In addition, data are published for one Pacific Islander group, Hawaiian (including part-Hawaiian), with the rest of Asian Americans and Pacific Islanders making up the residual category (National Center for Health Statistics, 1984). In 1992, the NCHS expanded the racial detail included in mortality statistics. The new coding scheme expanded the subcategories under Asian and Pacific Islander to include Chinese, Japanese, Hawaiian, Filipino, Asian Indian, Korean, Samoan, Vietnamese, Guamanian, and other (Yu & Liu, 1992). Because intercensal estimates of population are available only for the Asian and Pacific Islander population as a whole (e.g., Hollman, 1993), however, mortality estimates for Asian- and Pacific Islander-origin subgroups are possible only around the time of the Decennial Censuses.

The lack of national-level data on health conditions among Asians and Pacific Islanders has meant that evidence on health conditions among them have mostly come from smaller-scale epidemiologic investigations. State- and national-level vital statistics data in turn have provided the basis for mortality estimates (Barringer et al., 1993; Yu & Liu, 1992). Next, I examine national-level mortality estimates among Japanese, Chinese, Filipinos, and Other Asians and Pacific Islanders in reference to White Americans around the time of the 1990 Decennial Census.

Mortality Estimates Based on Vital Statistics and Census Data

Data for mortality estimates come from 1989-1991 vital statistics data on deaths and the 1990 Census of Population. Death rates are obtained in a conventional manner, using deaths from vital statistics in the numerator and the Census Bureau's estimates of population in the denominator. Information on deaths is obtained from 1989-1991 NCHS Mortality Detailed Files, which differentiate deaths among Whites, Blacks, American Indians, Chinese, Hawaiians (including part-Hawaiians), Japanese, Filipinos, Other Asians or Pacific Islanders, and "Others" (National Center for Health Statistics, 1992, 1993a, 1993b).[4] Based on place-of-birth information, I further estimate mortality among the foreign-born. Because place of birth is not fully reported in the Mortality Detail Files, a range of estimates is shown for the foreign-born; first, deaths for which place-of-birth information is missing are assumed to be deaths of the native-born and, second, these deaths are assigned to the foreign-born.

The population data for the denominator in the construction of mortality estimates are based on the 1990 Census of Population. The 100% count data are employed in the estimation of mortality for the Asian and Pacific Islander population as a whole and for selected Asian American subgroups in the comparison of their mortality to that of White Americans (U.S. Bureau of the Census, 1992). To examine mortality among the foreign-born Asian and Pacific Islanders, I had to rely on population estimates based on sample data from the 1990 Census (U.S. Bureau of the Census, 1993). Data on place of birth are not available from the 100% census count. Although sampling error throws some uncertainty on the exact level of mortality among the foreign-born, the size of the error is unlikely to alter the broader conclusions.[5] Because the Census of Population was taken on April 1, 1990, I have further adjusted the population counts used in the denominator in the construction of mortality rates to July 1, 1990. To make these adjustments, I use the ratios of the estimated resident population on July 1, 1990 to that of April 1, 1990 by age group for the entire Asian/Pacific Islander population (Hollman, 1993). Separate estimates for Asian/Pacific Islander subgroups are not available. The population data used in the calculation of death rates have not been adjusted for census undercount. No estimates of census undercount are available for Asian and Pacific Islanders. The lack of adjustment has the effect of slightly overestimating death rates at younger ages, particularly for males, where the estimated net census undercount rates are the highest (Robinson, Ahmed, Das Gupta, & Woodrow, 1993).[6]

To examine cause-specific mortality differentials among Asian Americans and Pacific Islanders relative to White Americans, age-standardized, cause-specific mortality rates were calculated for the three most important causes of death at ages 45 and above—namely diseases of the heart, malignant neoplasms, and cerebrovascular diseases—and for all other causes combined.[7] Age-standardized death rates are calculated for the age interval 45 through 84. The standard population used in these calculations is the estimated total U.S. resident population on July 1, 1990 (Hollman, 1993). The death rates shown for the open-ended age interval, 85+, have not been age-standardized.

Results

Death rates for White Americans, Chinese, Filipinos, Japanese, other Asians and Pacific Islanders, and for the Asian and Pacific Islander population as a whole are shown in Tables 3.2, 3.3, and 3.4, and Figures 3.1 and 3.2. Relative to White Americans, mortality among Asian and Pacific Islanders appears to be extremely low. For the group as a whole, the advantage appears greater at younger than at older ages. Estimated death rates for Asian and Pacific Islander males, for example, are less than half of the White rates below age 50. At ages 75+ they are 32% to 36% below those of White males. The advantage of Asian and Pacific Islander females relative to White females appears to be somewhat less but nevertheless substantial; death rates for Asian and Pacific Islander females are 37% to 46% below White female rates at ages 25 to 29 through 80 to 84; and 29% below the White rates at ages 85+.

As noted above, Asian Americans and Pacific Islanders residing in the United States represent a composite of numerous subpopulations that are likely to have very different health profiles. Some of this potential variability is evident when we examine death rates among the three largest Asian-origin populations relative to all Other Asian and Pacific Islanders combined. According to my tabulations, mortality is lower among the Chinese, Japanese, and Filipinos at all, except at the very highest ages, than among Other Asians and Pacific Islanders combined (Tables 3.2 and 3.3, and Figures 3.1 and 3.2). Little is known about the level of mortality among the many subpopulations that make up the "All Other" category. The only population in this group for which separate mortality estimates are available is the Hawaiian-origin subgroup. Mortality among Hawaiians has been estimated to be higher than among Japanese, Chinese, and Filipinos. Estimates of life expectancies at birth for 1980 in Hawaii, for example, show life expectancy at birth to be lowest for Hawaiians, 74.0, and highest for Chinese, 80.2, with intermediate values recorded for Japanese, 79.7, and Filipinos, 78.8 (Barringer et al., 1993, table 3.5).

Estimates of age-specific death rates for Chinese, Japanese, and Filipinos shown in Tables 3.2 and 3.3 and in Figures 3.1 and 3.2 are also well below those of Whites. The age-specific rates for Filipino males are 34% to 59% below White male rates; the respective figures are 36% to 72% for Chinese males and 37% to 78% for Japanese males. The figures for females range from 39% to 55% below White rates for Filipinos, 34% to 61% for Chinese, and 30% to 55% for Japanese. The differences in death rates are much smaller among the three Asian subgroups.

Age-specific death rates for the foreign-born in most instances are lower than the overall age-specific death rates (Table 3.4). For the entire Asian and Pacific Islander population, the age-specific death rates for the foreign-born are lower than for the group as a whole, except at the oldest ages; the same is true for individuals who fall within the category "Other Asian and Pacific Islander." For Chinese and Filipinos, age-specific death rates for the foreign-born are not consistently lower or higher than the overall rates. In general, the differences in overall death rates and those of the foreign-born are not large, which is expected given that a very substantial proportion of Other Asians and Pacific Islanders, Chinese, and Filipinos are foreign-born.

TABLE 3.2 Death Rates Based on Vital Statistics and Census Data: White and
Asian and Pacific Islander Males, 1989-1991 (death rates per 1,000)

			Males			
			Death Rates (per 1,000)			
Age Group	Whites	Asian/ Pacific Islanders	Chinese	Japanese	Filipino	Other Asian/ Pacific Islander
25–29	1.70	0.83	0.47	0.68	0.71	1.09
30–34	2.03	0.81	0.57	0.46	0.88	1.00
35–39	2.47	1.11	0.94	0.84	1.08	1.29
40–44	3.09	1.44	1.23	1.23	1.48	1.61
45–49	4.46	2.19	1.65	2.01	1.83	2.63
50–54	7.03	3.61	3.00	3.05	3.21	4.27
55–59	11.52	6.05	5.56	5.40	5.13	7.14
60–64	18.47	9.98	8.44	9.81	8.88	12.37
65–69	27.63	16.01	14.48	14.98	14.23	20.36
70–74	42.84	24.75	23.34	24.09	21.85	29.85
75–79	65.13	41.67	41.45	40.86	37.44	48.96
80–84	101.35	65.18	64.90	61.12	66.46	66.31
85+	181.05	123.32	123.64	132.47	122.39	110.49
		Ratios of Asian American and Pacific Islander Rates to White Rates				
25–29		0.49	0.28	0.40	0.42	0.64
30–34		0.40	0.28	0.22	0.44	0.49
35–39		0.45	0.38	0.34	0.44	0.52
40–44		0.47	0.40	0.40	0.48	0.52
45–49		0.49	0.37	0.45	0.41	0.59
50–54		0.51	0.43	0.43	0.46	0.61
55–59		0.53	0.48	0.47	0.45	0.62
60–64		0.54	0.46	0.53	0.48	0.67
65–69		0.58	0.52	0.54	0.51	0.74
70–74		0.58	0.54	0.56	0.51	0.70
75–79		0.64	0.64	0.63	0.57	0.75
80–84		0.64	0.64	0.60	0.66	0.65
85+		0.68	0.68	0.73	0.68	0.61

SOURCES: National Center for Health Statistics (1992, 1993a, 1993b); U.S. Bureau of the Census (1992).

The largest fraction of native-born individuals is found among the Japanese.
A comparison of overall death rates to those of the foreign-born among the
Japanese show higher mortality among the foreign-born women in all but one

TABLE 3.3 Death Rates Based on Vital Statistics and Census Data: White and
Asian and Pacific Islander Females, 1989-1991 (death rates per 1,000)

| | | | *Females* | | | |
| | | | *Death Rates (per 1,000)* | | | |
Age Group	*Whites*	*Asian/ Pacific Islanders*	*Chinese*	*Japanese*	*Filipino*	*Other Asian/Pacific Islander*
25–29	0.57	0.35	0.26	0.31	0.31	0.41
30–34	0.73	0.41	0.29	0.40	0.36	0.51
35–39	0.98	0.61	0.50	0.44	0.60	0.72
40–44	1.48	0.88	0.63	0.77	0.81	1.08
45–49	2.43	1.42	0.98	1.29	1.21	1.79
50–54	4.04	2.43	1.89	2.84	1.96	2.88
55–59	6.52	3.98	3.11	3.79	3.32	5.25
60–64	10.29	5.60	4.50	5.56	4.85	7.28
65–69	15.38	8.63	7.55	7.91	7.28	11.59
70–74	24.26	13.49	12.71	11.69	11.26	17.67
75–79	38.08	23.80	25.29	23.86	17.12	27.94
80–84	63.46	40.19	41.55	39.52	30.35	46.86
85+	141.91	100.05	100.10	114.25	73.50	90.81
	Ratios of Asian American and Pacific Islander Rates to White Rates					
25–29		0.61	0.46	0.55	0.55	0.73
30–34		0.57	0.39	0.55	0.49	0.70
35–39		0.62	0.51	0.45	0.61	0.73
40–44		0.59	0.43	0.52	0.55	0.73
45–49		0.59	0.40	0.53	0.50	0.74
50–54		0.60	0.47	0.70	0.48	0.71
55–59		0.61	0.48	0.58	0.51	0.80
60–64		0.54	0.44	0.54	0.47	0.71
65–69		0.56	0.49	0.51	0.47	0.75
70–74		0.56	0.52	0.48	0.46	0.73
75–79		0.63	0.66	0.63	0.45	0.73
80–84		0.63	0.65	0.62	0.48	0.74
85+		0.71	0.71	0.81	0.52	0.64

SOURCES: National Center for Health Statistics (1992, 1993a, 1993b); U.S. Bureau of the Census (1992).

of the age intervals shown. For Japanese males, the death rates of the foreign-
born are lower than the overall rates at ages 35 to 44 through 65 to 74 and
higher at the youngest and the oldest ages. The above conclusions are unaf-

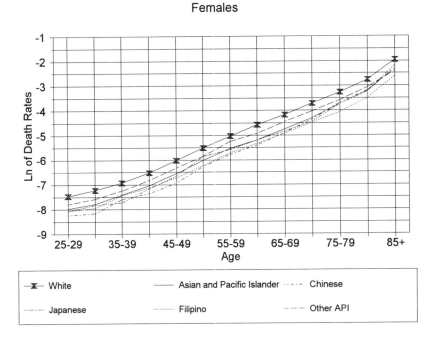

Figure 3.1. Death Rates, Whites and Asian and Pacific Islanders, Females 1989-1991

fected by whether deaths for which place of birth is missing are assigned to the native- or the foreign-born category.

Estimates of age-specific mortality rates presented here are similar to findings from previous, less detailed studies based on vital statistics and census data, except for the foreign-born (Yu, Chang, Liu, & Kan, 1985; U.S. Department of Health and Human Services, 1985, figs. 6 and 7). Yu et al. (1985), for example, estimated mortality among Chinese, Japanese, and Filipinos from 1979 to 1981; no sex-specific tabulations were shown. All estimated age-specific rates above age 25, shown for 10-year age intervals, were well below the rates for Whites, with the estimates for Filipinos showing strikingly low mortality. In addition, state-level studies from California and Hawaii have found mortality to be lower for Japanese and Chinese than for White Americans. In 1960, life expectancies at birth were estimated to be 72.9 for Chinese and 77.9 for Japanese, compared to 71.8 for Whites. In the 1979-1981 period, estimated life expectancy at birth for Japanese and Chinese combined was 82.5 versus 74.9 for Whites (Barringer et al., 1993, table 3.5). Similarly, based on 1980 data from Los Angeles County, estimated age-

Males

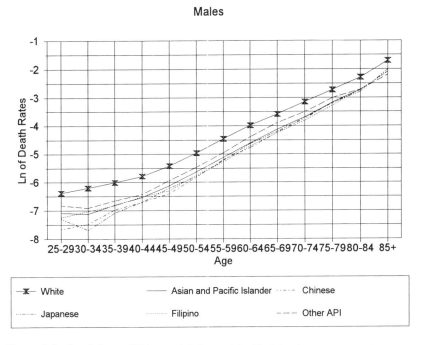

Figure 3.2. Death Rates, Whites and Asian and Pacific Islanders, Males 1989-1991

adjusted mortality rates for Japanese, Chinese, Koreans, and Filipinos were all well below those estimated for White Americans, with lowest rates recorded for Filipinos. Japanese had the highest estimated age-adjusted rate among Asian Americans, followed by Koreans, Chinese, and Filipinos (Frerichs, Chapman, & Maes, 1984).

Mortality estimates for Fiscal Year (FY) 1992 for Asians and Pacific Islanders, prepared by the Bureau of the Census in conjunction with its population projections from 1993 to 2050, also place Asian and Pacific Islander death rates well below those of Whites for both men and women (Day, 1993). In the age range from 25-29 to 80-84, the death rates for Asian/Pacific Islander males are 30% to 45% below White male rates; for females, the relative advantage ranges from 19% to 50%, except at ages 35 to 39 where the Asian and Pacific Islander rate is only 3% below the White rate, an obvious aberration from the general pattern (U.S. Bureau of the Census, unpublished tabulations). The Bureau's estimates are also based on vital statistics and census data, although the definition of Asian and Pacific Islander differs from that used in Tables 3.2 and 3.3. For the calculation of age-specific death rates,

TABLE 3.4 Death Rates (per 1,000), Asian and Pacific Islanders, Total and Foreign-Born, 1989-1991

Age	Asian/Pacific Islander		Chinese		Japanese		Filipino		Other Asian/Pacific Islander	
	All	Foreign-Born	All	Foreign-Born	All	Foreign-Born	All	Foreign-Born	All	Foreign-Born
Males										
25-34	0.83	0.80-0.82	0.52	0.47-0.52	0.53	0.55-0.55	0.79	0.81-0.81	1.07	0.97-1.00
35-44	1.26	1.15-1.19	1.05	0.96-1.02	0.99	0.78-0.79	1.26	1.21-1.22	1.46	1.27-1.32
45-54	2.74	2.53-2.61	2.23	2.24-2.36	2.36	1.90-1.96	2.34	2.24-2.26	3.28	2.85-2.94
55-64	7.92	7.16-7.33	6.97	6.69-6.91	7.61	6.97-7.20	6.84	6.46-6.48	9.54	7.98-8.17
65-74	20.14	19.05-19.50	18.38	18.53-19.06	18.67	14.68-15.86	18.58	18.18-18.35	25.34	20.79-21.32
75-84	52.88	52.82-53.78	51.28	52.17-53.44	50.02	53.87-54.37	51.30	51.90-52.31	61.38	55.93-57.70
85+	125.99	127.78-129.05	128.12	125.00-127.35	138.84	158.31-158.51	116.61	117.06-117.51	125.64	130.46-133.92
Females										
25-34	0.38	0.38-0.39	0.27	0.27-0.29	0.34	0.40-0.40	0.33	0.35-0.35	0.47	0.44-0.46
35-44	0.72	0.70-0.71	0.55	0.55-0.57	0.57	0.60-0.60	0.68	0.66-0.67	0.88	0.81-0.82
45-54	1.81	1.64-1.68	1.36	1.29-1.35	1.94	1.89-1.89	1.48	1.38-1.39	2.19	1.94-1.97
55-64	4.78	4.40-4.48	3.85	3.60-3.71	4.51	4.66-4.66	4.04	3.79-3.81	6.40	5.40-5.50
65-74	10.74	10.23-10.48	9.72	9.29-9.68	9.23	9.39-9.39	9.09	8.79-8.91	14.71	12.79-13.06
75-84	30.62	29.67-30.21	31.94	31.82-32.64	29.49	33.31-33.31	22.01	22.21-22.36	37.69	34.19-34.88
85+	102.27	107.70-108.83	108.35	110.72-112.92	107.14	121.78-121.78	72.77	75.04-75.70	101.91	100.97-102.29

SOURCE: National Center for Health Statistics (1992, 1993a, 1993b); U.S. Bureau of the Census (1993).

NOTES: In the calculation of age-specific death rates shown here, the 1990 Census sample data are used in the denominator. Because of sampling variability, the rates differ somewhat from those shown in Tables 3.2 and 3.3 where 100% count data are employed. The two rates shown for the foreign-born allocate all deaths of unknown place of birth first to native-born and then to foreign-born.

the estimated number of deaths was obtained by subtracting deaths of American Indians, provided by the Indian Health Service, from the deaths of "other races." This procedure was employed because NCHS death data were available only for Whites, Blacks, and "other races" for the time period of interest. Thus, deaths of the Asian and Pacific Islander population are a residual category once deaths for Whites, African Americans, and American Indians are excluded (Day, 1993, p. xxxvii). The denominator data come from the 1990 Census with adjustment for net census coverage error using demographic analyses. Despite the differences in methodology, these results are consistent with the results shown here for 1989 through 1991. As noted previously, the Census Bureau's most recent population projections also show very low mortality among Asians and Pacific Islanders compared to White Americans. Estimated life expectancies at birth for 1995 imply a 5.7-year advantage for Asian and Pacific Islander males relative to White males (e_0 = 79.3 vs. e_0 = 73.6) and a 4.8 year advantage for Asian and Pacific Islander females relative to White females (e_0 = 84.9 vs. e_0 = 80.1; Day, 1996, table B-1).

Yu et al. (1985) also examined mortality among the foreign-born Chinese, Filipinos, and Japanese, both sexes combined, with vital statistics and census data from the 1979-1981 period. The authors' findings stand in contrast to those recorded here. Age-adjusted death rates apparently were higher among the foreign- than the native-born in 1979-1981, as were age-specific death rates in all age intervals examined. At ages 25 to 34 through 65 to 74, the ratio of age-specific death rates of the foreign-born to the native-born ranged from 5.78 to 1.50 for Chinese, 4.78 to 1.59 for Japanese, and 2.86 to 0.89 for Filipinos. No estimates are available for Other Asian/Pacific Islanders or for the Asian/Pacific Islander population as a whole. In Table 3.4, mortality estimates for the foreign-born are contrasted to the overall death rates for Japanese, Chinese, and Filipinos. The death rates among the foreign-born between 1989 and 1991 for these Asian-origin subgroups do not appear to be consistently lower or higher than the overall age-specific death rates estimated for each of three Asian-origin populations, suggesting that neither are they consistently lower or higher than those of the native-born.

What could account for the differences in the results from 1979-1981 to 1989-1991 is not clear. The higher mortality among foreign-born Chinese, Filipinos, and Japanese in 1980 stands in contrast to other recent studies that have documented lower mortality among the foreign- than the native-born adults in the United States, most notably among Hispanics (Elo & Preston, in press; Kestenbaum, 1986; Rosenwaike, 1987). The results from 1990 appear somewhat more consistent with previous studies in this regard. Both sets of estimates, however, may be biased by inconsistencies in the reporting of place of birth in vital statistics and census data. Results from the 1960 Matched Records Study, which linked death certificates registered in the May-August period in 1960 to the 1960 Census of Population, found a tendency for individuals described as foreign-born on death records to be enumerated as native-born in the 1960 Census. This tendency had the effect of overestimating mortality among the foreign-born relative to the native-born (Kitagawa & Hauser, 1973). It is thus possible that estimates of mortality among the foreign-born Chinese, Filipinos, Japanese, and other Asians and Pacific Islanders are similarly biased. It is also possible that the degree of discrepancy in reporting of place of birth in vital statistics and census data has changed over time, which could lead to the above differences in estimated mortality among foreign-born Chinese, Japanese, and Filipinos in 1980 and 1990. Alternatively, changes in the health status of Chinese, Japanese, and Filipino immigrants over time could be partly responsible. Without further detail it is impossible to know the reasons for these differentials in findings. They do suggest, however, that we should be cautious in drawing conclusions about the relative mortality differentials between the foreign- and native-born Asian Americans and Pacific Islanders.

Problems With Mortality Estimates
Based on Vital Statistics and Census Data

The quality of mortality estimates based on vital statistics and census data for Asian Americans and Pacific Islanders is unquestionably worse than for Whites or African Americans. An indication of potential problems is evident in the estimates of age-specific death rates for Japanese males, which suggest a lower death rate at ages 30 to 34 than 25 to 29 (see Table 3.2). The main difficulty in estimating mortality for Asian Americans and Pacific Islanders from dual data sources stems from problems of comparability in the reporting of race in the two sources. The complication arises in part from differences in the way information on race is collected in each source. On the death certificate, information on the decedent's race is provided by the death certificate informant, typically by the next of kin, who is simply asked to identify the race of the decedent as "American Indian, Black, White, etc. (Specify)" (NCHS, 1994a, p. 7-3). This information is then filled in on the death certificate by the funeral director, who is responsible for completing all personal information on the death certificate. In the absence of an informant, race of the decedent is recorded by the funeral director by observation. To what extent funeral directors make independent assessments of race of the decedent is not known (e.g., National Center for Health Statistics [NCHS], 1969). The NCHS, then, provides death tabulations for the following groups: White, Black, American Indian, Chinese, Hawaiian, Japanese, Filipino, Other Asian or Pacific Islander, and Other. On the 1990 Census questionnaire, on the other hand, an individual's racial identity is self-reported. As discussed above, on the 1990 Census form nine distinct categories for Asian or Pacific Islanders are listed with a separate category for "Other API." As noted above, individuals who identify themselves as "Other API" are asked to specify further their origin (for a detailed listing of the responses considered by the Bureau of the Census to fall under the Asian American and Pacific Islander group, see U.S. Bureau of the Census, 1993, pp. B29-B30).

Thus, there is considerable room for inconsistencies in the classification of race in the two sources. We might expect, for example, a more complete enumeration of the Asian and Pacific Islander population in the Census than on death certificates, at least in part due to the fact that distinct categories for various Asian populations are listed separately on the census form but not on the death certificate. The reporting of race is likely to be particularly problematic for individuals of mixed racial parentage. Furthermore, the large influx of Asian immigrants since the mid-1960s and the increasing diversity of the Asian and Pacific Islander population as a whole undoubtedly has contributed to the problems of racial identification in various sources of government data. Recent immigrants, for example, may have had little exposure to the concept of race/ethnicity as understood in the United States, and thus may not be prepared to answer questions on race on survey forms or to provide such information at the time of death. It has also been suggested that a person's group identity may change over time and vary by context (e.g., Hahn, 1992; Hahn & Stroup, 1994; McKenney & Bennett, 1994; Yu & Liu, 1992).

Several recent studies have examined agreement in the reporting of race on death records and in population data, on birth records, or both, the usual sources of denominator data in the calculation of mortality estimates. Findings of all such studies suggest that mortality is underestimated for Asian Americans and Pacific Islanders when dual data sources are used. Most of these studies have focused on estimates of infant mortality and revealed substantial discrepancies in the coding of race in the two sources for Asian Americans. Hahn, Mulinare, and Teutsch (1992), for example, reported in a study based on linked birth and infant death records from 1983 to 1985 that

"almost as many infants classified as Filipino and Japanese at birth were classified as White at death (44.9% and 40.4%, respectively) as were consistently
classified as Filipino and Japanese at both birth and death (47.6% and 45.9%,
respectively)" (p. 261). Similarly, only 52.4% of the Chinese and 54.6% of
Other Asian and Pacific Islander births were classified as Chinese and Other
Asian and Pacific Islander at death. Most of the remainder were classified as
White. Consistent classification of infants by race at birth and at death increased infant mortality rates by 33.3% for Chinese, 48.8% for Japanese,
78.7% for Filipinos, and 37.7% for Other Asian/Pacific Islanders. Nevertheless, estimates of infant mortality based on consistent racial classification at
birth and at death were lower for Chinese (7.6 per 1,000), Japanese (6.4), and
Filipinos (8.4) than for Whites. Only Other Asians and Pacific Islanders (9.5)
had higher infant mortality rates than did White Americans (9.3). The pattern
of misreporting found in the Hahn et al. (1992) study is similar to that reported elsewhere (e.g., Frost & Shy, 1980; Norris & Shipley, 1971; Yu, 1984).

       Two other studies have examined possible biases in mortality estimates
for Asians and Pacific Islanders resulting from misclassification of race in the
numerator and denominator data. The most recent of these studies is by Sorlie, Rogot, and Johnson (1992). This study covers the entire age range but is
limited to the Asian and Pacific Islander group as a whole and is based on a
linkage of records from 12 Current Population Surveys (CPS) with the National Death Index for 1979-1985. The discrepancies between the baseline
race identification taken from the CPS and the matching death certificate
were larger for Asians and Pacific Islanders than for Whites, African Americans, or Hispanics. The percentage agreement for Asian and Pacific Islanders
was only 82.4%, and the race of the decedent was classified more often as
White on the death certificate than in the CPS. No detail by age or sex was
available, although the authors noted that "rates of agreement did not vary
much by sex or age group of the decedent" (Sorlie et al., 1992, p. 182). The
total number of deaths classified as Asian/Pacific Islander on the CPS survey
was 272, versus 242 on the matching death records, leading the authors to
conclude that death rates for Asians/Pacific Islanders calculated from vital
statistics and census data are likely to be underestimated by 12% (272/242 =
1.12). Multiplying the Asian and Pacific Islander death rates in Tables 3.2 and
3.3 by 1.12, however, would still leave the rates well below those of White
Americans.

       The only national-level study that has examined the comparability of
reporting of race for selected Asian subpopulations is the 1960 Matched

Records Study mentioned above. This study revealed high agreement in the reporting of race in the two sources for Japanese (97.0%), somewhat lower for Chinese (90.3%), and very low for Filipinos (72.6%). The estimated net difference rates were –1.4 for Japanese, –6.8 for Chinese, and –22.0 for Filipinos.[8] The most common source of discrepancy was for the person to be reported as White on the death certificate and non-White on the census record (NCHS, 1969). Adjusting the age-specific death rates of Japanese, Chinese, and Filipinos in Tables 3.2 and 3.3 by the above misreporting tendencies would still leave their death rates below those of White Americans.

A comparison of adjusted mortality indexes based on the 1960 study suggested that mortality among the Japanese was particularly low in comparison to White Americans; "the corrected mortality indexes for Japanese males and females 5 and over were about one-third lower than the corresponding indexes for White males and females" (Kitagawa & Hauser, 1973, p. 101). Estimated life expectancies at birth, based on uncorrected death rates, were 74.4 for Japanese males and 80.4 for Japanese females, the respective figures for White males and females were 67.6 and 74.7. On the other hand, the corrected mortality index at ages 5 and above was around 10% higher for Chinese males than for White males; for Chinese females, the corresponding index was 9% below of that for White females. Estimates of life expectancies at birth for Chinese were not reported, and no mortality estimates were presented for Filipinos (Kitagawa & Hauser, 1973). The above results for Japanese are consistent with findings for 1960 from Hawaii and California, mentioned previously, that similarly documented lower mortality for the Japanese than for Whites, Chinese, or Filipinos.

Thus, based on the results from the Kitagawa and Hauser study, we would expect the death rates for the Japanese shown in Tables 3.2 and 3.3 to be fairly accurate. These results show age-specific death rates for the Japanese to be well below the White rates, by 27% to 60% for males, ignoring ages 30-34 and 35-39 where the male rates for Japanese seem particularly low, and by 19% to 48% below the White rates for females. Based on the Kitagawa and Hauser results, the data for Chinese would appear to be somewhat less accurate than for the Japanese, particularly for males, although corrections for coding discrepancies would still probably leave their death rates below those of Whites. Data quality for Filipinos seems to be particularly problematic and casts doubt on the accuracy of mortality estimates shown in Tables 3.2 and 3.3.

Another potential problem with the use of vital statistics and census data is inconsistency in the reporting of age on death certificates and census records. I know of no studies that have examined consistency of age reporting in vital statistics and census data for Asian Americans and Pacific Islanders. However, a strong emphasis on age in East Asian cultures appears to be associated with unusually accurate age reporting, and thus potential biases caused by age misreporting are likely to be less important than those produced by inconsistencies in the reporting of race (Coale & Bannister, 1994). Finally, mortality estimates can be affected by population undercount in the Decennial Censuses. Although the Bureau of the Census provides estimates of net census undercounts based on demographic analyses (Robinson et al., 1993), undercount estimates are not available for Asian/Pacific Islanders. As noted above, the population data used here have not been adjusted for under-enumeration in the 1990 Census of Population. The effect on estimated mortality, however, again is likely to be much smaller than the distortions introduced by the lack of comparability in the reporting of race in vital statistics and census data.

Mortality Estimates Based on Linked Data Files

Estimates of mortality based on data sources in which information for deaths and population at risk come from a single file avoid the racial and ethnic classification problems created by dual data sources discussed above. Data sources of this type available for estimating mortality among older Americans are Social Security and Medicare files, the National Longitudinal Mortality Survey, the National Health Interview Survey files linked to the National Death Index, and subnational studies. These data sources are, however, less useful for analyses of mortality among Asians and Pacific Islanders than other population subgroups.

I know of no studies that have used Social Security/Medicare data to estimate mortality among Asian and Pacific Islander Americans. The racial detail available in these data do not permit the classification of individual records into the Asian and Pacific Islander category. The only way to investigate mortality among Asian Americans in these data would be to use a classification system based on surnames (e.g., Choi, Hanley, Holowaty, & Dale, 1993) or to identify individuals by place of birth.[9]

An alternative source of data for estimating mortality among Asians and Pacific Islanders as a whole is the National Longitudinal Mortality Survey (NLMS). Next, I show mortality estimates obtained from the NLMS Public Use File, Release 2, which is based on five Current Population Surveys (CPS) conducted between March 1979 and March 1981. The NLMS contains 637,162 individual records that have been linked to the National Death Index (NDI) for the years 1979 through 1989.[10] This record linkage identified 42,919 deaths that had occurred within the 9-year maximum follow-up period following the date of the CPS interview to members of the five CPS cohorts (for details on the linkage procedure, see Rogot, Sorlie, & Johnson, 1986).[11] Because no other follow-up of individuals in the five CPS cohorts was attempted, all individuals who were not linked to the NDI were considered to be alive at the end of the follow-up period. These procedures are likely to result in some deaths being missed because of a lack of perfect detection of deaths in the NDI. Rogot, Sorlie, Johnson, and Schmitt (1992) have noted that "there is some ascertainment loss, of perhaps 5%, occurring in the matching process because of recording errors in the files being matched" (p. 2).

There are reasons to suspect that the success in matching to the NDI differs by characteristics of the decedent, including his or her race. Curb et al. (1985) found, for example, significant variation by race and sex in the identification of known deaths in the NDI in 1979-1981. Deaths of African Americans and women were less likely to be located in the NDI than those of Whites and men. The main explanation given for this finding was Social Security number discrepancies in the NDI and in the identifying information of the decedent used in the match. We do not know whether the linkage rates varied by race or ethnicity in the NLMS, but it is possible that they were more complete for Whites than for Asian/Pacific Islanders. As noted above, a missing Social Security number is one reason for a failure to link to the NDI. At ages 45 through 89, the age range on which the following estimates are based, Social Security numbers were missing for 12.2% of Whites in contrast to 13.1% of Asian and Pacific Islanders in the NLMS. The difference is not large and suggests only a very slight possibility that deaths of Asian and Pacific Islanders were more likely to be missed in the linkage to the NDI than those of Whites due to differences in the presence of a Social Security number on the CPS record. Another reason for a linkage failure is that deaths of the foreign-born may not be recorded in the U.S. death records because some of these individuals may have died abroad. The percentage of the population that is foreign-born is extremely high among Asian and Pacific Islanders compared to Whites, and thus it is possible that a larger proportion of deaths of the former are not captured in U.S. vital statistics records.

The NLMS data on socioeconomic and demographic characteristics come from the interview data from the CPS surveys, in which the interviewer contacts, through personal interview or by telephone, the most knowledgeable adult member of the household, who provides information on all house-hold members. Our samples for these analyses consist of 79,689 males and 94,983 females aged 45 through 89, of whom 18,359 and 15,623, respec-tively, had died during the 9-year follow-up period. Because of the small number of deaths for Asian and Pacific Islanders, direct calculation of death rates is not possible. There were only 197 male and 105 female deaths among Asian and Pacific Islanders during the 9-year follow-up period (based on un-weighted data). Therefore, to assess ethnic differences in mortality, I estimate a logit regression model in which the dependent variable is the log odds of the probability of dying during the 9-year follow-up period. The estimated coefficients are then translated into age-specific death rates by 5-year age groups. Race/ethnicity distinguishes between Whites and Asian and Pacific Islanders.

Table 3.5 presents the estimated coefficients from the logit models. Model 1 presents the main effect for Asian and Pacific Islanders relative to Whites; Model 2 further distinguishes between native- and foreign-born Asian/Pacific Islanders. Because place of birth was missing for a sizable frac-tion of the sample, I have further distinguished this group from the foreign- and native-born Asians and Pacific Islanders. The purpose of Model 2 is to investigate the hypothesis that the relatively low mortality of Asian and Pa-cific Islanders reflects the fact that many of these individuals are recent mi-grants to the United States. Table 3.6 presents the age-specific death rates by 5-year age groups up to age 85-89 that are predicted from the coefficients shown in Table 3.5, Model 1.[12]

The results based on the NLMS suggest that mortality among Asian and Pacific Islander Americans is low relative to Whites and that a portion of the low mortality of Asian and Pacific Islanders is in part attributable to the low mortality of the foreign-born. We should, however, be somewhat cautious in drawing firm conclusions concerning the relative advantage of the foreign-versus native-born Asian and Pacific Islanders. As noted above, it is possible that the advantage of the foreign-born reflects in part difficulties in following them up in U.S. death records, since some may have died abroad. Thus, it is possible that the linkage of the CPS cohorts to the NDI was more successful for native- than for foreign-born Asian and Pacific Islanders, an outcome that would lead to an underestimate of mortality among the foreign-born. At the same time, however, the findings for the native-born Asian and Pacific Is-lander Americans imply that their mortality is also lower than that of White Americans.

TABLE 3.5 Coefficients of Equations Predicting the Log Odds of Dying in a Nine-Year Period: Males and Females Aged 45-89, 1979-1989, National Longitudinal Mortality Survey

	Males		Females	
	Model 1	*Model 2*	*Model 1*	*Model 2*
Age	0.1029	0.1029	0.1028	0.1028
	(0.001)	(0.001)	(0.001)	(0.001)
Race/Ethnicity				
White	—	—	—	—
Asian/Pacific Islander	−0.5384		−0.5384	
	(0.098)		(0.1198)	
Asian/Pacific Islander Native-Born		−0.5289		−0.4026
		(0.1935)		(0.233)
Asian/Pacific Islander Foreign-Born		−0.6937		−0.5442
		(0.1333)		(0.154)
Asian/Pacific Islander Birth Place Unknown		−0.1068		−0.7420
		(0.2090)		(0.321)
Constant	−7.6465	−7.6493	−8.3447	−8.3449
	(0.063)	(0.063)	(0.066)	(0.066)
Log-Likelihood	−35,945.4	−35,942.7	−35,192.0	−35,191.7
Sample Size	79,689	79,689	94,983	94,983

NOTE: — = reference category; standard errors in parentheses.

The results from the NLMS further indicate that mortality estimates based on vital statistics and census data exaggerate the relative mortality advantages of Asian and Pacific Islander males in comparison to White males. Ratios of Asian and Pacific Islander male death rates to those of White males range from 0.59 to 0.71 in Table 3.6, compared to a range of 0.49 to 0.68 in Table 3.2. This exaggeration is most likely the result of underestimation of mortality for this ethnic group based on data obtained from dual data sources. As noted previously, the consistency of race reporting for this subpopulation in death statistics and census records is low, much lower than for other racial and ethnic groups. The respective figures for females in Tables 3.6 and 3.3 are similar, ranging from 0.59 to 0.67 in Table 3.6 and 0.59 to 0.71 in Table 3.3.

An analyses of the linked National Health Interview Survey-National Death Index (NHIS-NDI) files by Rogers, Hummer, Nam, and Peters (1996)

TABLE 3.6 Predicted Death Rates: Whites and Asians and Pacific Islanders, National Longitudinal Mortality Survey, 1979-1989 (death rates per 1,000)

| | Death Rates (per 1,000) | | | |
| | Males | | Females | |
Age Group	Whites	Asian/Pacific Islanders	Whites	Asian/Pacific Islanders
45–49	4.13	2.43	2.07	1.21
50–54	6.83	4.04	3.44	2.02
55–59	11.20	6.67	5.69	3.36
60–64	18.14	10.94	9.35	5.55
65–69	28.87	17.75	15.23	9.14
70–74	44.77	28.27	24.40	14.88
75–79	67.16	43.90	38.23	23.87
80–84	96.75	65.96	58.08	37.45
85–89	133.43	95.22	84.96	56.99
	Ratios of Asian and Pacific Islander Rates to White Rates			
45–49		0.59		0.59
50–54		0.59		0.59
55–59		0.60		0.59
60–64		0.60		0.59
65–69		0.61		0.60
70–74		0.63		0.61
75–79		0.65		0.62
80–84		0.68		0.64
85–89		0.71		0.67

SOURCES: National Center for Health Statistics (1992, 1993a, 1993b); U.S. Bureau of the Census (1992).

are consistent with my results from the NLMS; both indicate that mortality among Asian/Pacific Islanders is well below that of Whites. Although potential linkage problems to the NDI may lead to underestimates of mortality based on data linked to the NDI, it is unlikely that such problems would account for all of the estimated mortality differences between Whites and Asian and Pacific Islanders obtained from the NLMS and NHIS-NDI. That mortality of native-born Asian and Pacific Islanders also appears lower than that of Whites lends further credence to the finding that mortality among this population subgroup is indeed lower than that of White Americans.

TABLE 3.7 Age-Standardized Death Rates for Selected Major Causes of Death: White and Asian and Pacific Islander Males, 1989-1991 (deaths per 1,000)

Age and Cause	White	Chinese	Japanese	Filipino	Other API	All API
45-84						
All Causes	25.24	14.07	14.22	13.70	17.42	14.95
Diseases of the heart	9.21	4.22	4.11	4.89	5.73	4.81
Cerebrovascular diseases	1.31	1.11	1.17	1.47	1.40	1.28
Malignant neoplasms	7.21	4.47	4.46	3.35	4.86	4.31
All other causes	7.51	4.28	4.49	3.98	5.43	4.55
85+						
All Causes	181.04	123.64	132.48	122.40	110.69	123.32
Diseases of the heart	75.11	46.77	43.89	50.24	39.73	46.21
Cerebrovascular diseases	15.40	11.55	18.50	13.18	10.47	13.58
Malignant neoplasms	26.74	17.37	19.65	16.15	18.24	17.61
All other causes	63.79	47.96	50.44	42.83	42.25	45.92

SOURCES: National Center for Health Statistics (1992, 1993a, 1993b); U.S. Bureau of the Census (1992).

Cause-Specific Mortality

The major causes of death for individuals aged 45 and above are diseases of the heart, malignant neoplasms, and cerebrovascular diseases. It would be surprising if differences in death rates from all causes combined between Whites and Asian and Pacific Islanders were not principally attributable to differences in death rates from these causes. Tables 3.7 and 3.8 present age-standardized death rates at ages 45 through 84 and the overall rate at 85+ from the above causes and all other causes combined in the 1989-1991 period for Whites, Chinese, Japanese, Filipinos, other Asians and Pacific Islanders, and the Asian and Pacific Islander group as a whole. These estimates are based on vital statistics and census data; the sample size for Asian and Pacific Islanders in the NLMS is too small for an examination of cause-specific mortality differentials.

Asian and Pacific Islander Americans have lower estimated age-standardized death rates than White Americans from heart disease, cancer, and all other causes combined. Heart disease and cancer account for a majority of the all-cause discrepancy between Whites and the various Asian and Pacific Islander subgroups and the API group as a whole (Tables 3.7 and 3.8).

TABLE 3.8   Age-Standardized Death Rates for Selected Major Causes of Death:
White and Asian and Pacific Islander Females, 1989-1991 (deaths
per 1,000)

Age and Cause	White	Chinese	Japanese	Filipino	Other API	All API
45-84						
All Causes	14.64	8.22	8.38	6.90	10.80	8.70
Diseases of the heart	4.67	2.21	2.27	2.29	3.45	2.58
Cerebrovascular diseases	1.04	0.94	0.88	0.84	1.27	1.00
Malignant neoplasms	4.60	2.71	2.82	1.84	2.87	2.60
All other causes	4.33	2.36	2.42	1.92	3.22	2.52
85+						
All Causes	141.91	100.09	114.25	73.51	90.80	100.05
Diseases of the heart	64.90	41.73	43.83	31.98	37.86	40.53
Cerebrovascular diseases	16.66	11.43	18.92	8.27	11.48	13.71
Malignant neoplasms	13.54	12.42	10.82	7.32	8.18	10.40
All other causes	46.81	34.52	40.67	25.94	33.29	35.41

SOURCES: National Center for Health Statistics (1992, 1993a, 1993b); U.S. Bureau of the Census (1992).

In contrast, differences in cerebrovascular disease mortality are minor and not
always consistent in direction. The age-standardized death rate from stroke,
for example, is lower for White males than for Filipino and Other Asian Pacific Islander males at ages 45 through 84 and lower than that of Japanese
males at ages 85+. Among women, White females have lower stroke mortality
than Other Asian/Pacific Islander females at ages 45 through 84 and lower
than Japanese females at ages 85+. In other cases, cerebrovascular diseases
account for only between 0.3% to 10.1% of the differential in death rates from
all causes combined between Whites and Japanese, Chinese, Filipinos, and
other Asians and Pacific Islanders (Tables 3.7 and 3.8).

Cerebrovascular disease thus appears to be a more important cause of
death among Asian Americans and Pacific Islanders than White Americans.
Its contribution to all-cause mortality ranges from 7.9% to 16.6% among Chinese, Japanese, Filipinos, and Other Asian/Pacific Islander males and females
at ages 45 through 84 and 85+. The respective figures for Whites are 5.2%
and 11.7%. On the other hand, heart disease is a less important contributing
factor to all-cause mortality among Chinese and Japanese than Filipinos,
Other Asians/Pacific Islanders, or White Americans, particularly at ages 45
through 84. The contribution of heart disease to all-cause mortality at these

ages ranges from 26.9% to 30.0% among Chinese and Japanese males and females in contrast to between 31.9% and 35.6% among Filipinos and Other Asians and Pacific Islanders and between 31.9% and 36.5% among Whites. Despite much lower age-standardized death rates from cancer among Chinese and Japanese than Whites, cancer mortality makes a larger contribution to all-cause mortality among Chinese and Japanese at ages 45 through 84 than among Whites, Filipinos, and Other Asians and Pacific Islanders (calculations based on death rates shown in Tables 3.7 and 3.8).

Analyses of cancer incidence and mortality by specific site further reveal that the distribution of various cancer types differs among Whites, Chinese, Japanese, and Filipinos. Gardner (1994) cites results of a National Cancer Institute study that show age-adjusted site-specific death rates for Chinese, Japanese, and Filipinos as well as White Americans. Age-adjusted cancer mortality rates for the three Asian-origin populations were below the estimated rates for Whites; 131.5 per 100,000 for Chinese, 104.2 for Japanese, 69.7 for Filipinos, and 163.6 for White Americans (Table 3.9; see also table 3.3 in Gardner, 1994). Despite the lower overall mortality from malignant neoplasms, age-standardized death rates for some specific sites were nonetheless higher for Japanese and Chinese than for White Americans. These sites included cancer of the rectum, corpus uteri, and esophagus among Chinese; lung cancer among Chinese females; and most important, stomach cancer, particularly among Japanese for whom the age-adjusted death rate from stomach cancer was more than 3 times as high as that for White Americans. Other sites for which differentials were relatively small between Whites and Japanese and Chinese involved cancer of the cervix uteri, colon, and pancreas. In contrast, death rates from breast and prostate cancer appeared low relative to the White rates. For Filipinos, age-adjusted death rates for all specific sites were lower than those of White Americans and lower than or similar to the estimated rates for Japanese and Chinese Americans (Table 3.9). No estimates were presented for other Asian or Pacific Islander Americans, except for Hawaiians, whose age-adjusted cancer death rate (200.5 per 100,000) was higher than that of Whites (Gardner, 1994).

It is important to keep in mind that the above estimates based on vital statistics and census data are subject to the same numerator-denominator bias as death rates from all causes combined. Moreover, the National Cancer Institute data have not been examined for possible ethnic classification inconsistencies (Gardner, 1994). Thus, estimated cause-specific mortality rates for Asian Americans and Pacific Islanders are also likely to be biased downward.

TABLE 3.9 Average Annual Age-Adjusted Cancer Mortality Rates per 100,000 by
Primary Site and Ethnicity, United States, 1978 to 1981

Primary Site	Whites	Japanese	Chinese	Filipinos
All Sites	163.6	104.2	131.5	69.7
Bladder	3.9	1.8	1.7	1.5
Breast, female	26.6	9.9	13.0	8.0
Ages <40	1.6	1.1	0.8	0.9
Ages 40+	70.2	25.2	34.6	20.6
Cervix uteri	3.2	2.7	2.9	1.6
Colon and Rectum	21.6	17.2	19.3	8.1
Colon	18.1	13.6	15.5	5.8
Rectum	3.5	3.6	3.8	2.3
Corpus uteri	3.9	3.9	4.3	2.0
Esophagus	2.6	1.9	3.3	1.9
Larynx	1.3	0.2	0.7	0.4
Lung, male	69.3	32.7	48.2	20.0
Lung, female	20.2	8.6	21.2	6.8
Multiple myeloma	2.4	1.2	1.2	1.2
Ovary	8.1	4.3	4.2	2.8
Pancreas	8.4	7.0	7.4	3.3
Prostate	21.0	8.8	7.5	8.2
Stomach	5.3	17.5	7.8	3.3

SOURCE: Gardner (1994, table 3.14).

There is no reason to suspect, however, that the relative importance of various causes of death is seriously distorted. As long as the inconsistency in race reporting in vital statistics and census data does not vary by cause of death, the cause-specific mortality data should provide a general picture of the relative importance of the major causes of death.

The results discussed above are in general agreement with what is known about cause-of-death patterns among Chinese and Japanese populations more generally and what is known about cause-specific mortality among Chinese and Japanese Americans from epidemiological investigations. Campbell (1995), for example, has noted certain similarities in noncommunicable disease mortality among ethnic Chinese populations worldwide. These include "1) extremely high death rates from cancers of the nasopharynx and esophagus . . . ; 2) relatively high death rates from cancers of the liver, stomach and among females, the lung; 3) relatively low death

rates from cancers of the colon, and among females the breast . . . ; 4) relatively low death rates from many forms of heart disease . . . ; 5) relatively high
death rates from hemorrhagic stroke" (Campbell, 1995, pp. 334-335; also see
Hanley, Choi, & Holowaty, 1995). These observations are in general agreement with the relative importance of various causes of death among Chinese
residing in the United States discussed above. The main exception is colon
cancer, in which case changes in dietary habits, that is, increased intake of
meats and saturated fats, among Chinese immigrants to the United States may
have played a role. Since a very large proportion of Chinese Americans are
recent arrivals to the United States, it is not surprising that the cause of death
patterns among them would resemble those of their countries of origin.[13] Factors that are hypothesized to be related to the prevalence of particular site-specific cancers among ethnic Chinese include diet (Armstrong, 1980;
Hildesheim & Levine, 1993), environmental factors such as domestic air pol-
lution, and infectious agents (Nomura et al., 1991; Parsonnet et al., 1991; see
the discussion of the role of the various factors in Campbell, 1995). Diet has
also been implicated in low heart disease and high stroke mortality among
elderly Chinese Americans (Choi et al., 1990).

Supporting evidence for the role of environmental factors, including
diet, in patterns of cause-specific mortality among Chinese comes from studies that have compared mortality among foreign-born and native-born Chinese Americans. These results are consistent with studies of other migrants to
the United States that have suggested that the level of acculturation has a
potential influence on health outcomes through changes in lifestyles and
health habits (e.g., Espino & Maldonado, 1990; Mitchell, Stern, Haffner,
Hazuda, & Patterson, 1990). The studies of Chinese migrants have shown
first-generation Chinese to have higher mortality from stomach, esophagus,
and liver cancer, and especially from cancer of the nasopharynx, in comparison to second-generation Chinese. Prostate cancer, which remains a relatively
minor cause, tended to be somewhat lower in first- than second-generation
Chinese males, while mortality from breast cancer was low among both first-
and second-generation Chinese females (Hanley et al., 1995; King & Haenszel,
1973; King & Locke, 1980; King, Locke, Li, Pollack, & Tu, 1985). It has been
further suggested that mortality from heart disease is higher among Chinese
immigrants to the United States than those in the countries of origin, but
lower than among U.S. Whites (King & Locke, 1987). A recent study of elderly Chinese immigrants residing in Boston further found that their risk profiles for heart disease and stroke resembled those of mainland Chinese living

in urban areas, predisposing them to mortality from hemorrhagic stroke while being protective against heart disease (Choi et al., 1990).

The most extensively studied Asian American population in the United States is the Japanese. The results of these studies are similar to those of the Chinese in that a mortality gradient between Japanese in Japan and Japanese in the United States has been documented for selected causes of death (e.g., Gardner, 1994). Among the best known studies of Japanese in the United States are the Ni-Hon-San studies based on a collaborative epidemiological investigation of Japanese males in Japan, Hawaii, and California. Reed and Yano (1994) summarized the results of these studies with respect to cardio-vascular disease mortality as follows: "there is a two to three fold higher risk of CHD among Japanese in the US compared to those in Japan, and that this difference can be accounted for largely by differences in the major risk factors, especially serum cholesterol, serum glucose, blood pressure, smoking and alcohol intake" (p. 12). According to Reed and Yano (1994), the key factor in elevated heart disease mortality among Japanese Americans compared to Japanese in Japan is "change from traditional Japanese life style involving high physical activity and an Asian diet low in animal fat and protein to a sedentary lifestyle combined with a high calorie Western diet leading to obesity, hypertension, diabetes and high serum cholesterol" (p. 13). Despite the higher death rates from heart disease among Japanese residing in the United States than in Japan, heart disease remains a less important cause of death among Japanese than White Americans, with Japanese in the United States having intermediate rates between Japanese in Japan and U.S. Whites (Haenszel & Kurihara, 1968; Kasl & Berkman, 1983).

In contrast, mortality from cerebrovascular diseases shows an opposite gradient, with the highest rates recorded in Japan. A comparison of stroke mortality in Tables 3.7 and 3.8 shows similar rates between Japanese and Whites at ages 45 to 84 and somewhat elevated rates among the Japanese at ages 85+, where the proportion of foreign-born among the Japanese is higher than at younger ages. It has also been suggested that diet, such as high intake of salt and low intake of fat, may be related to differences in stroke mortality among Japanese Americans and Japanese in Japan (Goldman & Takahashi, 1996; Reed, 1990). Similarly, the prevalence of specific cancers among Japanese Americans reflects patterns observed in Japan with relatively high death rates from stomach cancer and low death rates from breast cancer (see Gardner, 1994).

Among Filipinos, heart disease appears to be a more important cause of death than among either Japanese or Chinese. This finding is consistent with studies that have examined cardiovascular risk factors among Asian and Pacific Islander Americans, which have documented a higher prevalence of hypertension among Filipinos than either Chinese or Japanese (Klatsky & Armstrong, 1991; Stavig, Igra, & Leonard, 1988). In general, however, relatively little is known about risk factor distributions or cause-specific mortality differentials among Asian Americans and Pacific Islanders other than Chinese and Japanese. Further studies are needed to gain a better understanding of the variation in risk profiles among them. We could expect substantial variation among the various Asian and Pacific Islander subgroups, and we must be cautious in generalizing findings from one group to another (see Zane, Takeuchi, & Young, 1994).

Conclusions

All mortality estimates for Asian and Pacific Islanders, including Chinese, Japanese, and Filipinos, place their level of mortality well below that of White Americans. Except for estimates based on the National Longitudinal Mortality Survey, all others rely on vital statistics and census data. Results from studies that have examined discrepancies in the coding of race for Asian and Pacific Islanders in these data sources suggest that mortality estimates based on them for this population subgroup are too low. It is difficult to know the precise extent of underestimation in the recorded rates, which also is likely to vary by Asian and Pacific Islander subgroup. The most recent study that has compared the discrepancies in coding of race between death certificates and census records concludes that death rates for Asian and Pacific Islanders based on vital statistics and census data are likely to be underestimated by 12%. If the 1989-1991 Asian and Pacific Islander death rates are adjusted by this amount, they would still be 20% to 39% below the White rates for males and 17% to 34% below the White rates for females at ages 25+.

Among the Asian American subgroups, the data for Japanese are likely to be of highest quality. The 1960 Match Records Study showed very little discrepancy in the coding of Japanese ethnicity in vital statistics and census data. This is the only study that has examined coding inconsistencies among Asian American subgroups at adult ages. It is, of course, possible that the

1960 results no longer accurately reflect coding discrepancies for Japanese. One of the principal reasons why this might be the case relates to the increase in the proportion of individuals of mixed racial parentage. Such an increase would not affect the older cohorts, however. The proportion foreign-born is also low among Japanese relative to other Asians and Pacific Islanders, which should increase the probability that their deaths are captured by the U.S. vital statistics system. The 1989-1991 mortality estimates place the level of mortality among Japanese Americans well below that of Whites. At ages 45 and above, the ratio of Japanese age-specific death rates to those of Whites range from 0.43 to 0.73 for males and 0.48 to 0.81 for females. A comparison of mortality of Japanese Americans to that in Japan further suggest that mortality among Japanese Americans is very low. At ages 45 to 49 through 75 to 79, the ratio of 1989-1991 age-specific death rates of Japanese Americans to 1990 rates in Japan range from 0.60 to 0.71 for males and from 0.69 to 1.15 for females (Japan Aging Research Center, 1996). Even if the estimated death rates for Japanese are slightly underestimated, we can be confident in concluding that their level of mortality is low and below that of Whites.

We have less confidence in the results for Chinese and Filipinos. The Kitagawa and Hauser (1973) study showed coding discrepancies to be somewhat greater for Chinese and substantially larger for Filipinos than for Japanese. The Chinese rates are thus likely to be underestimated by a somewhat larger amount than the rates for Japanese, while I put little confidence in the mortality estimates for the Filipinos. Without additional studies of consistency of reporting of race in vital statistics and census data that could be used to correct mortality estimates based on these data, at present it seems impossible to provide accurate mortality estimates for Asian and Pacific Islander subgroups with the possible exception of Japanese. The use of indirect estimation techniques, developed to estimate mortality among populations with poor quality data, are also not suitable for the problem at hand, the principal reason being the very high net migration rates among Asian Americans and Pacific Islanders.

At the same time, however, mortality estimates based on the NLMS suggest that the level of mortality among Asians and Pacific Islanders as a whole is well below that of Whites. These results are consistent with recent estimates based on the NHIS-NDI linked files. In both data sources, information for deaths and population at risk come from a single source and thus the racial classification problem created by dual data sources is avoided. These data, however, are not without limitations. It is not known, for example, to what extent the success in linkage to the NDI differs by race/ethnicity. A very large fraction of Asians and Pacific Islanders is foreign-born, which in turn may result in deaths being missed in U.S. death records as individuals may have died abroad. Such linkage problems would have to be substantial, however, to raise the mortality estimates for Asians/Pacific Islanders to the level estimated for Whites. The NLMS results further suggest that mortality of native-born Asians and Pacific Islanders is lower than that of Whites. These estimates show that male mortality (the log odds of dying during the 9-year follow-up period) among native-born Asians and Pacific Islanders is 37% below that of Whites ($e^{-0.4601} = 0.63$; Table 3.5), the respective figure for females is 30% ($e^{-0.3567} = 0.70$; Table 3.5). Because the proportion foreign-born is extremely high among all Asian Americans other than Japanese, mortality among the native-born reflects in large part the mortality experience of Japanese Americans. These results are consistent with the notion that mortality among the Japanese is below that of Whites.

A comparison of cause-specific mortality differentials at ages 45+ between Whites and Asians and Pacific Islanders suggest that heart disease and cancer, the two leading causes of death at ages 45+, account for the majority of all-cause discrepancy. Only death rates from cerebrovascular diseases appear similar between Whites and Asians and Pacific Islanders and in some cases are higher among select Asian and Pacific Islander subgroups than among White Americans.

In this chapter, I have attempted to distinguish among the various Asian and Pacific Islander populations to the extent permitted by available data. At present, however, separate estimates are only possible for Japanese, Chinese, Filipinos, Hawaiians, and all other Asians and Pacific Islanders combined. We can only speculate about how mortality may vary among the many subgroups that make up the Other Asian and Pacific Islander category, and the variation may well be substantial. Health conditions among Southeast Asian refugees, for example, are likely to differ from those of Koreans and Asian Indians, the two largest population subgroups in this category. Studies focusing on specific populations are needed to gain a better understanding of health conditions among them. National-level data presently available will not help us in this regard.

Notes

1. According to the 1990 Census, there were, for example, 815,447 Asian Indians, 798,849 Koreans, 614,547 Vietnamese, 147,411 Cambodians, 90,082 Hmong, 149,014 Laotians, and 91,275 Thais living in the United States (U.S. Bureau of the Census, 1992, table 23).

2. This foreign-born percentage seems particularly low, but appears consistent with the enumeration in the 1980 Census of Population, which shows that at ages 55+ 23.9% of the Japanese population was foreign-born (U.S. Bureau of the Census, 1988, table 30). In 1990, the percentage foreign-born is lower at ages 65 through 84 (12.1%) than 85+ (70.0%) (U.S. Bureau of the Census, 1993).

3. Reporting of whether an individual is of Hispanic origin is also required.

4. When more than one race is listed on the death certificate, the following rules apply in the classification of the death into a particular racial category. Whenever Hawaiian origin is indicated on the death certificate, the death is coded as Hawaiian. When a mixture of White and any other race is listed, the death is coded to the relevant non-White race. When only non-White races are listed, the death is coded to the first race specified. When the race listed on the death certificate is either unknown, not stated, or unclassifiable, these records are assigned as either Black or White. In 1989, only 0.2% of death certificates fell into this last category. In both 1990 and 1991, the respective figure was 0.3% (National Center for Health Statistics, 1993c, 1994a, 1996).

5. A comparison of total age-specific death rates, that is, the native- and foreign-born combined, based on sample and 100% count data, show differentials in the range of 2% to 3%, with somewhat larger differentials for the oldest age group.

6. A comparison of the estimated death rates for Whites with the 1990 life table estimates reveals that the rates shown here are slightly higher below age 65 and slightly lower at ages 85+ than the 1990 life table rates (National Center for Health Statistics, 1994b). A similar comparison is not possible for the Asians and Pacific Islanders.

7. The ICD-9 codes associated with the cause of death categories are the following: diseases of the heart (390-398, 402, 404-429), cerebrovascular diseases (430-438), and malignant neoplasms (140-208). All other causes of death are included in the residual category "all other causes combined" (National Center for Health Statistics, 1992, 1993a, 1993b).

8. The net difference rate has as its numerator the difference between the total number of responses in a given category on the death and census record, and as its denominator the census record total (National Center for Health Statistics, 1969, pp. 2-3).

9. Mortality among Hispanic-origin individuals based on Social Security/Medicare data has been investigated in conjunction with the Census Bureau's projections of the Hispanic population (Spencer, 1986).

10. The NLMS Public Use File is a subset of the larger NLMS database, consisting of 12 census samples numbering about 1.3 million persons in the United States. Eleven of the 12 cohorts were taken from Current Population Surveys conducted during the period from March 1973 through March 1985, and one sample was drawn from the 1980 Census of Population. Sample individuals were then matched to the National Death Index (NDI) beginning in 1979, when the NDI was established, with plans to continue mortality follow-up through March 1993 (Rogot et al., 1992).

11. The five CPS surveys were conducted in March 1979; April, August, and December 1980; and March 1981.

12. The coefficients were translated into age-specific death rates as follows: $[\ln(E^k + 1)]/9 = {}_5\mu_{a+2}$; where k represents the sum of appropriate coefficients from Model 1 in Table 3.5. The calculations use more precision than the coefficients shown in Table 3.5.

13. This is not to say that the cause-of-death structures among Chinese populations everywhere are identical, only that the contribution of various causes of death to all-cause mortality has historically differed from that found in most Western countries in ways suggested in the text. Recent evidence indicates a growing similarity in the cause-of-death patterns in Singapore, Taiwan, Hong Kong, and in Western countries (Campbell, 1995).

References

Armstrong, B. (1980). The epidemiology of cancer in the People's Republic of China. *International Journal of Epidemiology, 9*(4), 305-315.

Barringer, H. R., Gardner, R. W., & Levin, M. J. (1993). *Asians and Pacific Islanders in the United States* (The Population of the United States in the 1980s. A Census Monograph Series). New York: Russell Sage.

Campbell, C. (1995). *Chinese mortality transitions: The case of Beijing, 1700-1990.* Unpublished doctoral dissertation, University of Pennsylvania. Ann Arbor, MI: UMI Dissertation Information Service.

Choi, B. C. K., Hanley, A. J. G., Holowaty, E. J., & Dale, D. (1993). Use of surnames to identify individuals of Chinese ancestry. *American Journal of Epidemiology, 138*(9), 723-734.

Choi, E. S. K., McGandy, R. B., Dallal, G. E., Russell, R. M., Jacob, R. A., Schaefer, E. J., & Sadowski, J. A. (1990). The prevalence of cardiovascular risk factors among elderly Chinese Americans. *Archives of Internal Medicine, 150,* 413-418.

Coale, A. J., & Bannister, J. (1994). Five decades of missing females in China. *Demography, 3*(3), 459-479.

Curb, J. D., Ford, C. E., Pressel, S., Palmer, M., Babcock, C., & Hawkins, C. M. (1985). Ascertainment of vital status through the National Death Index and the Social Security Administration. *American Journal of Epidemiology, 121*(5), 754-766.

Day, J. C. (1993). *Population projections of the United States, by age, sex, race, and Hispanic origin: 1993 to 2050* (U.S. Bureau of the Census, Current Population Reports, P25-1104). Washington, DC: Government Printing Office.

Day, J. C. (1996). *Population projections of the United States by age, sex, race, and Hispanic origin: 1995 to 2050* (U.S. Bureau of the Census, Current Population Reports, P25-1130). Washington, DC: Government Printing Office.

Elo, I. T., & Preston, S. H. (in press). Racial and ethnic differences in American mortality at older ages. In L. Martin & B. Soldo (Eds.), *Racial and ethnic differences in the health of older Americans.* Washington, DC: National Academy Press.

Espino, D. V., & Maldonado, D. (1990). Hypertension and acculturation in elderly Mexican Americans: Results from 1982-84 Hispanic HANES. *Journal of Gerontology, 45*(6), M209-213.

Frerichs, R. R., Chapman, J. M., & Maes, E. F. (1984). Mortality due to all causes and to cardiovascular diseases among seven race-ethnic populations in Los Angeles County, 1980. *International Journal of Epidemiology, 13*(3), 291-298.

Frost, F., & Shy, K. K. (1980). Racial differences between linked birth and infant death records in Washington State. *American Journal of Public Health, 70*(9), 974-976.

Gardner, R. (1994). Mortality. In N. W. S. Zane, D. T. Takeuchi, & K. N. J. Young (Eds.), *Confronting critical health issues of Asian and Pacific Islander Americans* (pp. 53-104). Thousand Oaks, CA: Sage.

Goldman, N., & Takahashi, S. (1996). Old-age mortality in Japan: Demographic and epidemiological perspectives. In G. Caselli & A. D. Lopez (Eds.), *Health and mortality among elderly populations.* Oxford, UK: Oxford University Press.

Haenszel, W., & Kurihara, M. (1968). Studies of Japanese migrants: I. Mortality from cancer and other diseases among Japanese in the United States. *Journal of the National Cancer Institute, 40,* 43-68.

Hahn, R. A. (1992). The state of federal health statistics on racial and ethnic groups. *Journal of the American Medical Association, 267*(2), 268-271.

Hahn, R. A., Mulinare, J., & Teutsch, S. M. (1992). Inconsistencies in coding of race and ethnicity between birth and death in US infants. *Journal of the American Medical Association, 267*(2), 259-263.

Hahn, R. A., & Stroup, D. F. (1994). Race and ethnicity in public health surveillance: Criteria for the scientific use of social categories. *Public Health Reports, 109*(1), 7-15.

Hanley, A. J. G., Choi, B. C. K., & Holowaty, E. J. (1995). Cancer mortality among Chinese migrants: A review. *International Journal of Epidemiology, 24*(2), 255-265.

Hildesheim, A., & Levine, P. H. (1993). Etiology of nasopharyngeal carcinoma: A review. *Epidemiologic Reviews, 19*(2), 466-485.

Hollman, F. (1993). *U.S. population estimates by age, sex, race, and Hispanic origin: 1980 to 1991* (U.S. Bureau of the Census. Current Population Reports P-25, No. 1095). Washington, DC: Government Printing Office.

Japan Aging Research Center. (1996). *Statistical abstract of aging in Japan.* Tokyo: Japan Aging Research Center.

Kasl, S. V., & Berkman, L. (1983). Health consequences of the experience of migration. *Annual Review of Public Health, 4,* pp. 69-90.

Kestenbaum, B. (1986). Mortality by nativity. *Demography, 23*(1), 87-90.

King, H., & Haenszel, W. (1973). Cancer mortality among foreign-born and native-born Chinese in the United States. *Journal of Chronic Diseases, 26,* 623-646.

King H., & Locke, F. B. (1980). Cancer mortality risk among Chinese in the United States. *Journal of the National Cancer Institute, 65,* 1141-1148.

King, H., & Locke, F. B. (1987). Health effects of migration: U.S. Chinese in and outside China-town. *International Migration Review, 21,* 555-575.

King, H., Locke, F. B., Li, J.-Y., Pollack, E. S., & Tu, J. T. (1985). Patterns of site-specific displacement in cancer mortality among migrants: The Chinese in the United States. *American Journal of Public Health, 75,* 237-242.

Kitagawa, E. M., & Hauser, P. M. (1973). *Differential mortality in the United States: A study of socioeconomic epidemiology.* Cambridge, MA: Harvard University Press.

Klatsky, A., & Armstrong, M. A. (1991). Cardiovascular risk factors among Asian Americans living in Northern California. *American Journal of Public Health, 81*(11), 1423-1428.

McKenney, N., & Bennett, C. E. (1994). Issues regarding data on race and ethnicity: The Census Bureau experience. *Public Health Reports, 109*(1), 16-25.

Mitchell, B. D., Stern, M. P., Haffner, S. H., Hazuda, H. P., & Patterson, J. K. (1990). Risk factors for cardiovascular mortality in Mexican Americans and non-Hispanic Whites: The San Antonio Heart Study. *American Journal of Epidemiology, 131*(3), 423-433.

National Center for Health Statistics. (1969). *Comparability of marital status, race, nativity, and country of origin on the death certificate and matching census record, United States—May-August 1960* (Vital and Health Statistics, Series 20, No. 18). Washington, DC: Government Printing Office.

National Center for Health Statistics. (1984). *Vital statistics of the United States. 1979: Vol. 2. Mortality. Part A.* Washington, DC: Government Printing Office.

National Center for Health Statistics. (1992). *Mortality detail files 1989: Vol. 8, Part 27* [Electronic data file]. Hyattsville, MD: U.S. Department of Health and Human Services, National Center for Health Statistics [Producer]. Ann Arbor, MI: Inter-university Consortium for Political and Social Research [Distributor], 1993.

National Center for Health Statistics. (1993a). *Mortality detail files 1968-1991: Part 28, 1990 data* [Electronic data file]. Hyattsville, MD: U.S. Department of Health and Human Services, National Center for Health Statistics [Producer]. Ann Arbor, MI: Inter-university Consortium for Political and Social Research [Distributor], 1994.

National Center for Health Statistics. (1993b). *Mortality detail files 1968-1991: Part 29, 1991 data* [Electronic data file]. Hyattsville, MD: U.S. Department of Health and Human Services, National Center for Health Statistics [Producer]. Ann Arbor, MI: Inter-university Consortium for Political and Social Research [Distributor], 1994.

National Center for Health Statistics. (1993c). *Vital and health statistics in the United States, 1989: Vol. 2. Mortality, Part A.* Washington, DC: Government Printing Office.

National Center for Health Statistics. (1994a). *Vital statistics of the United States, 1990: Vol. 2. Mortality, Part A.* Washington, DC: Government Printing Office.

National Center for Health Statistics. (1994b). *Vital statistics of the United States, 1990: Vol. 2, Section 6. Life tables.* Washington, DC: Public Health Service.

National Center for Health Statistics. (1996). *Vital statistics of the United States, 1991: Vol. 2. Mortality, Part A.* Washington, DC: Public Health Service.

Nomura, A., Stemmermann, G. N., Chyou, P.-H., Kato, I., Perez-Perez, G. I., & Blaser, M. J. (1991). Heliobacter pylori and gastric carcinoma among Japanese-Americans in Hawaii. *New England Journal of Medicine, 325*(16), 1132-1136.

Norris, F. D., & Shipley, P. W. (1971). A closer look at race differentials in California's infant mortality, 1965-67. *HSMHA Health Reports, 85*(9), 810-814.

Office of Management and Budget. (1978). Directive No. 15: Race and Ethnic Standards for Federal Statistics and Administrative Reporting. In *Statistical policy handbook* (pp. 37-38). Washington, DC: U.S. Department of Commerce, Office of Federal Statistical Policy and Standards.

Parsonnet, J., Friedman, G. D., Vandersteen, D. P., Chang, Y., Vogelman, J. V., Orentreich, N., & Sibley, R. K. (1991). Heliobacter pylori infection and the risk of gastric carcinoma. *New England Journal of Medicine, 325*(16), 1127-1131.

Reed, D. M. (1990). The paradox of high risk of stroke in populations with low risk of coronary heart disease. *American Journal of Epidemiology, 131,* 579-588.

Reed, D., & Yano, K. (1994, December). *Cardiovascular disease among elderly Asian-Americans: Lessons from the Ni-Hon-San studies.* Paper presented at the National Research Council Workshop on Racial and Ethnic Differences in Health in Late Life, Washington, D.C.

Robinson, J. G., Ahmed, B., Das Gupta, P., & Woodrow, K. A. (1993). Estimation of population coverage in the 1990 United States census based on demographic analysis. *Journal of the American Statistical Association, 88*(423), 1061-1079.

Rogers, R. G., Hummer, R. A., Nam, C. B., & Peters, K. (1996). Demographic, socioeconomic, and behavioral factors affecting ethnic mortality by cause. *Social Forces, 74*(4), 1419-1438.

Rogot, E., Sorlie, P., & Johnson, N. J. (1986). Probabilistic methods in matching census samples to the national death index. *Journal of Chronic Diseases, 39*(9), 719-734.

Rogot, E., Sorlie, P. D., Johnson, N. J., & Schmitt, C. (1992). *Mortality study of 1.3 million persons by demographic, social, and economic factors: 1979-1986 follow up* (NIH Publication No. 92-3297). Washington, DC: National Institutes of Health.

Rosenwaike, I. (1987). Mortality differentials among persons born in Cuba, Mexico, and Puerto Rico residing in the United States, 1979-81. *American Journal of Public Health, 77*(5), 603-606.

Sorlie, P. D., Rogot, E., & Johnson, N. J. (1992). Validity of demographic characteristics on the death certificate. *Epidemiology, 3*(2), 181-184.

Spencer, G. (1986). *Projections of the Hispanic population: 1983 to 2080* (U.S. Bureau of the Census, Current Population Reports P-25, No. 995). Washington, DC: Government Printing Office.

Stavig, G. R., Igra, A., & Leonard, A. R. (1988). Hypertension and related health issues among Asian and Pacific Islanders in California. *Public Health Reports, 103,* 28-37.

U.S. Bureau of the Census. (1973). *1970 census of population. Detailed characteristics. United States summary* (PC[1]-D1). Washington, DC: Government Printing Office.

U.S. Bureau of the Census. (1983). *1980 census of population. General population characteristics. United States summary* (PC80-1-B1). Washington, DC: Government Printing Office.

U.S. Bureau of the Census. (1988). *1980 census of population. Asian and Pacific Islander population in the United States: 1980* (PC80-2-1E). Washington, DC: Government Printing Office.

U.S. Bureau of the Census. (1992). *1990 census of population. General characteristics. United States.* Washington, DC: Government Printing Office.

U.S. Bureau of the Census. (1993). *1990 census of population. Asian and Pacific Islanders in the United States.* (1990 CP-3-5). Washington, DC: Government Printing Office.

U.S. Department of Health and Human Services. (1985). *Report of the Secretary's Task Force on Black and Minority Health: Vol. 2. Crosscutting issues in minority health.* Washington, DC: Author.

Yu, E. (1984). The low mortality rates of Chinese infants: Some plausible explanatory factors. *Social Science and Medicine, 16,* 253-262.

Yu, E., Drury, T. P., & Liu, W. T. (1982). Using National Health Interview Survey data in secondary analysis of health characteristics of Asian/Pacific Americans: Problems and prospects. In *Proceedings of the Annual Meeting of the American Statistical Association.* Detroit, MI: American Statistical Association.

Yu, E. S., Chang, C.-F., Liu, W. T., & Kan, S. H. (1985). Asian-White mortality differences: Are there excess deaths. In *Report of the Secretary's Task Force on Black and Minority Health: Vol. 2. Crosscutting issues in minority health* (pp. 209-251). Washington, DC: Department of Health and Human Services.

Yu, E. S., & Liu, W. T. (1992). US national health data on Asian Americans and Pacific Islanders: A research agenda for the 1990s. *American Journal of Public Health, 82*(12), 1645-1652.

Yu, E. S., & Liu, W. T. (1994). Methodological issues. In N. W. S. Zane, D. T. Takeuchi, & K. N. J. Young (Eds.), *Confronting critical health issues of Asian and Pacific Islander Americans* (pp. 22-50). Thousand Oaks, CA: Sage.

Zane, N. W. S., Takeuchi, D. T., & Young, K. N. J. (1994). *Confronting critical health issues of Asian and Pacific Islander Americans.* Thousand Oaks, CA: Sage.

Aging and Mortality Among American Indians

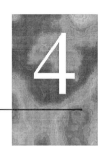

Concerns About the Reliability of a Crucial Indicator of Health Status

Robert John

Writing a chapter on mortality among American Indian[1] elders would appear to be a simple matter, given the certainty of the event and the substantial bureaucratic procedures designed to enumerate and classify each death that occurs in the United States. Yet mortality figures for American Indians are subject to three primary sources of error, some of which are a bigger problem for the American Indian population than for larger populations. The first major problem is a misclassification in the underlying cause of death. A second major problem is the misidentification of the race of the decedent. Finally, mortality figures are influenced by the accuracy of the American Indian population estimates.

Death certificates are the source of all mortality data in the United States. These data are collected by each state and seven other registration

AUTHOR'S NOTE: Partial support for this research was provided by the National Institute on Aging grant number R01-AG11294. I am indebted to Aaron Handler, Chief, Demographic Statistics Branch, Indian Health Service, who provided the most current mortality and population data for American Indians, and provided guidance in their use and interpretation. I would also like to acknowledge the substantive assistance of Heather Goggans, Staff Editor in the University of North Texas Minority Aging Research Institute, Patrice H. Blanchard, Economic Security Representative, American Association of Retired Persons, Vanessa Gilbert, Research Scientist in the University of North Texas Minority Aging Research Institute, and Catherine H. Hennessy, Epidemiologist, Centers for Disease Control and Prevention.

areas and are reported to the National Center for Health Statistics (NCHS) for compilation. Characterized as a "cooperative effort" (National Center for Health Statistics [NCHS], 1986, p. 1), each state can determine what information to collect and can design its own forms and procedures, including the qualifications of the individuals eligible to certify deaths. Because the federal government provides payment to the states for the data, the NCHS is able to ensure that a minimum amount of uniform data is collected and reported by each state through the design and adoption of standard certificates, the content of which is reviewed and revised periodically.

Questions about the accuracy of the medical information on the death certificate have been the subject of research for some time (Gittlesohn & Royston, 1982). There is a general consensus that physicians and other certifiers do not receive adequate training in how to complete the certificate and that this leads to a number of errors (Adams & Herrmann, 1995; Comstock & Markush, 1986; Glasser, 1981; Hanzlick, 1993; Kircher, 1990, 1992; Kleinman, 1982; NCHS, 1986). Typically, this lack of training has lead to inaccurate, incomplete, or misleading information. Kircher (1990, 1992) and Kircher, Nelson, and Burdo (1985) identified the current state of medical knowledge, incompleteness of the information available at the time of death, the various ways that death certificates are completed, and how the underlying cause of death is classified in vital records offices as pervasive problems. Comstock and Markush (1986) noted that physicians rarely amend the death certificate to improve the accuracy of the medical cause of death information to reflect data contained in clinical records or the results of postmortem examinations. However, other problems with the medical cause of death have also been documented.

Three types of studies challenge confidence in the accuracy of mortality figures: comparison of medical information in the death certificate with the results of an autopsy (Engel, Strauchen, Chiazze, & Heid, 1980; Goldman et al., 1983; Kircher et al., 1985; Schottenfeld, Eaton, Sommers, Alonso, & Wilkinson, 1982), comparison of the death certificate with a thorough review of clinical records (Gittlesohn & Senning, 1979; Guariglia & Abrahams, 1985; Heller, Friedlander, & Geller, 1985; Holmes & Baer, 1986), and quality assurance studies of death certificates conducted by states (Stein, 1992).

Probably the most disturbing type of error has been documented by studies that compare the clinical diagnosis of the underlying cause of death contained in the death certificate with the results of an autopsy. Unfortunately, the ability to conduct this type of study is in jeopardy because the rate of autopsy in the United States has declined steadily since the post-World War II era from around 50% (Geller, 1983; Roberts, 1978) to approximately 10% of deaths in 1994 (Singh, Kochanek, & MacDorman, 1996). Furthermore, there are large discrepancies in the likelihood of autopsy based on the presumed cause of death as well as the age and gender of the decedent. In comparison to the high rate of autopsy for homicide (97.2%), suicide (55.1%), and accidents and adverse effects (48.4%), the rate of autopsy is much lower for the leading causes of mortality among the aged, including chronic and degenerative diseases such as cardiovascular disease (6.6%), malignant neoplasms (2.3%), cerebrovascular diseases (2.9%), chronic obstructive pulmonary disease (3.1%), pneumonia and influenza (5.6%), and diabetes mellitus (3.3%) (Singh et al., 1996). The National Center for Health Statistics (NCHS; 1996a) has documented that autopsy declines with age—from 12.0% of deaths among 55- to 64-year-old decedents to 1.8% among decedents 85 years and over—and is lower at all ages for females than for males.

Based on a comparison with the results of an autopsy, Schottenfeld et al. (1982) found that 15% of death certificates required a recoding of the underlying medical cause of death. These researchers found the most errors in the death certificates of women, of individuals 70 years of age and over, and among patients who had been in the hospital longer than 28 days. Goldman et al. (1983) found that autopsy revealed a major diagnosis—one that, if known and treated, could have resulted in longer survival—had been missed in approximately 10% of the deaths. They also documented that diagnostic errors were more common among patients aged 65 years and over.

Kircher et al. (1985) found 29% and Engel et al. (1980) found 19% major disagreement between the death certificate and autopsy that shifted the underlying cause of death to another major disease category. Less dramatic changes that shifted the cause of death only within major disease categories were even more common. Unfortunately, several studies have shown that the premortem diagnostic accuracy also varies by disease and that the discrepancies are not random and "do not cancel each other out" (Engel et al., 1980, p. 107). However, these studies (Engel et al., 1980; Goldman et al., 1983; Kircher et al., 1985; Schottenfeld et al., 1982) fail to agree about which diseases are over- or underdiagnosed at the time of death. Fortunately, the leading causes of death are less sensitive to these errors than less common causes of death.

Attribution of each death to a single underlying cause is another major problem with published mortality data, especially for anyone who studies an aging population (Israel, Rosenberg, & Curtin, 1986; Kircher, 1990). Citing Israel et al. (1986), Kircher (1990) points out:

> For many years, descriptions of cause-specific mortality data have been presented almost entirely in terms of a single underlying cause for each death. This characterization of mortality was probably adequate as long as the major public health problems involved acute infectious disease. It has, however, become less appropriate as an increasing proportion of deaths have been the result of chronic disease. Deaths due to chronic diseases are often not well-characterized by a single cause; rather, they are more likely to represent a number of coexisting conditions among which there may be no direct etiologic chain to facilitate the identification of a single underlying cause. (p. 170)

Although the NCHS (1996a) is in the process of implementing an automated system to improve the availability of, quality of, and ability to use multiple-cause-of-death information, the impact of this innovation is yet to be realized.

Other problems also compromise the usefulness of existing mortality data. For example, Gittlesohn (1982) noted the increased use of nonspecific terminology to characterize the cause of death (e.g., neoplasms unspecified site, unspecified septicemia) and geographic differences in diagnostic labeling that have resulted in inordinately high concentrations of rare or unusual causes of mortality in certain localities (e.g., other myocardial insufficiency in Maryland).

A closely related problem is the disproportionate number of Indian deaths that are classified as the result of symptoms, signs, or ill-defined conditions (Becker, Wiggins, Key, & Samet, 1993). The NCHS (1996a) considers the proportion of deaths assigned to symptoms, signs, or ill-defined conditions a measure of the specificity of medical diagnoses at the time of death as well as an indication of the quality of the cause-of-death information contained in death certificates. Approximately 1.4% of deaths among American Indian elders aged 65 years and over between 1990 and 1992 were assigned to this residual category.

The second major source of error in American Indian mortality data is the misclassification of race on the death certificate (Frost, Tollestrup, Ross, Sabotta, & Kimball, 1994; Poe et al., 1993; Sorlie, Rogot, & Johnson, 1992), which almost always results in an underestimation of American Indian death rates (Sugarman, Holliday, Lopez, & Wilder, 1993). In most states, assignation of the race of the decedent is left to the funeral director. Hahn (1992) noted that funeral directors ask the next of kin about the race of the decedent or make independent judgments, but the degree to which funeral directors make independent judgments is not known. According to Querec (1994), "the race item is often completed based simply on personal observation by the funeral director" (p. 3). A small number of interviews with funeral directors in Washington State revealed that "the question about the race of the deceased is usually not asked unless there is uncertainty about the race" (Frost et al., 1994, p. 293).

Within the past several years, a number of studies on the accuracy of mortality data collected on American Indians have been conducted. Most studies of the accuracy of the coding of Indian deaths have focused on infant mortality (Frost & Shy, 1980; Hahn, Mendlein, & Helgerson, 1993; Hahn, Mulinare, & Teutsch, 1992; Kennedy & Deapen, 1991; Querec, 1992, 1994; Sugarman et al., 1993; Watson, Bennett, Reed, McBroom, & Helgerson, 1993). The most comprehensive nationwide study using linked birth and death records (Querec, 1994) found that American Indian infant mortality between 1983 and 1987 was 20% higher than reported when racial misclassifications were corrected. Other research (Hoyert, 1994) has corroborated this magnitude of error in American Indian infant mortality rates. Based on recent changes in how race is assigned in instances of infant mortality, Hoyert (1994) calculated that American Indian infant mortality between 1987 and 1989 was 24% greater when the race of the infant is determined solely by the race of the mother. Hahn et al. (1993) documented that, except for California and Oklahoma, race classification is more accurate in states with the largest number and greatest proportion of Indians in the population. A study of Oklahoma (Kennedy & Deapen, 1991) documented substantially higher infant mortality among American Indians because of racial misclassification of Indian deaths between 1975 and 1988. Using matched birth and death records, Kennedy and Deapen found that only 65.7% of Indian deaths were correct on the death certificate, and that 97.2% of the mistakes were classified as White. The revised estimate of American Indian infant mortality was 1.8 times the reported rate.

In order to ascertain the reliability of demographic information contained in death certificates of adults, the NCHS conducted the National Mortality Followback Survey (NMFS) in 1986. The NMFS compared information obtained from next of kin with the information in the death certificate of a nationally representative sample of 18,448 individuals aged 25 years and over who died in 1986. All American Indian deaths ($N = 422$) were included in the study because of the small number of American Indian deaths in any given year. Analysis of the NMFS data (Poe et al., 1993) revealed substantial problems with the accuracy of the race coding of American Indian deaths. These authors found that there was only 93% agreement for American Indian deaths, compared to 98% agreement for both Whites and Blacks. Of those deaths identified as American Indian on the death certificate but as another race by the next of kin, 80% were identified as White. Of those misclassified decedents identified as American Indian by the next of kin, 71% were identified as White and 28% were identified as Black on the death certificate. Unfortunately, this comparison revealed that there were 92 (21.8%) more American Indian deaths than were recorded in the death certificates. A larger study of the accuracy of demographic data contained in the death certificate (Sorlie et al., 1992) showed that only 73.6% American Indian deaths were correctly classified. These authors also concluded that mortality rates for American Indians are underestimated between 22% and 30%.

A more circumscribed study from Washington State (Frost et al., 1994) corroborated problems of American Indian racial misclassification on death certificates. Based on a comparison with the Indian Health Service (IHS) patient registry system records—a much more stringent criteria than self-identification—the accuracy of the racial coding item on Washington State death certificates from 1985 to 1990 was only 87.2%. As with the NMFS, Frost et al. (1994) found that most of these misclassifications (95%) were listed as White on the death certificate.

Frost et al. (1994) also investigated the personal characteristics that were associated with correct racial classification as well as those associated with incorrect classification. Multivariate analysis revealed that correct racial classification was significantly more likely if the deceased had more than 50% American Indian ancestry, was born in Washington State, or was a member of a large Washington State tribe. In fact, the race of individuals with more than 50% American Indian ancestry was correctly identified more than 90% of the time compared to 74% among those with 25% to 49% American Indian ancestry and 63.2% of individuals with less than a quarter American Indian ancestry. In addition, Frost et al. (1994) discovered that individuals who died of cancer were significantly less likely to be coded as American Indian whereas individuals who died from alcohol-related conditions were significantly more likely to be correctly identified as American Indian. Additional analysis of a small subset of the sample suggested that correct racial classification was significantly more likely if the informant was registered as an American Indian with the IHS.

The Indian Health Service (IHS; 1995b) has acknowledged that American Indian deaths are underreported in the seven states that compose the California, Oklahoma (Kansas, Oklahoma, and Texas), and Portland (Idaho, Oregon, and Washington) IHS Service Areas. Based on IHS estimates for 1996, these three service areas contain 39.5% of the IHS service population. Using these findings, the IHS (1995a) has produced two sets of figures for age-adjusted mortality and several derivative measures of health status (life expectancy at birth and years of productive life lost). These figures reveal that age-adjusted mortality rates for the leading causes of death and the derivative measures of health status are uniformly poorer when the data from the three IHS Service Areas with known reporting problems are excluded.

The full extent of the misidentification of American Indian deaths is not known. However, a major study of racial misclassification of Indian deaths between 1986 and 1988 (Indian Health Service [IHS], in press) has found that misclassification exceeded 10% in 12 of 33 Reservation States (36.4%). This study also found four IHS Service Areas with misclassification of Indian deaths that exceeded 10%, with substantially larger problems in some areas: California (30.4%), Oklahoma (28.0%), Bemidji (16.1%), and Nashville (12.1%). To make matters worse, the biggest discrepancies were found for American Indian elders aged 85 and over (15%), 65 to 74 years of age (14%), and 75 to 84 years old (13%).

In addition to basic problems created by the underreporting of Indian deaths because of racial misclassification, the third major source of error in establishing mortality rates is the lack of accurate American Indian population figures. For various reasons, accurate demographic information has been difficult to obtain for American Indians in general and for American Indian elders in particular, and the accuracy of census data has been an area of debate among demographers for some time (Harris, 1994; Passel, 1976, 1996; Passel & Berman, 1986; Snipp, 1989). There is general consensus that self-identification of race by the respondent in U.S. Decennial Census efforts is the primary reason for discrepancies in population counts since 1970. Passel (1996) has estimated that one third of the total Indian population in 1990 had adopted a new self-identification as an American Indian between 1960 and 1990. However, Harris (1994) has shown that, unlike other age groups, the 1990 Census contains an undercount of American Indian elders.

These inaccurate population estimates have influenced the calculation of recent American Indian mortality rates. In particular, intercensal projections of the size of the IHS service population that were made by the IHS during the 1980s and early 1990s were substantially smaller than the American Indian population figures compiled in the 1990 Decennial Census. Subsequent revisions of 1990 American Indian population figures by the Census Bureau have resulted in three consecutive years of recalculations of American Indian mortality rates by the IHS (1995b). The third recalculation appeared in the 1994 edition of IHS publications.

The IHS has also introduced several refinements in the way vital event statistics are calculated. The refinement with the greatest impact on mortality data, which was introduced by the IHS in 1992 publications, changed the method of calculating American Indian mortality rates. Prior to this date, mortality rates were calculated using American Indian population figures for Reservation States (which included urban Indians as well as those actually residing in IHS service areas). The new method uses population figures based only on the number of Indians residing in the counties in which IHS provides services. All mortality data in this chapter were calculated using the IHS method and refer only to the IHS service population.

Life Expectancy at Birth

Life expectancy at birth is a common measure of the overall health status of a population. Figure 4.1 depicts the steady increase in life expectancy at birth among Whites and American Indians since 1940. The precise gain in life expectancy among American Indians is somewhat unclear, although the increase has been substantial, even if the more conservative 1991 figures that exclude the IHS service areas with documented underreporting of Indian deaths are used as the basis of comparison. The difference between the high and low figures for life expectancy at birth for American Indians in 1991 is 4.5 years for Indian males and 4.8 years for Indian females.

Based on the more conservative calculations, life expectancy at birth (Indian Health Service [IHS], 1991, 1995a) increased by 19.3 years for American Indians—from 51 years to 70.3 years—during the 50-year period between 1940 and 1991. In comparison, life expectancy at birth for the White population (IHS, 1991; U.S. Department of Health and Human Services, 1995) increased by only 12.1 years (to 76.3 years) during the same period. For both populations, this increase in life expectancy has been greater for

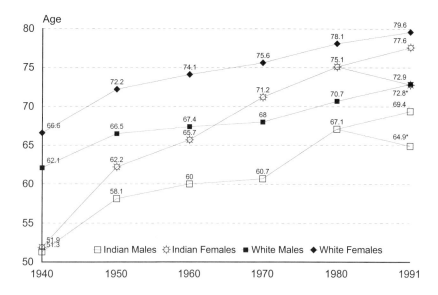

Figure 4.1. Life Expectancy at Birth Among American Indians and Whites by Sex
SOURCES: Indian Health Service (1991, 1995); U.S. Department of Health and Human Services (1995).
NOTE: * Excludes IHS Areas with documented underreporting of Indian deaths.

females than for males. By 1991, life expectancy at birth for American Indian females had increased by 20.9 years (to 72.8 years), whereas American Indian male life expectancy had increased by approximately 14.6 years (to 64.9 years). The gap between American Indian and White life expectancy at birth has narrowed so that life expectancy at birth was only 8.0 years less for American Indian males and 6.8 years less for American Indian females in 1991. Moreover, life expectancy at birth among American Indian females is now the same as among White males.

The remarkable improvement in life expectancy at birth for American Indians is largely attributable to the efforts of the IHS to eliminate infectious disease and to meet the acute-care needs of the Indian population, including aggressive efforts to improve maternal and child health. Over the past 40 years since the IHS assumed responsibility for American Indian health care, the shift from acute and infectious diseases to chronic and degenerative diseases has prompted several researchers to conclude that the American Indian population is undergoing an epidemiologic transition (Broudy & May, 1983; Kunitz, 1983; Manson & Callaway, 1990; Young, 1994). Consistent with this

interpretation, Johnson and Taylor (1991) documented that chronic and degenerative diseases are rising among the IHS American Indian service population. This change in morbidity is leading to a change in the mortality profile
of American Indian elders.

Deaths by Age and Sex

Despite recognizable health improvements that have resulted in increasing
life expectancy at birth, far fewer American Indians than Whites live to old
age. Among the general population, death usually occurs in old age, and most
Americans associate death with advanced age. According to the IHS (1995b),
74.9% of all deaths in the White population in 1991 occurred after 65 years
of age. In contrast, only 45% of deaths among the American Indian population between 1990 and 1992 occurred among elders over age 65. Moreover,
85.9% of all deaths in the White population, compared to only 59.3% of the
deaths among American Indians, occurred among individuals aged 55 years
and over. This discrepancy is associated with differential mortality among
males and females over the life course. For example, only 39.2% of American
Indian male deaths between 1990 and 1992 were among elders aged 65 and
over. In comparison, 53.5% of deaths among American Indian females were
among elders aged 65 and over.

Average Remaining Years of Life

A more useful and accurate estimate of life expectancy takes into consideration the current age of the individual and his or her current risk of mortality.
It is possible to estimate the average number of years of life that remain for
people who have achieved a particular age, based on the assumption that their
mortality experience will be the same as current age-specific mortality rates.
As seen in Table 4.1, differences between Whites and American Indians are
greatest in the younger age groups and for women. In fact, the 2.7-year difference between Indian and White women between the ages of 55 and 59
years declines gradually but does not fully disappear. In comparison, the gap
between Indian and White men is smaller, and after age 75, Indian men have
nearly the same life expectancy as White men. Overall, Table 4.1 reveals that
Indian female life expectancy in old age is approximately 20% longer than
Indian male life expectancy.

TABLE 4.1 Average Number of Years of Life Remaining by Age and Sex
for American Indians (Nine IHS Service Areas) 1991-1993 and
Whites 1992

	American Indian			White		
Age	*Male*	*Female*	*Both Sexes*	*Male*	*Female*	*Both Sexes*
55–59	20.7	24.8	22.9	22.9	27.5	25.3
60–64	17.6	21.1	19.4	19.1	23.2	21.3
65–69	14.5	17.6	16.2	15.5	19.3	17.6
70–74	11.7	14.2	13.1	12.4	15.6	14.2
75–79	9.3	11.4	10.5	9.6	12.2	11.2
80–84	6.8	8.6	7.9	7.2	9.2	8.5
85+	5.2	6.3	5.8	5.3	6.6	6.2

SOURCE: Indian Health Service, Division of Program Statistics; National Center for Health Statistics (1996b).

Comparative Mortality Rates

All Cause Mortality

Although it is one of the most general indicators of the health status of a population, mortality from all causes eliminates one source of potential error in vital events data: the misclassification of the underlying cause of death. The mortality rate among American Indian elders aged 65 years and over from all causes of death was lower than the rate for White elders. Based on age-specific mortality rates, Table 4.2 indicates that a "mortality crossover" occurs by age 75 (IHS, 1995b, p. 55). Up to age 65, the American Indian population has higher mortality than the White population. From age 65 to 74, the age-specific mortality rates are very much the same. After age 75, however, American Indians have lower age-specific mortality rates than the White population. These figures suggest that the mortality crossover now occurs approximately 10 years later than previous research had shown as occurring at age 65 (Espey, Samet, Wiggins, & Becker, 1993; Indian Health Service [IHS], 1992; John, 1995; John & Baldridge, 1996; Stinson & Plantz, 1986; U.S. Department of Health and Human Services, 1985). The rise in the age of the mortality crossover was first documented (without comment) in American Indian mortality figures for 1987 to 1989 (Indian Health Service [IHS], 1993).

TABLE 4.2   Age-Specific Mortality From All Causes Among American Indians Residing in IHS Service Areas (1990-1992) and Whites (1991): Rate per 100,000 Population

Age	American Indian			White		
	Male	Female	Both Sexes	Male	Female	Both Sexes
55–64	1,712.1	1,080.8	1,374.1	1,443.7	821.9	1,118.8
65–74	3,225.0	2,127.4	2,613.0	3,349.7	1,909.4	2,545.1
75–84	6,467.7	4,139.6	5,077.1	7,641.5	4,752.8	5,842.4
85+	13,844.3	10,452.1	11,696.7	18,020.9	14,188.1	15,239.0

SOURCE: Indian Health Service, Division of Program Statistics; National Center for Health Statistics (1996a).

Leading Causes of Mortality

American Indian elders over age 65 have lower overall mortality than the White elderly population, but the cause-specific mortality rates of the White elderly population differ substantially from the cause-specific mortality rates of American Indian elders. American Indian elders have lower death rates than the White elderly population for the top four leading causes of death, including diseases of the heart, cancer, cerebrovascular diseases, and chronic obstructive pulmonary disease. However, American Indian elders experienced higher mortality rates for all other major causes of mortality (IHS, 1995b; John, 1995). In particular, American Indian elders had higher mortality from diabetes mellitus, accidents and adverse effects, and pneumonia and influenza.

The leading causes of death between 1990 and 1992 among American Indian elders aged 65 and over are presented in Table 4.3. The seven leading causes of death for American Indian elders were diseases of the heart, malignant neoplasms, cerebrovascular diseases, pneumonia and influenza, diabetes mellitus, chronic obstructive pulmonary disease, and accidental injuries. Approximately 77% of all deaths among American Indian elders aged 65 and over during 1990 to 1992 were the result of these seven causes.

Heart Disease

Approximately one third of all deaths among American Indian elders aged 65 and over between 1990 and 1992 were attributable to cardiovascular diseases. Ischemic heart disease accounted for 61% of deaths attributable to diseases

TABLE 4.3 Leading Causes of Mortality for American Indian Elders Aged 65 and Over: 1990-1992

Cause	Rate per 100,000	Proportional Mortality (%)	Total Number of Deaths
Diseases of the heart	1,315.4	32.0	2,806
Malignant neoplasms	787.6	19.2	1,680
Cerebrovascular diseases	296.7	7.2	633
Pneumonia and influenza	237.7	5.8	507
Diabetes mellitus	232.1	5.7	495
Chronic obstructive pulmonary diseases	158.9	3.9	339
Accidental injuries	142.0	3.5	303
Nephritis, nephrotic syndrome, and nephrosis	86.7	2.1	185
Chronic liver disease and cirrhosis	71.3	1.7	152
Septicemia	59.5	1.4	127
All other causes		17.5	1,534

SOURCE: Indian Health Service, Division of Program Statistics.

of the heart. Approximately one third (30.7%) of all cardiovascular disease deaths among Indian elders 65 years and over were the result of acute myocardial infarction. Another 28.9% of cardiovascular disease deaths were the result of old myocardial infarction and other forms of chronic ischemic heart disease. Table 4.4 documents that American Indians have higher rates of mortality from heart disease than Whites between the ages of 55 and 64, and the rates are nearly identical in the 65-74 age group. However, after age 75, White mortality from cardiovascular disease accelerates. For all age groups, male mortality among both Indians and Whites is higher than female mortality. Although cardiovascular diseases are the cause of considerable mortality among American Indian elders, research on trends in mortality (John, 1995) has shown that mortality from cardiovascular diseases remained relatively stable between 1977 and 1988. According to Coulehan and Welty (1990), reduction of the major risk factors, including smoking, serum cholesterol levels, and hypertension, would decrease the prevalence of heart disease among American Indian elders.

Malignant Neoplasms

Nearly one fifth of all deaths among American Indian elders are the result of cancer. From 1990 to 1992, more than half of all cancer deaths among

TABLE 4.4 Age-Specific Mortality From Diseases of the Heart Among American Indians Residing in IHS Service Areas (1990-1992) and Whites (1991): Rate per 100,000 Population

	American Indian			White		
Age	Male	Female	Both Sexes	Male	Female	Both Sexes
55–64	551.6	235.2	382.2	499.4	188.2	336.8
65–74	1,068.2	560.4	785.0	1,198.6	567.4	846.0
75–84	2,262.5	1,244.0	1,654.2	2,858.2	1,814.7	2,208.3
85+	4,895.2	3,528.4	4,029.9	7,411.2	6,447.3	6,710.6

SOURCE: Indian Health Service, Division of Program Statistics; National Center for Health Statistics (1996a).

American Indian elders over age 65 were the result of malignant neoplasms of the digestive organs and peritoneum (31%) or the respiratory and intrathoracic organs (24%). Deaths attributable to cancer of the digestive organs increased with age, while deaths attributable to respiratory cancers peaked among elders in the 75-84 age group and declined somewhat among elders over age 85.

Among elders aged 65 and over, Indian female death rates from cancer are lower than among American Indian male elders (71% of the male rate). As seen in Table 4.5, American Indians over age 55 have significantly lower mortality from malignant neoplasms than Whites. However, there is evidence to suggest that cancer incidence among American Indians is underreported. In a study of a Surveillance, Epidemiology, and End Results (SEER) cancer registry in Washington State, Frost, Taylor, and Fries (1992) discovered substantial misclassification of race among individuals documented as American Indian in the IHS patient registry. These authors found that 30% of Indian cancer deaths were misclassified. As has been found in other studies, 93% of the racial misclassifications were identified as White. According to Frost et al. (1992), "the only independent predictor of racial misclassification in the SEER registry was blood quantum" (p. 961).

Cancer death rates among American Indian elders bear monitoring because cancer deaths increased by 19% among American Indian elders from 1977 to 1988, according to mortality trends (John, 1995). Moreover, Boss (1990) reported that American Indians had the worst 5-year survival rate for lung, stomach, breast, and prostate cancer of the eight ethnic groups on which comparative information was available. Although Rhoades (1990, p. 56) has

TABLE 4.5 Age-Specific Mortality From Malignant Neoplasms Among American Indians Residing in IHS Service Areas (1990-1992) and Whites (1991): Rate per 100,000 Population

Age	American Indian			White		
	Male	*Female*	*Both Sexes*	*Male*	*Female*	*Both Sexes*
55–64	339.0	280.3	307.6	505.0	374.7	436.9
65–74	721.8	541.4	621.2	1,091.5	673.8	858.2
75–84	1,228.8	778.5	959.8	1,866.4	1,018.7	1,338.5
85+	1,835.7	1,152.5	1,403.2	2,733.0	1,391.7	1,760.7

SOURCE: Indian Health Service, Division of Program Statistics; National Center for Health Statistics (1996a).

mentioned that biologic factors may contribute to mortality, the weight of the available evidence suggests that environmental and cultural factors (Boss, 1990; U.S. Department of Health and Human Services, 1985; Young, 1994) and lack of timely medical intervention in the disease process (Black & Wiggins, 1985) are important reasons for poor cancer survival rates. Results from the only nationwide survey of the IHS service population revealed that more extensive preventive and routine clinical services are also needed. Lefkowitz and Underwood (1991) documented that American Indian and Alaska Native women over age 60 were substantially less likely than their age peers in the general population to have ever had a clinical breast exam, mammogram, or Pap test.

Cerebrovascular Diseases

Hemorrhages, cerebral thrombosis and other occlusions of the cerebral arteries, and cerebral embolisms are the primary identifiable conditions in this disease category. However, the residual classification—all other and late effects of cerebrovascular diseases—accounted for 76.5% of cerebrovascular deaths among American Indian elders aged 65 and over between 1990 and 1992. Furthermore, the proportion of deaths attributed to this residual classification increased with age. Table 4.6 shows that the mortality rate from cerebrovascular diseases increases rapidly with age for American Indian elders (more than doubling with each successively older age group), but the rate of increase is much higher among Whites. Until age 75, American Indian elders have higher death rates from cerebrovascular diseases than Whites. After age

TABLE 4.6 Age-Specific Mortality From Cerebrovascular Diseases Among
American Indians Residing in IHS Service Areas (1990-1992) and
Whites (1991): Rate per 100,000 Population

Age	American Indian			White		
	Male	Female	Both Sexes	Male	Female	Both Sexes
55–64	58.5	43.3	50.4	44.2	34.1	38.9
65–74	171.5	130.6	148.7	150.5	110.5	128.1
75–84	382.3	402.4	394.3	516.4	439.1	468.3
85+	1,193.2	957.5	1,044.0	1,499.5	1,640.8	1,601.3

SOURCE: Indian Health Service, Division of Program Statistics; National Center for Health Statistics
(1996a).

75, the mortality rate among American Indian elders attributable to cerebrovascular diseases is substantially lower than among the White population.
Indeed, for elders over age 85, the mortality rate from cerebrovascular diseases among the White population is 1.5 times the rate among American
Indians.

Little research on the epidemiology of cerebrovascular diseases among
American Indians has been conducted. According to John (1995), mortality
rates from cerebrovascular diseases among American Indian elders decreased
by approximately 26% during the period between 1977 and 1988. Based on
the results of a descriptive analysis of a small sample of non-reservation adult
American Indians, Gillum (1995) has suggested that the high prevalence of
diabetes, smoking, and obesity contribute to mortality from cerebrovascular
diseases. Gillum recommended hypertension detection and treatment, and
smoking cessation and prevention as measures to reduce cerebrovascular
mortality.

Pneumonia and Influenza

Together, pneumonia and influenza are the fourth leading cause of death
among American Indian elders aged 65 and over. Of the two conditions, pneumonia accounted for 98.6% of deaths in this disease category between 1990
and 1992 for Indian elders over 65 years of age. Moreover, Table 4.7 shows
that the mortality rate associated with pneumonia and influenza among Indian
elders increases markedly with age. Among elders over 85 years old, the mortality rate is 4 times the rate among elders between 75 and 84 years of age.

TABLE 4.7 Age-Specific Mortality From Pneumonia and Influenza Among
American Indians Residing in IHS Service Areas (1990-1992)
and Whites (1991): Rate per 100,000 Population

	American Indian			White		
Age	*Male*	*Female*	*Both Sexes*	*Male*	*Female*	*Both Sexes*
55–64	45.7	25.8	35.1	20.8	11.9	16.1
65–74	109.7	59.9	81.9	70.8	40.5	53.9
75–84	421.3	202.5	290.6	324.4	185.9	238.2
85+	1,621.5	957.5	1,201.1	1,398.2	992.2	1,103.7

SOURCE: Indian Health Service, Division of Program Statistics; National Center for Health Statistics (1996a).

Indeed, among Indian elders over age 85, pneumonia is the third leading cause of death. With the single exception of females aged 85 and over, mortality from pneumonia and influenza among American Indians is higher than among Whites. Although John (1995) has shown that death rates attributable to pneumonia and influenza fell by approximately 14% between 1977 and 1988 among American Indian elders, a targeted vaccination effort, especially among elders over age 85, would continue to reduce mortality from these two causes of death.

Diabetes Mellitus

Diabetes appears to be a growing health problem among American Indian elders. According to John (1995), death rates attributable to diabetes increased by approximately 11% among American Indian elders between 1977 and 1988. This research also revealed that diabetes mellitus became the fifth leading cause of death during that period. Almost all diabetes mellitus among the American Indian population is adult-onset, non-insulin dependent diabetes (NIDDM), and obesity is widely recognized as a leading risk factor. Table 4.8 shows that between 1990 and 1992 the mortality rate from diabetes mellitus among Indian elders was substantially greater than the mortality rate among the White elderly population. However, the difference between the two populations decreases with age. Unlike other leading causes of mortality, American Indian female mortality is substantially greater than among American Indian male elders, and the difference increases greatly after age 85.

TABLE 4.8 Age-Specific Mortality From Diabetes Mellitus Among American
Indians Residing in IHS Service Areas (1990-1992) and Whites
(1991): Rate per 100,000 Population

	American Indian			White		
Age	Male	Female	Both Sexes	Male	Female	Both Sexes
55–64	107.3	124.5	116.5	30.7	26.2	28.4
65–74	174.9	210.8	194.9	74.2	63.1	68.0
75–84	226.3	286.7	262.3	146.6	124.3	132.7
85+	229.5	496.5	398.5	253.5	238.1	242.3

SOURCE: Indian Health Service, Division of Program Statistics; National Center for Health Statistics
(1996a).

There is evidence to suggest that the high prevalence of diabetes may
have a genetic cause. Notwithstanding any genetic predisposition, it is clearly
linked to high-fat, low-fiber diets and a sedentary lifestyle. Adult-onset diabetes can be controlled by diet, exercise, and medication. But, according to
Gohdes (1990), American Indian patient compliance has not been good.

The long-term health consequences of diabetes are renal failure; amputations; heart, kidney, and eye damage; and periodontal disease (Gohdes,
1990). Indeed, Rhoades et al. (1990) reported that 76% of all IHS hospitalizations for lower extremity amputations are because of diabetes. Within the
Indian diabetic population, however, the kidney is the prime target for end-
stage organ damage in contrast to cardiac complications within the U.S. general elderly population. The cost of medical interventions to deal with end-
stage renal disease among elderly American Indian diabetics is a major
problem for the IHS.

Chronic Obstructive Pulmonary Disease

The sixth leading cause of death among American Indian elders is the complex of disease processes known as chronic obstructive pulmonary disease
(COPD) that causes decreased capacity of the lungs to function. Chronic
bronchitis, pulmonary emphysema, and chronic asthma are the most familiar
diseases in this category, but other chronic obstructive pulmonary diseases
and allied conditions accounted for 77% of COPD deaths among American
Indian elders between 1990 and 1992. As seen in Table 4.9, except among
females aged 85 and over, Whites have higher death rates from COPD than

TABLE 4.9 Age-Specific Mortality From Chronic Obstructive Pulmonary
Disease and Allied Conditions Among American Indians Residing
in IHS Service Areas (1990-1992) and Whites (1991): Rate per
100,000 Population

Age	American Indian			White		
	Male	*Female*	*Both Sexes*	*Male*	*Female*	*Both Sexes*
55–64	39.3	27.7	33.1	57.8	44.7	50.9
65–74	128.6	73.5	97.9	206.7	127.0	162.2
75–84	327.7	139.4	215.2	511.8	238.3	341.5
85+	520.1	345.7	409.7	867.4	311.6	464.6

SOURCE: Indian Health Service, Division of Program Statistics; National Center for Health Statistics (1996a).

Indians. Moreover, the death rates of American Indian male elders are higher at all ages than the rate of their Indian female age peers.

Accidents and Adverse Effects

Death rates due to accidental injuries decreased by approximately 18% between 1977 and 1988 among the American Indian elderly population (John, 1995), and this cause of mortality has lost rank to diabetes mellitus and COPD since 1977. This trend is encouraging, but despite continued improvement in mortality from accidents and adverse effects, accidents were the seventh leading cause of death among American Indian elders between 1990 and 1992. As seen in Table 4.10, mortality as the result of accidents and adverse effects is uniformly higher among American Indian males than American Indian females. The accidental death rate among American Indian male elders aged 65 and over (227.6) is nearly triple the rate among American Indian female elders (79.0). American Indian death rates from accidental causes are uniformly higher than death rates among Whites, except among females aged 85 and over.

Motor vehicle accidents accounted for approximately 30% of accidental deaths among both Indian male and female elders between 1990 and 1992. Previous research (John, 1995) has shown that approximately 20% of injury deaths between 1986 and 1988 were due to falls, most of which resulted in a fracture. According to an Indian Health Service (IHS, 1990) study of injuries, between 1981 and 1985 female American Indian elders over 65 years old were more likely to die from a fall than were their Indian male age peers.

TABLE 4.10 Age-Specific Mortality From Accidents and Adverse Effects Among
American Indians Residing in IHS Service Areas (1990-1992) and
Whites (1991): Rate per 100,000 Population

	American Indian			White		
Age	Male	Female	Both Sexes	Male	Female	Both Sexes
55–64	148.8	53.5	97.8	42.7	17.4	29.5
65–74	195.5	46.3	112.3	58.2	30.6	42.7
75–84	245.8	110.5	164.9	130.5	78.5	98.1
85+	443.6	186.2	280.6	353.8	225.4	260.7

SOURCE: Indian Health Service, Division of Program Statistics; National Center for Health Statistics
(1996a).

As with other leading causes of mortality, many accidents are preventable. According to Smith (1990), death rates due to accidents were significantly higher where reservations were more rural and roads less improved. Elderly American Indians may be more at risk than the general population due to the higher number of miles driven in more isolated reservation communities. Poor housing conditions among American Indian elders probably also increase the risk of accidental death, especially from falls and burns. However, alcohol abuse was identified as the major risk factor associated with all types of accidental injuries (Smith, 1990).

Other Leading Causes of Mortality

Nephritis, nephrotic syndrome, and nephrosis are the eighth leading cause of mortality among American Indian elders over age 65. This category of diseases produces degenerative changes in kidney functioning caused by a variety of infectious or toxic agents, metabolic abnormalities, immunologic disorders, or alcohol abuse. Among American Indian elders, renal failure is the primary medical condition associated with this cause of mortality. Between 1990 and 1992, 96.8% of deaths in this disease category among American Indian elders were the result of renal failure. Age-specific mortality rates among American Indian elders from this category of diseases is approximately double the rate among Whites between the ages of 65 and 84. After age 85, the mortality rates are about the same.

Chronic liver disease and cirrhosis are the ninth leading cause of death among American Indian elders over age 65. Unlike all of the other leading causes of death among American Indian elders, mortality from chronic liver disease and cirrhosis declines with age. Death rates from this cause were consistently higher among Indian elders than the White elderly population between the ages of 65 and 84. Overall, after age 85 there is very little difference between Indian and White mortality rates. However, this similarity in the overall mortality rate masks significant gender differences. After age 85, Indian males have less than half the mortality rate of White males while the rate among Indian females is 1.4 times the rate among White females.

Because chronic liver disease and cirrhosis are closely associated with alcohol abuse, it is useful to know the mortality rate when all alcoholism deaths are grouped together. Prior to 1993, the IHS calculated alcoholism death rates using figures from three causes of death: alcoholic psychoses, alcohol dependence syndrome, and alcoholic liver disease. Since 1993, however, the IHS has expanded the way alcoholism death is defined and mortality rates are calculated. The new definition added alcohol overdose, alcoholic cardiomyopathy, alcoholic gastritis, elevated blood alcohol level, and accidental poisoning by alcohol to the calculation of alcoholism death rates. According to the IHS (1995b), this expanded definition resulted in a 25% increase in the number of deaths attributed to alcohol. Among American Indians, deaths from alcoholism peak between age 55 and 64 for males and between 45 and 54 for females (IHS, 1995b). After age 65, the alcoholism mortality rate among male elders is consistently more than twice the rate among Indian female elders. Moreover, after age 65, American Indian mortality from alcoholism is consistently 3 times the rate among Whites.

Septicemia, more commonly known as blood poisoning, is a systemic infection caused by pathogenic bacteria or their toxins in the blood. American Indian elders have uniformly higher age-specific mortality from septicemia than Whites. Overall, after age 65 American Indian males have higher mortality from septicemia than Indian females. However, the gender difference is greatest among American Indian elders between the ages of 65 and 74, and the difference decreases with age until there is no gender difference in mortality rates after age 85.

Conclusion

As one of the most widely used measures of the health status of a population, mortality data are indispensable in health care planning and delivery.

However, uncertainty about the accuracy of American Indian mortality data make it difficult to design appropriate public health measures and target health resources so that they will provide the greatest benefit to American Indian elders. Vital events data collection efforts remain one of the few attempts to obtain information on the entire American Indian population. Without doubt, American Indians will benefit from general improvements in the creation, collection, and compilation of mortality data, including implementation of the multiple cause of death procedures. However, greater emphasis must be placed upon ensuring the accuracy of American Indian mortality data.

Of the three problems with American Indian mortality data that were discussed in this chapter, the misclassification of race on the death certificate is the most serious, and new procedures for collecting and verifying American Indian mortality data are needed. Unfortunately, unless care is taken to improve the quality of American Indian mortality data now and in the future, we can expect the quality of mortality data to decline. Several studies (Frost et al., 1992; Frost et al., 1994) have shown that the accuracy of Indian race in mortality data depends on degree of Indian blood of the decedent. Previous research (U.S. Congress, 1986), however, has projected a rapid diminution of the degree of Indian blood during the next century because of high rates of intermarriage with other groups.

The routine misclassification of Indian deaths in this relatively small but rapidly growing population makes the mortality experience among American Indians more difficult to determine and more sensitive to the various sources of error than it is for Whites or large minority populations. The best research using national data (IHS, in press; Poe et al. 1993; Querec, 1994; Sorlie et al., 1992) suggests that American Indian mortality is underestimated by at least 20%. If these estimates are correct, American Indian elders have far less of a mortality advantage compared to Whites than previous research has suggested. In fact, if these estimates are true, the "mortality crossover" and many differences in cause-specific mortality rates may simply be an artifact of poor data.

Because of what we know about the problems with American Indian mortality data, our current understanding of American Indian mortality and other indicators of health status, such as life expectancy, must be interpreted with caution. Research on systematic problems in the reporting of Indian deaths and technical improvements in the method of calculating measures of health status have the potential to change our understanding of American Indian health, mortality, and longevity—perhaps substantially. Despite technical difficulties, there is no doubt that American Indian health status has improved dramatically since the IHS assumed responsibility for American Indian health care in 1955. However, the American Indian population is undergoing an epidemiologic transition that is continuing to shift mortality (and morbidity) from acute and infectious diseases to chronic and degenerative illnesses. These changing health problems require new health care initiatives for the American Indian population. Without accurate mortality data, resources cannot be allocated appropriately to deal with the growing chronic health problems of the aging American Indian population.

Note

1. For the purpose of this study, the terms *Indian* and *American Indian* are used interchangeably and refer to American Indians and Alaska Natives (Eskimos and Aleuts).

References

Adams, V. I., & Herrmann, M. A. (1995). The medical examiner: When to report and help with death certificates. *The Journal of the Florida Medical Association, 82*(4), 255-260.

Becker, T. M., Wiggins, C., Key, C. R., & Samet, J. M. (1993). Symptoms, signs, and ill-defined conditions: A leading cause of death among minorities. In T. M. Becker, C. Wiggins, R. Elliott, C. R. Key, & J. M. Samet (Eds.), *Racial and ethnic patterns of mortality in New Mexico* (pp. 145-159). Albuquerque: University of New Mexico Press.

Black, W. C., & Wiggins, C. (1985). Melanoma among southwestern American Indians. *Cancer, 55,* 2899-2902.

Boss, L. (1990). Cancer. In *Indian health conditions* (pp. 23-69). Washington, DC: Indian Health Service.

Broudy, D. W., & May, P. A. (1983). Demographic and epidemiologic transition among the Navajo Indians. *Social Biology, 30*(1), 7-19.

Comstock, G., & Markush, R. (1986). Further comments on problems in death certification. *American Journal of Epidemiology, 124*(2), 180-181.

Coulehan, J. L., & Welty, T. K. (1990). Cardiovascular disease. In *Indian health conditions* (pp. 71-98). Washington, DC: Indian Health Service.

Engel, L. W., Strauchen, J. A., Chiazze, L., Jr., & Heid, M. (1980). Accuracy of death certification in an autopsied population with specific attention to malignant neoplasms and vascular diseases. *American Journal of Epidemiology, 111*(1), 99-112.

Espey, D. K., Samet, J. M., Wiggins, C. L., & Becker, T. M. (1993). All-cause mortality. In T. M. Becker, C. Wiggins, R. Elliott, C. R. Key, & J. M. Samet (Eds.), *Racial and ethnic patterns of mortality in New Mexico* (pp. 12-22). Albuquerque: University of New Mexico Press.

Frost, F., & Shy, K. K. (1980). Racial differences between linked birth and infant death records in Washington State. *American Journal of Public Health, 70,* 974-976.

Frost, F., Taylor, V., & Fries, E. (1992). Racial misclassification of Native Americans in a surveillance, epidemiology, and end results cancer registry. *Journal of the National Cancer Institute, 84*(12), 957-961.

Frost, F., Tollestrup, K., Ross, A., Sabotta, E., & Kimball, E. (1994). Correctness of racial coding of American Indians and Alaska Natives on the Washington State death certificate. *American Journal of Preventive Medicine, 10*(5), 290-294.

Geller, S. A. (1983). Autopsy. *Scientific American, 248*(3), 124-136.

Gillum, R. F. (1995). The epidemiology of stroke in Native Americans. *Stroke, 26,* 514-521.

Gittlesohn, A. (1982). On the distribution of underlying causes of death. *American Journal of Public Health, 72*(2), 133-140.

Gittlesohn, A., & Royston, P. N. (1982). *Annotated bibliography of cause-of-death validation studies.* Hyattsville, MD: National Center for Health Statistics.

Gittlesohn, A. M., & Senning, J. (1979). Studies on the reliability of vital and health records: I. Comparison of cause of death and hospital record diagnosis. *American Journal of Public Health, 69*(7), 680-689.

Glasser, J. H. (1981). The quality and utility of death certificate data. *American Journal of Public Health, 71*(3), 231-233.

Gohdes, D. (1990). Diabetes. In *Indian health conditions* (pp. 99-112). Washington, DC: Indian Health Service.

Goldman, L., Sayson, R., Robbins, S., Cohn, L. H., Bettman, M., & Weisberg, M. (1983). The value of the autopsy in three medical eras. *New England Journal of Medicine, 308,* 1000-1005.

Guariglia, P., & Abrahams, C. (1985). The impact of autopsy data on DRG reimbursement. *Human Pathology, 16*(12), 1184-1186.

Hahn, R. A. (1992). The state of federal health statistics on racial and ethnic groups. *Journal of the American Medical Association, 267*(2), 268-271.

Hahn, R. A., Mendlein, J. M., & Helgerson, S. D. (1993, January). Differential classification of American Indian race on birth and death certificates, U.S. reservation states, 1983-1985. *The Provider,* pp. 8-11.

Hahn, R. A., Mulinare, J., & Teutsch, S. M. (1992). Inconsistencies in coding of race and ethnicity between birth and death in U.S. infants: A new look at infant mortality, 1983 through 1985. *Journal of the American Medical Association, 267*(2), 259-263.

Hanzlick, R. (1993). Death certificates: The need for further guidance. *The American Journal of Forensic Medicine and Pathology, 14*(3), 249-252.

Harris, D. (1994). The 1990 Census count of American Indians: What do the numbers really mean? *Social Science Quarterly, 75,* 580-593.

Heller, J., Friedlander, D., & Geller, S. A. (1985). Autopsy findings as a modifier of diagnosis-related group classification and hospital reimbursement. *The Mount Sinai Journal of Medicine, 52*(5), 311-314.

Holmes, J., & Baer, D. M. (1986, September). Autopsy diagnoses can increase DRG reimbursement. *Pathologist,* pp. 36-39.

Hoyert, D. L. (1994). *Effect on mortality rates of the 1989 change in tabulating race.* Hyattsville, MD: National Center for Health Statistics.

Indian Health Service. (1990). *Injuries among American Indians and Alaska Natives.* Rockville, MD: Author.

Indian Health Service. (1991). *Trends in Indian health—1991.* Rockville, MD: Author.

Indian Health Service. (1992). *Trends in Indian health—1992.* Rockville, MD: Author.

Indian Health Service. (1993). *Trends in Indian health—1993*. Rockville, MD: Author.

Indian Health Service. (1995a). *Regional differences in Indian health—1995*. Rockville, MD: Author.

Indian Health Service. (1995b). *Trends in Indian health—1995*. Rockville, MD: Author.

Indian Health Service. (in press). *Final report: Methodology for adjusting IHS mortality data for inconsistent classification of race*. Rockville, MD: Author.

Israel, R. A., Rosenberg, H. M., & Curtin, L. R. (1986). Analytical potential for multiple cause-of-death data. *American Journal of Epidemiology, 124*(2), 161-179.

John, R. (1995). *American Indian and Alaska Native elders: An assessment of their current status and provision of services*. Rockville, MD: Indian Health Service.

John, R., & Baldridge, D. (1996). *The NICOA report: Health and long-term care for American Indian elders* (A Report by the National Indian Council on Aging to the National Indian Policy Center). Washington, DC: National Indian Council on Aging.

Johnson, A., & Taylor, A. (1991). *Prevalence of chronic diseases: A summary of data from the survey of American Indians and Alaska Natives* (AHCPR Publication No. 91-0031). Rockville, MD: Public Health Service, Agency for Health Care Policy and Research.

Kennedy, R. D., & Deapen, R. E. (1991). Differences between Oklahoma Indian infant mortality and other races. *Public Health Reports, 106*(1), 97-99.

Kircher, T. (1990). The autopsy and vital statistics. *Human Pathology, 24*(2), 166-173.

Kircher, T. (1992, March 4). Autopsy and mortality statistics: Making a difference. *Journal of the American Medical Association, 267*(9), 1264-1265.

Kircher, T., Nelson, J., & Burdo, H. (1985). The autopsy as a measure of accuracy of the death certificate. *New England Journal of Medicine, 313,* 1263-1269.

Kleinman, J. C. (1982). The continued vitality of vital statistics. *American Journal of Public Health, 72,* 125-127.

Kunitz, S. J. (1983). *Disease change and the role of medicine: The Navajo experience*. Berkeley: University of California Press.

Lefkowitz, D. C., & Underwood, C. (1991). *Personal health practices: Findings from the survey of American Indians and Alaska Natives* (AHCPR Publication No. 91-0034). Rockville, MD: Public Health Service, Agency for Health Care Policy and Research.

Manson, S. M., & Callaway, D. G. (1990). Health and aging among American Indians: Issues and challenges for the biobehavioral sciences. In M. Harper (Ed.), *Minority aging: Essential curricula content for selected health and allied health professions* (pp. 63-119). Washington, DC: Government Printing Office.

National Center for Health Statistics. (1986). *Report of the Panel to Evaluate the U.S. Standard Certificates and Reports*. Hyattsville, MD: Author.

National Center for Health Statistics. (1996a). *Vital statistics of the United States, 1991: Vol. 2. Mortality, Part A*. Hyattsville, MD: Author.

National Center for Health Statistics. (1996b). *Vital statistics of the United States, 1992: Life tables*. Hyattsville, MD: Author.

Passel, J. S. (1976). Provisional evaluation of the 1970 Census count of American Indians. *Demography, 13,* 397-409.

Passel, J. S. (1996). The growing American Indian population, 1960-1990: Beyond demography. In G. D. Sandefur, R. R. Rindfuss, & B. Cohen (Eds.), *Changing numbers, changing needs: American Indian demography and public health* (pp. 79-102). Washington, DC: National Academy Press.

Passel, J. S., & Berman, P. A. (1986). Quality of 1980 Census data for American Indians. *Social Biology, 33,* 163-182.

Poe, G. S., Powell-Griner, E., McLaughlin, J. K., Placek, P. J., Thompson, G. B., & Robinson, K. (1993). *Comparability of the death certificate and the 1986 National Mortality Followback Survey*. Hyattsville, MD: National Center for Health Statistics.

Querec, L. (1992). *A study of infant mortality among American Indians & Alaska Natives from the 1983 linked birth/infant death data set*. Rockville, MD: Indian Health Service.

Querec, L. (1994). *Measuring underreporting of American Indian infant mortality: Methodology and findings*. Rockville, MD: Indian Health Service.

Rhoades, E. R. (1990). Profile of American Indians and Alaska Natives. In M. Harper (Ed.), *Minority aging: Essential curricula content for selected health and allied health professions* (DHHS Publication No. HRS [P-DV-90-4]; pp. 45-62). Washington, DC: Government Printing Office.

Rhoades, E. R., Hammond, J., Welty, T. K., Handler, A. O., Amler, R. W., D'Angelo, A. J., & Kaufman, S. (1990). The Indian burden of illness and future health interventions. In *Indian health conditions* (pp. 1-21). Washington, DC: Indian Health Service.

Roberts, W. C. (1978). The autopsy: Its decline and a suggestion for its revival. *New England Journal of Medicine, 299*, 332-338.

Schottenfeld, D., Eaton, M., Sommers, S. C., Alonso, D. R., & Wilkinson, C. (1982). The autopsy as a measure of accuracy of the death certificate. *Bulletin of the New York Academy of Medicine, 58*(9), 778-794.

Singh, G. K., Kochanek, K. D., & MacDorman, M. F. (1996). Advance report on final mortality statistics, 1994. *Monthly and Vital Statistics Report, 45*(3, Suppl.). Hyattsville, MD: National Center for Health Statistics.

Smith, R. (1990). Unintentional injuries. In *Indian health conditions* (pp. 285-299). Washington, DC: Indian Health Service.

Snipp, C. M. (1989). *American Indians: The first of this land*. New York: Russell Sage.

Sorlie, P. D., Rogot, E., & Johnson, N. J. (1992). Validity of demographic characteristics on the death certificate. *Epidemiology, 3*(2), 181-184.

Stein, E. (1992, January). Death certificates: Fill them out carefully (and correctly). *Colorado Medicine*, p. 19.

Stinson, F. S., & Plantz, M. C. (1986). *Comparative health service indicators for the IHS and U.S. populations* (Final report of the Indian Health Service Data Comparison Project). Washington, DC: CSR, Inc.

Sugarman, J. R., Holliday, M., Lopez, K., & Wilder, D. (1993). *Improving health statistics among American Indians by data linkages with tribal environment registries*. Washington, DC: National Center for Health Statistics.

U.S. Congress, Office of Technology Assessment. (1986). *Indian health care* (Publication No. OTA-H-290). Washington, DC: Government Printing Office.

U.S. Department of Health and Human Services. (1985). *Report of the Secretary's Task Force on Black and Minority Health: Vol. 3. Cancer*. Washington, DC: Government Printing Office.

U.S. Department of Health and Human Services. (1995). *Health United States: 1994*. Washington, DC: Government Printing Office.

Watson, C. C., Bennett, T., Reed, F. W., McBroom, W. H., & Helgerson, S. D. (1993, April 2). Classification of American Indian race on birth and infant death certificates—California and Montana. *Morbidity and Mortality Weekly Report*, 220-223.

Young, T. K. (1994). *The health of Native Americans: Towards a biocultural epidemiology*. Oxford, UK: Oxford University Press.

PART  II

Chronic Diseases and Disability

Race, Age, Chronic Disease, and Disability

Daniel O. Clark
Rose C. Gibson

Disability associated with chronic disease and aging is responsible for substantial societal and familial costs (Schneider & Guralnik, 1990) and plays a central role in health-related quality of life (Patrick & Bergner, 1990). Attempting to understand the source and impact of disability is thus very important, particularly among groups at relatively high risk of disability. It is generally accepted that disability prevalence, however measured, is more common among older African Americans than among Whites, although we are aware of one study that found African Americans to be no more disabled than Whites. Data of that study were on respondents residing in Cleveland in the late 1970s (see Ford, Haug, Jones, Roy, & Folmar, 1990). There is evidence that the size of the race difference, and perhaps the direction, is dependent on the age of the sample. In some data sets, race differences are apparent up to, but not after, age 80 years (see Gibson, 1991a; Clark, Maddox, & Steinhauser, 1993). After age 80, African Americans may experience a more favorable disability prevalence than Whites. In other data sets, a substantial African American disadvantage is apparent across all of the older age ranges (Clark, 1997; Mendes de Leon et al., 1995). As discussed later, the discrepancy across data sets may be due to different measures of disability.

Although many individual and environmental factors can and do affect disability (Verbrugge, 1990), the primary pathway is through chronic disease (Johnson & Wolinsky, 1993; Nagi, 1990; Wilson & Cleary, 1995). To date, however, there is very little information available on whether a greater rate of disability among African Americans is due to chronic disease prevalence, severity, or impact. In this chapter, we present the most recent nationally representative data available on the prevalence of chronic conditions, lower body limitation, and activities of daily living (ADL) disability among African Americans and Whites of three age groups (50 to 64 years, 65 to 74 years, and 75 years and over). Our primary intent is to show race differences and their pattern across the age groups. We then draw on regional and disease-specific studies to consider the severity and disability- and mortality-impact of particular chronic conditions, and make age group comparisons where possible.

Before beginning our review, definitions of the terms used and their theoretical associations are needed. The conceptual model of chronic disease and disability shown in Figure 5.1 is adapted from the recent work of Johnson and Wolinsky (1993), Nagi (1990), Patrick and Bergner (1990), Verbrugge (1990), and Wilson and Cleary (1995). Chronic disease represents the primary starting point, although we have also incorporated trauma and senescence (see Fries, 1992). Impairment represents the main pathway from chronic disease, or trauma and senescence, to disability, and is often identified through biological and physiological assessments (Wilson & Cleary, 1995). The results of these and other assessments (e.g., cognitive and sensory assessments) can be called signs. Symptoms, which are defined as the patient's perception of an abnormal state, are also important indications of impairment (e.g., pain, health problems, or sensations; see Patrick & Bergner, 1990).

The chronic disease-disability process is affected at every step by genetic endowment, culture, behavior, or social and physical environments and resources, or combinations of these. These four broad, interdependent categories of factors only summarize the many and very complex associations they have with one another and each stage of the process. For example, the impact of chronic disease on impairment is partially determined by the quality of and access to health services, including rehabilitation and management (Verbrugge, 1990). Similarly, the impact of impairment on disability may be influenced by health services, as well as individual physical and psychological resources. Indeed, the expression of disability itself is dependent on many of these same factors.

Disability has been variously measured, and a few conceptual issues must be addressed prior to review. The first is the distinction between functional limitation (e.g., lower body or mobility) and disability (ADL; see Figure 5.1). Function represents difficulty in body movements, whereas disabil-

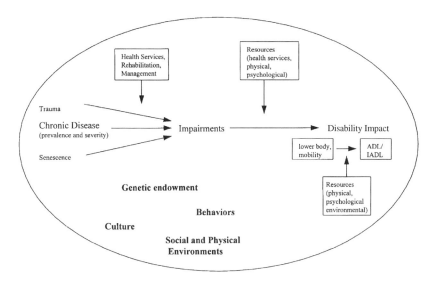

Figure 5.1. Chronic Disease and Disability

ity represents difficulty in daily tasks or social performance, such as ADLs and Instrumental ADLs (Nagi, 1976, 1990). Theoretically, lower and upper body function are determinants of ADL and IADL disability, and this causal association has been supported by recent studies (Guralnik, Ferrucci, Simonsick, Salive, & Wallace, 1995). The second distinction is within ADL and IADL disability. To provide more detail, the ADL and IADL disability items can be broken into either specific tasks (e.g., eating, bathing, grocery shopping) or groups of tasks containing similar objectives and skill requirements (e.g., self-care, home-care, and cognitive; Johnson & Wolinsky, 1993; Wolinsky & Johnson, 1991).

The separation of ADL items or groups of items is important and has improved understanding of disability, but there are several reasons why ADL disability measures may not be optimal for racial comparisons. First, the percentage of community-dwelling older adults with an ADL or IADL disability is quite low (i.e., less than 20%; see Manton, Corder, & Stallard, 1993b), which leaves a very crude indication of no functional disability for up to 80% of older adults. Also, for those who have an ADL disability, proxy response rates can be quite high (15% to 20%; Manton et al., 1993b), introducing a potential source of error. Second, disability prevention will be most effective when those at high risk of ADL or IADL onset are distinguished (Guralnik et al., 1995). And, third, there is some evidence that ADLs and IADLs are not reported with the same level of accuracy among African Americans and Whites (Gibson, 1991b; Johnson & Wolinsky, 1994), and particular concern for ADL reports among African American males may be warranted (Clark, Mungai, Stump, & Wolinsky, 1997; Johnson & Wolinsky, 1994). Reports are few and preliminary, but African American males appear to have quite unique ADL reporting patterns, which could be influenced by a host of factors including symptoms (i.e., impairments), cultural schemas, and social and physical environments. An example of the latter would be work-related trauma, which Leigh and Fries (1992) have shown to have important implications for disability. All of this points to the importance of data on function limitation, particularly lower body function, which has a substantially greater association with ADL and IADL disability, perceived health, and depression, than upper body function (Johnson & Wolinsky, 1993, 1994; Stump, Clark, & Wolinsky, 1996).

Fortunately, there have been a few studies of race differences in disability that have incorporated the distinction between functional limitation and disability. In this review, we draw on data for persons 51 to 61 years of age from the 1992 Health and Retirement Survey (HRS), and persons aged 70 years or over from the 1984 Longitudinal Study on Aging (LSOA) and the 1993 Assets and Health Dynamics (AHEAD) study. We also use these data in our review of chronic disease and impairment, as well as data from the 1990-1992 National Health Interview Survey (NHIS). The samples for these surveys are all based on multistage area probability samples, and all included an oversample of African Americans (generally 2:1). Thus, all of these data sets contain relatively large samples of African Americans (approximately 600 in the LSOA, 800 in the AHEAD, 1,600 in the HRS, and 3,000 in the NHIS).

We use Figure 5.1 as a heuristic device, and focus in this chapter on two factors: chronic disease and disability. Health care access and quality is not the focus of this chapter, and racial comparisons on impairment have generally not been done. A few measures of impairment have been incorporated into the most recent national surveys, and we provide a brief look at race differences in vision and hearing impairments, crude reports of pain, and impaired memory. Although we focus on just two of the factors shown in Figure 5.1, we keep this model in mind to structure our presentation of findings. We also come back to Figure 5.1 as we discuss the implications of and gaps in the studies we review in this chapter.

Impairment and Chronic Conditions

Impairment

In the 1990-1992 NHIS, between 5% and 6% of African Americans and Whites less than 75 years of age report vision impairments. The percentage goes up to between 10% and 15% for those over 75, but race differences remain nonexistent (Cohen & Van Nostrand, 1994). In contrast, 24% of African Americans aged 51 to 61 years in the 1992 HRS rated their eyesight as fair or poor, whereas 9% of Whites reported fair or poor eyesight. Among the 71- to 81-year-old African American respondents to the AHEAD, 30% reported fair or poor eyesight, whereas 20% of the White AHEAD respondents rated their eyesight fair or poor (Clark, Mungai, et al., 1997). In the case of hearing, Whites of all ages in the NHIS were more likely than African Americans to report difficulty hearing in one or both ears. In the HRS and AHEAD data, however, Whites were no more likely than African Americans to report fair or poor hearing. The NHIS asked if persons were blind, had cataract, glaucoma, or diseases of the retina. For hearing, the NHIS asked if persons were deaf or had tinnitus. The HRS and AHEAD data were based on perceived hearing and eyesight. The inconsistency across data sets may be due to access to information and medical care. Knowledge of disease or specific impairment as solicited in the NHIS, may be greater among Whites who tend to have greater information and medical care access.

Data on pain are uncommon in national data sets, but a broad question was included in both the HRS and the AHEAD. In both data sets, a little less than one third of the respondents stated they were often bothered by pain. There was very little variation by race. In regard to memory, however, there was considerable race variation. Scores on tests of immediate and delayed word recall were about one-third lower among African Americans, and perceived memory was rated as fair or poor 1.5 to 2 times more frequently among African Americans, regardless of age (Clark, Mungai, et al., 1997).

Chronic Conditions

Data on the prevalence of conditions generally come from self-report survey data. There are reliability and validity problems with virtually all sources of data on prevalence (see, e.g., Nordstrom, Remington, & Layde, 1994), although

self-reports are likely to be somewhat less valid than estimates based on medical records (see, e.g., Andersen, Mullner, & Cornelius, 1987; Heliovaara
et al., 1993; Teschke et al., 1992). Most important, there are no indications to
date that African Americans' self-reports of chronic disease contain any more
or less error than Whites' (see Andersen et al., 1987; Gibson, 1991a; Giles,
Croft, Keenan, Lane, & Wheeler, 1995).

The chronic conditions data are adapted from tables published in Cohen
and Van Nostrand (1994) using the 1990-1992 NHIS. We provide additional
data on chronic conditions using the 1993 AHEAD and the 1992 HRS (Clark,
Mungai, et al., 1997). There are conditions for which the prevalence estimates
from the different sources of data do not agree. This results in part from the
questions being phrased differently across the data sets. The NHIS asked persons whether they have the condition, and the HRS and AHEAD asked persons whether they have ever been told by a doctor that they have the condition. It is interesting to note that, even though the prevalence estimates often
differ across data sets, the African American to White ratios were very similar.
The exceptions were for arthritis and lung disease, although even with these
the ratios were in the same direction and differed by 35% or less. In the HRS
and AHEAD, arthritis prevalence was based on positive responses to the
question, "Have you seen a doctor for arthritis or rheumatism in the past 12
months." The NHIS simply asked persons whether they have arthritis. Questions about lung disease were less specific in the HRS and AHEAD than in
the NHIS. The NHIS asked specifically about emphysema and chronic bronchitis, whereas the HRS and AHEAD asked, "Has a doctor ever told you that
you have chronic lung disease such as chronic bronchitis or emphysema."

We have broken the data into three age groups (50-64, 65-74, and 75
and over), which approximately match the age groups used in the reports that
have been drawn upon to create Table 5.1. That table shows the prevalence of
conditions for African Americans and Whites, and the African American to
White ratios by age group and condition. The ratios were calculated by divid-
ing the African American prevalence by the White prevalence. Hypertension
is the most prevalent condition among African Americans, followed by arthritis, adult-onset diabetes (non-insulin dependent diabetes mellitus), and heart
disease. More than one half of African Americans 50 to 64 years of age have
hypertension, and two out of five have arthritis. One out of six have diabetes
or heart disease.

As is well known, African Americans have substantially higher rates of
hypertension in comparison to same-age Whites (Anderson, 1987), and this

TABLE 5.1 Condition Prevalence Estimates by Race and Age Cohort, NHIS, HRS, AHEAD, ca. 1992

Condition	50-64 Years			65-74 Years			75 Years and Over		
	African American	White	African/ White Ratio	African American	White	African/ White Ratio	African American	White	African/ White Ratio
Hypertension	57.5	35.8	1.61	48.0[a]	35.5[a]	1.35	41.2[a]	36.6[a]	1.13
Arthritis	41.4	38.4	1.08	43.9	43.7[a]	1.00	54.5[a]	55.1[a]	0.99
Diabetes	14.9	6.3	2.37	20.1[a]	9.7[a]	2.07	14.1[a]	8.8[a]	1.60
Heart disease	14.3	13.3	1.08	16.7[a]	19.7	0.85	22.2[a]	27.1[a]	0.82
Chronic lung disease (not asthma)	6.1	9.0	0.68	7.6[a]	11.1[a]	0.68	3.5[a]	10.0[a]	0.35
Cerebrovascular disease	4.9[a]	2.3[a]	2.13[a]	7.7[a]	5.6[a]	1.38	10.7[a]	7.9[a]	1.35
Cancer (not skin)	4.3	6.1	0.70	10.0	14.6	0.68	9.0	16.3	0.55
Obesity (% ideal BMI ≥ 140)	34.5	20.9	1.65	22.7	12.1	1.88	17.1	7.1	2.41

NOTE: a. Data come from 1990-1992 NHIS.
Standard errors for NHIS reported in U.S. Department of Health and Human Services (1995), as cited in Kochanek & Hudson (1995).
Standard errors for HRS and AHEAD reported in Clark, Mungai, Stump, & Wolinsky (1997).

is apparent in Table 5.1. The African American to White ratio is about 1.6 in the youngest age group, and declines with age cohort. The ratio in the 75-and-over age cohort is about 1.1. A similar pattern across age cohorts is apparent for arthritis, diabetes, heart disease, chronic lung disease, cerebrovascular disease, and cancer. In fact, the older age cohort of African Americans has a more favorable prevalence ratio than the younger age cohort for each condition of Table 5.1 except obesity. African American to White ratios for obesity prevalence are 1.6 in the younger age cohort, 1.9 in the middle cohort, and 2.4 in the oldest cohort. The prevalence of obesity declines with age cohort, but more quickly among Whites than African Americans. The prevalence of hypertension also decreases with age cohort among African Americans, but increases from youngest to oldest among Whites. Arthritis, heart disease, cancer, and cerebrovascular disease all increase with age cohort among both African Americans and Whites, but more quickly among Whites.

Disability

Each of the studies reviewed uses slightly different methods of scoring functional limitation, and so comparisons of prevalence across age groups that have originated from different surveys is difficult. It is therefore instructive to calculate ratios, where African American estimates are divided by White estimates. In doing this, we find that the African American to White ratio of lower body limitation ranges between 1.25 and 1.45 for those who are less than 85 years of age (Clark et al., 1993; Clark, Mungai, et al., 1997). The ratio is roughly 1.0 for those who are 85 years or over (Clark et al., 1993; unpublished AHEAD data). Although small samples are an important concern in the latter age group, the age pattern is apparent in both the LSOA and the AHEAD data.

In contrast, African American to White ratios of ADL disability range from 1.3 to 1.6 for all ages over 65, including 85 and up. This is true in the 1984 LSOA (Clark et al., 1993), the 1982 New Haven study of the Established Populations for the Epidemiologic Study of the Elderly (EPESE), the 1986 North Carolina Study of the EPESE (Mendes de Leon et al., 1995), and the 1989 National Long-Term Care Survey (NLTCS; Clark, 1997). A study of the Piedmont (North Carolina) Health Survey of the Elderly (PHE) data presents a slightly different, but potentially instructive, perspective on the race pattern noted above. Using data on 1-year transitions, rather than point prevalence estimates, Guralnik and colleagues (1995) calculated the average remaining number of ADL-disability-free years of life, or active life expectancy (ALE), and provided racial comparisons. The African American to White ratio for ALE was approximately 1.0 at age 65, 1.1 at age 75, and 1.4 at age 85. In other words, African Americans aged 75 and over have a greater average ALE than Whites. This finding appears at odds with the higher prevalence of ADL disability among African Americans shown in the above cited studies. The authors state that this discrepancy may be due to African Americans surviving longer in a disabled state, but that this is offset by a longer total life expectancy for African Americans at the oldest ages.

This, however, may not be a plausible explanation of the discrepancy. In 1991, Whites' life expectancy at age 65 years was 2 years greater than African Americans', 17.5 versus 15.5. At age 75 years, life expectancy differed by about 1 year, 11.1 and 10.2, for Whites and African Americans, respectively. At age 85 years, there was no difference, and life expectancy was about 6.0 years for both races (Kochanek & Hudson, 1995). Thus, it does not appear that greater total life expectancy for African Americans would offset a greater rate of survival with disability to explain the discrepancy between ADL disability prevalence and ALE. It is possible, and even likely, that the disability characteristics of either African American or White populations vary by region (Miles & Bernard, 1992). Mendes de Leon et al. (1995) found that the African Americans of the North Carolina EPESE site had only slightly higher ADL disability rates than Whites, whereas African Americans of the New Haven EPESE site had considerably higher rates of ADL disability than Whites. Given these discrepancies, greater efforts to document geographic variability in race differences in health and disability may be necessary.

In sum, functional limitation and disability are more prevalent among African Americans than among Whites at ages less than 80. After age 80, disability appears to remain more prevalent among African Americans, but functional limitation does not. We do not believe this pattern has been noted elsewhere, and reasons for it have not been previously considered. Potential explanations include race differences in proxy response rates and their validity, the measurement validity of self-reports, and access to environmental resources. As Manton, Corder, and Stallard (1993a) showed, the use of prosthetics in the maintenance of ADL independence increased in the decade of the 1980s. Use depends on information and financial resources, and these resources are unequally distributed by race. Greater use of prosthetics could give Whites an ADL advantage, even when they do not have a functional limitation advantage. Reasons for a racial cross-over in functional limitation and disability at age 80 or so may be the same as those for a mortality cross-over. Briefly and simplistically, selective survival results when the sicker and more disabled members of a socially disadvantaged population (e.g., African Americans) die before reaching old age. Only the healthy or physiologically robust members of the disadvantaged population reach old age (see Markides & Keith, 1995; Markides & Machalek, 1984).

Disease Severity, and Disability- and Mortality-Impact

There are very few reports or data available to address race differences in disease severity and impact. In light of this, we must draw on disease- and geographically specific data to form a review of race differences in disease severity and impact. We organize the following section by looking first at indications of race differences in disease severity, and then move to a consideration of the disability- and mortality impact of particular conditions.

In many ways, disease severity and impact could be thought of as synonymous. The two can be separated, however, by defining severity as the signs (manifestations perceived by a physician) and symptoms (manifestations perceived by a patient; see Berguss & Hamm, 1995) of a condition, and impact as the outcomes attributable to the condition. At times the distinction between symptoms and outcomes can blur, but generally we think of symptoms as specific complaints, and outcomes as general, observable consequences of symptoms (e.g., disability, mortality, health services use).

Unfortunately, with the limited amount of data available, we are able to review severity comparisons for only a few conditions. Moreover, comparisons of severity using clinical data are potentially biased, because these are affected by access to care. For this reason, there has been concern over findings of lower cardiac procedure rates among African Americans, who appear to have cardiac conditions of the same severity as Whites (Goldberg, Hartz, Jacobsen, Krakauer, & Rimm, 1992; Maynard et al., 1991; Wenneker & Epstein, 1989). The difficulty lies in determining whether these differential cardiac procedure rates are due to health care access, disease severity, comorbidity, or some combination. In comparing presenting symptoms and signs among 1,374 African American and 1,657 White emergency department patients with acute chest pain, Johnson, Lee, Cook, Rouan, and Goldman (1993) found reported symptoms (e.g., type and extent of chest pain) and signs (e.g., physical examination and electrocardiograph results) to be more severe among Whites. This was consistent with impact-indicators in the form of greater rates of coronary disease at discharge, complications, and death among Whites. Although another study also found lower rates of coronary disease among African Americans in a sample of patients referred for coronary angiography, it did not find any race differences in the severity of coronary disease (Sorrentino, 1993).

A similar difficulty may exist for hypertension. The prevalence of untreated hypertension is at issue. Although race differences in self-reports of hypertension were not found, Giles et al. (1995) did find educated and obese African Americans to be more aware of their hypertension than their less educated and slimmer counterparts. This education- and weight-dependent knowledge of hypertension did not appear to exist among Whites (Giles et al., 1995). This may affect comparisons of the severity of hypertension, as well as estimates of its prevalence. Thus, broad screening programs with actual blood pressure readings will be most reliable. Although hypertensive and normotensive veterans were not separated, blood pressure readings were taken on nearly 12,000 men screened as part of the Veterans Administration Hypertension and Screening Program. These data did not indicate any substantial differences between African American and White mean systolic or diastolic blood pressure levels (Miller et al., 1994).

Although not an indication of diabetes severity, data on more than 6,000 men (428 African American) followed for 3 years as part of the Usual Care group of the Multiple Risk Factor Intervention Trial, showed that diabetes incidence was higher among African Americans (6.5%) than Whites (3.9%; Shaten, Smith, Kuller, & Neaton, 1993). A study that compared 110 subjects matched for age, sex, and duration of diabetes showed that joint mobility was *greater* and foot pressures were *lower* among diabetic African Americans compared to diabetic Whites. There were no race differences, however, in either self-reported symptoms of neuropathy (i.e., pain, cramps, numbness, hot or cold sensations) or clinically assessed signs of neuropathy (Veves et al., 1995).

If body mass index (BMI) is used as the sign of obesity, there is evidence that obesity is more severe among African Americans than Whites, although this difference is largely limited to women. A greater proportion of African American women compared to White women are not only obese, but more likely to be severely obese (Clark, Mungai, et al., 1997). Moreover, the 10-year incidence of major weight gain (i.e., more than 10 kg) has been found to be 50% higher among African American women (Williamson, Kahn, & Byers, 1991).

Impact

Both the severity and impact of a given disease is exacerbated by comorbidity. Verbrugge, Lepkowski, and Konkol (1991) found the disability impact of arthritis to be substantially elevated in the presence of other, comorbid conditions. Similarly, the severity and impact of diabetes is affected by the presence of hypertension, particularly in the case of vascular complications (Goldschmid, Domin, Ziemer, Gallina, & Phillips, 1995). With African Americans having higher rates of most chronic conditions, comorbidity likely plays a critical role in determining disability- and mortality impact. Thus, although proportional impact is important, to say that diabetes, for example, accounts for 60% of end-stage renal disease (Cowie, Port, & Wolfe, 1989), or that hypertension accounts for 33% of excess African American mortality (Otten, Teutsch, Williamson, & Marks, 1990), is somewhat crude. The interplay between diabetes and hypertension makes it very difficult to attribute death to one and not the other. The role of comorbidity is certainly complex, and its role and impact deserves greater empirical assessment (Wallace & Lemke, 1991).

Nonetheless, diabetes and hypertension are good examples of the importance of considering the impact of a disease. At any level of blood pressure, African Americans experience greater cardiovascular and renal damage than Whites (see Kaplan, 1994). Hypertension's impact is seen in African Americans' higher rates of death from stroke, cardiac arrest, and renal failure (see Kaplan, 1994). Although renal failure is affected by hypertension, diabetes is its leading cause (Goldschmid et al., 1995). With higher rates of diabetes and hypertension controlled, African Americans are still more than 4 times more likely to experience end-stage renal disease than Whites (Cowie et al., 1989; Pao, Whittle, Whelton, & Seidler, 1992). All of this suggests that the disease- and mortality impact of diabetes and hypertension is greater among African Americans.

Unfortunately, very few studies have attempted to determine whether disability impact varies by race. A recent report by Verbrugge and Patrick (1995) is the most systematic disability-impact assessment to date. They found arthritis to have the greatest impact on disability for persons 45 and over, with heart disease, hypertension, and diabetes having the second, third,

TABLE 5.2 Adjusted Standardized Regression Coefficients for Lower Body Impact of Chronic Conditions and Their Rank by Race and Age

Condition	51-61 Years		71-81 Years	
	African American	Caucasian	African American	Caucasian
Hypertension	.036 (6)	.053 (5)	.013 (8)[a]	.056 (6)
Arthritis	.111 (1)	.068 (3)	.156 (1)	.144 (2)
Diabetes	.061 (4)	.046 (6)	.127 (4)	.036 (8)
Heart disease	.099 (2)	.121 (1)	.145 (2)	.131 (3)
Chronic lung disease	.064 (3)	.120 (2)	.056 (5)[a]	.156 (1)
Cerebrovascular disease	.054 (5)	.037 (7)	.136 (3)	.113 (4)
Cancer	.029 (7)	.030 (8)	.035 (6)[a]	.047 (7)
Obesity	.026 (8)	.065 (4)	.029 (7)[a]	.066 (5)

NOTE: a. Estimate is not significant at $p < .05$. All other coefficients significant at $p < .05$.

Coefficients adjusted for age, gender, geographic region, marital status, working status, income, net worth, education, insurance status, smoking status, alcohol use, perceived eyesight and hearing, pain, perceived memory, and immediate word recall (adjusted R^2 = .36 to .48).

Standard errors reported in Clark, Mungai, Stump, & Wolinsky (1997).

and fourth greatest impacts, respectively, depending on gender and age. Disability was essentially defined as dependence in ADLs or IADLs. Unfortunately, race was not considered in that report (data not shown in a table). Another recent report that investigated the impact of disease on lower body limitation was stratified by race, and Table 5.2 shows standardized regression coefficients for the diseases included in that study. The coefficients have been adjusted by sociodemographic characteristics, insurance status, health behaviors, and impairments (see Clark, Mungai, et al., 1997). For both the 51-to-61 and 71-to-81 age cohorts, there were differences in the impact order of diseases (see Table 5.2). In the younger age cohort, for example, arthritis had the greatest impact among African Americans, but the third greatest impact among Whites. There were not, however, any race differences in the impact of particular diseases (unstandardized regression coefficients [not shown] were compared) on lower body limitation that were considered statistically and substantively significant (Clark, Stump, & Wolinsky, 1997). The same is true of the older age cohort. There were differences in the order of impact, but it was concluded that the magnitude of impact was not statistically or substantively significant. This suggests that the disability impact of these eight diseases may be approximately equal across race groups. It is important to note

TABLE 5.3 Rates (per 100,000) for the Ten Leading Causes of Death, and Their
Rank, by Race and Broad Age Group, 1992

	45-64 Years		65 Years and Over	
Condition	African American	Caucasian	African American	Caucasian
Cancer	397.6 (1)	265.5 (1)	1333.8 (2)	1113.7 (2)
Heart disease	379.3 (2)	200.4 (2)	2009.8 (1)	1849.7 (1)
Accidents	46.0 (5)	26.8 (3)	87.4 (9)	82.4 (7)
Chronic lung disease	27.7 (8)	26.0 (4)	155.2 (6)	253.2 (4)
Cerebrovascular disease	74.9 (3)	24.8 (5)	467.0 (3)	384.3 (3)
Chronic liver disease (cirrhosis)	32.7 (7)	20.3 (6)	—	—
Diabetes	51.8 (4)	18.0 (7)	213.5 (4)	107.3 (6)
Suicide	—	16.0 (8)	—	—
HIV infection	45.7 (6)	12.2 (9)	—	—
Pneumonia and influenza	22.3 (9)	9.3 (10)	190.3 (5)	212.3 (5)
Hardening of arteries (atherosclerosis)	—	—	—	51.0 (9)
Homicide/legal intervention	21.0 (10)	—	—	—
Hypertension	—	—	61.6 (10)	—
Kidney disease (nephritis)	—	—	104.0 (7)	54.3 (8)
Blood infection (septicemia)	—	—	93.2 (8)	45.8 (10)
Residual	210.8	86.6	800.1	717.2
All causes	1747.3	706.0	6727.0	4871.2

SOURCE: Data from U.S. Department of Health and Human Services (1995), as cited in Kochanek & Hudson (1995).
NOTE: Dash indicates disease is not one of top 10 causes of death.

again that the estimates shown in Table 5.2 were adjusted for many covariates, including obesity and comorbid conditions. Without these controls, the impact of diseases may vary considerably by race due to the greater rates of obesity, hypertension, diabetes, and coronary heart disease among African Americans.

A consideration of mortality impact will offer some insight as well. Condition-specific cause of death data from 1992 are shown in Table 5.3. Two broad age groups are shown for both African Americans and Whites. It is important to note that much of the differential mortality is associated with disease prevalence and cannot be attributed to differential disease impact. Nonetheless, the mortality data of Table 5.3 clearly show higher rates of death for African Americans. Although African American to White ratios are not shown, it is again apparent that African American disadvantages are greatest in the younger age group. For all four age-by-race groups, cancer and heart disease represented the leading and second leading causes, respectively, of death. Within the 45-to-64-year age group, cancer and heart disease accounted for 44% and 66% of the deaths among African Americans and Whites, respectively. Within the 65-years-and-over age group, cancer and heart disease accounted for 50% and 61% of deaths among African Americans and Whites, respectively.

The remaining leading causes of death vary considerably by age group and race. Cerebrovascular disease is the 3rd leading cause of all groups except 45- to 64-year-old Whites, where accidents represented the 3rd leading cause and cerebrovascular disease the 5th. For African Americans of both age groups, diabetes was the 4th leading cause of death, and for Whites, chronic lung disease was the 4th. In the older age group, pneumonia and influenza were the 5th leading cause of death for both races. There is no obvious age or race pattern from the 6th through 10th leading causes of death.

Summary

A relatively large African American disadvantage in chronic conditions and disabilities is apparent in the young-old age groups. For most of these chronic conditions and disabilities, however, African Americans of the older age groups (roughly 80 and over) have less substantial disadvantages and, in some cases, have no disadvantage relative to Whites. The exceptions to this pattern are obesity and ADL disability, where African Americans have substantial disadvantages across all age groups. A clear African American disadvantage in mortality rates is apparent in Table 5.3, but it is impossible to separate mortality due to greater disease impact versus greater disease prevalence in that table. Conclusions about race differences in the severity and impact of chronic conditions would be very tentative with the data available. Nonetheless, it does appear that the impact of hypertension and diabetes on disease-related outcomes may be greater among African Americans. Reports assessing the impact of other conditions were not identified. Reviewing the disability- and mortality impact of chronic conditions, it is apparent that heart disease has the greatest impact. Heart disease is a leading cause of death and a leading cause of disability for all groups. Cancer is a leading cause of death, but has a relatively modest impact on disability. Diabetes and cerebrovascular disease represent the middle ground on both disability and mortality. Thus, for overall impact, heart disease leads the way.

Discussion

It has been concluded that about one third of excess mortality among African Americans is due to hypertension, another third is due to low socioeconomic status, and another third remains unexplained (Otten et al., 1990). We are not aware of a similar statement regarding disability, but several authors have suggested that differential access to social and physical environments and resources accounts for at least one half of the race disparity (Clark & Maddox, 1992; Rogers, Rogers, & Belanger, 1992). To say that race differences in mortality are due to socioeconomic status does not provide an understanding, but redirects the focus of the problem from race to socioeconomic status. The race disparity is certainly related to differences in the prevalence of chronic disease, particularly obesity, diabetes, cerebrovascular disease, and hypertension. The role of chronic disease is not in addition to the role of access to resources, however, because much of that impact is likely to occur through chronic disease. Behaviors certainly play a role, but that role is not independent of the role of resources or culture. Culture is certainly not independent of resources or environments, but rather shapes and is shaped by such factors (see Link & Phelan, 1995, and Williams & Collins, 1995, for comprehensive discussions of race, socioeconomic status, and health).

Similarly, genetic endowment cannot be considered independent of resources, culture, or behavior. The nature-nurture controversy has been rejected and replaced with more complex views of human development. Genetic expression does not occur in a vacuum; social and physical environments affect all expressions and behaviors. The opposite is also true. Thus, we cannot attribute any particular outcome solely to environment or genetics (Lewontin, Rose, & Kamin, 1984). This conclusion is certainly applicable to chronic disease and disability. Any attempt to understand race differences must recognize this fact. This is exemplified particularly well in hypertension research, which has looked to interdependent biological, nutritional, sociological, and psychological forces for a better understanding of excess hypertension among African Americans (see Anderson, 1987). Truly interdisciplinary models may be the only way to approach an understanding of group disparities in chronic disease and its impact.

By documenting chronic disease and disability differences between African Americans and Whites and not going into any detail regarding the source of these differences, this chapter has been somewhat limited in its focus. We also have not presented data on cognitive disorders, although they too are considerably more prevalent among African Americans (Callahan, Hendrie, & Tierney, 1995). Documenting differences is important, but studying the causes of particular diseases and how they vary by race and environment represents the primary path to understanding race differences in disability. The potentially very important issue of race differences in the distribution and impact of risk factors, for example, has recently been highlighted (Gibson, 1994). This is an area that has received some empirical attention (e.g., Clark, Stump, & Wolinsky, 1997; Harris-Hooker & Sanford, 1994; Keil et al., 1995; Lipton, Liao, Cao, Cooper, & McGee, 1993), and may provide valuable insights into differential causes of chronic diseases and methods of prevention.

As Fries (1992) has noted, the preservation of health or the prevention of disease has not been systematically integrated into the health care system and this has cost much in human and economic measures. Many diseases and processes of senescence can be postponed or even prevented, and the risk factors for many diseases are known and modifiable. A concerted effort by researchers, health care providers, and the public will be needed to address these modifiable risk factors effectively among those with high disease and disability prevalence. In the current political climate, it may be most effective to focus attention on diseases with the greatest combined prevalence and disability impact among African Americans. Based on the data of this chapter, these would be arthritis, heart disease, diabetes, and hypertension, with chronic lung disease and cerebrovascular disease closely following.

References

Andersen, R. M., Mullner, R. M., & Cornelius, L. J. (1987). Black-White differences in health status: Methods or substance? *The Milbank Quarterly, 65*(Suppl. 1), 72-99.
Anderson, N. A. (1987). Understanding the prevalence of hypertension among Black Americans. *Center Reports on Advances in Research, 10,* 1-8.
Berguss, G. R., & Hamm, R. M. (1995). Clinical practice: How physicians make medical decisions and why medical decision making can help. *Primary Care, 22,* 167-179.
Callahan, C. M., Hendrie, H. C., & Tierney, W. M. (1995). Documentation and evaluation of cognitive impairment in elderly primary care patients. *Annals of Internal Medicine, 122,* 422-429.
Clark, D. O. (1997). Trends in disability and institutionalization among older Blacks and Whites. *American Journal of Public Health, 87,* pp. 438-440.
Clark, D. O., & Maddox, G. L. (1992). Racial and social correlates of age-related changes in functioning. *Journal of Gerontology: Social Sciences, 47,* S222-S232.
Clark, D. O., Maddox, G. L., & Steinhauser, K. (1993). Race, aging, and functional health. *Journal of Aging and Health, 5,* 536-553.

Clark, D. O., Mungai, S. M., Stump, T. E., & Wolinsky, F. D. (1997). Prevalence and impact of risk factors for lower body difficulty among Mexican-Americans, African-Americans, and Whites. *Journal of Gerontology: Medical Sciences, 52A,* M97-M105.

Clark, D. O., Stump, T. E., & Wolinsky, F. D. (1997). A race and gender-specific replication of dimensions of disability and functional status. *Journal of Aging and Health, 9,* 28-42.

Cohen, R. A., & Van Nostrand, J. F. (1994). Trends in the health of older Americans: United States, 1994. *Vital and Health Statistics* (DHHS Publication No. PHS 93-1413, 3, 1-65). Hyattsville, MD: U.S. Department of Health and Human Services.

Cowie, C. C., Port, F. K., & Wolfe, R. A. (1989). Disparities in incidence of diabetic and end-stage renal disease according to race and type of diabetes. *New England Journal of Medicine, 321,* 1074-1079.

Ford, A. B., Haug, M. R., Jones, P. K., Roy, A. W., & Folmar, S. J. (1990). Race-related differences among elderly urban residents: A cohort study, 1975-1984. *Journal of Gerontology: Social Sciences, 45,* S163-S171.

Fries, J. F. (1992). Strategies for reduction of morbidity. *American Journal of Nutrition, 55,* 1257S-1262S.

Gibson, R. C. (1991a). Age-by-race differences in the health and functioning of elderly persons. *Journal of Aging and Health, 3,* 335-351.

Gibson, R. C. (1991b). Race and the self-reported health of elderly persons. *Journal of Gerontology: Social Sciences, 46,* S235-S242.

Gibson, R. C. (1994). The age-by-race gap in health and mortality in the older population: A social science research agenda. *The Gerontologist, 34,* 454-462.

Giles, W. H., Croft, J. B., Keenan, N. L., Lane, M. J., & Wheeler, F. C. (1995). The validity of self-reported hypertension and correlates of hypertension awareness among Blacks and Whites within the stroke belt. *American Journal of Preventive Medicine, 11,* 163-169.

Goldberg, K. C., Hartz, A. J., Jacobsen, S. J., Krakauer, H., & Rimm, A. A. (1992). Racial and community factors influencing coronary artery bypass graft surgery rates for all 1986 Medicare patients. *Journal of the American Medical Association, 267,* 1473-1477.

Goldschmid, M. G., Domin, W. S., Ziemer, D. M., Gallina, D. L., & Phillips, L. S. (1995). Diabetes in urban African-Americans. *Diabetes Care, 18,* 955-961.

Guralnik, J. M., Ferrucci, L., Simonsick, E. M., Salive, M. E., & Wallace, R. B. (1995). Lower-extremity function in persons over the age of 70 years as a predictor of subsequent disability. *New England Journal of Medicine, 332,* 556-561.

Harris-Hooker, S., & Sanford, G. L. (1994). Lipids, lipoproteins and coronary heart disease in minority populations. *Atherosclerosis, 108*(Suppl.), S83-S104.

Heliovaara, M., Aromaa, A., Klaukka, T., Knekt, P., Joukmaa, M., & Impivaara, O. (1993). Reliability and validity of interview data on chronic diseases. *Journal of Clinical Epidemiology, 46,* 181-191.

Johnson, P. A., Lee, T. H., Cook, E. F., Rouan, G. W., & Goldman, L. (1993). Effect of race on the presentation and management of patients with acute chest pain. *Annals of Internal Medicine, 118,* 593-601.

Johnson, R. J., & Wolinsky, F. D. (1993). The structure of health status among older adults: Disease, disability, functional limitation, and perceived health. *The Journal of Health and Social Behavior, 34,* 105-121.

Johnson, R. J., & Wolinsky, F. D. (1994). Gender, race, and health: The structure of health status among older adults. *The Gerontologist, 34,* 24-35.

Kaplan, N. M. (1994). Ethical aspects of hypertension. *The Lancet, 344,* 450-452.

Keil, J. E., Sutherland, S. E., Hames, C. G., Lackland, D. T., Gazes, P. C., Knapp, R. G., & Tyroler, H. A. (1995). Coronary disease mortality and risk factors in Black and White men. *Archives of Internal Medicine, 155,* 1521-1527.

Kochanek, K. D., & Hudson, B. L. (1995). Advance report of final mortality statistics. *Monthly Vital Statistics Report, 43*(6, Suppl). Hyattsville MD: National Center for Health Statistics.

Leigh, J. P., & Fries, J. F. (1992). Disability in occupations in a national sample. *American Journal of Public Health, 82,* 1517-1524.

Lewontin, R. C., Rose, S., & Kamin, L. J. (1984). *Not in our genes: Biology, ideology, and human nature.* New York: Pantheon.

Link, B. G., & Phelan, J. (1995). Social conditions as fundamental causes of disease. *Journal of Health and Social Behavior* [Extra issue], pp. 80-94.

Lipton, R. B., Liao, Y., Cao, G., Cooper, R. S., & McGee, D. (1993). Determinants of incident of non-insulin-dependent diabetes mellitus among Blacks and Whites in a national sample. *American Journal of Epidemiology, 138,* 826-839.

Manton, K. G., Corder, L. S., & Stallard, E. (1993a). Changes in the use of personal assistance and special equipment from 1982 to 1989: Results from the 1982 and 1989 NLTCS. *The Gerontologist, 33,* 168-176.

Manton, K. G., Corder, L. S., & Stallard. E. (1993b). Estimates of change in chronic disability and institutional incidence and prevalence rates in the U.S. elderly population from the 1982, 1984, and 1989 National Long-Term Care Survey. *Journal of Gerontology: Social Sciences, 48,* S153-S167.

Markides, K. S., & Keith, V. M. (1995). Race, aging and health in the USA. *Reviews in Clinical Gerontology, 5,* 339-345.

Markides, K. S., & Machalek, R. (1984). Selective survival, aging and society. *Archives of Gerontology and Geriatrics, 3,* 207-222.

Maynard, C., Litwin, P. E., Martin, J. S., Cerqueira, M., Kudenchuk, P. J., Ho, M. T., et al. (1991). Characteristics of Black patients admitted to coronary care units in metropolitan Seattle: Results from the myocardial infarction triage and intervention registry (MITI). *American Journal of Cardiology, 67,* 18-23.

Mendes de Leon, C. F., Fillenbaum, G. G., Williams, C. S., Brock, D. B., Beckett, L. A., & Berkman, L. F. (1995). Functional disability among elderly Blacks and Whites in two diverse areas: The New Haven and North Carolina EPESE. *American Journal of Public Health, 85,* 994-998.

Miles, T. P., & Bernard, M. A. (1992). Morbidity, disability, and health status of Black American elderly: A new look at the oldest-old. *Journal of the American Geriatrics Society, 40,* 1047-1054.

Miller, J. P., Perry, H. M., Rossiter, J. E., Baty, J. D., Carmody, S. E., & Sambhi, M. P. (1994). Regional differences in mortality during 15-year follow-up of 11,936 hypertensive veterans. *Hypertension, 23,* 431-438.

Nagi, S. Z. (1976). An epidemiology of disability among adults in the United States. *Milbank Memorial Fund Quarterly, 54,* 439-468.

Nagi, S. Z. (1990). Disability concepts revisited: Implications for prevention. In A. M. Pope & A. R. Tarlov (Eds.), *Disability in America: A national agenda for prevention* (Appendix A). Washington, DC: National Academy Press.

Nordstrom, D. L., Remington, P. L., & Layde, P. M. (1994). The utility of HMO data for the surveillance of chronic diseases. *American Journal of Public Health, 84,* 995-997.

Otten, M. W., Teutsch, S. M., Williamson, D. F., & Marks, J. S. (1990). The effect of known risk factors on the excess mortality of Black adults in the United States. *Journal of the American Medical Association, 263,* 845-850.

Pao, C. I., Whittle, J. C., Whelton, P. K., & Seidler, A. J. (1992). The excess incidence of diabetic end-stage renal disease among Blacks: A population-based study of potential explanatory factors. *Journal of the American Medical Association, 268,* 3079-3084.

Patrick, D. L., & Bergner, M. (1990). Measurement of health status in the 1990s. *Annual Review of Public Health, 11,* 165-183.

Rogers, R. G., Rogers, A., & Belanger, A. (1992). Disability-free life among the elderly in the United States: Sociodemographic correlates of functional health. *Journal of Aging and Health, 4,* 19-42.

Schneider, E. L., & Guralnik, J. M. (1990). The aging of America: Impact on health care costs. *Journal of the American Medical Association, 263,* 2335-2340.

Shaten, B. J., Smith, G. D., Kuller, L. H., & Neaton, J. D. (1993). Risk factors for the development of Type II diabetes among men enrolled in the usual care group of the multiple risk factor intervention trial. *Diabetes Care, 16*(10), 1331-1339.

Sorrentino, M. J. (1993). Racial disparities in coronary artery disease prevalence. *Annals of Internal Medicine, 119,* 861.

Teschke, K., Hertzman, C., Hershler, R., Wiens, M., Ostry, A., & Kelly, S. (1992). Reproducibility of self-reports of chronic disease. *Canadian Journal of Public Health, 83,* 71-72.

Verbrugge, L. M., & Patrick, D. L. (1995). Seven chronic conditions: Their impact on US adults' activity levels and use of medical services. *American Journal of Public Health, 85,* 173-182.

Verbrugge, L. M., Lepkowski, J. M., & Konkol, L. L. (1991). Levels of disability among U.S. adults with arthritis. *Journal of Gerontology: Social Sciences, 46,* S71-S83.

Verbrugge, L. M. (1990). The iceberg of disability. In S. Stahl *(Ed.), The legacy of longevity* (pp. 55-75). Newbury Park, CA: Sage.

Veves A., Sarnow, M. R., Giurini, J. M., Rosenblum, B. I., Lyons, T. E., Chrzan, J. S., & Habershaw, G. M. (1995). Differences in joint mobility and foot pressures between Black and White diabetic patients. *Diabetic Medicine, 12,* 585-589.

Wallace, R. B., & Lemke, J. H. (1991). The compression of comorbidity. *Journal of Aging and Health, 3,* 237-246.

Wenneker, M. B., & Epstein, A. M. (1989). Racial inequalities in the use of procedures for patients with ischemic heart disease in Massachusetts. *Journal of the American Medical Association, 261,* 253-257.

Williams, D., & Collins, C. (1995). U.S. socioeconomic and racial differences in health: Patterns and explanations. *Annual Review of Sociology, 21,* 349-386.

Williamson, D. F., Kahn, H. S., & Byers, T. (1991). The 10-y incidence of obesity and major weight gain in Black and White U.S. women aged 30-55 years. *American Journal of Clinical Nutrition, 53,* 1515S-1518S.

Wilson, I. B., & Cleary, P. D. (1995). Linking clinical variables with health-related quality of life. *Journal of the American Medical Association, 273,* 59-65.

Wolinsky, F. D., & Johnson, R. J. (1991). The use of health services by older adults. *Journal of Gerontology: Social Sciences, 46,* S345-S357.

Aging, Chronic Disease, and Physical Disability in Hispanic Elderly

Helen P. Hazuda
David V. Espino

It is generally well known that Hispanics, comprising more than 22 million people in 1991, are the second largest and most rapidly growing ethnic minority group in the United States (Day, 1996; Grebler et al., 1970). Less well known is that Hispanic elderly, 65 years of age and over, represented 5.2% of the total 1995 U.S. Hispanic population (more than one million people) (Day, 1996; U.S. Bureau of the Census, 1992). Of these Hispanic elderly, 55.1% were of Mexican origin, 15.6% Cuban origin, 9.8% Puerto Rican origin, 8.9% Central and South American origin, and 9.8% other Hispanic origin (Garcia, 1993). Increases in the Hispanic elderly will account for 13% of the total Hispanic population growth over the next 25 years (Day, 1996). Moreover, Hispanic elderly comprise the most rapidly growing segment of the total U.S. elderly population. By the year 2020, the Hispanic elderly population will grow by 76% compared to a growth rate of 38% for non-Hispanic White elderly and 34% for Black elderly (Day, 1996). By the year 2050, Hispanics will constitute 15.3% of all U.S. elderly (U.S. Bureau of the Census, 1992). Thus, maintenance of functional independence among elderly Hispanics is of increasing public health concern.

AUTHORS' NOTE: This work was supported in part by grants from the National Institute on Aging (1-R01-AG10444, 1-R01-10939, 1-P20-AG12044) and by the Mexican American Medical Treatment Effectiveness Research Center funded by the Agency for Health Care Policy and Research (1-U01-HS07397).

This chapter addresses that concern by assessing what is currently known about chronic disease and physical disability in Hispanic elderly and identifying areas in critical need of further research. This assessment is organized around the disablement process model first outlined by Nagi (Nagi, 1965, 1979, 1991) and further elaborated by Verbrugge and Jette (1994). According to this model, there are four stages in the main pathway from disease to disability: pathology (i.e., physiological and biochemical abnormalities that are detected and labeled as disease), impairments (i.e., significant structural abnormalities and dysfunctions in specific body systems such as the cardiovascular or musculoskeletal system), functional limitations (i.e., restrictions in basic physical and mental actions used in daily life by an individual's age-sex group), and disability (i.e., difficulty in doing activities in any domain of one's regular daily life due to a health or physical problem). Disease drives the disablement process through the mediating stages of impairments and functional limitations. Personal and environmental factors outside the main disease-disability pathway can slow, speed, or reverse the disablement process. These factors include predisposing risk factors, such as lower socioeconomic status or cigarette smoking; intrapersonal factors, such as lifestyle and behavior changes, psychosocial attributes and coping, and activity accommodations; and extra-personal factors, such as medical care and rehabilitation, medications and other therapeutic regimens, external supports, and built physical and social environment. The disablement process model thus provides the basis for a comprehensive and systematic approach to the epidemiology and prevention of disability (Verbrugge & Jette, 1994).

In reviewing the available data, we focused on national surveys that provide comparative data about the disablement process for Hispanics, the general population, or both. Most data are from the mid-1980s and provide information about Hispanics as a whole (Guralnik, LaCroix, Everett, & Kovar, 1989; U.S. Bureau of the Census, 1986, 1990; Vital and Health Statistics, 1990). The only data available across all Hispanic subgroups are from 1978 to 1980 (Treviño & Moss, 1984). Data on Mexican American only elderly have been reported from the Hispanic Health and Nutrition Examination Survey (HHANES: 1982-1984) (Espino, Burge, & Moreno, 1991). Some data have also been reported from the ongoing Mexican American Established Populations for the Epidemiological Study of the Elderly (Hispanic EPESE) survey based on a probability sample of approximately 3,000 Mexican Americans, 65+ years old, residing in the five southwestern states (Markides et al., 1996). Measures vary considerably across surveys. Conceptual terms are frequently defined in a manner that is not consistent with the terms and definitions of the disablement process model. Any information about the total disablement process must be pieced together from multiple studies across multiple time points.

Chronic Disease

Studies have shown that a variety of chronic diseases are associated with functional limitations, disability, or both, among the elderly (Boult, Kane, Louis, Boult, & McCaffrey, 1994; Furner, Rudberg, & Cassel, 1995; Guccione et al., 1994; Guralnik et al., 1989; Guralnik et al., 1993; Pinsky et al., 1985; Pinsky, Jette, Branch, Kannel, & Feinleib, 1990). These diseases include arthritis (Boult et al., 1994; Furner et al., 1995; Guccione et al., 1994), hypertension (Boult et al., 1994; Pinsky et al., 1990), heart disease (Furner et al., 1995; Guccione et al., 1994; Guralnik et al., 1993; Pinsky et al., 1985), diabetes (Furner et al., 1995; Guccione et al., 1994; Guralnik et al., 1993; Pinsky et al., 1990), cancer (Guralnik et al., 1993), hip fracture or osteoporosis (Guccione et al., 1994; Guralnik et al., 1993), and stroke (Boult et al., 1994; Furner et al., 1995; Guccione et al., 1994; Guralnik et al., 1993). The prevalence of these diseases among the general U.S. population and Mexican-origin Hispanics can be estimated from four major surveys: (a) the Supplement on Aging to the National Health Interview Survey (NHIS-SOA), (b) the Medicare Current Beneficiary Survey (MCBS), (c) the Hispanic Health and Nutrition Examination Survey (HHANES), and (d) the Hispanic EPESE. The NHIS is an annual survey of the civilian noninstitutionalized population conducted by the National Center for Health Statistics (NCHS) since 1956. It is the primary source of "official" statistical data on health and health service utilization in the United States (Johnson & Wolinsky, 1993). In 1984, the SOA was included as a supplement to the NHIS to collect information on the health, social functioning, and living arrangements of individuals aged 55 and older. About 60% of the sample is female, and more than 90% is White. The MCBS is a longitudinal panel survey begun by the Health Care Financing Administration in 1991. Samples are drawn from the Medicare enrollment to be representative of the Medicare population as a whole and by age group. The 1991 sample was 57% female, 84% White, and 83% elderly (65+ years old). HHANES was conducted by NCHS in 1982-1984 to provide estimates of health and nutritional status for the three major Hispanic subgroups (Mexican Americans, Puerto Rican Americans, and Cuban Americans) comparable to that obtained for the general population in the National Health and Nutrition Examination Survey (Espino et al., 1991). Data on Mexican Americans were obtained from a probability sample of the five southwestern states (California, Arizona, New Mexico, Colorado, and Texas), which included approximately 84% of all Mexican Americans in the United States (Vital and Health Statistics, 1985). The age range was 6 months to 74 years. The Hispanic EPESE is a 2-year longitudinal study based on a probability sample of Mexican Americans aged 65 years and over residing in the five southwestern states. First wave data were collected from 1993 to 1994. The sample had a mean age of 72.9 years and 5.1 years of education; 56.7% were female, 46.8% were foreign-born, and 72.6% were interviewed in Spanish. In the HHANES, disease diagnoses were based on a physician's medical history, physical examination, and laboratory results; in the other three surveys, disease diagnoses were based on self-report.

Prevalence data are shown in Table 6.1. Data on some diseases are not available across all studies. Within the general population, arthritis and hypertension are the two most prevalent chronic diseases, afflicting about 40% to 50% of elderly. This is also the case among Mexican Americans, although the prevalences are somewhat lower than in the general population, 30% for hypertension and about 4% to 40% for arthritis. Heart disease is the third most prevalent chronic disease among general population elderly, ranging from 14% to 20%. Among Mexican American elderly, the corresponding prevalence (16.5%) falls within the general population range, but diabetes is more prevalent than heart disease. About 22% of Mexican American elders report diabetes, a prevalence rate 1.5 to 2 times higher than the rate among general population elderly (about 10%-15%). Cancer prevalence among Mexican American elderly (6.4%) is almost identical to that among general population elderly (6.6%), while hip fracture or osteoporosis is slightly lower (Mexican Americans, 4.1% vs. general population, 5.5%). Stroke prevalence among older Mexican Americans (7.4%) is within the range among general population elderly (5.4% to 8.6%). Thus, the prevalence of leading chronic diseases among Mexican American elderly is the same or lower than that among general population elderly with the single, striking exception of diabetes.

The excess diabetes prevalence among Mexican American elderly may be particularly significant. A recent prospective study of predominantly White elders has shown that diabetes is a powerful predictor of successful aging (Strawbridge, Cohen, Shema, & Kaplan, 1996). More specifically, per-

TABLE 6.1 Prevalence (%) of Selected Chronic Conditions Among
Noninstitutionalized Persons 65 Years of Age and Older
According to Four U.S. Surveys[a]

Selected Conditions	NHIS SOA 60+ yrs 1984	MCBS 65+ yrs 1991	MA HHANES 65-74 yrs 1982-1984	Hispanic EPESE 65+ yrs 1993-1994
Arthritis or rheumatism	49.0	—	4.1	40.8
Hypertension	41.8	48.5	30.0	—
Heart disease[b]	14.0	20.0	16.5	9.2
Diabetes	9.5	14.7	21.6	22.2
Cancer	6.6	—	—	6.4
Hip fracture or osteoporosis	5.5	—	—	4.1
Stroke	5.4	8.6	—	7.4

SOURCES: Espino, Burge, & Moreno (1991); Guralnik, LaCroix, Everett, & Kovar (1989); Markides, Stroup-Benham, Goodwin, Perkowski, Lichtenstein, & Ray (1996); National Heart, Lung, and Blood Institute (1995, table 66).

NOTES: a. Abbreviations: NHIS, SOA = National Health Interview Survey, Supplement on Aging; MCBS = Medicare Current Beneficiary Survey; MA HHANES = Mexican Americans in the Hispanic Health and Nutrition Examination Survey; and Hispanic EPESE = the Hispanic Establishing Population for Epidemiologic Studies of the Elderly Survey. Diagnoses in all surveys except HHANES were based on self-report. HHANES diagnoses were based on a clinical examination by a physician.

b. Heart disease is not defined consistently across the four surveys. In the NHIS, SOA, and MCBS, heart disease includes self-reported coronary heart disease, heart attack, or angina; in the HHANES, heart disease was diagnosed by a physician following a complete medical and physical examination and included the specific disease entities of hypertensive heart disease, heart failure, ischemic heart disease, rheumatic heart disorders, and other forms of heart disease; and in the Hispanic EPESE, heart disease includes only self-reported heart attack.

sons with diabetes at baseline were 90% less likely to have aged successfully at 6-years' follow-up than persons free of diabetes at baseline (OR = 0.10, 95% confidence interval = 0.01-0.79) (Strawbridge et al., 1996). A person was considered to have aged successfully if he or she ". . . could do all the basic physical activities expected of an adult with little difficulty and had no more than a little difficulty on selected physical performance measures" (Strawbridge et al., 1996, p. 136). Furthermore, estimates of diabetes prevalence based on self-reports underestimate the true prevalence by about half (Haffner, Rosenthal, Hazuda, Stern, & Franco, 1984; Harris, 1985). In the San Antonio Longitudinal Study of Aging (SALSA) (Escalante, Lichtenstein, White, Rios, & Hazuda, 1995), for example, the prevalence of self-reported diabetes among Mexican American elderly was very similar to that observed in the Hispanic EPESE (25.1% and 22.2%, respectively), but the prevalence of diabetes based on World Health Organization blood glucose criteria (World

Health Organization, 1985) was about twice as high (47.4%) (unpublished data). In addition, diabetes frequently leads to a number of complications, including peripheral vascular disease, retinopathy, nephropathy, and neuropathy as well as heart attack and stroke (Stern & Haffner, 1990).

Functional Limitations

Within the disablement process model, functional limitations are restrictions in basic physical and mental actions used in daily life by an individual's age-sex group (Verbrugge & Jette, 1994). We were able to find one national report that provided race-/ethnic-specific data on the following sensory and physical functional limitations: seeing, hearing, speaking, lifting or carrying, walking, using stairs, getting around inside, getting around outside, and getting into and out of bed (U.S. Bureau of the Census, 1986). Persons were considered to have a functional limitation if they had difficulty performing one or more of these actions, and were considered to have a severe functional limitation if they were unable to perform one or more of these actions or if they needed the help of another person in order to perform one or more of the actions. Race-/ethnic-specific data for individual actions were not provided.

The prevalence of functional limitations by sex and race/ethnic origin is shown in Table 6.2. Among elderly men, the prevalence of functional limitation is appreciably lower among Hispanics than among Whites generally (Hispanic, 42% vs. White, 52%). However, the prevalence of severe functional limitation is nearly identical among the two race/ethnic groups (Hispanic, 20.2% vs. White, 21.2%). In contrast, among elderly women the prevalence of functional limitation is appreciably higher among Hispanics than Whites generally (Hispanic, 72.6% vs. White, 60.3%). Furthermore, the prevalence of severe functional limitation is 1.5 times higher among Hispanic women than among White women generally (Hispanic, 31.7% vs. White, 48.7%). Almost three quarters of elderly Hispanic women have a functional limitation, and almost half have a severe functional limitation. These rates are about twice as high as those observed in elderly Hispanic men. In addition, the rates of functional limitation in elderly Hispanic men are substantially lower than the corresponding rates in Blacks, whereas the rates of functional limitation in elderly Hispanic women are very similar to the corresponding rates in Blacks.

TABLE 6.2 Functional Limitation in Sensory and Physical Activities of Persons 65 Years of Age and Over by Sex and Race/Ethnic Origin: United States, 1984-1985

Sex and Level of Limitation[a]	White	Black	Hispanic[b]
MEN			
Total number	9,757,000	859,000	312,000
% with a limitation	52.0	69.0	42.0
% with a severe limitation	21.2	30.0	20.2
WOMEN			
Total number	14,165,000	1,321,000	372,000
% with a limitation	60.3	78.9	72.6
% with a severe limitation	31.7	49.0	48.7

SOURCE: U.S. Bureau of the Census (1986, table B).

NOTES: a. Persons were considered to have a functional limitation if they had difficulty performing one or more of the following sensory and physical activities: seeing, hearing, speaking, lifting or carrying, walking, using stairs, getting around inside, getting around outside, and getting into and out of bed. Persons were considered to have a severe functional limitation if they were unable to perform one or more of these activities *or* if they needed the help of another person in order to perform one or more of the activities.

b. Hispanics can be of any race.

Disability

Disability, as defined within the disablement process model, refers to difficulty in doing activities in any domain of one's regular daily life due to a health or physical problem (Verbrugge & Jette, 1994). Typically, these activities are defined as basic activities of daily living (ADLs) involving personal care (e.g, eating, dressing, bathing, grooming, toileting, transferring in and out of bed/chair) and instrumental activities of daily living (IADLs) necessary for maintaining a household in a particular social setting (e.g, preparing meals, doing housework, managing money, using the telephone, shopping for personal items). Some researchers also include advanced activities of daily living (AADLs; Reuben, Laliberte, Hiris, & Mor, 1990) or discretionary activities of daily living (Verbrugge & Jette, 1994) that involve other valued domains common for one's age-sex group (e.g., sports and physical recreation, socializing with friends and relatives, caring for grandchildren).

We were able to find no national reports containing separate data for Whites and Hispanic on disability as defined in the disablement process model. Most reports instead provide data about dependency (i.e., having or needing someone's help to do an activity) (Markides et al., 1996; U.S. Bureau of the Census, 1990; Verbrugge & Jette, 1994; Vital and Health Statistics, 1990). As Verbrugge and Jette (1994) point out, however, dependency measures a buffer, or intervention, to reduce disability rather than disability per se. Data from the 1984 NHIS-SOA indicate that the prevalence of self-reported difficulty in performing ADLs is 2 to 3 times higher than self-reported need for assistance in performing ADLs (Guralnik et al., 1989). Thus, the reports reviewed here provide no information about the proportion of Hispanics at risk of dependency by virtue of present disability.

The only comparative data for the major Hispanic subgroups on any aspect of the disablement process are disability-related data from the NHIS, 1978-1980 (Treviño & Moss, 1984). Table 6.3 shows the proportion of persons with limitations of activity due to chronic conditions by Hispanic origin, gender, and age (45-64 years and 65+ years). Whites (including Hispanic-origin Whites) are included as a comparison group. Persons limited in major activity are those unable to carry out their usual activity (i.e., working, keeping house, or going to school) and those restricted in the amount or kind of major activity for their age-sex group. Persons limited in any activity are those limited in major activity plus those restricted in other activities (e.g, recreational, civic, church, or other leisure activities).

Across all groups, the proportion with activity limitations (major or any) is about twice as high among those aged 65+ years as those aged 45 to 64 years. Limitations of major activity account for about 76% of all activity limitations in 45- to 64-year-olds, increasing to about 90% in those 65 years and over. The proportion of elderly Hispanics with major activity limitation is somewhat higher than the corresponding proportion of elderly Whites (men: Hispanics, 45.9% vs. Whites, 42.5%; women: Hispanics, 39.9% vs. Whites, 34.2%). Among elderly Hispanics, Cuban Americans have the lowest proportion of major activity limitation (men 37.7%, women 36.7%), and Puerto Rican Americans have the highest (men 57.7%, women 50.0%). The proportion of elderly Mexican Americans limited in major activity (men 49.2%, women 44.1%) is intermediate between these two subgroups, but is closer to that of Puerto Rican Americans than Cuban Americans. Data for all Hispanics combined, then, masks substantial variations among the major Hispanic subgroups.

Two reports provide comparative data on functional dependency in ADLs and IADLs for White, Black, and Hispanic elderly (U.S. Bureau of the Census, 1990; Vital and Health Statistics, 1990). In the first report, based on the 1984 NHIS-SOA (Vital and Health Statistics, 1990), functional dependen-

TABLE 6.3 Percentage of Persons With Limitations of Major Activity and Limitations of Any Activity Due to Chronic Conditions by Hispanic Origin, Gender, and Age: United States, 1978-1980

Type of Limitation,[a] Gender and Age	White	All Hispanics	Mexican American	Puerto Rican American	Cuban American	Other Hispanic
Limitation of major activity						
Men						
45-64 yrs	19.3	19.1	16.6	23.3	24.0	18.4
65+ yrs	42.5	45.9	49.2	57.7	37.7	48.2
Women						
45-64 yrs	16.4	19.2	19.7	24.8	16.7	17.1
65+ yrs	34.2	39.9	44.1	50.0	36.7	34.1
Limitation of any activity						
Men						
45-64 yrs	24.5	23.1	21.1	26.3	27.2	23.2
65+ yrs	47.6	49.4	54.0	57.7	40.3	50.0
Women						
45-64 yrs	21.8	25.0	25.6	33.1	20.6	23.9
65+ yrs	41.9	45.9	51.0	50.0	43.3	46.9

SOURCE: Treviño & Moss (1984).
NOTE: a. Persons limited in major activity are those unable to carry out their usual activity, whether it is working, keeping house or going to school, and those restricted in the amount or kind of major activity for their age-sex group. Persons limited in any activity are those limited in major activity plus those restricted in other activities, such as recreational, civic, church, or other leisure activities.

cy is considered present if a person (a) is having difficulty performing specific activities because of a health or physical problem *and* receives the help of another person in performing the activity or (b) is unable to perform the activity without special equipment and does not have the equipment. ADL activities included: bathing, eating, getting in or out of bed or chair (transferring), mobility, using the toilet, and continence. IADL activities included: preparing meals, shopping for personal items, managing their own money, using the telephone, doing light housework, doing heavy housework, and going outside. The proportion of persons reporting functional dependency in either ADLs or IADLs was somewhat higher among Hispanic elderly than among White elderly in general (27.1% and 24.7%, respectively) but lower than the corresponding proportion among Black elderly (34.1%). Though the direction and magnitude of the White-Hispanic difference is similar to that

TABLE 6.4 Number and Percentage Distribution of Persons 65 Years of Age
and Over Needing Personal Assistance With Instrumental Activities
of Daily Living Because of a Health Condition Lasting 3 Months or
Longer, by Race/Ethnic Origin: United States, 1986

| | | Needed Assistance With | | | |
Race/ Ethnic Origin[a]	All Persons	Personal Care[b] %	Getting Around Outside %	Preparing Meals %	Doing Light Housework %
White	25,022,000	6.2	11.0	8.4	10.5
Black	2,273,000	12.0	15.6	16.6	19.4
Hispanic†	803,000	6.5	11.6	11.7	11.8

SOURCE: U.S. Bureau of the Census (1990 [tables A & B], 1992).
NOTES: a. Hispanic includes any race.
b. Includes such things as dressing, eating, and personal hygiene.

reported above for limitations of major activity, the proportions who are functionally dependent in ADLs or IADLs are lower in both race/ethnic groups
than the proportions who are limited in major activity. Thus the prevalence of
dependency reported among Hispanics in national surveys varies appreciably
according to the definitions and measures used.

Table 6.4 shows the proportion of White, Black, and Hispanic elderly
needing assistance with selected ADLs and IADLs. Data are from the 1986
NHIS (U.S. Bureau of the Census, 1990). The percentage needing assistance
in personal care, getting around outside, and doing light housework is very
similar for Whites and Hispanics (personal care: 6.2% vs. 6.5%; getting
around outside: 11.0% vs. 11.6%; doing light housework: 10.5% vs. 11.8%).
However, the proportion of Hispanics needing assistance in preparing meals
is about 40% higher than the corresponding proportion among Whites (11.7%
vs. 8.4%). Across the four activities, the proportion of Blacks needing assistance compared with Whites is about 40% to 95% higher and compared with
Hispanics is about 30% to 85% higher.

Data on the need for assistance with individual ADLs and IADLs are
available for Mexican Americans from the Hispanic EPESE (Markides et al.,
1996; Markides, Rudkin, Espino, & Angel, in press). Comparative data on
Whites and all other races are available from the 1986 NHIS Supplement on
Functional Limitations (Prohaska, Mermelstein, Miller, & Jack, 1993). It
should be noted, however, that the definition of needing assistance differed in
the two studies. The NHIS report (Prohaska et al., 1993) considered persons

TABLE 6.5 Percentage of Persons Needing Assistance in Activities of Daily Living (ADLs) and Instrumental Activities of Daily Living (IADLs) Among Noninstitutionalized Persons 65 Years of Age and Over by Race/Ethnic Origin in Two Major Surveys[a]

	NHIS 1996		Hispanic EPESE 1993-94
Activity	White[b] (N = 24,753,000)	All Other (N = 2,784,000)	Mexican American (N = 3,050)
ADL			
Bathing	5.6	9.4	11.7
Dressing	4.2	6.1	9.5
Eating	1.1	0.6[c]	5.4
Transferring	3.0	5.2	8.8
Using toilet	2.3	3.5	7.5
IADL			
Meal preparation	5.9	11.6	14.0
Shopping	11.4	17.0	22.3
Using the telephone	2.9	4.6	11.2
Light housework	6.6	10.9	15.6

SOURCE: Based on data from Prohaska, Mermelstein, Miller, & Jack (1993, chap. 2, tables 3 and 6, pp. 23-39), and from Markides, Stroup-Benham, Goodwin, Perkowski, Lichtenstein, & Ray (1996).

NOTES: a. NHIS = National Health Interview Survey, Hispanic EPESE = Mexican American Establishing Populations for Epidemiologic Studies of the Elderly survey.

b. Includes Hispanics.

c. Unstable estimate.

Needing assistance is defined somewhat differently in the two reports. For the NHIS report, needing assistance was considered present if, because of a health problem, a person reported difficulty performing an activity alone *and* received help from another person. The MA EPESE does not specifically tie the need for assistance to a health or physical problem and defines it as needing help from a person or device *or* being unable to perform the activity.

as needing assistance if they reported that, because of a health problem, they had difficulty performing an activity by themselves *and* received help from another person. The Hispanic EPESE (Markides et al., 1996; Markides et al., in press) did not tie the need for assistance to a health problem, and defined needing assistance as needing help from a person *or* a device *or* being unable to perform the activity. Data from the two studies are shown in Table 6.5.

The NHIS data indicate that the percentage of persons needing assistance in individual ADLs and IADLs is substantially higher among all other races than among Whites generally. Furthermore, data from the Hispanic EPESE suggest that the proportion of Mexican American elderly needing assistance in these activities is consistently higher than both the proportion of Whites and of all other races needing assistance. The Mexican American to White ratio ranges from 1.96 for shopping to 4.91 for eating. For transferring and using the toilet, the need for assistance is about 3 times higher in Mexican American than White elderly, and for using the telephone the need for assistance is almost 4 times higher. With the exception of eating, for which the prevalence estimate is unstable in all other races, the ratio of Mexican Americans to all other races needing assistance ranges from 1.21 for meal preparation to 2.43 for using the telephone. Most ratios indicate a 20% to 50% excess in need for assistance among Mexican Americans relative to all other races.

These findings are in contrast to those reported previously (U.S. Bureau of the Census, 1990), which found that Hispanics as a group had rates of dependency in specific ADLs and IADLs that were similar to those of Whites generally (except for eating) but lower than those of Blacks. The greater need for assistance observed among Mexican American elderly in the Hispanic EPESE compared with White and other elderly in the NHIS may be the result of one or a combination of several factors: (a) differences in the definition of need for assistance used in the two studies (i.e., the NHIS definition was more restrictive); (b) differences in socioeconomic status between the two study samples (i.e., median education among Mexican American elders in the Hispanic EPESE was only 5.1 years, substantially below median education in the general population); and (c) variation in rates of dependency among Hispanic subgroups (i.e., Mexican Americans may have higher rates of dependency in ADLs and IADLs than Hispanics as a total group).

Chronic Disease, Functional Limitations, and Disability

The only published information that we were able to find on the association of specific chronic diseases with functional limitations or disability in Hispanics is data from the Hispanic EPESE (Markides et al., 1996) on physical function in Mexican Americans. These data are shown in Table 6.6, which gives the odds ratios for the association of six specific chronic conditions with ADLs and two lower body physical actions after adjustment for age, gender, and the other five chronic conditions. It should be noted that these data actually provide information about dependency (i.e., need for assistance from a device or person) in performing physical actions and activities of daily living

TABLE 6.6   Age- and Gender-Adjusted Odds Ratios and 95% Confidence Intervals for Indicators of Physical Function Regressed on Six Selected Chronic Conditions: Hispanic EPESE, 1993-1994

	Physical Function		
Selected Chronic Condition	*Any ADL Dependency*	*Climbing Stairs*	*Walking Half Mile*
Arthritis	1.451	2.030	2.198
	(1.053, 2.002)	(1.600, 2.576)	(1.692, 2.856)
Heart attack	1.954	2.078	2.137
	(1.237, 3.088)	(1.304, 3.313)	(1.415, 3.229)
Diabetes	1.577	2.081	2.104
	(1.122, 2.217)	(1.565, 2.767)	(1.631, 2.714)
Cancer	2.112	1.576	1.119
	(1.328, 3.361)	(1.015, 2.448)	(0.699, 1.792)
Hip fracture	4.857	6.008	6.314
	(2.739, 8.676)	(3.571, 10.109)	(3.625, 10.997)
Stroke	4.865	3.775	3.936
	(3.008, 7.869)	(2.405, 5.924)	(2.422, 6.394)
(*N*)	2,983	2,943	2,915

SOURCE: From "The Effect of Medical Conditions on Functional Limitation in Mexican American Elderly," by K. S. Markides, C. A. Stroup-Benham, J. S. Goodwin, L. C. Perkowski, M. J. Lichtenstein, & L. A. Ray, *Annals of Epidemiology, 6,* 1996. Used with permission.

rather than physical functional limitations and disability (i.e., difficulty in performing physical actions and activities of daily living) as defined in the disablement process model.

The six chronic conditions have a differential effect on ADL dependency (any vs. none) and dependency in the two lower body physical actions (i.e., climbing stairs and walking one half mile). Arthritis and diabetes are significantly associated with both ADL dependency and dependency in lower body physical actions, but the association with lower body physical actions (odds ratios about 2) is greater than the association with ADL dependency (odds ratios 1.4 to 1.6). Cancer, on the other hand, is more strongly associated with ADL dependency (odds ratio about 2) than with dependency in lower body physical actions (odds ratios about 1.1 to 1.6) and, in fact, is not significantly associated with walking one half mile. In contrast with these three chronic conditions, heart attack has a similar association with ADL dependency and dependency in lower body physical actions (odds ratios about 2). As previously reported for the general population (Verbrugge, Lepkowski, & Imanaka, 1989), hip fracture and stroke have the strongest associations with both ADL dependency (odds ratios about 5) and lower body dependency (odds ratios about 4 to 6). However, hip fracture is more strongly associated with lower body dependency (odds ratios about 6) than with ADL dependency (odds ratio about 5), while stroke is more strongly associated with ADL dependency (odds ratio about 5) than with lower body dependency (odds ratios about 4).

Differential effects of chronic conditions on dependency in specific ADLs were also observed in the MA EPESE (data not shown) (Markides et al., 1996). There were marked differences in the specific ADL activities associated with different chronic conditions. Only stroke was significantly associated with all seven ADLs. This finding of differential effects of individual chronic diseases on specific activities of daily living is consistent with previously reported findings in the general population (Furner et al., 1995; Verbrugge et al., 1989).

Sociocultural Factors and the Disablement Process

The major Hispanic subgroups differ markedly in their migration experiences, socioeconomic status, and degree of assimilation into American society (Bean & Tienda, 1987; Jaffe, Cullen, & Boswell, 1980). Furthermore, the major subgroups themselves are becoming more heterogeneous both socioeconomically and culturally (Jaffe et al., 1980; Keenan, Murray, & Truman, 1992). Thus, it is important to consider whether sociocultural factors, including socioeconomic status, assimilation into the broader American society, and migration, impact significantly on the disablement process.

Published national data related to socioeconomic status and disability across major Hispanic subgroups are available from the NHIS, 1978-1980 (Treviño & Moss, 1984). Table 6.7 shows the proportion of persons with limitations of major activity and any activity by age (45-64 years and 65+ years), family income (< $10,000 and ≥ $10,000), and Hispanic origin. Whites (including Hispanic-origin Whites) are included as a comparison group. As noted previously, persons limited in major activity are those unable to carry out their usual activity (i.e., working, keeping house, or going to school) and those restricted in the amount or kind of major activity for their age-sex

TABLE 6.7 Percentage of Persons With Limitations of Major Activity and Limitations of Any Activity Due to Chronic Conditions by Hispanic Origin, Family Income, and Age: United States, 1978-1980

Type of Limitation,[a] Family Income, and Age	White	All Hispanics	Mexican Americans	Puerto Rican Americans	Cuban Americans	Other Hispanic
Limitation of major activity						
<$10,000						
45-64 years	36.8	31.1	26.3	42.1	30.3	34.1
65+ years	41.8	45.0	47.8	57.5	42.9	37.5
>$10,000						
45-64 years	13.1	13.2	14.0	13.2	16.0	9.7
65+ years	32.6	38.9	44.6	45.5[b]	28.3	41.1
Limitation of any activity						
<$10,000						
45-64 years	42.6	36.3	31.3	50.5	34.3	39.0
65+ years	49.0	50.0	54.5	57.5	47.1	43.1
>$10,000						
45-64 years	18.5	18.0	18.5	17.1	18.5	17.0
65+ years	38.7	42.4	47.7	45.5[b]	35.0	44.6

SOURCE: Treviño & Moss (1984).

NOTE: a. Persons limited in major activity are those unable to carry out their usual activity, whether it is working, keeping house, or going to school, and those restricted in the amount or kind of major activity for their age-sex group. Persons limited in any activity are those limited in major activity plus those restricted in other activities, such as recreational, civic, church, or other leisure activities.
b. Unstable estimate.

group. Persons limited in any activity are those limited in major activity plus those restricted in other activities (e.g, recreational, civic, church, or other leisure activities).

For both Whites generally and all Hispanics, the proportion of persons with limitation of major or any activity is lower among those with family incomes greater than $10,000 per year than among those with family incomes less than $10,000 per year. For persons with family incomes less than $10,000 per year and aged 45 to 64 years, all Hispanics have a lower prevalence of activity limitation than their White counterparts (major activity limitation: all Hispanics, 31.1% vs. Whites, 36.8%; any activity limitation: all Hispanics, 36.3% vs. Whites, 42.6%). This relative advantage is shared by all Hispanic subgroups except Puerto Ricans. Among persons aged 65+ years old with family incomes less than $10,000 per year, an almost opposite pattern is

observed: All Hispanics have a higher or similar proportion of activity limitation compared with Whites (major activity limitation: all Hispanics, 45%
vs. Whites, 41.8%; any activity limitation: all Hispanics, 50% vs. Whites,
49.0%). For persons with family incomes greater than $10,000 and aged 45
to 64 years old, there is little difference between Whites and all Hispanics in
the prevalence of activity limitation (major activity limitation, all Hispanics,
13.2% vs. Whites 13.1%; any activity limitation: all Hispanics, 18.0% vs.
Whites, 18.5%). This pattern holds fairly consistently across all Hispanic subgroups. For persons aged 65+ years old with family incomes greater than
$10,000, the prevalence of activity limitation is greater among all Hispanics
than Whites (major activity limitation: all Hispanics, 38.9% vs. Whites,
32.6%; any activity limitation, all Hispanics, 42.4% vs. Whites 38.7%). This
relative disadvantage is observed for all Hispanic subgroups except Cuban
Americans. In both income groups, then, there is a reversal in the pattern of
ethnic differences in rates of disability (defined by activity limitation) from
middle to older age. Middle-aged Hispanics (except Puerto Rican Americans)
have lower disability rates than Whites generally, but elderly Hispanics (except Cuban Americans) have higher disability rates than Whites generally.
Examining the life experiences of middle-aged Hispanics may provide some
clues to the cause of this reversal.

   National data concerning the role of migration and assimilation into the
broader American society in the disablement process have been published
from the 1988 National Survey of Hispanic Elderly People, sponsored by the
Commonwealth Fund Commission (Angel & Angel, 1992; Davis, 1990).
About 2,000 Hispanic elderly (65+ years old) screened from 85,404 households in regions of the United States with high concentrations of Hispanics
participated in the study. Almost all Cuban American and Puerto Rican
American elderly were born outside the U.S. mainland (99% and 98%, respectively) compared with only 42% of Mexican American elderly. A high
proportion of Hispanic elderly spoke no English (Mexican Americans: 32%,
Cuban Americans: 57%, and Puerto Rican Americans: 37%). Disability was
measured by a modified ADL scale, with one point given for reported difficulty in each of seven activities (bathing, dressing, toileting, getting outside,
transferring, walking, and feeding oneself). Hispanic elderly who migrated to
the United States in late adulthood reported more disability than those who
migrated earlier in life. This excess was explained in part by the lower prevalence of social networks among late-life migrants. That is, social networks
were found to be protective against disability; and the later the age at migra-

tion, the more difficult it was for migrants to form social networks, probably because the adaptive capacity of the elderly is lower than that of younger individuals (Angel & Angel, 1992). Cuban American elderly relative to Mexican Americans and Puerto Rican Americans seemed to be protected against the negative effects of lower levels of assimilation (as measured by migration status) because of the well-established ethnic enclaves in which late-life arrivals resided (Angel & Angel, 1992).

Additional data about the effects of socioeconomic status and assimilation on the disablement process among Mexican-origin Hispanics are becoming available from the San Antonio Longitudinal Study of Aging (SALSA), carried out from 1992 to 1996 in San Antonio, Texas. Participants were 833 elderly Mexican American and European American subjects (65+ years old) residing in households randomly selected from three socioculturally distinct neighborhoods: a low-income, almost exclusively Mexican American section of town; a middle-income, ethnically balanced section of town; and a high-income, predominantly non-Hispanic White section of town. Multiple measures of socioeconomic status (education, occupation, household income) were administered, along with the Hazuda Assimilation Scales (Hazuda, Haffner, & Stern, 1988) that measured three independent dimensions of adult assimilation: Functional Integration With the Broader Society, a measure of structural assimilation (Gordon, 1975); Value Placed on Preserving Mexican Cultural Origins, a measure of cultural assimilation (Gordon, 1975); and Attitude Toward Traditional Family Structure and Sex-Role Organization, a second measure of cultural assimilation. Preliminary analyses (Hazuda, 1995) suggest that socioeconomic status (SES) and assimilation generally have a beneficial effect on all stages of the disablement process; that is, higher levels of SES and assimilation are associated with lower levels of chronic disease, functional limitations, and disability. However, both SES and assimilation appear to be more strongly and consistently associated with functional limitations and disability than with chronic disease. Among SES indicators, the effects of household income seem to be stronger and more pervasive than the effects of education or occupation. Among assimilation indicators, the effects of structural assimilation appear to be stronger than the effects of either dimension of cultural assimilation. This finding of a differential effect of various SES and assimilation indicators on the disablement process may provide clues about more proximate, mediating factors (e.g., medical care utilization, therapeutic regimens, adaptive strategies) that influence the development of functional limitations and disability in Hispanics.

Gaps in Current Research

There is much that we need to learn about chronic disease and physical disability in older Hispanics. First, there are no published data documenting the relative prevalence of chronic diseases, impairments, or functional limitations across the three major Hispanic subgroups. Although comparative data related to disability have been published for these subgroups, the data are not current (1978-1980) and, like the other reports on all Hispanics combined or on Mexican Americans, deal with dependency rather than disability (Treviño & Moss, 1984). These data nonetheless clearly indicate that failure to treat Hispanic subgroups separately masks wide differences among them and that findings based on all Hispanics or on a single Hispanic subgroup are not generalizable to all subgroups.

Second, although systematic tests of the disablement process model in general population elderly have begun to appear in the literature (Pinsky et al., 1985), little or no attention has been given to this area in Hispanics. The Hispanic EPESE has examined the direct effects of specific chronic diseases on ADL dependency and dependency in lower body physical actions (Markides et al., 1996), and this is an important contribution to the field. But the disablement process model defines disability and functional limitations as difficulty in performing activities or actions rather than as dependency and further posits that the association between chronic disease and disability is mediated by impairments and functional limitations, yet none of the published reports reviewed in this chapter have examined the direct effects of chronic disease on impairments or of functional limitations on disability. Nor have they examined the indirect effects of chronic disease on disability via the pathway of impairments, functional limitations, or both. Yet, effective decisions about where to intervene in the main disease-disability pathway to prevent, slow, or reverse the disablement process require such information.

Third, little attention has been given to identifying the points of impact within the disablement process of factors outside the main disease-disability pathway that may alter its course. Some of the data reviewed here do make a contribution in this area. We know, for example, that age at migration is a risk factor for disability among all Hispanic subgroups (Angel & Angel, 1992) and that social networks mediate the association between assimilation (as measured by migrant status) and disability by protecting against the apparently harmful effects of lower assimilation on disability (Angel & Angel,

1992). We also have some clues that socioeconomic status and assimilation may impact primarily on functional limitations and disability rather than on chronic disease (except for diabetes) (Hazuda, 1995). More information about these sociocultural factors and other potential modifier-variables is needed to know how to intervene to prevent, slow, or reverse the disablement process. For example, depression has been linked to poorer physical functioning in non-Hispanic elderly (Vega & Rumbaut, 1991). Higher rates of depression have been observed among Puerto Rican Americans in New York than among Puerto Ricans on the island or among Mexican Americans (Vega & Rumbaut, 1991), while very low rates of depression have been observed among Cuban Americans in Miami (Vega & Rumbaut, 1991). Are these differences in the rates of depression among Hispanic subgroups related to the similar pattern of subgroup differences in rates of activity limitation observed in the NHIS (Treviño & Moss, 1984)?

Fourth, all of the published data currently available are cross-sectional. There are no data on the incidence of chronic disease, impairments, functional limitations, or disability in elderly Hispanics nor can we test longitudinally causal pathways in the disablement process. Data from the Hispanic EPESE and several other longitudinal studies currently underway with funding from the National Institute on Aging should help fill this gap in the near future.

Finally, with the exception of disease diagnoses in the HHANES (Espino et al., 1991), all of the information available on stages of the disablement process in Hispanics are based on self-report. Disease prevalences thus may be underestimated (Ettinger et al., 1994; Haffner et al., 1984; Harris, 1985), and, to the extent that health care access, reporting, or both, differ, estimates of race/ethnic differences in chronic disease may be biased. Similar concerns can be raised for impairments, functional limitations, and disability. It is also not clear whether observed associations between disease and disability based on self-reports differ from those based on direct or performance-based measures of disease and disability.

Recommendations for Future Research

Several steps can be taken to improve our knowledge base as well as the quality of science related to chronic disease and physical disability in older Hispanics:

1. Utilize the standardized terms and definitions included in the disablement process model in all future research.
2. Design research to test the disablement process model systematically. Include variables within the main disease-disability pathway as well as variables outside that pathway that may prevent, slow, or reverse the disablement process. Measure disease, impairments, functional limitations, and disability not only by self-report, but by direct and performance-based measures as well.
3. Examine the disablement process in-depth for specific diseases, especially diabetes. Look for multiplicative effects on functional limitations and disability when diabetes occurs in the presence of other comorbid conditions, such as peripheral vascular disease, retinopathy, nephropathy, or neuropathy. Look for differential effects on discrete functional limitations, ADLs, and IADLs.
4. Design individual research projects so the information they provide is specific enough to guide the development of interventions to reduce disability.
5. Utilize complementary survey and clinical approaches to advance the field.
6. Expand research to target all Hispanic subgroups separately and to ensure that diversity within subgroups (based on migration status, urban-rural residency, socioeconomic status, assimilation, etc.) is adequately represented.

References

Angel, J. L., & Angel R. J. (1992). Age at migration, social connections, and well-being among elderly Hispanics. *Journal of Aging and Health, 4*(44), 480-499.

Bean, F. D., & Tienda, M. (1987). *The Hispanic population of the United States.* New York: Academic Press.

Boult, C., Kane, R. L., Louis, T. A., Boult, L., & McCaffrey, D. (1994). Chronic conditions that lead to functional limitation in the elderly. *Journal of Gerontology: Medical Science, 49*(1), M28-M36.

Davis, K. (1990). *National Survey of Hispanic Elderly People, 1988.* Ann Arbor, MI: Interuniversity Consortium for Political and Social Research.

Day, J. C. (1996). *Population projections of the United States by age, sex, race, and Hispanic origin: 1995 to 2050* (U.S. Bureau of the Census, Current Population Reports, P-25).Washington, DC: U.S. Department of Commerce, Bureau of the Census.

Escalante, A., Lichtenstein, M. J., White, K., Rios, N., & Hazuda, H. P. (1995). A method for scoring the pain map of the McGill Pain Questionnaire for use in epidemiological studies. *Aging Clinical Experimental Research, 7,* 358-366.

Espino, D. V., Burge, S. K., & Moreno, C. (1991). The prevalence of selected chronic diseases among the Mexican American elderly: Data from the 1982-1984 Hispanic Health and Nutrition Examination Survey. *Journal of the American Board of Family Practice, 4,* 217-222.

Ettinger, W. H., Fried, L. P., Harris, T., Shemanski, L., Schulz, R., & Robins, J. (1994). Self-reported causes of physical disability in older people: The Cardiovascular Heart Study. *Journal of the American Geriatric Society, 42,* 1035-1044.

Furner, S. E., Rudberg, M. A., & Cassel, C. K. (1995). Medical conditions differentially affect the development of IADL disability: Implications for medical care and research. *The Gerontologist, 35*(4), 444-450.

Garcia, J. M. (1993). The Hispanic population in the United States: March 1992. *U.S. Bureau of the Census, Current Population Reports, P20.* Washington, DC: U.S. Department of Commerce, Bureau of the Census.

Gordon, M. M. (1975). Toward a general theory of ethnic and racial group relations. In N. Glazer & D. P. Moynihan (Eds.), *Ethnicity: Theory and experience* (pp. 84-110). Cambridge, MA: Harvard University Press.

Grebler, L., Moore, J. W., Guzman, R. C., et al. (1970). *The Mexican-American people: The nation's second largest minority.* New York: Free Press.

Guccione, A. A., Felson, D. T., Anderson, J. J., Anthony, J. M., Zhang, Y., Wildon, P. W. F., Kelly-Hayes, M., Wolf, P. A., Kreger, B. E., & Kannel, W. B. (1994). The effects of specific medical conditions on the functional limitations of elders in the Framingham study. *American Journal of Public Health, 84*(3), 351-358.

Guralnik, J. M., LaCroix, A. Z., Abbott, R. D., Berkman, L. F., Satterfield, S., Evans, D. A., & Wallace, R. B. (1993). Maintaining mobility in late life. *American Journal of Epidemiology, 137*(8), 845-868.

Guralnik, J. M., LaCroix, A. Z., Everett, D. F., & Kovar, M. G. (1989). Aging in the eighties: The prevalence of comorbidity and its association with disability. *Advance Data From Vital and Health Statistics of the National Center for Health Statistics, Series 16.*

Haffner, S. M., Rosenthal, M., Hazuda, H. P., Stern, M. P., & Franco, L. J. (1984). Evaluation of three potential screening tests for diabetes mellitus in a biethnic population. *Diabetes Care, 7,* 347-353.

Harris, M. I. (1985). *Prevalence of non-insulin dependent diabetes and impaired glucose tolerance* (85-1468, VII-31). Washington, DC: U.S. Department of Health and Human Services.

Hazuda, H. P. (1995). Acculturation and socioeconomic status in healthy aging and disease. *American Journal of Human Biology, 7,* 136.

Hazuda, H. P., Haffner, S. M., & Stern M. P. (1988). Acculturation and assimilation among Mexican Americans: Scales and population-based data. *Social Science Quarterly, 69*(3), 687-705.

Jaffe, A. J., Cullen R., & Boswell, T. D. (1980). *The changing demography of Spanish Americans.* New York: Academic Press.

Johnson, R. J., & Wolinsky, F. D. (1993). The structure of health status among older adults: Disease, disability, functional limitation, and perceived health. *Journal of Health and Social Behavior, 34,* 105-121.

Keenan, N. L., Murray, E. T., & Truman, B. I. (1992). Hispanic Americans. In Centers for Disease Control and Prevention (Ed.), *Chronic disease in minority populations* (pp. 5.1-5.32). Atlanta: Centers for Disease Control.

Markides, K. S., Rudkin, L., Espino, D. V., & Angel, R. J. (in press). Health status of Hispanic elderly in the United States. In L. J. Martin, B. Soldo, & K. Foote (Eds.), *Ethnic differences in late life health.* Washington, DC: National Academy Press.

Markides, K. S., Stroup-Benham, C. A., Goodwin, J. S., Perkowski, L. C., Lichtenstein, M. J., & Ray, L. A. (1996). The effect of medical conditions on functional limitation in Mexican American elderly. *Annals of Epidemiology, 6,* 386-391.

Nagi, S. Z. (1965). Some conceptual issues on disability and rehabilitation. In M. B. Sussman (Ed.), *Sociology and rehabilitation* (pp. 100-113). Washington, DC: American Sociological Association.

Nagi, S. Z. (1979). The concept and measurement of disability. In E. D. Berkowitz (Ed.), *Disability policies and government programs* (pp. 1-15). New York: Praeger.

Nagi, S. Z. (1991). Disability concepts revisited: Implications for prevention. In A. M. Pope & A. R. Tarlov (Eds.), *Disability in America: Toward a national agenda for prevention* (pp. 309-327). Washington, DC: National Academy Press.

Pinsky, J. L., Branch, L. G., Jette, A. M., Haynes, S. G., Feinleib, M., Cornoni-Huntley, J. C., & Bailey, K. R. (1985). Framingham Disability Study: Relationship of disability to cardiovascular risk factors among persons free of diagnosed cardiovascular disease. *American Journal of Epidemiology, 122*(4), 644-656.

Pinsky, J. L., Jette, A. M., Branch, L. G., Kannel, W. B., & Feinleib, M. (1990). The Framingham Disability Study: Relationship of various coronary heart disease manifestations to disability in older persons living in the community. *American Journal of Public Health, 80*(11), 1363-1368.

Prohaska, T., Mermelstein, R., Miller, B., & Jack, S. (1993). Functional status and living arrangements. In J. F. Van Nostrand, S. E. Furner, & R. Suzman (Eds.), *Health data on older Americans: United States, 1992* (pp. 23-39). Hyattsville, MD: National Center for Health Statistics.

Reuben, D. B., Laliberte, L., Hiris, V., & Mor, V. (1990). A hierarchal exercise scale to measure function at the advanced activities of daily living (AADL) level. *Journal of the American Geriatrics Society, 38,* 855-861.

Stern, M. P., & Haffner, S. M. (1990). Type II diabetes and its complications in Mexican Americans. In *Diabetes/metabolism reviews* (pp. 29-45). New York: John Wiley.

Strawbridge, W. J., Cohen, R. D., Shema, S. J., & Kaplan, G. A. (1996). Successful aging: Predictors and associated activities. *American Journal of Epidemiology, 144,* 135-144.

Treviño, F. M., & Moss, A. J. (1984). Health indicators for Hispanic, Black and White Americans. In *Vital and Health Statistics* (DHHS Publication No. [PHS] 84-1576, Series 10). Hyattsville, MD: National Center for Health Statistics.

U.S. Bureau of the Census. (1986). *Disability, functional limitation, and health insurance coverage: 1984/85* (Current Population Reports, Series P-70). Washington, DC: U.S. Department of Commerce, Bureau of the Census.

U.S. Bureau of the Census. (1990). *The need for personal assistance with everyday activities: Recipients and caregivers* (Current Population Reports, Special Studies, P-23). Washington, DC: U.S. Department of Commerce, Bureau of the Census.

U.S. Bureau of the Census (1992). *Sixty-five plus in America* (Current Population Reports, Special Studies, P-23). Washington, DC: U.S. Department of Commerce, Bureau of the Census.

Vega, W. A., & Rumbaut, R. G. (1991). Ethnic minorities and mental health. In M. A. Winkleby, S. P. Fortmann, & B. Rockhill (Eds.), *Annual Review of Sociology.*

Verbrugge, L. M., & Jette, A. M. (1994). The disablement process. *Social Science and Medicine, 38*(1), 1-14.

Verbrugge, L. M., Lepkowski, J. M., & Imanaka, Y. (1989). Comorbidity and its impact on disability. *Milbank Memorial Quarterly, 67*(3-4), 450-484.

Vital and Health Statistics. (1985). *Plan and operation of the Hispanic Health and Nutritional Examination Survey.* Hyattsville, MD: National Center for Health Statistics.

Vital and Health Statistics. (1990). *Long term care for the functionally dependent elderly* (Data from the National Health Survey No. 104. DHHS Publication No. [PHS] 90-1765, Series 13). Hyattsville, MD: National Center for Health Statistics.

World Health Organization. (1985). *Diabetes mellitus. Report of a WHO study group* (Tech. Rep. Series No. 727). Geneva: World Health Organization.

Aging, Chronic Conditions, and Physical Disabilities in Asian and Pacific Islander Americans

Marjorie Kagawa-Singer
Nancy Hikoyeda
Sora Park Tanjasiri

General Demographics

Asian and Pacific Islander American (APIA) elderly constitute the fastest growing ethnic group 65 years and older in the United States today, but the diversity within the single federally designated APIA category is vast. Prior to the 1990 Census, the U.S. Census Bureau identified only 20 different APIA groups within the Asian category. The category of Asian Pacific Islanders, however, actually includes more than 60 different nationalities, a few of which are listed in Table 7.1.

Addressing the needs of APIA elderly as a homogenous population creates a misperception. Such a monolithic approach indicates that APIA elderly are healthier than others of the same age and masks the health needs of specific groups within this aggregate of highly diverse cultures (Chen & Hawks, 1995). Knowledge of the health status and disease incidence and prevalence of the majority of APIA groups is, however, presently largely unknown because of two major limitations: (a) low interest in APIA groups due to misperceptions of the lack of health problems within this population and (b) methodological difficulties in sampling, coupled with linguistic differences. Thus, few studies exist on older APIAs, and of those studies most focus on a

149

TABLE 7.1 Population Characteristics–Asian and Pacific Islander Classification

Asian	Pacific Islander
Chinese	Hawaiian
Filipino	Samoan
Japanese	Guamanian
Asian Indian	Other Pacific Islander[a]
Korean	Carolinian
Vietnamese	Fijian
Cambodian	Kosrean
Hmong	Melanesian[b]
Laotian	Micronesian[b]
Thai	Northern Mariana Islander
Other Asian[a]	Paulauan
Bangladeshi	Papua New Guinean
Bhutanese	Ponapean (Pohnpeian)
Borneo	Polynesian[b]
Burmese	Solomon Islander
Celebesian	Tahitian
Ceram	Tarawa Islander
Indochinese	Tokelauan
Indonesian	Tongan
Iwo-Jiman	Trukese (Chuukese)
Javanese	Yapese
Malayan	Pacific Islander, not specified
Maldivian	
Nepali	
Okinawan	
Pakistani	
Sikkim	
Singaporean	
Sri Lankan	
Sumatran	
Asian, not specified[c]	

SOURCE: U.S. Bureau of the Census (1990).

NOTE: a. In some data products, specific groups listed under "Other Asian" or "Other Pacific Islander" are shown separately. Groups not shown are tabulated as "All other Asian" or "All other Pacific Islander," respectively.

b. Polynesian, Micronesian, and Melanesian are Pacific Islander cultural groups.

c. Includes entries such as Asian American, Asian, Asiatic, Amerasian, and Eurasian.

few of the larger, more acculturated or more prominent populations, disregarding smaller subgroups (e.g., Southeast Asian [SEA] refugees, Asian Indians, Guamanians, Pacific Islanders). These APIA elderly studies tend to be descriptive or limited to specific diseases; data tend to be aggregated and/or not available by age, or age groupings are inconsistent; samples tend to be small and regional/local; and, therefore, studies are difficult to compare.

The bimodal distribution of health status indicators in this population indicates potential health-promoting assets and health risk factors in beliefs, behaviors, and resources. It is only when the data are disaggregated by specific subgroups that populations at high risk for disease become identifiable. For example, data collected on Korean and Vietnamese elderly highlight a higher proportion of uninsured and self-reports of health status as poorer than any other ethnic group (Tanjasiri, Wallace, & Shibata, 1995).

Each APIA ethnic group possesses a distinct language, culture, and social structure within the community. Consequently, the health care behaviors of APIA elderly differ substantially, largely due to variations in immigration histories, acculturation levels and language abilities, cohort experiences, and socioeconomic status. This chapter provides a broad and brief review of the existing literature on the health status of APIA elderly and makes recommendations for future efforts in research and practice. Because so little research has been conducted on this population, much of the information presented here makes inferences from the studies conducted to their implications on the elderly. Readers are further encouraged to use the major resources referred to in this chapter published by the Stanford Geriatric Education Center, the National Asian Pacific Center on Aging, and the University of California at Los Angeles/RAND Medical Treatment Effectiveness Program (UCLA/RAND/MEDTEP).

Population Size and Growth

Awareness of cultural differences among APIA populations has risen in the past 25 years due primarily to their increasing size and growth. In 1990, there were 7,273,662 APIAs of all ages, constituting 2.9% of the total U.S. population (U.S. Bureau of the Census, 1993a). Growth of the APIA population of all ages from 1980 to 1990 measured 107.8%. During this same time period, APIAs 65 years of age and older numbered 454,458, an increase of 114.6%. By 2020, the total population of APIAs is estimated to be 20.2 million, of which 2.1 million (10%) will be elderly (Asian Pacific Health Care Venture, 1993).

Currently, the Japanese American population has the highest proportion of elderly, primarily because their recent immigration rates from Japan have

TABLE 7.2 Size and Percentage of API Elderly 65 Years and Older, by Ethnic
Group, in the United States, 1990

	Total Population	65+ Years Old	Percentage of Group 65+ Years Old	Group-Specific 65+ as Percentage of All API 65+ Years Old
United States	248,709,873	31,241,831	12.5	NA[a]
All APIs	7,273,662	454,458	6.2	100.0
Chinese	1,645,472	133,977	8.1	29.5
Japanese	847,562	105,932	12.5	23.3
Filipino	1,406,770	104,206	7.4	22.9
Korean	794,849	35,247	4.4	7.8
Asian Indian	815,447	23,004	2.8	5.1
Vietnamese	614,547	18,084	2.9	4.0
Cambodian	147,411	3,724	2.5	0.8
Laotian	149,014	3,697	2.5	0.8
Hmong	90,082	2,535	2.8	0.5
Thai	91,275	1,416	1.6	0.3
Other Asian	302,209	7,901	2.6	1.7
Hawaiian	211,014	10,233	4.8	2.3
Samoan	62,964	2,047	3.3	0.5
Guamanian	49,345	1,523	3.1	0.3
Other Pacific Islander	41,701	932	2.2	0.2

SOURCE: U.S. Bureau of the Census (1990); Tanjasiri, Wallace, & Shibata (1995).
NOTE: a. Not applicable.

been low and they have had longer residency in the United States compared
to the other APIA groups. Although the Chinese American and Filipino
American communities are also of multiple generations in the United States
and each of these populations is larger than the Japanese American population, the proportions of elderly are smaller because of the larger numbers of
recent and younger immigrants (Table 7.2).

Immigration and Acculturation Status

The APIA elderly consist of two cohorts of immigrants (Tanjasiri et al.,
1995). Immigrants who arrived in the late 19th and early 20th centuries make

up the first cohort of APIA elders. Although documented immigration from the Pacific Rim dates as far back as the mid-1800s, APIA immigration was negligible during two-thirds of the 20th century because of numerous discriminatory immigration laws, such as the 1882 Chinese Exclusion Act, the 1924 Immigration Exclusion Act, and the 1934 Tydings-McDuffie Act (Morioka-Douglas & Yeo, 1990; U.S. Immigration & Naturalization Service, 1981). The second cohort consists of elderly APIAs who immigrated to this country since passage of the 1965 Immigration Act, which allowed entry of relatives of U.S. citizens and permanent residents. For instance, in 1990, the four leading Asian countries of documented elderly immigrants (the Philippines, mainland China, Korea, and Vietnam) constituted more than 30% (14,481 of 42,810) of elderly immigrants from all countries who came to the United States (U.S. Immigration & Naturalization Service, 1991).

Acculturation and Language

The proportion of APIA populations of all ages who are foreign-born (63.1%) remains the highest of all major racial and ethnic groups. By APIA ethnic group, Southeast Asians (SEAs) possess the largest proportions of foreign-born elderly, undoubtedly reflecting the large waves of recently arriving refugees. The populations with high proportions of foreign-born are Cambodian (98.4%), Laotian (98.2%), Vietnamese (98.0%), Thai (95.5%), Hmong (95.3%), Asian Indian (94.9%), Filipino (94.4%), and Korean (91.5%). In contrast, only 32.4% of Japanese 65 years of age and older are foreign-born (U.S. Bureau of the Census, 1992b).

Compounding the difficulties that occur with immigration status is the issue of language fluency. Many APIA elders live in households in which no adult speaks English (i.e., "linguistically isolated"), thus they have limited ability to interact with most public service agency staffs. According to the 1990 Census, 30.6% of all APIA 65 years of age and older are linguistically isolated, second only to elderly of Hispanic origin (33.8%) (U.S. Bureau of the Census, 1993a). Again, the percentage of linguistically isolated elderly varies considerably by APIA ethnic group: 55.8% Hmong, 54.9% Cambodian, 54.5% Korean, 53.3% Laotian, 50.0% Vietnamese, 46.5% Chinese, 40.8% Thai, 18.5% Japanese, 17.0% Filipino, and 14.2% Samoan (U.S. Bureau of the Census, 1993b).

Income, Education, and Gender

APIA populations, including elders over the age of 65, display a unique "bimodal" distribution in socioeconomic characteristics that points to a disproportionate representation at both tails of the distribution curves for income and educational attainment (Asian American Health Forum, 1990; Lin-Fu, 1993; Tanjasiri et al., 1995). In terms of income level, at one end of the spectrum 32% of married APIA elders have annual incomes of $50,000 and more, compared to 20% of married householders of all ethnicities age 65 to 74 in the United States. Similarly, a higher proportion of APIA elderly living alone have annual incomes of $35,000 and higher (U.S. Bureau of the Census, 1993a). At the lower end of the spectrum, 10.1% of APIA families with a person 65 years of age and older fell below the federal poverty level (FPL) ($14,335 for a family of four) compared to 5.4% of Whites, and furthermore, 12.0% of APIA elderly themselves had annual incomes below the FPL compared to 10.8% of Whites (U.S. Bureau of the Census, 1993b). The makeup of the APIA elderly 65 years of age and older with incomes below the FPL varies considerably by ethnic subgroup, with the highest rates among Southeast Asians (47% Hmong, 29% Cambodian, and 28% Laotians) while the lowest poverty rates are 8% for Filipino and 5% for Japanese.

Similar paradoxes exist for educational attainment. Overall, elderly APIA have a higher proportion of college graduates (13%) compared to the general U.S. population (11%) (Young & Gu, 1995). By ethnic group, Asian Indians (21%), Filipinos (16%), and Chinese (15%) have the highest educational attainment of all APIA elders. However, at the lower end of the education spectrum, 12.7% of APIA elders possess no education compared to only 1.4% and 5.7% of the nation's White and Black older populations, respectively (U.S. Bureau of the Census, 1992a). SEA elderly typically have less than a ninth grade education (92% for Hmong, 80% for Laotians, and 56% for Vietnamese) and most (59%) Pacific Islander American elders do not have a high school degree.

Finally, important gender differences exist for APIA elders in the aggregate and within specific APIA subgroups. With regard to educational attainment, the disparities by gender are wide: 16.3% of APIA females have no education, compared to 8.4% of males (Tanjasiri et al., 1995). By specific group, large male/female differentials can be seen among Vietnamese women, with a median of 5.9 years of education compared to 9.6 years for men, and Korean women, with a median of 6.9 years of education compared to 12.1 for men (McBride, Morioka-Douglas, & Yeo, 1996). Whereas the median annual income for APIA male heads of household 65 years of age and older was $9,295 in 1990, APIA females in the same age group with no spouse had a median annual income of only $7,731. The highest percentages of such APIA elderly females were among the Hmong (62%) and Cambodian (45%) women (Young & Gu, 1995). These differences in education, income, and gender hold important implications for understanding the health behaviors and outcomes of APIA elderly, especially for the women.

Health Promotion and Disease Prevention Behaviors

Exercise

Physical activity is an important factor in the prevention or modification of many chronic conditions such as heart disease, which is a leading cause of death in some APIA communities (Tamir & Cachola, 1994). Few studies, however, have examined levels of exercise among APIA elders. Moreover, inconsistent definitions and measures for exercise and physical activity make existing studies difficult to compare.

One study on exercise in the Korean population reported that only 17% of Koreans exercise, with 23% of men and 11.5% of women reporting regular exercise, compared to regular exercise rates of 69% among Anglo-American males and 57.5% among females (Han, 1990). Choi et al. (1990) found that among elderly Chinese in Boston, the proportion of males who exercised regularly increased with age (34% for ages 60-69 and 44% for 80+), while the proportion decreased among females of the same age (from 29% to 21%). The Hawaii State Department of Public Health (1988) looked at activity levels among Filipinos, Japanese, Hawaiians, and part-Hawaiians. Relative to the younger age groups, older adults were less likely to lead sedentary lifestyles if they were older than 65 (46.4%), retired (40.8%), or not living with their spouses (41.5%).

Physical activity and active lifestyles may be protective against thromboembolic and hemorrhagic strokes in older middle-aged men. Despite the variances found in existing studies, APIA older men and women appear to exercise less than their Anglo-American counterparts (Abbott, Rodriguez, Burchfiel, & Curb, 1994). Thus, further studies, clarification of definitions in physical activity and exercise, community education, and intervention programs would appear to be needed for more accurate assessment and improvement of levels of physical activity among the older APIA groups at risk.

Diet

Although the role of healthy diets in the prevention and management of chronic diseases is well established, little is known about the nutritional intake of APIA elders. Traditional APIA diets are felt to be "healthier" than the traditional White American diet because they are high in complex carbohydrates and grain proteins and low in animal fats and proteins. Sodium content, however, can be high, especially in many traditional Asian sauces and pickled foods. One example of a traditional diet intervention was the Waianae Diet Program ($N = 20$) conducted at the Waianae Clinic in Hawaii for obese Native Hawaiians 25 to 64 years of age (Shintani, Hughes, Beckman, & O'Conner, 1991). After 21 days on a traditional Native Hawaiian diet that consisted of a caloric distribution of 7% fat, 78% complex carbohydrates, and 15% protein, the average weight loss was 17.2 pounds. More important, follow-up revealed that all chronic disease indicators decreased significantly (Crews, 1994). The findings of this study demonstrate that adherence to a traditional APIA diet might have positive effects on the incidence and mortality from certain chronic diseases in the elderly.

It is difficult to analyze APIA diets for their nutritional content because the nutritional data on specific Asian foods are not readily available (G. Harrison, personal communication, September 1995). In addition, the style of cooking, serving, and eating may be very different from Western diets. Many APIA dishes are a combination of food sources (e.g., mixture of vegetables, meat or fish, and noodles) rather than discrete entities. Foods may be eaten "family style," from serving bowls placed in the center of the table, and individuals often select foods from the mixture according to their personal and gender preferences. An example of the latter is the habit of women who serve their families with the more desirable portions of a mixed meal and then eat the remaining elements. Such practices make calculating individual portions and nutritional analyses difficult.

Nonetheless, existing studies highlight potential areas of nutritional deficiencies for APIA elders. Kim, Yu, Liu, Kim, and Kohrs (1993) studied 169 Chinese American, 90 Korean American, and 50 Japanese American elders in a Chicago senior housing facility, using food composition tables from Taiwan, Japan, and Korea for their analyses. The authors found many respondents at risk for poor nutritional status, with an overall tendency of respondents to be underweight rather than overweight. Korean elders had the poorest diets and Japanese elders had the best. Nearly 70% of Korean and 49% of Chinèse females and 50% of Korean males were consuming less than 67% of the Recommended Daily Allowance of calcium. Older Koreans consumed inadequate amounts of protein and vitamins A and C. However, Chinese and Korean males consumed more basic nutrients than females of the same age.

In a current national study of transmenopause among women of several ethnicities (ages 42-52), a food frequency questionnaire and a nutritional analysis program have been developed for Japanese American and Chinese American women. Results of the nutritional analyses, however, will not be available until late in 1996 (G. Harrison & G. A. Greendale, personal communication, 1996). An understanding of the food habits, preferences, and beliefs of the various older APIA subgroups is needed for accurate assessment of their nutritional status and its impact on health.

Smoking

Smoking is a major cause of coronary heart disease (CHD) in the United States and has been implicated as a risk factor for bladder, pancreas, liver, and lung cancer. APIA smoking rates vary by a number of sociocultural characteristics such as age, gender, nativity, education, and level of acculturation. Smoking rates tend to be higher among younger age groups, males, and recent immigrants, particularly from countries in which smoking is socially acceptable. Rates tend to decline with higher acculturation (Tamir & Cachola, 1994).

Only one study could be found that looked specifically at smoking rates in older APIAs. Choi et al. (1990) studied 346 Chinese adults over age 60 in Boston and found a smoking prevalence of 39% among elderly Chinese American males compared to 20% among elderly White males. Overall, the U.S. adult smoking prevalence is 30%; Japanese have a rate of 37%; Chinese, 28%; and Filipino, 20%. High smoking rates among SEA men also exist. Laotians have a smoking rate of 92%; Kampucheans, 70.7%; and Chinese-Vietnamese, 54.5%. Not surprisingly, data indicate an 18% higher rate of lung cancer among SEA men than for the White population. Tamir and Cachola (1994) report that surveys of SEA men revealed a striking lack of knowledge and awareness of the relationship between smoking and associated diseases. Unless immediate and effective antismoking programs are instituted and supported, researchers agree that the rate of lung cancer in many elderly APIA ethnic populations will increase to a distressing magnitude, especially in the Chinese and SEA populations (Han, Kim, Lee, et al., 1989; Jenkins, McPhee, Ha, Nam, & Chen, 1995; Levin, 1985; McPhee et al., 1995; Rumbaut, 1989; Sasao, 1992).

Alcohol

Despite the growing numbers and diversity of the APIA populations, empirical data that document alcohol and other drug (AOD) use/abuse problems are lacking (Sasao, 1992). This lack of data is exacerbated in studies that highlight the status of APIA elders. Existing studies document significant use of alcohol by APIA males, but again rates vary by group and level of acculturation. Recent immigrants from Japan have a much higher proportion of heavy drinkers than Whites (Kitano, Hatanaka, Yeung, & Sue, 1985). In contrast, later-generation Chinese were likely to consume more alcohol than immigrant Chinese (Sue, Zane, & Ito, 1979). Similarly, alcohol consumption among Japanese Americans has been positively correlated with being male, unmarried, and third or fourth generation (Nakawatase, Yamamoto, & Sasao, 1993). Finally, Lubben, Chi, and Kitano (1989) explored drinking behavior in a sample of 280 Koreans in Los Angeles. In their sample, 12.5% were over age 60 and only 20% reported drinking any alcohol.

A number of studies have reported "facial flushing" among some Asians when alcohol is consumed. This may be accompanied by headache, nausea, tachycardia, dyspnea, and anxiety attributed to a deficiency in acetaldehyde dehydrogenase Type I (ALDH-1) (Nakawatase et al., 1993). In a study of drinking levels among 200 community-dwelling Japanese Americans in Los Angeles, those who experienced facial flushing were more likely to drink less. More than half of this sample were second or third generation and over age 40 (Nakawatase et al., 1993). This physiologic effect may account for some of the lower alcohol use in APIAs.

Sociocultural factors have also played a role in alcohol abuse, however. Chin, Lai, and Rouse (1991) examined alcoholism among 132 male clients in a New York City Chinatown alcoholism services agency. More than 53% of their clients were over age 50. About 75% of these men were born in China, had lived in the United States at least a decade, and worked in Chinese restaurants. Half of the men had less than a high school education and most were monolingual Chinese and estranged from their families. The high-pressure

TABLE 7.3 Differences in Health Risks for APIA Elders Compared to All U.S. Elders (+ = increased risk; − = decreased risk)

Condition	Chinese American	Japanese American	Filipino American	Korean American	Asian Indian American	S.E. Asian American	Pacific Islander American
HEART & CV							
Hypertension	−	−	+				+
Coronary heart disease		− ma.					
DIABETES	+ fe.	+	+	+			+
CANCER							
Breast	− fe.	− fe.					
Ovarian	− fe.	− fe.					
Prostate	− ma.	− ma.					
Esophageal	+	+					
Nasopharyngeal	+ ma.						
Colon	− fe.						
Liver/cirrhosis	+	+		+ ma.			
Stomach		+					
Pancreas	+ fe.						
HIP FRACTURE		−					
OSTEOPOROSIS		+					
INFECTIOUS DISEASES	+ HBV + TB		+ TB	+ HBV		+ HBV + TB	

SOURCE: This table was adapted with permission from the Stanford Geriatric Education Center.
NOTES: fe. = established only for females; ma. = established only for males; HBV = hepatitis B.

working environments, along with long hours, low pay, and free drinks, were believed to be causal factors for the alcohol abuse.

Disease Prevalence

Two notable infectious diseases in segments of the APIA population are discussed first, followed by the patterns of prevalence of the major chronic diseases. Overall, APIA populations suffer from the same three major causes of death as Whites: heart disease, cancer, and cardiovascular disease. Aggregated rates are generally lower in the APIA population; however, when rates are disaggregated, intragroup variation is considerable (see Table 7.3).

Infectious Diseases

Tuberculosis and Hepatitis B

Kitano (1994) found tuberculosis (TB) rates among Asian elderly were 12 times higher than among Whites. SEAs have 25 to 40 times the rate of TB, and this is highest among those over 45 (University of California Los Angeles/Veterans Affairs/RAND/Medical Treatment Effectiveness Program Outcomes Research Centers for API [UCLA/VA/RAND/MEDTEP], 1996). Moreover, increasing rates of multiple-drug-resistant strains of TB have been diagnosed in Chinese and SEA new immigrant populations, increasing the likelihood of death from poor adherence to the treatment regimen and ineffective drug regimens.

Hepatitis B is endemic throughout Southeast Asia and the Far East, where approximately 75% of the population are infected or are chronic carriers. The overall carrier rate in the United States is estimated to be about 0.2% of the U.S. population, but rates of 14% to 20% are found in the Chinese and SEA populations (Hann, 1994; Klontz, 1986). The Hepatitis B antigen carrier state (HBsAG) can lead to the development of hepatocellular carcinoma (HCC) in older individuals. The risk factors for HCC among HBsAG carriers are cirrhosis, male gender, age 40 years and older, Asian background, serum ferritin levels ≥ 300 mg/ml, chronic hepatitis, IgM anti-HBc titers, and alcoholism (Hann, 1994). Many American medical practitioners are often unaware of this health risk in APIA immigrants, especially among SEA refugees and Chinese immigrants.

Chronic Diseases

Thalassemias

Anemia is a common debilitating disorder in the elderly. For APIAs, however, practitioners should be aware of underlying genetic variants in hemoglobin synthesis that may be involved in the anemia: alpha and beta thalassemia and hemoglobin E carrier states (Powers, 1989; see also Table 7.4). These disorders are not responsive to the usual dietary modifications or vitamin supplements to correct anemia. Some vitamins, like C, may actually be contraindicated. It should also be noted that tea, commonly consumed in most traditional Asian diets, is known to interfere with the absorption of inorganic

TABLE 7.4 Prevalence of Thalassemia Trait

In Asia	Alpha %	Beta %
China	4-15	1-1.5
Taiwan	1.4	—
Thailand	20-30	5-10
Laos	44	—
Cambodia	—	—
U.S. Studies	*Alpha %*	*Beta %*
Chinese	4.9-9	3.5-4.8
Samoan	1.9	—
Filipino	6.4	0.7
Laotian	7.5-14	—
Mien	12	6.1
Vietnamese	8	8
Cambodian	12	3
Laotian	14	3

SOURCE: Table modified from Chen, Ng, Sam, Ng, Abe, Ott, Lim, Chan, & Winston (1993).

but not haem iron (the latter is mainly from meat). Elderly Asians whose diet consists mainly of vegetables and who drink tea with every meal, may be iron deficient as well (Modell & Berdoukas, 1984). Families and clinicians should be made aware of the high prevalence of thalassemia in South and Southeast Asian patients.

Heart and Cardiovascular Disease

Heart disease is the leading cause of death among APIAs in California, where Japanese have the highest death rate and Filipinos have the highest actual numbers of deaths (Tamir & Cachola, 1994). Except for studies of Japanese Americans in Hawaii, Seattle, and San Francisco, little effort has been made to study risk factors for heart disease in older APIAs. The results that do exist are conflicting. Surveys have been done among U.S. Filipino, Chinese, Japanese, Hawaiian, Indochinese, Vietnamese, and other Asian sub-populations; however, the samples have usually consisted of younger age groups and have been very small (Tamir & Cachola, 1994).

Tamir and Cachola (1994) noted that a positive correlation has been found between age and blood pressure levels across all APIA subgroups. The American Heart Association (1991) reports that overall blood pressure levels among Japanese Americans were lower than for Whites, but rates varied when socioeconomic and demographic characteristics were considered. In California, Japanese American men, aged 18 to 49, had a higher prevalence rate of hypertension (19%) than White males (15%); but in the 50+ age group, the rate for Japanese Americans (29%) was lower than for Whites (39%). When compared to White women, Japanese American women had a lower prevalence in both age groups.

Studies generally indicate high rates of hypertension among specific older APIA groups. Among Chinese immigrants in Boston, aged 60 to 96, Choi et al. (1990) found a 30% prevalence rate for hypertension among males and 34% among females, which was similar to rates in mainland China and lower than U.S. White rates. Lui and Yu (1985) reported that with increasing Westernization and acculturation, Chinese Americans show an increased risk of coronary artery disease.

The 1979 California Hypertension Survey found that Filipino men and women age 50+ had the highest prevalence rates, 60% and 65%, respectively, while Japanese American males (32%) and women (18%) had the lowest rates of all the ethnic groups (Stavig, Igra & Leonard, 1988). Curb et al. (1991) surveyed 257 Native Hawaiians in Hawaii. They found that 36% of those aged 40 to 59 ($n = 125$) had hypertension. Furthermore, the respondents exhibited low levels of awareness, education, control, or combinations of these, regarding cardiovascular risk factors. The respondents were also suspicious of the researchers based on adverse past experiences.

The health status of older Japanese Americans has been meticulously followed in a large longitudinal prospective study, the Honolulu Heart Program (HHP), that began in the 1960s and continues to the present. It has provided valuable epidemiological data on more than 8,000 men of Japanese ancestry born between 1900 and 1919 on the island of Oahu in Hawaii, who were age 45 to 68 at the inception of the study (Yano, Reed, & Kagan, 1985). In general, the Japanese American men in Hawaii are long-lived and appear to have a low incidence of CHD when compared to White males. Overall, CHD prevalence in the HHP was twice that of White males who participated in the Framingham study. The Japanese American men were at higher risk for CHD and lower risk for stroke when compared to males in Japan. Reed, McGee, and Katsuhiko (1982) reported an overall prevalence of hypertension

Asian and Pacific Islander Americans 163

of 17% from 1965 to 1968 among men in the program aged 45 to 49, and 23% in 1974 for those 50 and older. Curb, Reed, Miller, and Yano (1990) studied the health status and lifestyles in a sample of 1,379 men ages 60 to 81 from the HHP, who participated in three subsequent examinations between 1970 and 1982. Their data revealed an unexplainable trend of increasing prevalence at the oldest age groups for hypertension, heart attack, and stroke. The authors speculated that these higher rates may have been due to the influence of past life experiences on health, such as racial discrimination.

Few studies have examined serum cholesterol levels among older APIA subgroups. Reed et al. (1982) reported a 23.6% hypercholesterolemia rate from 1965 to 1968 for males and females aged 45 to 69 in Hawaii, and Curb et al. (1991) reported a rate of 40% for Native Hawaiian males and females aged 50 to 59. Hawaiian, Filipino, and SEA Americans exhibit a particular lack of knowledge and awareness about the role of cholesterol in CHD that needs to be addressed (Tamir & Cachola, 1994).

Diabetes

Diabetes causes major damage to the heart and cardiovascular system, retinas, kidneys, and lower extremities. Two important correlates to the development of diabetes are obesity and age (Crews, 1994). Detailed studies have been undertaken among Japanese Americans, who have been found to have twice the rate of Type II, or non-insulin dependent diabetes mellitus (NIDDM), as the White population and 4 times the rate of Japanese in Japan (Fujimoto et al., 1987). In the most comprehensive study of diabetes in an APIA population, Fujimoto et al. (1987) examined 229 second-generation (Nisei) men age 45 and older in King County, Washington. They estimated that 56% of Nisei men in the population had an abnormal glucose tolerance level and 20% had NIDDM. By comparison, the National Health and Nutrition Examination Survey showed diagnosed NIDDM prevalence rates for White males of 3.5% to 8.5% and 3.2% to 9% for undiagnosed NIDDM. Complications such as hypertension, CHD, retinopathy, neuropathy, and peripheral vascular disease were also reported to be higher among the Japanese Americans with diagnosed NIDDM. It was found that the Nisei men with diabetes consumed more fat and animal protein than those with no diabetes (Tsunehara, Leonetti, & Fujimoto, 1990). In the Los Angeles area, Japanese Americans in the same age group also had a 20% to 22% rate for diabetes (Lipson & Kato-Palmer, 1988).

Empirical data for diabetes among other APIA subpopulations is very limited, and studies vary considerably by age group and region (Crews, 1994); however, significant studies have been conducted on APIAs in Hawaii. Curb et al. (1991) reported a prevalence rate of 23% among Native Hawaiians aged 50 to 59. The Samoan rate of diabetes is 3 times the rate of the White population (Crews, 1994). Crews (1994) and Sloan (1963) also reported an age-adjusted prevalence rate of obesity of 48.8% for native Hawaiians compared to 7.3% for Whites. Obesity and "modern" U.S. diets may well be significant risk factors among these high-risk APIA elders. Further studies are needed to delineate the extent and outcomes of diabetes in older APIA populations as well as to ascertain the relationship of NIDDM to sociocultural factors, diet, exercise, environment, and access to health care.

Menopause

Menopause is technically the normal physiologic state in a woman when her ovaries cease to function, estrogen and progesterone production is markedly reduced, and fertility ends. Recent research indicates that the 4 to 8 or more years in which this transition occurs is a physiologically dynamic period with significant health consequences (Greendale & Judd, 1993). Conditions associated with menopause include hot flashes, lower genito-urinary tract atrophy, possible disruption in sexual functioning, possible mild psychological dysfunction, and disordered sleep. Longer-term health risks include increased likelihood of fracture and higher cardiovascular disease risk (Barrett-Connor, 1992). These reports, however, have been largely based upon studies of White women.

Studies in Asia indicate that the sequelae of menopause appear to be quite different from the United States. Rates of fracture are lower and symptom reporting is significantly lower and different than in American reports. For example, about 80% of White women report hot flashes, but in Japan, the rate was roughly 10% (Lock, Kaufert, & Gilbert, 1988). Alterations in mood, menstruation, and overall symptom reporting and sexual function appear significantly reduced (Lock, 1993). No research presently exists on the physiologic or psychosocial effects of the perimenopause or postmenopause on APIA women. One national study is currently ongoing to study the effects of perimenopause on Japanese American (G. Greendale & M. Kagawa-Singer, personal communication, 1994) and Chinese American women (E. Gold, B. Sternfeld, & S. Adler, personal communication, 1994).

Osteoporosis

Osteoporosis is the physiologic process of decrease in bone mineral content and normally occurs with aging. This condition occurs in men and women due to decreased physical activity, increased bone resorption, decreased muscle tensile strength affecting bone density, and the catabolic effects on metabolism of aging itself. The effects of osteoporosis are most pronounced in women, due to the lack of protective hormone effects during and following menopause. Osteoporosis is predicted to be a new burden to public health in Asia and in unacculturated elderly APIAs. Currently, the incidence of osteoporosis-related fractures is less than in most Western countries. However, by 2050, 50% of the 6.3 million hip fractures that occur worldwide will be in Asians as a result of the increasing aging population, a decrease in physical activity, and Westernization of lifestyles (Kao & P'eng, 1995).

There is a dramatic increase in the incidence of hip fracture with age. For example, hip fracture incidence is 350 times greater in women aged 85 years and over compared to women between 35 and 44 years of age. The mortality rate in the 12 months following hip fracture is 20% to 25% (Magaziner, Simonsick, Kashner, Hebel, & Kenzora, 1989). In one study of frail elderly Chinese, the mortality rate was 24% (Eng, 1994).

Silverman and Madison (1988) examined hip fractures reported in the California Hospital Discharge Data. Their analysis revealed that the incidence of hip fracture among APIAs was one-half to three-fourths that of Whites, but this was higher than for Hispanics and Blacks. Elderly APIAs have been found to have bone mass values similar to Whites, but only half the incidence of fractures (Cummings & Cauley, 1994; Hagiwara & Miki, 1989; Russell-Aulet & Wang, 1991). Further studies are necessary to determine incidence and prevalence of hip fractures in elderly APIAs and protective factors that could be supported to maintain the independence of this large and increasing APIA population (Cummings et al., 1994; Tobias, Cook, Chambers, & Dalzell, 1994).

Cancer

The relatively greater number of studies on cancer among APIA populations allows us to discuss this disease as a prototype of a chronic disease in the elderly for which ethnicity, gender, and cultural lifestyles have clearly been demonstrated to affect the disease incidence, trajectory, and prognosis. Overall, liver cancer is 12 times more prevalent in Asians, and both stomach cancer (Japanese) and nasopharyngeal cancer (Chinese) are 7 times more prevalent in the Asian population than in the general American population (Henderson, 1990; Muir, Waterhouse, Mack, Powell, & Whelan, 1987). By the second generation after immigration, however, the rates of all three sites of cancer begin to match the levels of the host country. Breast cancer incidence rates also mirror those of White American women in the Japanese American and Chinese American population after one generation, from levels one-fourth to one-seventh of those rates in their native countries (Ziegler et al., 1993).

For Chinese elders in North America, prostate, colon, and breast cancer appear to increase with acculturation, but rates are lower than White rates (Whittemore, 1989; Ziegler et al., 1993). Comparing age-adjusted rates in the United States and China, Whittemore (1989) found comparable colon cancer rates between Chinese American and White males, but rates were 3 times higher among Chinese males in Shanghai. Colon cancer rates for Chinese American women were four-fifths the U.S. White rates and twice as high as Shanghai. Nearly one-third of the mortality among Chinese Americans over 65 was due to malignant neoplasms.

Native Hawaiians have the highest rates of cancer of all organ sites of almost all other ethnic groups, except for Japanese Americans in Hawaii, who have higher stomach cancer rates than Whites or Native Hawaiians. Japanese Americans on the mainland have a higher incidence of stomach and esophageal cancer (American Cancer Society, 1997), but lower rates of breast, ovarian, and prostate cancer compared to Whites (Office of Minority Health, 1988).

The problems of aggregated APIA data are clearly evident in cancer studies. For example, by disaggregating the data, breast cancer rates are variant in the APIA population. According to the American Cancer Society (ACS), California Division (1991), the rates of breast cancer are considerably lower for Asians than Whites (55/100,000 compared to 115/100,000, respectively). When within-group differences are identified, however, the rates among Native Hawaiians is 111/100,000 and the Japanese 58/100,000 (American Cancer Society, 1990). The level of risk is significantly different between the two groups, and Native Hawaiians would clearly be a high-risk target population. Interpretation of rates is dependent upon who is included in aggregated data and whether or not disaggregated data are available.

The stage of disease at diagnosis also varies considerably among the APIA women. Seventy-five percent of Japanese American women were diagnosed with localized disease, compared to 62% of Filipino women (ACS, California Division, 1991). Native Hawaiian women are also diagnosed later in the disease course, when the cancer is more widespread (Kagawa-Singer & Chung, 1994).

Chinese, as an aggregate group, usually have health statistics showing better status than the White population. Lovejoy, Jenkins, Wu, Shankland, and Wilson (1989) studied 109 non- and limited English-speaking Chinese American women ages 35 and older to provide mammography and clinical breast examinations. They reported that 89% of these women had never had a mammogram, 47% had no doctor, and 21% had never had a breast exam. These results indicate that low socioeconomic status and low acculturation produce significant barriers and clearly identified this population as at need for high-risk intervention programs.

It should be noted, however, that when 5-year survival rates are compared among APIA women who present with advanced disease and White women, the variation is not as stark (American Cancer Society, 1991). The White population has a survival rate of about 75%, Japanese a little more than 80%, and most notably, Native Hawaiians have an almost 70% survival rate despite their late stage at presentation. Perhaps cultural *protective* factors are also involved. No studies have been done to date in cancer care using the perspective of studying cultural *assets* in health beliefs and practices among ethnic minorities.

Screening Barriers

Barriers to utilization of cancer (and other health) care for APIA elderly fall into two categories: structural and conceptual (Jenkins & Kagawa-Singer, 1994). Structural barriers include more widely acknowledged factors, such as availability, accessibility, acceptability, risks/benefits, cost and insurance coverage, as well as lack of knowledge and information about the disease and services. For APIA elders, specific structural barriers include a lack of: availability of competent services with bilingual and bicultural staff (e.g., breast self-examination instructors and patient information); outreach programs or sites in older APIA communities; accessible and/or affordable transportation; insurance coverage or little or no reimbursement for Pap tests and breast exams. Other barriers include illiteracy due to low educational attainment (e.g., among SEA refugees); daunting administrative procedures and paperwork; discrimination and exclusion in service delivery; and lack of a regular health care provider (Lui & Yu, 1985).

Conceptual (Lonner & Berry, 1986) barriers are acknowledged less often, but these factors create equally formidable barriers to adequate health care for APIA elders. Examples of conceptual barriers are demographic and sociocultural factors; past experiences with the health care system; screening knowledge; and attitudes toward diseases such as cancer (McCoy, Nielsen, Chitwood, et al., 1991).

Conceptual barriers also include cultural differences such as (a) concepts of health (e.g., role integrity vs. physiologic integrity (Kagawa-Singer, 1996); (b) beliefs about the causes of illness (e.g., retribution for transgression of sins); (c) variations in body concepts (e.g., meanings of different body parts, modesty, function); and (d) different meanings of the disability or lifestyle changes necessitated by the disease. For example, in breast cancer, APIA women have the lowest rate in selecting breast conserving therapy for early stage disease for all ethnicities, and instead, choose modified mastectomies (ACS, California Division, 1995). The selection of therapy seems based upon a concept of the breasts as less essential to their sense of femininity and integrity than for Anglo-American women (Kagawa-Singer, Wellisch, & Durvasula, in press).

Other examples of cultural barriers to cancer screening for older APIA women include: (a) a reluctance to touch their own bodies or have them seen or touched by strangers; (b) lack of awareness of cancer detection and prevention services because they are not advertised in their language; (c) avoidance of medical care unless the elder "feels" ill; (d) distrust for the health care system; (e) a need for endorsement of early detection and screening programs by recognized leaders in the APIA community; and (f) lack of insurance because of a belief that it would invite trouble.

Psychosocial Response to Cancer

Relatively little research has been conducted on the emotional and social responses of APIA elders to health problems. Cancer again will be used as a prototype to demonstrate the difference between disease (the pathophysiologic process) and illness (the meaning of the disease to the individual and the family), because the social aura of cancer as a dreaded disease puts into high relief the cultural mechanisms used to cope with all aspects of the response to cancer including: the meaning of the diagnosis; the impact of the side effects; perspectives on disability and impairment as sequelae to the treatment; concepts of death; and different patterns of response in the family dynamics that are mobilized to cope with each of these areas.

The concepts of suffering and help-seeking behavior discussed below are associated with more traditional APIA cultural values. APIA elderly tend to hold more traditional beliefs and behaviors and are thus more likely to express these responses to illness and disease, but again, these vary among and between the APIA subgroups. For example, APIA elders may be very reticent to ask for assistance from family members or professionals. The dominant U.S. health care system, however, is based upon the concept of "help-seeking behavior"—if something is wrong, individuals should assert themselves to find a remedy and verbalize their needs to both professionals and significant others. Both assertive behaviors and asking for assistance may be alien practices to elderly APIAs (Kagawa-Singer, 1988; Kagawa-Singer et al., in press).

Shame and Stigma

The threat of loss of face, for elders and their immediate and extended families, can be a major barrier to seeking care. Cancer, and some of the other diseases discussed in this chapter, such as tuberculosis, carry a psychological stigma that mitigates against disclosure of the diagnosis. Exposure of the stigmatized illness can cause shame or loss of face for the elder, as well as the family. "Face" and self-sacrifice are fundamental concepts in Asian cultures to maintain social respectability, public family image, as well as individual persona, and are poorly measured by Western conceptualizations (Zane, 1994).

The Asian sociopsychological ethos of face and self-sacrifice are powerful forces molding behavior in interpersonal interactions. One of the consequences of this structure is the belief that elders must hide negative emotions in order to maintain the harmony and welfare of the group (Kagawa-Singer, 1988). They should not appear selfish by preoccupation with their own dysphoric emotions. In conjunction with self-sacrifice is also an underlying belief that negative social situations among one's significant group are less amenable to change than is the more common perspective in Western society. Instead, it is assumed that one must endure the inevitable emotional friction created in tightly knit social groups. Thus public expression of self-reflection is discouraged, selflessness and self-sacrifice encouraged, and the expectation of changing a distressful situation (such as depression after mastectomy) may not exist.

A related Western concept is that of individual dignity. Face, however, is much more inclusive for Asians, for an individual is seen primarily as a representative of first the natal family, then the community. Individualism is viewed within the context of the group's integrity. Thus, face-saving opportunities are extremely significant. APIA elders have been socialized to be exquisitely aware of the impact of their actions on family face, given that individuals are seen as reflections of their families and social groups rather than as autonomous persons. Seeking help for emotional distress outside the immediate family might be interpreted by family and others as lack of response to family training and thereby result in loss of face. In a group society, self-sufficiency is highly valued. Elders must carry their share of the responsibility for the well-being of the group. If an elder seeks help outside the family, he or she might then be viewed as weak and incapable. In addition, this may also be interpreted as saying that the family is not competent to provide for the needs of its elders, which would be shameful.

Another, less talked about phenomenon is the implicit concept of self and individualism, upon which U.S. health care support services are based (Chang, 1988). Much effort is spent in the socialization process to nurture the ability to declare clear ego boundaries between self and other and to assert one's rights in seeking health care. Individual empowerment is often the focus of public health messages and patient education efforts. Inherent in the concept of the APIA individual, however, is dependency upon others (Kagawa-Singer & Chung, 1994). This discrepancy in basic belief structures foreshadows possible miscommunications, misunderstandings, and suboptimal use of the health care system among APIA elderly.

Alternative Therapies and Practices

The meaning of the diagnosis of a chronic life-threatening disease such as cancer to an APIA elder is determined by cultural and individual concepts of the cause of the disease. The cause may be physical (e.g., infection, accident); or metaphysical (e.g., bad winds, excessive emotions, other causes of imbalance in the energy forces that constitute health); or supernatural (e.g., soul loss, bad spirits, retribution for bringing shame upon an ancestor). The appropriate and rational treatment for the disease would then be based upon the etiology. The cosmology of the worldview of most APIA cultures is based upon the duality present in the Yin and Yang concept of balance between opposing elements, such as light and dark, wet and dry, hot and cold. The rationale of the therapies used by these cultures is based upon reestablishing balance. It has served to maintain "health" for members of these cultures for 6,000 years, and most practitioners of the various forms of healing, such as acupuncturists and herbalists, serve long and intensive training periods analogous to medical training in the United States. These practitioners may play an integral role in the health beliefs and practices of the traditional APIA communities, particularly for the more recent older immigrants and refugees.

Restrictiveness of Research Paradigm

Overall, the limited chronic disease research among APIA elders has focused primarily on identification of population risk groups and related cultural risk-promoting behaviors. Although this approach has successfully highlighted selected areas of need, it has also resulted in a restrictive research paradigm for the planning of future research and interventions. First and foremost, a fundamental change must occur in the mind-set of both dominant culture researchers and many minority researchers to remove the deficit theory as the basis for the study of APIA elderly. Implicit in much of the research on APIA elders is a focus upon the problems that result from barriers to access and use of health care due to acculturation or socioeconomic discrepancies. Less focus has been on the macro-societal structural barriers that promote these "problem" behaviors, but *little to no* focus has been brought to bear on the positive strengths of APIA elders that may account for the *lower* incidence of various acute and chronic diseases. These protective practices of older APIA subgroups could be supported more widely across APIA communities, as well as in other populations, to maintain low disease incidence and to reduce morbidity and mortality of diseases such as heart disease and some cancers.

Summary

Providing an overview of the health status of the APIA elderly is hampered by the dearth of studies on this population. The myth of the model minority as healthy, wealthy, and wise and the aggregation of more than 60 different nationalities as one homogeneous group create formidable barriers to uncovering the health needs of this population. For example, compared to other APIA groups, Japanese tend to be more acculturated and American-born; Koreans are commonly associated with the church; Chinese come from diverse parts of the world; Filipinos have a strong Spanish influence on their cultural background; and SEAs are more likely to be refugees and to suffer from post-traumatic stress disorder and sustain the health risks imposed by poverty, such as suboptimal nutrition, poor housing, and employment in high-risk jobs. On the other hand, many APIA cultures also share common philosophic heritages rooted in Hinduism, Buddhism, and Confucian traditions. A significant Muslim population also exists among many South Asian cultures such as Malaysians, Thai, and Asian Indians. These traditional cultures share an ethos of appropriate behavior and conduct. Group harmony, collectivity rather than individualism, and hierarchical familial/social roles are valued to an extent not found in Western cultures, particularly among the traditional APIA elderly. We must be careful, however, not to stereotype APIA elders based on these differences and commonalities.

What is apparent from the limited data is that significant health risks exist for particular subgroups in this highly heterogeneous federal category of APIA elderly for all major diseases and a few ethnic-specific diseases such as the thalassemias, Hemoglobin E, and hepatitis B. A significant portion of APIA elders live below the FPL and are more likely to rate their health as fair or poor, to have activity limitations, and to be uninsured when compared to any other ethnic group. The adult APIA population is also at risk due to rapid Westernization and its accompanying unhealthy health habits, such as sedentary lifestyles and high-fat, low-fiber diets. Studies indicate that after 10 to 15 years in the United States, immigrants begin to exhibit some of the same health risk indicators as the host population due to these lifestyle issues. This trend indicates that the incidence and mortality from preventable chronic diseases such as hypertension, diabetes, cardiovascular disease, and cancer will be a growing problem in the elderly APIA population.

Future Directions for Research and Practice

Currently, we have limited ability to (a) make broad generalizations about APIA elderly as an aggregated group or as specific subgroups. We must be able to identify specific factors that constitute health risk factors for older APIA as well as health protective cultural practices; and (b) develop ethnic-specific intervention programs for older APIA both to reduce health risk factors, and to identify, support, and disseminate information about positive cultural practices. To address the first need, the following summarizes specific methodological limitations found in studies of APIA elderly that result in conflicting and sometimes misleading results due to the distinct variability of the subgroups:

- *Aggregation:* Aggregating all older APIAs as "other" or as one homogeneous group without considering subgroups or age differentials
- *Validity:* Measuring concepts or constructs that may not be valid in APIA cultures
  Instrumentation: (a) Failing to use bilingual/bicultural measures or assessments specific to older APIAs; (b) Using translated measures or assessment instruments with little or no test of conceptual equivalence or attention to cultural differences that may affect self-report or self-disclosure with respect to social desirability
- *Sampling bias:* Focusing on the larger and more acculturated APIA elders such as Chinese and Japanese rather than the smaller populations due to English-speaking ability or ease of recruitment
- *Representativeness:* Rarely examining those who may be at highest risk, for example, substance abuse (e.g., older sea refugees)
- *Reliability:* Using disproportionately small sample sizes
- *Control:* Seldom controlling for socioeconomic and other demographic variations that may be confounded with ethnicity
- *Trained personnel:* Lack of bilingual and bicultural researchers and staff

Future research addressing these barriers would provide the database needed to document accurately the health status of APIA elderly.

The second objective, optimal delivery of care to the elderly APIA population, requires bilingual, bicultural staff who are culturally competent to reduce health risk behaviors and to promote positive ethnic health practices within the populations of focus. Greater public health benefit could accrue from this double-pronged approach. If those positive health practices and cultural lifestyles among APIA elders that result in lower disease rates were identified, health practitioners and policymakers could support these practices in high-risk populations of all ethnic groups.

There are large gaps in the research regarding APIA elders that will have major implications for the provision of health and long-term care services in the future. Research on APIA elders is sorely needed to study the effects of culture, environment, and biological factors on health. This research should include studies of chronic diseases (e.g., dementia, arthritis) and resultant disabilities; needs, preferences, and utilization of long-term care services and programs; explanatory models of illness and health behaviors; APIA lifestyles; the influence and role of families on health and coping; and the use of traditional versus Western medicine.

A skeleton infrastructure is now in place that must be strengthened to train individuals necessary to conduct the research to document the needs of the APIA elderly and produce the programs to support health-promoting behaviors. Many successful programs already exist for the various cultural groups within APIA community health centers. Information about these programs, however, is primarily anecdotal. Funding has been for implementation of programs rather than research. Rarely do community grants include enough funds to compensate time or staff to document the outcomes or disseminate the findings of the projects in professional journals. Efforts are being made to rectify this situation by national community health organizations such as the Association of Asian Pacific Community Health Organizations (AAPCHO), information clearinghouses and dissemination programs such as the Asian and Pacific Islander Americans Health Forum and the National Research Center for Asian American Mental Health (funded through NIMH) and most recently MEDTEP (funded by Agency for Health Care Policy and Research; UCLA/CA/RAND MEDTEP Center, 1992). MEDTEP was formed expressly to conduct research on elderly APIA. Moreover, two nationally recognized organizations serve as resource and training centers for information specifically on APIA elders and health: (a) the Stanford Geriatric Education Center in Palo Alto, California, specializes in ethnogeriatrics or minority aging and health, and (b) the National Asian Pacific Center on Aging in Seattle, Washington, expressly addresses specific issues, including demographics and delivery of health and social services.

The Office of Management and Budget Directive No. 15 (1995) is revising the federal designations for ethnic categories. The 1990 Census listed 11 APIA categories and allowed a fill-in category for "Other." National Database studies must be encouraged to adopt a similar breakdown for the APIA racial and ethnic category, as well as by age, in order to collect data that will be more valid and relevant to program and policy development (Chen & Hawks, 1995).

The agenda for research among the APIA elderly must focus upon all of these conceptual and methodological issues in order to chronicle and assess the health status of APIA elders more accurately and to develop and implement more culturally appropriate and effective policies and programs. These strategies would enable practitioners and policy developers to meet the long-term health care needs of APIA elderly and enable them to enjoy a more dignified and higher quality of life.

References

Abbott, R. D., Rodriguez, B. L., Burchfiel, C. M., & Curb, J. D. (1994). Physical activity in older middle-aged men and reduced risk of stroke: The Honolulu Heart Program. *American Journal of Epidemiology, 139*(9), 881-893.

American Cancer Society. (1990). *Cancer facts and figures for minority Americans.* Atlanta: Author.

American Cancer Society. (1991). *Cancer facts and figures for minority Americans.* Atlanta: Author.

American Cancer Society. (1997). *Facts and figures.* Atlanta: Author.

American Cancer Society, California Division, and California State Tumor Registry. (1991). *Cancer facts and figures.* Oakland: Author.

American Cancer Society, California Division, and California State Tumor Registry. (1995). *Cancer facts and figures.* Oakland: Author.

American Heart Association. (1991). Cardiovascular diseases and stroke in African Americans and other racial minorities in the United States: Special report. *Circulation, 83,* 1463-1480.

Asian American Health Forum. (1990). *Asian and Pacific Islander American California proportionate mortality rates* [Monograph Series 2]. San Francisco: Author.

Asian Pacific Health Care Venture. (1993). *Report on Asian Pacific health issues in Los Angeles County: Diversity and growth, current issues and challenges for the future.* (Available from: Asian Pacific Health Care Venture, 1530 Hillhurst Avenue, Los Angeles, CA 90027. fax: 213-644-3892; phone: 213-346-0370)

Barrett-Connor, E. (1992). Risks and benefits of replacement estrogen. *Annual Review of Medicine, 43,* 239-251.

Chang, S. C. (1988). The nature of the self: A transcultural view. *Transcultural Psychiatric Research Review, 25,* 169-203.

Chen, M. S., & Hawks, B. L. (1995). A debunking of the myth of healthy Asian Americans and Pacific Islanders. *American Journal of Health Promotion, 9*(4), 261-268.

Chen, A., Ng, P., Sam, P., Ng, D., Abe, D., Ott, R., Lim, W., Chan, S., & Winston, W. (1993). Special health problems of Asians and Pacific Islanders. In R. Matzen & R. Lang (Eds.), *Clinical preventive medicine.* St. Louis, MO: C. V. Mosby Year Book.

Chin, K.-I., Lai, T.-F., M., & Rouse, M. (1991). Social adjustment and alcoholism among Chinese immigrants in New York City. *International Journal of Addictions, 25,* 709-730.

Choi, E., McGandy, R., Dallal, G., Russell, R. M., Jacob, R., Schaefer, E. J., & Sadowski, J. A. (1990). The prevalence of cardiovascular risk factors among elderly Chinese Americans. *Archives of Internal Medicine, 150,* 413-418.

Crews, D. E. (1994). Obesity and diabetes. In N. W. S. Zane, D. T. Takeuchi, & K. N. J. Young (Eds.), *Confronting critical health issues of Asian and Pacific Islander Americans* (pp. 174-208). Thousand Oaks, CA: Sage.

Cummings, W. R., & Cauley, J. A. (1994). Racial differences in hip axis length might explain racial differences in rates of hip fracture. *Osteoporosis International, 4,* 226-229.

Cummings, S. R., Xu, L., Chen, X., Ahzo, X., Yu, W., & Ge, Q. (1994). Bone mass, rates of osteoporotic fractures, and prevention of fractures: Are there differences between China and Western countries? *Chinese Medical Sciences Journal, 9*(3), 197-200.

Curb, J. D., Aluli, E., Kautz, J. A., Petrovitch, H., Knutsen, S. F., Knutsen, R., O'Conner, H. K., & O'Conner, W. E. (1991). Cardiovascular risk factor levels in ethnic Hawaiians. *American Journal of Public Health, 81,* 164-167.

Curb, J. D., Reed, D. M., Miller, D., & Yano, K. (1990). Health status and life style in Japanese men with long life expectancy. *Journal of Gerontology: Social Sciences, 45,* S206-S211.

Eng, C. (1994, January). *Risk factors and outcomes of hip fracture in Asian American frail elderly.* Paper presented at the On Lok Senior Health Services/Asian American Health Forum Pilot Project Symposium. UCLA/MEDTEP Outcomes Research Center for Asians and Pacific Islanders, Los Angeles, CA.

Fujimoto, W. Y., Leonetti, D. L., Kinyoun, J. L., Newell-Morris, L., Shuman, W. P., Stolov, W. C., & Wahl, P. W. (1987). Prevalence of diabetes mellitus and impaired glucose tolerance among second-generation Japanese-American men. *Diabetes, 36,* 721-729.

Greendale, G. A., & Judd, H. L. (1993). The menopause: Health impact and clinical management. *Journal of American Geriatric Society, 41,* 426-436.

Hagiwara, S., & Miki, T. (1989). Quantification of bone mineral content using dual-photon absorptiometry in a normal Japanese population. *Journal of Bone Mineral Research, 4*(2), 217-222.

Han, E. (1990, November). *Korean health survey in Southern California: A preliminary report on health status and health care needs of Korean immigrants* [Abstract]. Paper presented at the Third Biennial Forum of the Asian American Health Forum, Inc.: API: Dispelling the Myth of a Healthy Minority, Bethesda, MD.

Han, E. E. S., Kim, S. H., Lee, M. S., et al. (1989). *Korean Health Survey: A preliminary report.* (Available from Korean Health Education, Information and Referral Center, 981 S. Western Avenue #404, Los Angeles, CA 90006; phone: 213-732-5648)

Hann, H. W. L. (1994). Hepatitis B. In N. W. S. Zane, D. T. Takeuchi, & K. N. J. Young (Eds.), *Confronting critical health issues of Asian and Pacific Islander Americans* (pp. 148-173). Thousand Oaks, CA: Sage.

Hawaii State Department of Health, Health Promotion and Education Office. (1988). *Hawaiians' health and risk behaviors, 1987.* Honolulu: Author.

Henderson, B. E. (1990). Commentary: Summary report of the Sixth Symposium on Cancer Registries and Epidemiology in the Pacific Basin. *Journal of the National Cancer Institute, 82,* 1186-1190.

Jenkins, C. N. H., & Kagawa-Singer, M. (1994). Cancer. In N. W. S. Zane, D. T. Takeuchi, & K. N. J. Young, (Eds.), *Confronting critical health issues of Asian and Pacific Islander Americans* (pp. 105-147). Thousand Oaks, CA: Sage.

Jenkins, C. N. H., McPhee, S. J., Ha, N. T., Nam, T. V., & Chen, A. (1995). Cigarette smoking among Vietnamese immigrants in California. *American Journal of Health Promotion, 9*(4), 254-256.

Kagawa-Singer, M. (1988). *Bamboo and oak: Differences in adaptation to cancer by Japanese-Americans and Anglo-Americans.* Unpublished doctoral dissertation, University of California at Los Angeles, Department of Anthropology.

Kagawa-Singer, M. (1996). Cultural systems related to cancer. In R. McCorkle, M. Grant, M. Frankstromborg, & S. Baird (Eds.), *Cancer nursing: A comprehensive textbook* (2nd ed., pp. 38-52). Philadelphia: W. B. Saunders.

Kagawa-Singer, M., & Chung, R. C.-Y. (1994). A paradigm for culturally based care in ethnic minority populations. *Journal of Community Psychology, 2*(2), 192-208.

Kagawa-Singer, M., Wellisch, D. K., & Durvasula, R. (in press). Impact of breast cancer on Asian women. *Culture, Medicine and Psychiatry.*

Kao, P. C., & P'eng, F. K. (1995). How to reduce the risk factors of osteoporosis in Asia. *Chung-Hua I Hsueh Tsa Chich Chinese Medical Journal, 55*(3), 209-213.

Kim, K. K., Yu, E. S., Liu, W. T., Kim, J., & Kohrs, M. B. (1993). Nutritional status of Chinese, Korean-, and Japanese-American elderly. *Journal of the American Dietetic Association, 93*(12), 1416-1422.

Kitano, H. (1994). Health and Asian American elderly: Research and policy issues. In C. M. Baressi (Ed.), *Health and minority elders: An analysis of applied literature.* Washington, DC: American Association of Retired Persons.

Kitano, H. H. L., Hatanaka, H., Yeung, Y. T., & Sue, S. (1985). Japanese-American drinking patterns. In L. A. Bennett & G. M. Ames (Eds.), *The American experience with alcohol: Contrasting cultural perspectives* (pp. 335-357). New York: Plenum.

Klontz, K. C. (1986, May 23). Analysis of a program for the prevention of perinatal hepatitis B. *California Morbidity,* p. 20.

Levin, B. L. (1985). *Cigarette smoking habits and characteristics in the Laotian refugee: A perspective pre- and post-resettlement.* Abstract presented at Refugee Health Conference, San Diego, CA.

Lin-Fu, J. S. (1993). Asian and Pacific Islander Americans: An overview of demographic characteristics and health care issues. *Asian American and Pacific Islander Journal of Health, 1*(1), 20-36.

Lipson, L. G., & Kato-Palmer, S. (1988). Asian Americans. *Diabetes Forecast, 41,* 48-51.

Lock, M., Kaufert, P., & Gilbert, P. (1988). Cultural construction of the menopausal syndrome: The Japanese case. *Maturitas, 14*(4), 317-332.

Lock, M. M. (1993). *Encounters with aging: Mythologies of menopause in Japan and North America.* Berkeley: University of California Press.

Lonner, W. J., & Berry, J. W. (1986). *Field methods in cross-cultural research.* Newbury Park, CA: Sage.

Lovejoy, N. C., Jenkins, C., Wu, T., Shankland, S., & Wilson, C. (1989). Developing a breast cancer screening program for Chinese-American women. *Oncology Nursing Forum, 16*(2), 131-187.

Lubben, J. E., Chi, I., & Kitano, H. H. L. (1989). The relative influence of selected social factors in Korean drinking behavior in Los Angeles. *Advances in Alcohol & Substance Abuse, 8,* 1-17.

Lui, W. T., & Yu, E. S. H. (1985). Asian/Pacific American elderly: Mortality differentials, health status and use of health services. *Journal of Applied Gerontology, 4,* 35-64.

Magaziner, J., Simonsick, E. M., Kashner, T. M., Hebel, J. R., & Kenzora, J. E. (1989). Survival experience of aged hip fracture patients. *American Journal of Public Health, 79*(3), 274-278.

McBride, M., Morioka-Douglas, N., & Yeo, G. (1996). *Aging and health: Asian/Pacific Islander American elders* (2nd ed.). Palo Alto, CA: Stanford Geriatric Education Center.

McCoy, C. B., Nielsen, B. B., Chitwood, D. D., et al. (1991). Increasing the cancer screening of the medically underserved in South Florida. *Cancer, 67,* 1808-1813.

McPhee, S. J., Jenkins, C. N. H., Wong, C., Fordham, D., Lai, K. Q., Adair, J., & Moskawitz, J. M. (1995). Smoking cessation intervention among Vietnamese Americans: A controlled trial. *Tobacco Control, 4*(Suppl. 1), S16-S24.

Modell B., & Berdoukas, V. (1984). *The clinical approach to thalassemia.* London: Grune & Stratton.

Morioka-Douglas, N., & Yeo, G. (1990). *Aging and health: Asian/Pacific Island American elders* (Working Paper Series No. 3). Stanford, CA: Stanford Geriatric Education Center.

Muir, C., Waterhouse, J., Mack, T., Powell, J., & Whelan, S. (Eds.). (1987). *Cancer incidence in five continents, Vol. V* (IARC Scientific Publications No. 88). Lyon, France: International Agency for Research on Cancer.

Nakawatase, T. V., Yamamoto, J., & Sasao, T. (1993). The association between fast-flushing response and alcohol use among Japanese Americans. *Journal of Studies on Alcohol, 54*(1), 48-53.

Office of Management and Budget. (1995). *Directive No. 15: Race and ethnic standards for federal statistics and administrative reporting. "Research to evaluate new federal categories for race and ethnicity reporting."* Paper presented at the 94th annual meeting of the American Anthropological Association, Washington, DC.

Office of Minority Health Resource Center. (1988). *Closing the gap: Cancer and minorities: Cancers of the cervix, stomach, esophagus run high for some.* Washington, DC: U.S. Department of Health and Human Services, Public Health Service.

Powers, L. W. (1989). *Diagnostic hematology.* St. Louis, MO: C. V. Mosby.

Reed, D., McGee, D., & Katsuhiko, Y. (1982). Biological and social correlates of blood pressure among Japanese men in Hawaii. *Hypertension, 4,* 406-414.

Rumbaut, R. G. (1989). Portraits, patterns and predictors of the refugee adaptation process: Results and reflections from the IHARP Panel Study. In D. W. Haines (Ed.), *Refugees as immigrants–Cambodians, Laotians, and Vietnamese in America.* Totowa, NJ: Rowman & Littlefield.

Russell-Aulet, M., & Wang, J. (1991). Bone mineral density and mass by total-body dual-photon absorptiometry in normal White and Asian men. *Journal of Bone Mineral Research, 6*(10), 1109-1113.

Sasao, T. (1992). *Statewide Asian drug service needs assessment.* Sacramento: California State Department of Health.

Shintani, T. T., Hughes, C. K., Beckman, S., & O'Conner, H. K. (1991). Obesity and cardiovascular risk intervention through the ad libitum feeding of the traditional Hawaiian diet. *American Journal of Clinical Nutrition, 53,* 1647s-1651s.

Silverman, S. L., & Madison, R. E. (1988). Decreased incidence of hip fracture in Hispanics, Asians, and Blacks: California hospital discharge data. *American Journal of Public Health, 78,* 1482-1483.

Sloan, N. R. (1963). Ethnic distribution of diabetes mellitus in Hawaii. *Journal of the American Medical Association, 183,* 123-128.

Stavig, G. R., Igra, A., & Leonard, A. R. (1988). Hypertension and related health issues among Asians and Pacific Islanders in California. *Public Health Reports, 103*(1), 28-37.

Sue, S., Zane, N., & Ito, J. (1979). Alcohol drinking patterns among Asian and Caucasian Americans. *Journal of Cross-Cultural Psychology, 10,* 41-56.

Tamir, A., & Cachola, S. (1994). Hypertension and other cardiovascular risk factors. In N. W. S. Zane, D. T. Takeuchi, & K. N. J. Young (Eds.), *Confronting critical health issues of Asian and Pacific Islander Americans* (pp. 209-246). Thousand Oaks, CA: Sage.

Tanjasiri, S. P., Wallace, S. P., & Shibata, K. (1995). Picture imperfect: Hidden problems among Asian Pacific Islander elderly. *The Gerontologist, 35,* 753-760.

Tobias, J. H., Cook, D. G., Chambers, T. J., & Dalzell, N. (1994). A comparison of bone mineral density between Caucasian, Asian and Afro-Caribbean women. *Clinical Science, 87*(5), 587-591.

Tsunehara, C. H., Leonetti, D. L., & Fujimoto, W. Y. (1990). Diet of second-generation Japanese-American men with (and without non-insulin-dependent diabetes. *American Journal of Clinical Nutrition, 52*(4), 731-738.

UCLA/CA/RAND MEDTEP Center. (1992). [Funded by Agency for Health Care Policy and Research, September].

University of California Los Angeles/Veterans Affairs/RAND/Medical Treatment Effectiveness Program Outcomes Research Centers for API. (1996). What's been going on? *Asian and Pacific Islander American Health Outcomes Update, 1*(3), 1-2.

U.S. Bureau of the Census. (1990). *1990 Census of population and housing-guide: Population characteristics* (pp. 19-48). Washington, DC: U.S. Department of Commerce, Bureau of the Census.

U.S. Bureau of the Census. (1992a). *Census of the population, 1990 (U.S.): General population characteristics, CP-1-1.* Washington, DC: U.S. Department of Commerce, Bureau of the Census.

U.S. Bureau of the Census. (1992b). *Current population survey.* Washington, DC: U.S. Department of Commerce, Bureau of the Census.

U.S. Bureau of the Census. (1993a). *Census of the population, 1990 (U.S.): Social and economic characteristics, CP-2-1.* Washington, DC: U.S. Department of Commerce, Bureau of the Census.

U.S. Bureau of the Census. (1993b). *Racial and ethnic diversity of America's elderly population. Profiles of America's elderly* (No. 3). Washington, DC: U.S. Department of Commerce, Bureau of the Census.

U.S. Immigration and Naturalization Service. (1981). *1980 statistical yearbook of the immigration and naturalization service.* Washington, DC: Government Printing Office.

U.S. Immigration and Naturalization Service. (1991). *1990 statistical yearbook of the immigration and naturalization service.* Washington, DC: Government Printing Office.

Whittemore, A. S. (1989). Colorectal cancer incidence among Chinese in North America and the People's Republic of China: Variation with sex, age, and anatomical site. *International Journal of Epidemiology, 18*(3), 563-568.

Yano, K., Reed, D. M., & Kagan, A. (1985). Coronary heart disease, hypertension and stroke among Japanese-American men in Hawaii: The Honolulu Heart Program. *Hawaii Medical Journal, 44,* 297-325.

Young, J. J., & Gu, N. (1995). *Demographic and socio-economic characteristics of elderly Asian and Pacific Island Americans.* Seattle: National Asian Pacific Center on Aging.

Zane, N. (1994). *An empirical examination of loss of face among Asian Americans.* Unpublished manuscript, Graduate School of Education, University of California, Santa Barbara, CA 93106.

Ziegler, R. G., Hoover, R. N., Pike, M. D., Hildesheim, A., Nomura, A. M. Y., West, D. W., Wu-Williams, A. H., Kolonel, L. N., Horn-Ross, P. L., Rosenthal, J. F., & Hyer, M. B. (1993). Migration patterns and breast cancer risk in Asian American women. *Journal of the National Cancer Institute, 85,* 1819-1826.

Chronic Disease in American Indian Populations

B. Josea Kramer

The prevalence of chronic disease in American Indian and Alaskan Native populations has increased over the 20th century and represents substantial health care costs and social costs. The increasing burden of chronic disease reflects the interaction of demographic, sociocultural, and environmental factors. The successful effort by the Indian Health Service to reduce infectious disease was the single most important factor leading to an increase in life expectancy at birth for American Indians and Alaskan Natives from 51 years, in 1940, to 71 years in 1980. During the last half of this century, changes in technology, diet, exercise, and lifestyle have introduced new risk factors for disease. In parallel to Western society as a whole, chronic cardiovascular disease, diabetes, and cancer are now major health problems in Indian communities and have become the leading causes of mortality for all ages and for those over age 65.

The great diversity characteristic of the hundreds of native American cultures and societies is reflected in the startling variation reported in health status, health behaviors, and disease prevalence rates. This chapter reviews current data on the overall health of American Indians and Alaskan Natives, as well as on studies conducted in specific tribes. First, diversity is discussed relative to health care, and databases are described. The next sections review recent research on diabetes and associated complications, hypertension, rheumatoid diseases, and cancer, including research foci on epidemiology, genetics,

---

EDITOR'S NOTE: The terms *white* and *black* are used in lower-case, following the author's preference.

181

environmental factors, health beliefs, and culture change. The next section focuses on interventions. The majority of diseases affecting American Indians have preventable risk factors. Most health education in Indian communities has been devoted to weight reduction, diet, and exercise, the health behaviors that have positive effects on diabetes, heart disease, hypertension, and cancer. Finally, consideration is given to the social meaning of chronic disease in aging.

American Indian Diversity: Cultural, Social, and Access to Health Care

American Indians and *Alaskan Natives* are collective terms describing more than 500 nations, tribes, bands, and native villages. At first contact with Europeans, an estimated 300 languages were spoken and, despite the decimation of aboriginal peoples, about 150 indigenous languages are used today. Indigenous cultures inhabited every climatic zone on this continent, with economies based on exploitation strategies as diverse as hunting and gathering to sedentary agriculture, and with political structures as varied as stratified, ranked societies to egalitarian bands. Not surprisingly, then, contemporary American Indian societies also vary in culture, lifestyle, and health. Regional trends in morbidity and mortality (Indian Health Service [IHS], 1993) reflect these cultural differences. Culture and social organization affect expression and experience of aging with chronic disease, including reports of unexpected continuity of activities despite functional impairments (Hendrie et al., 1993). Other researchers have noted risks associated with social structure. Among Navajo, a matrilineal and matrilocal society, unmarried men are far more likely to be isolated from kin; and being an elderly unmarried man is predictive of increased risk of death (Kunitz & Levy, 1988).

    Access to health care varies with residential location and governmental recognition of tribal status. Members of federally recognized tribes, living on federal reservations, trust territories, historic Indian areas in Oklahoma, and Alaskan villages, are provided free, universal access to health care by the Indian Health Service (IHS), a branch of the U.S. Public Health Service. Generally, however, the IHS has allocated insufficient resources for chronically disabled children or adults and for long-term care (John, 1994). In 1995, the IHS established the Elder Health Care Initiative to promote in-service training of its health care providers in principles of geriatric health care, to improve access for elders, and to target prevention programs (Stenger, 1996). Currently, more than half of the total American Indian population, including those over age 65, live in urban areas (U.S. Bureau of Commerce, 1990) where health care is generally provided on the basis of ability to pay, or, for the indigent, by state and local health departments, supplemented by Medicaid or Medicare for those who qualify. Urban American Indians and Alaskan Natives of all ages experience poorer health and functional status, across virtually all measures, than both the general population and their reservation counterparts (Grossman, Krieger, Sugarman, & Forquera, 1994; Kramer, 1992).

Prevalence of Chronic Disease: Databases

Prevalence data on American Indian health is available from a number of databases. Inconsistencies among the databases relate both to the heterogeneity of American Indian and Alaskan Native populations and to the limitations of the databases. The IHS produces an annual comprehensive report of American Indian and Alaskan Native morbidity and mortality as recorded by ICD-9 codes at IHS hospitals and clinics. This database incidentally captures sociocultural variation because the IHS service areas tend to represent cultural groups as well as geographic areas. Unfortunately, the IHS database represents only about 40% of the total American Indian and Alaskan Native population living on federal reservations or native areas. The IHS partially funds urban health clinics, but data from these clinics are not systematically collected. Information about urban Indian health is generally available only from isolated research reports, generally focusing on a single city or county. Most of this work is based on cross-sectional surveys and, to date, there has been little comparability among sampling methods or survey instruments.

Local, state, and regional disease and death registries tend to underestimate prevalence for American Indians because they are not properly classified. Racial misclassification of American Indians has been documented in surveillance registries for end-stage renal disease (Sugarman & Lawson, 1993), cancer (Frost, Taylor, & Fries, 1992), AIDS (Lieb, Conway, Hedderman, Yao, & Kerndt, 1992), injuries (Sugarman, Soderberg, Gordon, & Rivara,

1993), and mortality except alcohol-related deaths (Frost, Tollestrup, Ross, Sabotta, & Kimball, 1994).

American Indians represent about 1% of the total U.S. population, making sampling strategies difficult and costly. Special surveys of American Indian and Alaskan Native health have concentrated on the population living on reservations, those eligible for IHS care, or both. For instance, the Survey of American Indians and Alaskan Natives (SAIAN), conducted to compare the Indian population to the U.S. general population through data collected by the National Medical Expenditure Survey (NMES), was limited to IHS eligible populations. Unlike black and Hispanic populations, American Indian populations are not routinely oversampled to account for the variation in the population. Although surveys conducted in small, isolated communities, such as reservations, may account for most of the variation in that specific population, the enormous variation among tribes precludes generalizations based on a single tribal health survey. Finally, the health profile of American Indians and Alaskan Natives has changed dramatically during the last half of the 20th century, as have social, environmental, and technological factors.

Diabetes and Diabetes-Associated Complications

Health records of the early years of the 20th century indicate that diabetes was an uncommon disease among American Indians. Today, Type II, non-insulin-dependent diabetes mellitus (NIDDM) is widely endemic. The reported rate of diabetes is higher for American Indians in each age group than for any other U.S. ethnic group surveyed by the National Health Interview Survey, and these high rates are confirmed through comparison of IHS and NHANES II findings. For instance, while NHANES II reports that 9.3% of the population aged 65 to 74 years have been diagnosed with diabetes, the IHS reports that 20.3% of all American Indians aged 65+ years have been diagnosed with diabetes (Gohdes, Kaufman, & Valway, 1993).

The increased prevalence of diabetes has been well documented, especially among Pima and Tohono O'odham living on the Gila River Reservation in Arizona. By the 1940s, the diabetes rate was similar to that of whites, by the 1950s the rate among Pima exceeded the white rate, and by the 1960s the Pima had the highest recorded prevalence and incidence of NIDDM for any culturally or geographically defined population, with half of all adults over age 35 years having diabetes (Bennett, Burch, & Miller, 1971; Knowler, Bennett,

Hamman, & Miller, 1978). The longitudinal study, ongoing since 1965, has shown an increase in incidence of diabetes over the past 25 years and rates still appear to be rising in men over age 35 years (Knowler, Saad, Petit, Nelson, & Bennett, 1993). Like the Pima, other tribes also experienced dramatic increases in the prevalence and incidence of diabetes, including Oklahoma Cherokee, Oklahoma Seminole, Creek, Kiowa, Comanche, North Carolina Cherokee, Florida Seminole, Alabama Coushatta, Mississippi Choctaw, Seneca, Passamaquody, Mandan, Arikara, Hidatsa, and Alaskan Natives (Brosseau, 1993; Schraer, Bulkow, Murphy, & Lanier, 1993; Schraer, Lanier, Boyko, Gohdes, & Murphy, 1988; Wiedman, 1987).

Much of the literature reporting diabetes prevalence probably underestimates rates, because most studies are based on diagnosed cases gathered from chart reviews or from current clinic visits. Comparisons across published reports should be made with caution because (a) prevalence and incidence has increased through this century, so studies do not indicate stable rates at any point in time; and (b) diagnostic standards may vary, and studies do not use the same criteria to determine incidence and prevalence. With those caveats, there is considerable tribal variation in incidence and prevalence rates (Carter et al., 1989; Gohdes & Bennett, 1993). Peak prevalence is reported to occur at age 65+ years among Mohawk, Sioux, Chippewa, Ute, and Navajo; at middle age (45-64 years) among Chippewa, Eastern Band of Cherokee, Apache, and Mississippi Choctaw, and there is a disturbing rise in diabetes in younger age cohorts of Mississippi Choctaw and Eastern Band of Cherokee (Gohdes & Bennett, 1993). These differences suggest several causes that may be acting singly or in combination: a genetic link that is, as yet, undiscovered; variations in lifestyle that have yet to be operationally defined; different factors leading to obesity; increasing exposure to nontraditional diets and technology; or a combination of these. Furthermore, this variation implies differential costs of care for this chronic disease and its complications. Higher health care costs are anticipated with longer duration of NIDDM in individuals, which, in turn, is associated with increased likelihood for diabetes-related complications.

At one time, "Indian diabetes" was considered a benign disease and long-term complications were therefore not considered to be a significant cost. However, it is now clear that the microvascular and macrovascular complications of diabetes in American Indian populations are at least as common as in non-Indian patients with diabetes, and often occur with greater frequency. The higher incidence is most likely related to the longer duration of diabetes resulting from earlier on-set and the higher proportion of persons with diabetes, as well as to possible exposure to different or more intense risk factors. Dramatic differences are documented among Pima, where essentially all (95%) end-stage renal disease (ESRD), as well as first lower-extremity amputation, occurs in persons with diabetes (Nelson, Gohdes, et al., 1988; Nelson, Newman, et al., 1988). Although there are difficulties in comparing the complication rates among Indian populations because no standard method was used (e.g., registry information, community survey, case review, cross-section of clinic users), overall, ESRD is 6.8 times higher in American Indian patients with diabetes than in whites with diabetes (Muneta, Newman, Stevenson, & Eggers, 1993). There are age-related differences in frequencies of complications based on duration of NIDDM. For instance, Pima aged 45 to 64 years are reported to have a 14-fold greater incidence of ESRD, while Pima age 65 years and older are reported to have a 10-fold greater incidence than the U.S. population with diabetes. Most (85%) nontraumatic lower-extremity amputations in IHS facilities from 1983 to 1986 were performed on patients with diabetes, and most tribes far exceed the rate of non-Indians for lower-extremity amputations (Valway, Linkins, & Gohdes, 1993). The incidence of a first lower-extremity amputation associated with diabetes among American Indians increases with age, from young adults (48.1/10,000), through middle-age (85.9/10,000), to elders aged 65+ years (104.1/10,000), evidence of the challenge for health care systems to provide appropriate care for persons with long-term complications of diabetes.

Since the 1940s, a rapid increase in the prevalence of obesity and diabetes has occurred among indigenous populations of North America, Central America, the Pacific Islands, and Australia. An evolutionary explanation for the high prevalence of both obesity and non-insulin-dependent diabetes has been proposed as the "thrifty genotype" hypothesis (Neel, 1962, 1982). This hypothesis proposes that, because hunter-gatherers had a periodic and unpredictable food supply, those who were able to store surplus food calories efficiently in body fat during times of plenty and use this energy when food was scarce had real survival advantage. However, when diet and technology changed toward a sedentary industrialized economy with a year-round food supply that is high in fatty foods, calories, and processed foods, the advantage became detrimental. The resulting obesity should be regarded as a metabolic disease rather than a behavioral disorder (Ravussin, 1993). The former evolutionary advantage of an efficient and lower metabolic rate has not adjusted to the lower energy demands of the 20th century, particularly following World

War II. Home cultivation and preservation of subsistence foods was replaced by purchase of refined and highly caloric foods (e.g., refined, degermed, and enriched cornmeal has 13% more calories per cup than does ground meal); exercise associated with walking long distances, gardening, chopping wood, and hand-processing of foods was severely reduced or eliminated. Poverty generally restricts purchases to inexpensive processed foods that are high in fat and calories and these foods are also typical of the government's commodity food distribution program to low-income persons. Other reasons for the high rate of obesity seen in native peoples since the 1940s are the positive cultural value placed on adiposity as an indication of health and prosperity (Wiedman, 1987).

Culturally specific interpretations of diabetes affect treatment decisions and self-care. For instance, among Seneca, illness is considered to be the result of malevolent aggression and no personal blame is attached to development of a health condition (Judkins, 1978). The patient, alone, must combat the condition and is responsible for health improvement. Given this ideology, Seneca patients with diabetes become highly effective in controlling diet and weight and adhering to treatment plans. Seeking available and reasonable effective treatment (in this case, Western medicine) in no way conflicts with traditional values. In contrast, from the perspectives of Sioux and Navajo, diabetes is a "new" disease or a "white man's disease" negatively associated with non-Indian lifestyles. Sioux perceive the reason that so many families have diabetes is that the community is out of balance with its traditions and diabetes is an example of the destruction of their society and culture by non-Indians (Lang, 1989). Given the Sioux etiology, traditional healing methods are not considered fully effective and non-Indian treatment is required. Navajo discourse on diabetes involves metaphors of "doing battle" (Huttlinger et al., 1992). Episodes of care are described as battles in a war that eventually cannot be won against a degenerative disease that transforms Navajo into helpless captives. Nevertheless, adherence to a treatment plan is considered a major weapon. Diabetes also serves as a metaphor for struggling to maintain traditional culture in the face of strong social and economic forces that have disrupted Navajo society.

A key diabetes intervention is diet and, in all societies, food has special social and cultural meanings that go beyond its nutritional value. Food of the American frontier—such as flour, lard, beef, sugar, bacon, coffee, crackers—that was distributed as rations to Indians has been transformed to modern-day pan-tribal "Indian food." Fry breads, rich soups, and stews are now associated with cultural social and ritual events (Joe, Gallerito, & Pino, 1976; Lang, 1989; Powers & Powers, 1984; Primeaux & Henderson, 1981). Urging people to restrict or eliminate these foods, which have been invested with cultural meanings, is counterproductive and generally ignored in favor of participating in the social and cultural life of their communities. For instance, among Northern Ute, the message that food was a causal element in diabetes was discounted as just another example of non-Indians denigrating Ute cultural values because the people, whether traditional or Christian, blessed their meals, thereby rendering the food devoid of harmful substance. Targeting dietary interventions only to individuals with diabetes may be counterproductive if other family members are responsible for home economics and for imparting the domestic knowledge and skills to maintain good health of the family.

Future avenues for biomedical, behavioral, and health services research are evaluation of strategies to delay or prevent the onset of NIDDM and efficacy of early treatment to control diabetes and reduce complications (Fajans & Nutting, 1993; Kuller, 1993; Wilson & Horton, 1993). Basic science and epidemiological studies would define risk in American Indian populations, including age of onset, risk factors for diabetes and for obesity, diet, energy expenditure, and environmental and other macrosocial factors. Prevention efforts would be greatly bolstered by applying rigorous methods to clinical trials of diet and exercise interventions, as well as new drug therapies. Even if diabetes cannot be prevented, delaying onset would reduce morbidity and mortality associated with duration of disease.

Heart Disease and Hypertension

Heart disease is the leading cause of death among American Indians and Alaskan Natives, as it is for the general U.S. population (IHS, 1993a). The prevalence of heart disease among American Indians and Alaskan Natives is on the rise (Hoy, Light, & Megill, 1994; Klain, Coulehan, Arena, & Janett, 1988; Sievers, 1977), as would be expected in a population recently experiencing the transition to chronic disease from infectious disease as the major cause of mortality. Risk factors associated with coronary heart disease have become more common: obesity, diabetes, smoking, high cholesterol, hypertension, and sedentary lifestyles (Alpert, Goldberg, Ockene, & Taylor, 1991). However, specific risk factors vary across tribal and regional areas (Howard et al., 1992). Although age-adjusted mortality attributed to heart disease among all American Indian groups combined is 7% lower than for U.S. all races, there is considerable tribal variation, with tribes of the Northern Plains reporting morbidity and mortality rates as high or higher than the U.S. general population (Coulehan, 1992; Howard et al., 1992). The lower overall rate of cardiovascular disease masks the seriousness of this disease for American Indian populations. American Indians age 40 and younger have three to four times higher cardiovascular mortality than the general population (Sprafka, 1992).

Surprisingly, rates of hypertension are relatively low despite the high prevalence of obesity and diabetes among American Indians; nevertheless, morbidity from hypertension is significant, particularly among American Indians and Native Alaskans with diabetes (Broussard, Valway, Kaufman, Beaver, & Gohdes, 1992; Hoy, Light, & Megill, 1994, 1995). Generally, the prevalence of hypertension increases with age among both men and women. Other risk factors, such as social and economic stressors, have been suggested for Navajo to explain why the highest prevalence is among young men (Coulehan, 1992; DeStefano, Coulehan, & Wiant, 1979) and older Navajo women (Kunitz & Levy, 1986); in contrast, obesity is the strongest predictor of hypertension in young Navajo women. The interaction of hypertension and diabetes appears to have devastating impact, significantly increasing the risk for proliferative retinopathy, proteinuria, ESRD, cerebral vascular disease, and myocardial infarction. The high relative risk for hypertension among American Indian and Alaskan Native persons with diabetes represents a serious, and generally underestimated, health risk. Because of the strong relationship between hypertension and diabetes, health promotion activities to prevent both hypertension and diabetes are crucial to reducing the risk for heart disease in this population.

Several health promotion projects have found that awareness and control of hypertension are problematic. Only 50% of persons found to have hypertension among Penobscot (Deprez, Miller, & Hart, 1985), Navajo (DeStefano et al., 1979), and American Indians of the Northern Plains (Sharlin, Heath, Ford, & Welty, 1993) were aware of their disease. Yet self-reported hypertension tends to be overestimated in comparison to actual blood pressure (Gillum, Gillum, & Smith, 1984; Sharlin et al., 1993). A number of studies note the difficulty in management of hypertension with medication alone, suggesting the need for community-based programs to reduce risk factors.

Rheumatoid Disease

The prevalence of rheumatoid diseases is higher among many American Indian groups than Alaskan Natives or whites. The prevalence and incidence of rheumatoid arthritis has been documented as greater among Pima (Del

Puente, Knowler, Pettit, & Bennett, 1989), Chippewa (Harvey, Lotze, & Stevens, 1981), Tlingit (Boyer, Templin, & Lanier, 1991; Templin et al., 1994), and Yakima (Beasley, Wilkens, & Bennett, 1973). Furthermore, the age of onset may be earlier; half the Tlingit population with rheumatoid arthritis was diagnosed with the disease before age 35. Other rheumatoid diseases also occur with higher frequency among American Indians. The prevalence of systemic lupus erythematosus is high among Sioux, Arapaho, and Crow (Morton, Gershwin, Brady, & Steinberg, 1976), and Haida, Tlingit, and Tsimshian (Boyer et al., 1991). These studies of rheumatoid arthritis note the high frequencies of serum rheumatoid factor and HLA alleles, including DRB1 sequences and DR antigens associated with rheumatoid arthritis in other populations. Thus, American Indian populations may be unusually prone to autoimmune rheumatic disease.

Limited archaeological evidence suggests that, unlike diabetes, rheumatoid arthritis may be a New World disease (Rothschild, Turner, & DeLuca, 1988; Rothschild & Woods, 1990). Skeletal remains found in Northwestern Alabama and dating to 3,000-5,000 years ago, have been diagnosed with erosive polyarthritis characteristic of rheumatoid arthritis. Rheumatoid arthritis was not a recognized disease entity and does not appear in skeletal remains of European populations before the 18th century; in contrast, osteoarthritis, gout, and spondyloarthropathies are found in European archeological remains dating to 4,000 years before the present. Possible vectors spreading rheumatoid arthritis to Europe from America may be the result of a pathogen or allergen associated with either migration of peoples or transatlantic trade of tobacco, deer, rodents, dogs, or other trade goods.

Basic research on rheumatoid arthritis among these populations is limited by both the relatively small number of people in each study and by the lack of genetic variation. For instance, ANA seropositivity is estimated at 70% among Tlingit, in contrast to the 30% to 40% expected in Caucasian populations (Templin et al., 1994). Ninety percent of half- to full-blood Pima are characterized by HLA types with DR alleles characteristic of rheumatoid arthritis in other populations, yet only a fraction develop rheumatoid arthritis (Jacobsson et al., 1994). This genetic homogeneity greatly complicates identification of alleles associated with risk for rheumatoid arthritis (Calin, Bennett, Jupiter, & Terasaki, 1977; Templin et al., 1994).

Environmental factors need further consideration to explain the development of rheumatoid arthritis, or, as in the case of Pima, the steady decline in prevalence of rheumatoid arthritis over the past 25 years. Jacobsson and colleagues (1994) note the decline coincides with environmental factors such as the increase of diabetes, improved standard of living, reduction of infectious diseases including tuberculosis, and use of new drug therapies. Additional research is needed to understand environmental risk factors.

Little attention has been given to educational programs and culturally specific adaptive strategies to cope with rheumatoid diseases. The Canadian Arthritis Society (Arthritis Society, n.d.) has adapted the Arthritis Self-Management Program for the Canadian First Nations. Its widespread use throughout North America in both urban and reservation communities has yet to be evaluated. Use of validated self-reporting instruments to monitor disease progress have proved problematic in both urban (Fran Goldfarb, personal communication, 1996) and reservation communities (Templin et al., 1994) when questions have conflicted with culture-bound concepts relating to time, autonomy, and communication within a therapeutic setting. The social impact of living with a periodically disabling rheumatoid disease has received little attention, though one report indicates that withdrawal from shared labor in the community has negative consequences for both individuals and their families (Weiner, 1993).

Cancer

Cancer is the third leading cause of death among American Indians. Overall survival rates are dismal. American Indians experience the lowest cancer survival rate of any U.S. population (Burhansstipanov & Dresser, 1993). Only one third of American Indians diagnosed with cancer survive for 5 years, in comparison to about half of the majority population cancer patients. Although no single study has documented cancer incidence and mortality rates across American Indian and Native Alaskan populations, various regional studies and reports indicate that there is significant variation between indigenous populations and the general U.S. population. As in the general population, the most common cancer site is the lung. The most common cancer sites among whites (i.e., lung, prostate, colon, breast, uterus, urinary bladder) occur at lower rates among American Indians and Alaskan Natives. However, in comparison to whites, the incidence of cancers of the gallbladder, kidney, stomach, and cervix are relatively high in American Indians, as are cancers of the liver and nasopharynx in Native Alaskans (Nutting et al., 1993). Overall, among American Indian men, the incidence of kidney cancer is elevated, while among American Indian women the incidence for gallbladder, cervix, and kidney cancers is elevated (Mahoney & Michalek, 1991).

The occurrence of cancers also varies among indigenous culture areas and among cultural groups within a region. For instance, American Indian men living in Montana have higher incidence rates for kidney, lung, and prostate cancers than American Indian men living in the southwest. Although rates of cervical cancer are elevated in American Indian women in Montana and in New Mexico, the incidence for breast and lung cancer is higher among the Northern Plains than the southwestern women (Bleed, Risser, Sperry, Hellhake, & Helgerson, 1992). There is also variation within a region. In Alaska, for example, cancer frequencies vary among the three indigenous populations of Eskimo, American Indian, and Aleut (Lanier, Bulkow, & Ireland, 1989). Risk for cancer of the esophagus and liver is higher among Eskimo than Aleut or Indians; risk for gallbladder cancer is higher among Eskimo and Indians than Aleut; and risk for multiple myeloma is higher among Indians, with the rate among Indian men exceeding that of U.S. whites.

These differences in incidence and in site-specific cancers have been attributed to cultural heterogeneity associated with health behaviors, as well as to environmental factors. The frequency of lung cancer and cardiovascular disease risks have been linked to tribally specific patterns of cigarette smoking both on and off reservation (Bleed et al., 1992; Gillum et al., 1984; Welty, Zephier, Schweigman, Blake, & Leonardson, 1993). For instance, in the Southwest, where cigarette smoking tends to occur at low frequency, there are lower rates of lung cancer than have been noted among the tribes characterized by heavier smoking patterns on the Northern Plains.

High rates of cancer continue to be reported among Navajo who worked in uranium mines or lived nearby (Roscoe, Deddens, Salvan, & Schnorr, 1995). This occupational and environmental health hazard on the Navajo reservation was not mitigated by protective gear for workers nor by education of residents. Although hotly contested by tribal members, social and economic considerations to exploit the natural resource at the time outweighed cultural values to protect the land. Cancer is now seen by many Navajo as a culturally valid outcome for disturbing the sacred nature of the land by strip mining (Dawson, 1992). Therefore, families often have not aggressively pursued either treatment or legal options. The strong association between clans and their land base rules out voluntary relocation from the now environmentally hazardous zones. Navajo take the long view: In time the Earth will heal itself and the health problems will likewise diminish. Other indigenous beliefs about cancer and its etiology have received little attention.

Although cancer among American Indians and Alaskan Natives has received scant attention in the literature (Mahoney & Michalek, 1995), a number of research and intervention projects have recently focused on this health issue, particularly through the National Cancer Institute's Native American initiatives (Burhansstipanov, 1993) and the establishment of the AMC Native American Cancer Research Program at the AMC Cancer Research Center in Denver. Future research can be expected to identify more precisely why 5-year survival rates among American Indians are so poor even when controlling for age, ethnicity, cancer stage at diagnosis, or urban/rural residence (Becker et al., 1993; Sugarman, Dennis, & White, 1994). Other productive avenues of research may be identification of more effective prevention methods in communities where cervical cancer is more than 4 times the rate of U.S. whites (Welty et al., 1993), where annual community screenings using Pap smears alone have been proven ineffective in reducing high rates of invasive cervical cancers (Davidson et al., 1994), where current untargeted screening and standard follow-up care have not reduced excess mortality from cervical cancer (Gilbert, Sugarman, & Cobb, 1995), and where the cost/benefit ratio of community screening mammography is not favorable (Nutting, Calonge, Iverson, & Green, 1994).

Interventions

The leading causes of death for American Indians and Alaskan Natives over the age of 65 years are diseases of the heart, cancer, cerebrovascular diseases, diabetes mellitus, and pneumonia and influenza (IHS, 1993a). These five leading causes of death account for 71% of deaths reported by ICD-9 codes in Indian Health Service facilities during 1988, and the majority (58% of deaths) are attributable to heart disease, cancer, and diabetes. Culturally appropriate primary prevention wellness programs can reduce the risk factors for these diseases, and additional research may be needed to clarify certain population-specific risks. With high incidence rates indicating an earlier onset for some diseases, secondary prevention programs are essential to screen populations and provide early medical interventions. Most reported intervention programs have focused on tertiary prevention (e.g., education on exercise and diet) to minimize disability in persons already diagnosed with a disease process, such as diabetes. The challenge is to establish prevention programs while planning sufficient resources and services for the long-term medical complications of chronic diseases and for community-based support to assist persons aging with disabilities and impaired functional status. Intervention and prevention of chronic diseases ideally involve active partnerships among American Indian communities (tribal governments and urban multipurpose organizations), researchers, and health care systems (IHS and other public health systems, as well as health care agencies contracted to serve or targeting substantial American Indian populations).

In this chapter, the majority of recommended interventions have focused on behavioral interventions: (a) nutrition and exercise programs to control obesity and reduce the risk for diabetes, hypertension, cancer, and gallstones; and (b) smoking cessation and prevention programs to reduce preventable cancers and cardiovascular disease. There are quite a few health promotion and disease prevention projects initiated at the local level. A bibliography by the American Indian Health Care Association (1991) reports 93 projects, of which 26% relate to diabetes control, 9% relate to control of hypertension, and 5% relate to control of cervical and breast cancers. Only a few projects with strong evaluation components, however, are easily accessed in literature reviews (McMaster & Connell, 1994).

Community-based American Indian health interventions often share the common approach of defining health beliefs and behaviors (and thus promotion and prevention strategies) in relation to the community rather than the individual (DeJong, 1991). Smoking cessation is a good example. Urban American Indian smokers are knowledgeable about the health risk of smoking cigarettes, tolerant of other smokers, and are not experiencing peer pressure to quit (Barker & Kramer, 1993; Lando, Johnson, Graham-Tomasi, McGovern, & Solberg, 1992); it would not be culturally acceptable to offer *unsolicited* value judgments to peers about their personal behaviors, including smoking. A successful intervention strategy is to reconceptualize smoking from a personal behavior to a behavior that negatively impacts the health of the family and the community at large, such as the program slogan "Your problem, our future" (Hodge, 1992).

There is general agreement that successful diabetes intervention strategies will incorporate elements of traditional lifestyles modified for contemporary nutrition and activity patterns. However, behavior-based strategies are difficult to implement, maintain, and evaluate on a long-term basis. Nutrition education projects targeting persons with diabetes that recommend healthy diets based on local traditional foods or available substitutes (e.g., substituting store-bought fresh spinach for wild greens) for Pima (Boyce & Swinburn, 1993), Winnebago and Omaha (Stegmayer, Lovrien, Smith, Keller, & Gohdes, 1988), and Northern Ute (Tom-Orme, 1988) reported minimum or no short-term weight loss but improvement in self-care. Fitness programs that promote traditional activities have been enthusiastically embraced, and the Zuni community-based exercise program has received considerable public and media attention. The Zuni program combines traditional dance movements with aerobic exercise for less active or impaired older adults, and promotes other traditional activities, such as running for younger, active adults. On short-term evaluation, the fitness program was successful in decreasing weight, fasting blood sugar, and need for medications (Heath, Wilson, Smith, & Leonard, 1991). The difference in approaches between diet versus fitness and between individual-versus community-level interventions has not been assessed.

Culturally sensitive approaches in health education to reduce cancer risks have designed interventions for specific communities and trained lay health educators to deliver the program (Dignan et al., 1995). The Center for American Indian Research and Education in Berkeley, California, has developed two programs that use traditional storytelling in a Talking Circle format to discuss cervical cancer and nutrition and to empower women to take steps to promote good health and self-care. Media presentations using American Indian and Alaskan Native women as role models have been successful in promoting education about cervical cancer and the need for regular Pap screening (American Indian Health Care Association, 1993; Stillwater, Echavarria, & Lanier, 1995), as have media presentations targeting nonceremonial tobacco eradication (Hodge, 1990). Note that these methods engage traditional values of respect and authority for older role models and spokespersons, for oral transmission of knowledge, for nonintrusive guidance, and for the relationship of individuals to society.

The Burden of Chronic Disease on American Indian Societies and Future Approaches

The landmark study by the National Indian Council on Aging (1981) documented the dramatic difference in health and functional and social status of American Indian elders. By age 45 years, many people living on reservations (and at age 55 years for American Indians living in urban areas) were considered to be elders and were found to have the characteristics of other Americans aged 65 years. Gerontological researchers have accepted the American Indian and Alaskan Native definition of an "elder" as a person who has experienced a health or functional decline, fulfills a respected social role, or both, and these investigators have generally characterized subjects as 55+ years. Thus, chronic diseases and disability that are expressed in middle age also help define social personhood. Elders are honored and respected, providing cultural continuity through teaching, counseling, and example. The literature only incidentally mentions adaptive practices to compensate for disabilities, indicating that some elders remain more active than their non-Indian counterparts. Studies of American Indian elders have tended to focus on the process of aging rather than on the aged person.

The burden of chronic diseases, compromised health, and impaired functional status has a high economic cost for both health and human services. Congress has recently considered expanding Medicare coverage to include prevention of cancer and diabetes and its complications in order to avoid more costly treatments at advanced stages. In American Indian populations, in particular, the high prevalence of chronic disease indicates the need for prevention programs, as well as for health care allocations for management of chronic diseases over much of the adult life span. However, for the purposes of the IHS budget, mortality at age 65+ is not considered premature, so resources are not directed toward an aging American Indian population's needs (John, 1994).

The overall health status of American Indians challenges current policy that allocates resources on the basis of chronological age or minority status, rather than need. It appears that the burden of chronic disease falls disproportionately on American Indian populations and occurs at earlier ages than among other ethnic groups. The notion of "diversity in aging" can be refocused toward the variation in needs within and across population groups (Torres-Gil & Stanford, 1992; Wray, 1991). The diversity of needs for health and human services across American Indian and Alaskan Native societies and their variation in comparison to non-Indians exemplify this concept. The Older Americans Act, Title VI legislation recognizes the need to provide specialized aging services to middle-aged American Indian and Alaskan Native populations by allowing tribal contractors flexibility to serve elders who are younger than the 60-year age-eligibility criterion set by the Act for community-based long-term care services. In urban areas, this waiver does not apply, so in the County of Los Angeles, California (1989), where the median age for

American Indians elders was 58 years, community-based services were not planned for about half the elders living in the greater metropolitan area. In the absence of community-based senior services targeting this population, planners assume either that the need does not exist or that other resources would be tapped, such as families, other entitlement programs, or reverse migration to reservation communities.

The data reported in this chapter were derived from a variety of local and regional reports that generally exclude the majority of the American Indian population, which lives in urban areas. Future research efforts might systematically address the health conditions and utilization patterns of urban elders, as well as the more easily identified population living on reservations. Any national-level studies would need to develop methodological strategies for systematic oversampling of American Indian and Alaskan Native populations to compensate for past deficits, to account for the tremendous cultural variations and contemporary lifestyle differences, and to define the subject population (e.g., self-statement of ancestry, eligibility for federal or tribal benefits, or primary community of interaction). With the exception of ongoing studies among Pima, there is a lack of longitudinal and prospective studies on chronic disease. Future research might also develop a commitment for long-term evaluation of the many creative intervention demonstration projects that are generally funded with short-term grants. Additional research should also focus on adaptive practices and lived experience of chronic diseases within the sociocultural frameworks of American Indian societies to understand variation in risk factors, treatment preferences, and health care decision making. In summary, future biomedical, health services, and behavioral research foci should include: the identification of risk factors that account for the differences in health status between American Indians and non-Indians and among tribes; implementing and evaluating strategies to reduce risk; identification of cultural beliefs, practices, and preferences to develop appropriate intervention programs; documentation of the impact of chronic disease over the life course and the meaning of disease and disability in aging for these populations; and the initiation of policy measures and best practice models to better address the health and human service needs of this diverse population.

References

Alpert, J. S., Goldberg, R., Ockene, I. S., & Taylor, P. (1991). Heart disease in Native Americans. *Cardiology, 78,* 3-12.

American Indian Health Care Association. (1991). *Native American health promotion and disease prevention bibliography.* Saint Paul, MN: Author.

American Indian Health Care Association. (1993). Our voices. [Video]. (Available at $10 from American Indian Health Care Association, 1999 Broadway, Room 2530, Denver, CO).

The Arthritis Society. (n.d.). *The First Nations Arthritis Self-Management Program: Teacher's manual and reference materials, adapted for use in First Nations Communities.* Adapted from Kate Lorig, Arthritis Self-Management Program, NIH grant #AR20610. Distributed by the Arthritis Society (B.C. and Yukon Division), 895 W. 10th Ave., Vancouver BC, V57 117.

Barker, J. C., & Kramer, B. J. (1993, November). *Health risk assessment and cigarette use in older adults.* Paper presented at the meeting of the Gerontological Society of America, New Orleans.

Beasley, R. P., Wilkens, R. F., & Bennett, P. H. (1973). High prevalence of rheumatoid arthritis in Yakima Indians. *Arthritis and Rheumatism, 16,* 743-748.

Becker, T. M., Wheeler, C. M., McPherson, R. S., Parmenter, C. A., North, C. Q., & Miller, J. A. (1993). Risk factors for cervical dysplasia in southwestern American Indian women: A pilot study. *Alaska Medicine, 35,* 255-263.

Bennett, P. H., Burch, T. A., & Miller, M. (1971). Diabetes mellitus in American (Pima) Indians. *The Lancet, 2,* 125-128.

Bleed, D. M., Risser, D. R., Sperry, S., Hellhake, D., & Helgerson, S. D. (1992). Cancer incidence and survival among American Indians registered for Indian Health Service care in Montana, 1982-1987. *Journal of the National Cancer Institute, 84,* 1500-1505.

Boyce, V., & Swinburn, B. A. (1993). The traditional Pima diet. *Diabetes Care, 16*(Suppl. 1), 369-371.

Boyer, G. S., Templin, D. T., & Lanier, A. P. (1991). Rheumatic diseases in Alaskan Indians of the Southeast Coast: High prevalence of rheumatoid arthritis and systemic lupus erythematosus. *Journal of Rheumatology, 18,* 1477-1484.

Brosseau, J. (1993). Increasing prevalence of diabetes among the Three Affiliated Tribes. *Diabetes Care, 16*(Suppl. 1), 248-249.

Broussard, B. A., Valway, S. A., Kaufman, S., Beaver, S., & Gohdes, D. (1992). Clinical hypertension and its interaction with diabetes among American Indians and Alaskan Natives. *Diabetes Care, 16*(Suppl. 1), 292-296.

Burhansstipanov, L. (1993). National Cancer Institute's Native American cancer research projects. *Alaska Medicine, 35,* 248-254.

Burhansstipanov, L., & Dresser, C. M. (1993). *Native American Monograph No. 1: Documentation of the cancer research needs of American Indians and Alaskan Natives.* (National Cancer Institute. NIH Publication No. 93-3603). Washington, DC: Government Printing Office.

Calin, A., Bennett, P. H., Jupiter, J., & Terasaki, P. I. (1977). HLA B27 and sacroilitis in Pima Indians—Association in males only. *Journal of Rheumatology,* (Suppl.), 44-48.

Carter, J., Horowitz, R., Wilson, R., Sava, S., Sinnock, P., & Gohdes, D. (1989). Tribal differences in diabetes: Prevalence among American Indians in New Mexico. *Public Health Reports, 104,* 665-669.

Coulehan, J. (1992). Epidemiology of cardiovascular disease in American Indians: Research directions. In E. W. Haller & L. P. Aitken (Eds.), *Mashkiki: Old medicine nourishing the new* (pp. 31-37). New York: University Press of America.

County of Los Angeles. (1989). *The Urban American Indian Elders Outreach Project* (Final Report of Administration on Aging Demonstration Project 90 AMO273), J. Weibel-Orlando & B. J. Kramer, County of Los Angeles, Department of Community and Senior Citizens Services, Area Agency on Aging, Los Angeles.

Davidson, M., Bulkow, L. R., Lanier, A. P., Smith, R. A., Hawkins, I., Jensen, H., & Kiviat, N. B. (1994). Incidence of invasive cervical cancer preceded by negative screening in high-risk Alaska Native women. *International Journal of Epidemiology, 23,* 238-245.

Dawson, S. E. (1992). Navajo uranium workers and the effects of occupational illness: A case study. *Human Organization, 51,* 389-397.

DeJong, J. A. (1991, November). *Synopsis: Native American/Alaskan Native working group discussion: Visions of past, present and future.* Rockville, MD: U.S. Department of Health and Human Services, ADAMGHA, Office of Substance Abuse Programs.

Del Puente, A., Knowler, W. C., Pettit, D. J., & Bennett, P. H. (1989). High incidence and prevalence of rheumatoid arthritis in Pima Indians. *American Journal of Epidemiology, 129,* 1170-1178.

Deprez, R. D., Miller, E., & Hart, S. K. (1985). Hypertension prevalence among Penobscot Indians of Indian Island, Maine. *American Journal of Public Health, 75,* 653-654.

DeStefano, F., Coulehan, J. L., & Wiant, M. K. (1979). Blood pressure survey on the Navajo Indian reservation. *American Journal of Epidemiology, 209,* 335-345.

Dignan, M., Sharp, P., Blinson, K., Michielutte, R., Konen, J., Bell, R., & Lane, C. (1995). Development of a cervical cancer education program for Native American women in North Carolina. *Journal of Cancer Education, 9,* 235-242.

Fajans, S. S., & Nutting, P. (1993). Workshop report: Treating diabetes and its complications. *Diabetes Care, 16*(Suppl. 1), 378-379.

Frost, F., Taylor, V., & Fries, E. (1992). Racial misclassification of Native Americans in a surveillance, epidemiology, and end results cancer registry. *Journal of the National Cancer Institute, 84,* 957-962.

Frost, F., Tollestrup, K., Ross, A., Sabotta, E., & Kimball, E. (1994). Correctness of racial coding of American Indians and Alaskan Natives on the Washington state death certificate. *American Journal of Preventive Medicine, 10,* 290-194.

Gilbert, T. J., Sugarman, J. R., & Cobb, N. (1995). Abnormal Papanicolaou smears and colposcopic follow-up among American Indian and Alaska Native women in the Pacific Northwest. *Journal of the American Board of Family Practice, 8,* 183-188.

Gillum, R. F., Gillum, B. S., & Smith, N. (1984). Cardio-vascular risk factors among urban American Indians: Blood pressure, serum lipids, smoking, diabetes, health knowledge, and behavior. *American Heart Journal, 107,* 765-776.

Gohdes, D., & Bennett, P. H. (Eds.). (1993). Diabetes in Native Americans. *Diabetes Care, 16*(Suppl. 1).

Gohdes, D., Kaufman, S., & Valway, S. (1993). Diabetes in American Indians: An overview. *Diabetes Care, 16*(Suppl. 1), 239-243.

Grossman, D. C., Krieger, J. W., Sugarman, J. R., & Forquera, R. A. (1994). Health status of urban American Indians and Alaskan Natives: A population-based study. *Journal of the American Medical Association, 271,* 845-850.

Harvey, J., Lotze, M., & Stevens, M. B. (1981). Rheumatoid arthritis in a Chippewa band: I. Pilot screening of disease prevalence. *Arthritis and Rheumatism, 24,* 717-721.

Heath, G. W., Wilson, R. H., Smith, J., & Leonard, B. E. (1991). Community-based exercise and weight control: Diabetes risk reduction and glycemic control in Zuni Indians. *American Journal of Clinical Nutrition, 53,* 1642S-1646S.

Hendrie, H. C., Hall, K. S., Pillay, N., Rodgers, D., Prince, C., Norton, J., Brittain, H., Nath, A., Blue, A., Kaufert, J., Shelton, P., Postl, B., & Osuntokun, B. (1993). Alzheimer's disease is rare in Cree. *International Psychogeriatrics, 5,* 5-13.

Hodge, F. (1990). *It's your life* [Video]. (Available from the Center for American Indian Research and Education, 1918 University Ave., #2A, Berkeley, CA 94704)

Hodge, F. (1992). *It's your life—It's our future: Stop smoking guide* [Educational guidebook]. (Available from Center for American Indian Research and Education, 1918 University Avenue, #2A, Berkeley, CA 94704: American Indian Tobacco Control Project)

Howard, B. V., Welty, T. K., Fabsitz, R. R., Cowan, L. D., Oopik, A. J., Le, N., Yeh, J., Savage, P. J., & Lee, E. T. (1992). Risk factors for coronary heart disease in diabetic and non-diabetic Native Americans. *Diabetes, 41*(Suppl. 2), 4-11.

Hoy, W., Light, A., & Megill, D. (1994). Blood pressure in Navajo Indians and its association with type 2 diabetes and renal and cardiovascular disease. *American Journal of Hypertension, 7,* 321-328.

Hoy, W., Light, A., & Megill, D. (1995). Cardiovascular disease in Navajo Indians with type 2 diabetes. *Public Health Reports, 110,* 87-94.

Huttlinger, K., Krefting, L., Drevdahl, D., Tree, P., Baca, E., & Benally, A. (1992). Doing battle: A metaphorical analysis of diabetes mellitus among Navajo people. *The American Journal of Occupational Therapy, 46,* 706-712.

Indian Health Service. (1993). *Regional differences in Indian health.* Washington, DC: Government Printing Office.

Jacobsson, L. T. H., Hanson, R. L., Knowler, W. C., Pillemer, S., Pettitt, D. J., McCance, D. R., & Bennett, P. H. (1994). Decreasing incidence and prevalence of rheumatoid arthritis in Pima Indians over a twenty-five year period. *Arthritis and Rheumatism, 37,* 1158-1165.

Joe, J., Gallerito, C., & Pino, J. (1976). Cultural health traditions: American Indian perspectives. In M. F. Branch & P. P. Paxton (Eds.), *Providing safe nursing care for ethnic people of color* (pp. 81-98). New York: Appleton-Century-Crofts.

John, R. (1994). The state of research on American Indian elders' health, income security, and social support networks. In Gerontological Society of America (Ed.), *Minority elders: Five goals toward a public policy base* (2nd ed., pp. 46-58). Washington, DC: Gerontological Society of America.

Judkins, R. A. (1978). Diabetes and perception of diabetes. *New York State Journal of Medicine, 78,* 1320-1323.

Klain, M., Coulehan, J. L., Arena, V. C., & Janett, R. (1988). More frequent diagnosis of acute myocardial infarction among Navajo Indians. *American Journal of Public Health, 78,* 1351-1352.

Knowler, W. C., Bennett, P. H., Hamman, R. F., & Miller, M. (1978). Diabetes incidence and prevalence in Pima Indians: A 19-fold greater incidence than in Rochester, Minnesota. *American Journal of Epidemiology, 108,* 497-505.

Knowler, W. C., Saad, M. F., Petit, D. J., Nelson, R. G., & Bennett, P. H. (1993). Determinants of diabetes mellitus in the Pima Indians. *Diabetes Care, 16*(Suppl. 1), 216-227.

Kramer, B. J. (1992). Health and aging of urban American Indians. *Western Journal of Medicine, 157,* 281-285.

Kuller, L. H. (1993). Diabetes in American Indians: Reflections and future directions. *Diabetes Care, 16*(Suppl. 1), 380-383.

Kunitz, S. J., & Levy, J. E. (1986). The prevalence of hypertension among elderly Navajos: A test of the acculturative stress hypothesis. *Culture, Medicine & Psychiatry, 10,* 97-121.

Kunitz, S. J., & Levy, J. E. (1988). A prospective study of isolation and mortality in a cohort of elderly Navajo Indians. *Journal of Cross-Cultural Gerontology, 3,* 71-85.

Lando, H. A., Johnson, K. M., Graham-Tomasi, R. P., McGovern, P. G., & Solberg, L. (1992). Urban Indians' smoking patterns and interest in quitting. *Public Health Reports, 107,* 340-344.

Lang, G. C. (1989). Making sense about diabetes: Dakota narratives of illness. *Medical Anthropology, 11,* 305-327.

Lanier, A. P., Bulkow, L. R., & Ireland, B. (1989). Cancer in Alaskan Indians, Eskimos, and Aleuts, 1969-1983: Implications for etiology and control. *Public Health Reports, 104,* 658-664.

Lieb, L. E., Conway, G. A., Hedderman, M., Yao, J., & Kerndt, P. R. (1992). Racial misclassification of American Indians with AIDS in Los Angeles County. *Journal of Acquired Immune Deficiency Syndrome, 5,* 1137-1141.

Mahoney, M. C., & Michalek, A. M. (1991). A meta-analysis of cancer incidence in United States and Canadian native populations. *International Journal of Epidemiology, 20,* 323-327.

Mahoney, M. C., & Michalek, A. M. (1995). A bibliometric analysis of cancer among American Indians and Alaska Natives. *Alaska Medicine, 37*(2), 59-62, 77.

McMaster, P. L., & Connell, C. M. (1994). Health education interventions among Native Americans: A review and analysis. *Health Education Quarterly, 21,* 521-538.

Morton, R. O., Gershwin, M. E., Brady, C., & Steinberg, A. D. (1976). The incidence of systemic lupus erythematosus in North American Indians. *Journal of Rheumatology, 3,* 186-190.

Muneta, B., Newman, J., Stevenson, J., & Eggers, P. (1993). Diabetic end-stage renal disease among Native Americans. *Diabetes Care, 16*(Suppl. 1), 346-348.

National Indian Council on Aging. (1981). *American Indian elders: A demographic profile.* Albuquerque, NM: Author.

Neel, J. V. (1962). Diabetes mellitus: A "thrifty" genotype rendered detrimental by progress. *American Journal of Human Genetics, 14,* 353-362.

Neel, J. V. (1982). The thrifty genotype revisited. In J. Kobberling & R. Tattersall (Eds.), *The genetics of diabetes mellitus* (Serono Symposium No. 47). New York: Academic Press.

Nelson, R. G., Gohdes, D. M., Everhart, J. E., Hartner, J. A., Zwemer, F. L., Pettitt, D. J., & Knowler, W. C. (1988). Lower-extremity amputations in NIDDM—12 yr follow-up study in Pima Indians. *Diabetes Care, 11,* 8-16.

Nelson, R. G., Newman, J. M., Knowler, W. C., Sievers, M. L., Kunzelman, C. L., Pettit, D. J., Moffett, C. D., Teutsch, S. M., & Bennett, P. H. (1988). Incidence of end stage renal disease in type 2 (non-insulin dependent) diabetes mellitus in Pima Indians. *Diabetologia, 31,* 730-736.

Nutting, P. A., Calonge, B. N., Iverson, D. C., & Green, L. A. (1994). The danger of applying uniform clinical policies across populations: The case of breast cancer in American Indians. *American Journal of Public Health, 84,* 1631-1636.

Nutting, P. A., Freeman, W. L., Risser, D. R., Helgerson, S. D., Paisano, R., Hisnanick, J., Beaver, S. K., Peters, I., Carney, J. P., & Speers, M. A. (1993). Cancer incidence among American Indians and Alaska Natives, 1980 through 1987. *American Journal of Public Health, 83,* 1589-1598.

Powers, W., & Powers, M. (1984). Metaphysical aspects of an Oglala food system. In M. Douglas (Ed.), *Food in the social order: Studies of food and festivities in three American communities* (pp. 40-96). New York: Russell Sage.

Primeaux, M., & Henderson, G. (1981). American Indian patient care. In G. Henderson & M. Primeaux (Eds.), *Transcultural health care* (pp. 239-354). Menlo Park, CA: Addison-Wesley.

Ravussin, E. (1993). Energy metabolism on obesity: Studies in Pima Indians. *Diabetes Care, 16*(Suppl. 1), 232-238.

Roscoe, R. J., Deddens, J. A., Salvan, A., & Schnorr, T. M. (1995). Mortality among Navajo uranium miners. *American Journal of Public Health, 85,* 535-540.

Rothschild, B. M., Turner, K. R., & DeLuca, M. A. (1988). Symmetrical erosive peripheral polyarthritis in the late archaic period of Alabama. *Science, 241,* 1498-1501.

Rothschild, B. M., & Woods, R. J. (1990). Symmetrical erosive disease in archaic Indians: The origin of rheumatoid arthritis in the New World? *Seminars in Arthritis and Rheumatism, 19,* 278-284.

Schraer, C. D., Bulkow, L. R., Murphy, N. J., & Lanier, A. P. (1993). Diabetes prevalence, increase and complications among Alaska Natives 1987. *Diabetes Care, 16*(Suppl. 1), 257-259.

Schraer, C. D., Lanier, A. P., Boyko, E. J., Gohdes, D., & Murphy, N. J. (1988). Prevalence of diabetes mellitus in Alaskan Eskimos, Indians, and Aleuts. *Diabetes Care, 11,* 693-700.

Sharlin, K. S., Heath, G. W., Ford, E. S., & Welty, T. K. (1993). Hypertension and blood pressure awareness among American Indians of the Northern Plains. *Ethnicity and Disease 3,* 337-343.

Sievers, M. L. (1977). Historical overview of hypertension among American Indians and Alaskan Natives. *Arizona Medicine, 34,* 609-610.

Sprafka, J. M. (1992). The impact of lifestyle on cardiovascular disease in American Indians. In E. W. Haller & L. P. Aitken (Eds.), *Mashkiki: Old medicine nourishing the new* (pp. 38-50). New York: University Press of America.

Stegmayer, P., Lovrien, F. C., Smith, M., Keller, T., & Gohdes, D. M. (1988). Designing a diabetes nutrition education program for a native American community. *Diabetes Education, 14,* 64-66.

Stenger, P. (1996). *The Indian Health Care Service Elder Health Care Initiative.* Washington, DC: Public Health Service, Indian Health Service.

Stillwater, B., Echavarria, V. A., & Lanier, A. P. (1995). Pilot test of a cervical cancer prevention video developed for Alaska Native women. *Public Health Reports, 110,* 211-214.

Sugarman, J., Dennis, L. K., & White, E. (1994). Cancer survival among American Indians in western Washington state (United States). *Cancer Causes & Control, 5,* 440-448.

Sugarman, J., & Lawson, L. (1993). The effect of racial misclassification on estimates of end-stage renal disease among American Indians and Alaskan Natives in the Pacific Northwest. *American Journal of Ethnicity and Disease, 2,* 383-386.

Sugarman, J., Soderberg, R., Gordon, J. E., & Rivara, F. P. (1993). Racial misclassification of American Indians: Its effect on the injury rates in Oregon, 1989 through 1990. *American Journal of Public Health, 83,* 681-684.

Templin, D. W., Boyer, G. S., Lanier, A. P., Nelson, J. L., Barrington, R. A., Hansen, J. A., Harpster, A., & Carlsen, R. (1994). Rheumatoid arthritis in Tlingit Indians: Clinical characterization and HLA associations. *Journal of Rheumatology, 21,* 1238-1244.

Tom-Orme, L. (1988). Chronic disease and the social matrix: A Native American diabetes intervention. *Recent Advances in Nursing, 22,* 89-109.

Torres-Gil, F., & Stanford, E. P. (1992). *Diversity: New approaches to ethnic minority aging.* Amityville, NY: Baywood.

U.S. Department of Commerce, U.S. Bureau of the Census. (1990). *General population characteristics CP-1-1a.* Washington DC: Government Printing Office.

U.S. Department of Commerce, U.S. Bureau of the Census. (1993). *Social and economic characteristics* (Table 59, CP-2-1). Washington DC: Government Printing Office.

Valway, S. E., Linkins, R. W., & Gohdes, D. M. (1993). Epidemiology of lower-extremity amputations in the Indian Health Service, 1982-1987. *Diabetes Care, 16*(Suppl. 1), 349-353.

Weiner, D. (1993). Health beliefs about cancer among the Luiseño Indians of California. *Alaska Medicine, 34,* 285-296.

Welty, T. K., Zephier, N., Schweigman, K., Blake, B., & Leonardson, G. (1993). Cancer risk factors in three Sioux tribes: Use of the Indian-specific health risk appraisal for data collection and analysis. *Alaska Medicine, 35,* 265-272.

Wiedman, D. W. (1987). Type II diabetes mellitus, technological development and the Oklahoma Cherokee. In H. A. Baer (Ed.), *Encounters with biomedicine: Case studies in medical anthropology* (pp. 43-71). New York: Gordon & Breach Science Publishers.

Wilson, R., & Horton, E. (1993). Workshop report: Prevention and early treatment of NIDDM. *Diabetes Care, 16*(Suppl. 1), 376-377.

Wray, L. A. (1991). Public policy implications of an ethnically diverse elderly population. *Journal of Cross-Cultural Gerontology, 6,* 243-257.

PART III

Diet and Nutrition

Aging, Diet, and Nutrition in African Americans

Shiriki K. Kumanyika

Good nutrition is critical to successful aging (American Dietetic Association [ADA], 1996; Fischer & Johnson, 1990; Posner, Jette, Smith, & Miller, 1993). A high percentage of survivors ages 65 years and older report having at least one diet- or weight-related chronic condition (e.g., nearly 50% have arthritis, 36% have hypertension, 33% have heart disease, 11% have had a stroke, and 9% have diabetes) and many have several such conditions. From 5% to 8% of older adults may require assistance with one or more activities of daily living or personal care (Treas, 1995). These health problems may be caused or aggravated by dietary factors and can be ameliorated by nutrition intervention. However, constraints on the types of foods allowed on modified diets may disrupt established eating patterns or interfere with quality of life.

Consequences of chronic disease, such as loss of income, loss of independence, loss of social interaction due to physical disabilities or dementia, dental problems, loss of appetite, food intolerances, or other nutrition-related side effects of drug treatments or chemotherapy (Posner et al., 1993) may cause malnutrition. Manifestations of malnutrition may include impaired immune function, poor wound healing, and involuntary weight loss (Fischer & Johnson, 1990). Social circumstances, such as living alone or having an inadequate social network, may limit food access, particularly for older persons who are frail or have limited mobility. Loneliness, if present, may limit the desire to eat or the motivation to prepare meals.

EDITOR'S NOTE: The terms *white* and *black* are used in lower-case, following the author's preference.

Poverty continues to be the major determinant of food insufficiency in U.S. communities in spite of the existence of programs intended to address this problem (Life Sciences Research Office [LSRO], 1995). Even among older adults who are not poor, having fixed incomes may limit the ability to purchase food. Poverty predisposes to both chronic diseases and to malnutrition (LSRO, 1995).

Diet and nutrition issues for aging African Americans are exaggerated by the disproportionate prevalence of poverty (Treas, 1995) and of diet-related conditions such as hypertension, diabetes, stroke, obesity, knee osteoarthritis, end-stage renal disease, and functional impairments (Kumanyika, 1993a; Miles & Bernard, 1992; National Center for Health Statistics, 1995). Black-to-white mortality ratios for diet-related conditions such as heart disease, cancer, and diabetes are 1.3, 1.4, and 2.4, respectively (O'Hare, Pollard, Mann, & Kent, 1991). At ages 65 and over, the median income of African Americans (about $12,000) is lower than for whites by about $6,500 and lower by more than $1,000 than for Hispanic Americans (Treas, 1995). Median wealth of older African Americans, taking into account overall assets (rather than only current income), is only one quarter of that of white Americans (O'Hare et al., 1991).

This chapter reviews concepts and evidence related to dietary and nutritional problems among older African Americans and to the potential for ameliorating these problems through nutrition interventions. Of particular interest is whether the disadvantageous health status of older African Americans reflects customary African American eating patterns and, if so, how this can be remedied.

African American Eating and Physical Activity Patterns

Historical Influences and Trends

Eating patterns of African Americans derive from the combined historical influences of West Africa, slavery, and U.S. southern cuisines (Kittler & Sucher, 1989; Sanjur, 1982). A highly valued Sunday dinner menu in the post-slavery era has, thus, been described as: "Southern fried chicken, baked ham, stewed beef, steamed rice, baked macaroni and cheese, candied sweet potatoes, fresh string beans, green peas, garden butter beans, potato salad, sliced tomatoes, hot rolls, light bread, sweet potato pie, fried pies, and pound cake," all offered at the same meal (Sanjur, 1982). Other typical southern Black foods in African American diets included lima beans, rice, collard greens, ham hocks, stewed neck bones, gumbo, black-eyed peas, and cornbread. Pork and chicken, dark green leafy vegetables, and hominy grits are considered highly popular in traditional African American diets, while dislike for some milk products, possibly related to lactose intolerance, has been noted in some studies of African Americans (Kittler & Sucher, 1989). Frying and boiling are the most common food preparation methods in traditional African American cooking. Onions, green peppers, hot peppers, and various spices are commonly used to flavor foods.

Themes evident in descriptions of foods traditionally consumed by slaves have both positive and negative nutritional implications. One theme is that slaves were very resourceful in developing wholesome combinations of economical plant foods that could be prepared with minimal effort, for example, cooked slowly together in one pot over a long period while they were working in the fields (Kittler & Sucher, 1989). This aspect of African American food patterns is reflected in high consumption of soups and stews based on dried beans and peas, and various types of dark leafy greens (collards, turnips, mustards). Such eating patterns could be favorable to consumption of protective nutrients such as dietary fiber and antioxidants (carotenoids); however, long cooking times decrease dietary fiber and destroy certain vitamins. The practice of drinking or using in other dishes the "pot likker" left from cooking vegetables is nutritionally positive; this "recycles" heat stable nutrients that leach from vegetables into cooking water.

Many of the animal foods available to slaves were waste foods—foods of low or lesser nutritional value (e.g., ears, intestine, stomach, neck bones from pigs; organ meats such as heart, gizzard, and liver) than those consumed by plantation owners. These foods were used creatively by slaves to make filling and good-tasting dishes, and became part of an African American eating tradition that persisted long after more nutritious foods were available and affordable (Kittler & Sucher, 1989). Jerome (1982) noted that having a certain dish taste "right" is of central importance in African American eating traditions. Along with habits of eating heavy meals, eating large ceremonial meals on Sundays, and offering dual or triple selections within a food category, a strong preference for foods with high palatability would have an obvious potential for fostering overeating. This would be problematic under the current circumstances where levels of obligatory physical activity (agricultural

and domestic manual labor) have decreased and the food supply is more secure.

The survival value of cultural food patterns depends on the societal
context. Diets high in carbohydrates and plant sources of protein, supple-
mented minimally by fat and protein from animal products, are adaptive in
less industrialized societies where obligatory physical activity levels are high.
Food availability also fluctuates under such circumstances, and infectious
diseases are major determinants of mortality (Trowell & Burkitt, 1981). Protective elements of these dietary habits for the development of chronic diseases may be retained during initial stages of economic advancement, indus-
trialization, or urbanization. However, behavioral priming to "fill up" when
food is available, to value fat for its extra caloric and satiety value, and to
view previously inaccessible or unaffordable foods (e.g., meat, packaged
foods, or pastries) as rewards of an improved standard of living predispose to
overconsumption. Furthermore, as dietary composition changes to include
more meat and processed or pre-prepared foods, the traditional vegetable or
bean dishes flavored with salt-cured, fatty cuts of meat or the traditional
breads prepared and consumed with salt and fat or gravy become sources of
excess salt and fat.

Many more African Americans are employed in administrative and
managerial positions than in the past (O'Hare et al., 1991). In addition, the
price of the improved productivity that raises the standard of living is mecha-
nization of even the most menial jobs; less physical work is required, even
among the high proportion of African Americans with unskilled jobs. Auto-
mobiles and television have further increased the prevalence of physical in-
activity. In an analysis based on trends in England, James (1995) estimated
that energy expenditure has decreased by as much as 800 kilocalories (kcal)
per day. James (1995) notes that such reduced physical activity coupled with
the above-described types of changes in food patterns lead to obesity, even
though overall food consumption decreases, and eventually to the other diet-
related "diseases of Western societies" (Trowell & Burkitt, 1981). Conservative estimates now place dietary factors and sedentary activity patterns second only to tobacco among environmental or "lifestyle" exposures
contributing to U.S. deaths (McGinnis & Foege, 1993).

Popkin, Siega-Riz, and Haines (1996) have reported data confirming
that African Americans are falling behind the mainstream in progressing toward more healthful dietary patterns, based on national food consumption
survey data collected between 1965 and 1989-1991. They scored diets re-

ported by low- and high-socioeconomic status blacks and whites according to a composite of current dietary recommendations for consumption of fat, saturated fat, cholesterol, fruits and vegetables, carbohydrate, protein, and calcium. Looking back through this lens at diets in the mid-1960s, low-income-African Americans then had the healthiest diets: 16% of African Americans had diets meeting most current recommendations, compared to only 9% of low-income whites and 5% of high-income whites. In contrast, in the 1989-1991 period, the percentage of low-income African Americans whose diets met most recommendations had increased only modestly, to 24%, whereas the percentage among low- and high-income whites increased much more dramatically—to about 20% in both cases. Among a small number of higher-income African Americans for whom 1989-1991 data were available, only 3% now had diets meeting most recommendations. These findings may reflect a pattern in which relatively more African Americans and low-income persons are still aspiring to eating patterns associated with upward mobility, but which are now shunned by health conscious affluent whites (Kumanyika, 1996).

Food Consumption

Food consumption patterns of African Americans and whites ages 20 years and older were reported from the Continuing Survey of Food Intakes of Individuals (CSFII), conducted by the U.S. Department of Agriculture between 1989 and 1991 (LSRO, 1995). As observed previously (Jerome, 1988; Kittler & Sucher, 1989), African Americans and whites are accessing the same food sources and are consuming diets that are similar in many respects. For example, African Americans were equally likely to report consuming the most commonly used forms of grain products: yeast breads, rolls, cereals, and pasta. However, surveys also continue to show differences between food choices of African Americans and whites, often reflecting cultural practices. According to the CSFII data (LSRO, 1995), African Americans were less likely to consume grain-based desserts or snacks or mixtures (including pizza, spaghetti, noodles, rice and pasta mixtures, and quiche). More African Americans than whites report consumption of dark green vegetables and green beans, and fewer consume deep yellow vegetables, tomatoes, lettuce, and other vegetables. Overall fruit consumption is lower among African Americans. Beef, fish, and shellfish consumption are lower and pork and poultry consumption higher among African Americans than whites. Marked ethnic differences in dairy product consumption are also observed: African Americans consume fewer dairy products than whites except for whole milk, which African Americans consume more frequently. More African Americans than whites consume eggs and fewer report consumption of foods classified as legumes, nuts and seeds, or fats, oils, and sweets.

Beverage Consumption

CSFII data on consumption of nonalcoholic and alcoholic beverages indicate that African Americans are less likely to consume coffee and more likely to consume regular versus diet forms of fruit or soft drinks (LSRO, 1995). Higher drinking water consumption (tap water and spring water) among African Americans than whites at most ages and particularly among males was noted in the 1988-1991 National Health and Nutrition Examination Survey (NHANES III) data (LSRO, 1995). The proportion of African Americans who consume alcohol is lower than in whites (LSRO, 1995). Among females, wine and hard liquor consumption are lower among African Americans. Among men, African Americans are substantially less likely than whites to report consuming wine, but the percentages reporting beer and liquor consumption are relatively similar.

Food Sufficiency and Meals Away From Home

Among low-income persons (defined as households with gross incomes less than 131% of the Federal Poverty Income Guideline), black respondents in the CSFII were less likely than whites to report not having "enough of the kinds of foods we want to eat" (44% vs. 58%, respectively) and more likely to report having "enough but not always what we want" (43% vs. 34%, respectively) (LSRO, 1995). CSFII data also suggest that African Americans are less likely than whites to eat away from home. This latter finding may reflect both income and historical-cultural factors (discrimination and responses to discrimination) leading to a preference for eating in private, familiar surroundings (Airhihenbuwa et al., 1996).

In summary, diet-related health profiles of African Americans reflect an evolution from relatively protected to relatively disadvantaged with respect to chronic disease. Conditions for which African Americans had lower incidence or mortality than whites several decades ago are now equally or more common in African Americans (Kumanyika & Golden, 1991; Liao & Cooper,

1995). Once-protective aspects of traditional eating practices have been transformed into harmful aspects, due to societal changes. Although current eating patterns and food-related attitudes in the African American population are similar to those of white Americans, they retain some distinctive features suggestive of longstanding traditions and culturally influenced beliefs and practices dating back to slavery and post-slavery periods.

Eating Patterns, Weight, and Physical Activity Among Older African Americans

General Findings

National surveys and smaller-scale studies reviewed by Jerome (1988) suggested that older African Americans and whites have comparable dietary patterns, although with some noteworthy differences in the types of foods consumed and with more evidence of nutritional deficiencies among African Americans. Low intakes of calories and several nutrients among older African Americans may be attributable to the higher frequency of meal skipping, primarily breakfast or lunch, reported by older African Americans (Jerome, 1988). The Cardiovascular Health Study (CHS) also reported a higher frequency of meal skipping among the African American men and women in their population-based cohort of adults ages 65 and over (Kumanyika, Tell, Shemanski, Polak, & Savage, 1994). Only 48% of African Americans versus 74% of whites in the CHS reported consuming three meals per day. More breakfast skipping was also reported by older African American respondents in the 1990 National Health Intervention Survey (Piani & Schoenborn, 1993).

One would expect a high proportion of older African Americans to have changed their diets for management of one or more chronic diseases. Jerome (1988) reported qualitative data to this effect: At a 10-year follow-up, many of the older African Americans interviewed in a qualitative study in the Midwest had modified their diets. Changes made included reducing consumption of pork, wild game, alcohol, salt, sugar, fat, and citrus beverages and increasing use of special dietary foods. Food preparation methods were also changed, for example, less frying. In the CHS cohort (Kumanyika et al., 1994), approximately 25% of men and women were following special diets, of which about half were medically prescribed. However, in spite of a higher prevalence of cardiovascular diseases in the African Americans in the CHS cohort (Manolio et al., 1995), there was no difference in the proportion following medically prescribed diets by race. In fact, eating patterns (determined from food frequency scores) of the African American participants in the CHS were generally less healthful than those of white participants: higher consumption of meat, eggs, bacon, sausage, and fried foods (both overall and in fast food restaurants), and lower consumption of high-fiber cereals and fruits (Kumanyika et al., 1994). Higher fat dietary practices such as eating the fat on meat and skin on chicken were about 3 times more prevalent among the African American than white CHS participants.

Low Nutrient Intakes

The definition of dietary adequacy has evolved to include increasing dimensions of eating patterns (LSRO, 1995). As indicated in Table 9.1, some vitamins and minerals are now thought to have more roles in preventing disease and protecting health than was previously recognized. Traditional thresholds for nutrient adequacy, that is, the Recommended Dietary Allowances (RDAs), which are based on guidelines for preventing classical nutrient deficiency diseases, do not necessarily define intakes that are optimal for protection from cardiovascular diseases or cancer. Supplementary intakes of antioxidant vitamins such as ascorbic acid (vitamin C), β-carotene (a vitamin A precursor), or α-tocopherol (vitamin E) above RDA levels may be considered beneficial (LSRO, 1995).

Similar to the impression from Jerome's (1988) review, which was based on NHANES data from the 1970s, the NHANES III data (1988-1991) indicate low nutrient intakes among older African Americans compared both to younger African Americans and to older white Americans (LSRO, 1995). Table 9.2 shows several nutrients for which median intakes for African American men or women are at or below two thirds of the RDAs: energy; vitamins A, E, and B_6; calcium, magnesium, iron, and zinc. Zinc intake appears to be low among women in general. With the exception of vitamin A, median intakes among older African Americans were relatively lower than those of 20- to 59-year-old African Americans of the same sex. These low median intakes are of great concern, even taking into account the imprecision of dietary intake data and the margin of safety that is built into the RDAs. The contribution of poverty to the prevalence of low vitamin and mineral in-

TABLE 9.1 Nutrition and Health Issues in Aging

Dietary or Nutritional Status Variable	Associated Health Risks or Outcomes
Inadequate access to food or food intake (e.g. secondary to poverty, social circumstances, functional disability, depression, cognitive impairment, appetite, or dentition problems)	Malnutrition, involuntary weight loss, poor recovery from illness, failure-to-thrive
Excess energy intake and low level of physical activity	Obesity and obesity-related conditions
Obesity	Diabetes, hypertension, heart disease, dyslipidemias, gallbladder disease, knee osteoarthritis, sleep apnea, endometrial cancer, other cancers, mobility limitations
High fat diet	Atherosclerosis, heart disease, cancer
High sodium intake and possibly suboptimal intakes of potassium and magnesium	Hypertension
Suboptimal intakes of antioxidant nutrients such as vitamin C (ascorbic acid), vitamin E (α-tocopherol) or β-carotene	Possible lack of protection from certain types of cancer and cardiovascular disease and from ophthalmic problems such as cataracts and macular degeneration
Suboptimal intakes of calcium and vitamin D (either ingested vitamin D or vitamin D synthesis in skin through sunlight exposure)	Poor bone health and related increased risk of fracture
Suboptimal intake of vitamins B_6, B_{12}, and folic acid	High blood levels of homocysteine and related risks of cardiovascular disease
Inadequate fluid intake	Dehydration
Adherence to modified diets (e.g., low-sodium, low-protein, low-fat, or other diets prescribed in medical nutrition therapy)	Aggravation of diet-related chronic disease processes

SOURCES: Alpers, Clouse, & Stenson (1988); American Dietetic Association (1996); National Research Council (1989).

takes among older African Americans could not be determined from the data available.

Vitamin and mineral intake by older African Americans is less likely to be augmented by the use of vitamin and mineral supplements; supplement

TABLE 9.2 Evidence of Dietary Inadequacies Among African American Men and Women Ages 60 Years and Older, With Comparison Data for Older Whites and for Younger (Ages 20-59) African Americans

	Males			Females		
	African Americans 20-59 Years	African Americans 60+ Years[a]	Non-Hispanic White Americans 60+ Years[a]	African Americans 20-59 Years	African Americans 60+ Years[a]	Non-Hispanic White Americans 60+ Years[a]
Median daily nutrient intakes as percentage of 1989 recommended values, 1988-1991[b]						
Kilocalories	84	67	81	78	71	75
Vitamin A	53	55	91	52	63	104
Vitamin E	75	51	70	75	57	74
Vitamin B$_6$	89	65	89	74	73	88
Calcium	74	62	90	62	50	77
Magnesium	74	58	83	66	67	83
Zinc	75	57	72	65	55	62

SOURCE: Life Sciences Research Office (1995; Third Nutrition Monitoring Report, table 6-21).
NOTE: a. Recommendations for adults ages 51 years and older were used as the standard for this age group.
b. Recommended values based on 1989 Recommended Dietary Allowances.

use is lower among African Americans than whites at all ages (Figure 9.1). However, this does not necessarily mean that supplement use by African Americans should be increased. Current dietary guidance strongly favors reliance on foods to provide essential nutrients, because supplements may be lacking in other protective elements that occur in foods (U.S. Department of Agriculture [USDA], 1995).

The health consequences of suboptimal calcium intakes among African Americans are not well understood. Adequate calcium intakes in young adulthood favor the development of a peak bone mass that minimizes later risk of developing osteoporotic fractures secondary to bone losses. However, in spite of having calcium intakes substantially lower than recommended, African American men and women have heavier and denser bones and are less likely to develop fractures (LSRO, 1995). This more favorable bone status of African Americans was confirmed by bone mass measurements collected in NHANES III (Looker et al., 1995). The prevalence of osteoporosis (defined by World Health Organization criteria: bone mineral density more than 2.5 *SD* below that for 20- to 29-year-old white females) among women 50 years

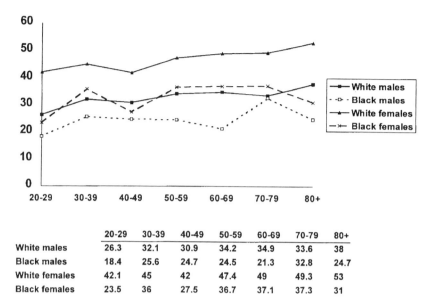

	20-29	30-39	40-49	50-59	60-69	70-79	80+
White males	26.3	32.1	30.9	34.2	34.9	33.6	38
Black males	18.4	25.6	24.7	24.5	21.3	32.8	24.7
White females	42.1	45	42	47.4	49	49.3	53
Black females	23.5	36	27.5	36.7	37.1	37.3	31

Figure 9.1. Percentage Reporting Use of Vitamin and/or Mineral Supplements in the Past Month, 1988-1991
SOURCE: Life Sciences Research Office (1995).

and older was 10% in African American women versus 21% in white women. Osteopenia (bone mineral density between 1 and 2.5 *SD* below reference levels) occurred in 29% of African American and 39% of white females ages 50 and over. Some of this advantageous bone status may reflect certain bone-protective aspects of being overweight, but there are other contributing factors that are still being identified. For example, bone status is affected by vitamin D status and metabolism, and vitamin D status is affected by sunlight exposure and skin pigmentation.

Dietary Composition

A diet that has no more than 30% of total kilocalories from fat, 8% to 10% of total kilocalories as saturated fat, at least 55% of kilocalories from carbohydrate sources (which limits protein kilocalories to about 15%), and less than 300 mg/day of cholesterol is recommended (LSRO, 1995; USDA, 1995). Fiber recommendations are not quantified in the U.S. Dietary Guidelines, but the National Cancer Institute has recommended consuming 20 to 30 grams of

TABLE 9.3 Median Intakes of Fat, Saturated Fat, Carbohydrate, Cholesterol, and Fiber Among African American and White Adults Ages 60 and Older, by Sex

	Males		Females	
Dietary Component	*African American*	*White*	*African American*	*White*
Total fat (% kcal)	33.6	33.8	32.8	32.5
Saturated fatty acids (% kcal)	11.0	11.1	10.2	10.6
Carbohydrate (% kcal)	47.8	49.3	51.9	52.3
Cholesterol (mg)	258	221	164	158
Dietary fiber (g)	10.8	15.0	11.0	12.8

SOURCE: Life Sciences Research Office (1995; Third Nutrition Monitoring Report, Vol. 1, table 6-18).

fiber per day (LSRO, 1995). Recommendations to increase consumption of grains, cereals, fruits, and vegetables are intended, in part, to improve the fiber composition of the diet. These recommendations are intended to reduce risks of developing cardiovascular diseases and cancer. They also coincide with diet therapy recommendations for management of cardiovascular disease and diabetes and are, therefore, highly relevant to many older African Americans.

Although many aspects of African American food patterns and food preparation would appear to predispose to a diet that is higher, on average, in fat and saturated fat, this is not reflected in either dietary or serum lipid data. Serum lipid profiles of African Americans tend to be similar to or somewhat more favorable than those of white persons of the same sex and age (LSRO, 1995). Total cholesterol levels are similar across race, and levels of protective high density lipoprotein (HDL) cholesterol are often found to be higher in African Americans than whites. The fat, saturated fat, carbohydrate, and protein content of the diets of African Americans and whites is rather similar. Relevant data for persons 60 years and older are shown in Table 9.3. Median intakes fall short of guidelines (are too high or too low) for both African American and white men and women. Median cholesterol intakes are higher for older African Americans than whites, but are within the recommendation of less than 300 mg per day. Fiber intakes are generally lower than recommended and are lower in African Americans than in whites in both sexes, but especially in males. The 1976-1980 NHANES II data indicate that the foods that provide dietary fiber (and, therefore, the type of dietary fiber) are different for African Americans and whites (Block & Lanza, 1987).

Differences in Dietary Composition by Age and Education

The National Heart Lung and Blood Institute (NHLBI) (1995) has tabulated NHANES III dietary data for U.S. adults by age, sex, race/ethnicity, and socioeconomic indicators. The utility of these data is limited by the small sample sizes for African American respondents ages 65 and older (e.g., estimates for those with ≥ 12 years of education have 40 respondents or less), but the overall picture provided by these data is still somewhat informative with respect to possible similarities or differences in dietary status among African Americans in different demographic groups.

According to the NHLBI (1995) analysis, total energy intake decreases across age. This decrease may be warranted if energy output declines with reductions in physical activity, but it also predisposes to consumption of an insufficient quantity of food. Low overall food intake can make it impossible to take in sufficient quantities of micronutrients. An association of higher education with higher energy intakes is evident in middle age (45 to 64) and among older men, suggesting that those with low socioeconomic status (SES) are most likely to have insufficient overall food intake. The percentage of fat calories in the diet shows little variation across age for men but among women appears to be better, that is, slightly lower, for those in the oldest age group. The breakdown by education suggests a U-shaped association of fat intake and education in some age groups such that those with the least and most education consume a higher fat diet than those in the middle. The same pattern is seen for saturated fat and for cholesterol. The types of high-fat foods consumed by low- versus high-income African Americans may differ. For example, higher fat intake among the best educated segment of the African American population might reflect consumption of high-fat "status foods," such as steaks or high-fat desserts. Higher fat intake among those in the lowest SES stratum might be related to a general lack of knowledge of fat sources, a lack of awareness of the need to reduce dietary fat, lack of available or affordable alternatives (e.g., low-fat dairy products or convenience foods) or a disproportionate incidental access to high-fat foods (e.g., store brands of packaged products; fast food restaurants). Among those with higher SES, other knowledge or motivational factors might be at work.

Intake of energy from carbohydrates is the mirror image of energy from fat, especially in those 65 and older. Protein intake increases with education in men between 25 and 64 years of age, but appears to decrease with increasing education in men and women ages 65 and older. Fiber intakes of older African Americans are as high as those of adults ages 25 to 44 among women

and, among men, are almost as high except among those with less than a high
school education. Education seems to have a favorable association with fiber
intake in older African Americans.

Dietary Sodium and Potassium

High intakes of dietary sodium are implicated in the development of hypertension, and sodium reduction is recommended as first-line and continuing
adjunctive therapy in hypertension management (National High Blood Pressure Education Program, 1993). The prevalence of hypertension is very high
in the U.S. population and is higher in African Americans than whites in all
adult age groups. At ages 50 years and older, up to 60% of white males and
74% of white females have hypertension (defined as elevated blood pressure
or taking drugs prescribed to lower blood pressure), versus 78% and 81%,
respectively, among African Americans (LSRO, 1995). NHANES III dietary
data, which do not include discretionary salt use, suggest that dietary sodium
intake is similar in African Americans and whites in the 20- to 59-year age
range, and lower in African Americans above age 60 (Table 9.4). The median
level estimated for African Americans from the dietary data is actually below
the recommended 2,400 mg upper limit but would exceed the limit if an allowance, such as an additional 15% (Mattes & Donnelly, 1991), were made
for discretionary salt. Lower salt intake in the older age group may be a valid
finding, reflecting the higher prevalence hypertension-related advice to reduce sodium intake.

Potassium intakes of African Americans are lower than in whites in
both age groups (Table 9.4), which is noteworthy given that a high dietary
sodium-to-potassium ratio may contribute to hypertension. The lower sodium
intake of older African Americans results in a sodium-to-potassium ratio
more favorable than that for younger African Americans; again, however,
whether the discretionary salt additions in older African Americans negate
this apparent advantage is unknown.

Overweight and Physical Activity

In order of public health and clinical priorities, obesity is the nutrition problem of the greatest urgency for aging African Americans. Obesity refers specifically to excess body fat; however, the terms *overweight* and *obesity* are
often used interchangeably when describing prevalence, because weight

TABLE 9.4 Median Daily Sodium and Potassium Intake of U.S. Adults, 1988-1991

	Males		Females	
	White	*Black*	*White*	*Black*
Sodium (median daily intake in mg)				
20-59 years	3,863	3,619	2,650	2,675
60+ years	3,083	2,355	2,315	1,988
Potassium (median daily intake in mg)				
20-59 years	3,208	2,507	2,305	1,822
60+ years	2,801	2,039	2,344	1,809

SOURCE: Life Sciences Research Office (1995; Third Report on Nutrition Monitoring in the United States).
NOTE: Sodium intake data do not include discretionary additions of salt.

rather than fatness is what is usually measured, and because most excess weight in adults is excess fat, especially among women. By the typical definitions—body mass index (BMI) greater than or equal to 27.3 kg/m^2 (BMI = weight divided by the square of height in meters) for men and more than or equal to 27.8 kg/m^2 for women—approximately a third of African American men and 50% to 60% of African American women between the ages of 50 and 79 years are at least moderately overweight (Figure 9.2). African American women are from 1.5 to more than 2 times as likely as African American men to be overweight at ages 30 and above. At ages 70 and above, a third to a half of African American women are above a weight considered moderately overweight. Our understanding of the health significance of being overweight in the oldest age groups is limited, however.

The prevalence of overweight in the U.S. population has increased since the 1960s. Trends differ by age cohort (i.e., by generation) and sex, as shown in Figures 9.3a and 9.3b for selected age groups. Compared to 1960-1962, overweight prevalence in 1988-1991 was approximately 8% higher among African American men 20 to 29 years of age but nearly doubled among African American women in that age group over the same time period. Cohorts of African American men and women aged 50 to 59 had a prevalence of overweight 10% to 13% higher in 1988-1991 than in 1960-1961. Data are shown for both African Americans and whites in the 60- to 74-year age group. Among 60- to 74-year-old men, the increase in overweight prevalence was dramatic, and moreso for African American than for white men. In contrast, the prevalence of overweight among African American and white women ages 60 to 74 years either remained relatively stable or declined.

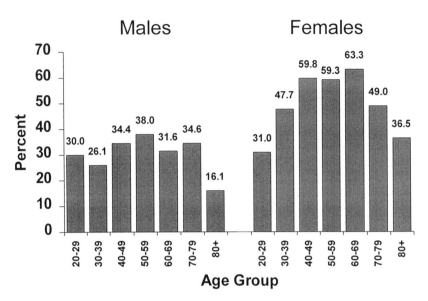

Figure 9.2. Overweight Prevalence in African American Males and Females by Ten-Year Age Groups. Overweight is defined as body mass index ≥ 27.8 kg/m^2 for men and ≥ 27.3 kg/m^2 for women.
SOURCE: Life Sciences Research Office (1995).

Only 1 in every 4 or 5 African American men or women ages 65 and over reports regular exercise (Figure 9.4). These low activity levels undoubtedly contribute to the prevalence of obesity. They may also contribute to insufficient overall energy intake (i.e., by limiting energy requirements) leading to micronutrient deficiencies.

Most data on the association of SES with overweight in African Americans suggest weak positive associations in men and inverse associations in women. However, social transitions may alter these associations across generations (Kumanyika, 1994a). This holds true for all industrialized societies. How poverty predisposes to obesity in low-income women is unclear. Along lines discussed previously, low leisure-time physical activity may contribute to this problem disproportionately in the current circumstances where obligatory activity is almost universally low, and only the affluent can afford or arrange significant discretionary activity in leisure time (James, 1995).

In summary, data on the dietary and nutritional status of older African Americans suggest concurrent under- and overnutrition. Intakes of many

Males

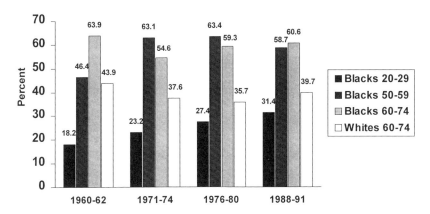

Figure 9.3a. Trends in Overweight Prevalence Among Males Between 1960 and 1991

SOURCE: Life Sciences Research Office (1995).

Females

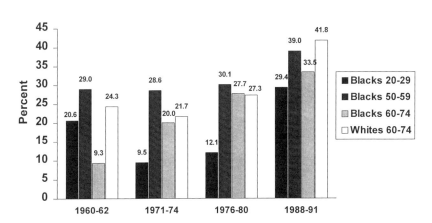

Figure 9.3b. Trends in Overweight Prevalence Among Females Between 1960 and 1991

SOURCE: Life Sciences Research Office (1995).

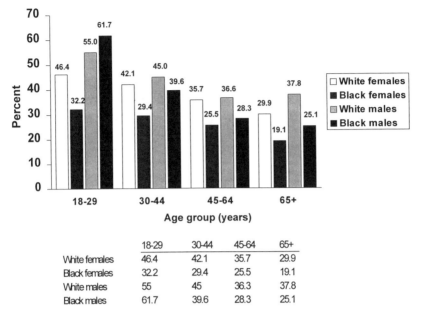

	18-29	30-44	45-64	65+
White females	46.4	42.1	35.7	29.9
Black females	32.2	29.4	25.5	19.1
White males	55	45	36.3	37.8
Black males	61.7	39.6	28.3	25.1

Figure 9.4. Percentage Who Exercised or Played Sports Regularly
SOURCE: 1990 National Health Interview Survey.

nutrients are suboptimal and are associated with relatively low overall energy intake. At the same time, overnutrition problems become more prominent with the increasing prevalence in aging of diet-related chronic conditions such as obesity, hypertension, diabetes, and osteoarthritis. Decreasing physical activity with aging worsens this picture both by decreasing caloric needs (and, therefore, intake of micronutrients) and by increasing the tendency to be overweight. Only a small chronic excess of calorie intake versus expenditure maintains or perpetuates overweight. Osteoporosis and osteopenia are the only major diet-related chronic conditions common in aging populations for which older African Americans appear to have some advantage, but this advantage cannot be linked to any positive aspects of diet or activity patterns. With the possible exception of decreased salt intake, available data on the dietary patterns of older African Americans do not imply widespread dietary modifications for chronic disease management. Some aspects of dietary composition appear to be more favorable for older than for younger African American adults; these may be generation effects reflecting, for example, continued relatively high consumption of certain high-fiber foods among African Americans born in the earlier decades of the 20th century. Having higher education does not necessarily improve dietary status, at least with respect to high-fat, high-cholesterol diets.

Nutrition Intervention and Lifestyle Change in Older African Americans

General Issues

Neither traditional dietary adequacy issues nor the more recently emerging diet and chronic disease issues are as well defined for older as for younger populations. Although it is recognized that some nutrient needs may decrease in aging while others increase, standards of nutritional adequacy have not been well developed with specific reference to older adults, particularly at the end of the life span. RDAs for adults "51 years and older" are thus used with limited confidence. Furthermore, dietary interventions (which are most often expressed as food restrictions) may compromise overall food intake or otherwise diminish quality of life for older adults in a way that is not compensated by the potential health benefits of such modifications.

The validity of generalities about diet and health decreases as the longevity and heterogeneity of the older population increase. Thus, the applicability of advice related to overnutrition and risk reduction when a person has already survived to an older age can be challenged under the assumption that such persons may have "outlived" any diet-related risks. Referring to whether older persons would benefit from following cholesterol-lowering diets, Grover, Gray-Donald, Joseph, Abrahamowicz, and Coupal (1994) concluded that *"the elderly should . . . be left to chose their foods as they please, as the predicted benefits of dietary change would be negligible."* However, in data for African Americans and whites ages 65 and older in the Cardiovascular Health Study (CHS), survival to advanced ages did not rule out further susceptibility to clinical cardiovascular disease (Manolio et al., 1995): African Americans in the CHS cohort were at higher risk than whites for both prevalent and subclinical cardiovascular disease.

The view that older survivors are nonsusceptible to diet-related risks on hereditary grounds is also difficult to support. Heredity is definitely a factor in determining whether individuals exposed to certain dietary factors eventually develop disease, but there are no means at present to clearly characterize people as "nonsusceptible" to chronic conditions. Family history is probably more useful for identifying than ruling out susceptibility. Furthermore, as suggested by the CHS data, for some types of diseases it is difficult to identify an age at which susceptibility has passed and after which diet would no longer matter (Manolio et al., 1995). Heart attacks and cancer are identified for the first time after the age of 60 or 65 in many individuals. In this sense, survivorship to older ages may reflect only a lack of susceptibility to what is termed "premature" onset of chronic disease, where "premature" in fact implies that many are at risk of developing the condition during their aging years.

Another argument against intervening on diet at older ages may be that drug therapy is easier to administer than dietary approaches (e.g., taking a diuretic instead of restricting sodium intake to reduce hypertension-related risks). However, drug therapies do not necessarily compensate for disease-related metabolic or functional problems. Dietary modifications are, therefore, helpful adjunctives to drug therapy and may also help to minimize the drug dose needed (American Diabetes Association, 1997; National High Blood Pressure Education Program, 1993, 1994a, 1994b).

Even when the potential health benefits of making dietary changes at older ages are acknowledged, the wisdom of making such changes at older ages may be questioned on the grounds that eating patterns have strong social and psychological values. Dietary modifications are viewed generally as deprivations rather than as potential ways to enhance the quality of life. As in the Grover et al. (1994) analysis, potential health benefits tend to be defined by life expectancy rather than functional status or other quality-of-life variables. Cost and feasibility issues are also raised with respect to dietary interventions in older adults. Feasibility of dietary modifications may be particularly problematic for older African Americans given the extent of informal food sharing through churches and other social networks in African Americans communities (Bailey & Walker, 1982).

Much of the argument for diet and health associations relies on population-level indicators. Among white populations, there are also extensive data based on studies of individuals from which to evaluate specific risks attributable to dietary factors and, in some cases, to evaluate nutrition interventions to reduce risk factors. There is a paucity of individual-level diet and health data in African Americans (Hargreaves, Baquet, & Gamshadzahi, 1989; Kumanyika, 1993b, 1994b). In addition, available data raise questions as to whether dietary risk factors identified in white populations apply to African

Americans in the same manner (Correa et al., 1985; Forgan et al., 1993; Kumanyika, 1994b; Stevens, 1993; Whittemore et al., 1995). Even for cardiovascular disease, where data on intermediate outcomes such as blood pressure and blood lipids have been collected for African Americans, few studies involve older adults, and those that do have small sample sizes or limited assessment of dietary practices.

Special Issues for African Americans

The African American population is increasingly diverse. However, eating pattern differences between African Americans and whites have been observed across socioeconomic strata and to some extent across regions (although diets of African Americans and whites in the South have many similarities); that is, there are some persistent cultural differences in eating patterns (Kittler & Sucher, 1989). To decide whether dietary changes should address those aspects of African American eating patterns that are closer to the mainstream diet (these may be the majority of food selections and preparation methods) or those that are more unique (those cultural practices most likely to perpetuate high fat or high salt intakes) requires further study of the relevant behavioral and cultural issues.

Several surveys suggest less adequate knowledge of current diet and health issues among African Americans compared to whites (Ford & Jones, 1991; Hyman, Simons-Morton, Ho, Dunn, & Rubovits, 1993; Jepson, Kessler, Portnoy, & Gibbs, 1991; Stewart, DeForge, Reese-Carter, Pecukonis, & Roberts, 1995), particularly among African Americans with low educational attainment. This may relate, in part, to the existence of opposing beliefs about "healthy foods"; for example, the need for balanced meals or of "eating properly"—perceived as important for maintaining resistance to colds and flu or other acute health problems (White & Maloney, 1990). Such beliefs may have been carried over from the not-too-distant period when nutritional adequacy was the primary emphasis in dietary guidance. At one time, foods such as meat and dairy products or liver, now de-emphasized because of their fat or cholesterol content, were emphasized as good sources of protein, vitamins, and minerals, and federal programs were put in place to ensure adequate consumption of these foods. The related general beliefs about "healthy" diets are not incorrect and are still relevant to those who have marginal dietary intake. A high prevalence of low literacy skills among African Americans may also limit access to health information (Williams et al., 1995).

Social norms in the African American community may limit recognition and acceptance of this reversal in dietary advice toward de-emphasis of animal products. For example, positive perceptions of "soul foods" as symbolic of the resourcefulness and survival of an oppressed people might render current derivatives of these foods particularly important in African American cultural identity and may foster the perpetuation of even those foods clearly perceived as unhealthful. This problem might be particularly acute for the current generation of older African Americans. Older African American women may also feel some responsibility, as guardians of tradition, to perpetuate certain eating patterns for cultural reasons, in spite of health-related knowledge to the contrary, and may prepare these foods for others even if they "can't eat them." On the other hand, older African Americans who desire to distance themselves from traditions associated with slavery and poverty may shun traditional foods precisely because they are symbols of the past. These possibilities do not appear to have been well studied, at least not in the biomedical literature. Available studies of dietary intake or compliance with medically prescribed diets are exploratory, superficial, or silent (Bell, Summerson, & Konen, 1995; Berg & Berg, 1989; Kumanyika & Adams-Campbell, 1991) with respect to capturing the influence of cultural dimensions or symbolic meanings of food. Folk practices involving dietary supplementation have been little studied as diet and health variables in African Americans, although some reports suggest that such practices are prevalent and directly influence compliance with medical advice (Brown & Segal, 1996; Heurtin-Roberts, 1990; Mathews, 1987).

Data relevant to dietary change perspectives of African Americans have been reported from a qualitative study by Airhihenbuwa et al. (1996). Certain foods, both wholesome and less so, were identified as typically African American and associated with survival under difficult circumstances. The authors' premise that African Americans might be reluctant to relinquish these foods to preserve culture was not borne out by comments from focus group participants. Practical factors such as availability and affordability of alternatives, cross-cultural exposures influencing food preferences, the "non-cooking" lifestyles of younger cohorts of African Americans, and health problems proscribing intakes of fat and salt were viewed as determinants of whether African Americans would be eating "soul food" 50 years from now. The perception among many of those interviewed that survival depends on adaptability to one's environment suggests, however, that African Americans would be more likely to respond to changes in the food environment than to initiate them. If this responsiveness to the food environment is indeed a characteristic of African American eating patterns, it may limit the prospects for accelerating the pace of dietary changes in African American communities in order to close the diet-related morbidity/mortality gap. Changes in the environment would have to come first.

Physical activity levels are lower among less-educated older Americans, among both African Americans and whites (Clark, 1995). However, cultural beliefs related to historical circumstances of African Americans may influence physical activity attitudes and practices of older African Americans in unique ways (Airhihenbuwa, Kumanyika, Agurs, & Lowe, 1995). Probing about the relative importance of exercise and rest yielded strong perceptions that getting enough rest would be considered a higher priority than exercising and that, in some cases, exercise would be viewed as a stressor. Respondents also perceived themselves as more physically active at work than whites. Survey results from 239 African Americans enrolling in a cardiovascular nutrition education study indicated a higher prevalence of such beliefs about exercise among the less-educated subset (Airhihenbuwa, Kumanyika, TenHave, & Adams-Campbell, 1995). Similar beliefs have been reported in qualitative and quantitative studies in other populations (U.S Department of Health and Human Services, 1986, 1992).

Cultural differences between African Americans and whites in their perspectives on obesity or overweight are better documented (Kumanyika, 1993b; Kumanyika, Wilson, & Guilford-Davenport, 1993; Rand & Kuldau, 1990). Although weight preoccupation is relatively high among both African Americans and whites and at all ages, differences in body image and related psychosocial variables have been documented between black and white girls and women and men of various ages: attitudes toward obesity are less negative among African Americans; and self-concept and self-esteem are less tightly linked to weight status in African Americans compared to whites. These types of attitudes tend to be characteristic of populations undergoing economic and epidemiologic transitions from circumstances in which starvation and wasting diseases predominated. Concern about obesity also tends to be less in older persons (Harris & Furukawa, 1986; Rand & Kuldau, 1990) and, among older persons, less in African Americans than whites (LSRO, 1995; Rand & Kuldau, 1990; Stevens, Kumanyika, & Keil, 1994; Stevens, Kumanyika, Keil, & Seibert, 1994). This may be partly a cohort effect, in that older generations are more likely to have experienced food shortages, and partly a change with age in the cosmetic values related to body size. The image of a vulnerable, frail elderly person may predispose older adults to a reactive, greater appreciation for having some excess weight.

Intervention Approaches

There are relatively few dietary intervention studies involving African Americans or from which ethnic comparisons can be made. However, it is relatively clear that conventional dietary counseling and nutrition behavior change programs meet with less success in African Americans than whites (Kumanyika, Hebert, et al., 1993; Kumanyika & Morssink, 1997). Initial dietary changes are less successful in African Americans or changes are not maintained as successfully, for example, in weight or sodium reduction for hypertension prevention or treatment and weight reduction for diabetes treatment Kumanyika, Obarzanek, Stevens, Hebert, & Whelton, 1991; Stevens, Corrigan, et al., 1993; Wing & Anglin, 1996; Wylie-Rosett et al., 1993).

Reports of cultural adaptations of nutrition interventions in African Americans relate primarily to weight reduction programs. McNabb, Quinn, and Rosing (1993) achieved an average weight loss of 9.8 lb in 10 of 13 inner-city African American women with non-insulin-dependent diabetes mellitus (NIDDM), ages 41 to 60, who participated in a culturally adapted, 18-week counseling program and were followed for 1 year. Comparison subjects gained 3 lb on average during the same period. Interviews with culturally similar women had been used to identify obstacles to adoption of dietary and exercise change programs, and the resulting information was used to design an educational program geared toward relevant problem-solving. The authors attributed the success of the program to their emphasis on active-discovery learning in which participants were helped to identify their own learning needs and to develop personally relevant strategies to meet those needs. In addition, the authors pointed out that the program did not focus initially on calorie reduction or increases in activity, in order to allow participants' motivation to make changes to evolve internally and independently.

Agurs-Collins, Kumanyika, TenHave, and Adams-Campbell (in press) conducted a randomized, controlled trial of a nutrition, weight, and physical activity program designed to be effective with older African Americans with NIDDM. Cultural adaptations in this study included the use of program materials depicting African American individuals, families, or communities; incorporation of language, values, and foods relevant to African Americans; and encouraging participants to discuss and work through dietary adherence issues relevant to their personal day-to-day situations. In addition, participant involvement and group dynamics were fostered by asking participants to develop a name for themselves; this name was then printed on T-shirts and used for group identity. Weight loss achieved was modest (approx. 5 lbs.) but was comparable to that observed in studies of older populations of whites.

It is difficult to synthesize data from these types of intervention studies, partly because there are so many different ways to implement behavioral interventions. In addition, it is both difficult and potentially invalid to compare across programs that have different levels of client-centered adaptations and that are tested in different populations and settings. Programmatic features employed (such as involvement of participants on a partnership basis, involving staff with cultural and life experiences similar to those of participants, and working with an ethnically or socially homogeneous participant population) may introduce sufficient changes to render the programmatic approach qualitatively different from another program designed to achieve the same objectives.

Conclusions

Any population, for which nutrition problems are important at a given time and place depends on the relevant social, economic, and health circumstances. This review of dietary and nutritional status issues of aging African Americans has focused on persons presumably born and raised in the United States, and issues have been reviewed in the context of current U.S. national nutrition monitoring priorities (LSRO, 1995). These priorities clearly emphasize chronic disease-related nutritional risks, in contrast to prior decades when the major focus was on nutritional adequacy issues. Highlighted problems relate to chronic conditions that affect older adults disproportionately, and several (overweight, hypertension, and other overweight-related conditions such as diabetes) are notably more prevalent among older African Americans than older white Americans.

Dietary data for older African Americans suggest numerous, potential nutritional problems. Some are in the area of overnutrition, that is, high-fat, low-fiber diets that cause or aggravate chronic diseases; others relate to suboptimal intake of food, overall, and of certain vitamins and minerals. Data specifying health outcomes of older African Americans that can be directly tied to dietary problems are limited. However, on theoretical grounds, the existence of suboptimal nutrient intakes in large subsets of the older African American population suggests a need for corrective interventions.

The problem of poverty as a pervasive social force predisposing to both inadequate food intake and to chronic disease is a core aspect of poor nutritional status in the older African American population. Whether sociocultural characteristics of African American families (e.g., intergenerational households, food sharing, church networks) compensate for poverty-related influences on food intake is unclear, primarily because of the absence of studies linking these variables. Dependency on others for food may complicate adherence to dietary modifications unless the food preparer or institutional food provider understands not only the dietary modifications needed but also ways in which these modifications can be implemented without compromising appetite or related quality of life; or, the ability to depend on others for food may be a factor enabling some older African Americans to live in the community.

Although the existing literature does provide some insights about cultural considerations in modification of eating and activity patterns among older African Americans, this is an area requiring much more systematic study using approaches that ask valid and meaningful questions. More understanding is needed regarding the behavioral determinants of community and individual behavior change and of differences in dietary and behavioral change perspectives across generations. Traditional African American eating habits may be more relevant to older African Americans than to younger cohorts of African Americans who have matured during the era of "fast food" and television commercials, but some aspects of the eating patterns of the current cohort of older African Americans may also be generalizable to younger cohorts as they enter their aging years. Data on cultural aspects of diet, lifestyle, and behavioral change are currently lacking for African Americans across the life span.

References

Agurs-Collins, T. D., Kumanyika, S. K., TenHave, T. R., & Adams-Campbell, L. L. (in press). *A randomized, controlled trial of weight reduction and exercise for diabetes management in older African Americans.*

Airhihenbuwa, C. O., Kumanyika, S., Agurs, T. D., & Lowe, A. (1995). Perceptions and beliefs about exercise, rest, and health among African Americans. *American Journal of Health Promotion, 9,* 426-429.

Airhihenbuwa, C. O., Kumanyika, S., Agurs, T. D., Lowe, A., Saunders, D., & Morssink, C. B. (1996). Cultural aspects of African American eating patterns. *Ethnicity and Health, 1*(3), 245-260.

Airhihenbuwa, C. O., Kumanyika, S. K., TenHave, T. R., & Adams-Campbell, L. A. (1995, May/June). *An assessment of culturally-relevant exercise attitudes of African Americans.* Paper presented at the Second International Heart Health Conference, Barcelona, Spain.

Alpers, D. H., Clouse, R. E., & Stenson, W. F. (1988). *Manual of nutritional therapeutics* (2nd ed.). Boston: Little, Brown.

American Diabetes Association. (1997). Nutrition recommendations and principles for people with diabetes mellitus. *Diabetes Care, 20*(1), S14-S17.

American Dietetic Association. (1996). Position of the American Dietetic Association: Nutrition, aging and the continuum of care. *Journal of the American Dietetic Association, 96,* 1048-1052.

Bailey, F. E., & Walker, M. L. (1982). Socio-economic factors and their effects on the nutrition and dietary habits of the Black aged. *Journal of Gerontological Nursing, 8*(4), 203-207.

Bell, R. A., Summerson, J. H., & Konen, J. C. (1995). Dietary intakes by levels of glycemic control for Black and White adults with non-insulin dependent diabetes mellitus. *Journal of the American College of Nutrition, 14,* 144-151.

Berg, J., & Berg, B. L. (1989). Compliance, diet and cultural factors among Black Americans with end-stage renal disease. *Journal of the Black Nurses Association, 3*(2), 16-28.

Block, G., & Lanza, E. (1987). Dietary fiber sources in the United States by demographic group. *Journal of the National Cancer Institute, 79,* 83-91.

Brown, C. M., & Segal, R. (1996). The effects of health and treatment perceptions on the use of prescribed medication and home remedies among African American and White American hypertensives. *Social Science and Medicine, 43,* 903-917.

Clark, D. O. (1995). Racial and educational differences in physical activity among older adults. *The Gerontologist, 354,* 472-480.

Correa, P., Fontham, E., Pickle, L. W., Chen, V., Lin, Y., & Haenszel, W. (1985). Dietary determinants of gastric cancer in South Louisiana inhabitants. *Journal of the National Cancer Institute, 75,* 645-654.

Fischer, J., & Johnson, M. A. (1990). Low body weight and weight loss in the aged. *Journal of the American Dietetic Association, 90,* 1697-1706.

Ford, E. S., & Jones, D. H. (1991). Cardiovascular health knowledge in the United States. Findings from the National Health Interview Survey, 1985. *Preventive Medicine, 20,* 725-736.

Forgan, J. F., Ziegler, R. G., Schenberg, J. B., Hartge, P., McAdams, M. J., Falk, R. T., Wilcox, H. B., & Shaw, G. L. (1993). Race and sex differences in associations of vegetables, fruits, and carotenoids with lung cancer risk in New Jersey (United States). *Cancer Causes and Control, 4,* 173-281.

Grover, S. A., Gray-Donald, K., Joseph, L., Abrahamowicz, M., & Coupal, L. (1994). Life expectancy following dietary modification or smoking cessation. *Archives of Internal Medicine, 154,* 1697-1704.

Hargreaves, M. K., Baquet, C., & Gamshadzahi, A. (1989). Diet, nutritional status, and cancer risk in American Blacks. *Nutrition and Cancer, 12,* 1-28.

Harris, M. B., & Furukawa, C. (1986). Attitudes toward obesity in an elderly sample. *The Journal of Obesity and Weight Regulation, 15*(1), 5-16.

Heurtin-Roberts, S. (1990). Health beliefs, compliance—Hypertension. *Journal of the American Medical Association, 264*(22), 2864.

Hyman, D. J., Simons-Morton, D. G., Ho, K., Dunn, J. K., & Rubovits, D. S. (1993). Cholesterol-related knowledge attitudes and behaviors in a low-income, urban patient population. *American Journal of Preventive Medicine, 9,* 82-89.

James, W. P. T. (1995). A public health approach to the problem of obesity. *International Journal of Obesity, 19*(Suppl. 3), S37-S45.

Jepson, C., Kessler, L. G., Portnoy, B., & Gibbs, T. (1991). Black-White differences in cancer prevention knowledge and behavior. *American Journal of Public Health, 81,* 501-504.

Jerome, N. W. (1982). Diet and acculturation. The case of Black Americans in-migrants. In N. W. Jerome, R. F. Kandel, & G. H. Pelto (Eds.), *Nutritional anthropology. Contemporary approaches to diet and culture* (pp. 275-325). Pleasantville, NY: Redgrave Press.

Jerome, N. W. (1988). Dietary intake and nutritional status of older U.S. Blacks. An overview. In J. S. Jackson, P. Newton, A. Ostfield, D. Savage, & E. L. Schneider (Eds.), *The Black American elderly: Research on physical and psychosocial health.* New York: Springer.

Kittler, P. G., & Sucher, K. (1989). Black Americans. In *Food and culture in America* (pp. 171-199). New York: Van Nostrand Reinhold.

Kumanyika, S. K. (1993a). Diet and nutrition as influences on the morbidity/mortality gap. *Annals of Epidemiology, 3,* 154-158.

Kumanyika, S. K. (1993b). Special issues for obesity in minority populations. *Annals of Internal Medicine, 119,* 650-654.

Kumanyika, S. K. (1994a). Obesity in minority populations. An epidemiologic assessment. *Obesity Research, 2,* 166-182.

Kumanyika, S. K. (1994b). Racial and ethnic issues in diet and cancer epidemiology. In M. Jacobs (Ed.), *Diet and cancer: Markers, prevention, and treatment* (pp. 59-70). New York: Plenum.

Kumanyika, S. K. (1996). Improving our diet—Still a long way to go. *New England Journal of Medicine, 335,* 738-740.

Kumanyika, S. K., & Adams-Campbell, L. L. (1991). Obesity, diet and psychosocial factors contributing to cardiovascular disease in Blacks. In E. Saunders & A. Brest (Eds.), Cardiovascular diseases in Blacks [Special issue]. *Cardiovascular Clinics, 21*(3), 47-73.

Kumanyika, S. K., & Golden, P. M. (1991). Cross-sectional differences in health status in U.S. racial and ethnic minority groups. *Ethnicity and Disease, 1,* 50-59.

Kumanyika, S. K., Hebert, P. R., Cutler, J. A., Lasser, V. A., Sugars, C. P., Steffen-Batey, L., Brewer, A. A., Cameron, M., Shepek, L. D., Cook, N. R., & Miller, S. (1993). Feasibility and efficacy of sodium reduction in the Trials of Hypertension Prevention, Phase I. *Hypertension, 22,* 504-512.

Kumanyika, S. K., & Morssink, C. B. (1997). Cultural appropriateness of weight management programs. In S. Dalton (Ed.), *Overweight and weight management* (pp. 69-106). Gaithersburg, MD: Aspen Publishing.

Kumanyika, S. K., Obarzanek, E., Stevens, V. J., Hebert, P. R., & Whelton, P. K. (1991). Weight loss experience of Black and White participants in NHLBI-sponsored clinical trials. *American Journal of Clinical Nutrition, 53,* 1631S-1638S.

Kumanyika, S. K., Tell, G. S., Shemanski, L., Polak, J., & Savage, P. J. (1994). Eating patterns of community-dwelling older adults. The Cardiovascular Health Study. *Annals of Epidemiology, 4,* 404-415.

Kumanyika, S. K., Wilson, J. E., & Guilford-Davenport, M. (1993). Weight-related attitudes and behaviors of Black women. *Journal of the American Dietetic Association, 93,* 416-422.

Liao, Y., & Cooper, R. S. (1995). Continued adverse trends in coronary heart disease mortality among Blacks: 1980-81. *Public Health Reports, 110,* 572-579.

Life Sciences Research Office. (1995). *Third report on nutrition monitoring in the United States* (Prepared for the Interagency Board for Nutrition Monitoring and Related Research, 1995). Washington, DC: Government Printing Office.

Looker, A. C., Johnston, C. C., Wahner, H. W., Dunn, W. L., Calvo, M. S., Harris, T. B., Heyse, S. P., & Lindsay, R. L. (1995). Prevalence of low femoral bone density in older U.S. women from NHANES III. *Journal of Bone Mineral Research, 10,* 796-802.

Manolio, T. A., Burke, G. L., Psaty, B. M., Newmann, A. B., Haan, M., Powe, N., Tracy, R. P., & O'Leary, D. H., for the CHS Collaborative Research Group. (1995). Black-White differences in subclinical cardiovascular disease among older adults. The Cardiovascular Health Study. *Journal of Clinical Epidemiology, 48,* 1141-1152.

Mattes, R. D., & Donnelly, D. (1991). Relative contributions of dietary sodium sources. *Journal of the American College of Nutrition, 10*(4), 383-393.

Mathews, H. F. (1987). Rootwork: Description of an ethnomedical system in the American South. *Southern Medical Journal, 80,* 885-891.

McGinnis, J. M., & Foege, W. H. (1993). Actual causes of death in the United States. *Journal of the American Medical Association, 270,* 2207-2212.

McNabb, W. L. (Ed.), Quinn, M. T., & Rosing, L. (1993). Weight loss program for inner-city Black women with non-insulin dependent diabetes mellitus: Pathways. *Journal of the American Dietetic Association, 93*(1), 75-77.

Miles, T. P., & Bernard, M. A. (1992). Morbidity, disability and health status of Black American elderly: A new look at the oldest-old. *Journal of the American Geriatric Society, 40*(10), 1047-1054.

National Center for Health Statistics. (1995). *Health United States, 1994* (DHHS Publication No. [PHS] 95-1232). Hyattsville, MD: Public Health Service.

National Heart, Lung, and Blood Institute. (1995). *Chartbook of U.S. national data on socioeconomic status and cardiovascular health and disease.* Bethesda, MD: Author.

National High Blood Pressure Education Program. (1993). The fifth report of the Joint National Committee on Detection, Evaluation, and Treatment of High Blood Pressure. *Archives of Internal Medicine, 153,* 154-183.

National High Blood Pressure Education Program. (1994a). National High Blood Pressure Education Program working group report on hypertension in diabetes. *Hypertension, 23,* 145-158.

National High Blood Pressure Education Program. (1994b). National High Blood Pressure Education Program working group report on hypertension in the elderly. *Hypertension, 23,* 275-285.

National Research Council, Committee on Diet and Health, Food and Nutrition Board, Commission of Life Sciences. (1989). *Diet and health.* Washington, DC: National Academy Press.

O'Hare, W. P., Pollard, K. M., Mann, T. L., & Kent, M. M. (1991). African Americans in the 1990s. *Population Bulletin, 46*(1), 1-40.

Piani, A. L., & Schoenborn, C. (1993). Health promotion and disease prevention: United States, 1990. *Vital Health Statistics, 10,* 185.

Popkin, B. M., Siega-Riz, A. M., & Haines, P. S. (1996). A comparison of dietary trends among racial and socioeconomic groups in the United States. *New England Journal of Medicine, 335,* 716-720.

Posner, B. M., Jette, A. M., Smith, K. W., & Miller, D. R. (1993). Nutrition and health risks in the elderly. The Nutrition Screening Initiative. *American Journal of Public Health, 83,* 973-978.

Rand, C. S. W., & Kuldau, J. M. (1990). The epidemiology of obesity and self-defined weight problems in the general population: Gender, race, age and social class. *International Journal of Eating Disorders, 9*(3), 329-343.

Sanjur, D. (1982). *Social and cultural perspectives on nutrition.* Englewood Cliffs, NJ: Prentice Hall.

Stevens, J. (1993). Future directions in obesity research. In E. O. Voit & Z. Zhang (Eds.), *Festschrift for Millage Clinton Miller, III, Ph.D.* (pp. 115-122). Charleston: Medical University of South Carolina Press.

Stevens, J., Kumanyika, S. K., & Keil, J. E. (1994). Attitudes toward body size and dieting: Differences between elderly Black and White women. *American Journal of Public Health, 84,* 1322-1325.

Stevens, J., Kumanyika, S. K., Keil, J. E., & Seibert, L. (1994). Body size perceptions and eating attitudes in elderly men. *Obesity Research, 2,* 127-134.

Stevens, V. J., Corrigan, S. A., Obarzanek, E., Bernauer, E., Cook, N. R., Hebert, P. R., Mattfeldt-Beman, M., Oberman, A., Sugars, C., Dalcin, A. T., & Whelton, P. K., for the TOHP Collaborative Research Group. (1993). Weight loss intervention in Phase I of the Trials of Hypertension Prevention. *Archives of Internal Medicine, 153,* 849-858.

Stewart, D. L., DeForge, B. R., Reese-Carter, S., Pecukonis, E. V., & Roberts, H. (1995). Knowledge of blood cholesterol reduction in community residents. *Journal of the National Medical Association, 87,* 533-536.

Treas, J. (1995). Older Americans in the 1990s and beyond. *Population Bulletin, 50*(2), 1-46.

Trowell, H. C., & Burkitt, D. P. (Eds.). (1981). *Western diseases. Their emergence and prevention.* Cambridge, MA: Harvard University Press.

U.S. Department of Agriculture, Agricultural Research Service. Dietary Guidelines Advisory Committee. (1995). *Report of the Dietary Guidelines Advisory Committee on the Dietary Guidelines for Americans, 1995, to the Secretary of Health and Human Services and the Secretary of Agriculture.* Springfield, VA: National Technical Information Service.

U.S. Department of Health and Human Services. (1986). *Public perceptions of high blood pressure and sodium* (NIH Publication No. 86-2730). Washington, DC: Author.

U.S. Department of Health and Human Services, Office of Health Promotion and Disease Prevention. (1992). *Promoting healthy diets and active lifestyles to lower-SES adults.* Washington, DC: Author.

White, S. L., & Maloney, S. K. (1990). Promoting healthy diets and actives lives to hard-to-reach groups. Market research study. *Public Health Reports, 105,* 224-231.

Whittemore, A. S., Kolonel, L. N., Wu, A. H., John, E. M., Callagher, R. P., Howe, G. R., Burch, J. D., Hankin, J., Dreon, D. M., West, D. W., Teh, C.-Z., & Paffenbarger, R. S. (1995). Prostate cancer in relation to diet, physical activity, and body size in Blacks, Whites and Asians in the United States and Canada. *Journal of the National Cancer Institute, 87,* 652-661.

Williams, M. V., Parker, R. M., Baker, D. W., Parikh, N. S., Pitkin, K., Coates, W. C., & Nurss, J. R. (1995). Inadequate functional health literacy among patients at two public hospitals. *Journal of the American Medical Association, 274,* 1677-1682.

Wing, R. R., & Anglin, K. (1996). Effectiveness of a behavioral weight control program for Blacks and Whites with NIDDM. *Diabetes Care, 19,* 409-413.

Wylie-Rosett, J., Wassertheil-Smoller, J., Blaufox, M. D., Davis, B. R., Langford, H. R., Oberman, A., Jennings, S., Hataway, H., Stern, J., & Zimbaldi, N. (1993). Trial of antihypertensive intervention and management. Greater efficacy with weight reduction than with a sodium-potassium intervention. *Journal of the American Dietetic Association, 93,* 408-415.

Nutrition Among Hispanic Elders in the United States

Katherine L. Tucker
Luis M. Falcón
Odilia Bermúdez

Although recent research has contributed exciting advances in our understanding of the role of nutrition in health and disease, the nutrient requirements of the elderly population, and some of the factors associated with risk of poor diets, very little research has been conducted specifically among minority groups. For Hispanic elders, a fast-growing segment of the Hispanic population, this scarcity of knowledge is a critical problem. There are several reasons why elderly Hispanics may be expected to be at greater risk of nutrition problems than the general population, the most obvious being their greater rates of poverty. High poverty rates are marked among Puerto Ricans and Dominicans; but even among Cuban Americans, who exhibit the highest socioeconomic status among Hispanic groups, we find very high rates of poverty among the elderly. Many of the latter migrated to the United States late in life, without the protection of a pension or Social Security.

Hispanics share a common language and, to some extent, a general region of origin, but have variations in culture and life experiences in the United States that are reflected in their dietary patterns. Because the term *Hispanic* encompasses a population characterized by diverse experiences, it is essential to emphasize specific subgroups to the extent possible.

In this chapter, we examine available data on the diet and nutrition status of Hispanic elders, utilizing results predominantly from the Hispanic Health

AUTHOR'S NOTE: Blood lipids were analyzed by Ernst Schaefer and Wanda Carrasco.

and Nutrition Examination Survey (HHANES) for Mexican American, Puerto Rican, and Cuban adults aged 60 to 74; from the more recent National Health and Nutrition Examination Survey (NHANES III) data—for Mexican Americans only, but without an upper age restriction; and from an ongoing study of Hispanic elders (mainly Puerto Ricans and Dominicans) living in the state of Massachusetts. In addition, we note published results from other studies on the diet, nutritional status, or both, of Mexican American elders, most notably, from the San Antonio Heart Study.

The chapter is organized in six sections. The first briefly reviews important issues regarding recent research on nutrition and aging; the second section describes the main sources of data presented. The third, fourth, and fifth sections focus on dietary intake patterns, anthropometric status (obesity and underweight), and biochemical indicators, respectively; and the sixth contains a summary.

Nutrition and Aging

With the rapid growth of the oldest segments of the general population, and the associated concerns for the costs of medical and long-term care, the past two decades have seen more research focused on the potential role of diet and nutritional status in the preservation of health and function. Consequently, we now have a greater understanding of the importance of diet in the prevention of the leading causes of death and disability; but much remains to be done. Recent advances include new understanding of the importance of antioxidant and B complex vitamins in the prevention of heart disease and stroke; and of the role of differing fat sources. A variety of vitamins and minerals appear to play a role in prevention of cancer, in improving immune function, in bone status and fracture prevention, preservation of cognitive function, prevention of cataracts, and more. The importance of a good diet throughout life and into the elder years is more evident than ever.

Obtaining a nutrient-rich diet is of particular importance for the elderly population for several reasons. Because of decreased function in many systems, elders tend to be less efficient in the absorption and processing of some nutrients. Metabolic studies have shown that, contrary to some earlier beliefs, nutrient requirements do not decrease for most nutrients—in fact there is evidence that the elderly have increased requirements for many vitamins and minerals when compared with younger persons (Russell & Suter, 1993;

Wood, Suter, & Russell, 1995). In addition, elders are the heaviest users of medications, many of which cause further increases in nutrient requirements; and the burdens of diseases themselves may lead to increased nutrient needs (Roe, 1989). Nutrients of particular concern include vitamin B_{12}, the absorption of which is greatly affected by a common condition called atrophic gastritis (Russell & Suter, 1993) and vitamin D, which has been shown to be less available due to the decreased efficiency of several steps in its synthesis and conversion to an active form (McLaughlin & Holick, 1985). Vitamin B_{12} is needed for maintenance of nerve function and vitamin D for bone density. Though nutrient requirements are high, total food intakes tend to be significantly lower for most elderly persons due to lower activity levels. This means that the nutrient density of the diet is critical.

At the same time, a variety of health and social factors make obtaining a nutrient-dense diet particularly difficult for elders. Decreased mobility means that getting to the store for the fresh fruits, vegetables, dairy products, and meats that contain needed nutrients is difficult; cooking is more difficult for those with arthritis and mobility problems; appetites may suffer in association with illness, including depression—a common problem among the elderly; chewing problems associated with ill-fitting dentures and swallowing problems limit intakes of certain foods; and, for many, low incomes limit access to adequate and high-quality foods. Nutrients consistently seen to be consumed in amounts below the recommended dietary allowances (RDA) in large proportions of free-living elderly subjects include: calcium, zinc, magnesium, vitamin D, riboflavin, vitamin B_6, vitamin B_{12}, and folate (Tucker, Jacques, & Rush, 1995). Studies examining factors associated with poor diets among elderly groups have identified income, education level, number of medications, use of dentures, living alone—particularly among men—and non-White race as key variables (Davis, Murphy, & Neuhaus, 1988; Dwyer, White, Ham, Lipschitz, & Wellman, 1991; The Nutrition Screening Initiative, 1991; Tucker, Jacques, & Rush, 1995).

A well-documented phenomenon in the United States is the increase in obesity among all age groups. There is a clear tendency toward weight gain with age, making obesity among the elderly a major health risk. The associations between obesity and hypertension, diabetes, heart disease, and disability levels are well known, and control of obesity is a key but stubborn factor in the fight to control the effects and outcomes of chronic disease. In addition to the risks that obesity imposes in its own right, high weight level may exist concurrently with nutrient deficiency. This combination may easily occur as a consequence of energy dense, but low micronutrient diets, along with low physical activity. For the elderly, there is also a subset on the other end of the spectrum—the underweight. Often associated with illness, but also apparent in extreme cases of food insecurity, the correction of undernutrition—or wasting—is another key challenge.

The limited research available on Hispanics suggests that nutritional risk factors, particularly obesity and poor diet quality, are of major concern. In the following sections we will present some of the data that describe the extent of these problems and the apparent differences in risk seen among different Hispanic subgroups.

Sources of Data on Nutrition of Hispanic Elders

National Surveys

Because historically, Hispanics—like many other immigrant groups—have been a young population, very little was known about the nutrition of Hispanic elders in the United States. The limited data available for Hispanics have focused on mothers and children, traditional risk groups of concern (Sanjur, 1995). The first major survey to include measures of diet and nutrition status of U.S. Hispanics was the Hispanic Health and Nutrition Examination Survey (HHANES), conducted between 1982 and 1984 (Woteki, 1990). This national survey selected probability samples of three Hispanic groups: Mexican Americans in the Southwest; Cubans in Dade County, Florida; and Puerto Ricans in the Metro New York-New Jersey area. As in earlier NHANES surveys, subjects between the ages of 3 months and 74 years were included. The survey consisted of two main parts—a household interview and an examination during a visit to a mobile center. For the adult (20-74 years) subset, the examination included a medical and dental exam, dietary interview, anthropometric measures (height, weight, skinfolds, and circumferences), and laboratory tests on blood and urine samples (Fanelli-Kuczmarski & Woteki, 1990). Among the eldest segment (aged 60-74 years), 457 Mexican Americans, 242 Cubans, and 203 Puerto Ricans aged 60 to 74 years were interviewed—and 367, 177, and 144, respectively, examined (Woteki, 1990). Consequently, most of the published research on elderly Hispanics generated from that national survey has been done with the Mexican American subsample only. Response rates for completion of the interview ranged from 74% for Cubans 60 to 69 years of age to 88% for Puerto Ricans aged 70 to 74 years. For examinations, response rates were considerably lower—from 48% for the 70- to 74-year-old Puerto Ricans to 69% for the 70- to 74-year-old Mexican Americans (Woteki, 1990).

Recognizing the need for more data on persons older than age 74, the Third National Health and Nutrition Examination Survey (NHANES III) was designed without an upper age limit, and with an oversample of elderly subjects. It also includes an oversample of Mexican Americans, but not other Hispanic groups (Woteki, Briefel, Hitchcock, Ezzati, & Maurer, 1990). Data for NHANES III were collected between 1988 and 1995, in two phases. Nutrient intake data and selected other results from Phase I (1988-1991) have been published and will be referred to below.

National surveys like HHANES and NHANES III contribute tremendously to our understanding of nutritional status among Hispanic groups, particularly for Mexican Americans. The NHANES III will provide much needed data on the elder segment of the general U.S. population. With few exceptions, non-national studies designed to look specifically at the health of Hispanic elders have also been conducted among the Mexican American population, such as the San Antonio Heart Study. Several newer studies of Mexican American and other elders of Spanish descent living in the southwestern United States are currently under way. They include the New Mexico Aging Process Study (Lindeman), the San Luis Valley Health and Aging Study (Hammon), and the Mexican American EPESE (Markides). While data on the health and nutrition of Mexican American elders are becoming more available, data for other Hispanic elder groups remain scant or nonexistent. This lack of information is of particular concern in the context of high poverty rates, particularly among Hispanic groups living predominantly in the northeastern United States. A report of 1990 National Census data found that Puerto Ricans and Dominicans were the Hispanic subgroups most likely to be in poverty, with approximately 30% and 33%, respectively, of families below the poverty level, compared with 23% of Mexican American, 11% of Cuban, and 10% of non-Hispanic families (U.S. Department of Commerce, 1993). Levels of poverty vary substantially by age group and gender. Among Puerto Rican subjects in HHANES, 32% of males and 50% of females aged 55 to 74 years were living below the poverty level (Bermúdez, 1994). Lower levels of education, lower income, and limited ability to speak English have been proposed as factors behind the disadvantaged position of Puerto Rican elderly relative to other elderly Hispanics (Andrews, 1989; Bastida, 1988; Korte & Villa, 1988).

The Massachusetts Hispanic Elders Study

The Massachusetts Hispanic Elders Study was designed to address the need for data among non Mexican-American Hispanic groups living in the Northeast. The composition of the Massachusetts Hispanic elderly population is approximately 61% Puerto Rican, 15% Dominican, 9% Cuban, 7% Central American, 5% South American, and 3% other Hispanic, including Mexican American. Using state counties and census blocks, a two-stage cluster design with sampling proportional to size was used in order to generate a sample that approximates the population of Hispanic elders in the state. Neighborhood non-Hispanic White (NHW.) controls were also selected from the same census blocks. Because, as noted above, the Hispanic population in Massachusetts is largely low income, the NHW neighborhood subjects also tend to be from low-income households and are therefore representative of NHWs living in these neighborhoods, but are not representative of NHW in Massachusetts.

Home interviews were designed to contain information that, in part, parallels that collected in the NHANES III, although physical examinations were not conducted. The home visit includes an extensive sociodemographic interview; a brief health history; a depression scale; questions on disability, medication use, health behaviors, health services, and program participation; a 24-hour dietary recall; a specially developed food frequency questionnaire; and measures of height, weight, knee height, circumferences of waist, hip, and arm, and triceps skinfold. The interview is followed, usually a few days later, by a fasting blood draw—which is scheduled during the interview. Blood samples are analyzed for glucose, lipids, and hemoglobin levels. During Phase I of data collection, from 1993 to 1995, 600 interviews were completed, with useable dietary information for 549 and blood samples for 418. Of those identified as target subjects and invited to participate, 85% of the Hispanic sample and 70% of the NHW sample agreed to be interviewed. This study is currently undergoing a Phase II of data collection to increase the sample size sufficiently to present subgroup data reliably. In the following sections, we present preliminary data on nutritional status obtained from the 600 Phase I subjects.

Dietary Intake

Food Patterns

There are few data available on diets of Hispanic elders. Information on younger adults, however, shows some similarities stemming from a common Spanish influence, but also considerable differences in the food patterns of different Hispanic groups (Sanjur, 1995). Among Mexican Americans, the major staple food is tortilla made from corn or wheat. When following the traditional diet, tortillas tend to be consumed daily with frijoles (pinto beans) either stewed or refried, with meat, or both. Salsas made with tomatoes, onions, and chili peppers are frequent accompaniments. Among Puerto Ricans, the staple is rice, generally consumed with stewed pink beans, chicken, or meat. Plantains are also an important starchy food, as are a variety of potato-like root crops. The Cuban American diet is closer to the Puerto Rican than the Mexican; rice is the main staple, consumed with beans or meats.

Studies of Mexican American food intake patterns in Texas have found differing results in comparison to the NHW population. In a comparison of food intakes of adults aged 20 to 60 years in Texas, Borrud et al. (1989) found that Mexican Americans consumed a greater proportion of their intakes of saturated fat and cholesterol from meats than did African Americans or NHWs. They also found that the Mexican Americans used flour tortillas 3 times more often than they used corn tortillas. The authors noted that this population of Mexican Americans appears to be in transition, with "adherence to traditional foods, such as beans and tortillas, but also . . . a substantial use of beef, a change from earlier reports" (Borrud et al., 1989, p. 1068). In contrast, investigators in the San Antonio Heart Study found that Mexican Americans consumed less beef than did NHWs (Bartholomew, Young, Martin, & Hazuda, 1990). They also found that Mexican Americans consumed more eggs, poultry, legumes, organ meats, avocados, tortillas, and sugar; and less skim milk, ice cream, fruits, juices, vegetables, breads, and margarine than did NHWs. More research on the dietary patterns and factors associated within the Mexican American population may help to explain these apparently contradictory findings.

Differences in food pattern across the three major groups represented in the HHANES are illustrated in Figure 10.1. The sources of total energy intake for the three groups were identified and the 10 contributing the highest percentage of energy for any of the three groups are presented. For Mexican

242   DIET AND NUTRITION

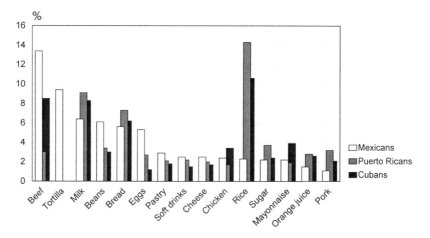

Figure 10.1. Food Contribution to Energy Intake, HHANES Elders (60-74 yrs)

American elders, the greatest contributors to total energy intake are beef
(13%), followed by tortilla (9%), milk (6%), beans (6%), bread (6%), eggs
(5%), pastries (3%), soft drinks (3%), and cheese (3%). They consume much
more tortilla, beef, egg, and beans than the other groups; and much less rice,
pork, orange juice, milk, and bread. Rice comprises approximately 2% of
their intake. In contrast, rice is the leading source of energy for the Puerto
Ricans (14%) and Cubans (11%). In addition to rice, Puerto Rican elders consume more milk (9% of total energy), bread (7%), sugar (4%), and pork (3%)
than the other groups. Other major contributors for the Puerto Ricans are
beans (3%), beef (3%), orange juice (3%), and eggs (3%). For the Cuban
subset, rice intake is followed by beef (9%), milk (8%), bread (6%), salad
dressing including mayonnaise (4%), chicken (3%), and orange juice (3%).

Using the same method with our study of Massachusetts elders, we see
smaller food intake differences across groups (Figure 10.2). Our results for
Puerto Ricans strongly resemble those from the HHANES Puerto Rican sample, showing dominant intakes from rice (15%), milk (11%), beans (4%),
bread (4%), and sugar (3%). Foods that appear somewhat more important in
the Massachusetts, as compared with the HHANES, Puerto Rican samples
include oil (9%), chicken (6%), potato (3%), and plantain (2%). The appear-
ance of oil as an important energy source in the Massachusetts study may be

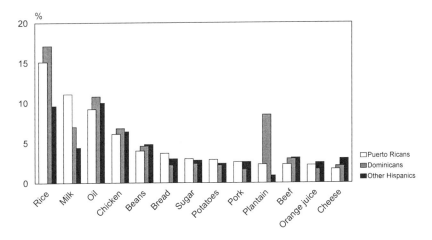

Figure 10.2. Food Contribution to Energy Intake, Massachusetts Elders (60-98 yrs)

due to a difference in coding of intake data—recipe ingredients, including oil, were coded separately whenever possible. Among the groups in Massachusetts, Dominican elders consume larger proportions of rice, oil, and plantain than do the other groups; other Hispanics (Cubans, Central and South Americans) tend to consume considerably less rice, oil, milk, and plantain than the Puerto Ricans or Dominicans.

Macronutrient Intake

Available evidence suggests marked differences in average total energy consumption across Hispanic groups. Table 10.1 presents energy intakes as reported from the HHANES (Loria et al., 1995), and from the NHANES III (McDowell et al., 1994), based on 24-hour dietary recalls. These results show that among Hispanic subgroups, total energy intakes tend to be greatest for Cuban and lowest for Puerto Rican elders. Furthermore, at all age groups 60 years and above, total energy intakes are considerably lower among Mexican Americans than among NHW elders. Comparable data from Massachusetts also show lower average energy intake for Hispanic elders when compared to NHW neighborhood controls (Table 10.1). Among Hispanic subgroups,

TABLE 10.1 Daily Energy Intake by Sex and Ethnic Group Among Elders in HHANES, NHANES III, and Massachusetts, From One-Day Dietary Recalls

	Men		Women	
Elder Group	n	Mean ± SE	n	Mean ± SE
HHANES (60-74 years)				
Mexican Americans	ns	1,840 ± 57	ns	1,339 ± 36
Cubans	ns	1,921 ± 106	ns	1,353 ± 47
Puerto Ricans	ns	1,727 ± 89	ns	1,126 ± 58
NHANES III				
Non-Hispanic Whites				
60-69 years	247	2,118 ± 59	246	1,602 ± 45
70-79 years	285	1,924 ± 45	253	1,431 ± 32
80 yrs and over	250	1,802 ± 45	251	1,335 ± 31
Mexican Americans				
60-69 years	152	1,963 ± 79	153	1,297 ± 47
70-79 years	60	1,660 ± 111	51	1,280 ± 110
80 yrs and over	19	1,460 ± *	23	1,251 ± *
Massachusetts (60-98 years)				
Puerto Ricans	110	1,738 ± 65	158	1,378 ± 42
Dominicans	22	1,543 ± 109	44	1,469 ± 95
Other Hispanics	42	1,858 ± 121	59	1,463 ± 83
Non-Hispanic Whites	61	2,028 ± 92	97	1,541 ± 67

SOURCE: HHANES: From "Macronutrient Intakes Among Adult Hispanics: A Comparison of Mexican Americans, Cuban Americans, and Mainland Puerto Ricans," by C. M. Loria, T. L. Bush, M. C. Carrol, A. C. Looker, M. A. McDowell, C. L. Johnson, & C. T. Sempos, *American Journal of Public Health, 85,* 1995. Used with permission.
NHANES: McDowell, Briefel, Alaimo, Bischof, Caughman, Carroll, Loria, & Johnson (1994).
NOTE: * Figure does not meet standard of reliability or precision; ns = not specified.

"Other Hispanics" tend to have the highest intakes, with more variation across groups for men than for women. Energy requirements depend on body size, metabolic efficiency, and physical activity. It is therefore difficult to interpret the meaning of differing energy intakes across groups without further information. Much of the lower intake among Hispanic compared with NHW groups is likely to be due to shorter stature, and therefore, lower requirement; some may also be associated with differences in physical activity.

Based on accumulated research findings on risk of heart disease and cancer, national dietary guidelines suggest that macronutrient intake be partitioned so that total fat intake is less than 30% of energy intake and saturated fat is less than 10%. It is also recommended that dietary cholesterol intakes be below 300 mg/day (National Cholesterol Education Program, 1991). Macronutrient intakes as a percentage of total energy are presented in Table 10.2 for the HHANES elders (Loria et al., 1995). Mexican Americans appear to have lower carbohydrate intake (46% of energy vs. 51%) and higher total fat (36% vs. 30%-31%), saturated, and monounsaturated fat intakes than do Puerto Ricans or Cubans, consistent with their higher beef intakes, discussed above. Loria et al. (1995) also reported that Mexican Americans aged 60 to 74 had significantly higher cholesterol intakes than did Puerto Ricans or Cubans (men: 441 mg vs. 306 and 279, respectively; women: 302 mg vs. 200 and 211, respectively). Table 10.2 presents the more recent NHANES III data for men and women, showing slightly higher carbohydrate (50%-53%) and lower fat intakes (32%) among Mexican Americans, compared with those seen earlier in the HHANES (above). With the exception of greater reported alcohol intakes among NHWs, the NHANES III macronutrient proportions do not appear to differ greatly across these two ethnic groups for either men or women. Macronutrient intakes for Hispanic elders living in Massachusetts are also presented in Table 10.2.

Highest carbohydrate intakes are seen among Dominican men and women (58%-57%) with 54% to 55% among Puerto Ricans and 53% to 56% among "Other" Hispanics. In contrast, the diets of NHW neighborhood controls contain 48% to 54% carbohydrates. The Hispanic-NHW contrast is even greater for type of carbohydrate. For example, Dominicans are consuming 40% to 43% of their energy intakes from complex carbohydrate and 14% to 18% from sugars, compared with 26% to 29% complex and 23% to 25% sugars for NHWs. Total, saturated, and monounsaturated fat intakes also appear to be considerably lower among Massachusetts Hispanics (28%-31% for total fat) than among neighborhood NHWs, HHANES, and NHANES III elders. Figure 10.3 presents the proportion of subjects from each subgroup in the Massachusetts study with intake levels greater than the recommended 30% of energy from fat, 10% from saturated fat, and more than 300 mg of cholesterol. For all of these, much higher proportions of the NHW neighborhood control sample have high intakes, while lowest levels are seen, for most, in the Dominican subgroup. Still, substantial proportions of all groups have high fat intakes, which may place them at increased risk for high blood cholesterol levels and heart disease.

Among Hispanic groups, Mexican Americans appear to be most likely to have high total and saturated fat intakes. Results from the San Antonio

TABLE 10.2 Macronutrient Percentage Contribution to Energy Intake: HHANES, NHANES III, and Massachusetts

| | HHANES (60-74 Years)[a] | | | NHANES III (60+ Years)[b] | | | | Massachusetts (60-98 Years) | | | | | | | |
| | MA | PR | Cuban | MA | | NHW | | NHW[c] | | PR | | Dominican | | Other | |
Macronutrient	Both Sexes N=298	Both Sexes N=109	Both Sexes N=138	M N=231	F N=227	M N=782	F N=750	M N=61	F N=98	M N=110	F N=158	M N=22	F N=44	M N=42	F N=59
Carbohydrates	46.0	51.4	51.2	50.4	52.7	49.7	52.7	48.4	53.8	54.3	55.4	57.5	57.3	53.3	55.9
Mean and (SE)	(0.60)	(0.80)	(0.60)	(0.99)	(0.91)	(0.42)	(0.47)	(1.48)	(1.14)	(0.95)	(0.83)	(2.00)	(1.41)	(1.32)	(1.18)
Protein	18.3	17.8	18.7	16.9	16.9	16.0	16.2	16.1	16.5	15.5	15.7	15.9	15.2	17.7	17.1
Mean and (SE)	(0.40)	(0.40)	(0.30)	(0.32)	(0.38)	(0.17)	(0.17)	(0.66)	(0.54)	(0.42)	(0.33)	(0.77)	(0.80)	(0.75)	(0.72)
Total fats	35.9	31.3	29.8	32.4	31.7	33.7	32.2	34.2	30.6	30.6	29.8	28.0	28.4	28.6	28.3
Mean and (SE)	(0.90)	(0.70)	(0.60)	(0.77)	(0.69)	(0.35)	(0.39)	(1.36)	(1.03)	(0.82)	(0.67)	(1.62)	(1.24)	(1.11)	(1.04)
Saturated fats	13.0	11.3	10.8	10.9	10.9	11.6	10.9	12.0	11.2	10.1	10.3	9.0	8.5	10.0	9.8
Mean and (SE)	(0.30)	(0.20)	(0.20)	(0.38)	(0.38)	(0.16)	(0.16)	(0.64)	(0.50)	(0.37)	(0.34)	(0.78)	(0.51)	(0.52)	(0.52)
Mono-unsaturated fats	14.0	11.5	11.5	11.9	11.4	12.7	11.8	12.7	11.0	10.1	10.0	8.2	9.7	10.2	9.6
Mean and (SE)	(0.30)	(0.20)	(0.20)	(0.32)	(0.32)	(0.17)	(0.17)	(0.58)	(0.42)	(0.33)	(0.28)	(0.50)	(0.49)	(0.44)	(0.39)
Polyunsaturated fats	6.2	6.2	5.4	6.9	6.5	6.7	7.0	6.7	5.9	8.1	7.1	8.7	7.9	5.9	6.6
Mean and (SE)	(0.20)	(0.20)	(0.10)	(0.24)	(0.23)	(0.12)	(0.14)	(0.48)	(0.30)	(0.43)	(0.29)	(0.95)	(0.71)	(0.43)	(0.54)
Alcohol	NS	NS	NS	1.5	0.3	2.6	1.1	3.0	0.7	0.4	0.0	0.0	0.9	1.7	0.2
Mean and (SE)				(0.28)	(0.14)	(0.26)	(0.16)	(1.07)	(0.25)	(0.27)	(0.00)	(0.00)	(0.86)	(0.81)	(0.13)

SOURCE: a. HHANES: From "Macronutrient Intakes Among Adult Hispanics: A Comparison of Mexican Americans, Cuban Americans, and Mainland Puerto Ricans," by C. M. Loria, T. L. Bush, M. C. Carrol, A. C. Looker, M. A. McDowell, C. L. Johnson, & C. T. Sempos. *American Journal of Public Health, 85,* 1995.

b. NHANES III: Modified from McDowell, Briefel, Alaimo, et al. (1994).

NOTE: ns = not specified.

c. NHW elders living in same neighborhoods as randomly selected Hispanic elders.

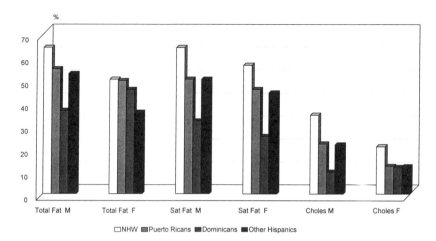

Figure 10.3. Percentage With High Intake of Fat and Cholesterol, Massachusetts Elders (60-98 yrs)
NOTE: High intake defined as: Greater than 30% energy from fat; greater than 10% energy from saturated fat; and, greater than 300 mg of cholesterol.

Heart Study demonstrated that Mexican Americans consumed more carbohydrates and more cholesterol than did NHWs; more total energy (women only); less protein (women only); and more saturated fat (men only) (Haffner, Knapp, Hazuda, Stern, & Young, 1985). The same group (Knapp, Hazuda, Haffner, Young, & Stern, 1988) constructed a scale to assess the avoidance of six dietary sources of saturated fat and cholesterol. They found no significant difference in overall score across ethnic groups, with both non-Hispanic White and Mexican American women more likely to avoid high saturated fat/cholesterol foods than men. However, Mexican Americans were less likely to recognize whole milk, eggs, and visible fat on meat as foods that contained saturated fat and cholesterol, suggesting that nutrition education in this area may be of benefit.

Micronutrient Intake

Table 10.3 presents mean intakes of vitamins and minerals for Mexican American and NHW men and women, aged 60+ years for the first phase of NHANES III (Alaimo et al., 1994), and for the subgroups in the Massachusetts

TABLE 10.3 Daily Intake of Selected Micronutrients Among Elders From One-Day Dietary Recalls: Mean (SE)

| | NHANES III (≥ 60 Years) | | | | Massachusetts Study (≥ 60 Years) | | | | | | | | | | |
| | MA | | NHW | | NHW[a] | | PR | | Dominican | | Other Hispanic | | | | |
Micronutrient N	M 231	F 227	M 782	F 750	M 61	F 98	M 110	F 158	M 22	F 44	M 42	F 59
Vitamin A (µg)	1,138 (135)	870 (56)	1,298 (59)	1,117 (42)	1,282 (125)	1,133 (139)	749 (120)	909 (118)	723 (249)	656 (116)	1,049 (240)	873 (152)
Vitamin C (mg)	110 (10)	83 (5)	102 (3)	105 (3)	129 (28)	103 (9)	79 (9)	90 (7)	71 (18)	96 (18)	126 (18)	107 (13)
Vitamin E (µg)	7.2 (0.47)	6.0 (0.57)	9.4 (0.37)	8.1 (0.39)	7.3 (0.56)	4.8 (0.29)	7.5 (0.54)	5.6 (1.36)	10.8 (2.16)	10.8 (1.47)	6.6 (0.66)	5.3 (0.48)
Thiamin (mg)	1.5 (0.06)	1.1 (0.05)	1.7 (0.03)	1.4 (0.03)	1.6 (1.09)	1.3 (0.06)	1.5 (0.07)	1.2 (0.04)	1.4 (0.12)	1.2 (0.12)	1.7 (0.16)	1.2 (0.08)
Riboflavin (mg)	1.8 (0.08)	1.4 (0.06)	2.1 (0.04)	1.7 (0.03)	2.0 (0.11)	1.6 (0.07)	1.4 (0.07)	1.2 (0.59)	1.2 (0.14)	1.1 (0.10)	1.7 (0.13)	1.3 (0.08)
Niacin (mg)	18.4 (0.79)	14.1 (0.76)	23.3 (0.49)	18.3 (0.38)	22.4 (1.24)	17.8 (1.09)	16.5 (0.82)	13.7 (0.51)	14.5 (1.27)	15.3 (1.34)	20.5 (1.55)	15.6 (1.01)
Folates (mg)	300 (15)	205 (12)	318 (9)	272 (8)	317 (33)	244 (15)	259 (15)	220 (11)	282 (29)	257 (27)	240 (38)	257 (21)
Vitamin B_6 (mg)	1.6 (0.08)	1.3 (0.06)	2.0 (0.05)	1.6 (0.04)	2.1 (0.11)	1.5 (0.09)	1.6 (0.08)	1.3 (0.05)	1.7 (0.16)	1.6 (0.16)	2.0 (0.15)	1.4 (0.10)
Vitamin B_{12} (mg)	5.6 (0.54)	4.0 (0.27)	5.9 (0.29)	3.6 (0.16)	7.6 (2.96)	3.7 (0.55)	3.2 (0.50)	3.0 (0.60)	2.2 (0.41)	2.0 (0.28)	4.8 (1.44)	2.8 (0.46)
Calcium (mg)	777 (39)	602 (30)	823 (18)	675 (16)	726 (47)	631 (36)	654 (38)	558 (28)	582 (78)	442 (37)	679 (61)	625 (46)
Magnesium (mg)	290 (10)	209 (8)	308 (6)	244 (4)	314 (16)	253 (13)	256 (10)	207 (7)	266 (22)	242 (16)	316 (30)	235 (14)
Iron (mg)	14.4 (0.68)	10.6 (0.60)	16.5 (0.40)	12.6 (0.34)	16.9 (1.48)	11.6 (0.68)	11.8 (0.60)	9.7 (0.42)	11.5 (0.83)	9.8 (0.63)	15.2 (1.57)	10.0 (0.68)
Zinc (mg)	10.3 (0.44)	8.0 (0.38)	12.2 (0.35)	8.8 (0.24)	11.8 (0.92)	8.0 (0.40)	8.6 (0.44)	6.8 (0.28)	8.8 (1.04)	7.0 (0.51)	10.6 (0.88)	7.5 (0.52)

SOURCE: NHANES modified from Alaimo, McDowell, Briefel, et al. (1994).
NOTE: a. NHW elders living in same neighborhoods as randomly selected Hispanic elders.

elders study. Intakes of most vitamins and minerals appear to be slightly lower for the Mexican American elders, when compared with NHWs in NHANES III. These differences are particularly great for vitamin E, riboflavin, niacin, vitamin B_6, calcium, and zinc for both genders and also for vitamin C, folate, and magnesium for women. In the San Antonio Heart Study of adults aged 25 to 64 years, Knapp et al. (1985) also saw lower intakes of vitamins A and C, niacin, and calcium among Mexican Americans when compared with NHWs. Among Mexican Americans in that study, higher calcium intakes were associated with higher level of socioeconomic status.

Similarly, most micronutrient intakes appear to be lower among Hispanic elders, particularly Dominican and Puerto Rican elders, in Massachusetts when compared with NHWs living in the same neighborhoods. Among men, the "Other Hispanics" tend to have micronutrient intakes that are closer to the NHWs' than to the other two Hispanic groups. This is particularly true for vitamins A, C, B_6, niacin, calcium, magnesium, iron, and zinc; all three Hispanic groups of men tended to have lower average intakes of folate and vitamin B_{12}. For most of these nutrients, average intakes also appear to be lower than those of the Mexican American men in NHANES III. These relative intake patterns are similar for women. Mexican American women have lower average intakes of all the micronutrients, when compared with NHW women in NHANES III. Among the Massachusetts subgroups, average intake of vitamins A and B_{12}, riboflavin, and calcium were lowest for the Dominican women; intakes of vitamin B_6, niacin, folate, magnesium, and zinc were lowest for the Puerto Rican women. Average intakes of riboflavin, niacin, vitamin B_{12}, calcium, and zinc also appear to be lower among Puerto Rican and Dominican women, when compared with Mexican American women. An exception to the pattern of lower intakes among Dominicans and Puerto Ricans is seen for vitamin E intake, which is highest among both Dominican men and women.

A report using data from the HHANES also showed that calcium intakes were lowest among Puerto Ricans, when compared with Mexican Americans and Cuban Americans (Looker, Loria, Carrol, McDowell, & Johnson, 1993), and those intake levels (701 and 557 mg for men and women aged 55-74, respectively) are similar to our Massachusetts results for Puerto Ricans. Reported calcium intakes for Mexican American elders in HHANES were 743 and 582 mg for men and women, respectively; and for Cubans, 792 and 616 mg (Looker et al., 1993). Another report from HHANES also showed relatively low intakes of other micronutrients for their small sample of Puerto

Rican elders (Interagency Board for Nutrition Monitoring and Related Research, 1993). Analyses of HHANES data on frequency of food consumption for adults aged 20 to 74 years revealed poorer dietary quality scores for Puerto Ricans than for other Hispanic groups (Marks, Garcia, & Solis, 1990), and lower use of vegetables, breads, cereals, and protein rich foods, including beef (Kuczmarski, Kuczmarski, & Najjar, 1991).

It therefore appears that despite macronutrient profiles that may be considered more "heart healthy" than those of NHWs, Hispanic elders—particularly Puerto Ricans and Dominicans—tend to have lower intakes of micronutrients. This seems to be associated with limited diversity of diet, with lower use of fruits, vegetables, and animal products by these groups. Given the importance of many of these micronutrients to health maintenance, including the protective effects of several B vitamins on heart disease, antioxidant vitamins (vitamins C, E, and β-carotene) on cancer, and vitamin D and calcium on bone density, efforts to improve the dietary quality of Hispanic elders, particularly the Puerto Ricans and Dominicans, should lead to improved health outcomes.

Acculturation

Because Hispanics are a relatively recent immigrant group, and their immigration still continues in large scale, the question of acculturation and how it affects the diets and nutrition patterns of these groups is an interesting one. For many ethnic groups in the United States, the maintenance of food patterns associated with their home countries is one of the last remnants of their culture of origin. Acculturation, or the adoption by an immigrant-origin group of cultural patterns more commonly associated with the majority culture, has been documented to be related to health outcomes. Only a few studies have examined the effects of acculturation on diet and related health outcomes among Hispanics.

Limited data on acculturation and diet suggest major differences between Mexican Americans and Puerto Ricans. In a study of younger Mexican American women in California (aged 19-44 years), Romero-Gwynn et al. (1993) found large decreases in the use of traditional foods, both as reported before and after immigration to the United States and across first- and second-generation immigrants. They noted that although these changes included some positive trends (decreased use of lard, cream, and sausage; increased use of milk and salads), they also contained negative aspects (decreased use of homemade fruit drinks and vegetable noodle soup; increased use of butter, margarine, vegetable oil, mayonnaise, and cookies). On balance, the authors conclude that the changes are more negative than positive, leading to increased intake of fat and sugar and lower intake of food sources of β-carotene than the traditional diet. A more recent and larger comparison of first- and second-generation Mexican American women, using data from the HHANES, also found that first-generation Mexican American women had higher average intakes of protein, vitamins A and C, folate, and calcium than did second-generation women, again suggesting negative effects of acculturation on diet (Guendelman & Abrams, 1995).

In contrast, an analysis of HHANES data by one of the authors (O.B.) found that among elderly Puerto Ricans, dietary quality, as measured by a score based on consumption of a variety of food groups, was better among the more acculturated (Bermúdez, 1994). An earlier study of Puerto Rican women also showed that, after control for socioeconomic variables, those women who had migrated to the United States had better nutrient intakes than did women living in Puerto Rico (Immink, Sanjur, & Burgos, 1983). In a review of cultural influences on food-related behavior, Axelson (1986) points out that "culture is learned," but that "individuals participate differentially in their culture" (p. 346). While it is clear that the foods traditionally included in the diets of these Hispanic subgroups differ considerably, more research is needed to determine the reasons for these apparent differences in dietary change with acculturation and what implications these changes may have for health status.

Measurement Issues

One of the limiting factors in studying the diets of Hispanics has been the lack of reliable data on the nutrient value of foods commonly consumed by these groups. Much progress has been made in this area, largely as a result of efforts made to improve the database for use with the HHANES, although more remains to be done. Loria, McDowell, Johnson, and Woteki (1991), for example, point to the differences in Mexican American foods such as tacos, where the Americanized versions included in the U.S. Department of Agriculture (USDA) database differ from those frequently consumed by the Mexican American population. For example, the database taco includes a fried tortilla and lettuce, while Mexican versions include a tortilla cooked without fat and served without lettuce. Also, the database version of tomato-chili sauce contains greater energy and sodium levels than does uncooked Mexican salsa, and lower fat levels than does cooked Mexican salsa.

Another problem, particularly for relating diet measures to health, is the need for specifically designed food frequency questionnaires when collecting data from a group with different eating patterns. Given adequate nutrient databases, the 24-hour recall is a very useful tool for quantifying mean intakes for groups, and comparing these across groups. However, substantial day-to-day variation in dietary intake makes a single 24-hour recall a poor representation of an individual's usual diet. This leads to serious misclassification in the ranking of nutrient intakes that, in turn, leads to the attenuation of correlation and regression coefficients when the variable (nutrient or food intake) is related to health outcomes or other variables. Because many days of intake are needed to achieve a relatively reliable measure of usual intake (Hartman et al., 1990)—which demands a heavy respondent burden and considerable expense—food frequency instruments are commonly used in epidemiologic studies. The use of this type of instrument has contributed greatly to recent progress in our understanding of long-term usual dietary intake and disease outcomes. Major food frequency questionnaires in use have been designed to rank individuals in terms of their usual nutrient intakes. Their design has depended on a variety of assumptions related to the dominant patterns in the population. These include the food list, which includes the major sources of nutrients in the total population; the nutrient database, in which the weighted contribution of specific foods to the total food group represented by the line item (e.g., apples, pears, and applesauce) is based on the frequency of consumption within the reference population; and in the portion size assumptions, again based on mean values from the reference population. To collect data from a population subgroup with a distinctly different eating pattern, special instruments must be designed. Given the diversity in diet patterns across Hispanic subgroups discussed above, it is clear that the adaptations needed for use with Mexican Americans will differ from those needed for use with Puerto Ricans. When an objective is direct comparison across subgroups, or with the majority population, this adaptation requires carefully designed compromises to avoid bias toward greater precision in measurement for one versus other groups of interest. This poses a challenge as we expand our study of diet and disease into differing ethnic groups and subgroups.

Anthropometric Status

Obesity

The prevalence of obesity has been increasing among the U.S. population at alarming rates. The clearly established negative effect of obesity on the incidence and severity of a variety of serious chronic diseases, including hypertension, diabetes, and heart disease (Lew & Garfinkel, 1979; Manson et al., 1995; Rissanen et al., 1989), make this a serious public health problem. Anthropometric data from NHANES III Phase I, presented by Kuczmarski, Flegal, Campbell, and Johnson (1994), show large increases in the prevalence of overweight in relation to the NHANES II data. This is true for all age groups, including the elderly. Men aged 60 to 74 years were estimated to have a prevalence of overweight of 40.9% in the 1988-1991 period, versus 26.8% in the earlier survey; and women, 41.3% versus an earlier 37.3%.

Data from HHANES show that obesity is even more prevalent among Hispanics than among the NHW population, particularly for women. Table 10.4 summarizes the results for a measure of weight that is calculated to be independent of height—the body mass index (BMI = weight in kg/height in m^2) for Hispanic groups in the HHANES. Among Hispanic adults aged 65 to 74 years, Puerto Ricans had the highest average BMIs (26.3 kg/m^2 for men and 28.5 for women). According to standards determined by the 85th and 95th percentiles of weight for 20- through 29-year-olds in the NHANES II survey (National Center for Health Statistics, 1987), individuals are considered to be overweight if they are at or above BMIs of 27.8 for men or 27.3 for women, and to be severely overweight at BMIs greater than or equal to 31.1 for men and 32.3 for women. Based on these criteria, Puerto Ricans also have the greatest percentages classified as overweight (31.6% for men and 61% for women) and as severely overweight (10.2% for men and 23.9% for women) among the HHANES groups (Najjar & Kuczmarski, 1989).

In parallel with the overall increases in the general U.S. population, Kuczmarki and colleagues (1994) report large increases in obesity prevalence among Mexican Americans from the HHANES to the NHANES III—from 30.9% to 39.8% for men and 41.5% to 48.1% for women. Among older groups in NHANES III, overweight was more common among Mexican American men, when compared to NHW and non-Hispanic Black (NHB) men; and among Mexican American women compared with NHW women.

TABLE 10.4 Overweight and Severe Overweight Among Elders in HHANES and Massachusetts

HHANES (Ages 65-74 Years)		Puerto Ricans	Cubans	Mexicans
MEN				
N		25	41	82
BMI ($\bar{x} \pm SD$)		26.3 ± 3.6	26.0 ± 3.9	25.8 ± 3.6
Overweight (%)		31.6	31.1	30.3
Severe Overweight (%)		10.2	5.0	7.4
WOMEN				
N		53	64	118
BMI ($\bar{x} \pm SD$)		28.5 ± 6.1	26.7 ± 3.8	27.8 ± 5.0
Overweight (%)		61.0	39.6	49.7
Severe Overweight (%)		23.9	7.7	21.3

Massachusetts (Ages 60-98 Years)	NHW[a]	Puerto Ricans	Dominicans	Other Hispanics
MEN				
N	58	104	21	40
BMI ($\bar{x} \pm SD$)	27.8 ± 7.2	26.5 ± 4.7	25.0 ± 3.6	26.8 ± 3.5
Overweight (%)	43.1	37.5	19.0	42.5
Severe Overweight (%)	20.7	13.5	9.5	7.5
WOMEN				
N	94	152	44	56
BMI ($\bar{x} \pm SD$)	28.2 ± 7.1	29.5 ± 6.3	29.7 ± 5.4	29.1 ± 6.6
Overweight (%)	53.2	61.8	65.9	55.4
Severe Overweight (%)	25.5	31.6	27.3	28.6

SOURCE: HHANES: Najjar & Kuczmarski (1989).

NOTE: Overweight: BMI equal to or greater than the 85th percentile for subjects 20-29 years examined in NHANES II (men ≥ 27.8; women ≥ 27.3).

Severe overweight: BMI equal to or greater than the 95th percentile for subjects 20-29 yrs. examined in NHANES II (men ≥ 31.1; women ≥ 32.3).

a. NHW elders living in same neighborhoods as randomly selected Hispanic elders.

Non-Hispanic Black women were somewhat more likely to be overweight than the Mexican American women (Kuczmarski et al., 1994).

Findings from the Massachusetts study are also presented in Table 10.4. Puerto Rican and Dominican women have the highest prevalence of obesity, with rates for Puerto Rican women similar to those in HHANES (61.8% in

Massachusetts vs. 61% in the HHANES); however, the prevalence of severe overweight is much greater in the Massachusetts sample (31.6% vs. 23.9%). Dominican women also have alarmingly high obesity rates. In contrast, the men with the highest obesity rates in this study were the NHW neighborhood controls. Still, the rates for Puerto Rican men in Massachusetts exceed those seen in HHANES (37.5% vs. 31.6% for overweight; and 13.5% vs. 10.2% for severe overweight). As our study was conducted more recently than the HHANES, these figures are consistent with other trend indicators, which suggest that obesity prevalence has increased dramatically over the past decade.

Given the important negative health effects associated with obesity, it is important to understand the factors associated with these high obesity rates among Hispanics, but few studies have examined this. Pawson, Martorell, and Mendoza (1991), using HHANES data, performed multiple regressions of BMI on age, gender, poverty, language spoken, and, for Mexican Americans only, geographic location. For Puerto Ricans and Mexican Americans, greater age and female gender were associated with greater BMI; poverty was associated with greater BMI for Mexican Americans only.

The San Antonio Heart Study examined adult Mexican Americans and NHWs, aged 25 to 64 years, living in two distinct areas for NHWs and three areas for Mexican Americans—an urban "transitional" middle-income neighborhood, and a higher-income suburban area; plus a group of low-income Mexican Americans living in "barrio" neighborhoods. They saw significantly greater BMIs and subscapular skinfolds among Mexican Americans when compared to NHWs, with no differences for either ethnic group across living area among men, but clearly higher levels of obesity among women in the urban versus suburban areas (Malina, Little, Stern, Gaskill, & Hazuda, 1983). In an examination of attitudes and behavior in relation to obesity, investigators from the San Antonio Heart Study found few ethnic differences in knowledge about obesity, but greater "fatalism" about obesity among Mexican American women (Stern, Pugh, Gaskill, & Hazuda, 1982). Mexican Americans were also much less likely to report avoidance of sugar or dieting behavior than were NHWs. These differences were stronger in the urban neighborhoods than in the suburban study area. Mexican Americans in both areas were more likely to say that "Americans are too concerned about weight loss" (Stern et al., 1982, p. 925), which, the authors suggest, indicates that Mexican Americans have not "fully accepted the American cultural ideal of leanness" (p. 926). In further work with these data, the authors found that among Mexican Americans, increased acculturation was associated with a linear decline in obesity for both men and women, while socioeconomic status was associated with less obesity only for women (Hazuda, Haffner, Stern, & Eifler, 1988). Even among women, acculturation was more closely associated with obesity than was socioeconomic status, indicating, the authors conclude, that culturally mediated factors are more important than socioeconomic factors.

Given its importance as a disease risk factor, the evidence of increasing rates of obesity in the general population (Kuczmarski et al., 1994) and the extremely high rates of obesity, including severe obesity, among Hispanic elders, it is clear that this problem is of major public health concern. That Puerto Ricans, the most socioeconomically disadvantaged of all Hispanic groups, show the highest prevalence of obesity is troubling given all the other problems associated with poverty. The suggestion that acculturation has been shown in some studies to be inversely associated with obesity is an intriguing finding that awaits further corroboration.

Underweight

There is currently no accepted standard cutoff point for estimating prevalence of underweight among elderly groups. Sichieri, Everhart, and Hubbard (1991) estimated the prevalence of underweight using several different cutoff points and showed that prevalence rates may vary greatly when different standards are used. Using the National Center for Health Statistics (NCHS) 15th percentile for subjects in NHANES II aged 20 to 29 years, cutoff points for underweight are 20.8 for men and 19.1 for women (Sichieri et al., 1991). The World Health Organization and the Canadian standards have defined BMI less than 20 as a cutoff point for underweight; (Canada Health Promotion Directorate, 1988; World Health Organization, 1990) and some have used a cutoff point as high as less than 22 BMI (Posner, Jette, Smigelski, Miller, & Mitchell, 1994).

Underweight among Hispanic elders has been poorly documented. Using data from the NHANES II and the HHANES for all adults aged 19 to 74 years, Sichieri et al. (1991) found that women were more likely than men to be underweight when uniform cutoff points were used; but with the NHANES II 15th percentile (which differentiates between men and women), men were more likely to be underweight. Among males, African American men were most likely to be underweight (13.4%), followed by Puerto Rican men

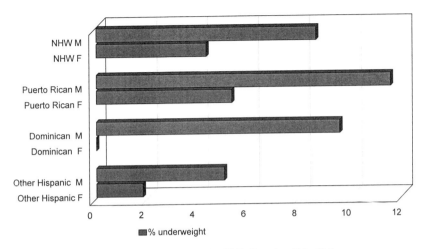

Underweight: Men, BMI < 20.7, Females. B<I <19.1

Figure 10.4. Prevalence of Underweight, Massachusetts Elders (60-98 yrs)
NOTE: Underweight: Males, BMI < 20.7; Females, BMI < 19.1.

(11.2%). Among females in the NHANES II and HHANES, NHW and Puerto Rican women were most likely to be underweight (8.3 and 8.1%, respectively). Prevalence of underweight was 9.2% and 7.6% for Mexican American and Cuban men, respectively; and 3.8% and 5.9% for Mexican American and Cuban women, respectively (Sichieri et al., 1991).

Following the method used by Sichieri et al. (1991), we used the NHANES II 15th percentiles for subjects 20 to 29 years of age to define cutoff points for underweight. Results from the Massachusetts study (Figure 10.4) show that, in addition to obesity, underweight appears to be a problem in a significant proportion of this population, with the highest rates among Puerto Rican men (11.5%—almost the same rate as that seen in HHANES) and Dominican men (9.5%). On the other hand, the prevalence of underweight is very low among women in this study, with the highest rate, for Puerto Rican women (5.3%), somewhat lower than the rates seen among Puerto Rican women in the HHANES.

The reasons for undernutrition among free-living elders are difficult to assess cross-sectionally. Low weights are often due to underlying disease processes, and they are predictive of future hospitalization (Mowé, Bøhmer, &

Kindt, 1994). They may also be due to inadequate dietary intake, which in turn may be due to a variety of factors including disability, depression, poverty, low education level, poor dental status, and lack of social support (Davis et al., 1988; Posner et al., 1994; Tucker, Spiro, & Weiss, 1995). Both overweight and underweight may contribute to deterioration in health and level of independence. Further research is needed for a better understanding of how to intervene to improve weight maintenance at a healthy level.

Biochemical Indices

Lipids

High total cholesterol and triglyceride levels have long been known to be risk factors for heart disease. In addition, low level of one type of cholesterol—HDL, or high density lipoprotein cholesterol—is now known to be even more predictive of future heart disease. Despite the presence of several risk factors for heart disease, including high rates of obesity, one paradox has been lower observed rates of heart disease among Mexican Americans when compared with NHWs. Researchers from the San Antonio Heart Study (Mitchell, Stern, Haffner, Hazuda, & Patterson, 1990) found that, for both men and women, triglycerides were higher and high density lipoprotein (HDL) cholesterol lower for Mexican Americans than for NHWs. These authors suggest that some genetic or unmeasured lifestyle factor must be present in Mexican Americans or absent in NHWs to explain the differences in risk. In contrast, prevalence of high cholesterol (more than 240 mg/dl) in HHANES adults was lower than that reported for NHWs and non-Hispanic African Americans in NHANES II; but among Hispanic subgroups, was highest for Puerto Rican women, at 22.7% (vs. 20% for Mexican American and 16.9% for Cuban women). Among Hispanic men, the percentage with high cholesterol levels was greatest for Mexican Americans (18.8% vs. 17.1% for Puerto Ricans and 16.9% for Cubans; Fanelli-Kuczmarski & Woteki, 1990).

Data from the Massachusetts Hispanic Elders Study show few differences in these indicators across the three Hispanic subgroups or in comparison with the NHW group (Table 10.5). As in the HHANES versus NHANES II data described above, highest average cholesterol levels are seen in the NHW women, followed by the Puerto Rican women. "Other Hispanics" tend

TABLE 10.5 Serum Levels of Triglycerides, Cholesterol, HDL, Cholesterol/HDL Ratio Among Elders in Massachusetts

Indicator Mean (SE)	NHW[a]		Puerto Rican		Dominican		Other Hispanic	
	Men	Women	Men	Women	Men	Women	Men	Women
N	Mean (SE) 39	Mean (SE) 58	Mean (SE) 87	Mean (SE) 115	Mean (SE) 16	Mean (SE) 36	Mean (SE) 27	Mean (SE) 40
Triglyceride	156 (11.0)	172 (12.0)	152 (8.6)	155 (7.4)	127 (13.0)	165 (12.4)	161 (13.8)	190 (12.8)
Total cholesterol	191 (5.8)	222 (5.4)	187 (4.2)	208 (3.6)	184 (11.0)	204 (6.8)	198 (7.6)	204 (6.6)
HDL cholesterol	42 (1.6)	55 (2.3)	43 (1.8)	49 (1.3)	38 (2.3)	46 (2.8)	43 (2.2)	46 (1.9)
LDL cholesterol	118 (5.4)	133 (4.9)	114 (3.9)	127 (3.2)	120 (10.3)	125 (5.9)	122 (6.2)	120 (6.2)
Cholesterol/HDL Ratio	4.8 (0.2)	4.4 (0.2)	4.8 (0.2)	4.5 (0.1)	4.9 (0.4)	4.8 (0.2)	4.8 (0.2)	4.6 (0.2)

NOTE: a. NHW elders living in same neighborhoods as randomly selected Hispanic elders.

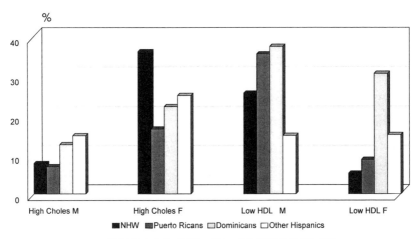

Figure 10.5. Percentage With High Blood Cholesterol and With Low HDL Cholesterol Levels, Massachusetts Elders (60-98 yrs)
NOTE: High total cholesterol > 240 mg/dl; Low HDL cholesterol < 35 mg/dl.

to have highest triglyceride levels. Figure 10.5 presents the proportions of the subgroups with low levels of HDL, the so-called good cholesterol, and with high total cholesterol. Low HDLs are more prevalent among men than women, while high total cholesterol levels are more prevalent among women than men. Puerto Rican men and Dominican men and women are most likely to have low HDL; NHW women are most likely to have high total cholesterol.

Nutrient Status

Only limited data are available on nutrient status of Hispanic groups. Using data from the HHANES, Looker, Johnson, and Underwood (1988) presented serum retinol levels for men and women aged 45 to 74 years. Vitamin A deficiency (serum retinol less than 0.35 mmol/L) was not seen to be a problem for these adult Hispanics. Among men, mean levels were highest among the Cubans (2.05 mmol/L) and lowest for Mexican Americans and Puerto Ricans (1.87 and 1.96, respectively). Among women, they were also highest among the Cubans (1.77), followed by the Puerto Ricans (1.72) and Mexican Americans (1.68).

Folate status is of considerable interest among elders due to recently accumulating evidence of its preventive effects on vascular disease (Selhub et al., 1995; Stampfer et al., 1992) and possibly on cognitive function (Jacques & Riggs, 1995; Riggs, Spiro, Tucker, & Rush, 1996). Both serum and red blood cell (RBC) folate levels were measured in the HHANES only for women aged 18 to 44 years (Fanelli-Kuczmarski, Johnson, Elias, & Najjar, 1990). The RBC folate measure is considered to reflect longer-term folate status more accurately. Among these women, the prevalence of low RBC folate was high for all groups, but was greatest for the Cubans (16.7%), followed by the Puerto Ricans (13.6%) and Mexican Americans (7.8%). More research is needed to determine the extent of this potentially serious problem among older Hispanics.

Another nutrient of considerable interest among elders, due to its antioxidant properties and proposed cancer prevention effects, is vitamin E. Again, few data are available to assess the status of this nutrient in Hispanic groups. Serum α-tocopherol levels were analyzed for HHANES subjects aged 4 to 74 years (Looker, Underwood, Wiley, Fulwood, & Sempos, 1989). Among the eldest group presented (aged 45-74 years), mean values were lowest for the Puerto Rican group (25.8 μmol/L, vs. 27.9 and 29.2 for Cubans and Mexican Americans, respectively). Puerto Ricans also tended to have lower α-tocopherol/lipid (cholesterol + triglycerides) ratios than did other groups. The latter were examined because blood levels of vitamin E, a fat soluble vitamin, are influenced by serum lipid concentrations (Vatassery, Krzowski, & Eckfeldt, 1983); thus, this ratio provides an additional measure of vitamin E status. The reasons for the apparently lower vitamin E status among Puerto Ricans requires further investigation.

Iron status was measured among subjects in the HHANES, using the three-variable mean corpuscular volume (MCV) model developed for use with NHANES II (Pilch & Senti, 1984), where impaired iron status for adults was defined by abnormal values for at least two of the following parameters: transferrin saturation (less than 16%), erythrocyte protoporphyrin (greater than 1.14 μmol/L of red blood cells) and MCV (less than 80 fl). Using this model, the prevalence of poor iron status among Hispanics aged 65 to 74 years was greatest for Cuban women (5.9%), followed by Mexican American and Puerto Rican women (both 1.9%). Among younger women, rates were greatest among Puerto Ricans. Mexican American men had a prevalence of 1.5%. No cases of impaired iron status were seen among a sample of 38 Cuban men; the Puerto Rican sample was deemed too small to present an estimate (Looker, Johnson, McDowell, & Yetley, 1989). In comparison, the percentages of NHANES II NHW men and women aged 65 to 74 with impaired iron status were 2.9% and 3.4%, respectively.

In the Massachusetts study, low iron status, as measured by hemoglobin less than 11.5 g/dl, was greater among Puerto Rican elders than that seen in HHANES; 5.8% for men and 7.1% for women. It was higher still for "Other Hispanic" women (10%), but lower for Dominican women (2.9%). No cases of low hemoglobin were seen among our small samples of Dominican and "Other Hispanic" men. The NHW neighborhood control group had rates of 2.6% for men and 7% for women. Iron deficiency among elders is often due to bleeding disorders. Deficiency in this age group due to inadequate diet is unusual, but may occur. Further information is needed to determine the specific causes, and thereby the appropriate treatments, for poor iron status in elders.

Summary

There are many reasons for concern about the diet and nutrition status of Hispanic elders. Differences in diet patterns across groups include much greater use of rice and starchy staples like potatoes, other root crops, and plantains by Puerto Ricans, Dominicans, and Other Hispanics, whereas Mexican American diets include much greater use of beef, tortillas, and eggs, with associated high intake of total fat, saturated fat, and cholesterol. The recent NHANES III show slightly lower—but still higher than recommended—fat intakes among Mexican American elders, when compared with the HHANES.

Despite macronutrient profiles that may be considered more heart healthy than those consumed by the Mexican American population, average micronutrient intakes appear to be lowest for Puerto Rican and Dominican elders, particularly for vitamin C, riboflavin, calcium, iron, and zinc. Although Mexican Americans in the NHANES III tend to have somewhat higher intakes for most vitamins and minerals than do the Puerto Ricans and Dominicans in the Massachusetts study, their intakes of most nutrients are lower than the NHWs in NHANES III. Low micronutrient intake is therefore an important concern for all the Hispanic subgroups.

A major problem in the U.S. population, and which is particularly prevalent among Hispanics, is obesity. Women in particular suffer from excessive rates of obesity, which, in turn, is a risk factor for a variety of serious chronic diseases and for increased mortality. On the other hand, these groups also have subsets with low weight, or wasting, which may be due largely to advanced disease processes, but which may also be related to food insecurity.

Data on blood lipids across groups are less consistent. Although somewhat lower than in non-Hispanic groups in NHANES II, data from HHANES adults show relatively high rates of high cholesterol levels, particularly among Puerto Rican women. The Massachusetts women also have higher average cholesterol rates than the men but, in contrast to other findings, the Puerto Rican women were less likely to have high cholesterol than women in other groups. Low HDL levels appear to be a particular problem among Massachusetts Hispanics.

Only very limited data are available on blood nutrient levels for Hispanic adults, and far fewer for elders. The sample sizes for all of these are quite limited. From what is available, there is no evidence of vitamin A deficiency among Hispanic adults. Folate status is reported only for 18- to 44-year-old women in HHANES, but among these, low levels are not uncommon (8%-17%). Given its importance to homocysteine levels, heart disease, and possibly other chronic conditions, the assessment of folate status among Hispanic elders needs to be addressed in future research. Impaired iron status has been seen, particularly among Cuban women in HHANES and among "Other Hispanic" women and Puerto Rican women and men in Massachusetts.

Like many investigations, these early findings on diet and nutrition of Hispanic elders raise more questions than they answer. Obesity, underweight, low micronutrient intake, and possibly low folate and iron status are all important problems among Hispanic elders. Prevalence and severity rates appear to differ substantially across Hispanic subgroups, highlighting the real differences that exist and emphasizing the need to examine these groups separately. Factors that may explain these differentials include poverty and education levels, migration and acculturation histories, and cultural patterns of diet and health attitudes, beliefs, practices, and access, as well as some possible genetic components. Research is needed to better understand the causation and consequences of these nutrition problems among Hispanic subgroups and to develop culturally appropriate education and interventions to improve nutrition and associated health status among the growing population of Hispanic elders in the United States.

References

Alaimo, K., McDowell, M. A., Briefel, R. R., Bischof, A. M., Caughman, C. R., Loria, C. M., & Johnson, C. L. (1994). *Dietary intake of vitamins, minerals, and fiber of persons ages 2 months and over in the United States: Third National Health and Nutrition Examination Survey, Phase 1, 1988-91* (Advance data from Vital and Health Statistics, No 258). Hyattsville, MD: National Center for Health Statistics.

Andrews, J. (1989). *Poverty and poor health among elderly Hispanic Americans.* Report of the Commonwealth Fund Commission on Elderly People Living Alone, Baltimore, MD.

Axelson, M. L. (1986). The impact of culture on food-related behavior. *Annual Review of Nutrition, 6,* 345-363.

Bartholomew, A. M., Young, E. A., Martin, H. W., & Hazuda, H. P. (1990). Food frequency intakes and sociodemographic factors of elderly Mexican Americans and non-Hispanic Whites. *Journal of the American Dietetic Association, 90,* 1693-1696.

Bastida, E. (1988). Reexamining assumptions about extended familism: Older Puerto Ricans in a comparative perspective. In M. Sotomayor & H. Curiel (Eds.), *Hispanic elderly: A cultural signature* (pp. 163-183). Edinburg, TX: Pan American University Press.

Bermúdez, O. (1994). *Relationship of acculturation, health, and socioeconomic factors to dietary status of Puerto Rican elderly.* Unpublished doctoral dissertation, University of Massachusetts, Amherst.

Borrud, L. G., Pillow, P. C., Allen, P. K., McPherson, R. S., Nichaman, M. Z., & Newell, G. R. (1989). Food group contributions to nutrient intake in Whites, Blacks, and Mexican Americans in Texas. *Journal of the American Dietetic Association, 89,* 1061-1069.

Canada Health Promotion Directorate. (1988). *Canadian guidelines for healthy weights* (Report of an expert group convened by Health Promotion Directorate, Health Service and Promotion Branch). Ottawa: Minister of National Health and Welfare.

Davis, M. A., Murphy, S. P., & Neuhaus, J. M. (1988). Living arrangements and eating behaviors of older adults in the United States. *Journal of Gerontology, 43,* S96-S98.

Dwyer, J., White, J., Ham, R. J., Lipschitz, D., & Wellman, N. S. (1991, September/October). Screening older Americans' nutritional health: Future possibilities. *Nutrition Today,* pp. 21-25.

Fanelli-Kuczmarski, M. T., Johnson, C. L., Elias, L., & Najjar, M. F. (1990). *Folate status of Mexican American, Cuban, and Puerto Rican women. American Journal of Clinical Nutrition, 52,* 368-372.

Fanelli-Kuczmarski, M. T., & Woteki, C. E. (1990, May/June). Monitoring the nutritional status of the Hispanic population: Selected findings for Mexican Americans, Cubans and Puerto Ricans. *Nutrition Today,* pp. 6-11.

Guendelman, S., & Abrams, B. (1995). Dietary intake among Mexican American women: Generational differences and a comparison with White non-Hispanic women. *American Journal of Public Health, 85,* 20-25.

Haffner, S. M., Knapp, J. A., Hazuda, H. P., Stern, M. P., & Young, E. A. (1985). Dietary intakes of macronutrients among Mexican Americans and Anglo Americans: The San Antonio Heart Study. *American Journal of Clinical Nutrition, 42,* 1266-1275.

Hartman, A. M., Brown, C. C., Palmgren, J., Pietinen, P., Verkasalo, M., Myer, D., & Virtamo, J. (1990). Variability in nutrient and food intakes among older middle-aged men. Implications for design of epidemiologic and validation studies using food recording. *American Journal of Epidemiology, 132,* 999-1012.

Hazuda, H. P., Haffner, S. M., Stern, M. P., & Eifler, C. W. (1988). Effects of acculturation and socioeconomic status on obesity and diabetes in Mexican Americans. *American Journal of Epidemiology, 128,* 1289-1301.

Immink, M. D., Sanjur, D., & Burgos, M. (1983). Nutritional consequences of US migration patterns among Puerto Rican women. *Ecology of Food and Nutrition, 13,* 139-148.

Interagency Board for Nutrition Monitoring and Related Research, Ervin, B., & Reed, D. (Eds.). (1993). *Nutrition monitoring in the United States: Chartbook I. Selected findings from the National Nutrition Monitoring and Related Research Program.* Hyattsville, MD: Public Health Service.

Jacques, P. F., & Riggs, K. M. (1995). B vitamins as risk factors for age-related diseases. In I. H. Rosenberg (Ed.), *Nutritional assessment of elderly populations: Measure and function* (pp. 234-251). New York: Raven.

Knapp, J. A., Haffner, S. M., Young, E. A., Hazuda, H. P., Gardner, L., & Stern, M. P. (1985). Dietary intakes of essential nutrients among Mexican-Americans and Anglo-Americans: The San Antonio Heart Study. *American Journal of Clinical Nutrition, 42,* 307-316.

Knapp, J. A., Hazuda, H. P., Haffner, S. M., Young, E. A., & Stern, M. P. (1988). A saturated fat/cholesterol avoidance scale: Sex and ethnic differences in a biethnic population. *Journal of the American Dietetic Association, 88,* 172-177.

Korte, A., & Villa, R. F. (1988). Life satisfaction of older Hispanics. In M. Sotomayor & H. Curiel (Eds.), *Hispanic elderly: A cultural signature* (pp. 65-95). Edinburg, TX: Pan American University Press.

Kuczmarski, R. J., Flegal, K. M., Campbell, S. M., & Johnson, C. L. (1994). Increasing prevalence of overweight among US adults. The National Health and Nutrition Examination Surveys, 1960 to 1991. *Journal of the American Medical Association, 272,* 205-211.

Kuczmarski, R. J., Kuczmarski, M. F., & Najjar, M. F. (1991). Food group usage of Hispanics residing in selected areas of the US [Abstract]. *Journal of the American Dietetic Association, 91*(Suppl.), A-80.

Lew, E. A., & Garfinkel, L. (1979). Variations in mortality by weight among 750,000 men and women. *Journal of Chronic Disease, 32,* 563-576.

Looker, A. C., Johnson, C. L., McDowell, M. A., & Yetley, E. A. (1989). Iron status: Prevalence of impairment in three Hispanic groups in the United States. *American Journal of Clinical Nutrition, 49,* 553-558.

Looker, A. C., Johnson, C. L., & Underwood, B. A. (1988). Serum retinol levels of persons aged 4-74 years from three Hispanic groups. *American Journal of Clinical Nutrition, 48,* 1490-1496.

Looker, A. C., Loria, C. M., Carrol, M. D., McDowell, M. A., & Johnson, C. L. (1993). Calcium intakes of Mexican Americans, Cubans, Puerto Ricans, non-Hispanic Whites, and non-Hispanic Blacks in the United States. *Journal of the American Dietetic Association, 93,* 1274-1279.

Looker, A. C., Underwood, B. A., Wiley, J. A., Fulwood, R., & Sempos, C. T. (1989). Serum alpha-tocopherol levels on Mexican Americans, Cubans and Puerto Ricans aged 4-74y. *American Journal of Clinical Nutrition, 50,* 491-496.

Loria, C. M., Bush, T. L., Carrol, M. D., Looker, A. C., McDowell, M. A., Johnson, C. L., & Sempos, C. T. (1995). Macronutrient intakes among adult Hispanics: A comparison of Mexican Americans, Cuban Americans, and Mainland Puerto Ricans. *American Journal of Public Health, 85,* 684-689.

Loria, C. M., McDowell, M. A., Johnson, C. L., & Woteki, C. E. (1991). Nutrient data for Mexican-American foods: Are current data adequate? *Journal of the American Dietetic Association, 91*(8), 919-922.

Malina, R. M., Little, B. B., Stern, M. P., Gaskill, S. P., & Hazuda, H. P. (1983). Ethnic and social class differences in selected anthropometric characteristics of Mexican American and Anglo adults: The San Antonio Heart Study. *Human Biology, 55,* 867-883.

Marks, G., Garcia, M., & Solis, J. M. (1990). Health risk behavior of Hispanics in the United States: Findings from HHANES, 1982-84. *American Journal of Public Health, 80*(Suppl.), 20-26.

Manson, J. E., Willet, W. C., Stamper, M. J., Colditz, G. A., Hunter, D. J., Hankinson, S. E., Hennekens, C. H., & Speizer, F. E. (1995). Body weight and mortality among women. *New England Journal of Medicine, 333,* 677-685.

McDowell, M. A., Briefel, R. R., Alaimo, K., Bischof, A. M., Caughman, C. R., Carroll, M. D., Loria, C. M., & Johnson, C. L. (1994). *Energy and macronutrients intakes of persons ages 2 months and over in the United States: Third National Health and Nutrition Examination Survey, Phase 1, 1988-91* (Advance data from Vital and Health Statistics, No. 255). Hyattsville, MD: National Center for Health Statistics.

McLaughlin, J. A., & Holick, M. G. F. (1985). Aging decreases the capacity of human skin to produce vitamin D_3. *Journal of Clinical Investigation, 76,* 1536-1538.

Mitchell, B. D., Stern, M. P., Haffner, S. M., Hazuda, H. P., & Patterson, J. K. (1990). Risk factors for cardiovascular mortality in Mexican Americans and non-Hispanic Whites. The San Antonio Heart Study. *American Journal of Epidemiology, 131,* 423-433.

Mowé, M., Bøhmer, T., & Kindt, E. (1994). Reduced nutritional status in an elderly population (< 70 y) is probable before disease and possibly contributes to the development of disease. *American Journal of Clinical Nutrition, 59,* 317-324.

Najjar, M. F., & Kuczmarski, R. J. (1989). *Anthropometric data and prevalence of overweight for Hispanics: 1982-84. National Center for Health Statistics* (Vital and Health Statistics, Series 11, No. 239). Hyattsville, MD: U.S. Department of Health and Human Services, Public Health Service.

National Center for Health Statistics. (1987). *Anthropometric reference data and prevalence of overweight, United States, 1976-80* (Vital and Health Statistics, Series 11, No. 238; DHHS Publication No. [PHS] 87-1688). Washington, DC: Government Printing Office.

National Cholesterol Education Program. (1991). Report of the Expert Panel on Population Strategies for Blood Cholesterol Reduction. *Circulation, 83,* 2154-2232.

The Nutrition Screening Initiative. (1991). *Report of Nutrition Screening 1: Toward a common view* [Executive summary] (pp. 1-12). Washington, DC: Author.

Pawson, I. G., Martorell, R., & Mendoza, F. E. (1991). Prevalence of overweight and obesity in U.S. Hispanic populations. *American Journal of Clinical Nutrition, 53,* 1522S-1528S.

Pilch, S. M., & Senti, F. R. (Eds.). (1984). *Assessment of the iron nutritional status of the U.S. population based on data collected in the second National Health and Nutrition Examination Survey, 1976-1980.* Bethesda, MD: Federation of American Societies for Experimental Biology.

Posner, B. M., Jette, A., Smigelski, C., Miller, D., & Mitchell, P. (1994). Nutritional risk in New England elders. *Journal of Gerontology, 49,* M123-M132.

Riggs, K. M., Spiro, A., III, Tucker, K. L., & Rush, D. (1996). Relations of vitamin B_{12}, vitamin B_6, folate, and homocysteine to cognitive performance in the Normative Aging Study. *American Journal of Clinical Nutrition, 63,* 306-314.

Rissanen, A., Heliovaara, M., Knekt, P., Aromaa, A., Reunanen, A., & Maatela, J. (1989). Weight and mortality in Finnish men. *Journal of Clinical Epidemiology, 42,* 781-789.

Roe, D. A. (1989). *Diet and drug interactions.* New York: Van Nostrand Reinhold.

Romero-Gwynn, E., Gwynn, D., Grivetti, L., McDonald, R., Stanford, G., Turner, B., West, E., & Williamson, E. (1993, July/August). Dietary acculturation among Latinos of Mexican descent. *Nutrition Today,* pp. 5-12.

Russell, R. M., & Suter, P. M. (1993). Vitamin requirements of elderly people: An update. *American Journal of Clinical Nutrition, 58,* 4-14.

Sanjur, D. (1995). *Hispanic foodways, nutrition & health.* Needham Heights, MA: Allyn & Bacon.

Selhub, J., Jacques, P. F., Bostom, A. G., D'Agostino, R. B., Wilson, P. W., Belanger, A. J., O'Leary, D. H., Wolf, P. A., Schaefer, E. J., & Rosenberg, I. H. (1995). Association between plasma homocysteine concentrations and extracranial carotid-artery stenosis. *New England Journal of Medicine, 332,* 286-291.

Sichieri, R., Everhart, J. E., & Hubbard, V. S. (1991). Relative weight classifications in the assessment of underweight and overweight in the United States. *International Journal of Obesity, 16,* 303-312.

Stampfer, M. J., Malinow, M. R., Willet, W. C., Newcomer, L. M., Upson, B., Ullmann, D., Tishler, P. V., & Hennekens, C. H. (1992). A prospective study of plasma homocysteine and risk of myocardial infarction in U.S. physicians. *Journal of the American Medical Association, 268,* 877-881.

Stern, M. P., Pugh, J. A., Gaskill, S. P., & Hazuda, H. P. (1982). Knowledge, attitudes, and behavior related to obesity and dieting in Mexican Americans and Anglos: The San Antonio Heart Study. *American Journal of Epidemiology, 115*(6), 917-927.

Tucker, K. L., Jacques, P., & Rush, D. (1995). Characteristics associated with poor dietary intakes among elderly Boston residents. *Age & Nutrition, 6*(3), 149-154.

Tucker, K. L., Spiro, A., & Weiss, S. T. (1995). Variation in food and nutrient intakes among older men: Age, and other socioeconomic factors. *Nutrition Research, 15*(2), 161-176.

U.S. Department of Commerce, Bureau of the Census. (1993). *We the American Hispanics* (WE-2). Washington, DC: Government Printing Office.

Vatassery, G. T., Krzowski, A. M., & Eckfeldt, J. H. (1983). Vitamin E concentrations in human blood plasma and platelets. *American Journal of Clinical Nutrition, 37,* 1020-1024.

Wood, R. J., Suter, P. M., & Russell, R. M. (1995). Mineral requirements of elderly people [Review]. *American Journal of Clinical Nutrition, 62*(3), 493-505.

World Health Organization. (1990). *Diet, nutrition and the prevention of chronic diseases* (WHO Tech. Rep. Series 797) (pp. 69-71). Geneva: World Health Organization.

Woteki, C. E. (1990). The Hispanic Health and Nutrition Examination Survey (HHANES 1982-1984): Background and introduction. *American Journal of Clinical Nutrition, 51,* 897S-901S.

Woteki, C. E., Briefel, R., Hitchcock, D., Ezzati, T., & Maurer, K. (1990). Selection of nutrition status indicators for field surveys: The NHANES III design. *Journal of Nutrition, 120*(11S), 1140-1145.

PART IV

Mental Health

Hispanic Aging, Social Support, and Mental Health

Does Acculturation Make a Difference?

María P. Aranda
Manuel R. Miranda

Although a number of recent reviews on Hispanic aging (Aranda, 1995/1996; Miranda, 1991; Sotomayor, 1991) have appeared in the literature, information pertaining to the nature and rates of mental disorders in this population as well as effective practice interventions remain extremely limited. Previous efforts to determine the rates and correlates of psychological distress in older Hispanic populations have pointed to contradictory results due to both conceptual and methodological issues. A conspicuous omission has been the exclusion of acculturation as a potential determinant of psychological well-being in later life, especially as it pertains to subgroups of older Hispanics and their families residing in the United States. The purpose of this chapter is to provide additional insights into the role that acculturation may play in the mental health of Hispanic elderly and the effects of acculturation on their social supports. Implications for future research and clinical practice will be discussed.

Background

Based upon current demographic projections, our society is becoming increasingly aged and ethnically diverse. First, it is expected that by the year 2030, 22% of the population will be 65 years of age or older compared to 11%

in 1980 (U.S. Department of Health and Human Services, 1991). Second, although the relative proportion of older adults among the White elderly will still be higher than the percentage for minorities, the older ethnic minority population is expected to grow at an even greater rate. For example, between 1990 and 2030, the older White population will grow by 92%, much slower than the projected rate of 247% growth for older Blacks and 395% for older Hispanics (U.S. Department of Health and Human Services, 1991). Not surprisingly, national public and private organizations devoted to the study of, and service to, older ethnic minorities call for immediate attention to this population and the systematic infusion of racial and ethnic minority content in research, practice, and curriculum development on aging (American Society on Aging, 1992; Gerontological Society of America, 1994; U.S. Department of Health and Human Services, 1990).

The Hispanic elderly in particular represent the fastest growing segment of the 65 and over older adult group in the United States (Miranda, 1991). Their numbers will grow dramatically to projected levels of 12.5 million for the 65+ group by 2050, and 4.5 million for those 85 years of age and older (U.S. Bureau of the Census, 1993). Far from being a monolithic group, the Hispanic elderly represent a diverse population along several social, economic, political, and ethnic variables.

Beyond the demographic imperative facing our country, the clinical practice literature also points to the growing numbers of Hispanic elderly who are coming to the attention of service providers (Applewhite, 1988; Aranda, 1990). Unfortunately, little has been documented regarding possible service and treatment modalities appropriate for this group in spite of the fact that older Hispanics have been shown to become more functionally disabled at an earlier age due to medical illnesses than their non-Hispanic White counterparts (Villa, Cuellar, Gamel, & Yeo, 1993). Inasmuch as functional disability is linked to assaults on one's personal coping resources as well as social relationships, we can expect functionally disabled older Hispanics to be afflicted by a multiplicity of psychosocial problems directly affecting their psychological well-being, social supports, and capacity to utilize formal mental health services.

Acculturation and Hispanic Mental Health

Psychological well-being in later life is a function of a multiplicity of factors that develop and change over the life span of the individual. Acculturation, which is one source of variation in human development and behavior, is defined here as:

> those phenomena which result when groups of individuals having different cultures come into continuous first-hand contact, with subsequent changes in the original cultural patterns of either or both groups. (Redfield, Linton, & Herskovits, 1936, p. 149)

For older ethnic minorities, the process of cultural change in the areas of language, ethnic identity, values, beliefs, customs, interactional ties, and so forth, presents a tremendous opportunity for adjustment to life's challenges. The relationship of acculturation to psychological well-being and social supports is the focus of the remainder the chapter.

The majority of studies on Hispanic mental health have focused primarily on the adult population of younger Hispanics. Using this cadre of studies as a baseline for comparison, we can begin to formulate hypotheses regarding acculturation and mental health for older Hispanics.

Several hypotheses have been proposed regarding the relationship between acculturation and psychopathology among Hispanics. The relationship between acculturation and mental health has been summarized by Rogler, Cortes, and Malgady (1991) as to relate in either a (a) positive linear direction, (b) negative linear direction, or (c) curvilinear fashion.

The hypothesis that a positive linear relationship exists between acculturation and mental health suggests that individuals high in acculturation will suffer from higher levels of psychological distress. Studies rendering support for the positive relationship between acculturation and mental disorder are documented in the literature (Burnam, Hough, Karno, Escobar, & Telles, 1987; Caetano, 1987; Escobar, Randolph, & Hill, 1986; Fernandez-Pol, Bluestone, Morales, & Mizruchi, 1985; Gilbert, 1987; Graves, 1967; Markides, Krause, & Mendes de Leon, 1988; Neff, 1986).

Perhaps the studies most indicative of the direct positive relationship hypotheses have been those that examined alcohol and drug consumption and abuse. Inasmuch as the findings point to a direct relationship, it is conjectured that increases in acculturation expose the person ecologically and socially to increased use of alcohol and drugs (Rogler et al., 1991). First, the more acculturated person internalizes self-deprecating attitudes and stereotypes from the dominant culture that result in self-destructive behaviors. Second, exposure to situations in which drugs and alcohol are more accessible increases the risk of consumption and abuse for the more acculturated individual.

Other studies that focus on the rates of psychopathology in Hispanic populations have suggested that rates of distress and disorder are highest in the low acculturated groups. Because of the psychosocial stresses secondary to the immigration process and adaptation to a new host society, a foreign-born person is seen as being at risk for developing psychological distress in comparison to later-generation individuals. In other words, the hypothesis of a direct negative relationship predicts that immigrants low in acculturation have higher rates of psychological distress and disorder. Various studies examined support the direct negative relationship between low acculturation and high psychopathology (Burnam et al., 1987; Escobar et al., 1986; Griffith, 1983; Inclan, 1983; Linn, Hunter, & Perry, 1979; Moscicki, Locke, Rae, & Boyd, 1989; Ortiz & Arce, 1984; Roberts, 1980; Salgado de Snyder, 1987a, 1987b; Torres-Matrullo, 1976).

Although the preponderance of studies point to a linear relationship between acculturation and psychopathology, still another class of outcomes appears. More specifically, some support exists for a curvilinear relationship between acculturation and psychological distress and disorder: that members of the biculturated group are more likely to experience lower levels of psychological distress than either the low or high acculturated groups (Lang, Munoz, Bernal, & Sorenson, 1982; Ortiz & Arce, 1984; Warheit, Vega, Auth, & Meinhardt, 1985). The notion that bilingualism has protective effects against psychosocial stressors has gained some acceptance in both the practice and research literature (Burnam et al., 1987; Keefe & Padilla, 1987; Ortiz & Arce, 1984; Ramirez, 1988; Smart & Smart, 1992).

How do these theoretical assumptions relate to older Hispanics residing in the United States? First, as a group, older Hispanics are considered to be the least acculturated in comparison to younger cohorts of Hispanics, due at least in part to their generational status and relatively lower levels of assimilation. Second, acculturation and its measurement specifically in older Hispanic groups have eluded systematic, theoretical refinements, although more recent attempts have begun to address this problem (Baxter, Caldwell, Shetterly, & Hamman, 1993; Hazuda, Stern, & Haffner, 1988). Third, the effects of confounding variables such as gender, income, education, and health status may be accentuated in this population and are likely to play a significant role in the interrelationships of variables on certain mental health outcomes. Finally, acculturation may not only have a direct effect on mental health status, but may demonstrate indirect effects vis-à-vis its effect on other moderating variables such as the older adult's social supports.

Mental Health and the Hispanic Elderly

The mental health literature in the area of ethnic aging commonly evokes the "social stress" or "social causation" hypothesis to predict greater psychopathology among ethnic elderly (see Markides & Mindel, 1987). The original hypothesis has been used to explain the higher rates of psychological distress in those individuals with lower socioeconomic status. The social stress hypothesis has since been extended to ethnic minority groups that can be expected to experience more stressful life change events as a result of migration, acculturative stress, discrimination, and exclusionary practices from the mainstream culture (Markides & Mindel, 1987). The social causation hypothesis has some conceptual similarities to the negative linear relationship hypotheses discussed earlier in that less-acculturated groups are hypothesized as having higher rates of psychological distress.

Using the social stress perspective, we can begin to explain why older Hispanics may be at risk for developing psychological disorders as a result of both migration and acculturation as well as minority group status. Migration is likely to disrupt attachments to supportive networks in the society of origin and to impose on the Hispanic immigrant the difficult task of incorporation into the primary groups of the host society. Yet, depending on such factors as generational status and length of residency in the United States, the individual's life stresses may vary. For example, a new immigrant from the indigenous regions of Guatemala may experience cultural dissonance as a result of the initial contact with a host society that is culturally distinct from his or her birthplace. A second-generation Mexican American elderly individual who was born and raised in the Venice-Mar Vista area of Los Angeles County, on the other hand, does not experience the initial culture dissonance characterized by recent immigrants and refugees.

Notwithstanding, some researchers contend that other forms of acculturative stress may abound even for the U.S.-born or those who have lived in the United States for many years. The stress related to culture change or acculturative stress inherent in post-immigration adjustment may be persistent and cumulative (Burnam et al., 1987; Griffith, 1983; Lang et al., 1982; Salgado de Snyder, 1987a; Sorenson & Golding, 1988; Warheit et al., 1985). For some subgroups of older Hispanics, such as the Mexican American elderly, nonmigratory acculturative stress is especially germane given that the majority are not immigrants but U.S.-born (Lacayo, 1980).

Still another class of stressors is associated with minority group status. This is based on the notion that for some U.S. ethnic minority groups, the stress of immigration and culture change is compounded by membership in a minority group. Minority groups are those groups that have unequal access to power and are considered unworthy of sharing power equally in a society and are often stigmatized because of assumed inferior traits or characteristics (Greene, 1994). Women, ethnic minorities, gays and lesbians, and the physically challenged are examples of such groups. For ethnic groups such as the Hispanic elderly, the stress of immigration, culture change, and acculturative stress is compounded by minority group status. For example, the older Hispanic may experience barriers to the use of formal services as a result of minority group status factors, e.g., agency staff resistance to dealing with underserved and hard-to-reach populations; lack of adequate health insurance. In summary, the social stress hypothesis may account for the increased vulnerability of older Hispanics as the result of stress-producing events emanating from migration, acculturation, and minority group status.

Nevertheless, it is suggested that variations in acculturation can account for differential outcomes in terms of mental disorders. For instance, biculturated older Hispanics may actually have acquired characteristics and skills that enhance their competencies in navigating their bicultural existence. In other words, biculturated individuals may "have the best of both worlds" and as such retain the psychic, emotional, and spiritual strength of their culture-of-origin, yet are also able to gain entry to Anglo-dominated institutions in the areas of health care, education, politics, media, and other informational transfers. Thus, it is plausible that a bicultural existence along several dimensions may be a protective factor in the older Hispanic's mental well-being. Unfortunately, the dynamics by which this might occur have not been investigated.

Rates of Mental Disorders Among Older Hispanics

Studies on older Hispanics have only superficially begun to address the mental health profile of this group. The few studies comparing Hispanic and Anglo elderly rates of psychological distress in general not only point to competing results, but are narrow in scope and examine different psychological outcomes such as life satisfaction (Andrews, Lyons, & Rowland, 1992), depressed and positive affect (Krause & Goldenhar, 1991), psychological distress (Markides & Lee, 1990), depressive symptomatology (Mendes de Leon & Markides, 1988; Zamanian et al., 1992), and major depression and dysphoria (Kemp, Staples, & Lopez-Aqueres, 1987).

In the first survey documenting prevalence data on the Hispanic elderly in Los Angeles County ($N = 703$), Kemp and his associates (1987) reported the prevalence of depression and dysphoria as measured by the subset of items on the Comprehensive Assessment and Referral Evaluation (CARE), which identifies the psychiatric problems of community-dwelling older adults. The data pointed to high rates of two major affective disorders: dysphoria and depression (about 26%). But when medical disability was held constant, the rate of depression decreased to 5.5%, which more closely approximates the rates of depression in the general elderly population. Thus, the authors stated that physical health status was strongly correlated with depressive disorders in this elderly Hispanic sample.

Another study examined depressive symptoms among three generations of Mexican Americans in Texas ($N = 1,125$; 375 subjects in each generation; Mendes de Leon & Markides, 1988). Using the Center for Epidemiologic Studies Depression Scale (CES-D), the researchers reported that the sample as a whole experienced comparatively low levels of depressive symptoms (mean scores for older males and females were 7.5 and 12.1, respectively). Nevertheless, the rate of high depressive symptoms (score of 16 or higher) among older females was significantly higher than for older males. In fact, older females had the largest proportion of high depressive symptomatology rates of all age groups studied (26% reported 16 symptoms or more on the CES-D). These differences remained after adjusting for marital status, education, and employment.

In the only longitudinal, comparative study on the psychological well-being of older Mexican Americans and Anglos, predictors of functioning and well-being over an 8-year period were examined ($N = 254$) in San Antonio, Texas (Markides & Lee, 1990). First, the researchers found that psychological well-being at Time 2 was significantly predicted by Time 1 values on psychological well-being. Second, that less educated subjects were also more likely to report increased psychological distress. Third, that declines in life satisfaction were associated with higher initial levels of psychological distress. In terms of ethnic comparisons on psychological distress, the Mexican American group was less likely to experience increases in distress over time than their Anglo counterparts. The authors caution that the relatively smaller number of Anglos sampled may account for this finding.

Only three studies reviewed extended the analysis to examine the relationship between acculturation and psychological well-being among older Hispanics. In the first study to look at Hispanic subgroup differences, Krause and Goldenhar (1991) studied data from a nationwide survey of older Mexican Americans, Puerto Ricans, and Cubans ($N = 2,299$) and found that levels of psychological distress tended to vary across Hispanic ethnic groups, and that these differences could be attributed to the interrelationships among (a) language acculturation, (b) educational attainment, (c) financial strain, and (d) social isolation. Using LISREL analyses to assess the relative direct, indirect, and total effects of language acculturation on psychological well-being, the data suggested that language acculturation did not exert a significant direct effect on depressed or positive affect (no rates were reported). Nevertheless, the indirect effects of other intervening variables suggested that acculturation had "a beneficial effect on well-being primarily because more acculturated Hispanics tend to experience fewer financial problems and less social isolation" (p. S286).

The suggestion that more highly acculturated groups of older Hispanics report less depression was corroborated by another study based on random telephone interviews in Fresno, California ($N = 259$; Zamanian et al., 1992). Mexican American elderly 60 years of age and older were administered the CES-D, the Geriatric Depression Scale (GDS), and the Acculturation Rating Scale for Mexican Americans (ARSMA). The relationships between acculturation and the two depression scores were significant even after controlling for socioeconomic status. Minimally acculturated individuals reported higher depression levels than their highly acculturated or biculturated counterparts, whose scores were quite similar to one another.

A positive relationship between language acculturation and psychological well-being was also found in a subsequent study. Language acculturation, that is, self-rated items of both English and Spanish ability, was significantly related to better psychological status in a national random survey of older Hispanics ($N = 632$; Tran, 1994). The subjective well-being measure was operationalized by the concepts of positive affect and lack of negative affect. The findings indicated that those who had a stronger bilingual ability had a better psychological status. Unfortunately, no data were included in this study regarding monolingual English-speaking Hispanics.

Although certainly not conclusive, the last three studies reviewed seem to indicate that, at least for older Hispanics, acculturation may prove to be a protective factor against psychological disorders, at least in the area of depression or depressive symptomatology. Moreover, the dimension of language usage and preference seems to dominate in terms of the operationalization of acculturation in these studies. This is not surprising given the function of language in the development of an individual's and group's ethnicity, culture, and degree of assimilation. Although English-speaking ability is but one indicator of acculturation, previous research indicates that English-speaking ability generally accounts for at least 55% to 60% of the variance in most acculturative scales (Baxter et al., 1993; Burnam et al., 1987; Cuellar, Harris, & Jasso, 1980; Deyo, Diehl, Hazuda, & Stern, 1985; Griffith, 1983; Keefe & Padilla, 1987; Lubben & Becerra, 1987; Olmedo & Padilla, 1978; Padilla, 1980). Subsequent work by Hazuda and her associates (Hazuda, Haffner, Stern, & Eifler, 1988; Hazuda, Stern, & Haffner, 1988) specifically addresses the fact that acculturation is multidimensional and that different dimensions may be differentially related to various health outcomes. How this notion may relate to psychological well-being in older adults remains to be examined.

Another important consideration is that the majority of studies reviewed focused primarily on the experience of older Mexican Americans which is not surprising given the fact that this subgroup constitutes about 60% of all Hispanic elderly in the United States (Commonwealth Fund Commission, 1989). Thus, the few studies that examine the rates of mental disorders among the Hispanic elderly have essentially studied the phenomenon of depressive symptomatology in older Mexican Americans. The importance of these findings for other subgroups of older Hispanics needs further attention.

Social Support, Acculturation, and Hispanic Aging

Previous literature reviews have already surveyed an impressive cadre of studies on the relationship of social support to physical and psychological health (see Vaux, 1988). Social ties are said to be connected in complex sets of relationships among members of social systems in what is referred to as the person's social network. A social network, in other words, is the locus or network that encompasses all of a person's social contacts and through which social support is proffered. For the purpose of the chapter, social support is defined as those resources, tangible or intangible, that are exchanged among members of a social network and that can span across a full range of network members: family, friends, neighbors, co-workers, church members, and so forth (Aranda, 1995). Social support is not only comprised of the social network, but of the supportive functions that are proffered by the social network, such as providing tangible goods and services to expressing affection, feedback, and esteem building (Cohen & Syme, 1985; Gottlieb, 1978).

The link between stressful life events and disease or disorder, although consistently observed in the systematic research studies of the 1970s, was weak and pointed to the attenuating effects of other factors, namely social support. How is social support implicated in the health outcome process? First, social support acts to protect individuals from the effects of stressful life conditions (the stress buffering model). Second, social support also has the effect of providing a protection against potentially deleterious life events independent of the stress process (the direct effect model). Although more empirical evidence exists in favor of the direct effect model, attempts to test both theories have been problematic due to inconsistencies across studies in terms of definitions of constructs and diversity of measures, and reliance on cross-sectional research (Cohen & Syme, 1985; Vaux, 1988). Moreover, social support encompasses the appraisals of the availability and adequacy of the social network and its potential support functions.

A conspicuous omission from the social support literature has been the examination of acculturation as a major variable in the stress-coping-outcome models of health- and mental health-related functioning. Such information could enrich the explanatory power of our analytic models and provide alternative hypotheses for differential rates of disorders across groups. Second, interventions to prevent, reduce, or eliminate psychological disabilities could be developed and implemented with more precision for the older Hispanic population and their caregivers.

That the elderly are a heterogeneous population is gaining more acceptance. The sources of that heterogeneity include differences in the patterns of social involvement and attachments among elderly groups such as older ethnic minorities, including those of the Hispanic elderly. How does acculturation affect the social embeddedness, enacted support, and importance applied to these supports among Hispanics residing in the United States? Do social relationships moderate the effects of acculturation on mental health? To begin examining these questions, let us turn to the literature on the social supports of the Hispanic elderly and the effects of acculturation on social supports.

Support within Hispanic families may be higher than in the general population, partly as a function of the sheer number of persons that constitute the older Hispanic's social network. Hispanic families have larger social networks, live in households with multiple members, and are more likely to report intergenerational living arrangements (Bean & Tienda, 1987). To begin, the average size of the Hispanic household is larger (3.48) compared to the non-Hispanic White household (2.58). About 12% of Hispanic households have six or more members compared with 3% of non-Hispanic White households (U.S. Bureau of the Census, 1991). Second, aside from having larger households, Hispanic families are larger on the average than non-Hispanic White families (3.80 vs. 3.13 persons, respectively). It is important to note that subgroup differences do exist in terms of national origin, U.S. region, rural versus urban, and so forth. For example, Mexican Americans have the largest families on average (4.06) compared to 3.37 for Puerto Ricans and 2.81 for Cubans.

Hispanic kinship networks are an important source of social support for the older Hispanic and a key mediator of stressful life events (Aranda & Knight, 1997; Bastida, 1988; Sotomayor & Applewhite, 1988; Sotomayor & Randolph, 1988; Szapocznik & Hernandez, 1988; Valle & Vega, 1980). Part of the reason for the availability of support may be due to the co-living arrangements and close geographical proximity of family. For example, the Hispanic elderly appear to be more likely than other elderly groups to live in multigenerational households, with three out of four of these households headed by their adult children (Cubillos & Prieto, 1987). It also appears that older Hispanics, in comparison to their non-Hispanic White counterparts, are much more likely to be married and much more likely to rely on family for support than on friends (Commonwealth Fund Commission, 1989; Lacayo, 1980; Lubben & Becerra, 1987). Again, some caution should be exercised before making generalizations, at least in part due to increasing evidence regarding regional variations between Hispanics and non-Hispanic Whites in social relationships. For example, in a study of the social support of elderly Hispanics and non-Hispanic Whites in southern Colorado (Baxter, Hoag, & Hamman, 1994), both groups had similar sized social networks, similar patterns of frequency of contact, and similar patterns in club and church participation. Differences were found between the groups, on the other hand, in terms of composition: Hispanic networks were comprised mostly of family while the non-Hispanic Whites were comprised of friends.

The importance of the social network as a resource in promoting the health and welfare of individuals has long been recognized in Hispanic communities. Yet, the perception of the traditional extended family orientation as a major source of support among Hispanic elderly has been modified due to urbanization and modernization. The extended family structure is being modified to fit changing economic, social and cultural conditions (Becerra & Greenblatt, 1983; Maldonado, 1975). The process of acculturation and modernization, and its concomitant changes in informal caregiving patterns, faces many older Hispanics today. For example, older Hispanics already are the most urbanized subgroup of elderly in the United States (Cubillos & Prieto, 1987). Thus, it is clear that the assumption that the Hispanic elderly always have an existing, readily accessible, and beneficial social network is no longer a given.

Some researchers purport, on the other hand, that Hispanics still espouse the cultural value of familism despite variations due to acculturation, modernization, and sociodemographic status (Sabogal, Marin, Otero-Sabogal, Marin, & Perez-Stable, 1987). The cultural value of *la familia* or familism was first identified by Hispanic writers in the 1970s. Maldonado (1979) defines familism as the centrality of the family among its members. According to Maldonado, the Hispanic individual develops a sense of self through the family. Thus, self-identification is equated with family identification. This is reminiscent of recent theoretical writings by Landrine (1992), who argues that ethnic minority groups are more likely to develop an "indexical self." In other words, the concept of self is embedded in relationships with significant others rather than in the more Anglo tradition of the "referential self." The degree to which the individual adheres to the value of familism may be in part indicative of the level of acculturation.

Evidence exists to contradict the decline of Hispanic familism or at least to define the conditions that may lead to differences in social relationships among differing acculturation groups. Sabogal et al. (1987) studied the effects of acculturation on familism in a Hispanic sample made up of Mexican, Central, and Cuban American respondents in San Francisco, California. Three specific dimensions of familism were identified, as well as the relative resiliency of each dimension: family obligations, perceived support from the family, and the family as referent. Perceived support from the family showed the most resiliency with increased acculturation. Yet high acculturated Hispanics still scored higher than their non-Hispanic White counterparts on both adherence to attitudes regarding family obligations and family as referent.

Earlier work by Keefe and her associates (Keefe & Padilla, 1987) also studied family ties across generations in California. Keefe (1980) found that usage of primary kin networks was positively correlated with generation level. Mexican Americans, whether born in the United States or Mexico, had the same cultural preference for interacting with relatives, but the potential number of local social ties increased with generational level as the U.S.-born Mexican American counted on more primary and secondary kinship ties. Utilizing their acculturation scale of ethnic loyalty and cultural awareness, the researchers found that both ethnic identity and extended familism were the two most significant cultural factors that persisted over time to later-generation Mexican Americans.

An early attempt at studying the effects of acculturation and familial attitudes toward the elderly was undertaken by Zuniga de Martinez (1979), who undertook an exploratory study in San Diego, California, to describe the relationship between acculturation factors and the attenuation of attitudes toward familial reliance as a supportive mechanism for the Mexican American elderly. She found that as acculturation increased, traditional attitudes toward familial support for the aged decreased. Correlated with weakened family reliance were a departure from identification with Mexican cultural heritage, loss of contact with relatives in Mexico, longer U.S. residency, and English-language ability. Thus, Zuniga de Martinez posits that although Mexican culture is maintained by the closeness to Mexico for many Mexican Americans, for those most impacted by acculturation processes, there will be a trend toward less familial support of the elderly.

These findings were corroborated by other researchers (Diaz-Guerrero & Szalay, 1991; Jenerson-Madden, Ebersole, & Romero, 1992) who examined the perception of the role of family in younger Hispanic age groups. For example, Mexicans in Mexico and first-generation Mexican Americans were studied in terms of their beliefs toward the family (Diaz-Guerrero & Szalay, 1991). The researchers found that the Mexican subjects were more likely to reflect the ideals of interdependence, unity, and cohesion of the family above the individual. For the Mexican American subjects, the family was regarded as important, highly valued, but with the independence and autonomy of the individual overriding the interests of the family as a whole. Still another study found statistically significant differences between first generation Mexicans and non-Hispanic Whites on their responses regarding the family as the most important source of meaning in life. Seventy percent of the Mexican American group reported family as the most important in comparison to 47% of the non-Hispanic group (Jenerson-Madden et al., 1992).

Lubben and Becerra (1987), in their study of the social support of Black, Mexican, and Chinese elderly in the Los Angeles area, found a relationship between language acculturation and living arrangements. Using English-speaking ability to divide their Mexican sample into two acculturation groups—monolingual Spanish-speakers (MSS), and bilinguals (BIL)—the authors reported cultural differences with regard to social networks. According to the researchers, the non-Hispanic Whites were more likely to live alone than the two Mexican American groups, yet the BIL group was still less likely to live with family than the MSS group. Although the trend for higher acculturated individuals was toward less contact with children, there was no significant difference between the groups in terms of family interaction.

In the next section of studies reviewed, the notion of support expectations arose as an element of analysis. For example, in a three-generation study that examined language differences on intergenerational support (Levitt, Guacci, & Weber, 1992), it was found that Spanish-speaking respondents in the older and middle generations viewed their relations with the younger generation women less positively compared to English-speaking respondents. The researchers posit that the results are consistent with previous research indicating intergenerational tension in acculturating groups. As stated by the authors, "relational discord across generations may reflect a clash of cultural support expectations" (p. 478).

The issue of unmet support expectations of family support has also been documented in the literature by Markides and his associates (Markides, Boult, & Ray, 1986; Markides, Martin, & Sizemore, 1980) and remains a focus of debate. More specifically, although the expectation of support and assistance may be present among elderly Mexican Americans, the ability and willingness to deliver may not be present on the part of the children. In terms of the Mexican American elderly, Zuniga de Martinez (1979) and Markides and Martin (1983) found evidence of considerable mutual support between older Mexican Americans and their adult children, with high levels of daily contact and high expectations that children should provide support to the elderly. Evidence on the effects of race and ethnicity on filial expectations of support for the elderly has been equivocal in other minority group studies. For example, Black race was unrelated to filial responsibility expectations and realizations (Seelbach, 1978), while White respondents actually had stronger support for filial norms (Hanson, Sauer, & Seelbach, 1983). At least for specific subgroups of Mexican Americans, being female, widowed, and having more chronic illnesses have been associated with a lesser likelihood of perceiving that a caregiver would be available if needed (Talamantes, Cornell, Espino, Lichtenstein, & Hazuda, 1996).

Cultural influences aside, other factors may serve as explanatory variables for the family relationship patterns of Hispanic families. To begin, socioeconomic factors such as education and income, sociohistorical forces, generational differences, increasing urbanization and modernization, and the like, can contribute to the variations in family patterns that exist today. For example, it is not clear whether the Hispanic elderly are living with family as a result of cultural preference, economic necessity, or both. A nationwide survey of older Hispanics (Commonwealth Fund Commission, 1989) reports that the majority of those Hispanic elderly who live with family members are monolingual Spanish-speakers and have per capita incomes below the poverty level. Other studies have refuted the overreliance on cultural explanations as the basis for intergenerational support and have called on controlling for important structural factors in future research (De la Cancela & Martinez, 1983; Gratton & Wilson, 1988; Mutran, 1985).

The fact that the Hispanic elderly are more likely to live in multigenerational households with their adult children as heads of household may be a result of other factors related to the health and socioeconomic status of the Hispanic elderly. Do older Mexican Americans live with their children because of their frail health and need for assistance? What are the factors that lead to the co-living arrangements, and what are the factors that maintain those living arrangements over time? At least for females, there is growing evidence that for both Hispanic and Black elderly women, economics are more significant than health in determining whether a woman co-resides with her children (Worobey & Angel, 1990). Thus, fewer alternatives may exist for older ethnic minorities' living arrangements in the event of diminished health in comparison to their non-Hispanic White counterparts.

Age at migration was also found to have a significant effect on social contacts of older Hispanics, and subsequently on well-being (Angel & Angel, 1992). In other words, Hispanics who moved to the United States as older adults are less likely than earlier immigrants to have been involved in social activities and more likely to report disability and lower life satisfaction than the native-born or those who migrated earlier than age 12. This has implications for the Hispanic elderly in general, who are considered to be heterogeneous in terms of their nativity.

In summary, the social supports of the Hispanic elderly as we see them today are the result of a combination of sociodemographic, sociohistorical, and ethnic change and health status variables that are complexly related to one another. The notion that acculturation may have a direct influence on mental health as well as an indirect effect through its effect on social support is in need of further examination.

Research Implications

As more Hispanics enter their senior years, service providers will need to critically evaluate the assumptions and existing program components that constitute their mental health services in terms of their relevance to the Hispanic elderly. Toward this end, it is critically important to identify and measure with precision those variables that potentially influence mental health outcomes within this population. For example, how is adjustment to aging influenced by differences in the country/area of origin or residence (United States vs. Central or South America; the Southwest vs. other U.S. regions; urban vs. rural); by differences in language skills (monolingual vs. bilingual, language dominance, level of literacy); by differences in years and quality of education; by general life experiences (including both common and unique stressors) and the resulting coping mechanisms developed; by physical health; and by a host of other variables that directly affect the validity of diagnostic and treatment procedures for the Hispanic elderly?

Certainly, some of these issues apply to most elderly individuals. The specificity of these issues in relation to the Hispanic elderly, however, stems from the cultural or racial vulnerability to stress, coping resources, and social support that may influence as well as mediate the rates of mental disorders in the population. For example, late-life depression occurs in the context of co-existing medical disorders (cancer, heart disease, stroke, arthritis), biological vulnerabilities (age-related physiological and brain structure changes; genetic risks for illnesses such as diabetes), and psychosocial factors (bereavement, physical illness, retirement, family conflicts). Are older Hispanics at higher risk for late-life depression given their increased exposure to psychosocial stressors due to poverty, discrimination, community violence and disasters, lower functional status, and so forth? Are acquired biological vulnerabilities to late-life depression elevated in this population as a result of higher alcohol consumption, especially among Hispanic men (Caetano, 1987; Markides et al., 1988), exposure to work-related hazards (environmental toxins, traumatic head injuries) in a population that is overrepresented in agriculture and industrial occupations, and so on? In other words, can ethnic-specific differences in biological vulnerabilities and stressors explain differences in rates and features of specific mental disorders such as depression among older adults? Applying research efforts to these areas of inquiry can prove fruitful in identifying those populations at greater risk.

The fact that various forms of depression were featured so prominently in the mental health literature reviewed above points to two realities regarding depression: (a) its ubiquitous nature, and (b) its conceptual relationship to stress. Perhaps for other psychiatric disorders such as schizophrenia and bipolar disorders, which are far less common in the population and typically begin earlier in life, a genetic propensity features more prominently. Thus, the conceptual link between stress and these disorders is even more muddled by the issue of genetic vulnerability. Unfortunately, no national population-based studies exist that specifically examine the rates of severe psychiatric disorders or the expression of psychological distress in older, community-residing Hispanic populations.

Future research should continue to look beyond single-variable determinants of mental disorders in older Hispanics, such as acculturation, life-change events, socioeconomic status, social support, and so forth. Rather, it is important that a multifactorial, transactional approach to the study of mental disorders be used in order to evaluate how separate factors interact with one another to contribute to psychological distress. For instance, the stress-coping-outcome paradigm, as outlined extensively by previous writers (Aranda & Knight, 1997; Miranda & Castro, 1985; Pearlin, Lieberman, Menaghan, & Mullan, 1981), is a model that can be applied to older Hispanic populations and that has significant implications for the delivery of mental health services. Briefly described, the model conceptualizes psychological distress as a response to stress that is mitigated or buffered by the person's coping resources, such as personal resources and social supports.

Recommendations for future research directions include the following:

- Pursue population-based studies to determine the incidence and prevalence of psychiatric disorders in older Hispanics.
- Study the differential occurrence of specific psychiatric disorders among subgroups in the Hispanic elderly population with a special focus on acculturation, and its multiple dimensions, as a major variable.
- Include prospective studies to identify general risk factors, for example, life stress events, specific illnesses and functional disabilities, and their relationship to psychiatric disorders.

- Improve diagnosis and identification of Hispanic elderly suffering from mild to severe psychiatric disorders by health and mental health care providers. Develop innovative case-finding research protocols.
- Develop linguistically and culturally appropriate instruments for use in research and clinical settings. Improve the conceptualization and measurement of acculturation among older Hispanics to include different dimensions of acculturation.
- Improve the dissemination of information on depression, its diagnosis and treatment, and service delivery models to consumers and their families, professionals, and other staff engaged in the provision of services to older Hispanics.
- Include studies to examine possible cultural expressions of psychological symptomatology in older Hispanics, using both qualitative and quantitative research methods.
- Develop demonstration projects focused on innovative models of care delivery with focus on targeting at-risk groups of older Hispanics and on developing partnerships of care with health and human service agencies.
- Develop and evaluate intervention-based studies linked to the special circumstances of the Hispanic older adult and that test the effectiveness of both biological and psychosocial treatment strategies.

Practice Implications

Any discussion of intervention strategies in alleviating stress and improving competencies in the Hispanic elderly requires a consideration of mediating variables such as coping styles, personal assets, and social support. Although these mediating variables are important in understanding the relationship between life stress and mental health status in any population, they are critical to understanding the phenomenological impact of cultural values and behaviors on the mental health status of Hispanic elderly persons.

In studying the relationship among stress, mental health status, and coping resources, it is important to identify potential interventions, on both a biological and psychosocial level, to prevent or mitigate psychological distress in this population. What are some of these interventions? Aside from the usual recommendations for working with the mental health needs of older adults (see Hersen & Hasselt, 1996), several additional recommendations are in order.

First, as presented earlier, acculturation is a major source of variation in older adults, a crucial factor in the assessment of social supports, and an important link in the cultural expression of adaptation to stress. The service provider is in a crucial position to evaluate the person's level of acculturation as well as that of others in the social network. Although numerous issues related to the conceptualization and measurement of acculturation still abound, several standardized instruments are available and have been reviewed elsewhere in the literature (Cuellar et al., 1980; Deyo et al., 1985; Hazuda, Stern, & Haffner, 1988; Keefe & Padilla, 1987; Marin, Sabogal, Marin, Otero-Sabogal, & Perez-Stable, 1987; Padilla, 1980; Szapocznik, Scopetta, Kurtines, & Aranalde, 1978). Knowledge of the person's acculturation level can assist the service provider in crafting a culturally sensitive treatment plan by assessing the following: (a) expression of the presenting problem(s); (b) reliance on specific forms of coping behaviors (internal vs. external; emotional vs. cognitive; Hispanic vs. non-Hispanic themes); (c) appraisals of availability of social support and its helpfulness; (d) attitudes and behaviors toward the interviewer or service provider; (e) help-seeking and help-receiving behaviors; (f) attitudes toward Western versus indigenous health practices and treatments; and so forth.

Second, the family support system is also a viable source of assistance to the older Hispanic, not only during times of stress but as a prophylactic factor against disease and psychological distress. Treatment strategies should include family members or other non-kin caregivers as part of an integrated treatment plan. Thus, family therapy and psychoeducational approaches with the family as a key co-consumer of services should be integrated with other forms of treatment.

Third, practitioners should be trained in the principles and strategies of crisis intervention. This is a result of the reality that most older Hispanics do not readily seek out professional mental health services, even less so than their White counterparts (Lopez-Aqueres et al., 1984). Consequently, when the older Hispanic does come to the attention of the mental health provider, it is usually when the symptoms of psychological distress are acute and in need of crisis intervention.

To mitigate the effects of minority group status, the service provider can assist the older Hispanic in developing personal competencies to effect change in his or her life. Empowerment-producing strategies as explained by Gutierrez (1990) and Sotomayor (1991) can enhance the personal, interpersonal, or political power so that individuals, families, and communities can take action to improve their situation and reduce their sense of powerlessness. National aging organizations such as the National Hispanic Council on

Aging, the Asociacion Nacional Pro Personas Mayores, the American Society on Aging, and the Gerontological Society of America sponsor numerous programs describing effective empowerment and social action strategies for older Hispanic populations (American Society on Aging, 1992; Gerontological Society of America, 1994; Sotomayor, 1991; U.S. Department of Health and Human Services, 1990).

Conclusion

As we witness the continued aging of the U.S. population, numerous issues in terms of the psychological well-being of older ethnic minorities can no longer elude our research, service delivery, and policy agendas. The conceptualization and measurement of psychological health and distress and their determinants among older Hispanics are fertile areas of inquiry and in need of new theoretical formulations. Variations in acculturation can be measured and their effect in preventing or increasing psychosocial stress can be examined within transactional models of stress, coping, and mental health outcomes.

References

American Society on Aging. (1992). *Serving elders of color: Challenges to providers and the aging network.* Report prepared by the National Task Force on Minority Elders. San Francisco: Author.

Andrews, J. W., Lyons, B., & Rowland, D. (1992). Life satisfaction and peace of mind: A comparative analysis of elderly Hispanic and other elderly Americans. In T. L. Brink (Ed.), *Hispanic aged mental health* (pp. 21-42). New York: Haworth.

Angel, J. L., & Angel, R. J. (1992). Age at migration, social connections, and well-being among elderly Hispanics. *Journal of Aging and Health, 4*(4), 480-499.

Applewhite, S. (Ed.). (1988). *Hispanic elderly in transition.* Edinburg, TX: Pan American University Press.

Aranda, M. P. (1990). Culture friendly services for Latinos. *Generations, 14,* 55-57.

Aranda, M. P. (1995-1996). *Acculturation and social relationships as predictors of health, mental health, and service utilization among older Mexican Americans and non-Latino Whites.* Doctoral dissertation, School of Social Work, University of Southern California.

Aranda, M.P., & Knight, B.G. (1997). The influence of ethnicity and culture on the caregivers stress and coping process: A sociocultural review and analysis. *The Gerontologist, 37,* 342-354.

Bastida, E. (1988). Reexamining assumptions about extended familism: Older Puerto Ricans in a comparative perspective. In M. Sotomayor & H. Curiel (Eds.), *Hispanic elderly: A cultural signature* (pp. 163-183). Edinburg, TX: Pan American University Press.

Baxter, J., Caldwell, E., Shetterly, S. M., & Hamman, R. F. (1993, November). *Performance of acculturation scales in a rural, Hispanic elderly population.* Paper presented at the annual meeting of the Gerontological Society of America, New Orleans.

Baxter, J., Hoag, S., & Hamman, R. F. (1994, November). *San Luis Valley Hispanic health and aging study.* Paper presented at the annual meeting of the Gerontological Society of America, Atlanta, GA.

Bean, F. D., & Tienda, M. (1987). *The Hispanic population of the United States.* New York: Academic Press.

Becerra, R. M., & Greenblatt, M. (1983). *Hispanics seek health care: A study of 1,088 veterans of three war eras.* Rockville, MD: University Press of America.

Burnam, M. A., Hough, R. L., Karno, M., Escobar, J. I., & Telles, C. A. (1987). Acculturation and lifetime prevalence of psychiatric disorders among Mexican Americans in Los Angeles. *Journal of Health and Social Behavior, 28,* 89-102.

Caetano, R. (1987). Acculturation and drinking patterns among U.S. Hispanics. *British Journal of Addiction, 82,* 789-799.

Commonwealth Fund Commission. (1989). *Poverty and poor health among elderly Hispanic Americans.* Baltimore, MD: Commonwealth Fund Commission on Elderly People Living Alone.

Cohen, S., & Syme, L. S. (1985). *Social support and health.* New York: Academic Press.

Cubillos, H., & Prieto, M. (1987). *The Hispanic elderly: A demographic profile.* Washington, DC: National Council of La Raza.

Cuellar, I., Harris, L. C., & Jasso, R. (1980). An acculturation scale for Mexican American normal and clinical populations. *Hispanic Journal of Behavioral Sciences, 2*(3), 199-217.

De la Cancela, B., & Martinez, I. Z. (1983). An analysis of culturalism in Latino mental health: Folk medicine as a case in point. *Hispanic Journal of Behavioral Sciences, 5*(3), 251-274.

Deyo, R. A., Diehl, A. K., Hazuda, H., & Stern, M. (1985). A simple language-based acculturation scale for Mexican Americans: Validation and application to health care research. *American Journal of Public Health, 75*(a), 51-55.

Diaz-Guerrero, R., & Szalay, L. B. (1991). *Understanding Mexicans and Americans: Cultural perspectives in conflict.* New York: Plenum.

Escobar, J. E., Randolph, E. R., & Hill, M. (1986). Symptoms of schizophrenia in Hispanic and Anglo veterans. *Culture, Medicine, and Psychiatry, 10,* 259-276.

Fernandez-Pol, B., Bluestone, H., Morales, G., & Mizruchi, M. (1985). Cultural influences and alcoholism: A study of Puerto Ricans. *Alcoholism: Clinical and Experimental Research, 9,* 443-446.

Gerontological Society of America. (1994). *Minority elders: Five goals toward building a public policy base* (2nd ed.). Washington, DC: Gerontological Task Force of Minority Issues in Gerontology.

Gilbert, M. J. (1987). Acculturation and changes in drinking patterns among Mexican American women: Implications for prevention. *Alcohol Health and Research World, 15*(3), 234-238.

Gottlieb, B. H. (1978). The development and application of a classification scheme of informal helping behaviors. *Canadian Journal of Behavioural Science, 10,* 105-115.

Gratton, B., & Wilson, V. (1988). Family support systems and the minority elderly: A cautionary analysis. *Journal of Gerontological Social Work, 13*(1/2), 81-93.

Graves, T. (1967). Acculturation, access, and alcohol in a tri-ethnic community. *American Anthropologist, 69,* 396-421.

Greene, R. (1994). *Human behavior theory: A diversity framework.* New York: Aldine De Gruyter.

Griffith, J. (1983). Relationship between acculturation and psychological impairment in adult Mexican Americans. *Hispanic Journal of Behavioral Sciences, 5*(4), 431-459.

Gutierrez, L. M. (1990). Working with women of color: An empowerment perspective. *Social Work, 35,* 149-154.

Hanson, S. L., Sauer, W. J., & Seelbach, W. C. (1983). Racial and cohort variations in filial responsibility norms. *The Gerontologist, 23*(6), 626-631.

Hazuda, H. P., Haffner, S. M., Stern, M. P., & Eifler, C. W. (1988). Effects of acculturation and socioeconomic status on obesity and diabetes in Mexican Americans. *American Journal of Epidemiology, 128,* 1289-1301.

Hazuda, H. P., Stern, M. P., & Haffner, S. M. (1988). Acculturation and assimilation among Mexican Americans: Scales and population-based data. *Social Science Quarterly, 69,* 687-706.

Hersen, M., & Hasselt, V. (1996). *Psychological treatment of older adults.* New York: Plenum.

Inclan, J. (1983). Psychological symptomatology in second generation Puerto Rican women of three socioeconomic groups. *Journal of Community Psychology, 11,* 414-417.

Jenerson-Madden, D., Ebersole, P., & Romero, A. M. (1992). Personal life meaning of Mexicans. *Journal of Social Behavior and Personality, 7*(1), 151-161.

Keefe, S. E., & Padilla, A. M. (1987). *Chicano ethnicity.* Albuquerque: University of New Mexico Press.

Kemp, B. J., Staples, F., & Lopez-Aqueres, W. (1987). Epidemiology of depression and dysphoria in an elderly Hispanic population. *American Geriatrics Society, 35,* 920-926.

Krause, N., & Goldenhar, L. M. (1991), Acculturation and psychological distress in three groups of elderly Hispanics. *Journal of Gerontology, 47*(6), S279-S288.

Lacayo, C. G. (1980). *A national study to assess the service needs of the Hispanic elderly* (Final report). Asociacion Nacional Pro Personas Mayores (National Association for Hispanic Elderly) (DHHS Publication No. 0090-A-1295). Washington, DC: Government Printing Office.

Landrine, H. (1992). Clinical implications of cultural differences: The referential versus the indexical self. *Clinical Psychology Review, 12,* 401-415.

Lang, J. G., Munoz, R. F., Bernal, G., & Sorensen, J. L. (1982). Quality of life and psychological well-being in a bicultural Latino community. *Hispanic Journal of Behavioral Sciences, 4,* 433-450.

Levitt, M. J., Guacci, N., & Weber, R. A. (1992). Intergenerational support, relationship quality, and well-being: A bicultural analysis. *Journal of Family Issues, 13*(4), 465-481.

Linn, M. M., Hunter, K., & Perry, P. R. (1979). Differences by sex and ethnicity in the psychosocial adjustment of the elderly. *Journal of Health and Social Behavior, 20,* 273-281.

Lopez-Aqueres, W., Kemp, B., Staples, F., & Brummel-Smith, K. (1984). Use of health care services by older Hispanics. *Journal of the American Geriatrics Society, 32,* 434-440.

Lubben, J. E., & Becerra, R. M. (1987). Social support among Black, Mexican, and Chinese elderly. In D. E. Gelfand & C. M. Barresi (Eds.), *Ethnic dimensions of aging* (pp. 130-144). New York: Springer.

Maldonado, D. (1975). The Chicano aged. *Social Work, 20,* 213-216.

Maldonado, D. (1979). Aging in the Chicano context. In D. E. Gelfand & A. J. Kutzik (Eds.), *Ethnicity and aging: Theory, research, and policy.* New York: Springer.

Marin, G., Sabogal, F., Marin, B. V., Otero-Sabogal, R., & Perez-Stable, E. J. (1987). Development of short acculturation scale for Hispanics. *Hispanic Journal of Behavioral Sciences, 9*(2), 183-205.

Markides, K. S., Boult, J. S., & Ray, L. A. (1986). Sources of helping and intergenerational solidarity: A three-generation study of Mexican Americans. *Journal of Gerontology, 41*(4), 506-511.

Markides, K. S., Krause, N., & Mendes de Leon, C. F. (1988). Acculturation and alcohol consumption among Mexican Americans: A three-generation study. *American Journal of Public Health, 78*(9), 1178-1181.

Markides, K. S., & Lee, D. J. (1990). Predictors of well-being are functioning in older Mexican Americans and Anglos: An eight-year follow-up. *Journal of Gerontology, 45*(1), 69-73.

Markides, K. S., & Martin, H. W. (1983). *Older Mexican Americans: A study in an urban barrio.* (Monograph of the Center for Mexican American Studies.) Austin: University of Texas Press.

Markides, K. S., Martin, H. W., & Sizemore, M. (1980). Psychological distress among elderly Mexican Americans and Anglos. *Ethnicity, 7,* 298-309.

Markides, K. S., & Mindel, C. H. (1987). *Aging and ethnicity.* Newbury Park, CA: Sage.

Martinez, M. Z. (1979). *Los Ancianos: A study of the attitudes of Mexican Americans regarding support of the elderly* (Doctoral dissertation, Brandeis University, 1979). Ann Arbor, MI: University Microfilms International.

Mendes de Leon, C., & Markides, K. (1988). Depressive symptoms among Mexican Americans: A three generation study. *Journal of Epidemiology, 127,* 150-160.

Miranda, M. R. (1991). Mental health services and the Hispanic elderly. In *Empowering Hispanic families: A critical issue for the '90s* (pp. 141-154). Milwaukee, WI: Family Service of America.

Miranda, M. R., & Castro, F. (1985). A conceptual model for clinical research on stress and mental health status: From theory to assessment. In W. Vega & M. R. Miranda (Eds.), *Stress and Hispanic mental health: Relating research to service delivery* (pp. 174-210). Rockville, MD: U.S. Department of Health and Human Services.

Moscicki, E. K., Locke, B. Z., Rae, D. S., & Boyd, J. H. (1989). Depressive symptoms among Mexican Americans: The Hispanic Health and Nutrition Examination Survey. *American Journal of Epidemiology, 130*(2), 348-360.

Mutran, E. (1985). Intergenerational family support among Blacks and Whites: Response to culture or to socioeconomic differences. *Journal of Gerontology, 40*(3), 382-389.

Neff, J. A. (1986). Alcohol consumption and psychological distress among U.S. Anglos, Hispanics, and Blacks. *Alcohol and Alcoholism, 21,* 111-119.

Olmedo, E. L., & Padilla, A. M. (1978). Empirical and construct validation of a measure of acculturation for Mexican Americans. *The Journal of Social Psychology, 105,* 179-187.

Ortiz, V., & Arce, C. H. (1984). Language orientation and mental health status among persons of Mexican descent. *Hispanic Journal of Behavioral Sciences, 6*(2), 127-143.

Padilla, A. (1980). The role of cultural awareness and ethnic loyalty in acculturation. In A. Padilla (Ed.), *Acculturation: Theory, models, and some new findings* (pp. 47-84). Boulder, CO: Westview.

Pearlin, L. I., Lieberman, M. S., Menaghan, E. G., & Mullan, J. T. (1981). The stress process. *Journal of Health and Social Behavior, 22,* 53-67.

Ramirez, A. G. (1988). Spanish in the United States. In E. Acosta-Belen & B. J. Sjostrom (Eds.), *The Hispanic experience in the United States* (pp. 187-206). New York: Praeger.

Redfield, R., Linton, R., & Herskovits, M. J. (1936). Memorandum for the study of acculturation. *American Anthropologist, 38,* 149-152.

Roberts, R. E. (1980). Prevalence of psychological distress among Mexican Americans. *Journal of Health and Social Behavior, 21,* 134-145.

Rogler, L. H., Cortes, D. E., & Malgady, R. G. (1991). Acculturation and mental health status among Hispanics. *American Psychologist, 46*(6), 585-597.

Sabogal, F., Marin, G., & Otero-Sabogal, R., Marin, B. V. O., & Perez-Stable, E. J. (1987). Hispanic familism and acculturation: What changes and what doesn't? *Hispanic Journal of Behavioral Sciences, 9*(4), 397-412.

Salgado de Snyder, V. N. (1987a). Factors associated with acculturative stress and depressive symptomatology among married Mexican immigrant women. *Psychology of Women Quarterly, 11,* 475-488.

Salgado de Snyder, V. N. (1987b). The role of ethnic loyalty among Mexican immigrant women. *Hispanic Journal of Behavioral Sciences, 9,* 287-298.

Seelbach, W. C. (1978, October). Correlates of aged parents' filial responsibility expectations and realizations. *The Family Coordinator,* pp. 341-350.

Smart, J. F., & Smart, D. W. (1992). Acculturation, biculturism, and the rehabilitation of Mexican Americans. *Journal of Applied Rehabilitation Counseling, 24*(2), 46-51.

Sorenson, S. B., & Golding, J. M. (1988). Suicide ideation and attempts in Hispanics and non-Hispanic Whites: Demographic and psychiatric disorder issues. *Suicide and Life-Threatening Behavior, 18,* 322-333.

Sotomayor, M. (1991). *Empowering Hispanic families: A critical issue for the '90s.* Milwaukee, WI: Family Service of America.

Sotomayor, M., & Applewhite, S. (1988). The Hispanic elderly and the extended multigenerational family. In S. Applewhite (Ed.), *Hispanic elderly in transition* (pp. 90-104). New York: Greenwood.

Sotomayor, M., & Randolph, S. (1988). A preliminary review of caregiving issues and the Hispanic family. In M. Sotomayor & H. Curiel (Eds.), *Hispanic elderly: A cultural signature* (pp. 137-160). Edinburg, TX: Pan American University Press.

Szapocnik, J., & Hernandez, R. (1988). The Cuban American family. In C. H. Mindel, R. W. Habenstein, & R. Wright (Eds.), *Ethnic families in America* (3rd ed., pp. 160-172). New York: Elsevier Science.

Szapocznik, J., Scopetta, M. A., Kurtines, W., & Aranalde, M. (1978). Theory and measurement of acculturation. *International Journal of Psychology, 12,* 113-130.

Talamantes, M., Cornell, J., Espino, D. V., Lichtenstein, J. J., & Hazuda, H. P. (1996). SES and ethnic differences in perceived caregiver availability among young-old Mexican Americans and non-Hispanic Whites. *The Gerontologist, 36,* 88-99.

Torres-Matrullo, C. (1976). Acculturation and psychopathology among Puerto Rican women in mainland United States. *American Journal of Orthopsychiatry, 46,* 710-719.

Tran, T. V. (1994). Bilingualism and subjective well-being in a sample of elderly Hispanics. *Journal of Social Service Research, 20*(1/2), 1-19.

U.S. Bureau of the Census. (1991). The Hispanic population in the United States: March 1991. *Current Population Reports* (Series P-20, No. 455). Washington DC: Government Printing Office.

U.S. Bureau of the Census. (1993). Racial and ethnic diversity of America's elderly population. *Profiles of America's Elderly, 3.* Washington, DC: Government Printing Office.

U.S. Department of Health and Human Services, Public Health Service. (1990). *Healthy people 2000. National health promotion and disease prevention objectives* (Series PHS-91-50213). Washington, DC: Government Printing Office.

U.S. Department of Health and Human Services. (1991). *Aging America: Trends and projections* (DHHS Publication No. [FCoA] 91-28001). Washington, DC: Government Printing Office.

Valle, R., & Vega, W. (Eds.). (1980). *Hispanic natural support systems: Mental health promotion perspectives.* Sacramento, CA: Department of Mental Health.

Vaux, A. (1988). *Social support: Theory, research, and intervention.* New York: Praeger.

Villa, M. L., Cuellar, J., Gamel, N., & Yeo, G. (1993). *Aging and health: Hispanic American elders* (2nd ed.) (Stanford Geriatric Education Center Working Paper Series, Ethnogeriatric Reviews, No. 5). Stanford, CA: Stanford Geriatric Education Center.

Warheit, G. J., Vega, W. A., Auth, J., & Meinhardt, K. (1985). Psychiatric symptoms and dysfunctions among Anglos and Mexican Americans: An epidemiological study. In J. R. Greenley (Ed.), *Research in community and mental health* (pp. 3-32). London: JAI.

Worobey, J. L., & Angel, R. J. (1990). Poverty and health: Older minority women and the rise of the female-headed household. *Journal of Health and Social Behavior, 31,* 370-383.

Zamanian, K., Thackery, M., Starrett, R. A., Brown, L. G., Lassman, D. K., & Blanchard, A. (1992). Acculturation and depression in Mexican American elderly. In T. L. Brink (Ed.), *Hispanic aged mental health* (pp. 109-121). New York: Haworth.

Asian American Elderly Mental Health

Harry H. L. Kitano
Tazuko Shibusawa
Kerrily J. Kitano

Research information on the mental health of elderly Asian Americans is scarce. As a consequence, stereotypes have filled the vacuum. For example, there is the perception that mental illness is not a major problem among Asian Americans, or if a problem, that they would rather take care of their own. Another perception is that there is such a degree of shame associated with mental problems that these remain hidden from the public. There is an image of Asian Americans doing well, especially in income and education, so that they do not have to depend on public support for their elderly. Because of the wide diversity among Asian Americans these images occasionally fit, but more often than not they remain as stereotypes.

The purpose of this chapter is to go beyond the stereotypes, the opinions, and guesses and cover the following:

1. To provide relevant demographic data as background for understanding different Asian American groups
2. To provide a heuristic model to assess the role of acculturation and ethnic identity
3. To summarize studies concerning mental health and mental illness
4. To provide suggestions for future studies

Prior to addressing the above goals, there are several other concerns. One deals with combining the various Asian American groups; there are more than 30 groups, each with its own history, culture, motives for immigration, reception by the host society, time of arrival, demographic factors, length of time in the country, acculturation, and ethnic identity. When the groups are combined, these many differences are obscured and present a distorted picture of each of the Asian American groups.

A common justification for this procedure is that each of the Asian American groups is too small. Another is that the grouping is convenient for statistical purposes, and data are often reported this way. There is even the old cliche—that because they look alike, they must be alike. But the generalizations drawn from such studies are suspect.

For example, Uehara, Takeuchi, and Smukler (1994) explored the implications of treating disparate Asian American ethnic groups as a single, undifferentiated category in a study of community functioning status. When treated as a single ethnic entity, the Asian Americans were found to have a lower level of functioning difficulty than White subjects. When treated as separate groups, however, only one of the five Asian American groups, the Chinese, had a significantly lower level of difficulty. The authors indicate that the analytic strategy of combining the diversity can lead to misleading research and treatment results. Moreover, in clinical practice there will be problems in routinely assigning a person of Japanese ancestry to an elderly Korean, without some knowledge of the past history of the groups (Uehara et al., 1994).

Demographic Data

Numbers

Table 12.1 shows the population of Asian Americans, based on the 1990 U.S. Census, in the United States. There were 14 Asian American and Pacific Islander (AA/PI) populations identified. The total Asian/Pacific count was 7,273,662, which nearly doubled the AA/PI count in 1980. The 5 most numerous groups were the Chinese at 1,645,472; the Filipinos at 1,406,770; the Japanese at 847,562; the Asian Indians at 815,447; and the Koreans at 798,849.

Even though the population growth over the past decade has been rapid, Asian Americans still constitute less than 3% of the total U.S. population. Because the majority live along the Pacific Coast, in Hawaii, and in metro-

TABLE 12.1 Largest Asian or Pacific Islander Groups in the United States, 1990

Group	Total	Share of U.S. Population (%)
Total Asian and Pacific Islander	**7,273,662**	**2.9**
Total Asian	6,908,638	2.8
Total Pacific Islander	365,024	0.1
Chinese	1,645,472	0.7
Filipino	1,406,770	0.6
Japanese	847,562	0.3
Indian	815,447	0.3
Korean	798,849	0.3
Vietnamese	614,547	0.2
Hawaiian	211,014	0.1
Laotian	149,014	0.1
Cambodian	147,411	0.1
Thai	91,275	0.0
Hmong	90,082	0.0
Samoan	62,964	0.0
Guamanian	49,345	0.0
Tongan	17,606	0.0

SOURCE: Asians in America (1991).

politan areas like New York and Chicago, they remain relatively invisible (or as stereotypes in the mass media) to most of the country.

Age, Immigration

A picture of the Asian Americans by age composition, native-born and immigrant, is shown on Table 12.2. The data, drawn from the 1990 U.S. Census, illustrate the differences between native-born and immigrant in terms of age. There were wide differences among the groups. The Japanese with 22% had the highest number in the 60-years-and-older category, followed by the Pacific Islanders with 7%, the Chinese with 6%, and the Koreans with 4%. All of the other AA/PI groups had less than 1% in the 60-years-and-older category. One reason for the paucity of research on the elderly is the small numbers.

There are differences between the native-born and the immigrant. Some of the new immigrants to the United States have come with older family members, whereas the earlier Asian Americans were primarily young, single, male laborers; therefore there are differences in acculturation and life experiences.

TABLE 12.2 Age Composition, Native-Born and Immigrant

NATIVE-BORN

Years of Age	Asian Indian (%)	Cambodian (%)	Chinese (%)	Filipino (%)	Hmong (%)	Japanese (%)	Korean (%)	Laotian (%)	Pacific Islander (%)	Thai (%)	Vietnamese (%)
0-9	57	91	38	39	90	13	55	90	26	48	76
10-19	31	7	21	28	8	11	27	7	20	44	20
20-29	7	1	14	15	1	15	8	1	18	5	2
30-39	2	*	12	8	*	17	3	1	14	1	1
40-49	1	*	8	5	*	12	2	*	9	1	*
50-59	1	*	3	3	*	10	1	*	6	*	*
60-69	*	*	3	2	*	13	2	*	4	*	*
70-79	*	*	2	*	*	7	1	*	2	*	*
80+	*	*	1	*	*	2	1	*	1	*	*
Total (%)	100	100	100	100	100	100	100	100	100	100	100

IMMIGRANT

Years of Age	Asian Indian (%)	Cambodian (%)	Chinese (%)	Filipino (%)	Hmong (%)	Japanese (%)	Korean (%)	Laotian (%)	Pacific Islander (%)	Thai (%)	Vietnamese (%)
0-9	5	15	3	3	19	7	10	10	7	3	4
10-19	11	23	11	11	27	7	15	27	16	10	23
20-29	22	19	20	18	21	18	19	22	26	20	25
30-39	26	20	25	23	14	24	22	21	23	27	24
40-49	21	12	17	20	8	17	17	11	13	30	14
50-59	9	6	11	11	5	15	10	5	8	7	7
60-69	4	3	8	7	3	8	4	2	4	2	3
70-79	*	1	4	5	2	1	2	1	2	*	*
80+	*	1	1	2	1	3	1	1	1	*	*
Total (%)	100	100	100	100	100	100	100	100	100	100	100

SOURCE: Information generated from 1990 Census of the Population, Five Percent Public Use Microdata Sample (PUMS).
NOTE: * Less than 1%

TABLE 12.3 Home and Ability to Speak English: 1990 (by percentage)

	Speak Asian or Pacific Islander at Home	Do Not Speak English "Very Well"	Linguistically Isolated
Total Asian	65.2	56.0	34.9
Chinese	82.9	60.4	40.3
Filipino	66.0	35.6	13.0
Japanese	42.8	57.7	33.0
Asian Indian	14.5	31.0	17.2
Korean	80.8	63.5	41.4
Vietnamese	92.5	65.0	43.9
Cambodian	95.0	73.2	56.1
Hmong	96.9	78.1	60.5
Laotian	95.6	70.2	52.4
Thai	79.1	58.0	31.8
Other Asian	21.0	49.9	30.2

SOURCE: U.S. Bureau of the Census (1993, p. 5).

NOTE: Linguistic isolation refers to persons in households in which no one 14 years old or over speaks only English and no one who speaks an language other than English speaks English "very well."

Language Facility

Table 12.3, based on the U.S. Census for 1990, shows the language spoken at home and the ability to speak English. Aside from Asian Indians and Filipinos, many of the AA/PI groups are linguistically isolated. This may be one of the reasons behind the lack of use of the social and psychological services in the community.

Poverty

Figure 12.1 shows poverty rates by ethnic group, drawn from the 1990 U.S. Census. There was a wide range of poverty by ethnic group. The Hmong had the highest rate at 63.6%, while the Filipino at 6.4% and the Japanese at 7.0%, had the lowest.

The demographic characteristics indicate differences between AA/PI groups in number, in place of birth, in English-speaking ability, and in poverty. This background is important for understanding some of the issues and problems facing Asian Americans. There are also many other differences, so that lumping all Asian Americans together under one category will provide erroneous impressions.

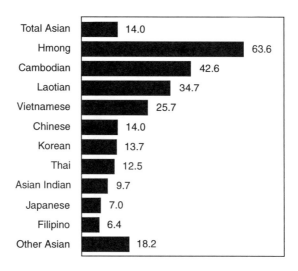

Figure 12.1. Poverty Rates for Asian Persons: 1989 (by percentage)
SOURCE: U.S. Bureau of the Census (1993, p. 7).

Asian Culture

The basic model for understanding Asian Americans is to assess what the immigrants brought with them; their encounter with the mainstream; and the subsequent changes, if any. Sandberg (1986) refers to this process as straight line theory, in which immigrants arrive in the United States with their culture of origin and in subsequent interactions acquire or acculturate to the dominant culture. Most European immigrants fit this model, so that over time and generations there is a straight line from the culture of origin or ancestral culture to the American culture. However, the process does not take into account barriers faced by Asians, such as prejudice, discrimination, and segregation, delaying or distorting the straight line. There may be other models that may provide more accurate pictures of Asian Americans.

There are some broad generalizations, contrasting the values and norms of "Asian cultures"[1] with the American, or dominant, culture. Asian cultures are different in that they give higher priority to the wishes of the family and community and less emphasis on individualism. Filial piety and the use of shame is a method of reinforcing expectations and proper behavior. Shame is also related to deviance, so that there is shame in having a member of the family with mental illness. There is also a fatalistic orientation to the world.

The basic family and societal structures represent a hierarchy, with fathers and sons holding dominant positions. Traditional Asians may be less verbal and more hesitant to express feelings than their American peers; therapeutic models that call for high verbal expression (including the language problem) may therefore be difficult.

It should be noted that most Asians are familiar with "traditional values," but there is seldom a one-to-one correlation between values and behavior.

The Kitano Model

For all immigrant groups, there are at least two interacting variables that provide a means for identification. One dimension of the Kitano model is acculturation and assimilation in the American culture. The other dimension is that of ethnic identity, which refers to the retention and identification of customs, attitudes, and beliefs of the culture of origin. The interaction of these two variables is shown on the two-by-two table (see Figure 12.2).

Four "ideal" types are developed from this model. Type A is high in assimilation and low in ethnic identity. Type B is high in assimilation and high in ethnic identity. Type C is high in ethnic identity and low in assimilation, and Type D is low in ethnicity and low in assimilation.

Type A, high in assimilation and low in ethnic identity, describes individuals who are for all intents and purposes "Americanized." Clothes, language, and culture resemble the mainstream model. The individual does not need bilingual help and can live, retire, and interact with the dominant culture. Third-, fourth-, and subsequent generations are most likely to belong to this category.

Type B, high in assimilation and high in ethnic identity, represents a bicultural adaptation. The individual feels comfortable in both the dominant and ethnic communities, with friends and contacts in both. Intellectuals and businesspeople are most likely to fall into this category. There is a high probability that the person has either professional or business ties to both cultures. Monolingual individuals may feel somewhat disadvantaged when dealing with Type B individuals.

Type C, high in ethnic identity and low in assimilation, is most characteristics of the Issei, or first-generation, immigrant. Individuals may be newly arrived, have immigrated at an advanced age, or have lived in ethnic communities for most of their lives. Many of the research findings from the "old" country may be relevant for Type C. These individuals may adhere more

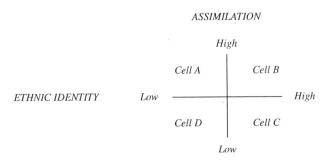

Figure 12.2. Assimilation and Ethnic Identity

closely to the "traditional culture," and their interaction with the dominant culture may reinforce stereotypes.

Type D, low in ethnic identity and low in assimilation, indicates a person alienated from both the ethnic and the dominant systems. Type D persons reject the ethnic role, yet may also feel rejected by the dominant culture. Alcoholism, delinquency, and other forms of deviance may be at the root of individuals in this category.

Review of Studies

Chae (1987) indicates that in order to understand older Asians, one must understand their Confucian heritage (see Type C in the model). The author states that numerous older Asians suffer from poverty and illness and are often ignored by their own families. Long hours and low wages require family members to work, so the elderly and the children are often left alone without adequate care and supervision. San Francisco's Chinatown has the highest suicide and tuberculosis rates in the nation, and many of the elderly there suffer from malnutrition.

This group of elderly Asians is in multiple jeopardy. They suffer from poverty, poor health, poor housing, racism, and loneliness. Yet few seek help from community agencies because of language and cultural barriers, including unfamiliarity with the available institutional arrangements in the community.

An illustration of the lack of understanding of the culture of the Asian elderly is that of a 72-year-old Japanese woman, probably an Issei or first-generation immigrant. She was eventually diagnosed as psychotic because she had isolated herself in her nursing home room and refused any personal contact, including members of her own family. Health care providers misinterpreted her behavior—instead of being hospitalized, she had expected to be taken care of by her children, in the family home, until death.

Chae (1987) concludes that it is important to know about the client's education, occupation, and formal social status when determining the mental health of AA/PI individuals. And we would add, the *level of acculturation and ethnic identity is equally significant.*

Asian Americans

Since the category of Asian Americans remains in use, this section will report on published material under that title. We limited our search to articles and books that were written in the 1990s.

Flaskerud and Akutsu (1993) studied 1,528 adult Asian American clients in the Los Angeles County mental health system. Those seen by Asian therapists at Asian-specific clinics were diagnosed with significantly lower percentages of psychotic and other major psychiatric disorders and with significantly higher percentages of nonpsychiatric disorders than were Asian clients seen by Asian and White therapists at mainstream facilities. It appears that clinics for Asians, staffed by Asian therapists, were much more aware of cultural nuances than mainstream agencies.

Grant (1995), in writing about interventions with ethnic minority elderly, emphasizes the importance of keeping aware of demographic trends, poverty, health, dementia, substance abuse, racism, ageism, and cultural differences. Other problems include assessment and diagnostic issues, intervention and treatment approaches, and guidelines for working with ethnic minority elderly.

Sakauye (1992) reviewed the clinical literature on mental health problems facing the Asian American elderly and discussed three major areas of concern. One dealt with diagnostic problems when dealing with the foreign-born; another focused on the major barriers toward treatment of both foreign-born and American-born Asians; and the third was the influence of biological differences. Topics included culture-bound syndromes and communication, acculturation stress, alternative treatments, and prejudice and value differences.

The Chinese

Cheung and Spears (1992) conducted a mail survey of psychiatric morbidity among Chinese women living in Dunedin, New Zealand. Sociodemographic variables associated with minor psychiatric morbidity included having no children and being either very highly or very poorly educated. Among migrants, higher psychiatric morbidity was found in those who were born in China and whose reason for migration was to follow the lead of their families. They also had problems with speaking English.

Ying and Miller (1992) investigated the psychological problems associated with the help-seeking behavior of Chinese Americans. Of 143 Chinese Americans, ranging in age from 19 to 85, 13.3% sought professional help. Those subjects seeking help had more physical symptoms, come close to having a nervous breakdown, had a relative who had been in treatment, and were American-born. Acculturation was an important predictor of both behavior and attitudes, with the less acculturated in greater need of education about the importance of mental health services

Kitano, Berkanovic, Chi, and Lubben (1993, 1994) surveyed a random sample of Chinese American and Japanese American elderly living in Los Angeles. The Chinese Americans, both male and female, scored significantly higher on the CES-D depression scale than the Japanese Americans (see Table 12.4).

The Filipinos

One of the few studies of the Filipino American is by Tompar-Tu and Sustento-Seneriches (1995), who present the results of a 5-year study on the mental health of Filipino Americans. Their volume includes a variety of vignettes and outlines, and discusses how treatment could be made more accessible to and effective for this ethnic group. Cultural adjustment included losses experienced in the immigration process, changes in male-female roles, and shame-evoking situations in the workplace. These changes are associated with depression, anxiety, and brief reactive psychoses. The authors hope that the book will be a tool for providing more accurate assessment of Filipino American mental health.

Asian Indians

Gupta (1992) conducted a follow-up study of 86 first-generation immigrants from the Indian subcontinent matched to an indigenous English-born control

TABLE 12.4 A Comparison of Chinese and Japanese American Elderly on the CES-D

Variables	Chinese American (%) (n = 204)	Japanese American (%) (n = 173)
CES-D Total (All)**		
0-5	46.3	70.6
6+	53.7	29.4
CES-D Total (Males)**		
0-5	48.7	76.4
6+	51.3	23.6
CES-D Total (Females)*		
0-5	43.2	64.2
6+	56.8	35.8

NOTE: * $p < 0.01$; **$p < 0.001$

group. All subjects had been diagnosed as suffering from a functional psychoses. Attempts to locate patients from 5 to 20 years later indicated that a significantly higher proportion of the immigrant group could not be traced to a general practitioner within the United Kingdom. Gupta suggests that the apparently low rates of use of inpatient psychiatric services by Asian immigrants may reflect a reticence to consult conventional practitioners about psychological problems.

The Japanese and Japanese Americans

Iwata, Okuyama, Kawakami, and Saito (1989) studied the prevalence of depressive symptoms in 2,190 Japanese tax workers, using the Japanese version of the CES-D. Although the study does not concentrate on the elderly, the findings are still of interest. A higher level of depressive symptoms was found in 15.2% of males and 10.6% of females. Males aged 50 years and older had more depressive symptoms than other males. Perceived stress, related to both family life and the workplace, was associated with a high level of depressive symptoms. The Japanese model of "long distance marriages," in which the head of household is sent away from home for occupational reasons, had little influence on depressive symptoms.

Maeda, Teshima, Sugisawa, and Asakura (1989) identified factors related to health in old age that appear to be different in Japan than in other developed countries. They cite the traditional culture of Japan and the longevity of the Japanese. Attention is drawn to the prevalence of dementia and suicide in old age.

Peterson, Rose, and McGee (1985) analyzed 1,098 Japanese and 873 Caucasian elderly based on Hawaii Department of Health data. Better health was predicted by younger age, higher family income, maintenance of work role, and Japanese ethnicity. The findings suggest the importance of ethnocultural supports in the maintenance of health.

Ishihara (1985) reports that in 1985 an estimated 64.5% of those over 65 in Japan were living with their children. In 1970, there were 76.9% of the elderly living with their children. In 1975, there were 72.5% and in 1980, there were 68.7%, reflecting a gradual trend for the elderly to live away from their family.

Rose (1982) investigated the role of family supports in aging between Japanese American and Caucasian families in Hawaii. The Japanese elderly had more family supports and more successful adjustment than the Whites.

The Koreans

Yamamoto, Rhee, and Chang (1994) examined the lifetime prevalence of various psychiatric disorders among 100 Korean elderly in Los Angeles, using the Diagnostic Interview Schedule, Version III (American Psychiatric Association, *Diagnostic and Statistical Manual of Mental Disorders* [*DSM III*], 1980). There was a relatively low prevalence of *DSM III* disorders with the exception of alcohol abuse and dependence, especially among Korean males. The lifetime prevalence of *DSM III* disorders among Koreans in Korea was reported to be higher than the Los Angeles sample.

Kim, Kim, and Hurh (1991) examined the life conditions of elderly Korean immigrants and their relationship with their married children in the context of filial piety. The traditional notion of filial piety has undergone modification—although married children and spouses are obligated to care physically for and provide comfort to their parents, the dominance of the marital bond is recognized.

Hurh and Kim (1990) investigated structural and situational variables of Korean immigrants and their mental health. Subjects who were married, highly educated, or currently employed in a high-status occupation had better mental health than others. There were gender differences. For men, work-related variables were the strongest correlates of mental health, whereas no distinctive set of variables was related to women's mental health. However, family life satisfaction and ethnic attachment were important for women.

Kim (1996) indicates that *haan* and its variations are an important dynamic in Korean society. The Korean use of the term emphasizes suppression of anger, indignation, and the holding of a grudge. Historical and political circumstances have lead to most Koreans having suffered war and political and social upheaval that has brought suffering, personal loss, unbearable pain, and woe. Most have struggled and survived, but with deep feelings of *haan*—suppressed anger, resentment, and underlying depression. Feelings of indignation and victimization have been suppressed by Confucian teachings of harmony, but the anger remains.

Haan is the Korean version of the Jewish Holocaust. A *haan*-ridden person feels that he or she is an innocent victim who suffers through the fault or mistake of others, such as a bad master, an abusive husband, a cruel mother-in-law, a corrupt government, or an invading foreign power.

From a clinical perspective, *haan* is considered a Korean culture-bound psychiatric syndrome called *Hwa-byung*. It manifests itself in a mixture of clinical depression, anxiety, and somatic symptoms characterized by a lump and pressure in the throat and chest. It is most common among women, especially married women who are beyond middle age and are of lower social-class standing.

Hwa-byung is now listed as one of the culture-bound syndromes in the appendix of the revised *Diagnostic Manual* (*DSM IV;* American Psychiatric Association, 1994). It is described as a Korean folk syndrome that includes insomnia, fatigue, panic, fear of impending doom, dysphoric affect, indigestion, anorexia, palpitation, and generalized aches and pains. There have been debates whether this is a Korean syndrome, or whether "anger disease" is more universal in nature and has different names in different cultures.

In a survey of Koreans and their possession of *Hwa-byung,* 72% said they were having troubles with their spouses over extramarital affairs, alcoholism, and domestic violence. Sixty-eight percent had in-law problems, and 35% felt their difficulties with children could be attributed to *Hwa-byung.* In addition, social factors were also cited; 65% were related to poverty, 58% to some form of life hardship, and 32% to unfair blame and criticism.

Southeast Asians

Lee (1990) provides a general chapter on Southeast Asians. She explored the impact of war, family interaction, and the effects of immigration on the Southeast Asian family system. Topics addressed include migration and acculturation stress, traditional and transitional cultural characteristics on the family system, and the clinical manifestations of mental health problems. There is an attempt to translate the refugee experience into effective clinical practice.

Hauff and Vaglum (1995) studied the prevalence and the course of mental disorders among 145 Vietnamese refugees who were personally interviewed on their arrival in Norway and 3 years later. At the 3-year follow-up, one in four suffered from a psychiatric disorder, and the prevalence of depression was 17.7%. Being female, experiencing extreme traumatic stress in Vietnam, negative life events in Norway, lack of a close confidant, and chronic family separation were identified as predictors of psychopathology. The effects of war and persecution were long-lasting and compounded by adverse factors while in exile.

Hinton, Chen, Du, Tran, and colleagues (1993) explored the prevalence of mental disorders in 201 adult, newly arrived ethnic Vietnamese and ethnic Chinese refugees from Vietnam. Overall, 18.4% had one or more current disorder; 8.5% had adjustment disorders and 5.5% had major depression. The Vietnamese had significantly higher post-traumatic stress disorder and generalized anxiety disorder when compared to the Chinese. The ethnic differences in psychopathology were largely explained by the Vietnamese having experienced more traumatic events, including separation from the family. Subjects who were married and veterans were more likely to have one or more psychiatric disorders.

Moore and Boehnlein (1991) described the treatment of 85 Mien refugees in a U.S. university psychiatric program. Cultural beliefs about illness and medication interfered with adherence to prescribed treatment. Subjects rarely volunteered their traumatic histories, psychiatric problems, or dissatisfaction with medications. The use of medication for somatic complaints and the continuing recognition of Mien health beliefs led to a trusting doctor-patient relationship and continued psychiatric care.

Although most of the studies on the Southeast Asians were not on the elderly, the information is of value in understanding the hardships suffered by this group.

Alzheimer's Disease

A report distributed by the Massachusetts Medical Society (1990) indicates that in California, of the 439 patients diagnosed with Alzheimer's, only

9, or 2.1%, were Asian. More than 77% were White, 9.1% were Black, and 7.5% were Hispanic.

A study by Homma and Niina (1988) in an epidemiological study in Japan, reports that dementia among the elderly was at the 4% to 5% level, and that for those 80 years and older, the rate was 20%. They cited a need for an acceptable international diagnosis for "dementia of the Alzheimer type."

Yu, Liu, Levy, and associates (1989) reported on a longitudinal study of Alzheimer's disease and dementia in China. About 4.1% of adults 55 years or older could be classified as having severe cognitive impairment, and 14.4% with mild impairment.

It is difficult to assess the prevalence of Alzheimer's disease in the various Asian American groups. However, the Chief Executive Officer[2] of a Japanese retirement home in Los Angeles indicates that although they have no person with Alzheimer's in their home, they are planning an Alzheimer's group in their agency. There is evidently a need for such a service.

Suicide

A common stereotype of Asians, especially the Japanese, is that they are prone to commit suicide. A review of studies concerning elderly Japanese in Japan and suicide includes the following: Hirayama (1986) wrote about a high incidence of suicide among elderly Japanese women. The suicide of elderly living with their children's family ranked first, followed by elderly living alone. Freed (1993) attributed the suicide of elderly females to role conflict, persistent religio-cultural factors, and role disintegration. Becoming dependent and helpless, with failing health, especially after becoming widowed, was an important cause. Maeda et al. (1989) reported that the suicide rate of Japanese women rises suddenly at age 65 and older; there is no adequate explanation for this rise. They comment that the suicide rate of the Japanese elderly before World War II was much higher than the present rate.

Araki and Murata (1986) cite the lessening chances of being taken care of by one's own children in old age, as well as not participating in productive work, as being responsible for increased suicides in old people. Shimizu (1992), Maeda (1992), and Dodge and Austin (1990) cite the loss of the traditional grandmother role, sickness and ill health, becoming a burden on the family, and financial failure as reasons behind elderly suicide. Suicide rates

TABLE 12.5 Suicide Rates for Asian Americans (per 100,000 per year)

	USA Rates		National Rates
White Americans	13.2		
African Americans	6.1		
Native Americans	13.3		
Chinese Americans	8.3	Taiwan	10.0
		Hong Kong	13.5
Japanese Americans	9.1	Japan	17.6
Filipino Americans	3.5	Philippines	8.3

SOURCE: From "Differences in Epidemiology of Suicide in Asian Americans by Nation of Origin," by D. Lester, in *Omega, 29*(2), 1994, p. 91. Used with permission.

appear substantially higher among Japanese elders living in multigenerational households than among those living in nuclear families. Watanabe, Hasegawa, and Yoshinaga (1995) found higher suicide rates among the elderly in the rural parts of Japan. They suggest that the more ingrained traditional values of rural elders place them at greater risk for demoralization, depressive disorders, and suicide.

Takahashi, Hirasawa, Koyama, and Asakawa (1995) indicate that in 1990 those over 65 accounted for 12% of the population in Japan, but this age group accounted for 29% of deaths.

Asian American Suicide

Suicide rates for Asian Americans were reported by Lester (1994). Table 12.5 shows that White and Native American suicide rates were higher than those of the Chinese-, Japanese-, and Filipino American populations. A comparison of the Asian American groups with the country of origin indicates that suicide rates were higher in the countries of origin.

Table 12.6 shows the suicide rates for various groups by sex, age, and marital status. The Chinese- (25.9%) and Japanese American (18.9%) rates were the highest in the 65-years-and-older group. Table 12.7 illustrates the methods used for suicide by the Chinese, Japanese, and Filipino Americans with other groups. Hanging was the major method for the Asian Americans, while use of firearms was the most common method in the White, African American, and Native American groups.

TABLE 12.6 Suicide Rates for Americans by Sex, Age, and Marital Status (per 100,000 per year)

	White	African	Native	Chinese	Japanese	Filipino
Sex						
Male	20.6	10.4	22.0	9.1	13.4	5.3
Female	6.1	2.2	4.9	7.5	5.5	1.7
Age						
15-24	13.7	7.3	26.5	6.8	8.3	5.6
25-34	17.3	12.5	24.7	8.8	10.6	5.0
35-44	16.8	9.6	17.6	5.8	9.8	1.7
45-54	17.4	7.0	11.4	16.6	10.9	6.4
55-64	17.2	6.5	7.9	9.7	11.2	7.1
65+	19.1	5.5	2.8	25.9	18.9	5.2
Marital Status						
Single	19.1	9.4	31.9	10.5	12.7	6.9
Married	12.7	7.1	10.5	7.4	8.5	3.3
Widowed	20.4	6.5	8.9	34.0	19.2	4.2
Divorced	41.8	12.5	24.3	32.8	15.8	5.0

SOURCE: From "Differences in Epidemiology of Suicide in Asian Americans by Nation of Origin," by D. Lester, in *Omega, 29*(2), 1994, p. 91. Used with permission.

TABLE 12.7 Methods for Suicide Used by Asian Americans (percentages)

	Solid/Liquid Poisons	Gas/Vapors	Hanging (etc.)	Firearms	Other
Whites	11.5	9.5	13.3	57.5	8.1
African Americans	7.6	1.8	16.4	58.8	15.4
Native Americans	7.7	1.6	26.4	57.1	7.1
Chinese Americans	10.4	4.5	43.3	10.4	31.3
Japanese Americans	7.8	3.1	37.5	23.4	28.1
Filipino Americans	11.1	7.4	29.6	29.6	22.2

SOURCE: From "Differences in Epidemiology of Suicide in Asian Americans by Nation of Origin," by D. Lester, in *Omega, 29*(2), 1994, p. 92. Used with permission.

Summary

Although there is diversity between and among all Asian and Asian American groups, several generalizations can be made from the studies. Perhaps the most common is that the elderly groups do not consistently use dominant community professional services, and prefer to use family and informal ethnic group resources. Elements of shame, cultural belief systems, English-language ability, lack of knowledge of services, and a host of other elements combine to keep elderly Asian Americans from using community services.

A second generalization is based on the diversity among and within the Asian American and Pacific Islander category. Issues range from recently arrived refugees to groups that have been here for more than a century. Therefore, the effects of history, acculturation, and ethnic identity present challenges for researchers, clinicians, and policymakers. Understanding a newly arrived refugee and a fifth-generation professional call for different models, even though they might belong to the same ethnic group.

Another issue relates to the background experiences of the different Asian groups. Elderly Chinese and Japanese were early victims of racism and oppression; many of the Japanese went through forced incarceration during World War II. The Vietnam War provided the impetus for the immigration of Vietnamese refugees.

It is important to recognize that because of the diversity in Asian American elderly, it will be impossible for any individual or organization to provide total coverage. Instead, it will be important to acknowledge that there are realistic limitations and that the prescription of being open, courteous, and treating all people with dignity may still be the best model.

Research

In terms of future research, specific ethnic group studies will be valuable. However, small samples will often present a problem; therefore the question to be addressed is, "Is it better to have Asians lumped together, or is it better not to conduct research that may be flawed?" One possible alternative is to conduct interviews and case studies with members of the various ethnic groups after they have been lumped together.

Studies concerning long-term care, the use of ethnic facilities, the role of the family, and housing arrangements will be valuable. The role of ethnic communities (e.g., resources, organizations, and geographic area) will be important to know as well as the use of dominant-culture community resources by generation and ethnic identity.

The use of standardized instruments (e.g., *DSM III*) and their translations will be important to monitor, including the development of norms for the various Asian American groups. Because Asian Americans represent one of the fastest growing populations, primarily through immigration, much of the data from the 1990 Census is obsolete. Data on numbers, distribution by ethnic group, and poverty will be important to gather.

Finally, because many of the Asian American groups are made up of newcomers, it will be important to understand the diagnosis and treatment of mental illness in their host cultures. The role of immigration and acculturation can account for some of the possible changes in the United States.

Notes

1. The term *Asian* here refers primarily to those with a Confucian background (e.g., Chinese, Japanese, and Korean).
2. Telephone conversation on May 7, 1996, with Shawn Miyake, Keiro Services, in Los Angeles. Keiro is a retirement home for elderly Japanese Americans.

References

American Psychiatric Association. (1980). *Diagnostic and statistical manual of mental disorders* (3rd ed.). Washington, DC: Author.

American Psychiatric Association. (1994). *Diagnostic and statistical manual of mental disorders* (4th ed.). Washington, DC: Author.

Araki, S., & Murata, K. (1986). Social life factors affecting suicide in Japanese men and women. *Suicide and Life-Threatening Behavior, 16*(4), 458-468.

Asians in America. (1991). *Asian Week,* p. 6.

Chae, J. (1987). Older Asians. *Journal of Gerontological Nursing, 13*(11), 11-17.

Cheung, P., & Spears, G. (1992). Psychiatric morbidity among Dunedin Chinese women. *Australian and New Zealand Journal of Psychiatry, 26*(2), 183-190.

Dodge, H. H., & Austin, R. L. (1990). Household structure and elderly Japanese female suicide. *Family Perspective, 24,* 83-97.

Flaskerud, J. H., & Akutsu, P. D. (1993). Significant influence of participation in ethnic-specific programs on clinical diagnosis for Asian Americans. *Psychological Reports, 72*(3), Pt. 2, 1228-1230.

Freed, A. O. (1993). *The changing worlds of older women in Japan.* Manchester, CT: Knowledge, Ideas and Trends.

Grant, R. W. (1995). Interventions with ethnic minority elderly. In J. F. Aponte, R. Y. Rivers, & J. Wohl (Eds.), *Psychological interventions and cultural diversity* (pp. 199-214). Boston: Allyn & Bacon.

Gupta, S. (1992). Psychosis in Asian immigrants from the Indian sub-continent: Preliminary find-ings from a follow-up study including a survey of general practitioners. *Social Psychiatry and Psychiatric Epidemiology, 27*(October), 242-244.

Hauff, E., & Vaglum, O. (1995). Organised violence and the stress of exile: Predictors of mental health in a community cohort of Vietnamese refugees three years after resettlement. *British Journal of Psychiatry, 166*(March), 360-367.

Hinton, W., Chen, Y. J., Du, N., Tran, C. G., et al. (1993). DSM IIIR disorders in Vietnamese refugees: Prevalence and correlates. *Journal of Nervous and Mental Disease, 181*(2), 113-122.

Hirayama, H. (1986). Public policies and services for the aged in Japan. *Journal of Gerontological Social Work, 9*(4), 39-52.

Homma, A., & Niina, R. (1988). Alzheimer disease and associated disorders. *International Views: Research on Alzheimer Disease in Japan, 2*(4), 366-374.

Hurh, W. M., & Kim, K. C. (1990). Correlates of Korean immigrants' mental health. *Journal of Nervous and Mental Disease, 178*(11), 703-711.

Ishihara, K. (1985). Structure of household involving the aged. In *Structure and issues of an aging society* [in Japanese]. Tokyo: Tokyo University Press.

Iwata, N., Okuyama, Y., Kawakami, Y., & Saito, K. (1989). Prevalence of depressive symptoms in a Japanese occupational setting: A preliminary study. *American Journal of Public Health, 79*(11), 1486-1489.

Kim, K. C., Kim, S., & Hurh, W. M. (1991). Filial piety and intergenerational relationship in Korean immigrant families. *International Journal of Aging and Human Development, 33*(3), 233-245.

Kim, L. (1996, March). Korean ethos: "Haan." *Association of Korean American Psychiatrists Newsletter, 7*(2), 6-9.

Kitano, H., Berkanovic, E., Chi, I., & Lubben, J. (1993). *The Chinese elderly in Los Angeles.* Paper presented at the International Conference on the Elderly, Hong Kong.

Kitano, H., Berkanovic, E., Chi, I., & Lubben, J. (1994). *A comparison of the Chinese and Japa-nese elderly in Los Angeles.* Paper presented at the International Conference on the Elderly, Singapore.

Lee, E. (1990). Family therapy and Southeast Asian families. In M. P. Mirkin (Ed.), *The social and political contexts of family therapy* (pp. 331-354). Boston: Allyn & Bacon.

Lester, D. (1994). Differences in epidemiology of suicide in Asian Americans by nation of origin. *Omega, 29*(2), 89-93.

Maeda, D., Teshima, K., Sugisawa, H., & Asakura, Y. S. (1989). Aging and health in Japan. *Jour-nal of Cross-Cultural Gerontology, 4*, 143-162.

Maeda, N. (1992). Long-term care for the elderly in Japan. In T. Schwab (Ed.), *Caring in an aging world* (pp. 246-264). New York: McGraw-Hill.

Massachusetts Medical Society. (1990, February 23). *Morbidity and Mortality Weekly Report, 49*(7), 105.

Moore, L. J., & Boehnlein, J. K. (1991). Posttraumatic stress disorder, depression, and somatic symptoms in U.S. Mien patients. *Journal of Nervous and Mental Disease, 179*(12), 728-733.

Peterson, M. R., Rose, C. L., & McGee, R. I. (1985). A cross-cultural study of Japanese and Caucasian elders in Hawaii. *International Journal of Aging and Human Development, 21*(4), 267-279.

Rose, C. L. (1982). Familial supports and well-being in Hawaii elders: A Japanese Caucasian comparison. *Pacific/Asian American Mental Health Research Center, 1*(3), 9-11.

Sandberg, N. (1996). *Jewish life in Los Angeles.* Lanham, MD: University Press of America.

Sakauye, K. (1992). The elderly Asian patient. *Journal of Geriatric Psychiatry, 25*(1), 85-104.

Shimizu, M. (1992). Suicide and depression in late life. In M. Bergener, K. Hasegawa, S. I. Finkel, & T. Nishimura (Eds.), *Aging and mental health disorders: International perspectives* (pp. 91-101). New York: Springer.

Takahashi, Y., Hirasawa, H., Koyama, K., & Asakawa, O. (1995). Suicide and aging in Japan: An examination of treated elderly attempters. *International Psychogeriatrics, 7*(2), 239-251.

Tompar-Tu, A., & Sustento-Seneriches, J. (1995). *Depression and other mental health issues: The Filipino American.* San Francisco: Jossey-Bass.

Uehara, E. S., Takeuchi, D. T., & Smukler, M. (1994). Effects of combining disparate groups in the analysis of ethnic differences: Variations among Asian American mental health service consumers in level of community functioning. *American Journal of Community Psychology, 22*(1), 83-99.

U.S. Bureau of the Census. (1993). *We the American Asians.* Washington, DC: U.S. Department of Commerce, Economics and Statistical Administration.

Watanabe, N., Hasegawa, K., & Yoshinaga, Y. (1995). Suicide in later life in Japan: Urban and rural differences. *International Psychogeriatrics, 7*(2), 253-261.

Yamamoto, J., Rhee, S., & Chang, D. (1994). Psychiatric disorders among elderly Koreans in the United States. *Community Mental Health Journal, 30*(1), 17-27.

Ying, Y., & Miller, L. (1992). Help-seeking behavior and attitude of Chinese Americans regarding psychological problems. *American Journal of Community Psychology, 20*(4), 549-556.

Yu, E., Liu, W. T., Levy, P., et al. (1989). Cognitive impairment among elderly adults in Shanghai, China. *Journal of Gerontology: Social Sciences, 44*(3), S97-S106.

PART  V

*Health Services and
Long-Term Care*

Health Care Use and Long-Term Care Among African Americans

Access and Quality Issues

Verna M. Keith
Carol O. Long

The ability to use health care services in a timely and appropriate manner remains an important quality-of-life issue for older African Americans. A combination of high chronic disease rates and low levels of economic resources means that some older Blacks spend a disproportionate share of their incomes on health care and that some do not get needed care. Although both Medicare and Medicaid soften the impact of out-of-pocket health care expenses among the African American elderly, they do not eliminate them (Davis et al., 1987). The evidence also suggests that older African Americans are still more likely than older Whites to receive care in practice settings such as hospital outpatient departments (Kotranski, Bolick, & Halbert, 1987; Petchers & Milligan, 1988), settings that are characterized by long waiting times and less continuity of care (Dutton, 1978). Moreover, some African American elders, especially those residing in the rural South, appear to have significant problems accessing technologically sophisticated diagnostic procedures (Escarse, Epstein, Colby, & Schwartz, 1993).

The purpose of this chapter is to examine issues related to the use of health care services among older African Americans. The first section reviews literature on the use of services since the inception of Medicare and Medicaid. The second discusses continuing inequities in utilization among Medicare beneficiaries. The third section presents some preliminary findings on factors

319

affecting use of preventive health care services for the purpose of identifying subgroups of older African American who underutilize screening tests for chronic disease. Next, we present some preliminary results from an analysis of provider perceptions and satisfaction with services among subgroups of African American elderly. The final section of the chapter reviews issues related to the use of long-term care services among older African Americans.

Use of Health Care Services: Positive Changes Over the Past 30 Years

Historically, access to health care services has been more problematical for African Americans than for Whites. In decades prior to the passage of Medicare and Medicaid, Blacks were less likely than Whites to visit a physician, be hospitalized, and to have preventive checkups (Aday & Eichorn, 1972). Racial differences in quality of care were also striking in that African Americans were more likely than Whites to be treated in hospital outpatient clinics and emergency rooms, and less likely to see a physician in a private office setting (Aday & Eichorn, 1972). These differences were generally attributed to lower rates of insurance coverage, racial discrimination, and segregated health care facilities. Obtaining insurance coverage was especially difficult for the elderly. Davis et al. (1987) note that, in 1963, about half had no private health insurance coverage because carriers viewed them as poor economic risks. Further, existing policies generally offered limited coverage and exempted preexisting conditions. Older African Americans were at exceptionally high risk for uncovered medical expenses owing to their lower incomes and lower levels of employer-related health benefits (Davis et al., 1987).

Medicare and Medicaid were established in the mid-1960s to improve access to health care services for medically underserved groups—the elderly, the poor, and minorities. Medicare was designed to reduce financial barriers to obtaining health care among Social Security beneficiaries 65 years of age or older and, since 1974, the disabled. The program provided inpatient hospital care, physician services, physician prescribed medical equipment and supplies, and limited posthospital care at home and in skilled nursing facilities (Chulis, Eppig, Hogan, Waldo, & Arnet, 1993; Garfinkel, Bonito, & McLeroy, 1987). Equally important for African Americans and other minorities, the Medicare program targeted racial barriers to health care by requiring participating hospitals to eliminate segregation policies (Smith, 1990). Medicaid, a jointly financed federal-state program, was designed to provide hospital and physician services to various categories of the poor including the aged, blind, and disabled covered under the Supplemental Security Income (SSI) program. The program also covered prescription drugs, long-term care, and other services selected by individual states (see Gurny, Baugh, & Davis, 1992). Medicaid was especially important in addressing the needs of extremely poor African American elderly. Many had been employed in agriculture and other industries that were not covered by Social Security legislation, which, in turn, disqualified them for Medicare coverage. Other African American elderly were eligible for Medicaid under SSI because frequent spells of unemployment qualified them for only the minimum Social Security benefit, a benefit well below federal poverty guidelines (see Chen, 1991). An added bonus for SSI recipients was the "buy-in" program that permitted states to pay the Medicare Part B (physician services) premiums, coinsurance, and deductibles for the aged and disabled on welfare. Thus, destitute Black elders benefited by falling into all three targeted groups.

Since the passage of Medicare and Medicaid, African Americans' access to health care has improved dramatically, and racial differences in the use of health services have narrowed markedly (Aday, Andersen, & Fleming, 1980; Aday, Fleming, & Andersen, 1984). These changes are especially notable among older Americans. Data indicate that contact with a provider, the number of provider visits, and rates of hospitalization are similar for White and African American elderly. In the 1985-1987 period, the average number of provider visits per person were 8.7 and 8.8 for African Americans and Whites, respectively (Reed, Darity, & Roberson, 1993). Studies using multivariate analyses generally show that race is not an independent determinant of utilization when racial differences in health status are factored in (e.g., Wolinsky et al., 1989; Wolinsky & Johnson, 1991). In other words, need for health care services appears to be the most important factor precipitating provider contact and number of visits. Although the relative health disadvantages of African American elderly suggests that they should exceed White elders in utilization of health care services, and even though the need for health care appears to be a stronger predictor of use among African Americans (Wolinsky et al., 1989), attaining parity on these indicators of access represents a remarkable achievement. In addition, racial differences in overall reimbursements as well as benefits for skilled nursing facility care, two long-standing inequities in Medicare, appear to have narrowed as Medicare has matured (Davis et al., 1987).

Continuing Concerns: Barriers and Issues of Quality

In spite of the progress made over the past several decades, ample evidence suggests that a significant number of African American elderly continue to encounter barriers when seeking medical care. In 1980, 15 years after the Medicare legislation, older Blacks were still more likely than older Whites to have clinics as their regular source of care, and waiting times in these settings were longer for Blacks than Whites (Schlenger & Corder, 1984). More recent data indicate that race continues to play a role in health care utilization through its effects on income and education. A survey of Medicare beneficiaries (Health Care Financing Administration [HCFA], 1994), for example, found that low-income respondents and those with less than 12 years of education were significantly less likely to report a physician visit in the past year, although the number of visits was similar for those able to gain access to the system. Contact with a physician was lowest for those without a regular source of care, and 10.5% of those with incomes of $10,000 or less reported no regular source of care compared to 7.1% of those with incomes of $35,000 or more. Having a regular source of care is important for managing chronic disease and avoiding delayed, and therefore more costly, treatment.

Some 8.8% of lower-income beneficiaries also reported unmet health care need—having a health problem and not receiving care in the previous year (HCFA, 1994). Of these, 63.3% reported a financial barrier. As expected, Medicare beneficiaries in poor health were more likely to have a physician visit and to have a greater number of visits per user than those in better health. However, those in poor health were also more likely to report unmet need for services (20.1%) than even those in fair health (12.6%). Of those reporting unmet need, respondents in poor health were more likely to cite financial barriers (59.8%) than those in fair health (51.9%). Similar to data reported in other studies, racial and ethnic differences in utilization were not significant when other factors such as health status and income were held constant. However, it is well documented that older minorities have more health problems and the highest poverty rates. In 1990, 45% of African American elderly were at or below 125% of the poverty threshold, compared to only 16.4% of the White elderly (Chen, 1991). Thus, race appears to have an effect on use of services through its effects on income and health. It must be noted that a disproportionate share of African American Medicare beneficiaries consist of the disabled non-elderly (about 35% compared to about 14% among Whites).

However, the larger share of younger beneficiaries is unlikely to alter the findings that many lower status African American elders still encounter barriers to care.

Increasingly, lack of insurance to supplement Medicare coverage poses a critical obstacle for older African Americans. Supplemental policies are needed to defray rising out-of-pocket expenses for Medicare deductibles and copayments and to pay for noncovered services. Those without supplemental health insurance are less likely to use Medicare reimbursed services (Chulis et al., 1993). In 1991, just under 29% of African American elderly Medicare beneficiaries had Medicare as the sole source of insurance compared to just under 10% of Whites. In contrast, 79% and 40.2% of older Whites and African Americans, respectively, had privately purchased policies, employer-sponsored policies, or some combination of both (Chulis et al., 1993). African Americans, on the other hand, were almost 3 times as likely as Whites (29.8% vs. 9.2%) to have supplemental insurance through Medicaid (Chulis et al., 1993). It is not clear if lack of supplemental coverage is voluntary or due to an inability to afford premiums. A voluntary choice seems unlikely, however, given that those without supplemental private policies tend to be older, sicker, and more poorly educated than those covered (Garfinkel et al., 1987). It is more likely that these differences reflect lower incomes among the African American elderly and the greater tendency of older Whites to be employed in jobs that carried retirement health benefits (Chulis et al., 1993; Davis et al., 1987).

The quality of medical care services also appears to vary substantially by race. Recent research raises disturbing questions regarding whether or not African Americans received highly specialized medical services at the same rates as Whites. Using 1986 physician claims data for a sample of Medicare beneficiaries aged 65 and older, Escarse and colleagues (1993) found that older Whites were more likely to receive 23 of 32 diagnostic medical procedures, sometimes exceeding Blacks at a 3:1 ratio. In contrast, Blacks exceeded Whites in only 7 services, and the differences were small. Moreover, Whites were especially advantaged in access to higher-technology and newer services. Racial differences in procedures were especially marked in rural areas, with most of the disparity occurring in the South. For example, rural Whites were 21 times as likely as rural Blacks to receive coronary angioplasty. Racial differences in financial barriers do not explain Blacks' underutilization. Even among Medicare-Medicaid beneficiaries of similar socioeconomic standing and low out-of-pocket costs, racial differences remained.

Differences in access to these services could also not be entirely accounted for by racial variation in clinical conditions. The authors note that patient preferences and health beliefs may play a role, but also suggest that race may influence physician and institutional treatment decision. Their strongest argument, however, is that older African Americans are more likely to receive treatment in overcrowded and underfunded hospitals that may provide limited access to costly medical procedures. In addition, they suggest that other barriers (e.g., long waiting times, less satisfactory patient-physician relationships, and less continuity of care) may hamper diagnostic evaluations and appropriate referrals and follow-ups. It is important to point out that racial differences in procedures are also found among younger persons (e.g., Wenneker & Epstein, 1989), findings that indicate that African Americans face serious quality issues over the life course.

Taken together, these studies of Medicare beneficiaries suggest that some African American elderly may not be able to afford supplemental Medicare coverage, do not have a regular source of care, have unmet medical needs due in large part to financial barriers, and are less likely to have contact with health care personnel. Moreover, older Blacks do not appear to have equitable access to technologically sophisticated diagnostic tools. Other evidence suggests that waiting time at physicians' offices and other sites of care are still considerably longer for African American elderly than younger African Americans and older Whites (Reed et al., 1993).

Use of Preventive Services

The early detection of chronic disease through screening tests is widely regarded as an effective strategy for reducing morbidity and mortality. Non-invasive procedures now exist for a number of chronic diseases, including colorectal cancer (fecal occult blood test), heart disease and stroke (screening for hypertension), and breast cancer (mammogram and breast examinations). As Weisman and colleagues point out, preventive procedures are a high priority among the elderly because the incidence of heart disease and many cancers is highest in this age group (Weisman, Celentano, Teitelbaum, & Klassen, 1989). With the exception of hypertension screening, the use of preventive health care measures by older Americans is lower than recommended under current guidelines (Burg, Lane, & Polednak, 1990; Chao, Paganini-Hill, Ross, & Henderson, 1987; Makuc, Fried, & Kleinman, 1989). Women age 65 and over are significantly less likely to have mammography, breast exams, and Pap tests than are younger women, and these procedures decline with age even among the elderly (Burg et al., 1990). African American women report fewer procedures than White women, although between 1973 and 1985 racial differences narrowed considerably (Makuc et al., 1989). In addition to age and race, several other factors appear to be associated with the use of screening procedures. Studies have consistently indicated that having a regular source of care increases the prevalence of screening in the general population and among older persons (see Chao et al., 1987; Rakowski, Julius, Hickey, & Halter, 1987). Using an index of preventive health care, Rakowski et al. also found that frequent interaction with family had a positive effect on health practices. Support for socioeconomic status differences in the probability of screening exams are mixed. Burg and colleagues (1987), using data from the Awareness of Breast Cancer Project, found that education and income were not significant determinants of having a breast exam or a mammogram in older women. In contrast, findings from the National Health Interview Survey indicate that poor women, both Black and White, are less likely to have breast exams and Pap smears (Makuc et al., 1989). Having checkups also appear to be important determinants of female-specific tests (Makuc et al., 1989). There is some indication, however, that even among women having more recent physical exams, preventive tests are not emphasized as strongly for those who are poor (Makuc et al., 1989).

The African American elderly have elevated risk of morbidity from chronic disease. At age 70 and over, Blacks are more than twice as likely as Whites to have diagnosed hypertension and diabetes (Manton, Patrick, & Johnson, 1987). Because hypertension and diabetes are risk factors for heart disease and stroke, they play a crucial role in accounting for the higher mortality rates among Blacks. Thus, screening is especially critical for African American elderly. The next section of this chapter examines some preliminary findings on the extent to which older Blacks receive preventive health care and documents subpopulation differences.

Data and Methods

Data from the 1991 National Health Interview Survey of Health Promotion and Disease Prevention (HIS-HPDP) are used to investigate the use of preventive health behaviors among African American elderly. The Health Interview Survey (HIS) is an ongoing annual survey that collects information on health care utilization in the noninstitutionalized U.S. population. The HIS uses multistage sampling that results in 52 weekly samples that are pooled to yield data on 110,000 persons in 42,000 households. The HIS-HPDP is a special supplement in which one person 18 years or older was randomly sampled from each household in the 1991 HIS. The analyses presented here are based on African Americans 65 years and older. Because we are primarily interested in the relationship among selected predictors of preventive health care use, unweighted data are used. The total of number of respondents is 944.

Independent Variables. In keeping with the purpose of identifying subgroups of African American elderly who encounter barriers in accessing preventive care services, the independent variables are primarily demographic characteristics—age (coded in actual years), gender (females coded 1), education (coded in actual years ranging from 0 to 18), living alone (coded 1), region (the four census regions with South as the reference category), and urban-rural residence (central city, rural, with suburban the uncoded category). Having a regular source of care (coded 1 for yes and 0 for no) is also a predictor. Health status (coded 1 for excellent, 2 for good, 3 for fair, and 4 for poor) is controlled because it is reasonable to assume that those with poor health status have more contact with physicians who prescribe screening for chronic disease. It is also likely that older persons in poor health receive screening, in part, for the management of chronic disease (Chao et al., 1987). Whether a respondent had a specific chronic condition and type of insurance coverage was not available in the supplement. Unfortunately, a large number of missing cases prevented the inclusion of income. These omissions represent unavoidable limitations.

Dependent Variables. For African Americans of both sexes, we examined whether in the past 12 months respondents had a checkup (coded 1 for yes) and a cholesterol check (coded 1 for yes). Given that large numbers of African Americans had experienced blood pressure screening in the past year, we examined months since last screening, truncating at 18 months to prevent skewing by respondents at the extreme end. Respondents who had a checkup in the past year were asked if they had the following tests—vision, hearing, urine, blood test, and stool. For brevity, these were summed into an index ranging from 0 to 5 and labeled as "tests." "Immunization" indicates whether respondents had flu, pneumonia, and tetanus shots in the past 12 months and ranges from 0 to 3. The reference period for the Pap test (coded 1 for yes) and breast exam (coded 1 for yes) is the past year, while the reference period for the mammogram (coded 1 for yes) is the past 2 years. Physician visit in the past year (coded 1 for yes) is also included for comparative purposes. If there is a large discrepancy in the proportions with a physician contact and a checkup, this may indicate that older African Americans are not being encouraged to have physicals and therefore have poorer quality health care.

Results

An examination of the sample characteristics (data not shown) indicates that the mean age of respondents is 73.6 and the mean educational attainment is 9.1 years. Females are 63.5% of the sample, and 55.5% of the sample report living alone. A majority of respondents (56.9%) live in the South, 15.7% in the Northeast, 18.4% in the Midwest, and 9% in the West. More than two thirds (67.4%) reside in central cities, followed by 17.6% in suburban areas and 17.6% in rural areas. Ten percent report excellent health, 50% good health, 25% fair health, and 14.6% report poor health. Just under 91% of the respondents have a regular source of care.

Logistic and ordinary least squares regression are used to analyze the data and the results for the indicators that are not female-specific are presented in Table 13.1. For the total sample, just under 86% report a physician visit in the past year. Having a usual source of care is the most important predictor. Converting the logistic coefficient (2.18) indicates that those with a regular source of care are 8.8 times as likely as those without a regular provider to have visited a physician or other health care provider in the past year. As health declines, respondents are more likely to report a visit. Living alone, being male, and being younger are associated with lower probabilities of having a visit. Mean number of flu, pneumonia, and tetanus shots were quite low, .62, indicating that on average respondents had less than one of these immunizations in the past year. Further analyses indicate that only 28% of these respondents were immunized for the flu, 14% for pneumonia, and 22% received tetanus shots. Being male, having higher education, residing in the Northeast versus the South, having a usual source of care, and poorer health are predictive of immunizations.

Only 54.6% of respondents report a cholesterol screening in the past year, a serious problem given the high rates of heart disease among older African Americans. The logistic regression indicates that females and those living with others are significantly more likely to have this test. Further, residents in

TABLE 13.1 Logistic and OLS Regression Analyses: Use of Preventive Care
Among African American Elderly: Health Interview Survey, 1991

	MD Visit	Immunization	Cholesterol	BP-Check[a]	Checkup	Tests[b]
	N = 928	N = 790	N = 786	N = 901	N = 895	N = 585
(Percentage/Mean)	(85.9)	(0.62)	(54.6)	(3.8)	(73.9)	(3.8)
Female	.65**	−.07*	.31*	−.14***	.51**	−.01
Age	.07***	−.03	.01	−.11***	.02	−.07
Education	.03	.16***	.01	.05	.03	.03
Live alone	−.46*	.00	−.33*	.05	−.27	−.02
Region						
Northeast	.20	.08*	.83***	−.05	.54*	.12**
Midwest	.47	.05	.54*	−.08**	.66**	.08
West	.39	.04	.38	−.02	.23	.01
Residence						
Central city	−.05	.07	.30	.06	.12	.16**
Rural	−.59	.02	.16	.07	−.05	−.01
Usual source	2.18***	.14***	1.61***	−.32***	2.26***	.09*
Health	.55***	.07*	.22*	.18***	.46***	−.05
Hypertensive	—	—	—	.00	—	—
Intercept	−7.06	.11	−3.21	21.43	−4.57	4.63
Chi-square	144.86	—	75.70	140.63	145.82	—
p	.001	—	.001	.001	.001	—
df	11	—	11	11	11	—
R^2 adjusted	—	.06	—	.19	—	.05

NOTE: a. Months since blood pressure check. Negative numbers indicate shorter elapsed time.
b. Tests among those having a checkup.
* $p < .05$; ** $p < .01$; *** $p < .001$

the Northeast and Midwest are significantly more likely than those in the
South to report a cholesterol screening. Those with a regular source of care
were 3 times as likely to be screened, and the probability of screening increases
as health declines. Months since the last blood pressure screening is 3.8
months on average. Elapsed time is lower for females, those with higher education, residence in the Midwest versus the South, those with a regular source
of care; elapsed time decreases as health status worsens. These differences
appear even when the presence of self-reported hypertension is controlled.[b]

   In contrast to the 86% who had a physician visit in the past year, only
73.9% of older African Americans report having a checkup. Similar to having

TABLE 13.2 Logistic Regression Analyses of Preventive Care Among Elderly
African American Women, Health Interview Survey, 1991

	Pap Test[a]	*Breast Exam*[a]	*Mammogram*[b]
	N = 549	*N = 552*	*N = 551*
(Percentage)	*(41.6)*	*(58.2)*	*(46.1)*
Age	−.04**	−.00	−.02
Education	.02	.01	−.01
Live alone	.33	.28	.24
Region			
Northeast	−.03	−.11	.46
Midwest	.42	.00	−.21
West	.42	.13	.84*
Residence			
Central city	−.01	.12	.59*
Rural	−.23	−.17	−.13
Usual source	1.67***	1.29**	1.57**
Health status	.02	.16	.03
Checkup	1.22***	1.38***	.93***
Intercept	−.31	−2.40	−.79
Chi-square	69.33	76.9	69.83
p	.001	.001	.001
df	11	11	11

NOTE: a. Months since blood pressure check. Negative numbers indicate shorter elapsed time.
b. Tests among those having a checkup.
* $p < .05$; ** $p < .01$; *** $p < .001$

a physician visit, the odds of having a checkup are 9 times higher for those
with a regular source of care. Being female and having poorer health also
increase the probability of a physical. Those residing in the Northeast and
Midwest are significantly more likely than those residing in the South to report having a checkup. Respondents who had checkups report 3.9 preventive
tests on average. Residents of the Northeast are significantly more likely to
have tests than those residing in the South, and those residing in central city
areas are surprisingly more likely to have exams or tests than those residing
in suburban areas. Having a usual source of care has a positive effect, but
there are no significant differences by health status.

Table 13.2 presents the results of the logistic regression for the female-
specific preventive measures. The data indicate that among African American

women, 41.6% had a Pap test, 58.2% had a breast exam, and 46.1% had a mammogram. This is consistent with studies that show rather low rates for these screening exams. Tessaro, Eng, and Smith (1994) found that reasons for the low use of mammograms among African American women include other health concerns, fear of finding cancer, and customs that dictate going to the doctor only when there is a problem. Whether or not respondents had a checkup in the previous year is assessed because past research indicates that this is an important predictor. Unlike other studies, age had a significant impact only on whether or not respondents had a Pap test. We did not control for having a hysterectomy, which could account for this finding. Thus, a significant proportion of older Black females do not get breast exams or mammograms, but the proportion not getting exams does not appear to increase as they age. Having a usual source of care and having a checkup are important determinants of having all three preventive measures. The probability of having a mammogram is higher for those residing in the West versus the South, and those residing in central city areas versus suburban areas. Mammograms are more technologically driven, and this may explain why geographical differences do not show up in the other screening tests.

In summary, the percentage of older African Americans who have not received various preventive screening within the past year is quite high, although a one-year interval may be too short for some of the screening tests. With the exception of cholesterol screening and mammograms, the reference period was one year. The data also indicate that there are differences among African Americans in use of preventive health care services. Males are at higher risk for not receiving preventive care, being significantly less likely than females to visit a physician, have a checkup, and to have cholesterol screens. Some regional differences also emerged, with southerners being less likely to be immunized, have cholesterol checks, have a checkup, and have preventive tests. The elderly in greatest need, those in poor health, appear to use these services more. However, we cannot tell whether these tests are administered for diagnostic purposes or if they are being used in the management of already existing chronic ailments. Having a regular source of care influences the probability of having all these screenings and the probability of having a checkup. For example, 90% of those with a regular source saw a provider in the year before the survey compared to only 40% of those who did not. The corresponding figures for a checkup were 78.9% and 23.5%, respectively, for those with and without a regular source. While those with a regular provider averaged 3.1 months since last blood pressure check, those without a regular source averaged 11.7 months. Further analyses indicated that those with higher education are more likely to have a regular source of care. These findings for education and health status may point to two groups of elders that are most likely to have a regular source of care—those who are fairly well educated and covered by private supplemental "Medigap" packages and another group in poor health who are covered by Medicare and Medicaid. The data, however, do not permit an assessment of this hypothesis. Overall, there appear to be some differences in use within the African American community on these indicators. Further analysis is needed to determine whether there are interaction effects and to determine how income and insurance coverage may affect use of these services.

Satisfaction With Health Care Services

Satisfaction with health care services is an important dimension of health care because it is assumed that dissatisfaction with services leads to poor compliance, unproductive switching between providers, and—ultimately—delay in seeking treatment (Fox & Storms, 1981). With the exception of cost and convenience, Americans generally have fairly high levels of satisfaction with health care services (Aday & Andersen, 1975). Satisfaction is also high for those in HMOs (Dolinsky & Caputo, 1990). Studies of factors related to patient satisfaction have produced mixed results, especially for demographic characteristics. Some studies find lower satisfaction rates for Blacks, males, the non-elderly, the unmarried, and low socioeconomic persons while other studies do not (see Aday & Andersen, 1975; Fox & Storms, 1981; Ware, Davies-Avery, & Stewart, 1978). Further research, however, indicates that demographic factors have indirect effects on overall satisfaction through their relationship to health care delivery characteristics—being able to see a general practitioner or specialists when needed (Dolinsky & Caputo, 1990) and having a regular source of care (Fox & Storms, 1981). Provider evaluations also have a strong effect on satisfaction (Cleary & McNeil, 1988; Larsen & Rootman, 1976; Zyzanski, Hulka, & Cassel, 1974). Persons who rate their provider high are more likely to be satisfied with health care in general.

Similar to the general population, Medicare beneficiaries in a recent survey revealed high satisfaction rates in this population (HCFA, 1994). Among elderly beneficiaries, well over 95% were satisfied with the quality of care, availability of care, and ease of getting to the doctor. However, only 80% were satisfied with costs. Multivariate analyses indicate that satisfaction rates were similar for African American and White beneficiaries; however, satisfaction with costs was lower for those in poor health, those with Medicare only, and those with lower incomes. Interestingly, those using a physician's office as a regular source of care were less satisfied than those without a regular source. Beneficiaries with 12 years of education or less were also less satisfied with the availability of care.

Because the African American elderly are more likely to live below the poverty line and to have poorer health profiles, we examined provider ratings and overall satisfaction with care among this group. Again, the purpose was to determine whether there are subgroups of Blacks aged 65 and over who have lower levels of satisfaction than others.

Data and Methods

The data for these analyses are drawn from the Medicare Current Beneficiary Survey (MCBS) and represent a sample of noninstitutionalized beneficiaries continuously enrolled during 1991 and 1992. The MCBS is a multipurpose survey designed to focus on economic issues for the Medicare population, including health care use, expenditures, and the factors that affect the ability to pay for health care services. These analyses are based on 829 African American persons 65 and over and include oversampling for those 85 and over. These analyses are for the unweighted data.

Independent Variables. Sex, age, living arrangements, region, and urban-rural residence are the demographic characteristics used in the analyses. Income is ordinal, ranging from 1 for those with incomes $5,000 or less to 11 for those with incomes of $50,000 or more. Age is coded as ordinal into 5-year age intervals as previously determined by the MCBS survey staff. Years of educational attainment range from 1 to 18 years, 6 years of college or more. A measure of whether respondents' regular provider was in a private (e.g., doctor's office, HMO, etc.) or in a public (e.g., hospital outpatient department, clinic, etc.) setting was also assessed. Perceived health status ranges from 1 for poor health to 5 for excellent. Functional health status is measured by the number of ADLs and IADLs. Three types of insurance coverage are included—Medicare and Private/Other (i.e., private, employer-supplemented, and other), Medicare plus Medicaid, and Medicare only. Evaluation of the regular provider/setting is measured by a series of 12 questions that ask respondents their perceptions of medical care received from the regular provider. These statements incorporate information on competency, understanding of the respondent's medical history, the thoroughness of examinations, explanations of medical problems, hurriedness, confidence placed in the physician, and communication skills. Responses range from strongly agree to strongly disagree, with the highest possible score being 48. The alpha coefficient for this scale is .82. One standard deviation below and above the mean is used to group respondents into low, medium, and high levels.

Dependent Variables. Satisfaction with health care is measured by a 7-item scale that assesses quality, availability, cost, location and convenience, general information imparted, and follow-up care. Responses ranged from very satisfied to very unsatisfied, with the highest possible score being 28. The alpha for this scale is .89. A factor analysis revealed that the provider/setting evaluation and satisfaction items represent distinct scales (results available on request[1]).

Results

An examination of the sample characteristics (data not shown) reveals that approximately 64% of the respondents are female, 60% reside in the South, and 27.5% reside in rural areas. The age distribution was 65 to 69 (26%), 70 to 74 (17.5%), 75 to 79 (20.7), 80 to 84 (19.5%), and 85 and older (16.2%). Mean years of education is 8.28 and mean income is 2.21 (i.e., on average, income fell into the $5,001-$10,000 category). Just over 32% of beneficiaries live alone, while 60% live with relatives and 15.6% live with unrelated persons. Elders averaged 11.14 ADLs and 12.07 IADLs. Poor health is reported by 11.1%, fair health by 26.1%, good health by 28.8%, very good health by 22.3%, and excellent health by 11.4%. Those with a private provider constitute 70% of the sample compared to 30% with a public provider. Slightly more than 24% are covered by Medicare only, 30.5% have Medicare and Medicaid, and 44.1% have Medicare plus private or other supplementation. Finally, 18.9% report low satisfaction with place of care, while 68.2 and 12.9% report medium and high levels of satisfaction, respectively.

The mean level of health care satisfaction for this group is 21.4. The data indicate that neither age, education, nor income have significant effects once other variables are controlled (data not shown). As the number of ADLs increased, satisfaction decreased. Thus, those with more disabilities are less satisfied with the system. Table 13.3 presents multiple classification results showing mean satisfaction levels for various groups of African Americans as defined by other demographic variables, type of regular provider, insurance coverage, and provider ratings. Males are significantly more satisfied with services than are females after adjustments for other variables. Satisfaction is also related to health status, with the mean level of satisfaction increasing from 20.64 for those in poor health to 22.25 for those in excellent health. As expected, those with Medicare only report lower levels of satisfaction than those with supplemental policies. Indeed, the Medicare-Medicaid population is slightly more satisfied that those with private policies, although the difference is not statistically significant. As expected, provider ratings influence overall satisfaction in the expected direction. Those who are most dissatisfied with their regular source of care are also least satisfied with overall health care.

Factors associated with regular provider/setting evaluations are presented in Table 13.4. In contrast to satisfaction with health care, females are more satisfied with their regular source of care than are males. Surprisingly, those residing in rural locations rated their usual provider/setting higher than those residing in urban areas. Consistent with the findings for satisfaction, ratings become more positive as health status improves. Those receiving care in a public setting rate their source more positively than those in private settings. Finally, insurance coverage has no effect on provider ratings.

These findings indicate that subpopulations within the African American elderly differ in their evaluations of health care services, with satisfaction being lower among females, those in poor/fair health, those with Medicare only, and those who rate their place of care lowest. Further, it is females, those living in rural locations, those with better health, and those receiving care in public sites that have the highest evaluations of their regular place of care. The finding that those in public sites have higher evaluations of providers than those receiving care in private settings is indeed puzzling. Thus, while we can point to interesting differences, further research is needed to explain these findings fully. As noted previously, the population aged 85 years and older is oversampled, and satisfaction tends to increase with age. More conclusive results must rely on the weighted sample.

TABLE 13.3 Multiple Classification Analysis of Satisfaction With Health Care Among African American Elderly—MCBS (Unweighted Data)

	Unadjusted Mean	Adjusted Mean[a]	Eta	Beta	F
Gender			.03	.08	4.055*
Male	21.55	27.67			
Female	21.34	21.25			
Region			.06	.04	.878
Non-South	21.61	21.53			
South	21.28	21.33			
Urban-rural residence			.08	.02	.302
Urban	21.48	21.36			
Rural	21.19	21.49			
Health status			.27	.22	7.885***
Poor	20.55	20.64			
Fair	20.87	20.98			
Good	21.26	21.31			
Very good	22.32	22.08			
Excellent	22.29	22.25			
Living arrangements			.07	.05	1.025
Lives alone	21.62	21.58			
Lives with kin	21.33	21.34			
Lives with non-kin	21.16	21.21			
Regular provider setting			.08	.02	2.320
Public	21.39	21.32			
Private	21.42	21.65			
Insurance coverage			.10	.13	5.251**
Medicare only	20.94	21.05			
Medicare-Medicaid	21.61	21.84			
Medicare-private\other	21.48	21.25			
Provider rating			.35	.37	44.038***
Low	20.43	21.35			
Medium	21.16	21.17			
High	23.30	23.39			

NOTE: a. Means adjusted for all other variables in table plus age, education, income, ADLS, and IADLs.
* $p < .05$; ** $p < .01$; *** $p < .001$

TABLE 13.4 Multiple Classification Analysis of Provider Ratings Among African American Elders—MCBS (Unweighted Data)

	Unadjusted Mean	*Adjusted Mean*[a]	*Eta*	*Beta*	*F*
Gender			.12	.10	6.373*
Male	36.26	36.33			
Female	37.22	37.19			
Region			.08	.03	.525
Non-South	33.37	36.64			
South	36.64	36.80			
Urban-rural residence			.16	.16	12.865***
Urban	35.87	35.87			
Rural	37.36	37.26			
Health status			.14	.15	3.725**
Poor	36.81	36.80			
Fair	36.12	36.08			
Good	36.96	36.95			
Very good	37.57	37.57			
Excellent	37.49	37.67			
Living arrangements			.03	.01	.059
Lives alone	37.05	36.83			
Lives with kin	36.76	36.90			
Lives with non-kin	36.98	36.99			
Regular provider setting			.08	.10	6.257*
Public	37.07	37.11			
Private	36.33	36.22			
Insurance coverage			.07	.03	.185
Medicare only	36.50	36.80			
Medicare-Medicaid	36.76	36.80			
Medicare-private/other	37.17	37.00			

NOTE: a. Means adjusted for all other variables in table plus age, education, income, ADLS, and IADLs.
* $p < .05$; ** $p < .01$; *** $p < .001$

Use of Long-Term Care Services

It is well documented that older African Americans are less likely than older Whites to reside in long-term care institutions (see Keith, 1987), although African Americans may use other long-term care services at somewhat greater rates than Whites (Wallace, Snyder, Walker, & Ingman, 1992). In

1985, utilization rates were 39 per 1,000 for elderly African Americans compared to 60 per 1,000 for elderly Whites (Jackson & Perry, 1989). Among the nursing home population, quality of care may vary by race. Older African Americans, although more impaired, are less likely to reside in skilled nursing facilities, and there is some evidence that nursing homes serving African American elderly provide a lower quality of care than those serving older Whites Americans (Belgrave, Wykle, & Choi, 1993). With few exceptions, similar factors appear to predict nursing home placement among African Americans and Whites, including marital status/living arrangements, disability, and availability of caregivers (e.g., Burr, 1990). Given that Black-White differences in these indicators do not explain differential placement rates, several explanations have been advanced.

Early speculation that lower institutionalization rates among African Americans stemmed from lower levels of need have not been supported in subsequent research. Compared to older Whites, older African Americans report higher rates of chronic conditions, poorer self-reported health, and higher disability rates (National Center for Health Statistics [NCHS], 1993a, 1993b). Until extreme old age, 85 and over, African American elderly have a higher probability of dying than older Whites, and this holds for almost all the major causes of death (NCHS, 1993b). It is reasonable to assume that selective survival at younger ages could produce a group of hearty African Americans age 85 and over who need less nursing and personal home care than similar aged Whites (see Markides & Machalek, 1984). However, this is unlikely. Gibson and Jackson (1992) found similar levels of disability among those Whites and Blacks aged 85 years and older, yet Whites are almost twice as likely to be institutionalized.

The Black disadvantage in economic resources may play a role in differential institutionalization. On average, nursing home costs are approximately $25,000 annually (Liu & Manton, 1989). In 1991, older African Americans were 3 times as likely as older Whites to live in poverty (33.8% vs. 10.1%), and the 1988 median net worth of older African Americans was $22,210 compared to $81,648 for older Whites (Chen, 1991). These differences in resources mean that a larger proportion of African Americans rely on Medicaid to finance nursing home placement. Because Medicaid reimburses at a lower rate, Medicaid patients may be less desirable than private-pay residents (Belgrave et al., 1993). Affordability is especially problematical for African Americans who live in the 20 states that do not provide Medicaid coverage for the medically needy—those who qualify for Medicaid because their income minus their medical expenses meets the eligibility quidelines. Thus, these individuals represent a "notch" population—unable to afford to finance private care and unable to qualify for Medicaid. Moreover, Harrington Meyer (1994) suggests that states with higher proportions of African Americans and Hispanics are less likely to offer medically needy coverage.

It is often argued that African Americans are less likely to use nursing homes because cultural preferences favor family care. Researchers have documented that older African Americans have a varied and strong social support system that provides assistance (e.g., Taylor, 1988). It remains unclear, however, whether older Blacks receive more support than older Whites. It is also not clear whether racial differences observed from study to study reflect cultural or economic factors. Mutran (1985), examining intergenerational transfers among Blacks and Whites, found that Blacks were more likely to give and receive support, but these differences declined when socioeconomic status was controlled. On the other hand, attitudes regarding caregiving were more important in explaining support among Blacks. More recently, Montgomery and Hirshorn (1991), using data from the National Survey of Families and Households, found that Black males and females in poor health were more likely than their White counterparts to report that they received no help from primary kin (spouse and children) with several household chores. However, the survey did not include help from the extended kin network, which is reported to be more prevalent among African American elders. When all health statuses were considered, however, Black women had the highest probability of receiving household help. Thus, racial differences in informal care varies depending on definitions of help, sources of help, and within subpopulations based on need. The extent to which preferences and cultural factors play a unique role remains an open question.

Racial discrimination in nursing home placement has long been discussed as one explanation of low use of nursing homes among older African Americans. Because discrimination is difficult to document, it is often inferred if racial differences do not disappear when other explanatory factors are controlled. For example, Falcone and Broyles (1994) make a strong case for discrimination in their study of patients in North Carolina hospitals awaiting nursing home placements. After controlling for demographic factors; behavioral, financial, and family problems; and special medical requirements, non-White patients faced an extended delay (time between when a patient is medically ready for discharge and when the patient is actually discharged). The mean number of days delayed was 8.0 for Whites and 20.0 for non-

Whites. They note that discrimination could take place in several forms in-cluding roommate matching—homes deferring to the racial preferences of their patients in selecting roommates—but argue that the more likely source is the preference of nursing home owners or operators. Although these data are confined to one state, the evidence suggests that this is a widespread phe-nomenon. Smith (1990), for example, notes that in Pennsylvania the bed popu-lation ratios are higher in counties with a higher proportion White. He argues that, unlike in the case of hospitals, the structure of Medicare and Medicaid has not exerted economic pressures on nursing homes to desegregate.

Conclusions

Medicare and Medicaid improved the use of health services care among African American elderly, especially as measured by general indicators such as annual contact with a provider and average number of visits per person per year. Yet there is ample evidence to suggest that obtaining health care poses problems for a significant minority of African American elderly. These prob-lems include inability to afford supplemental Medicare policies; care in non-private settings; unmet need; and less access to sophisticated diagnostic pro-cedures. The analyses presented indicate that subpopulations of African Americans do not use routine preventive screening at recommended rates, and the absence of a regular provider appears to be an important determinant. Further, close to 10% have no regular provider/source of care, a significant minority. Satisfaction with health care and provider is also not consistent across all groups of elderly with Medicare only, with those in the poorest health being the least satisfied. These findings are only tentative given the various limitations discussed earlier. However, they strongly suggest that re-search is needed to explore these topics more fully. An especially interesting research question is how use of preventive services varies by type of insur-ance coverage. We also need a more complete exploration of how the various components of satisfaction (e.g., costs and availability) are related to insur-ance coverage and place of care among African American elderly. African Americans continue to underutilize nursing homes and the debate over why this is the case is ongoing. Replication of the Falcone and Broyles (1994) study in other states would be helpful in determining whether or not African American elderly face discrimination in placements. Overall, these findings suggests that examining differences within the African American elderly population is a useful strategy for identifying subpopulations that have unique health care problems and for fine-tuning health care policy so that the needs of all elders are more effectively addressed.

Note

1. Available from Carol O. Long, College of Nursing, Arizona State University, Tempe, AZ 85287.

References

Aday, L. A., & Andersen, R. (1975). *Development of indices of access to medical care.* Ann Arbor, MI: Health Administration Press.

Aday, L. A., Andersen, R., & Fleming, G. (1980). *Health care in the U.S.: Equitable for whom?* Beverly Hills, CA: Sage.

Aday, L. A., & Eichorn, R. (1972). *The utilization of health services: Indices and correlates* (DHEW Publication No. [HSM] 73-3003). Rockville, MD: National Center for Health Services Research and Development.

Aday, L. A., Fleming, G., & Andersen, R. (1984). *Access to health care in the U.S.: Who has it, who doesn't.* Chicago: Pluribus.

Belgrave, L., Wykle, M., & Choi, J. (1993). Health, double jeopardy, and culture: The use of institutionalization by African Americans. *The Gerontologist, 33,* 379-385.

Burg, M. A., Lane, D., & Polednak, A. (1990). Age group differences in the use of breast cancer screening tests: The effects of health care utilization and socioeconomic variables. *Research on Aging, 2,* 514-530.

Burr, J. A. (1990). Race/sex comparisons of elderly living arrangements: Factors influencing the institutionalization of the unmarried. *Research on Aging, 12,* 507-530.

Chao, A., Paganini-Hill, A., Ross, R., & Henderson, B. (1987). Use of preventive care by the elderly. *Preventive Medicine, 16,* 710-722.

Chen, Y. (1991). Improving the economic security of minority persons as they enter old age. In *Minority elders: Longevity, economics, and health* (pp. 14-23). Washington, DC: The Gerontological Society of America—Task Force on Minority Issues.

Chulis, G. S., Eppig, F. P., Hogan, M. O., Waldo, D. R., & Arnet, R. H. (1993). Health insurance and the elderly: Data from MCBS. *Health Care Financing Review, 14*(3), 163-181.

Cleary, P., & McNeil, D. (1988). Patient satisfaction as an indicator of quality of care. *Inquiry, 25,* 25-36.

Davis, K., Lillie-Blanton, M., Lyons, B., Mullan, F., Powe, N., & Rowland, D. (1987). Health care for Black Americans: The public sector role. *The Milbank Quarterly, 65*(Suppl. 1), 213-247.

Dolinsky, A. L., & Caputo, R. K. (1990). The role of health care attributes and demographic characteristics in the determination of health care satisfaction. *Journal of Health Care Marketing, 10*(4), 31-39.

Dutton, D. (1978). Explaining the low use of health services by the poor: Costs, attitudes, or delivery system. *American Sociological Review, 43,* 348-368.

Escarse, J. J., Epstein, K. R., Colby, D. C., & Schwartz, J. S. (1993). Racial differences in the elderly's use of medical procedures and diagnostic tests. *American Journal of Public Health, 87*(3), 948-954.

Falcone, D., & Broyles, R. (1994). Access to long-term care: Race as a barrier. *Journal of Health Politics, Policy and Law, 19*(3), 583-595.

Fox, J. G., & Storms, D. M. (1981). A different approach to sociodemographic predictors of satisfaction with health care. *Social Science and Medicine, 15*(A), 557-564.

Garfinkel, S. A., Bonito, A. J., & McLeroy, K. R. (1987). Socioeconomic factors and Medicare supplemental health insurance. *Health Care Financing Review, 9*(1), 21-30.

Gibson, R. C., & Jackson, J. S. (1992). The Black oldest old: Health, functioning, and informal support. In R. M. Suzman, D. P. Willis, & K. G. Manton (Eds.), *The oldest old* (pp. 321-340). New York: Oxford University Press.

Gurny, P., Baugh, D., & Davis, A. (1992). Chapter 10: A description of Medicaid eligibility. *Health Care Financing Review,* Annual Supplement, pp. 207-234.

Harrington Meyer, M. (1994). Gender, race, and the distribution of social assistance: Medicaid use among the frail elderly. *Gender & Society, 8,* 8-28.

Health Care Financing Administration. (1994). *Report to Congress: Monitoring the impact of Medicare physician payment reform on utilization and access* (HCFA Publication No. 03358). Washington, DC: Government Printing Office.

Jackson, J. J., & Perry, C. (1989). Physical health conditions of middle-aged and aged Blacks. In K.S. Markides (Ed.), *Aging and health: Perspectives on gender, race, ethnicity, and class* (pp. 111-176). Newbury Park, CA: Sage.

Keith, V. M. (1987). Long-term care and the Black elderly. In W. Jones, Jr., & M. F. Rice (Eds.), *Health care issues in Black America* (pp. 173-209). New York: Greenwood.

Kotranski, L., Bolick, J., & Halbert, J. (1987). Neighborhood variations in the use of city-supported primary health care services by an elderly population. *Journal of Community Health, 12,* 231-245.

Larsen, D. E., & Rootman, I. (1976). Physician role performance and patient satisfaction. *Social Science and Medicine, 10*(1), 29-32.

Liu, K., & Manton, K. (1989). The effect of nursing home use on Medicaid eligibility. *The Gerontologist, 29,* 59-66.

Makuc, D., Freid, V., & Kleinman, J. (1989). National trends in the use of preventive health care by women. *American Journal of Public Health, 79*(1), 21-26.

Manton, K. G., Patrick, C. H., & Johnson, L. W. (1987). Health differentials between Blacks and Whites. *The Milbank Quarterly, 65*(Suppl. 1), 129-199.

Markides, K. S., & Machalek, R. (1984). Selective survival, aging and society. *Archives of Gerontology and Geriatrics, 3,* 207-222.

Montgomery, R., & Hirshorn, B. (1991). Current and future family help with long-term care needs of the elderly. *Research on Aging, 13*(2), 171-204.

Mutran, E. (1985). Intergenerational family support among Blacks and Whites: Responses to culture or to socioeconomic differences. *Journal of Gerontology, 40,* 382-389.

National Center for Health Statistics. (1993a). *Annual summary of births, marriages, divorces and deaths: United States 1992* (Monthly vital statistics report; 41[13]). Hyattsville, MD: Public Health Service.

National Center for Health Statistics. (1993b). *Health, United States, 1993.* Washington, DC: Government Printing Office.

Petchers, M. K., & Milligan, S. E. (1988). Access to health care in a Black urban elderly population. *The Gerontologist, 28,* 213-217.

Rakowski, W., Julius, M., Hickey, T., & Halter, J. (1987). Correlates of preventive health behavior in later life. *Research on Aging, 9,* 331-355.

Reed, W., Darity, W., & Roberson, N. (1993). *Health and medical care of African-Americans.* Westport, CT: Auburn House.

Schlenger, W. E., & Corder, L. S. (1984). Access to health care among aged Medicare beneficiaries. *National Medical Care Utilization and Expenditure Survey* (Series B—Report #3, DHHS Publication No. 84-20203). Washington, DC: Government Printing Office.

Smith, D. B. (1990). Population ecology and the racial integration of hospitals and nursing homes in the United States. *The Milbank Quarterly, 68*(4), 561-596.

Taylor, R. J. (1988). Aging and supportive relationships among Black Americans. In J. S. Jackson (Ed.), *The Black American elderly: Research on physical and psychosocial health* (pp. 259-281). New York: Springer.

Tessaro, I., Eng, E., & Smith, J. (1994). Breast cancer screening in older African-American women: Qualitative research findings. *American Journal of Health Promotion, 8*(4), 286-293.

Wallace, S., Snyder, J., Walker, G., & Ingman, S. (1992). Racial differences among users of long-term care: The case of adult day care. *Research on Aging, 14*(4), 471-495.

Ware, J. E., Davies-Avery, A., & Stewart, A. (1978). The measurement and meaning of patient satisfaction. *Health and Medical Care Services, 1*(1), 1-15.

Wenneker, M. B., & Epstein, A. M. (1989). Racial inequalities in the use of procedures for patients with ischemic heart disease in Massachusetts. *Journal of the American Medical Association, 261,* 253-257.

Weisman, C., Celentano, D., Teitelbaum, M., & Klassen, A. (1989). Cancer screening services for the elderly. *Public Health Reports, 104*(3), 209-214.

Wolinsky, F., Aguirre, B., Fann, L., Keith, V., Arnold, C., Niederhauer, J., & Dietrich, K. (1989). Ethnic differences in the demand for physician and hospital utilization among older adults in major American cities: Conspicuous evidence of considerable inequalities. *The Milbank Quarterly, 67*(4-5), 412-449.

Wolinsky, F., & Johnson, R. (1991). The use of health services by older adults. *Journal of Gerontology: Social Sciences, 46,* S345-S357.

Zyzanski, S., Hulka, B., & Cassel, J. (1974). Scale for the measurement of satisfaction with medical care: Modifications in content, format, and scoring. *Medical Care, 12,* 611-120.

Health Service Use and Long-Term Care Among Hispanics

Ronald J. Angel
Jacqueline L. Angel

Although our knowledge is increasing rapidly, as of yet we have limited information concerning either the patterns or predictors of acute or long-term health care use by older Hispanics. Only recently has the study of Hispanic health at any age moved from small, localized samples to large-scale epidemiological and health services research. Studies such as the ongoing Mexican American Epidemiologic Study of the Elderly (Markides, Rudkin, Angel, & Espino, in press) are beginning to provide basic information on health, functional status, and health care use among older Mexican Americans. The Hispanic oversample of preretirement age individuals in the Health and Retirement Survey (HRS) will provide much needed information on health transitions, as well as health care use and financing, among Hispanics as they retire and move into the later decades of life (Juster, 1993).

Perhaps the most serious gap in our understanding of health care use patterns among Hispanics, though, is an almost complete lack of information concerning the impact of the organization and financing of health services on utilization patterns for these groups. Most of our large-scale national data sets include too few Hispanics of any nationality to allow detailed analyses of their health care use. It is difficult, therefore, to test complex models of health service use that control for social class and cultural, organizational, and health factors simultaneously.

343

An Overview of Hispanic Health Care Use

Before proceeding, we offer an overview of what is to follow and briefly summarize what we know of the use of both acute and long-term care among Hispanics. In the remainder of the chapter we elaborate these patterns in greater detail. We begin by noting that the study of Hispanic health has gained momentum in the past two decades. Before the 1970s, even when researchers included Hispanics in their studies, they failed to differentiate among Hispanic groups in tests of more complex utilization models. Yet such differentiation is crucial if we are to determine the extent to which the need for medical care is being met for different groups and if we are to understand better the nature of the access barriers they face (Wolinsky et al., 1989).

The limited evidence we have shows roughly comparable rates of physician and hospital use among Hispanics and non-Hispanics in middle age and beyond, with the exception of Puerto Ricans and Mexican Americans who often see physicians and enter hospitals at lower rates than non-Hispanics (Treviño & Moss, 1984; Wolinsky et al., 1989). Other data, however, show that Puerto Ricans who receive Medicaid are twice as likely as are non-Hispanic Whites to spend at least one night in a hospital (Angel & Angel, 1994). We are not, therefore, in any position to definitively characterize Hispanic physician and hospital use as either excessively high or low. The association among the need for services, its financing and organization, and the actual use of services by different subgroups of Hispanics is far too complex for such characterizations. The data reveal very different levels of need for services among Hispanic groups, as well as differences in the association between need and the actual use of services (Wolinsky et al., 1989).

Although older Hispanics are, in general, as likely to see a physician during the year as are non-Hispanics, they are far less likely than non-Hispanic Whites to enter nursing homes, nor do they use community-based care services to any significant degree (Angel & Angel, 1997; Wallace, Campbell, & Lew-Ting, 1994; Wallace & Lew-Ting, 1992). One recent study found that severely functionally impaired and socially isolated Hispanics 70 years of age and over were less likely than non-Hispanics of similar age to use paid in-home care services (Wallace, Levy-Storms, & Ferguson, 1995).

We are able only to speculate as to the reasons for differences between Hispanics and non-Hispanics in the use of either acute or long-term care services. It has been suggested, for example, that the family may serve as an alternative to institutionalization for the frail Hispanic elderly, resulting in a decreased probability of using nursing homes. Language barriers and cultural distance between non-Hispanic providers and Hispanic patients may discourage general medical and mental health care use, as well as the use of long-term care services by Hispanics. In addition to these cultural barriers to the use of services, Hispanics face serious financial obstacles to the use of health and long-term care services. As we elaborate further below, Hispanics in general, and Mexican Americans in particular, are seriously underinsured for medical care at earlier ages, and after the age of 65 they are less likely than other groups to have supplemental "Medigap" coverage (Angel & Angel, 1996).

Low income also serves as a barrier to the use of nursing homes and formal in-home community services by older Hispanics (Angel & Angel, 1997; Wallace et al., 1994). Medicare provides only limited, post-acute, coverage for nursing home or community-based care, and the majority of such care must be paid for out of pocket (Schulz, 1995). Before an older individual who must enter a nursing home qualifies for Medicaid, both individuals and couples must liquidate most of their resources and "spend down" to Medicaid eligibility (Angel & Angel, 1996). As we elaborate below, even with universal Medicare coverage, the premiums, deductibles, and copayments that Medicare does not cover can represent significant barriers to health care use. It is clear, therefore, that low income and a lack of health insurance interact with cultural, social class, and system factors to discourage the use of both acute and long-term care services by Hispanics. As of yet we do not have a good idea of how these various factors interact to influence acute or long-term care use by older Hispanics. Given the current fragmented nature of information on health care use among these groups, then, this chapter is as much a call for research into new and important areas concerning health care use by older Hispanics as it is a review of our existing knowledge.

Minority Group Status and Health Care Use

Before we proceed to an examination of health care use by Hispanics, it is necessary to be clear about the role of group membership on the need for both acute and long-term care. Although all individuals age biologically, the rate at which they do so, and especially the rate at which they lose their functional capacities, is extremely variable, and the aging process and its consequences are influenced by numerous cultural and social class factors (Angel & Angel, 1997). The dramatic increase in life expectancy at older ages that we have witnessed during the 20th century clearly demonstrates that the aging process is not set in stone and that it is subject to numerous social and environmental influences (Angel, 1996). Social inequalities that increase a minority group's exposure to environmental risk factors and restrict access to medical care, therefore, can directly decrease active life expectancy and increase the portion of life spent in ill health (Angel & Angel, 1997).

The limited evidence we have indicates that Blacks spend fewer years free of functional limitations than do Whites (Crimmins, Hayward, & Saito, 1996). Since higher status older persons enjoy both longer lives and fewer inactive years than lower status individuals, these disadvantages are accounted for largely by social class (Crimmins et al., 1996). Hispanics, on the other hand, have longer expected life spans than Blacks (Angel & Angel, 1996) and it appears that certain aspects of traditional Mexican American culture may protect health (Bagley, Angel, Dilworth-Anderson, Lui, & Schinke, 1995). Social class factors that influence the length of life, as well as the timing of the onset of chronic disease, then, are also major determinants of the need for both acute and long-term care.

Disease and functional incapacity have both biological and social causes and consequences (Angel & Angel, 1997). As one moves from the strictly biological level to the more social and functional levels, the number of cultural, social, and institutional factors that structure the consequences of disease and illness increases. Figure 14.1 presents a model of the process through which disease is translated into illness and functional incapacity and, ultimately, into the need for both acute and formal long-term care. The model makes it clear that the use of both acute and long-term care are mediated by various social factors and that incapacity and the need for care are as much functions of environmental demands and of one's social context as of aging and disease themselves.

The model specifically emphasizes the cultural and social class context within which incapacity occurs. In this model, culture and social class are contextual factors that influence each stage in the process, both by affecting the probability of the occurrence of each stage and by influencing the timing of the transition to the next stage. The extent to which disease manifests itself as incapacity and the inability to carry out one's usual social roles directly affects the need for both acute and long-term care.

The model begins with disease, which is the actual pathological process that manifests itself as impairments such as heart disease or the loss of motor control. If these functional limitations are severe enough, they can result in

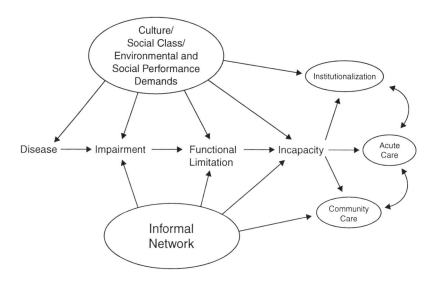

Figure 14.1. The Sociocultural Context of Long-Term Care

incapacity. Blacks and Hispanics have lower average socioeconomic statuses than non-Hispanic Whites, and the data clearly show that minorities and the poor have higher morbidity rates than the middle class (Centers for Disease Control, 1990; Franco et al., 1985; Frerichs, Chapman, & Maes, 1984; Jepson, Kessler, Portnoy, & Gibbs, 1991; Kittner, White, Losonczy, Wolf, & Hebel, 1990; Siegel, Deeb, Wolfe, Wilcox, & Mark, 1993). Mexican Americans experience very high rates of diabetes, which can lead to kidney failure, the loss of limbs, blindness, heart disease, and death (Samet, Coultas, Howard, Skipper, & Hanis, 1988). On the other hand, certain data indicate that Mexican Americans enjoy a mortality advantage over non-Hispanics from both heart disease and cancer (Bagley et al., 1995; Frerichs et al., 1984; Markides et al., in press; Mitchell, Stern, Haffner, Hazuda, & Patterson, 1990). Group membership, therefore, does not operate simply and can have both positive and negative consequences. It is clear, however, that in most contexts poverty increases the risk of disease and its negative health consequences.

    Once a disease has manifested itself, cultural and social class factors influence the probability that help will be sought (Angel & Thoits, 1987; Dutton, 1986; Mechanic, 1980). They also influence the quality of health care that one receives and one's compliance with recommended medical regimens. All of these factors operate to determine one's functional status. If one gets treatment for a chronic condition early in the course of disease, effective management is often possible. One very important cultural influence on functional capacity and the use of health care arises from differences in social support, as well as in individuals' ability to purchase care. These factors influence both the probability of health care use and the probability that a disease will progress to incapacity (Angel & Angel, 1992). This model is particularly useful in sensitizing us to the fact that the need for both acute and long-term care are as much a function of one's cultural and social context as of disease and functional limitations themselves.

What Do We Actually Know About Health Care Use by Older Hispanics?

Wolinsky et al. (1989) note that in the study of health care use, an appreciation of the unique status of Hispanics has increased since the 1960s, when it was common practice to drop groups other than Blacks or Whites from analyses of physician or hospital use. Today, researchers are aware of the need not only to include Hispanics, but to differentiate among nationality groups because the data reveal large differences in both the use of health services and the determinants of that use. In addition to an appreciation of differences among nationality groups, we are also becoming more aware of the heterogeneity within individual Hispanic subgroups in both health risks and health care use. Although this appreciation leads to more complex analyses and the need for more and better data, it is made necessary by very real differences between and among Hispanics and non-Hispanics. Although Hispanics may share a common Spanish heritage, they differ significantly in other economic and health-related factors and in the impact of those factors on health care use (Bagley et al., 1995; Eribes & Bradley-Rawls, 1978; Espino, Neufeld, Mulvihill, & Libow, 1988; Greene & Monahan, 1984; Holmes, Teresi, & Holmes, 1983; Morrison, 1983; Torres-Gil & Villa, 1993; Wallace et al., 1994).

Even with our greater appreciation of the need to disaggregate the Hispanic population in studies of health care use among the elderly, our ability to do so remains limited because we simply lack the data. The data that are available demonstrate great variability among Hispanic groups and also reveal similar, and sometimes greater, use of services by Hispanics than non-Hispanics (Treviño & Moss, 1984; Wolinsky et al., 1989). Data from the National Health Interview Survey, for example, show that among those 65 or older, Puerto Ricans, Cuban Americans, and Other Hispanics report more physician visits per year than do Mexican Americans or the population at large (Treviño & Moss, 1984). Data from the Survey of Elderly Hispanics confirm these findings and reveal a high mean number of physician visits for Puerto Ricans 65 or older. Puerto Rican elderly are 3 times as likely as non-Hispanic Whites to see a doctor, regardless of the type of health insurance coverage they are eligible for or receive (Angel & Angel, 1994).

Institutional and Community Care

The data also reveal differences between elderly Hispanics and non-Hispanics in the use of long-term care. Hispanics are underrepresented in nursing homes, and they use fewer home health care and community-based social services than non-Hispanics (Angel, 1991; Burr, 1990; Eribes & Bradley-Rawls, 1978; Espino et al., 1988; Greene & Ondrich, 1990; Morrison, 1983; Torres-Gil & Fielder, 1986-1987; Wallace & Lew-Ting, 1992; Worobey & Angel, 1990). Even when they suffer fairly serious functional impairments, older individuals of every race and ethnicity continue to live in the community, often alone (Angel, 1991; Angel & Angel, 1997; Angel, Angel, & Himes, 1992; Worobey & Angel, 1990). On any day, 3% of (65 years and over) older Mexican Americans and Puerto Ricans and 2% of older Cuban Americans are residents of nursing homes, while almost 5% of older Blacks and nearly 6% of elderly non-Hispanic Whites are in nursing homes.

Yet there are probably many individuals in the community who could use such services. A study by Espino and colleagues found that among nursing home residents in New York, Puerto Ricans were younger and had more disabilities than non-Hispanics (Espino et al., 1988). These data raise the possibility that although, overall, Hispanic life spans are similar to those of non-Hispanic Whites, they may suffer more serious functional limitations at earlier ages (Espino, Burge, & Moreno, 1991). It may also be the case that among Hispanics the family assumes the responsibility for the care of infirm individuals for a longer period and resorts to institutionalization only when the older person becomes an impossible caregiving burden.

Several reasons for the lower rates of nursing home use by Hispanics have been offered, including the lack of long-term care facilities in minority communities, cultural differences between the providers of care and minority group members, more powerful cultural norms among Hispanics concerning children's responsibility for the care of aging parents, and cultural differences in preferences in living arrangements (Angel, Angel, McClellan, & Markides, 1996; Eribes & Bradley-Rawls, 1978). Data from the Hispanic Established Population for Epidemiologic Study of the Elderly (H-EPESE; Markides et al., in press) indicate that relatively few Mexican Americans over the age of 65 would expect to enter a nursing home in the event of a serious decline in health. Poor Mexican Americans simply have no choice but to keep their aging parents at home and, consequently, because there is such low demand for nursing homes in Hispanic areas, potential providers may be discouraged from providing nursing home services. Although there has been a great deal of speculation about the extent to which culturally-based norms governing children's obligations to care for their aging parents account for the lower use of nursing homes by older Hispanics, it is still not clear how much of a role culture (independent of income) plays (Gratton, 1987; Oriol, 1994; Weeks & Cuellar, 1981; Williams, 1990).

Of course, Hispanics are not alone in avoiding nursing homes. Institutionalization is clearly a recourse of last resort for most families (Angel & Angel, 1997). For Hispanics, though, the unfamiliar physical and cultural environment, unpalatable food, difficulty with English, and staff whose behavior is governed by a different set of norms can make a nursing home a truly unappealing place. As of yet we know relatively little about the decision-making process involved in institutionalizing an older parent, yet the data make it clear that the decision-making process is influenced by numerous cultural and social class factors, in addition to fundamental family values and economic considerations (Groger, 1994). One of the major differences among groups that leads to their different rates of nursing home use is the availability of family support (Angel & Angel, 1997). Hispanics have more children on average than non-Hispanic Whites, and individuals with larger families are better able to remain in the community. This may also account for their low rates of use of formal in-home community-based services (Angel & Angel, 1997; Wallace et al., 1994; Wallace & Lew-Ting, 1992). It is clear, therefore, that for Hispanics, formal home-based care is not replacing the family in its role as the major caregiver to impaired elderly Hispanics.

Numerous barriers to the use of both acute and long-term care by Hispanics have been identified, or at least raised as possibilities. These span the range from those based on cultural distance between patient and provider (Chesney, Chavira, Hall, & Gary, 1982; Estrada, Treviño, & Ray, 1990), to those that focus on the serious lack of private health insurance among working-age Hispanics and the ineligibility for public insurance among recent immigrants (Angel & Angel, 1996, 1997). Other explanations focus on institutional factors, such as the lack of hospital and long-term care facilities in or near Hispanic communities (Angel & Angel, 1997; Treviño, Moyer, Burciaga Valdez, & Stroup-Benham, 1991). Yet it is becoming increasingly clear that none of these cultural, social, and economic factors operate alone. Rather, they interact to influence both health and the ability of Hispanics to gain access to care. Minority group status and low acculturation increase the risk of poverty, which itself increases one's exposure to health risks and raises barriers to health care. Let us examine those barriers in greater detail.

Economic and Health Insurance Barriers

Regardless of one's social group, the ability to pay for health care is a major determinant of its use. In the United States, most health care is paid for by either private or public insurance. A lack of insurance, therefore, represents a major barrier to health care (U.S. General Accounting Office, 1992). Hispanics are seriously underinsured for health care before age 65 (Angel & Angel, 1996; U.S. General Accounting Office, 1992; Valdez et al., 1993). In 1990, 52% of Blacks and 78% of non-Hispanic Whites reported owning private health insurance, while less than half of Hispanics (48%) reported any private insurance of any sort (National Council of La Raza, 1992). Hispanics are also less likely than non-Hispanics to use public insurance (U.S. General Accounting Office, 1992). In 1990, only 18% of Hispanics received Medicaid compared to 25% of Blacks (National Council of La Raza, 1992). Rates of health insurance coverage differ greatly, depending upon specific Hispanic subgroups. Central and South Americans and Mexican Americans have the lowest levels of coverage (approximately 60% and 64%, respectively, in 1990) and Puerto Ricans the highest (86%), with 74% of Cuban Americans and 79% of Other Hispanics reporting coverage (National Council of La Raza, 1992).

In conjunction with poverty and barriers related to language, culture, and geographic location, the lack of insurance has serious implications for the health and well-being of Hispanic Americans (Chesney et al., 1982; Estrada et al., 1990; Guendelman & Schwalbe, 1986; Wolinsky et al., 1989). Unfortunately, the situation is only getting worse: The number of uninsured Hispanics is increasing at the same time that the number of uninsured Blacks and non-Hispanic Whites is decreasing (National Council of La Raza, 1992).

Inadequate Medicare Supplemental Coverage

As a result of Medicare, the huge disparities in health insurance coverage between Hispanics and non-Hispanics is reduced greatly after the age of 65 (Angel & Angel, 1996). Yet older Hispanics still face significant financial barriers to care. The vast majority of Americans over the age of 65 have private Medigap policies to cover the physician and hospital charges that Medicare does not pay. For the most part, this coverage represents the extension of employer-sponsored plans or privately purchased Medigap policies. For the majority of retired Americans, therefore, their health insurance package consists of Medicare as the core, and supplemental private policies to pick up the slack. A certain fraction have privately purchased long-term care insurance policies, although these remain fairly rare.

The typical health insurance package of older Hispanics is rather different. A small fraction of Hispanics, and a surprisingly larger fraction of Mexican Americans, do not receive basic Medicare, probably because they are also less likely to participate in the Social Security program. In 1990, only 80% of Hispanics over the age of 65 reported receiving Social Security, compared to 88% of Blacks and 93% of non-Hispanic Whites (National Council of La Raza, 1992). Of those who do participate in Medicare, a smaller fraction have private health insurance to pay for the hospital, physician, and other services that Medicare does not cover (Angel & Angel, 1996).

Table 14.1 presents data from a survey of Hispanics 65 and older sponsored by the Commonwealth Fund during the mid-1980s (Davis, 1990). It shows that, in comparison to non-Hispanic Whites, a higher proportion of all Hispanic elderly report no health insurance. It also reveals great variation among Hispanic subgroups. Nearly 6% of older Mexican Americans report that they have no health insurance of any sort. In addition to this wide variation in coverage among groups, factors such as nativity result in large variations

TABLE 14.1 Health Insurance Coverage of Individuals Sixty-Five and Older by Race and Hispanic Ethnicity

Type of Insurance	Non-Hispanic White (%)	Non-Hispanic Black (%)	Mexican American (%)	Cuban American (%)	Puerto Rican (%)
No insurance	1.3	2.9	5.9	2.9	3.1
Any Medicaid	13.3	33.1	37.0	47.9	55.7
Medicare only	18.1	34.5	29.7	19.8	27.2
Private	67.3	29.5	27.5	29.4	14.1
Sample size	(2,016)	(139)	(819)	(653)	(327)
Total	100.0	100.0	100.1	100.0	100.1

SOURCE: Angel & Angel (1997).

TABLE 14.2 Health Insurance Coverage by Nativity for Mexican Americans Aged Sixty-Five and Older

Type of Insurance	Native-Born (%)	Foreign-Born (%)
No insurance	2.4	12.4
Any Medicaid	31.4	37.8
Medicare only	34.8	39.2
Private	31.4	10.6
Total	100.0	100.0
Sample size	(1,649)	(1,297)

SOURCE: Angel & Angel (1997).

within groups. Table 14.2, for example, which presents data for older Mexican Americans from the H-EPESE (Markides et al., in press), shows that the foreign-born have particularly low rates of coverage. More than 12% of older foreign-born Mexican Americans report that they have no insurance of any sort.

Table 14.1 also shows that even when they do participate in the Medicare program, Hispanics are more likely than non-Hispanic Whites to rely solely on Medicare and to report that they do not own Medicare supplemental insurance. This lack of private supplemental insurance has potentially serious consequences for health among Hispanics, because the difference between what Medicare pays and the actual cost of physician and hospital services can be quite substantial, especially for individuals on fixed incomes (Rowland & Lyons, 1987). For example, in 1992 under Medicare Part A, which covers hospital costs, an elderly individual was required to pay a deductible of $652 and to pay a portion of the cost of long stays as part of a cost-sharing provision. Under Part B of Medicare, which covers physician services and ambulatory care, a person had to pay an annual premium of $382 and a $100 deductible, as well as a 20% copayment for services used.

There are many other possible reasons for lower rates of participation in Medicare among older Mexican Americans and for the lack of private Medigap insurance among Hispanics generally. For Mexican Americans, citizenship status may represent a barrier to coverage (Estrada et al., 1990). Many older Mexican Americans have never become legal residents of the United States. For those who do not speak English, which is quite common among older cohorts, access problems may keep them from seeking medical care or participating in Social Security (Andersen, Zelman Lewis, Giachello, Aday, & Chiu, 1981). And, as is the case for insurance generally, private coverage is simply out of reach for the poor.

The consequence of a lack of Medicare supplemental insurance is that an older individual who lacks private health insurance is dependent on Medicaid to pay the deductibles and cost-sharing charges that Medicare does not cover (Angel & Angel, 1996). For the impoverished elderly, Medicaid covers the cost of long-term care and also provides Medigap insurance coverage that pays what Medicare does not cover (Burwell, Adams, & Meiners, 1990; Feder, Rowland, Holahan, Salganicoff, & Heslam, 1993; Liu, Doty, & Manton, 1990; Liu & Manton, 1991; Mor, Intrator, & Laliberte, 1993; Short, Kemper, Cornelius, & Walden, 1992; Spence & Wiener, 1990). Because of their economic profiles, Hispanics are disproportionately dependent on Medicaid, and it is clear that in the absence of the Medigap coverage provided by Medicaid, more individuals would forgo medical care and even fewer would enter nursing homes than is currently the case.

Physical and Cultural Barriers

The data, therefore, suggest various access barriers to both acute and long-term care among elderly Hispanics. Clearly, lower rates of insurance coverage and lower average incomes represent major barriers to care. Yet other significant nonfinancial barriers exist, among which transportation to care stands out. Data from the Mexican American EPESE show that older Mexican Americans are much less likely to drive than non-Hispanic Whites.

Foreign-born older Mexican American women, in particular, tend to rely on family members as their primary source of transportation (Angel et al., 1996). Family members who must work may be unable to provide this transportation (Kaiser, Gibbons, & Camp, 1993; Weeks & Cuellar, 1981; Williams, 1990). Public transportation systems, especially in rural areas of the United States, are often inadequate or nonexistent. The lack of transportation clearly reduces the access to some health care facilities. Access to services becomes especially difficult when multiple visits are required over limited periods of time.

Access is further hampered by the uneven geographical distribution of health care services (Kindig & Yan, 1993). In Texas, for example, the elderly Mexican American population is concentrated in the southern and western parts of the state while the major mental health and long-term care facilities are concentrated in the northern and eastern parts of the state. This lack of fit between facilities and prospective clients is bound to result in some degree of underutilization by Mexican Americans in need of inpatient mental heath care services.

Other aspects of the physical environment in which Mexican Americans live are likely to hamper the use of health services. In South Texas, for example, many elderly Mexican Americans live in densely populated *colonias* that, in spite of being formally urban as a function of the county's population size, share many of the social service resource deficits of more purely rural communities. The combined impact of a lack of personal resources and the limited availability of health care services on the use of services by seriously ill or disabled elderly Mexican Americans is clearly an issue that merits further research. Among Puerto Ricans, who live predominantly in highly urban areas in the Northeast, access barriers result from the lack of services in inner-city barrios.

Some older Hispanics, especially the more traditional, use folk medicine either as a substitute for regular care or, more commonly, as a complement to regular medical care (Kaiser et al., 1993; Torres-Gil & Fielder, 1986-1987). Elderly Mexican Americans living along the U.S.-Mexico border also travel to Mexico to receive care or to supplement the care they receive through Medicare, as well as to purchase pharmaceutical aids and products (Warner & Reed, 1993).

The data clearly show that traditional Mexican American families tend to have close family ties and to interact primarily with kin (Angel & Angel, 1992; Weeks & Cuellar, 1981, 1983). More acculturated individuals, like other middle-class Americans, have broader ties and interact more with friends, neighbors, and co-workers. Acculturation, therefore, potentially affects the use of medical services. We know that factors such as the lack of knowledge about available services reduces their use (Holmes et al., 1983). Those who have broader networks have more access to information about service availability.

The lack of English proficiency interferes both with Hispanic patients' access to care and, potentially, with their compliance with a physician's treatment plan. Unfortunately, although most patient education materials are available in Spanish, they are not always written at the literacy level of many older individuals. Although a bilingual family member or friend may be able to help translate the physician's instructions, that individual may him- or herself not clearly understand the instructions or fail to convey them completely to the older individual.

It is increasingly clear, then, that individual factors operate within specific cultural and organizational environments to influence both contact with, and passage through, the medical care system. It is also clear that rural areas, where many elderly Mexican Americans live, often lack easily accessible services (Angel, DeJong, Cornwell, & Wilmoth, 1995; Blazer, Landerman, Fillenbaum, & Horner, 1995). Ironically, this is also true for the inner city, in which many Puerto Ricans live. While substantial evidence shows that cultural factors influence the use of physicians and other health care services by Hispanics, the data make it clear that financial factors and the organization of services play an even more important role (Angel & Angel, 1997; Wallace et al., 1994).

Potential Data Sources for the
Study of Hispanic Health Care Use

Currently, there are several focused surveys sponsored by the National Institute on Aging and other federal foundations that will make a better understanding of the health and welfare of older Mexican Americans possible. The H-EPESE (Markides et al., in press), the San Antonio Heart Study (Hazuda et al., 1986), the Commonwealth Fund Study of Elderly Hispanics (Davis, 1990), the Health and Retirement Survey (Juster, 1993), the Public Use Microdata for persons 60 years and over (PUMS-O; U.S. Bureau of the Census, 1993), and the National Health and Nutrition Examination Survey-III (HANES-III; National Center for Health Statistics, 1992) will provide needed information on the mental, physical, and social well-being of older Hispanics. Yet as laudable as these new data collection and dissemination efforts are, they represent only a beginning, and more focused studies of specific subgroups and specific health conditions, as well as their consequences for health and illness behaviors among elderly, are necessary.

The National Institute on Aging funds the Hispanic Established Population for Epidemiologic Studies of the Elderly (H-EPESE), a large survey of Mexican American elderly who reside in five Southwestern states, Texas, California, New Mexico, Arizona, and Colorado (Markides et al., in press). This survey was modeled after the Established Populations for Epidemiologic Studies of the Elderly (EPESE) that were carried out in East Boston, Massachusetts; New Haven, Connecticut; two East Central Iowa counties in 1982; and five counties in Piedmont, North Carolina in 1984 (Cornoni-Huntley et al., 1986). The H-EPESE survey provides data from the 1993-1994 baseline survey of 3,050 individuals over the age of 65 and a 2-year follow-up. This project is truly unique because it is the first epidemiological survey of a large sample of elderly Mexican Americans and constitutes a benchmark in the study of the health of this population. All of the respondents were interviewed in their homes for approximately 2 hours by trained interviewers who obtained information on functional capacity, nativity status, basic demographic background, household structure, socioeconomic status, health insurance coverage, doctor and hospital visits, and medication use.

The Public Use Microdata Sample of Older persons (PUMS-O) consists of a 3% sample of individuals 60 years and older, and includes information available on the regular Census Bureau Public Use Microdata files (U.S. Bureau of the Census, 1993). These data can be combined with the regular 5% or 1% PUMS to increase the sample of elderly Hispanics, especially the very old. The 1990 file is stratified by age and consists of subsamples from three broad age ranges, 60 to 74; 75 to 89; and 90 and older. One of the distinct advantages of these data is that the large number of cases available permits a detailed analysis of the oldest-old, and the data are ideal for the comparison of specific Hispanic subgroups. These data can be used to make comparisons between Hispanics and non-Hispanics, as well as detailed comparisons among Hispanic groups. The data include information on institutionalization and functional capacity among older Hispanics, as well as indicators of cultural orientation, such as citizenship, ancestry, year of arrival in the United States, migration history, country of birth, language spoken at home, and English-language proficiency. Information is also available on mobility and self-care limitations. The PUMS-O contains codes that identify "planning service" areas identified by the states' health planning agencies. These identifiers make it possible in certain cases to append service area information to the file to control for aggregate service delivery system factors.

The third National Health and Nutrition Examination Survey, NHANES-III, provides information on the health status and health care use of a sample of noninstitutionalized persons in the United States (see NCHS, 1992, for details of sample design procedures). This survey includes oversamples of the oldest-old and of Hispanics that will make comparisons between Hispanics and non-Hispanics possible. The HANES-III is unique because it contains the results of a detailed physical examination in which abnormal findings are coded in terms of the International Classification of Diseases, ninth revision, categories. The physician examined all major physiological systems and evaluated them as normal or abnormal. The examination also included measurements of blood pressure, height, weight, body fat, bone density, tympanic impedance, audiometry, vision, glucose tolerance, and laboratory tests (e.g., X rays) for arthritis, diabetes, and anemia. The physician also administered a performance test to assess the degree of impairment in gross mobility functioning.

Besides the physician's examination, a detailed medical history was obtained from each examinee. The health interviews include questions concerning nutrition, physical activity, mental health, and health habits, as well as a question asking respondents to evaluate their general health level as excellent, very good, good, fair, or poor. Information on the respondent's access to a regular source of medical care, the number of hospitalizations, the reason for and location of the last visit to a health care provider, and sources of health care financing was obtained. In addition, the household survey gathered information on activities of daily living (ADLs) and on a number of specific health conditions, such as diabetes, gallstones, cardiovascular conditions, pain in the chest or abdomen, and dental problems. Although the number of older Hispanics will inevitably be limited, these data will allow us to assess the health and medical care use of middle-aged Hispanics and those in their late sixties and early seventies.

The Survey of Elderly Hispanics (SEH) consists of a telephone survey of 2,299 Hispanics (937 Mexican Americans, 368 Puerto Ricans, 714 Cuban Americans, and 280 Other Hispanics) aged 65 and over carried out in 1988 by Westat, Inc., for the Commonwealth Fund (Davis, 1990). It is one of the best available sources of data for assessing sources of formal and informal support as well as the health care needs of a national sample of older Hispanics in the United States.

One source of data that has not yet been exploited is the archives of the Health Care Financing Administration (HCFA), the federal agency in charge of administering Medicare. Every time an older person uses Medicare, information on the diagnosis, the procedures carried out, and the prescriptions made is recorded. These encounter data can be aggregated into a person file that provides a fairly complete history of an older person's health care use. Information aggregated to the person level is released publicly as the Medicare Provider Analysis and Review (MEDPAR) File (Lyman, 1996). As of yet, detailed Hispanic nationalities are not reported, but it is possible to compare Hispanics as a group to non-Hispanic Blacks and Whites. Of course, since information is provided only for those who use Medicare-covered services, individuals who are not in the system or those who do not use covered services are not included. Nonetheless, given nearly universal Medicare participation, these data hold out great promise for the study of differences between Hispanics and other groups in the actual care that they receive.

The Future of Health Care for Older Hispanics

Data on the predictors of health care use by older Hispanics are beginning to accumulate, and they make it clear that Medicare has played a crucial role in equalizing health care use between the poor, including poor Hispanics, and those who are better off. As a consequence, although there are some exceptions, older Hispanics use physician and hospital services at rates similar to those of non-Hispanics. The serious barriers to high-quality health care that exist in countries such as Mexico, which does not have the resources to devote to the care of the elderly, or the barriers that existed in the United States prior to Medicare, have largely been eliminated. Today, for those over the age of 65 we do indeed have comprehensive national health insurance.

Of course not everyone gets all of the care they need, and even among the elderly, differences in wealth translate into differences in quality of care, especially long-term care. To the extent that poverty among the elderly is concentrated among minority groups, older Hispanics in poverty are potentially affected by our incomplete system of health care financing. As we pointed out earlier, the premiums, deductibles, copayments, and cost-sharing provisions that are part of Medicare have their greatest health care impact on those who can least afford to pay these additional costs. An equitable system of health care would be one in which the remaining financial barriers to health care are eliminated, but of course such an equitable system would be far more expensive than one that rations health care on the ability to pay at least a portion of the real cost.

Although rough parity has been achieved in acute care services, in long-term care large differences between elderly Hispanics and non-Hispanic Whites emerge. Most long-term care is paid for by the older person him- or herself or by the family, and the cost of such care can be staggering. The average cost of nursing home care is more than $40,000 per year and the highest-quality specialized care can cost far more. Paying for such care requires that one draw upon savings and assets. Unfortunately, both Blacks and Hispanics have far fewer assets than non-Hispanic Whites (Angel & Angel, 1996). Relatively few, therefore, are able to afford high-quality private care, and when they do enter nursing homes they are more often than non-Hispanic Whites dependent on Medicaid from the very first. Because of its high cost and limited coverage, private long-term care insurance will never be a viable option for the vast majority of Hispanics.

Although gaps in coverage for both acute and long-term care remain, it is hard to imagine that we can expect much more in the way of individual Medicare or long-term care coverage given the rapid growth in the number of individuals over 65 and the increases in life expectancy at older ages that have occurred in recent decades. In the future, in fact, decreases in coverage and a greater shift of costs to the elderly themselves are probably inevitable, given the rate of increase in the size of the elderly population and the modest rates of economic growth that we are likely to experience. Even with attempts to ensure equity, it is likely that the negative consequences of the need to rein in medical care expenditures for the elderly will fall heaviest on poor and minority Americans, including Hispanics.

Even though the financial barriers to care have been largely overcome, other nonfinancial barriers remain. The maldistribution of health care, access barriers related to a lack of transportation, language and education barriers, and cultural distance between medical professionals and their patients all lower the ability of older Hispanics to receive the care they need. Overcoming these barriers in a cost-efficient and effective manner requires a new philosophy of both acute and long-term care delivery. Preventive care provided by bilingual, bicultural professionals in accessible locations holds the promise of increasing compliance and reducing the need for more expensive treatments, as well as for increasing an older person's quality of life.

Like the rest of the population, Hispanics have enjoyed large increases in life expectancy at older ages and, although they will continue to be a relatively young population because of their higher fertility, the number of old Hispanics will increase dramatically early in the 21st century. This aging population will require more long-term care. Even though Hispanics currently enter nursing homes at very low rates, in the future smaller families, the need for women to work, greater marital disruption, and increasing geographical mobility will strain the ability of Hispanic families to care for aging parents, just as they have for other groups. As a consequence, more elderly Hispanics will find themselves in need of institutional care. As this new market emerges, we could see growth in the number of nursing homes that are predominantly Hispanic and in which an older person can eat familiar foods, engage in familiar entertainment, and communicate in Spanish with bilingual staff members. Such nursing homes could provide older Hispanics a real option in nursing home care.

On the other hand, because older Hispanics are highly dependent on Medicaid for the financing of nursing home care, it is possible that they may be confined to low-quality Medicaid mills in which only minimal services are provided, especially if reimbursements under Medicaid are lowered or do not keep up with inflation. This possibility, and the desire of most older persons to remain in the community as long as possible, makes community-based long-term care a particularly appealing alternative. Because of Hispanics' typically larger families and apparent willingness to care for aging parents, the possibilities of community-based long-term care seem particularly promising. In the future, our task will be to provide assistance to the family in caring for its elderly members. Such an approach holds out great promise for combining formal and informal sources of support and of allowing infirm elderly persons to remain in the community while minimizing the caregiving burden on the family.

Furthering our understanding of health care use by Hispanics requires that we gain a better understanding of their health and more detailed assessments of specific health conditions and the barriers to health care that, not only Hispanics, but Blacks, Asians, and other minority Americans, face. There are numerous general models of the pathways to care that sensitize us to the complex cultural, social, financial, and organizational forces that affect the likelihood that an individual comes into contact with the medical care system and the route that he or she follows through that system once the role of patient is assumed. Some models place the entire process within a cultural context and incorporate the patient's and the family's understanding at the core of the help-seeking process (Angel & Thoits, 1987). The extension of such general models to the elderly could help us understand how social class and social support affect an older individual's response to specific health conditions within particular cultural and family contexts. Until we have such models and information on specific health conditions and the help-seeking response to them, comparisons of elderly Hispanics, or any other minority group, to the majority population run the risk of obscuring significant differences related to specific health conditions within similar aggregate patterns.

References

Andersen, R., Zelman Lewis, S., Giachello, A. L., Aday L., & Chiu, G. (1981). Access to medical care among the Hispanic population of the southwestern United States. *Journal of Health and Social Behavior, 22,* 78-89.

Angel, J. L. (1991). *Health and living arrangements of the elderly.* New York: Garland.

Angel, J. L., & Angel, R. J. (1992). Age at migration, social connections, and well-being among elderly Hispanics. *Journal of Aging and Health, 4,* 480-499.

Angel, J. L., Angel, R. J., McClellan, J. L., & Markides, K. S. (1996). Nativity, declining health, and preferences in living arrangements among elderly Mexican Americans: Implications for Long-Term Care. *The Gerontologist, 36,* 464-473.

Angel, J. L., DeJong, G. F., Cornwell, G. T., & Wilmoth, J. M. (1995). Diminished health and living arrangements of rural elderly Americans. *National Journal of Sociology, 9*(1), 31-57.

Angel, R. J. (1996, May). *Demography, health care policy, and aging.* Paper presented at the Population Association of America Meeting, New Orleans, LA.

Angel, R. J., & Angel, J. L. (1994, August). *The acute and long-term care of minority elderly: Implications of health care financing reform.* Paper presented at the American Sociological Association Meeting, Los Angeles.

Angel, R. J., & Angel, J. L. (1996). The extent of private and public health insurance coverage among adult Hispanics. *The Gerontologist, 36,* 332-340.

Angel, R. J., & Angel, J. L. (1997). *Who will care for us? Aging and long-term care in multicultural America.* New York: New York University Press.

Angel, R. J., Angel, J. L., & Himes, C. L. (1992). Minority group status, health transitions, and community living arrangements among the elderly. *Research on Aging, 14,* 496-521.

Angel, R. J., & Thoits, P. (1987). The impact of culture on the cognitive structure of illness. *Culture, Medicine, and Psychiatry, 11,* 23-52.

Bagley, S. P., Angel, R. J., Dilworth-Anderson, P., Lui, W., & Schinke, S. (1995). Adaptive behaviors among ethnic minorities. *Health Psychology, 14,* 632-660.

Blazer, D. G., Landerman, L. R., Fillenbaum, G., & Horner, R. (1995). Health services access and use among older adults in North Carolina: Urban vs. rural residents. *American Journal of Public Health, 85,* 1384-1390.

Burr, J. A. (1990). Race/sex comparisons of elderly living arrangements: Factors influencing the institutionalization of the unmarried. *Research on Aging, 12,* 507-530.

Burwell, B. O., Adams, E. K., & Meiners, M. R. (1990). Spend-down of assets before Medicaid eligibility among elderly nursing-home recipients in Michigan. *Medical Care, 28,* 349-362.

Centers for Disease Control. (1990). Trends in lung cancer incidence and mortality, United States, 1980-1987. *Morbidity and Mortality Weekly Report, 39,* 875-883.

Chesney, A. P., Chavira, J. A., Hall, R. P., & Gary, H. E., Jr. (1982). Barriers to medical care of Mexican-Americans: The role of social class, acculturation, and social isolation. *Medical Care, 20,* 883-891.

Cornoni-Huntley, J., Blazer, D. G., Lafferty, M. E., Everett, D. F., Brock, D. B., & Farmer, M. E. (1986). *Established populations for epidemiologic studies of the elderly, resource data book* (NIH Publication No. 86-2443). Bethesda, MD: National Institute on Aging.

Crimmins, E. M., Hayward, M. D., & Saito, Y. (1996). Differentials in active life expectancy in the older population of the United States. *Journal of Gerontology: Social Sciences, 51*(B), S111-S120.

Davis, K. (1990). *National survey of Hispanic elderly people, 1988* (ICPSR 9289). Ann Arbor, MI: Inter-university Consortium for Political and Social Research (P.O. Box 1248, Ann Arbor, MI 48106).

Dutton, D. B. (1986). Social class, health, and illness. In L. H. Aiken & D. Mechanic (Eds.), *Applications of social science to clinical medicine and health policy* (pp. 31-62). New Brunswick, NJ: Rutgers University Press.

Eribes, R. A., & Bradley-Rawls, M. (1978). The underutilization of nursing home facilities by Mexican-American elderly in the southwest. *The Gerontologist, 18,* 363-371.

Espino, D. V., Burge, S. K., & Moreno, C. A. (1991). The prevalence of selected chronic diseases among older Mexican Americans: Data from the Hispanic HANES. *Journal of the American Board of Family Practice, 4,* 217-222.

Espino, D. V., Neufeld, R. R., Mulvihill, M., & Libow, L. S. (1988). Hispanic and non-Hispanic elderly on admission to the nursing home: A pilot study. *The Gerontologist, 28,* 821-824.

Estrada, A. L., Treviño, F. M., & Ray, L. A. (1990). Health care utilization barriers among Mexican-Americans: Evidence from HHANES 1982-84. *American Journal of Public Health, 80,* 27-31.

Feder, J., Rowland, D., Holahan, J., Salganicoff, A., & Heslam, D. (1993). *The Medicaid cost explosion: Causes and consequences.* The Kaiser Commission on the Future of Medicaid. 624 North Broadway, Room 453, Baltimore, MD 21205.

Franco, L. J., Stern, M. P., Rosenthal, M., Haffner, S. M., Hazuda, H. P., & Comeaux, P. J. (1985). Prevalence, detection, and control of hypertension in a biethnic community. *American Journal of Epidemiology, 121,* 684-696.

Frerichs, R. R., Chapman, J. M., & Maes, E. F. (1984). Mortality due to all causes and cardiovascular diseases among seven race-ethnic populations in Los Angeles County. *International Journal of Epidemiology, 13,* 291-298.

Gratton, B. (1987). Familism among the Black and Mexican-American elderly: Myth or reality? *Journal of Aging Studies, 1,* 19-32.

Greene, V. L., & Monahan, D. J. (1984). Comparative utilization of community-based long-term care services by Hispanic and Anglo elderly in a case management system. *Journal of Gerontology, 39,* S730-S735.

Greene, V. L., & Ondrich, J. I. (1990). Risk factors for nursing home admissions and exits: A discrete-time hazard function approach. *Journal of Gerontology, 45,* S250-S258.

Groger, L. (1994). Decision as process: A conceptual model of Black elders' nursing home placement. *Journal of Aging Studies, 8,* 77-94.

Guendelman, S., & Schwalbe, J. (1986). Medical care utilization by Hispanic children. *Medical Care, 24,* 925-937.

Hazuda, H. P., Comeaux, P. J., Stern, M. P., Haffner, S. M., Eifler, C. W., & Rosenthal, M. (1986). A comparison of three indicators for identifying Mexican Americans in epidemiological research: Methodological findings from the San Antonio Heart Study. *American Journal of Epidemiology, 123,* 96-112.

Holmes, D., Teresi, J., & Holmes, M. (1983). Differences among Black, Hispanic, and White people in knowledge about long-term care services. *Health Care Financing Review, 5,* 51-67.

Jepson, C., Kessler, L. G., Portnoy, B., & Gibbs, T. (1991). Black-White differences in cancer prevention knowledge and behavior. *American Journal of Public Health, 81,* 501-504.

Juster, F. T. (1993). The Health and Retirement Survey. *ICPSR Bulletin, 14,* 1-2.

Kaiser, M. A., Gibbons, J. E., & Camp, H. J. (1993). Long-term care: Development of services for Latino elderly. In M. Sotomayor & A. Garcia (Eds.), *Elderly Latinos: Issues and solutions for the 21st century* (pp. 29-44). Washington, DC: National Hispanic Council on Aging.

Kindig, D. A., & Yan, G. (1993). Physician supply in rural areas with large minority populations. *Health Affairs, 12*(Suppl.), 177-184.

Kittner, S. J., White, L. R., Losonczy, K. G., Wolf, P. A., & Hebel, J. R. (1990). Black-White differences in stroke incidence in a national sample. *Journal of the American Medical Association, 264,* 1267-1270.

Liu, K., Doty, P., & Manton, K. (1990). Medicaid spenddown in nursing homes. *The Gerontologist, 30,* 7-15.

Liu, K., & Manton, K. (1991). Nursing home length of stay and spenddown in Connecticut, 1977-1986. *The Gerontologist, 31,* 165-173.

Lyman, R. (1996). *Medicare provider analysis and review (MEDPAR) file.* Health Care Financing Administration, 7500 Security Blvd., Baltimore, MD.

Markides, K. S., Rudkin, L., Angel, R. J., & Espino, D. V. (in press). Health status of Hispanic elderly in the United States. In L. G. Martin, B. J. Soldo, & K. Foote (Eds.), *Racial and ethnic differences in late life health in the United States.* Washington, DC: National Academy Press.

Mechanic, D. (1980). The experience and reporting of common physical complaints. *Journal of Health and Social Behavior, 21,* 146-155.

Mitchell, B. D., Stern, M. P., Haffner, S. M., Hazuda, H. P., & Patterson, J. K. (1990). Risk factors for cardiovascular mortality in Mexican Americans and non-Hispanic Whites. *American Journal of Epidemiology, 131,* 423-433.

Mor, V., Intrator, O., & Laliberte, L. (1993). Factors affecting conversion rates to Medicaid among new admissions to nursing homes. *Health Services Research, 28,* 2-25.

Morrison, B. J. (1983). Sociocultural dimensions: Nursing homes and the minority aged. In G. S. Getzel & M. J. Mellor (Eds.), *Gerontological social work practice in long-term care* (pp. 127-145). New York: Haworth.

National Center for Health Statistics. (1992). *Design and operation of the third Health and Nutrition Examination Survey.* Washington, DC: Government Printing Office.

National Council of La Raza. (1992). *Hispanics and health insurance.* Washington, DC: Labor Council for Latin American Advancement.

Oriol, W. (1994). Social policy and Mexican American aging. *Perspectives on Aging, 2,* 21-28.

Rowland, D., & Lyons, B. (1987). *Medicare's poor: Filling the gaps in medical coverage for low-income elderly Americans.* The Commonwealth Fund, 624 North Broadway, Room 492, Baltimore, MD 21205.

Samet, J. M., Coultas, D. B., Howard, C. A., Skipper, B. J., & Hanis, C. L. (1988). Diabetes, gallbladder disease, obesity, and hypertension among Hispanics in New Mexico. *American Journal of Epidemiology, 128,* 1302-1311.

Schulz, J. H. (1995). *The economics of aging* (6th ed.). Westport, CT: Auburn House.

Short, P. F., Kemper, P., Cornelius, L. J., & Walden, D. C. (1992). Public and private responsibility for financing nursing-home care: The effect of Medicaid asset spend-down. *The Milbank Quarterly, 70,* 277-298.

Siegel, P. Z., Deeb, L. C., Wolfe, L. E., Wilcox, D., & Mark, J. S. (1993). Stroke, mortality, and its socioeconomic, racial, and behavioral correlates in Florida. *Public Health Reports, 108,* 454-458.

Spence, D., & Wiener, J. (1990). Nursing home length of stay patterns: Results from the 1985 national nursing home survey. *The Gerontologist, 30,* 16-20.

Torres-Gil, F., & Fielder, E. (1986-1987). Long-term care policy and the Hispanic population. *Journal of Hispanic Studies, 2,* 49-66.

Torres-Gil, F., & Villa, V. (1993). Health and long-term care: Family policy for Hispanic aging. In M. Sotomayor & A. Garcia (Eds.), *Elderly Latinos: Issues and solutions for the 21st century* (pp. 45-58). Washington, DC: National Hispanic Council on Aging.

Treviño, F. M., & Moss, A. J. (1984). Health indicators for Hispanic, Black, and White Americans. *Vital and Health Statistics* (Series 10, 148. DHHS Publication No. [PAS] 84-1576). Washington, DC: Government Printing Office.

Treviño, F. M., Moyer, E., Burciaga Valdez, R., & Stroup-Benham, C. (1991). Health insurance coverage and utilization of health services by Mexican Americans, mainland Puerto Ricans, and Cuban Americans. *Journal of the American Medical Association, 265,* 233-237.

U.S. Bureau of the Census. (1993). *Public use microdata samples, United States* (1990 Census of Population and Housing, U.S. Technical Documentation). Washington, DC: U.S. Department of Commerce, Bureau of the Census.

U.S. General Accounting Office. (1992). *Access to health care—Significant gaps exist* (GAO/PEMD-92-6). Washington, DC: Government Printing Office.

Valdez, R. B., Morgenstern, H., Brown, E. R., Wyn, R., Chao, W., & Cumberland, W. (1993). Insuring Latinos against the costs of illness. *Journal of the American Medical Association, 269,* 889-895.

Wallace, S. P., Campbell, K., & Lew-Ting, C. (1994). Structural barriers to the use of formal in-home services by elderly Latinos. *Journal of Gerontology: Social Sciences, 49,* S253-S263.

Wallace, S. P., Levy-Storms, L., & Ferguson, L. R. (1995). Access to paid in-home assistance among disabled elderly people: Do Latinos differ from non-Latino Whites. *American Journal of Public Health, 85,* 970-975.

Wallace, S. P., & Lew-Ting, C. (1992). Getting by at home: Community-based long-term care of Latino elders. *Western Journal of Medicine, 157,* 337-344.

Warner, D. C., & Reed, K. (1993). *Health care across the border: The experiences of U.S. citizens in Mexico.* Austin, TX: Lyndon B. Johnson School of Public Affairs.

Weeks, J. R., & Cuellar, J. B. (1981). The role of family members in the helping networks of older people. *The Gerontologist, 21,* 388-394.

Weeks, J. R., & Cuellar, J. B. (1983). Isolation of older persons: The influence of immigration and length of residence. *Research on Aging, 5,* 369-88.

Westat, Inc. (1989). *A survey of elderly Hispanics. Final report to the Commonwealth Fund Commission on Elderly People Living Alone.* (1650 Research Boulevard, Rockville, MD 21205)

Williams, N. (1990). *The Mexican American family: Tradition and change.* Dix Hills, NY: General Hall.

Wolinsky, F. D., Aguirre, B. E., Fann, L., Keith, V. M., Arnold, C. L., Niederhauer, J. C., & Dietrich, K. (1989). Ethnic differences in the demand for physician and hospital utilization among older adults in major American cities: Conspicuous evidence of considerable inequalities. *The Milbank Quarterly, 67,* 412-449.

Worobey, J. L., & Angel, R. J. (1990). Functional capacity and living arrangements of unmarried elderly persons. *Journal of Gerontology: Social Sciences, 45,* S95-S101.

Long-Term Care Among American Indians

A Broad Lens Perspective on Service Preference and Use

E. E. Chapleski

Overview

Research is only beginning to emerge concerning the long-term care patterns of minority elders in the United States. American Indian[1] long-term care research is among the most recent and least well developed. Social scientists have been warned that attention to conceptual equivalence is critical to comparative cross-cultural research (Markides, Liang, & Jackson, 1990; Neugarten & Bengtson, 1968). Achieving equivalence, however, is an arduous, perhaps never-ending, task. A reasonable understanding of long-term care must therefore begin by exploring both the differences and the commonalties of long-term care within and between American Indians and the general population.

Chief Dan George said, "let no one forget it, we are a people with special rights . . . " It is that reminder that American Indians are not just another minority group, but a group of diverse tribes who, by virtue of treaties between sovereign nations, were promised education and health services in exchange for land (Rhoades, 1990). Thus, despite political treatment as just

AUTHOR'S NOTE: Support for this research was funded in part by the National Institute on Aging RO1-AG 11152.

another minority, many American Indians do not consider themselves *minority* but rather possessing a unique legal status with dual citizenship (McCabe & Cuellar, 1994). It is with respect for that truth that the opportunity to contribute to this volume is welcomed, with the hope that it will raise awareness and attention to the conditions of these forgotten elders of the United States.

The literature on American Indian long-term care is fraught with gaps reflecting the state of political, economic, and social affairs in U.S. Indian country. It is highly complex and presents a paradox between diversity and commonality. The purpose of this chapter is to inform the debate on long-term care by focusing on the differences as well as the similarities among American Indian and Alaska Native elders. Though all Natives share a common experience vis-à-vis the dominant society, their biocultural roots vary as evidenced by differences in language, areas of residence, lifestyles, and cultural beliefs (Young, 1994). The chapter begins with a description of American Indian elders, who they are, where they reside, and how political decisions affected migration and existing residential patterns. Need for long-term care is demonstrated through an examination of social, functional, physical, and mental health characteristics, followed by a discussion of competing models for defining and meeting these needs. Next, the inadequacy of existing data to document need is presented. The chapter concludes with a discussion of culture and options for the future based on what is currently known. Findings from recent research on American Indian elders of the Great Lakes region[2] will inform the discussion.

Historical Background: The Effects of Migration on Residence Patterns

The 1990 census reported more than 165,000 Indians over the age of 60 in the United States (National Indian Council on Aging, 1992). Although American Indian elders share many characteristics in common with other minority elders, including poor health, lower life expectancy, disproportionate numbers in poverty, and large extended families, these indigenous elders are both unique and heterogeneous (John, 1991), representing approximately 150 languages and 300 federally recognized tribes, nearly 200 Alaska Native villages, 100 state historical tribes, and several dozen with no formal recognition (Manson & Trimble, 1982). In 1990, two thirds of the American Indian elders lived in 10 states, and approximately 44% of the total 1.9 million American

Indian/Alaska Natives in the United States lived in Oklahoma, California, Arizona, or New Mexico. Approximately one fourth live east of the Mississippi River (U.S. Bureau of the Census, 1990).

The distribution of American Indians does not reflect ecological pressures as much as historical and political developments. The Indian Removal Bill of 1830, for example, forced relocation of eastern tribes to territories west of the Mississippi, primarily to official Indian Territory in Oklahoma. The more recent relocation effort of the Bureau of Indian Affairs (BIA) between 1952 and 1972, to designated urban relocation centers, stimulated urbanization for the purpose of employment and assimilation (Snipp, 1991) as evidenced by the 144% growth of the urban Indian population between 1960 and 1970 (Beale, 1973).

Although IHS (Indian Health Service) and BIA services may have originally flowed to locations perceived to hold tribal members, relocation policies created a redistribution of Indian people to areas less accessible to IHS or BIA services. Generally, IHS service areas consist of counties that have the reservation of a federally recognized tribe within or contiguous to their borders (exceptions to this general rule include the states of Alaska, Nevada, and Oklahoma) (U.S. Congress, Office of Technology Assessment, 1986). Hence, only 59% of American Indian and Alaska Native elders live in IHS service areas, and 87% of the IHS service population have used the services within the past 3 years (John, 1995). Furthermore, the fact of dual citizenship in a tribal government and the United States government (and therefore state governments) adds confusion and complexity to service availability, eligibility, and ultimately use.

The historic restriction of Indians to reservation areas or Indian territory is reflected in residential patterns. American Indian elderly, for example, are more likely to live in rural areas than their non-Native American counterparts. While more than 50% live in urbanized areas, a far greater proportion of Indian elderly live in rural areas than is true for any other racial or ethnic subgroup (Agree, 1988), although extreme rurality may be attenuated by urban encroachment. It is estimated that approximately 20% of American Indians live on tribal trust lands, 8% live on Historic Areas of Oklahoma, 3% live in Alaska Native Villages or rural areas, and more than half in urban areas (Burhansstipanov, 1993). While IHS in 1990 estimated that 61% of all Native Americans age 60 and over live in their service areas, these areas are confined to federally recognized reservations or Oklahoma trust territories and about 34 urban clinics across the entire country. Therefore, in states (such

TABLE 15.1 Projections of American Indians and Alaska Native Populations and Life Expectancy by Sex

	1995		2030		2050	
	Male	Female	Male	Female	Male	Female
Population age 60-64	27,000	30,000	62,000	82,000	82,000	88,000
Population age 65-74	37,000	45,000	103,000	116,000	115,000	130,000
Population age 75-84	16,000	25,000	56,000	70,000	70,000	83,000
Population age 85+	5,000	10,000	24,000	45,000	52,000	90,000
Life expectancy at birth (years)	72.5	82.1	76.3	85.8	78.1	87.7
Life expectancy at age 65 (years)	84.4	89.0	87.0	91.8	88.4	91.1

SOURCE: U.S. Bureau of the Census, Publication Number P25-1104, Summary Tape File 1 (STF1) [Electronic data tape]. Washington, DC: U.S. Bureau of the Census [Producer and Distributor].

as Michigan or California) where the majority live off the reservation, the percentage living in IHS service areas is much lower.

Little is known about long-term care among American Indians living in different locations (McCabe & Cuellar, 1994). What is known suggests need to be far in excess of use or availability (Kunitz & Levy, 1991; National Indian Council on Aging [NICOA], 1981). Research concerning the extent of relative disadvantage of urban versus rural Native Americans is inconsistent. Data from Los Angeles and Michigan show urban residents are especially disadvantaged (Chapleski, 1992; Kramer, Polisar, & Hyde, 1990), while other research demonstrates rural residents experience more health problems and greater perceived need for services (John, 1995). The extant research, however, does not differentiate for the most part among urban, rural on-reservation,[3] and rural off-reservation residential environments. A recent exception is Chapleski and Dwyer (1995), who found that in-home service use patterns among Great Lakes Indian elders varied significantly by area of residence, with reservation elders more likely to report knowledge and use of in-home services than their urban or rural off-reservation counterparts.

Sociodemographic Indicators of Present and Future Need

A demographic transition is occurring among American Indians, similar to that being experienced by other ethnic/racial minorities. Although Ameri-

TABLE 15.2 Selected Socioeconomic Characteristics of American Indians and Alaska Natives, Age 65 and Older

	Percentage
One-person household	32
Female household, no husband present	54
Housing lacks complete plumbing facilities	26
No vehicle available	38
No telephone	53
Income below poverty level	36
Persons living alone with income below poverty level	40
Less than high school education (age 60 and over)	63

SOURCE: U.S. Bureau of the Census, Publication 1990 CH-2-1a [Electronic data tape]. Washington, DC: U.S. Bureau of the Census [Producer and Distributor].

can Indians age 60 and older are a relatively small group in absolute numbers, they are among the fastest growing groups of racial/ethnic elders, exceeding growth rates of older Whites and Blacks in the decade between 1980 and 1990. American Indians age 65 and above experienced a 52% increase during that same decade, compared to 21.4% and 20.2% increases for Whites and Blacks, respectively (Barresi & Stull, 1993). In addition, Manson and Callaway (1988) have estimated a doubling of the American Indian population over 75 by the year 2000. National projections of population growth and life expectancy for American Indians and Alaska Natives in 1995, 2030, and 2050 are shown in Table 15.1.

Comprehensive data documenting social and economic characteristics of older American Indians are limited (McCabe & Cuellar, 1994). However, census data, although reputedly underreporting the indigenous population, provide the best estimates of selected characteristics associated with risk; for example, measures of isolation and lack of resources. Selected socio-economic characteristics of American Indians and Alaska Natives age 65 and older are shown in Table 15.2 (U.S. Bureau of the Census, 1990). Their housing frequently lacks plumbing (26%) or electricity. Poverty is widespread, with more than 30% of American Indians age 65 and over at or below the federal poverty level. On some reservations, more than half are below the official poverty level. Isolation is a factor for the 38% with no available vehicle and the 53% who have no telephone. These conditions are especially problematic when experienced by the 32% who live alone.

Clearly, should the severe social and economic conditions continue or increase, these growth projections suggest increased long-term care needs of American Indians and Alaska Natives living in different locations. Other major factors associated with predicting need for long-term care are discussed below.

Selected Predictors of Need for Care

Physical Health (Morbidity and Comorbidity)

With increasing age, the morbidity patterns of a population change from acute to chronic diseases. Documenting chronic illness is important because it affects disability, predicts mortality, and is associated with emotional distress and depression. American Indian elderly have higher rates of certain chronic diseases than other populations. For example, they continue to evidence higher incidence rates for a number of chronic illnesses: diabetes, liver and kidney disease, hypertension, arthritis, emphysema, and gallbladder problems (Agree, 1988; Chapleski, 1990, 1992; NICOA, 1981). The 1987 Survey of American Indians and Alaska Natives (SAIAN), a supplement to the National Medical Expenditure Survey, however, found no differences in age-/sex-adjusted rates for hypertension, emphysema, or arthritis (Johnson & Taylor, 1991). Table 15.3 shows comparisons among the Great Lakes sample of elders, the Survey of American Indians and Alaska Natives (SAIAN, 1987), and national samples along a number of chronic ailments.

Furthermore, it is not uncommon for older persons to have more than one disease or condition simultaneously, many combinations of which increase the odds of disability and mortality (Manton, 1988; Rice & LaPlante, 1988). The Great Lakes elders reported a mean of 3.90 ($SD = 2.46$) conditions per person. While 24.4% reported heart problems, for example, 22.2% have heart problems along with at least two other coexisting conditions. Overall, 7.2% had no chronic conditions, 25.1% had one or two conditions, 30.2% had three or four conditions, and 37.5% had five or more chronic conditions. If both chronic conditions and survival rates increase, these comorbid conditions may rise dramatically and have a major impact on long-term care.

Functional Abilities (ADLs and IADLs)

Given the relationship of functional limitations to determination of need for long-term care, the validation of measurement instruments—such as the

TABLE 15.3 Comparison of Great Lakes American Indian Chronic Conditions With National Samples

	Prevalence			
Condition	American Indian[a] 55 and Over %	U.S Population[b] 65 and Over (1993) %	SAIAN[c] 65 and Over %	SOA (1984)[d] 55 and Over %
1. Arthritis	61.3	49.3	48.6	43.7
2. High blood pressure	43.3	34.9	36.7	40.3
3. Diabetes	31.6	10.3	27.4	8.9
4. Obesity	28.4	13.2	25.2*	—
5. Hearing impairment	30.0	31.4	—	28.1
6. Vision problems	28.8	9.6	—	11.0
7. Heart	24.4	30.7	28.7	—
8. Allergies	20.5	7.3	—	—
9. Bronchitis/asthma	18.8	10.6	—	—
10. Kidney/prostate	12.1	10.4	—	—

SOURCE: a. Michigan LTC Study—1993 Data—American Indian Elders (weighted to adjust for stratification).

b. National Health Interview Survey, 1993.

c. National Medical Expenditure Survey, SAIAN, 1987.

d. Supplemental Survey on Aging, 1984.

NOTE: * Reported ≥ 120% deviation from ideal weight.

Older American Resources Survey (OARS)—with American Indian populations is critical (McCabe & Cuellar, 1994). The literature, however, holds few examples of such validation research. The National Indian Council on Aging (NICOA) used a modified version of the instrument (NICOA, 1981) but the purpose was needs assessment rather than validation of the instrument. Findings from the few reported studies of disability are inconsistent. The NICOA study reported higher functional ability among urban elders than rural elders (John, 1995), whereas Kramer (1991), on the other hand, has documented greater disability among urban elders.

Functional limitations were assessed in the Great Lakes Long Term Care study using seven *Activities of Daily Living (ADLs)* (eat, dress, groom, walk, get in/out of bed, bathe, toilet), and seven *Instrumental Activities of Daily Living (IADLs)* (telephone, get places out of walking distance, shop, prepare meals, do housework, take meds, handle money). Reliabilities (alpha coefficients) of both the personal and instrumental types of activities were .86 and .88, respectively. Seventy-seven percent of respondents (age 55 and older) had no limitation on ADLs and 70.9% had no limitation on IADLs. Combining personal and social functioning, 35.9% of respondents report one or more ADL/IADL difficulty, with 12.3% reporting four or more. There are no significant differences by area of residence. However, these findings show that even among a relatively young (mean = 68 years) sample of elders, functional limitations are greater than among older Whites. For example, the Longitudinal Study on Aging showed percentages with any IADL at 27.2% in 1986 and 30% in 1988 for a national sample of persons age 70 and over (Kovar, 1987).

Mental Health/Memory/Dementia

There is a scarcity of information about the epidemiology of major mental disorders among American Indians in general (Neligh & Scully, 1990). Diagnosis is often difficult because of the cultural factors influencing its presentation, and the lack of good diagnostic tools for Indian elderly (Neligh & Scully, 1990). Yet understanding depression among American Indians is critical for estimating prevalence as well as identifying just what is universal and what is culturally variable (LeVine, 1984). Western medicine has tended to partition physical from mental and body from mind while indigenous cultures share a more holistic and less partialized worldview. It is a serious error, therefore, to generalize from the Euro-American Westernized view of depression to Indian experiences and behavior (Shore & Manson, 1981). Using the Great Lakes elder sample, a confirmatory factor analysis was conducted to test the measurement structure of both the 20-item CES-D and a 12-item model previously tested on Mexican Americans by Liang, Van Tran, Krause, and Markides (1989). Multiple group comparisons among three residential strata, those living in an urban context, in rural off-reservation settings, and on the reservation, were conducted to examine threats to factorial invariance posed by varying cultural contexts. Results supported the expectation that the depression measure would not be invariant across area of residence. The shortened 12-item model fit the data better than the original 20-item model (Chapleski, Lamphere, Kaczynski, Lichtenberg, & Dwyer, 1996). These results support previous findings of an essentially unidimensional model that is useful in cross-cultural studies of depression in elderly persons (Baron, Manson, Ackerson, & Brenneman, 1990; Liang et al., 1989; McCallum, Mackinnon, Simons, & Simons, 1995; Roberts, 1980). Applying the 12-item scale and testing for mean differences among elders living in the three areas, the Great

Lakes study found significantly higher depression scores among urban residers than among either the rural or reservation populations.

Similarly, little is known about dementia among American Indian elders. Cognitive functioning has been associated with one of the most common health problems in the elderly, falling, and with recovery from falls. Moreover, converging research findings indicate that memory problems are significantly related to several Instrumental Activities of Daily Living Skills (IADLS), skills that are necessary for independent living and thus play a central role in the health and functional abilities of older adults. Cognitive impairment is the most frequently cited explanation for institutionalization of older adults in the United States, yet cognitive impairment is reported to be relatively low among Indian nursing home residents (Manson & Callaway, 1990). Once again, the implications of increased longevity become important. If American Indians are more likely to survive to older ages, will they, like Whites, be more at risk for organic brain syndrome? And what will this mean for long-term care?

Major Life Events

Stressful life events have been said to account for the excess of psychological symptoms in lower socioeconomic strata (Dohrenwend & Dohrenwend, 1969) and predict negative changes in physical health (Holmes & Rahe, 1967). Using a list of 19 life events, the Great Lakes elder study asked if any of the events had occurred within the past 6 months, then how much impact each of the identified events had (scored 0 not bad at all, 1 not too bad, and 2 very bad). Sixty-seven percent reported 1 or more event. A summary variable was created by weighting each reported life event by its respective impact rating and then summing across all weighted life events. Forty-eight percent reported at least 1 event that was bad or very bad. Elders who had more severe life event/impact scores had significantly higher depression scores (using the CES-D), significantly more chronic diseases, and higher ADL and IADL impairments, compared to elders with lower life event scores (Chapleski, Lichtenberg, Dwyer, Jankowski, & Tsai, 1995). Social support, measured by frequency of interaction with the native network, was also positively correlated with life event scores, suggesting that Native elders coped with these life events by seeking support from their Native network. Longitudinal analysis is needed, however, to identify the cause/effect relationships.

Competing Models of Long-Term Care

There is no clear consensus about what long-term care means, and this holds true regardless of race, culture, or ethnicity. Kane and Kane's (1987) assertion that decisions concerning the proper goals of long-term care are basically political and social decisions rather than empirical ones is especially germane for the American Indian elder. Most U.S. legislation defines the elderly by chronological age, usually 65. Policy that defines old age as exclusively chronological ignores race and class differences. Perhaps a fairer measure for entry into old age would be in terms of numbers of years remaining rather than numbers of years lapsed (Mangen & Peterson, 1984).

Furthermore, these political and social decisions have defined a long-term care system that is acute biased, institutionally based, and professionally oriented. The conceptualization of long-term care in the modern Western world is based on a medical model that takes precedence over a more holistic, social model. The pervasive influence of medicine on the United States led to the medicalization of many aspects of life, including aging (Estes & Binney, 1989) and long-term care (Henderson, 1995). An example of this viewpoint is that long-term care is often confused with where it is located, for example, a nursing home, and it is often associated solely with physical health parameters. Indian country is not unaffected by these decisions. In a study of 208 Indian Health Service (IHS) employees, health providers to American Indian tribes subscribed largely to this model and defined long-term care as a "health" problem provided for mainly in a nursing home setting. Social service professionals in this same study, however, were more likely to mention a range of settings for care and to perceive family and community-oriented personnel to be highly involved in the care (Manson, 1989).

Tribes and Indian aging agencies are beginning to examine and embrace much more comprehensive models with contextual frameworks that include the multiple dimensions of long-term care. These dimensions cross the boundaries of health and social services and contain elements of both (Kane & Kane, 1987). Furthermore, these dimensions may be influenced by culturally distinct worldviews. Policymakers and service providers have learned that the "one size fits all" approach is neither feasible nor acceptable. This recognition has led to an increase in comprehensive, culturally competent studies to define issues and problems among previously understudied groups. Understanding long-term care requires a dynamic, contextual, and cultural perspective much like a camera lens that captures the close-up as well as the wide angle, on multiple occasions across time.

McCabe and Cuellar (1994) report the recommendation (from the 1990 Roundtable for Long-Term Care for Indian Elders) of a long-term care definition specific to Indian elders that would include an age definition younger than the usual age 65, as well as other parameters, including chronic illnesses, disabilities, and a decrease in functional assessment measures. This recommendation is similar in concept to broad definitions generated from major gerontological sources. For instance, Kane and Kane (1987) provide a broad definition that appears to encompass these parameters but avoids chronological age limitations: "Long-term care is a set of health, personal care, and social services delivered over a sustained period of time to persons who have lost or never acquired some degree of functional capacity."

Long-term care definitions and attitudes among Native elders were explored recently in a number of contexts, including two Administration on Aging (AoA) funded conferences[4] and a series of elder focus groups in the Great Lakes region. Resounding consensus was expressed by leaders and elders for Indian-managed and -owned facilities that are community based; are intergenerational, involving entire families; provide assisted living and home-based care; and, most important, represent traditions, beliefs, and spirituality of Native people.

The Great Lakes elders illuminated attitudes toward "long-term care," reporting that, for the most part, the concept long-term care is foreign to the American Indian lexicon and way of thinking—families and tribal members take care of one another just because "it is the Indian way." It is a matter of communal tribal values and expectations of *interdependence* rather than *independence*. As one Michigan Ojibwa put it,

> Well, in general, long-term care is not the ideal situation according to the way an Indian community is supposed to work because the fact that we have long-term care means that the family's not able to perform or unwilling to perform that role.

The same informant recognized the influence of larger society, however:

> if society, if Indian society, continues to pattern non-Indian society, and define our quality of life as not having elders in our environment, which larger society does, then the need for long-term care will get larger and larger and larger. And to that extent we need to address it and make it as amenable to the needs of our elders as possible so they can maintain their dignity.

Clearly, divergent worldviews must be recognized and systems adapted to incorporate, it is to be hoped, the best of both.

Consensus Surrounding a Continuum of Services

Most definitions of long-term care suggest that the key is functioning and independence or lack thereof. Interventions to delay or ameliorate these dependencies form the mix of formal and informal services that make up the long-term care system in its broadest sense. The term *system* belies the piecemeal, fragmented, patchwork of services that make up the long-term care continuum in most communities nationwide. Manson and Callaway (1990) noted the underdeveloped continuum of care and overemphasis on institutionalization among American Indian communities. Although the usual array of health and social services described in a *continuum* are found throughout many [Indian] communities, all of the services are not found in any one community.

A long-term care continuum includes housing arrangements (from the elder's own home to nursing homes to many intermediate levels between) as well as transportation, services to aid in tasks of daily living, education services, nutrition services, companion services, respite care, hospice care, as well as health and mental health services. An American Indian continuum often includes other dimensions as well, such as the spiritual and religious, and use of traditional healers. Help may come from informal providers (family, friends, or neighbors) or formal providers such as Indian Health Service, the tribe, or other services offered to all older persons through entitlements, such as the Social Security Act (e.g., Title XX, Medicare, SSI, Medicaid), the Older Americans Act, the Housing and Community Development Act, or CETA.

The National Indian Council on Aging (NICOA) has proposed that establishment of a continuum of long-term care services is the most critical issue facing Indian elders. Yet long-term care has not been a priority for IHS despite the lengthened life expectancies and significantly higher rates of chronic ailments among Native elders (see John, Chapter 4, & Kramer, Chapter 8, in this volume). Manson and Callaway (1988) found, in a survey of IHS and tribal providers, that IHS and state government were perceived as principally responsible for ensuring the availability of long-term care services, with the BIA and the tribes perceived as moderately responsible. The IHS is predicated on an acute care model, however, and community-based or in-home supportive services are usually provided via other sources of funding, including Title III-C or Title VI of the Older Americans Act or Title XX of the Social Security Act (Manson & Callaway, 1988). Furthermore, many federally recognized tribes are choosing self-determination (P. L. 638), giving them full authority over how their IHS allocation will be spent.

> We've just gone with self governance for our IHS programs which means it's more like a block grant, we get the money and decide what to do with it and so that way it doesn't much matter to us what IHS does. (Reservation Informant)

Thus, there is no single agency with responsibility for long-term care and no formal coordination among IHS, BIA, NICOA, and the tribes (Brown, 1995; Manson & Callaway, 1988).

Hence, long-term care remains primarily a family and tribal responsibility, and many individual tribes *are* taking responsibility for planning and providing these services. For instance, the Tohono O'odham Nation (Arizona) plan is depicted in a comprehensive medicine wheel form, focusing primarily on home- or community-based provision. The tribe has allocated a percentage of profits from gaming to elderly programs (Brown, 1995). A more thorough understanding of how tribes are planning and providing long-term care services will be forthcoming from The National Resource Centers on Native American Aging study of home- and community-based services using a national sample of tribes.

Determinants of Service Utilization and the "4A" Model

There is little published research exploring the determinants of community-based in-home service utilization for American Indians. The utilization data that exist reveal a pattern of underutilization of formal services, whether health or social services (Agree, 1988; Heath, Ornelas, & Marquart, 1993; NICOA, 1981). The majority of Indian and Alaskan elderly rarely see a physician (Agree, 1988), and their use of outpatient services is lower than for the general U.S. older population (Heath et al., 1993). It is a fact that a continuum of services is a theoretical ideal at this point in time, and therefore it is critical to assess and plan for services that will be acceptable, accessible, and, in fact, used.

The Great Lakes elder research examined individual determinants of service utilization and found that availability and acceptability of needed services was limited and varied depending on area of residence. The availability of services is a necessary but not sufficient condition for their use. Other factors that impinge on service use can be viewed from a simple "4A" model. The four As are: *Availability* of services, *Awareness* of services, *Acceptability* of services, and *Accessibility* of services (Gelfand, 1994). Availability of services is an obvious prerequisite for any service utilization. If individuals are going to be clients of any program, they must have an awareness of the service and its availability. Awareness in regard to service use, however, must be seen as a multidimensional concept that includes an awareness on the part of older persons of their need for a particular service and some knowledge about what they have to do to receive the service. Psychosocial attitudes that have their roots in strongly held cultural beliefs may affect service utilization. For example, an Indian elder may prefer to use traditional healers solely or in conjunction with mainstream health-related services.

Past history of satisfaction or dissatisfaction with services can have a major impact on the willingness of older minority group members to use services or to trust their health to a system in which representatives from their own ethnic/racial background are very limited in number. There are also obvious issues related to such factors as quality of the service and its cost that affect the acceptability of a particular service among older individuals. Accessibility has been viewed as a major factor in service delivery utilization rates. Accessibility means not only the ability physically to reach a service center, but the ability of the older person to surmount some of the complicated eligibility requirements associated with many U.S. social welfare programs. Given the variety of eligibility criteria written into entitlements and services available through the complex of urban, rural, and reservation-based services, these complications may be heightened.

Furthermore, beliefs about the value of different forms of health care, as well as beliefs about the appropriateness of treating certain symptoms, are determinants of health behavior that may have their roots in long-standing ethnic traditions. For American Indians, native healers may be viewed as more appropriate sources of treatment than physicians for some illnesses. Herbal remedies may be preferred over costly prescription drugs.

Using a model of residence distinguishing among reservation, rural, and urban Great Lakes Indian elders, and using 1989 needs assessment data, Chapleski and Dwyer (1995) found that service utilization and its determi-

TABLE 15.4 Great Lakes American Indians Age 55 and Above: Use and Knowledge of Services by Area of Residence

Significance Variables	Means (Standard deviations in parentheses)				
	Total	Reservation	Urban	Rural	F-Test
Index of use of 11 services[a]	1.42	1.97	1.25	1.21	.004
	(1.65)	(1.68)	(1.54)	(1.83)	
Index of use of preventive health services[b]	0.67	1.04	0.57	0.53	.001
	(0.96)	(1.10)	(0.88)	(0.94)	
Index of use of in-home services[c]	0.29	0.46	0.24	0.20	.005
	(0.52)	(0.61)	(0.48)	(0.49)	
Index of service knowledge[c]	6.95	8.52	6.09	7.66	.000
	(3.81)	(2.99)	(4.09)	(2.95)	

NOTE: a. Index consists of the emergency, home health, health screening, hearing screening, vision screening, smoking cessation, nutrition, congregate meals, home repair, and food commodity variables.

b. Index consists of the nutrition, smoking cessation, and the vision, hearing, and over-all health screening variables.

c. Index consists of the chore and home health variables.

nants from both a supply and a demand perspective vary greatly among the three areas of residence. Reservation residers were significantly more likely than rural off-reservation or urban older American Indians to use several types of in-home service. For example, by employing a tripartite model of area of residence to examine in-home service use, they found that reservation dwellers were 4.1 times more likely to use home services, 3.8 times more likely to use a home health aid, and 5.55 times more likely to have a home visit than urban elders, controlling for other characteristics. Rural off-reservation elders were more than 4 times less likely to use home health services than their rural on-reservation counterparts. These findings suggest that the typical rural-urban or on-/off-reservation dichotomies are not sufficient to capture variation by area of residence.

Gelfand, Chapleski, and Pugh (1996) found results similar to the Chapleski and Dwyer (1995) study, with reservation residers most likely to utilize all types of service (see Table 15.4). Overall, 25.4% of the 309 respondents had used one or more home-based service (chore and home health aides); 39.5% had used one or more community-based service (home repair, emergency assistance, congregate meals, and food commodities), and 37.8% had used one or more health-related service (vision, hearing, overall health screening, nutrition, and smoking cessation) within the past year.

Controlling for sociodemographic factors, health, ADLs, social support, and area of residence, using OLS regression, area of residence (reservation) was found to be a major predictor of both knowledge and utilization of services. Results from a short survey of service providers, administered to augment respondents' reported use, show two basic factors may explain this difference—availability and acceptability. First, the federally recognized reservations, with considerably more resources than rural and urban communities, offer more services. Second, the services are more acceptable to recipients because they are, for the most part, provided by and for other American Indians. Many of these services are funded under Title VI of the Older Americans Act. Title VI recognizes the extraordinary need of older American Indians, and although it has not been revised in many years, the general thrust of its statements is still applicable to older American Indians in many communities. Unfunded and underfunded for many years, the future of Title VI remains uncertain. Whatever the outcome, it does not provide services in rural off-reservation or urban communities, where the majority of American Indians reside.

Ambivalence Toward Institutional Care

Whereas a nursing home is often feared and viewed as a "place to die," the existence of a home on a reservation can be a source of pride and viewed as a material manifestation of respect for elders (Cook, 1992). Many tribes are considering some type of facility, and their decisions are influenced by state licensure requirements, need for third-party reimbursement (Medicaid, etc.), as well as tribal economic resources (Tohm & Hart, 1995).

The data on nursing facilities is sparse and inconsistent, perhaps due to how they are counted and what level of care is available. Unlike in the general population, nursing home facilities are extremely rare in Indian communities (John, 1995). Only 3% of American Indian/Alaska Natives were institutionalized compared with 5% of the White elderly, 4% of African Americans, 3% of Hispanic Americans, and 2% of Asian/Pacific Americans in a portrait developed by the American Association of Retired Persons (1987). The first licensed Indian nursing home was built in 1969 in Arizona, and only 13 tribally operated nursing homes existed in 1993 (John, 1995). A 1993 report from AoA, however, listed 24 American Indian/Alaska Native facilities in the

50 states. Facilities vary in levels of care provided, with 20 reporting skilled care provision.

One facility run by the Menominee in Wisconsin chose not to seek state licensure or third-party reimbursements because they wanted to be allowed to practice traditional medicine and for residents to control their own care while involving the entire family. Another example of a unique model of culturally competent services to Indian elders is manifest in the Earthstar Project, Inc., which houses an Elders' Lodge located in an urban environment in St. Paul, Minnesota. Earthstar provides an array of services needed along a continuum of care, including housing, social services, respite care, and spiritual ceremonies.

The Great Lakes research explored attitudes and preferences concerning institutional care. Key informants at one reservation location reported community pride in their nursing facility—"it is nice just to have it there . . . for someone else." Survey findings show that a nursing home was the least preferred option for care, but if absolutely necessary and given no other choice, 70% of urban Indians would prefer to go farther away in order to be with other American Indian residents. Furthermore, nearly three fourths of the sample acknowledged that the presence of American Indian staff at such a facility was somewhat or very important. This is important information for tribes, as well as urban Indian agencies, to acknowledge in planning appropriate long-term care.

American Indian Social Networks Remain Strong

Native American family networks are much more firmly based on interdependence than Anglo-American families (John, 1988). The extended family and its traditional support system are viewed as the norm, yet the sparse research on American Indian families raises questions about the effects of migration from the reservation or the erosion of these networks. The Great Lakes research is examining migratory patterns. Twenty-six percent of the elders were actually born in the urban area, while 40.5% were born on or near reservations. A migratory propensity measure was constructed from questions asking where the respondents had lived during five periods of their lives and where they plan to spend their remaining years. Those currently living on reservations were significantly less likely than either rural or urban to have migrated during any of these periods. Most plan to spend the rest of their life "aging in place," but some urban elders do plan to move to an Indian settlement or reservation community. Anecdotal evidence supports this reverse migration:

A lot of [the elders] actually moved away from their traditional home
areas to the big cities . . . and got jobs in factories and raised their families
there. And now that they're getting older, we do see more coming back. I
think that's kind of a pattern and we see more young people coming back
too. Some of their children are coming with them, their adult children are
coming back to work for the tribe and the elders are you know, coming
back to be a part of the community again. So I think that's just a . . .
probably there were big migrations out in the fifties and sixties and now
we're seeing a migration back. (Reservation Ojibwa Informant)

Manson and Pambrun (1979) stated, "we have no definitive research to
give a measure of certainty to our knowledge of the status of American Indian
families or how American Indian families are changing." Although families
do provide the majority of care to American Indian elders, as in the case of
other minority elders, little is known about how that care varies by tribe
(McCabe & Cuellar, 1994) or by area of residence, or if it is changing with
younger generations. Longitudinal research, though currently unavailable, is
forthcoming from the Great Lakes study on the continuity of social networks
of American Indians, differences in social relations by area of residence, and
the long-term effects of social relations on long-term care.

Preliminary evidence suggests that Great Lakes American Indian elders
appear to enjoy good and supportive relations with their children and families. Measures of size and density indicate most of the older Indians have
large families and report at least two or three close friends with whom they
keep close contact. Findings by location are similar to those of older adults in
general, with rural elders reporting larger family networks. Overall, more
than half are married (50.8%), but this differs significantly depending on
where the elder lives, with 57% of reservation, 55% of rural, and 47% of
urban elders being married. This difference is explained largely by differences in divorce/separation, with the urban elder more than twice as likely to
be divorced or separated (20.5%) than the rural (9.5%) or reservation (2.9%)
elder. At the same time, the urban elder is least likely to live alone (20.6%
compared to 29% and 21.7% for reservation and rural, respectively). The
mean number of children per elder is 3.74, although the rural mean is 4.65 per
elder and 66% have at least one child living within 30 miles (Mean = 1.46).
While only a small number (4.5%) live alone and have no children, for those
few the long-term care options may be reduced.

An index of social integration was constructed using items related to
cultural embeddedness and degree of contact with other American Indians.

Differences by area of residence in mean scores on the Native Network Index were statistically significant ($F = .000$), with the reservation sample scoring highest (mean = 14.96, SD = 3.56), the rural intermediate (mean = 13.38, SD = 4.3), and the urban lowest (mean = 12.26, SD = 3.68).[5] The pattern of living arrangements, social networks, and support is similar to that seen among African American elders. While fewer live alone than reported among White elders, those who do live alone often live in close proximity to kin, whether defined as family, friends, or tribal members, and these kin check in on each other regularly:

> it's such a norm to take care of the family . . . its not a burden . . . something you know is just part of you. For example we were talking to an elder who is at least 60 and he said he was going to take food to his mother and every other day he checks on her. She's 80 some years old and still lives by herself. He said "I go check and take care of her." There is that constant closeness and we always try and check up on them too and see how they're doing and this type of thing so we know where they are, but most of them are just so independent . . . (Rural Odawa Informant)

American Indians traditionally placed high value on respect for their elders, although some literature suggests that many younger American Indians have adopted the dominant societal values, lost much of their cultural ethos, and that reverence for elders is more a stereotype than a reality (Campbell, 1989; John, 1988; Manson & Pambrun, 1979). Key informants in the Great Lakes study believe it is not a stereotype and yet not as much a reality as in the past, but that respect for elders certainly remains an ideal.

> There probably is an ideal, and probably true in most cases. In most cases the families do try to take care of their elders, regardless of what that takes. They want to do what the elder wants. As a community we respect elders. As a community we believe that because of the traditions, being mostly oral, that the elders know what their parents told them, which is what their grandparents told them. (Reservation Ojibwa Informant)

And not just a unidirectional ideal:

> My grandmother told me when I was young that you have to respect your elders, but they have to be worth the respect that you give them, which is really a responsibility that they have as elders, that they're supposed to earn that respect by living out their role as elders. So it's not a one-way street. (Reservation Ojibwa Informant)

Together, the demographic transition, poverty rates, and the clash of cultural values may significantly affect the American Indian family's ability to care for its elders and for those elders to be able to live out their role as elders.

The Importance of Culture

With increasing attention to disadvantaged ethnic minority populations, gerontologists point out the need to examine the *influence of culture and social context to build theory and influence policy* (Markides et al., 1990). More research is needed to examine the impact of changing environments and culture over time (McCabe & Cuellar, 1994). Recognition of the vast heterogeneity that exists both within and among tribal groups limits the generalizability of research findings that do not account for these differences. To what degree have assimilation efforts and forced acculturation affected conditions, attitudes, and behaviors of American Indian elders, and of younger cohorts as well? Do the more traditional have different preferences than those who are more acculturated? There are a number of markers of cultural embeddedness, including the giving of Indian names, participation in Native spiritual rituals, participation in cultural activities such as pow-wows, storytelling, educating children to indigenous ways, practicing and teaching of traditional arts and crafts (beadwork, quillwork, sculpting, etc.), degree of contact with other Native people versus non-Natives, and above all, language.

> If you understand the language, then within reason you could understand the secrets, the religion, and the insides, but without the language you don't have it. And you cannot go and learn a language, yes/no, you can't learn a culture. The only way to learn a culture is to live it. You know, a good number of Indians that did know, and did know when they were small, but don't know any longer because they've been acculturated. And people my age and older were acculturated with a stick or a heavy belt in a residential school, and my first day at school I was taken aside, along with a cousin of mine. We had one Indian nun and she took us aside and told us in no uncertain terms "never speak in Indian. Never. If you do, we'll thrash you." She stood there with the belt in her hand cracking it on her hand. . . . Anyway, so the way to get the Indian out of the Indian is to get rid of the language, because within the language is all the mysteries, religion, the mores, everything is there. The secrets. And without them you've got nothing. (Urban Odawa Elder)

The Great Lakes Indian elders study data show both loss and resurgence of these cultural markers, as well as a renewed pride in being Indian. Sixty-six percent of the elders have no Indian name that they can recall. Ten percent, 90% of whom are urban, are not enrolled in a tribe. Twenty-one percent never participate in any cultural activities and another 21% rarely participate. The two off-reservation groups (urban and rural) participate significantly more than the reservation elders, however. The most frequently mentioned cultural activities were pow-wows (36.9%), followed by arts and crafts (20%) and language (17%). However, half never attend any Native spiritual rituals. Half understand no Native language. Twenty-eight percent speak and understand a few words of their Native language, and only 10% speak fluently. However, language classes are cropping up in all three locations. Indian tribes are supporting their own schools in which the previously forbidden subjects of the BIA schools (language, culture, ritual, Indian history) are major curricular items.

> What's really important is the regeneration of the culture and of the language, the crafts, all of the things—the oral history, the stories, the things that are inside so many of the elders but have not necessarily been shared. This regeneration is not necessarily residing in any one generation, it is starting, in many cases, with the young in school and then sometimes certainly with the middle generation, and the elders. (Rural Odawa Informant)

Thus, while culture is important and has certainly not been eradicated, there is great variance in how it is observed. Remarks from the focus groups suggested that the effect of the Indian schools was to drive the traditional culture inward. Many who do not outwardly practice any of these cultural activities, still maintain a traditional attitude but it is very private and guarded. Major questions of concern for long-term care stem from the effects of culture. Does the resurgence of the Native culture pose positive outcomes for improving health behaviors? One of the Great Lakes informants believes that could be true.

> I think just the tribe in general, that having more pride in being Indian and in the community has kind of, in a sense, people doing those self-destructive behaviors that they did twenty-thirty year ago are aware that people are . . . kind of watching. The young people are watching them and the community is more aware of the Indians and that sense of pride makes them not want to engage in some of those things that happened twenty or thirty years ago.

Might cultural embeddedness then have positive affects on morbidity, well-being, and mortality even?

Data Sources Insufficient But Improving

A major problem in identification of conditions that constitute need is the lack of adequate data. There is no single source of data nationally that can capture either the unique residential statuses of North American Indians in their cultural context or the full range of social, health, and economic measures necessary to determine preferences and needs for services. McCabe and Cuellar (1994) reported having found significantly fewer references and more gaps than expected in a comprehensive computerized search of available literature on older American Indian/Alaska Natives' health and human service needs.

Major sources of data and their limitations include the following: (a) *The decennial census,* noted for its undercounts of the indigenous population, does not provide data that differentiate unique residential locations of tribes with federal recognition from tribes of other status and rural off-reservation Natives nor does it provide adequate information on functional health, mental health, or social support. (b) *The IHS* collects health data, but little social or functional status and no attitudinal data from IHS facilities and disseminates aggregate figures by region. These data do not include comprehensive national data from the 34 urban clinics or the many "undocumented" Indians in urban and non-federally recognized tribes (Kramer, 1991; McCabe & Cuellar, 1994) and therefore provide estimates for only 40% to 60% of North American Indians. (c) *AoA Long-Term Care Resource Centers* are currently collecting and analyzing data from a national sample of tribes, but the data are limited to tribal entities and based on expert informant information concerning service needs and usage. (d) The *Survey of American Indians and Alaska Natives (SAIAN),* a 1987 component of the National Medical Expenditure Survey (NMES), offers the largest national sample of North American Indians, but only 410 are age 65 or older and there are no questions concerning mental health, social service use, or vital status (LaVeist, 1995). Furthermore, the SAIAN sample was based on an IHS-constructed frame of counties of American Indians living on or near reservations, thus sustaining similar limitations noted in (b) above.

These do not constitute the universe of national data but rather the most recent. (e) NICOA in 1980 conducted the first comprehensive national research of American Indian elders' conditions and service structures. Although it did not use the multistage area probability sample design the SAIAN instituted, it may have a smaller noncoverage error by including urban areas and non-federally recognized tribes in the frame (NICOA, 1981). In any case, these data provided a baseline for comparisons across age and race as well as across time, but 16-year-old data may not provide a picture of what exists today. (f) Another comprehensive assessment of the status of American Indian/Alaska Native elders is available in a recent publication funded by the IHS and written by Robert John (1995). It too, however, suffers from old and inadequate data sources, often using 1980 Census data and a reanalysis of the 1980 NICOA data. There are numerous other state, local, and tribal data sources (for a more thorough coverage see McCabe & Cuellar, 1994) that provide partial pictures in specific locations.

Recent efforts to understand and improve long-term care among American Indian elders include:

1. AoA grants for developing a model paraprofessional home-care worker training program for American Indian colleges (John, 1993)
2. Native American Leadership Institutes on Aging (National Resource Center on Minority Aging Populations, 1991)
3. University of New Mexico's Center on American Indian Aging/Information
4. Two National Resource Centers for Older Indians, Native Alaskans, and Native Hawaiians (funded by the Administration on Aging)
5. Two special requests for applications from the National Institute on Aging address long-term care issues among two specific groups of American Indian elders: the Navajo (Robert John, P.I.) and Great Lakes (Elizabeth Chapleski, P.I.). NICOA, often in partnership with AoA's Indian desk, continues to be a major actor in all efforts to understand and improve the conditions of North American Indian elders.

Options for the Future

So, what implications and options emerge from what is known? What questions, if any, have been answered? What answers have raised new questions? For instance, who is responsible for planning and delivering long-term care to American Indians? Can projections of future need be based on current health behaviors and beliefs? Which of these findings are common to aging among all races and populations and which are unique? How do current cohorts of American Indian elders differ from future cohorts? How does residential location affect all of these?

A major purpose of this chapter was to describe the great heterogeneity of American Indian elders and to present a historical and cultural perspective. The data are just not available to speak with authority or generalize to the entire indigenous population. Perhaps that is an inappropriate goal and, in any case, given the political and structural constraints, perhaps an unattainable goal. Findings that show intragroup differences to be as great or greater than intergroup differences complicate matters. These factors must be taken into account, however, and research directed at understanding differences arising from varying degrees of acculturation, different residential locations, and differences in sociodemographic conditions.

It is crucial to understand cultural context and to capture the positive attributes of culture. Yet the dynamic, emergent nature of the interaction of culture and environment suggests fresh approaches are needed. Burton, Dilworth-Anderson, and Bengtson (1992) discussed the challenge of developing theory in the study of diversity and aging and the importance of moving beyond traditional methods and theories. They suggest three ways to do this: (a) using grounded theory, (b) using cultural resources and the humanities to enrich the interpretation of themes in the lives of ethnic/minority elderly, and (c) incorporating a life-course perspective relevant to the intergenerational interdependence typical in these elderly.

What theories have emerged from the themes or data presented in this chapter? Throughout this chapter the view of American Indian aging has been in a social and cultural context. The chapter incorporated a perspective recommended by Passuth and Bengtson (1988) as the most promising existing theoretical framework for studying diversity and aging, a combination of political economy theory and social phenomenology, the former capturing the macro and the latter, the micro perspective.

Research, in order to capture what it means to grow old as an American Indian in different environments, must be longitudinal and use multidisciplinary approaches and methods. Combinations recommended include focus groups; Talking Circles; qualitative interviews; observational techniques to understand cultural themes in art, history, music and ritual; as well as quantitative survey techniques.

Long-term care systems should reflect and capitalize on the strengths of the culture in both planning and delivery. Involve Native elders in planning, involve families in delivery. Services, including housing options, must be both flexible and culturally competent. The goal of any long-term care system is to maintain independence as long as possible. This requires matching functional need with the demands of the environment and the abilities of families or tribes to buffer these demands.

Notes

1. The terms *American Indian, Native American, Indian, Native,* and *Indigenous* are used interchangeably throughout this chapter and refer to American Indians and Alaska Natives (Eskimos and Aleuts) (IA/AN). A recent survey asked American Indian elders of the Great Lakes region how they would prefer to be addressed, and the results included a wide variety of preferences encompassing all of the above plus specific tribal identities and indigenous language choices, for example, *Anishnabe*. An equal percentage (38%) chose *American Indian* and *Native American*.

2. Based on comprehensive long-term care survey data collected from 309 urban-, rural-, and reservation-residing Michigan American Indians aged 55 and older, as well as focus group discussions and key informant interviews. The research was supported by a grant from the National Institutes of Health, National Institute on Aging (RO1-AG 11152).

3. The terms *on-reservation* or *reservation* in this chapter are limited to those reservations with federal recognition. *Off-reservation* or *rural off-reservation* may be state or historic tribes or bands of indigenous communities that no longer have (or never had) this political designation.

4. Advocacy for Community Based Long Term Care in Indian Country Roundtable, Washington, D.C., November, 1995; and National Resource Center on Native American Aging, First Annual Conference, Mesa, Arizona, December, 1995.

5. The Native Network Index was constructed from five variables (degree of contact with American Indian neighbors, of contact with American Indian relatives, of contact with American Indian friends within the past year, and the proportion of neighbors and friends who are Native or non-Native). Index scores ranged from 5 to 22 with an acceptable reliability coefficient (alpha = .72).

References

Agree, E. M. (1988). Portrait of Native American elderly. In *Hearing before the Select Committee on Aging, House of Representatives* (Comm. Publication No. 100-645). Washington, DC: Government Printing Office.

American Association of Retired Persons. Minority Affairs Initiative. (1987). *A portrait of older minorities: Minority elderly in California.* Washington, DC: American Association of Retired Persons.

Baron, A. E., Manson, S. M., Ackerson, L. M., & Brenneman, D. L. (1990). Depressive symptomology in older American Indians with chronic disease: Some psychometric considerations. In C. Attkisson & J. Zich (Eds.), *Screening for depression in primary care* (pp. 217-231). New York: Routledge, Kane.

Barresi, C. M., & Stull, D. E. (1993). *Ethnicity and long-term care.* New York: Springer.

Beale, C. L. (1973). Migration patterns of minorities in the United States. *American Journal of Agricultural Economics, 55,* 938-946.

Brown, E. (1995, November-December). *Preparing for the 21st century: Developing a continuum of care for American Indian elderly.* General Session Speaker, National Resource Center on Native American Aging, First Annual Conference for North American Indians on Aging, Health and Human Services, Mesa, AZ.

Burhansstipanov, L. (1993). *Documentation of the cancer research need of American Indians and Alaska Natives* (Monograph No. 1). Bethesda, MD: National Cancer Institute.

Burton, L. M., Dilworth-Anderson, P., & Bengtson, V. L. (1992). Creating culturally relevant ways of thinking about diversity and aging: Theoretical challenges for the twenty-first century. In E. P. Stanford & F. M. Torres-Gil (Eds.), *Diversity: New approaches to ethnic minority aging* (pp. 129-140). Amityville, NY: Baywood.

Campbell, A. R. (1989). The changing dimension of Native American health: A critical understanding of contemporary Native American health issues. *American Indian Culture and Research Journal, 13,* 3-4.

Chapleski, E. E. (1990). *Michigan needs assessment of the Native American 55 and over population.* Lansing: Michigan Office of Services to the Aging.

Chapleski, E. E. (1992, June). *Older minorities in Michigan: A profile of needs.* Detroit: Michigan Office of Services to the Aging and Wayne State University, Institute of Gerontology.

Chapleski, E. E., & Dwyer, J. W. (1995). The effects of on- and off-reservation residence on in-home service utilization among Great Lakes American Indians. *Journal of Rural Health, 11*(3), 204-216.

Chapleski, E. E., Gelfand, D. E., & Pugh, K. E. (1997). Great Lakes American Indian elders and service utilization: Does residence matter? *Journal of Applied Gerontology, 16*(3).

Chapleski, E. E., Lamphere, J. K., Kaczynski, R., Lichtenberg, P. A., & Dwyer, J. W. (1996). *Structure of a depression measure among American Indian elders: Confirmatory factor analysis of the CES-D.* Manuscript under review.

Chapleski, E. E., Lichtenberg, P., Dwyer, J., Jankowski, T., & Tsai, P. (1995, November). *Great Lakes American Indian elders: Residence and comorbidity as predictors of well-being.* Symposium Presentation, 48th Annual Scientific Meeting of the Gerontological Society of America, Los Angeles.

Cook, C. D. (1992). The village of Otabe: Tribal officials and service providers coordinate comprehensive support for elders. In E. P. Stanford & F. M. Torres-Gil (Eds.), *Diversity: New approaches to ethnic minority aging* (pp. 159-163). Amityville, NY: Baywood.

Dohrenwend, B. P., & Dohrenwend, B. S. (1969). *Social status and psychological disorder: A causal inquiry.* New York: John Wiley.

Estes, C. L., & Binney, E. A. (1989). The biomedicalization of aging: Dangers and dilemmas. *The Gerontologist, 29,* 587-596.

Gelfand, D. (1994). *Aging and ethnicity: Knowledge and services.* New York: Springer.

Heath, S. W., Ornelas, R., & Marquart, C. (1993). An action plan for Indian and Alaska Native elders. *The IHS Primary Care Provider, 18*(5), 81-86.

Henderson, J. N. (1995, November-December). *Forgetfulness and confusion among elders in Indian Country.* Keynote Speaker, First Annual Conference for North American Indians on Aging, Health and Human Services, Mesa, AZ.

Holmes, T. H., & Rahe, R. H. (1967). The social readjustment rating scale. *Journal of Psychosomatic Research, 11,* 213-218.

John, R. (1988). The Native American family. In C. H. Mindel, R. W. Habenstein, & R. Wright (Eds.), *Ethnic families in America* (3rd ed.). New York: Elsevier.

John, R. (1991). *Minority elders: Longevity, economics, and health.* Washington, DC: The Gerontological Society of America.

John, R. (Ed.). (1993, Spring). Three American Indian colleges receive grants to promote training. *Focus on American Indian Aging,* p. 2.

John, R. (1995). *American Indian and Alaska Native elders: An assessment of their current status and provision of services.* Washington, DC: U.S. Department of Health and Human Services, PHS, IHS, Office of Health Programs.

Johnson, A., & Taylor, A. (1991). *Prevalence of chronic disease: A summary of data from the Survey of American Indians and Alaska Natives* (AHCPR Publication No. 91-0031). Rockville, MD: Agency on Health Care Policy and Research.

Kane, R. A., & Kane, R. L. (1987). *Long-term care: Principles, programs and policies.* New York: Springer.

Kovar, M. G. (1987). *The longitudinal study of aging: The 1986 reinterview public use file: Proceedings of the 1987 Public Health Conference on Records and Statistics* (DHHS Publication No. 88-1214). Hyattsville, MD: National Center for Health Statistics.

Kramer, J. (1991). Urban American Indian aging. *Journal of Cross-Cultural Gerontology, 6,* 205-217.

Kramer, B. J., Polisar, D., & Hyde, J. C. (1990). *Study of urban American Indian aging* (Final Report to the Administration on Aging, Grant No. 90AR0118). City of Industry, CA: Public Health Foundation of Los Angeles County.

Kunitz, S. J., & Levy, J. E. (1991). *Navajo aging: The transition from family to institutional support.* Tucson: University of Arizona Press.

Liang, J., Van Tran, T., Krause, N., & Markides, K. S. (1989). Generational differences in the structure of the CES-D scale in Mexican Americans. *Journal of Gerontology, 44,* s110-s120.

LaVeist, T. A. (1995). Data sources for aging research on racial and ethnic groups. *The Gerontologist, 35,* 328-339.

LeVine, R. A. (1984). Properties of culture: An ethnographic view. In R. A. Shweder & R. A. LeVine (Eds.), *Culture theory essays on mind, self and emotion.* Cambridge, UK: Cambridge University Press.

Mangen, D. J., & Peterson, W. A. (Eds.). (1984). *Research instruments in social gerontology: Vol. 3. Health, program evaluation, and demography.* Minneapolis: University of Minnesota Press.

Manson, S. M. (1989). Long-term care in American Indian communities: Issues for planning and research. *The Gerontologist, 29,* 355-358.

Manson, S. M. (1993). Long term care of older American Indians: Challenges in the development of institutional services. In C. M. Barresi & D. E. Stull (Eds.), *Ethnicity and long-term care* (pp. 130-143). New York: Springer.

Manson, S. M., & Callaway, D. G. (1988). Health and aging among American Indians: Issues and challenges for the biobehavioral sciences, American Indian and Alaska. *Native Mental Health Research* (Monograph No. 1).

Manson, S. M., & Callaway, D. G. (1990). Health and aging among American Indians: Issues and challenges for the geriatric sciences. In M. S. Harper (Ed.), *Minority aging: Essential curricula content for selected health and allied health professions* (DHHS Publication No. HRS P-DV-90-4). Washington, DC: Government Printing Office.

Manson, S. M., & Pambrun, A. M. (1979). Social and psychological status of the Indian elderly: Past research, current advocacy, and future inquiry. In *The continuum of life: Health concerns of the Indian elderly.* Albuquerque, NM: National Indian Council on Aging.

Manson S. M., & Trimble J. E. (1982). American Indian and Alaska Native communities. In L. R. Snowden (Ed.), *Reaching the underserved: Mental health needs of neglected populations* (pp. 143-163). Beverly Hills, CA: Sage.

Manton, K. G. (1988). A longitudinal study of functional change and mortality in the United States. *Journal of Gerontological Social Science, 43,* S153-S161.

Markides, K. S., Liang, J., & Jackson, J. S. (1990). Race, ethnicity, and aging: Conceptual and methodological issues. In R. H. Binstock & L. K. George (Eds.), *Handbook of aging and the social sciences* (pp. 112-129). New York: Academic Press.

McCabe, M., & Cuellar, J. (1994). *Aging and health: American Indian/Alaska Native elders.* Stanford, CA: Stanford Geriatric Education Center.

McCallum, J., Mackinnon, A., Simons, L., & Simons, J. (1995). Measurement properties of the Center for Epidemiological Studies depression scale: An Australian community study of aged persons. *Journal of Gerontology: Social Science, 50B*(3), S182-S189.

National Indian Council on Aging. (1981). *American Indian elderly: A national profile.* Albuquerque, NM: National Indian Council on Aging.

National Health Interview Survey. (1993). National Center for Health Statistics, Department of Health and Human Services. Washington, DC: Government Printing Office.

National Indian Council on Aging. (1992). *Indian elder health care: NICOA's statement for a joint Senate/House staff briefing.* (Available from National Indian Council on Aging, 10501 Montgomery, Albuquerque, NM 87111)

National Resource Center on Minority Aging Populations. (1991). Native American leadership institutes on aging. *Minority Aging Exchange, 3*(5), 6-7.

Neligh, G., & Scully, J. (1990). Differential diagnosis of major mental disorders among American Indian elderly. In M. S. Harper (Ed.), *Minority aging: Essential curricula content for selected health and allied health professions* (DHHS Publication No. HRS [P-DV-90-4]). Washington, DC: Government Printing Office.

Neugarten, B. L., & Bengtson, V. L. (1968). *Cross-national studies of adulthood and aging: Interdisciplinary topics in gerontology.* Basel, Switzerland: Karger.

Passuth, P. M., & Bengtson, V. L. (1988). Sociological theories of aging: Current perspectives and future directions. In J. E. Birren & V. Bengtson (Eds.), *Emergent theories of aging* (pp. 333-355). New York: Springer.

Rhoades, E. R. (1990). Profile of American Indians and Alaska Natives. In M. S. Harper (Ed.), *Minority aging: Essential curricula content for selected health and allied health profession* (pp. 45-62) (DHHS Publication No. HRS [P-DV-90-4]). Washington, DC: Government Printing Office.

Rice, D. P., & LaPlante, M. P. (1988). Chronic illness, disability, and increasing longevity. In S. Sullivan & M. E. Lewin (Eds.), *The economics and ethics of long-term care and disability.* Washington, DC: American Enterprise Institute for Public Policy Research.

Roberts, R. E. (1980). Reliability of the CES-D scale in different ethnic contexts. *Psychiatry Research, 2,* 125-134.

Survey of American Indians and Alaska Natives. (1987). *National Medical Expenditure Survey supplement.* Rockville, MD: Public Health Service, Agency for Health Care Policy and Research.

Shore, J. H., & Manson, S. M. (1981). Cross-cultural studies of depression among American Indians and Alaska Natives. *White Cloud Journal, 2*(2), 5-12.

Snipp, C. M. (1991). *American Indians: The first of this land.* New York: Russell Sage.

Tohm, S., & Hart, F. (1995, December). *Long term care: Is a nursing home the answer?* Symposium conducted at the National Resource Center on Native American Aging's First Annual Conference for North American Indians on Aging, Health and Human Services, Mesa, AZ.

U.S. Bureau of the Census. (1990). *1990 census of population and housing: Summary of population and housing characteristics.* Washington, DC: Department of Commerce.

U.S. Congress, Office of Technology Assessment. (1986). *Indian health care* (OTA-H-290). Washington, DC: Government Printing Office.

Young, T. K. (1994). *The health of Native Americans: Towards a biocultural epidemiology.* New York: Oxford University Press.

PART VI

Health Policy

Caught in Hostile Cross-Fire

Public Policy and Minority Elderly in the United States

Steven P. Wallace
Valentine M. Villa

Minority elderly[1] in the United States at the end of the 20th century find themselves in a hostile cross-fire of social policy. Historically, racial and ethnic minorities have been exploited for cheap labor and scapegoated during periods of economic downturns. Public policy has alternatively encouraged immigration and the economic improvement of minority groups, only later to marginalize and penalize some of them. The 1990s is witnessing an antiminority policy space that blames non-European immigrants and minorities for the social and economic problems generated by multinational corporations and the globalization of the economy. Added to the punitive policies aimed at minorities and non-European immigrants is a historic attack in the public policy arena on the legitimacy of the elderly. Beginning in the late 1970s and accelerating in the 1980s there has been a growing effort to counter the image

AUTHORS' NOTE: The authors may be contacted as follows: Steven P. Wallace, UCLA School of Public Health, Box 951772, Los Angeles, CA 90095-1772, voice (310) 206-3578, fax (310) 825-5960, e-mail SWallace@ucla.edu; and Valentine M. Villa, UCLA School of Public Policy and Social Research, Department of Social Welfare, 3250 PPB, Box 951656, Los Angeles, CA 90095-1656, voice (310) 825-8092, fax (310) 206-7564, e-mail vvilla@ucla.edu.

of the elderly as a deserving group. The increasingly accepted public image of the elderly as generally healthy and well-off further marginalizes minority elderly who are disproportionately low-income and in poor health. Thus, policies that are punitive for minorities and immigrants are compounded by those that weaken public programs for the elderly.

In this context of hostility to immigrants and minorities and the shrinking legitimacy of the elderly, federal policy has become dominated by budget issues. The rising cost of health care has combined with a primary emphasis on reducing government spending to create pressures to reduce health care costs, resulting in policies that may decrease access to the health care services needed by minority elderly. The chapter concludes with an overview of likely policy and other trends into the 21st century that may influence access to care and the appropriateness of care for minority elderly.

The Invisibility of Minority Elderly in Public Policy

Throughout most policy discussions minority elderly remain invisible in the United States, even though the elderly are a central focus of public policy, as are racial and ethnic minorities. This invisibility is a consequence, in part, of demography, the role of race and immigration in labor market policies, and the role of older persons in minority communities.

Much of this volume has correctly emphasized the *growing* numbers of minority elderly. But, historically, the proportions of older persons in minority populations has been comparatively small. Table 16.1 shows that the non-Latino White population has the largest proportion of elderly, whereas minority populations have the highest proportions of children and youth. For politicians whose motivations are partly based on the reactions of voters, the relatively small numbers of minority elderly (4.9 million vs. 28.6 million older non-Latino Whites in 1995) and their lower voting rates make minority elderly a marginal constituency. Minority communities as a whole are similarly less likely to push the needs of the elderly in policy arenas. While the non-Latino White population has about 1.5 youths for each elder, most of the minority groups have about 4 youths per elder (Table 16.1). The Latino population is the youngest, with about 6 youths per elder! The needs of youth—education, employment, reproductive health services—are therefore more prominently experienced in minority communities. In addition, the social problems experienced by the young are more likely to be visible to the entire

TABLE 16.1 Demographic Composition of the Population, 1995

	Total Population Size (thousands)	Percentage Age 65 and Over	Percentage Age 17 and Under	Ratio Youth to Elderly
Non-Latino White	193,566	14.8	23.6	1.60
African American	31,598	8.4	32.2	3.85
Latino	26,936	5.6	35.6	6.38
Asian American	8,788	6.8	29.1	4.27
Native American	1,931	6.7	34.9	5.21

SOURCE: U.S. Bureau of the Census (1996).

community. Unemployment, gang violence, and drug abuse are more likely to involve the young and, in turn, affect many others in the community. In contrast, when older persons experience poverty, chronic illnesses, or inadequate housing, they are unlikely to be disruptive to those around them. Their problems become a liability for families, but not for the wider community in the same way as the problems of the young. Although the problems encountered by the young and old in minority communities often share a common *source,* the *symptoms* of those problems appear more in the private sphere among the old and more in the public sphere among the young.

To the extent that minority communities have limited resources to advocate for public policies, it is logical that prominent organizations such as the Urban League and the National Council of La Raza have not prioritized their policy efforts toward proportionally small numbers of elderly. The organizations that represent minority elderly policy interests, such as the National Center for Black Aged, the National Hispanic Council on Aging, and other minority-group-specific national senior organizations, grew out of federal funding designed to foster such centers rather than from grassroots organizing. On the other hand, the growing proportion of elderly in minority communities, combined with the aging of community activists who developed advocacy skills in the 1950s and 1960s, will likely increase the amount of minority community policy activity on aging policy in the coming years.

A second factor making minority elderly invisible in much social policy is their low labor force participation rates. Policymakers are interested in labor force issues of racial and ethnic minorities because high unemployment rates in many minority communities generate a number of social problems (Wilson, 1996). Similarly, the *employment* of recent immigrants is periodically viewed as a threat to native-born laborers, generating policy activity around issues of immigration (Portes & Bach, 1986; Rothstein, 1993). This contributes to research and policy attention to issues including the causes of unemployment, limited economic opportunity, and welfare dependency in immigrant and racial/ethnic minority communities. Once an individual reaches older ages, however, separation from the labor force is seen as normal and desirable. When absent from the labor force due to age, immigrant and minority elderly are no longer considered either problems or threats, and they fall out of consideration in the frequent policy activity focused on economic and labor policy.

Finally, the status of the elderly in most minority families likely contributes to the limited policy attention paid to minority elderly. The elderly in minority communities generally have higher levels of family support than non-Latino White older persons (Wallace, 1990; Wallace & Lew-Ting, 1992), indicating that the families are assuming the duty of providing for the care of disabled older relatives. While this provides the potential for family advocacy on policy issues, in practice family care is experienced as a private obligation. Expectations of family support by minority elders are also likely to lead elders to focus their efforts on strengthening family relations rather than moving to political action.

Political and Economic Change Drives Public Policy

This situation of invisible minority elders in the public policy arena occurs within a context that is increasingly hostile to minorities and older persons. Aging advocates often focus on the immediate threats to public programs for older persons—battling a cut in home-delivered meals here, increased Medicare premiums there, and all the while trying to decrease negative perceptions of aging that contribute to age discrimination (Wallace & Williamson, 1992). It is useful to take a step back, however, and look at some of the basic economic and political forces that frame these changes in public policy. In particular, we summarize some of the changes in the U.S. economy and the consequences of those changes on the public perception of immigrants and minorities. We then look at how the politics of health and aging policy shifted when the primary focus of federal policy making became dominated by budget debates. This will provide a better understanding of why aging policies that negatively impact minority elderly are being proposed, as well as the timing of their political popularity.

Changes in the economy and the growing importance of economics in public policy decisions are major factors driving aging and health policies. Much has been written about the economic restructuring in the United States during the 1980s and 1990s. During this time period the United States shifted away from manufacturing toward a service economy. The result has been an increasing bifurcation of the workforce into well-paid and poorly paid positions. Leading the decline in jobs that provided middle-class earnings were manufacturing positions (Rosenthal, 1995). It has become increasingly easy for manufacturing industries to move their production out of the United States to developing countries where wages are low, benefits nonexistent, and environmental and safety regulations lax. Some manufacturing jobs that have remained in the United States have relocated from the higher-waged upper Midwest and Northeast to the lower-waged South and Southeast. The new jobs being created are disproportionately upper- and lower-wage positions. Between 1983 and 1993, 21% of job growth occurred in the service sector in industries such as retail sales and food service. Similarly, the number of clerical and other administrative support positions grew rapidly during this period and had median earnings below the average for all occupations (Rosenthal, 1995). In addition, these positions are less likely to include health insurance, employer-paid pensions, or union protections. At the higher end of the wage scale, administrative specialty jobs increased rapidly, led by teachers and registered nurses (Rosenthal, 1995). In addition, the competition from international competitors and pressures to increase profits has pushed U.S. companies to become increasingly "lean," resulting in restructurings and reorganizations involving layoffs of previously secure white-collar middle-managers (Gardner, 1995). Even companies such as IBM, which for decades had a "no layoff" policy, fired thousands of workers during the 1990s to reduce expenses (Langberg, 1993). These and other pressures have resulted in an overall stagnation or decline of the purchasing power of family wages for more than 10 years, and increased insecurity among many about the long-term futures of their jobs, health insurance, and pensions.

Historically, when the general public faces increased economic insecurity there is increased public concern about threats to jobs and the standard of living. It is in these historical periods that immigrants and people of color are most vulnerable to punitive public policies. During the Depression, for example, thousands of persons of Mexican ancestry were rounded up and deported to Mexico, often without concern for whether they were permanent residents or even U.S. citizens, because of a publicized belief that they were taking jobs from (non-Latino White) citizens (McWilliams, 1948). In the 1990s the public debate has shifted from jobs, where it has become less convincing that low-skilled immigrants compete for well-paying jobs, to the costs of public benefits used by immigrants. Federal legislation passed in 1996 gives states the option of cutting off most public assistance benefits to noncitizen immigrants who have worked for less than 10 years in the United States. Depending on how taxes paid and public programs used are counted, research can show that immigrants provide a net *contribution* or a net *drain* on public resources (Fix & Passel, 1994). But the *politics* of immigration has emphasized only the use of health, education, and welfare programs by immigrants, with no attention to the taxes paid and other contributions of immigrants. As a result, nearly 55% of Americans believe that immigrants cause economic crisis by increasing the demand on government services (Moore, 1993). Anti-immigrant sentiment has been expressed in a number of public votes, such as Proposition 187 in California that would have made undocumented immigrants ineligible for almost all public services and required public services to identify and report possible undocumented immigrant users (Armbruster, Geron, & Bonacich, 1995). It is no accident that the anti-immigrant movement is strongest in the West, because workers in the West during the early 1990s were more likely than average to lose their jobs and not find another one (Gardner, 1995), and also lived in the region with the highest rates of immigration (Smith & Tarallo, 1995).

Anti-immigrant policies are not directed specifically at the elderly, but the elderly are often caught up in the effects of the broader policy changes. Limiting public benefits received by *legal* immigrants would penalize numerous older persons who depend on SSI (Supplemental Security Income) and Medicaid. About one quarter of SSI recipients nationally are noncitizen, legal immigrants (U.S. Social Security Administration, 1994). Some proposals aimed at reducing public assistance spending would prohibit most immigrant elderly from receiving any health or income support (Wallace & Manuel-Barkin, 1995). The undercurrent of anti-immigrant sentiment indirectly affects older persons who have family and other relatives who may be affected by proposed legislation. Some elderly are reluctant to use services that they are eligible for because they fear that they may bring government attention to others in their family, putting them at risk.

At the same time that immigrants are being scapegoated for problems with government finances and other economic problems, people of color in general are the subject of negative policy actions as exemplified by attacks on affirmative action. Some politicians have used affirmative action as a "wedge issue" to attract White voters who perceive minority workers as unfairly competing for jobs, as seen in the recent California proposition banning affirmative action in government programs (Pear, 1996). Efforts to overcome centuries of race-based discrimination began in the 1960s with programs designed to give minorities and women a chance to obtain jobs and education in areas from which they had been traditionally excluded. Public opinion polls in the 1990s document the public perception of Whites that race-based discrimination no longer exists (contrary to the findings in the academic literature; see, e.g., Massey & Denton, 1993), whereas African Americans continue to perceive an impact of race on the opportunity structure (Stall, 1996). Whites focus on how affirmative action may make it harder for them to obtain desirable jobs while overlooking the problem of the decreasing pool of desirable jobs resulting from economic processes. This reflects the fact that it is easier to blame social problems on persons than on social institutions or historical processes. This trend in public opinion serves to delegitimate programs that are believed to serve racial and ethnic minority populations disproportionately.

Similar attempts at scapegoating have occurred with the elderly. Since the 1980s there has been an organized effort to portray the elderly as uniformly wealthy and taking an unfair share of public resources. These groups worked to make the government role in pensions and health care for the elderly (via Social Security and Medicare) appear unnecessary (Quadagno, 1989) and have tried to frame policy debates within a context of intergenerational conflict (Binstock, 1995). High levels of poverty and lack of access to health care for children and low-income adults are erroneously attributed to the successes of Social Security and Medicare in preventing those problems among older persons. In particular, minority children are portrayed as particularly disadvantaged by the spending on older persons. Yet programs for the elderly are especially important in minority communities because of the interdependence of family units, and the causes of poverty among racial and ethnic minority communities (unemployment, single-headed households, etc.) are unrelated to spending on programs for older persons (Minkler, 1992).

There have also been significant political changes that have changed the *context* of aging and health policy. One of the most significant public policies that affects minority elderly is the federal budget process. During the 1980s, a series of taxing and spending changes occurred that has severely limited the ability of policymakers to respond creatively to social needs. First, then-

President Reagan led the fight for the largest tax cut in history. Cutting income taxes (which gets progressively higher as income from all sources, including investments, rises) while raising Social Security taxes (a regressive flat tax on wages only) provided tax relief primarily to those with the highest incomes while substantially reducing government revenues (U.S. House of Representatives, 1987). Second, this era saw an enormous peace-time military buildup that increased spending during a time of falling tax revenues. The result was that the federal deficit ballooned, making the deficit *the* central policy issue at the federal level (Wallace & Estes, 1989). Laws passed to reduce the deficit required that any new spending be offset by spending cuts elsewhere or by new taxes. These changes have resulted in federal planning being driven by budgetary rather than programmatic considerations (Waldivsky, 1992).

The economic uncertainties of the 1990s have contributed to the continued concern over the size of the budget deficit. When attempting to reduce the deficit, the politics of economic crisis has led most political discussions to involve cuts in programs (although tax hikes were also approved during the early 1990s). The largest federally funded programs are Social Security (22% of federal spending), Medicare and Medicaid (17%), the military (16%), and interest on the national debt (16%). Despite the large amount of public attention paid to them, all means-tested (welfare) programs account for only 6.0% and foreign aid for 1.4% of the federal budget (U.S. Office of Management & Budget, 1995). Even though Social Security and most of Medicare are self-funded (i.e., special, dedicated taxes support them and cannot be used for any other purpose), these two programs have been the special targets of many budget cutters. Cuts in these programs would, by and large, only postpone the deficit because the savings could only be loaned to reduce the deficit rather than actually to pay off some of the accumulated debt. But the cuts would be "real" for those low- and moderate-income elderly who rely on Social Security for most of their monthly income and have Medicare as their only form of health insurance. The next section identifies the key actors in health policy and discusses how these constraints result in specific types of health policies for minority elderly.

Elite Interests in the Health Policy Process

To understand the politics of health policy, it is essential to review briefly the key players in the health policy arena. Though minority elderly are largely invisible in public policy both as targets of policies and influences on policy, a set of powerful groups is clearly visible as central players in shaping and benefiting from health policy changes. Historically, elites such as the American Medical Association, the American Hospital Association, the insurance industry, and the pharmaceutical industry have held sway over American health policy (Starr, 1982). More recently, employers who pay for the health insurance of their employees have become a major player in health policy (Bergthold, 1991). Unfortunately, the interests of none of these groups overlaps with the health needs of minority elderly.

The corporate health sector's primary interests are in maximizing profits and minimizing government regulation of their business, although the drug companies, insurance companies, and hospitals often differ on the particulars of specific legislation. The other powerful private interest is organized medicine, which tries to support high physician incomes and professional autonomy. These medical interests were particularly visible in the 1993 battles over President Clinton's proposed national health care reform. One estimate is that more than $100 million was spent by over 650 groups on campaign contributions and advertising in attempts to influence the outcome of health care reform. Campaign donations in 1993 and 1994 by the American Medical Association (AMA) to members of Congress totaled $772,042; the American Hospital Association contributed $459,741; and the American Healthcare Association $215,025. In addition, the health insurance industry ran a $10 million TV campaign designed to undermine public support for any changes that would decrease the role of private insurance (Center for Public Integrity, 1994).

Business has been a key actor in health policy debates over the past 15 years. Both locally and nationally, businesses have formed "business coalitions on health" in response to the rising proportion of total compensation spent on medical benefits (Bergthold, 1990). Employers have a stake in the health policy for the elderly, both because they pay half of Medicare taxes (the other half being paid by the employee) and because many large employers offer retirees insurance that supplements Medicare ("Medigap" insurance). Most business efforts have been aimed at limiting their exposure to the rising costs of medical care, with no attention to the special needs of low-income or minority elderly. With health care policy regulating, subsidizing, and otherwise affecting the health care sector—which comprises as much as one seventh of the U.S. economy (Levit et al., 1994)—health policy is also caught up in the broader ideological and economic conflicts over the extent and direction of government involvement in the economy and society.

The federal bureaucracy has also been the site of a moderate amount of policy influence and initiative, though the federal health bureaucracy has not been as active in health issues as the Pentagon has in military issues. The Social Security Administration was instrumental in shaping the design and implementation of Medicare in the 1960s, the initial push to encourage health maintenance organizations (HMOs) in the 1970s came from the executive branch, and hospital and physician reimbursement changes of the 1980s were the result of administrative initiatives. The organizational tendency to enhance one's own department is evident in the multiple and overlapping programs focusing on long-term care for the elderly that are jealously guarded at the local level by the Area Agencies on Aging, Medicaid agencies, and state funded (through federal Social Service Block Grant money, for example) programs (Estes, 1979). Because no government office focuses specifically on minority elderly (such as the Department of Veterans Affairs focuses on vets, or the Administration on Aging focuses on all elderly), there is no institutional voice at the federal level that advocates for minority elderly policies.

None of the central interests in health care policy are particularly responsive to minority community needs, especially not among the elderly. The sector least interested in minority elderly is the corporate medical sector. Because the first concern of this sector is profits, and minority elderly are more likely to have lower incomes, the minority market is not a major concern. The history of the growth of for-profit hospitals, for example, has found them concentrating in growing, middle-class, White, suburban areas. This is where there are the highest concentrations of privately insured (i.e., most profitable) individuals. In contrast, inner cities have been losing hospitals because of the economics of serving inner-city residents, not because of a lack of need for medical care (Rice, 1987; Witeis, 1992).

The high level of social and economic segregation of most minorities, on the other hand, could make it possible for them to become an attractive "niche" market for some providers if the minority community has sufficient purchasing power. Enhancing purchasing power in a market system was the goal of Medicare, for example. It provided the equivalent of private insurance to all persons age 65 and over. The result was an increase in the use of the covered hospital and doctor services, reducing or eliminating earlier differences by race and income on the overall use of those services (Feder, 1977). Medicare also helped increase access to medical services by African American elderly by strictly enforcing antisegregation provisions against hospitals that accepted any Medicare. With Medicare's hospital reimbursement policies being exceptionally lucrative in the 1960s, and the elderly being the highest users of medical care services, hospitals that had been segregated had a powerful incentive to open their doors equally to Blacks and Whites.

The situation in the 1990s, however, has changed substantially. Medicare has reduced reimbursements to hospitals and doctors as a way to slow rising costs, making Medicare patients less attractive (Moon & Davis, 1995). Even less desirable are Medicaid patients. Comparatively low payments by Medicaid lead many physicians and nursing homes to avoid Medicaid patients (Institute of Medicine, 1986), and many hospitals view treating Medicaid patients as a cost rather than a revenue. To the extent that minority elderly are disproportionately concentrated in low-income and racially homogeneous areas (Wallace, 1990), the trends affecting the entire health care system hit them the hardest.

Without any institutional interests that have a vested interest in the needs of minority elderly, health policy takes shape with limited attention to their needs. The dominant issue in health policy at the end of the 20th century has been containing health care costs. The next section focuses on the strategies likely to be taken in that effort, and their consequences for minority elderly.

Cost Containment Policies and Minority Elderly

Most health policies that affect the elderly fail to take into account the differential impact of those policies on subgroups of the elderly. Cost-containment policy is a particularly important area that is receiving extensive policy attention, but with limited consideration of racial and ethnic populations. There are several areas of cost containment that have particularly severe impacts on minority elderly, including changing the out-of-pocket costs for health care, shifting toward managed care, and trying to discourage the use of nursing homes. In each of these areas, the impact on minority elderly is likely to be different than for the elderly population in aggregate.

Increasing Out-of-Pocket Costs

One common approach to reducing health care spending has been to increase out-of-pocket costs. Using classical economic models, it is assumed that the higher the cost of an item (medical care), the more judiciously an individual will make use of it. Medicare includes copayments and deductibles that are designed, in theory, to reduce the unnecessary use of services.

The deductibles paid under Medicare are amounts that the individual has to pay out of pocket (or with private insurance) before Medicare begins to pay for services. These are the equivalent of one day's hospital charge for inpatient care (in 1996 it was $736) and $100 for physician services (Health Care Financing Administration [HCFA], 1996). In addition, there is a copayment of 20% of physician charges. Finally, there is a premium charge for Medicare Part B (which covers physician care) of $42.50 in 1996 (HCFA, 1996), which has risen from $14.50 in 1984 (U.S. Congressional Budget Office, 1993). These costs, along with the costs for services not covered by Medicare, such as prescription drugs, dental care, and long-term care, can add up to quite high costs for an older person with a chronic illness. Excluding nursing home expenses, the average out-of-pocket costs (including insurance premiums) for older persons *living in poverty* was $1,860 in 1994, equivalent to more than one third of their income (American Association of Retired Persons [AARP], 1994).

These high costs motivate the majority of older persons to obtain private supplemental insurance in addition to Medicare. About 75% of the total population age 65 and over has private supplemental insurance, while only 15% rely exclusively on Medicare (Table 16.2). There are great disparities by race and ethnicity, however. African American and Hispanic elderly are 2 to 3 times more likely than Whites to have no insurance except Medicare (Table 16.2). Because minority elderly are also more likely to have low and middle incomes, changes in the financing of Medicare that increases out-of-pocket costs will disproportionately hurt minority elderly.

Proposals to increase the out-of-pocket costs dramatically for the elderly have been discussed for a number of years (Villers Foundation, 1987), but have been most clearly articulated by the 1994 Republican Congressional election platform that promised to roll back the role of government in the health and welfare of the country. Republican Congressional candidates ran on a platform of policy proposals they called the "Contract with America," based on the assumption that government had too large a role in the health and welfare of the population and that individuals should instead assume a greater "responsibility" for their own health and well-being. Under this Contract, premiums and out-of-pocket costs and deductibles under Medicare would have doubled. Cost sharing for Medicaid would also have increased, and states would have been given the option to limit the amount and scope of

TABLE 16.2 Health Insurance of Older Persons: United States, 1994

	Medicare & Private (%)	Medicare & Medicaid (%)	Medicare Only (%)
All older persons	75.1	5.3	14.8
White	80.3	3.7	12.3
African American	44.9	14.4	34.6
Hispanic	49.2	19.5	23.2

SOURCE: National Center for Health Statistics (1996).

assistance provided to recipients, such as eliminating existing protections against spousal impoverishment when one spouse requires nursing home care (Administration on Aging, 1995). Because of the increased spending by older persons for health care required under these proposals, they have the potential to increase economic vulnerability among minority elders and to decrease their access to health and long-term care.

Limited access to health and long-term care services for older minorities means that greater responsibility for their well-being would be shifted to minority families who, like their elderly members, are disproportionately economically and socially vulnerable. According to the Center on Budget and Policy Priorities (1989), about 1 in 4 Latino workers paid by the hour does not earn enough to keep a family of three out of poverty. In addition, African Americans and Latinos are more often in female-headed households, resulting in more families dependent on a single wage earner and more living in poverty (Garcia, 1993). Moreover, increases in teen pregnancy and increases in the prevalence of AIDS, HIV, and drug dependence found among younger members of minority populations has resulted in an increase in four-generation households in which, for the most part, middle-aged women are caring for parents, adult children, and grandchildren (Antonucci & Cantor, 1994; National Council of La Raza, 1992; Sotomayor, 1993). Accordingly, there is an increasing number of minority women age 55 and over who must quit their jobs to care for family members, while at the same time receiving no income from Social Security or private pensions (Garcia, 1993; Minkler & Roe, 1993). Clearly, minority families have accepted the "responsibility" of caring for family members, and indeed express a preference for caring for relatives in the home (Antonucci & Cantor, 1994; Kiyak & Hooyman, 1994). However, given the challenges of increased financial burdens for medical care, caring for family members without assistance from government programs is unrealistic.

Managed Care

The most significant trend in the health care system during the 1990s is the growth of managed care systems. Medicare, a relative latecomer to the managed care revolution, has more than 10% of its insured in managed care plans. Medicare HMO plans grew at a rate of 30% in 1995, and Congressional proposals would greatly increase that growth (U.S. General Accounting Office [GAO], 1995). In California, well over 40% of all Medicare recipients are in HMOs, accounting for more than one quarter of all Medicare HMO enrollees nationally (U.S. GAO, 1995). This rapid change in the organization of health care financing and delivery is occurring with only limited government involvement and oversight, despite the potential consequences of the shift for access to care and the quality of care for older persons.

Managed care takes a wide variety of different forms, all of which focus on containing costs. The only type of managed care currently being used by Medicare are prepaid, at-risk health maintenance organizations (HMOs). The archetypal HMO is the staff model in which the plan receives a fixed payment per enrollee regardless of the actual health care use (called capitation), the health care providers are on salary, and all health care facilities (hospitals, labs, offices) are owned by the organization. Other HMO models contract out for physician services to physician groups or individuals, usually capitating the physician care and often putting the physicians at some risk for hospitalization costs. These models generally limit patient choice to a limited number of physicians and hospitals chosen by the plan. It is this "closed panel" feature that older persons most often find objectionable because of the importance they place on their relationship with their current care providers (Frederick/ Schneiders, Inc., 1995).

At an organizational level, managed care moves medicine from a guild or craft model to more of an industrial or bureaucratic model. This new organizational model has the *potential* to increase accountability, continuity, and efficiency. The wide gulf in knowledge between providers and patients about disease and its treatment means that under the traditional individual practitioner model the patient was at the mercy of the abilities and prejudices of each individual provider. Under a more bureaucratic system it is possible to have more comprehensive checks and balances to prevent inappropriate care, lack of follow through, and other problems. In addition, most managed care plans require lower copayments and few or no deductibles compared with fee-for-service insurance, reducing the out-of-pocket costs of older persons and improving their financial access to care.

On the other hand, as organized systems, managed care introduces a new set of systemic incentives. The most widely discussed incentive under capitated systems is to undertreat patients in order to maximize profits because the plan receives a fixed premium payment per enrollee. Some HMOs make physicians personally at risk for above average hospital costs (regardless of whether the costs are justified), providing the greatest incentives to undertreat (Pauly, Hillman, & Kerstein, 1990). Other characteristics of some managed care organizations that patients are particularly sensitive to include the weaker commitment to a particular practice site by physicians, which increases provider turnover; reduced patient autonomy; and increasingly bureaucratized systems that are harder to negotiate (Frederick/Schneiders, Inc., 1995). Less visible to individual patients, but particularly important for access to care for minority elders, are incentives that exist in some large capitated systems to recruit preferentially or "skim" the healthiest patients who will be the lowest users of services, to avoid the chronically ill and disabled, and to enroll patients with little attention to whether the location and service mix are most appropriate for the enrollee (Moon & Davis, 1995). Press accounts of marketing problems are common, including marketers who split their commission with new enrollees, high pressure tactics, and misinformation (e.g., Olmos, 1996). These and other problems have led to an average of 20% of new enrollees dropping out of HMOs within one year (Brown, Bergerson, Clement, Hill, & Retchin, 1993).

One potentially worrisome trend in the managed field is the rapid growth of for-profit HMOs in the market. Generating profits to pay to shareholders and to pay the excessive salaries of some top executives (e.g., $6.1 million per year to the CEO of one HMO in 1995—see Mathews, 1995) exaggerates the incentives to undertreat patients. While nonprofit HMOs can be pressured to provide extra services, such as medical education or uncompensated care in exchange for their tax-exempt status, for-profit businesses have profits as their foremost goal. On the other hand, the behavior of nonprofit chains in other sectors of the health care industry has been little different than that of the for-profits because both operate under similar market conditions (Clarke & Estes, 1992).

As large organizations, it is reasonable to expect managed care systems to operate similarly to other large organizations in our society. Discrimination based on both race and age are common in many key institutions of our society. Research has shown how the educational system reinforces racial inequality, how the labor market perpetuates the disadvantaged positions of minorities and older workers (Farley & Allen, 1989), and how housing markets and the mortgage system perpetuate discrimination based on race (Massey & Denton, 1993). Each of these sectors—education, employment, and housing—is dominated by large institutions that rationalize and direct the operation of each sector, and in each sector there has been a continuing concern with access and equity. Although older persons may have faced racial barriers in education, employment, and housing earlier in their lives, the health care system is the most important public social institution with which they *currently* interact.

The quality of life of minority elderly is largely dependent on the *past* dynamics of social systems that have resulted in their current levels of knowledge, income, health status, and housing. Those conditions are combined with the *current* dynamics of the medical care system that influences their medical care use and outcomes of health care. There is ample evidence that minority elderly receive different patterns of care under the fee-for-service system (e.g., McBean & Gornick, 1994). The bureaucratic organization of managed care could serve to equalize the care received by different groups of older persons, or it could accentuate those differences in ways that have a substantial impact on the quality of life of minority elders. As long as the primary driving force of health care policy is cost containment, however, issues such as access to care, quality, and equity for racial and ethnic minority elderly will remain on the back burner (Wallace, Abel, & Stefanowicz, 1996), and the managed care-based health care system will evolve with little attention to minority elders.

Reducing the Use of Nursing Homes

Whereas Medicare pays for very little nursing home care, Medicaid pays for almost half of all nursing home expenses (Levit et al., 1994). Paying for this nursing home care consumed about 20% of *all* Medicaid spending in 1993 (U.S. GAO, 1995). As these costs continue to rise there have been a variety of policy approaches to reducing the high costs of care. On the supply side, changes were made starting in the 1970s in the way nursing homes were paid, effectively reducing the reimbursement rates. Many states have also placed restrictions on the construction of new nursing homes to reduce the supply of beds. On the demand side, the federal government allowed states, beginning in the 1980s, to expand home and community services (such as homemakers and adult day care) under their Medicaid programs as a way of helping older persons remain in their own homes. In addition, there have been a number of demonstration projects designed to make it more attractive for individuals to purchase private insurance that covers long-term care.

The primary motive in all of these policy changes has been to reduce the costs to the government of nursing home care (Wallace et al., 1996). On one level, the change in emphasis from institutional to community long-term care is beneficial to minority elderly since they are less likely than non-Hispanic Whites to use nursing homes. In 1990, about 26% of non-Hispanic Whites age 85 and over lived in nursing homes, compared with 17% of African Americans, 11% of Hispanics, and 12% of Asian Americans (Damron-Rodriguez, Wallace, & Kington, 1994). The high rates of the oldest-old minorities *outside* of nursing homes creates a special need for community-based services in minority communities. The extra funding and expanded programs for community care under Medicaid in all states are likely to benefit minority elderly especially, because they are also more likely than non-Hispanic Whites to receive Medicaid (see Table 16.2). Thus, the effort to reduce nursing home spending may have a positive (if unintended) benefit to minority elders.

On the other hand, the increasing restrictions on nursing home availability will make it increasingly difficulty for minority elderly who need nursing home care to obtain it. Nursing homes are an appropriate source of care for some. Their residents are most commonly persons with high levels of physical and cognitive disabilities and low levels of available family support. When Medicaid reduces reimbursements and makes it ever less financially attractive to admit Medicaid patients, minority elderly are the most likely to face discrimination based on their source of payment. While about 40% of older persons overall enter nursing homes on Medicaid, more than 70% of African American elderly enter nursing homes with Medicaid as their primary source of payment (Hing, 1987). The effort to increase the proportion of the population with private long-term care insurance for nursing homes will only exacerbate this problem. The high costs of private long-term care insurance result in no more that 20% of persons being able to afford it (Wiener, Illston, & Hanley 1994). The high incomes needed to make long-term care insurance affordable will result in a lower proportion of racial and ethnic minorities being able to afford it, and the higher payment rates of private insurance than

Medicaid will further disadvantage minority elderly when they compete for a nursing home bed.

For minority elders to benefit from expanded in-home and community-based services, their access to these programs must be improved. Studies of community-based long-term care use among minorities has found lower participation rates than needs would indicate (Hyde & Torres-Gil, 1991). Barriers to utilization include money, a lack of knowledge about services, English-language proficiency, the complexity of the application process, location of providers outside minority communities, and lack of bilingual staff (Moon, Lubben, & Villa, in press; National Council of La Raza, 1991; Wallace, Levy-Storms, & Ferguson, 1995). Improving access would require a commitment on the part of policymakers to develop legislation that mandates providers to create culturally appropriate and sensitive programs and develop information and outreach strategies that are targeted to minority communities.

Health Policy for the 21st Century

It has been said that individuals make their own history, but not under the conditions of their own choosing. Minority elderly have not chosen to be surrounded by an anti-immigrant and antiminority policy space, attacks on programs for the elderly, and powerful interests in the health care system that do not put a high priority on their needs. But minority elderly and their communities are *not* passive objects of health policy, either. Most take active roles in maintaining their physical and spiritual health and in managing their medical care needs. But the forces that shape health policy for the elderly take little notice of this group. The health problems and concerns of older minorities are largely invisible in the larger health policy context, and the interests of the most influential players in the health policy arena—medical providers and businesses that pay for employee health insurance—rarely include special attention to the elderly in racial and ethnic minority groups.

Even while health policy largely overlooks minority elderly, they are caught in the cross-fire of social trends that are separately attacking public policies for immigrants and minorities as well as older persons. Large, impersonal changes in the structure of the U.S. economy have increased income inequality and heightened racial, ethnic, and generational conflict, and the changing nature of the federal policy process has made budgetary issues the cornerstone of all other public policy. These trends can been seen in the health care cost-containment policies embodied in increased Medicare out-of-pocket costs, the increased reliance on managed care, and continuing efforts to reduce nursing home use.

If older minorities are being buffeted by policy changes that do not take them into account, is there any hope that policy in the 21st century may be more appropriate for minority elderly? Some changes are likely to increase the awareness of health policy to issues of minority aging, especially demographic changes, while other social changes such as continuing increases in the cost of health care may provide counterpressures on public policy to ignore the health care needs of minority elderly.

Perhaps the most significant change that will occur in the 21st century is the increasing diversity of the older population. Torres-Gil (1992) identifies three trends that will reshape aging policy in the future, one of which is growing diversity (including race/ethnicity, family structure, income distribution, etc). As the proportion of the older population that is minority grows from 14% of those age 65 and over in 1990 to 32% by 2050, it will be increasing difficult simply to ignore that segment of the older population. Moreover, as the older population becomes increasingly diverse, the working-age adult population will become more diverse as well. In California, for example, non-Latino Whites will make up less than half of the total population before the year 2000 (Hayes-Bautista, 1991). This historic demographic shift could increase attention to the needs of minority populations at all ages, or it could be used to increase the racial and ethnic tensions of the 1990s.

Demography alone will not influence public policy, however, as is shown by the political activity required by women (who constitute a majority of the population) in the early 1900s to obtain the right to vote (Skocpol, 1992)! Ensuring that health policy and long-term care policy is responsive to minority elderly populations, therefore, will require increased advocacy as the population grows. Minority elected officials and national aging organizations representing minority populations, in particular, need to make health and long-term care parts of their larger agendas and move toward developing proposals and platforms that are informed, visible, and best suited for the populations they represent. The development of proposals for the financing, development, and delivery of health and long-term care will also require minority scholars and service providers to play a key role in educating policymakers about the needs and experiences of aging minority elders. In addition, it is critical that communities, service providers, and advocacy groups work to empower older minorities to move toward self-advocacy. These kinds of activities can ultimately lead to policy agendas that not only dovetail better with needs, but are more proactive than reactive.

The other trend that could bode ill or well for minority elderly is the continued growth of medical care costs. The ever-growing share of the national economy devoted to medical services guarantees that efforts to rein in medical inflation will continue. The emphasis on managed care as a way to contain costs is helping to change the structure of our medical care system, although pressures continue to increase the out-of-pocket costs of the elderly and to restrict access to some services. If current dominant interests in health care policy reform continue to shape public policy in the coming years, changes in the medical care system are likely to protect corporate profits and existing medical care enterprises at the expense of adequate access to care for minority elderly. It is possible, however, that the efforts of minority communities and organizations representing the interests of minority elderly will be able to form effective coalitions with mainstream aging organizations, citizens' lobby groups, and organized labor to push for policy changes that prioritize the human needs of diverse populations (Binstock 1995; Wallace & Estes, 1989). One major step in that direction would be to bring the United States into step with the rest of the industrialized world and establish some form of national health insurance that provides equal financial access to health care for all older Americans and provides nondiscriminatory forms of cost control over the entire medical care system (Brown, 1994; Pepper Commission, 1990). Such a system of health insurance could be structured in a way that would minimize many of the problems facing minority elderly in access to care, the growing financial burdens of health services, and institutional barriers to appropriate care. As demonstrated in the efforts to reform health insurance in the early 1990s, powerful interests with a stake in the currently inequitable system will oppose many of the needed changes. Only a concerted effort by a broad coalition has a chance of enacting the types of broad health policy changes needed by minority elderly.

Note
_____

1. We intentionally use the term *minority* rather than *ethnic* elderly to emphasize the element of socially imposed stratification and inequality experienced by older African Americans, Asian Americans, Latinos, and Native Americans during their lifetimes. The concept is based on power relationships rather than numerical size. The term *ethnic elderly* is broader and encompasses the variation in cultural practices and heritages of different groups of older persons. Thus,

Irish American elderly may be an ethnic group to the extent that they hold distinct beliefs, family patterns, and behaviors, but are not a minority (during the 1990s) because they face no institutional barriers to their full participation in society that is based on their heritage.

References

American Association of Retired Persons (AARP). (1994). *Coming up short: Increasing out-of-pocket health spending by older Americans*. Washington, DC: AARP Public Policy Institute.

Administration on Aging. (1995, September). Medicaid block grants and OAA performance partnerships: Potential impacts on LTC for diverse communities. *Diversity and Long Term Care Newsletter*. Washington, DC: Author.

Antonucci, T. C., & Cantor, M. H. (1994). Strengthening the family support system for older minority persons. In *Minority elders: Five goals toward building a public policy base*. Washington, DC: Gerontological Society of America.

Armbruster, R., Geron, K., & Bonacich, E. (1995). The assault on California's Latino immigrants: The politics of Proposition 187. *International Journal of Urban and Regional Research, 19*(4), 655-663.

Bergthold, L. (1990). *Purchasing power in health*. New Brunswick, NJ: Rutgers University Press.

Bergthold, L. (1991). The fat kid on the seesaw: American business and health care cost containment, 1970-1990. *Annual Review of Public Health, 12,* 157-175.

Binstock, R. H. (1995). A new era in the politics of aging: How will old-age interest groups respond? *Generations, 19*(3), 68-74.

Brown, E. R. (1994). Should single-payer advocates support President Clinton's proposal for health care reform? *American Journal of Public Health, 84*(2), 182-187.

Brown, R., Bergerson, J., Clement, D., Hill, J., & Retchin, S. (1993). *The Medicare risk program for HMOs—Final summary report on findings from the evaluation*. Princeton, NJ: Mathematica Policy Research.

Center for Public Integrity. (1994). *Well-healed: Inside lobbying for health care reform*. Washington, DC: Author.

Center on Budget and Policy Priorities. (1989, June 26). Minimum wage veto hurts Latinos and Blacks. *Hispanic Link Weekly Report,* pp. 2-4.

Clarke, L., & Estes, C. L.. (1992). Sociological and economic theories of markets and nonprofits: Evidence from home health organizations. *American Journal of Sociology, 97,* 945-969.

Damron-Rodriguez, J., Wallace, S. P., & Kington, R. (1994). Service utilization and minority elderly: Appropriateness, accessibility and acceptability. *Gerontology and Geriatrics Education, 15*(1), 45-64.

Estes, C. L. (1979). *The aging enterprise*. San Francisco: Jossey-Bass.

Estes, C. L., Swan, J. H., & Associates. (1993). *The long term care crisis: Elders trapped in the no-care zone*. Newbury Park, CA: Sage.

Farley, R., & Allen, W. R. (1989). *The color line and the quality of life in America*. New York: Oxford University Press.

Feder, J. M. (1977). Medicare implementation and the policy process. *Journal of Health Politics, Policy, and Law, 2,* 173-189.

Fix, M. E., & Passel, J. S. (1994). Setting the record straight: What are the costs to the public? *Public Welfare, 52*(2), 6-15.

Frederick/Schneiders, Inc. (1995). *Analysis of focus groups concerning managed care and Medicare*. Prepared for the Kaiser Family Foundation. Washington, DC: Author.

Garcia, A. (1993). Income security and elderly Latinos. In M. Sotomayor & A. Garcia (Eds.), *Elderly Latinos: Issues and solutions for the 21st century* (pp. 17-28). Washington, DC: National Hispanic Council on Aging.

Gardner, J. M. (1995). Worker displacement: A decade of change. *Monthly Labor Review, 118*(4), 45-58.

Hayes-Bautista, D. E. (1991). Young Latinos, older Anglos, and public policy: Lessons from California. *Generations, 15*(4), 37-42.

Health Care Financing Administration. (1996). *Medicare fact sheet.* Baltimore, MD: Author.

Hing, E. (1987). *Use of nursing homes by the elderly: Preliminary data from the 1985 National Nursing Home Survey* (NCHS Advance Data No. 135). Hyattsville, MD: National Center for Health Statistics.

Hyde, J. C., & Torres-Gil, F. (1991). Ethnic minority elders and the Older Americans Act: How have they fared? *Generations, 15*(3), 57-62.

Institute of Medicine. (1986). *Improving the quality of care in nursing homes.* Washington, DC: National Academy Press.

Kiyak, H. A., & Hooyman, N. R. (1994). Minority and socioeconomic status: Impact on quality of life in aging. In R. P. Ables, H. C. Gift, & M. G. Ory (Eds.), *Aging and the quality of life* (pp. 295-315). New York: Springer.

Langberg, M. (1993, October 29). IBM cuts first S.J. workers. *San Jose Mercury News,* p. 1E.

Levit, K. R., Cowan, C. A., Lazenby, H. C., McDonnell, P. A., Sensenig, A. L., Stiller, J. M., & Won, D. K. (1994). National health spending trends, 1960-1993. *Health Affairs, 13*(5), 14-31.

Massey, D. S., & Denton, N. A. (1993). *American apartheid: Segregation and the making of the underclass.* Cambridge, MA: Harvard University Press.

Mathews, J. (1995, December 27). $6.1 million a year to run an HMO. *Washington Post, 119,* p. B1.

McBean, A. M., & Gornick, M. (1994). Differences by race in the rates of procedures performed in hospitals for Medicare beneficiaries. *Health Care Financing Review, 15*(4), 77-90.

McWilliams, C. (1948). *North from Mexico: The Spanish-speaking people of the United States.* New York: Greenwood.

Minkler, M. (1992). Generational equity or interdependence. In E. P. Stanford & F. M. Torres-Gil (Eds.), *Diversity: New approaches of ethnic minority aging* (pp. 65-72). Amityville, NY: Baywood.

Minkler, M., & Roe, K. (1993). *Grandmothers and caregivers: Raising children of the crack cocaine epidemic.* Newbury Park, CA: Sage.

Moon, A., Lubben, J., & Villa, V. M. (in press). Awareness and utilization of community long term care services by elderly Korean and non-Hispanic White Americans. *The Gerontologist.*

Moon, M., & Davis, K. (1995). Preserving and strengthening Medicare. *Health Affairs, 14*(4), 31-46.

Moore, D. W. (1993). Americans feel threatened by new immigrants. *Gallup Poll Monthly, 334,* 2-17.

National Center for Health Statistics. (1996). *Health, United States, 1995.* Hyattsville, MD: U.S. Public Health Service.

National Council of La Raza. (1991). *On the sidelines: Hispanic elderly and the continuum of care.* Washington, DC: Author.

National Council of La Raza. (1992). *The state of Hispanic America 1991: An overview.* Washington, DC: Author.

Olmos, D. R. (1996, June 25). HMO accused of marketing fraud, other improprieties. *Los Angeles Times, 115,* p. D2.

Pauly, M. V., Hillman, A. L., & Kerstein, J. (1990). Managing physician incentives in managed care. *Medical Care, 28,* 1013-1024.

Pear, R. (1996, November 7). In California, voters bar preferences based on race. *New York Times, 145,* p. B7.

Pepper Commission. (1990). *A call for action.* U.S. Bipartisan Commission on Comprehensive Health Care. Washington, DC: Government Printing Office.

Portes, A., & Bach, R. L. (1986). *Latin journey: Cuban and Mexican immigrants in the United States.* Berkeley: University of California Press.

Quadagno, J. (1989). Generational equity and the politics of the welfare state. *Politics and Society, 17*(3), 353-376.

Rice, M. F. (1987). Inner city hospital closures/relocations: Race, income status, and legal issues. *Social Science and Medicine, 24*(11), 889-896.

Rosenthal, N. H. (1995). The nature of occupational employment growth, 1983-93. *Monthly Labor Review, 118*(6), 45-55.

Rothstein, R. (1993). Immigration dilemmas. *Dissent, 40,* 455-463.

Skocpol, T. (1992). *Protecting soldiers and mothers: The political origins of social policy in the United States.* Cambridge, MA: Harvard University Press.

Smith, M. P., & Tarallo, B. (1995). Proposition 187: Global trend or local narrative? Explaining anti-immigrant politics in California, Arizona, and Texas. *International Journal of Urban and Political Research, 19*(4), 664-676.

Sotomayor, M. (1993). The Latino elderly: A policy agenda. In M. Sotomayor & A. Garcia (Eds.), *Elderly Latinos: Issues and solutions for the 21st century* (pp. 1-16). Washington, DC: National Hispanic Council on Aging.

Stall, B. (1996, October 31). Prop. 209's fate may hinge in two words. *Los Angeles Times, 115,* p. A1.

Starr, P. (1982). *The social transformation of American medicine.* New York: Basic Books.

Torres-Gil, F. M. (1992). *The new aging: Politics and change in America.* New York: Auburn House.

U.S. Bureau of the Census. (1996). *Population projections of the United States, by age, sex, race, and Hispanic origin: 1995 to 2050* (Current Population Reports, Series P25-1130). Washington, DC: U.S. Department of Commerce, Bureau of the Census.

U.S. Congressional Budget Office. (1993). *Changing the structure of Medicare benefits: Issues and options.* Washington, DC: Government Printing Office.

U.S. General Accounting Office. (1995). *Long-term care: Current issues and future directions.* Washington, DC: Author.

U.S. House of Representatives, Committee on the Budget. (1987). *President Reagan's fiscal year 1988 budget.* Washington, DC: Government Printing Office.

U.S. Office of Management and Budget. (1995). *The budget of the United States, 1996.* Washington, DC: Executive Office of the President.

U.S. Social Security Administration. (1994, March). *Aliens who receive SSI payments.* Baltimore, MD: Office of Supplemental Security Income.

Villers Foundation. (1987). *On the other side of Easy Street: Myths and facts about the economics of old age.* Washington, DC: Author.

Waldivsky, A. B. (1992). *The new politics of the budgetary process* (2nd ed.). New York: Harper-Collins.

Wallace, S. P. (1990). The political economy of health care for elderly Blacks. *International Journal of Health Services, 20*(4), 665-680.

Wallace, S. P., Abel, E. K., & Stefanowicz, P. (1996). Long-term care and the elderly. In R. Andersen, T. Rice, & G. Kominski (Eds.), *Beyond health care reform: Key issues in policy and management* (pp. 180-201). San Francisco: Jossey-Bass.

Wallace, S. P., & Estes, C. L. (1989). Health policy for the elderly: Federal policy and institutional change. In *Policy issues for the 1990s: Policy studies review annual, #9* (pp. 591-613). New Brunswick, NJ: Transaction Books.

Wallace, S. P., Levy-Storms, L., & Ferguson, L. R. (1995). Access to paid in-home assistance among disabled elderly people: Do Latinos differ from nonLatino Whites? *American Journal of Public Health, 85*(7), 970-975.

Wallace, S. P., & Lew-Ting, C. Y. (1992, September). Getting by at home: Community based long-term care of Latino elderly. *Western Journal of Medicine, 157*(3), 337-344.

Wallace, S. P., & Manuel-Barkin, C. (1995). Older immigrants in California: Health care needs & the policy context. (Final Report, November 1995).

Wallace, S. P., & Williamson, J. B. (1992). The senior movement in historical perspective. In *The senior movement: References and resources* (pp. vii-xxxvi). New York: G. K. Hall.

Wiener, J. M., Illston, L. H., & Hanley, R. J. (1994). *Sharing the burden: Strategies for public and private long-term care insurance*. Washington, DC: The Brookings Institution.

Wilson, W. J. (1996). *When work disappears: The world of the new urban poor*. Chicago: University of Chicago Press.

Witeis, D. G. (1992). Hospital and community characteristics in closures of urban hospitals: 1980-1987. *Public Health Reports, 107*(4), 409-416.

Index

EDITOR'S NOTE: Page references followed by *t* or *f* indicate tables or figures, respectively. Page references followed by "n" indicate endnotes.

National Resource Center on Minority Aging
    Populations, 389
National Asian Pacific Center on Aging,
    151, 174
National Cancer Institute, 67, 215-216
    Native American initiatives, 193
National Center for Black Aged, 399
National Center for Health Statistics
    (NCHS), 15, 39, 46, 50t-51t, 54t,
    56-57, 59, 74n4, 74nn6-8, 76-77,
    80-82, 103, 206, 233, 253, 266, 337,
    341, 356, 358, 364, 409t, 418
    Mortality Detailed Files, 47
    National Mortality Followback Survey
        (NMFS), 83-84
    vital statistics data, 46-47
    See also Hispanic Health and Nutrition
        Examination Survey (HHANES);
        National Health Interview Survey
        (NHIS)
National Cholesterol Education Program,
    245, 266
National Council of La Raza, 351-352, 364,
    399, 409, 414, 418
National Death Index (NDI), 60-61, 72,
    74n10
National Health and Nutrition Examination
    Survey (NHANES), 46
    NHANES II, 184, 216, 256-257, 263
    NHANES III, 210, 214, 217-218, 236,
        239, 243, 244t, 245, 246t, 248t,
        249-250, 253-254, 356, 358
National Health Interview Survey (NHIS),
    60, 110-112, 113t, 129, 184, 222f, 349,
    373t, 394
    functional limitations due to chronic
        conditions, 142
    persons needing assistance in ADLs and
        IADLs, 136-137, 137t
    Supplement on Aging (SOA), 129-131,
        131t, 373t
    Supplement on Functional Limitations,
        136-137
National Health Interview Survey-National
    Death Index (NHIS-NDI), mortality
    estimates fbased on, 63-64, 72
National Health Interview Survey of Health
    Promotion and Disease Prevention
    (HIS-HPDP), 325-326

National Heart, Lung, and Blood Institute
    (NHLBI), 131t, 217, 233
National High Blood Pressure Education
    Program, 218, 224, 233
National Hispanic Council on Aging, 290, 399
National Indian Council on Aging (NICOA),
    195, 201, 368, 370, 372-373, 378-379,
    389, 394
National Institute of Mental Health (NIMH),
    174
National Institute on Aging, 145, 357, 391n2
National Institutes of Health, 391n2
National Longitudinal Mortality Survey
    (NLMS), 17, 60-62
    death rates based on, 63, 64t
    mortality estimates based on, 62, 63t, 71-73
    Public Use File, 60, 74n10
National Long-Term Care Survey (NLTCS),
    114
National Medical Expenditure Survey
    (NMES), 184, 373t
    Survey of American Indians and Alaska
        Natives (SAIAN) component, 388
National Mortality Followback Survey
    (NMFS), 83-84
National Research Center for Asian
    American Mental Health, 174
National Research Council, 213t
    Committee on Diet and Health, Food and
        Nutrition Board, 233
National Resource Center on Minority Aging
    Populations, 394
National Resource Center on Native
    American Aging, 379, 391n4
National Survey of Families and Households,
    338
National Survey of Hispanic Elderly People,
    142
National surveys, 238-240
    See also specific surveys
Native Alaskans. See Alaska Natives
Native American initiatives (National Cancer
    Institute), 193
Native Americans. See American Indians
Native Network Index, 385, 391n4
Navajo:
    cancer among, 192
    diabetes among, 185, 187
    hypertension among, 189

About the Contributors

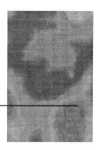

Jacqueline L. Angel received her Ph.D. from Rutgers University and is Assistant Professor of Public Policy at the Lyndon B. Johnson School of Public Affairs at the University of Texas at Austin. With Ronald Angel she is author of *Painful Inheritance: Health and the New Generation of Fatherless Families* (1993). She is an expert in long-term care policy and the community support of the minority elderly.

Ronald J. Angel received his Ph.D. from the University of Wisconsin, Madison and is Chair of the Department of Sociology at the University of Texas at Austin. He is editor of the *Journal of Health and Social Behavior* and, with Jacqueline Angel, is the author of *Who Will Care for Us: Aging and Long-Term Care in Multicultural America* (1997). He is the author of numerous articles on the health and living arrangements of older minority Americans.

María P. Aranda, Ph.D., is Assistant Professor at the School of Social Work, University of Southern California. Her research is in the areas of clinical social work practice with Hispanic older adults and their families, acculturation and health/mental health outcomes, services utilization, and caregiving to individuals with Alzheimer's disease and other dementing illnesses. She is a clinical social worker specializing in the treatment of mental disorders in primary health care settings. She currently serves on the State of California Governor's Committee on Alzheimer's Disease as well as on several local boards and committees dedicated to the enhancement of mental health service delivery to underserved populations.

Odilia Bermúdez is Research Associate at the Jean Mayer USDA Human Nutrition Research Center on Aging at Tufts University and Project Manager for the Massachusetts Hispanic Elders Study. She received her Ph.D. in nutrition from the University of Massachusetts at Amherst, where she participated in research on the diets of minority elders. Before coming to Massachusetts, she worked as a public health nutritionist in Panama and other Central American countries.

Elizabeth E. Chapleski is Assistant Professor of Research at Wayne State University, Institute of Gerontology, in Detroit. She received her Ph.D. in Sociology and Social Work from the University of Michigan-Ann Arbor, in 1991. Her research and teaching interests include American Indian culture and aging and survey research methods. She has extensive experience in survey research and has served as principal investigator for two statewide needs assessments of American Indians in Michigan. She was principal investigator of a NIA-funded longitudinal study of long-term care among American Indians of the Great Lakes. She is now analyzing these data, comparing the patterns of informal support networks and the influences of the networks on the long-term care preferences among older American Indians living in urban, rural off-reservation, and reservation locations.

Daniel O. Clark received a Ph.D. in Medical Sociology from Duke University in 1991 and subsequently completed a Postdoctoral Fellowship in Health Promotion and Disability Prevention at the Center for Health Studies in Seattle. He is Assistant Professor in the Department of Medicine at Indiana University School of Medicine and Research Scientist in the Regenstrief Institute for Health Care. His primary interests are health promotion and disability prevention among lower-income and minority adults. He is currently collecting health and physical activity data on approximately 1,000 older adults, studying risk factors for chronic disease and disability through public use data, and testing the effectiveness of a clinic- and community-based exercise intervention. His research is published regularly in gerontology, public health, and epidemiology journals.

Irma T. Elo received her Ph.D. in Public Affairs and Demography in 1990 from Princeton University. From 1990 to 1992, she was a Postdoctoral Fellow in the Population Studies Center, University of Pennsylvania. In 1992, she joined the Population Studies Center at the University of Pennsylvania as a

Research Associate and in 1994 she was appointed as an Adjunct Professor of Sociology at Penn. She has also served as Associate Director of Penn's Population Aging Research Center since 1995, and in 1996 she was appointed as Associate Director of Penn's Population Studies Center. She has conducted research on racial and ethnic differences in mortality in the United States with a focus on African Americans. Her research interests include social inequalities in health and mortality among both children and adults.

David V. Espino, MD, is Associate Professor of Family Medicine and Director of the Division of Community Geriatrics, Department of Family Practice at The University of Texas Health Science Center at San Antonio. He is a graduate of the University of Texas Medical Branch-Galveston. He completed a family practice residency at Memorial Medical Center–Corpus Christi, Texas, and a geriatric fellowship at Mount Sinai Medical Center, New York City. He has more than 40 publications in the area of Hispanic aging. His major research interests are centered on cognitive dysfunction in older Mexican Americans.

Luis M. Falcón is Associate Professor of Sociology and Director of Graduate Studies in the Department of Sociology at Northeastern University in Boston. He received his Ph.D. in sociology and population studies from Cornell University. He is a social demographer with a research focus on migration, labor force participation, and poverty among minority groups in the United States, and is currently Co-Principal Investigator of the Massachusetts Hispanic Elders Study.

Rose C. Gibson is Faculty Associate, Institute for Social Research and Institute of Gerontology, and Professor, at the University of Michigan where she teaches the Sociology of Aging and Research Methods. After receiving her Ph.D. from the University of Michigan, she was a Postdoctoral Fellow there in Statistics and Survey Research Design and Methodology on Minority Populations. She is the author of several books including *Different Worlds: Inequality in the Aging Experience* (with Eleanor Stoller), *Blacks in an Aging Society,* and *Health in Black America* (with James Jackson), and numerous articles and chapters on sociocultural issues in aging that appear in volumes such as *The Handbook of the Psychology of Aging,* the *Journals of Gerontology, The Milbank Quarterly,* the *ANNALS,* and the *Journal of Aging and*

Health. She is Editor-in-Chief of *The Gerontologist* and serves on several other editorial boards in the field of aging.

Helen P. Hazuda, Ph.D., is Professor of Medicine, Divisions of Clinical Epidemiology and Geriatrics, The University of Texas Health Science Center at San Antonio, Texas, where she joined the faculty in 1979. Trained in sociology and epidemiology, she focused her initial research on social and cultural aspects of cardiovascular disease and diabetes in Mexican American and European American populations. Her activities in this area led to the publication of an ethnic algorithm for classifying persons as Mexican American, European American, or other as well as a set of standardized scales for measuring multiple dimensions of acculturation and assimilation of Mexican-origin Hispanics. In recent years, she has directed her attention to the area of disability. She currently serves as Principal Investigator of the San Antonio Longitudinal Study of Aging (SALSA), co-directs the OH:SALSA Research Center on Oral Health in Aging, and chairs the Cross-Cultural Assessment Team of the Mexican American Medical Treatment Effectiveness Research Center, a minority MEDTEP center. As Director of the Hispanic Healthy Aging Center, she is also actively involved in the development of interventions to promote functional independence in Hispanic and European American elderly.

Nancy Hikoyeda, M.P.H., is in the doctoral program at the UCLA School of Public Health, Department of Community Health Sciences. She received her undergraduate degree in Education from the University of Utah. She received her M.P.H. in Health Education and a Certificate in Applied Social Gerontology from San Jose State University. Her research interests include ethnogerontology and ethnogeriatrics with a special emphasis on health services and long-term care utilization and end-of-life decision making by Asian and Pacific Islander American elders and their families. She has coauthored a number of publications and training materials on ethnogeriatrics. She previously served as the Program Assistant for the Stanford Geriatric Education Center.

Robert John, Ph.D., is Associate Professor in the Department of Applied Gerontology at the University of North Texas and Director of the Minority Aging Research Institute. His research and teaching interests include a variety of applied and social policy issues concerning aging minorities, families, and health. His latest major publication is a monograph coauthored with Dave Baldridge titled *The NICOA Report: Health and Long-Term Care for American Indian Elders,* a Report by the National Indian Council on Aging to the National Indian Policy Center, Washington, D.C.

Marjorie Kagawa-Singer, Ph.D., R.N., M.N., is Assistant Professor, UCLA School of Public Health and Asian American Studies. She is a nurse and anthropologist, and received her master's degree in nursing from UCLA School of Nursing and her master's and doctorate in anthropology from UCLA. Her research and publications focus on issues in cross-cultural health care and specifically multicultural issues in cancer care along the care continuum from prevention to end-of-life decision making. Her research focuses primarily on the Asian and Pacific Islander population. She has also lectured extensively on the influence of culture on patient and family responses to chronic diseases, the dynamics involved in multicultural staff interactions, and discrepancies in health outcomes by ethnicity.

Verna M. Keith is Associate Professor of Sociology and is affiliated with the Adult Development and Aging Program at Arizona State University. She completed her Ph.D. at the University of Kentucky and did postdoctoral work in the School of Public Health and the Institute of Gerontology at the University of Michigan. Her research focuses on minority health care issues and life stress and well-being and racial/gender stratification. Her work has appeared in the *American Journal of Sociology, Demography, Journal of Marriage and the Family,* and *Research of Aging.* She is currently investigating the impact of positive and negative social ties on depressive symptoms among the elderly.

Harry H. L. Kitano received his Ph.D. from the University of California, Berkeley and is currently Professor of Social Welfare and Sociology, Emeritus at UCLA. He was the initial holder of the Endowed Chair in Japanese American Studies, and his most recent books include *Race Relations,* 5th ed.; *Generations and Identity: Asian Americans*, 2nd ed. (with Roger Daniels); and an edited volume with Roger Daniels and Sandra Taylor titled *Japanese Americans: From Relocation to Redress.* He is currently working on a book titled, *The Impossible Dream: Japanese Americans and Redress,* with Mitchell Maki and Megan Berthold.

Kerrily J. Kitano, MSW, is currently a doctoral candidate in the School of Social Welfare, University of California, Berkeley. Her research has been on assessing the impact of HIV, and improving HIV-related services for Asian and Pacific Islander Americans. Her work experience includes teaching, case management, and behavioral research through a number of community-based organizations in the San Francisco Bay Area and with the University of Hawaii at Manoa. She is a third-generation Japanese American and a second-generation academician.

B. Josea Kramer, Ph.D., is Associate Director for Education and Evaluation at the Geriatric Research, Education and Clinical Center (GRECC), Sepulveda VA Medical Center and is Associate Research Anthropologist at the UCLA School of Medicine. She is responsible for developing national, regional, and local continuing medical education programs in geriatrics and extended care and is currently developing a national training program for the VA on evaluation of geriatrics and extended care programs. An anthropologist, she has made significant contributions in research and applied gerontology, especially on the topic of American Indian aging and the development of public-private partnerships for corporate elder care. She is on the editorial boards of *Gerontology and Geriatrics Education and Journal* and of *Aging and Ethnicity* and has served as guest editor for "Ethnic Diversity in Aging and in Aging Services in the U.S.," a special issue of the *Journal of Cross-Cultural Gerontology.* She also participated on task forces for the Gerontological Society of America and for the National Institute on Aging to develop public policy regarding minority health and aging.

Shiriki K. Kumanyika is a nutritionist and epidemiologist with a research focus on obesity and other diet-related chronic disease issues in African Americans and other minority populations. She holds a Ph.D. in Human Nutrition from Cornell University, a Master of Public Health from Johns Hopkins University, a master's degree in Social Work from Columbia University, and a B.A. in Psychology from Syracuse University. She is Professor of Nutrition and Epidemiology at the University of Illinois at Chicago and Head of the Department of Human Nutrition and Dietetics.

Carol Olson Long is Faculty Associate in the College of Nursing at Arizona State University. She completed her doctorate in sociology at Arizona State

University. Her research interests include patient satisfaction, issues related to health care access, and home health care.

Kenneth G. Manton, Ph.D., is Research Professor, Research Director, and Director of the Center for Demographic Studies at Duke University, and Medical Research Professor at Duke University Medical Center's Department of Community and Family Medicine. He is also a Senior Fellow of the Duke University Medical Center's Center for the Study of Aging and Human Development. His research interests include mathematical models of human aging, mortality, and chronic disease. He was the 1990 recipient of the Mindel C. Sheps Award in Mathematical Demography, presented by the Population Association of America; and in 1991 he received the Allied-Signal, Inc. Achievement Award in Aging administered by the Johns Hopkins Center on Aging.

Kyriakos S. Markides received his Ph.D. in sociology in 1976 from Louisiana State University. He is currently Professor and Director of the Division of Sociomedical Sciences, and faculty member of the Center on Aging at the University of Texas Medical Branch in Galveston. He is currently on the board of four professional journals, including *Research on Aging* and *Abstracts in Social Gerontology*. He is also Editor of the *Journal of Aging and Health,* which he founded in 1989. He is currently a member of the Council of the Behavioral Sciences Section of the Gerontological Society of America and a member of the Program Development board of APHA. His numerous publications include the chapter on race and ethnicity in the 1996 *Handbook on Aging and the Social Sciences,* the book *Aging and Ethnicity* (1987), and numerous recent articles on the health of Hispanic elderly. He is currently Principal Investigator of an NIA-funded study of the health of 3,050 older Mexican Americans in the five southwestern states.

Manuel R. Miranda, Ph.D., is the first occupant of the Edward R. Roybal Endowed Chair in Gerontology and Public Service at California State University, Los Angeles. He is currently on leave from the National Institute on Aging (NIA) in Washington, D.C., where he was involved in developing research resources and programs in the area of minority aging. Prior to his NIA position, he served as Staff Director for the U.S. House of Representatives Select Committee on Aging. He has had an extensive career in higher education that has included tenure at the University of California, Los Angeles

(UCLA). At UCLA, he held the position of Professor and Chair of the Doctoral Program in the School of Welfare. He was a Distinguished Visiting Scientist with the National Institute of Mental Health (NIMH) from 1984 to 1985. He has published extensively in the fields of gerontology, mental health, and health and welfare issues with a special emphasis on minority populations.

Tazuko Shibusawa received her doctorate in social welfare at the School of Public Policy and Social Research at the University of California, Los Angeles. She will join the Social Work faculty at Columbia University in the Fall of 1997. She has worked as a clinical and psychiatric social worker in both the United States and Japan and has published extensively in the areas of cross-cultural psychotherapy, family therapy, and women and mental health. She is currently engaged in conducting research on attitudes toward dependency and receiving care among elderly in both Japan and the United States.

Eric Stallard, A.S.A., M.A.A.A., is Research Professor and Associate Director of the Center for Demographic Studies at Duke University. He is a member of the American Academy of Actuaries and an Associate of the Society of Actuaries. He is a member of the American Academy of Actuaries' Committees on Long Term Care and Social Insurance. He also serves on the Society of Actuaries' Long Term Care Experience Committee. His research interests include modeling and forecasting for medical demography and health actuarial practice. He was the 1996 winner of the National Institute on Aging's James A. Shannon Director's Award. His research funded under this award focuses on forecasting models for acute and long-term care.

Sora Park Tanjasiri, Dr. P.H., is a lecturer in the School of Social Ecology, University of California, Irvine. She received her doctorate in Community Health Science at the UCLA School of Public Health. Her research focuses on cancer prevention among minority populations, and her dissertation explored tobacco control policy efforts in Asian and Pacific Islander American communities. Previously, she served as Project Director at the UCLA Jonsson Comprehensive Cancer Center for a multiethnic study of smoking among Latina and African American adolescents, and also participated on several breast and cervical cancer screening projects. Her publications cover multiethnic health promotion issues across the age spectrum.

Katherine L. Tucker is Director of Dietary Assessment in the Epidemiology Program of the Jean Mayer USDA Human Nutrition Research Center on Aging, and Associate Professor of Nutritional Epidemiology at the School of Nutrition Science and Policy at Tufts University. She received her Ph.D. from the International Nutrition Program at Cornell University. Her research focuses on the dietary intake and nutritional status of populations; and on relationships among diet, nutrition, and health. She is currently the Principal Investigator of the Massachusetts Hispanic elders study, funded by the National Institute on Aging to study diet, health, and disability among Hispanic elders in Massachusetts.

Valentine M. Villa, Ph.D., is Adjunct Assistant Professor in the Department of Social Welfare, UCLA School of Public Policy and Social Research. Her research interests include the investigation of health status differentials among minority and non-Hispanic White populations with an emphasis on the roles that socioeconomic status, culture, health care utilization, and health practices play in determining health status among older populations.

Steven P. Wallace, Ph.D., is Associate Professor in the Department of Community Health Sciences, UCLA School of Public Health. He is also the Borun Scholar of the UCLA Borun Center for Gerontological Research, and is Associate Director of the UCLA Center for Health Policy Research. He has published widely on access and policy issues involving long-term care and other health issues for racial and ethnic minority elderly, including articles on Latinos, African Americans, and Asian Americans. He has recently started a research program examining the consequences of managed care for minority elderly.